Lecture Notes in Computer Science 674

Edited by G. Goos and J. Hartmanis

Grzegorz Rozenberg (Ed.)

Advances in Petri Nets 1993

APN

93

Springer-Verlag
Berlin Heidelberg New York
London Paris Tokyo
Hong Kong Barcelona
Budapest

Series Editors

Gerhard Goos
Universität Karlsruhe
Postfach 69 80
Vincenz-Priessnitz-Straße 1
W-7500 Karlsruhe, FRG

Juris Hartmanis
Cornell University
Department of Computer Science
4130 Upson Hall
Ithaca, NY 14853, USA

Volume Editor

Grzegorz Rozenberg
Department of Computer Science, Leiden University
P.O. Box 9512, 2300 RA Leiden, The Netherlands

CR Subject Classification (1991): F.1-3, C.1-2, D.4, I.6

ISBN 3-540-56689-9 Springer-Verlag Berlin Heidelberg New York
ISBN 0-387-56689-9 Springer-Verlag New York Berlin Heidelberg

Printed in Germany

Typesetting: Camera ready by author/editor
45/3140-543210 - Printed on acid-free paper

Preface

The idea behind the series of volumes "Advances in Petri Nets" is to present to the general computer science community recent results which are the most representative and significant for the development of the area.

The main source of papers for the "Advances" is the annual International Conference on Applications and Theory of Petri Nets. Selected papers from the latest conferences are considered for the series. In addition, the "Advances" present also papers submitted directly for publication - potential authors are encouraged to submit papers directly to the editor of the "Advances". All contributions go through an independent refereeing process and, if accepted, they often appear in the "Advances" in a revised and extended form.

The main aims of the "Advances" are:

(1) to present to the "outside" scientific community a fair picture of recent advances in the area of Petri nets, and

(2) to encourage those interested in the applications and the theory of concurrent systems to take a closer look at Petri nets and then join the group of researchers working in this fascinating and challenging area.

"Advances in Petri Nets 1993" covers the 12th International Conference on Applications and Theory of Petri Nets held in Gjern, Denmark, in June 1991. I would like to thank the members of the program committee for their help in selecting papers from the workshop to be submitted to the "Advances".

Special thanks go to the referees of the papers in this volume who very often are responsible for considerable improvements of papers presented here. The referees were: M. Ajmone Marsan, C. André, F. Baccelli, G. Balbo, E. Best, R. Bhatia, J. Billington, G. Bruno, G. Chehaibar, L. Cherkasova, G. Chiola, F. de Cindio, R. Coelho, W. Damm, J. Desel, R. Devillers, M. Diaz, S. Donatelli, H. Ehrig, J. Esparza, C. Fernandez, A. Finkel, G. Franceschinis, H. Genrich, C. Girault, U. Goltz, R. Hopkins, P. Huber, M. Jantzen, K. Jensen, E. Kindler, M. Koutny, H.-J. Kreowski, M. Lindqvist, J. Martinez, G. De Michelis, T. Murata, S. Natkin, M. Nielsen, L. Ojala, C.-A. Petri, W. Reisig, U. Rhein, R. Shapiro, M. Silva, C. Simone, E. Smith, Y. Souissi, P. Starke, P.S. Thiagarajan, R. Valette, A. Valmari, W. Vogler, K. Voss, R. Walter. The editor is also indebted to Mrs. M. Boon-van der Nat for her help in the production of this volume.

Leiden, March 1993

G. Rozenberg
Editor

Contents

Replacement of Open Interface Subnets and Stable State Transformation Equivalence*

Ghassan CHEHAIBAR

BULL Corporate Research Center, Bldg F3.2G.28

Rue Jean Jaurès, 78340 Les Clayes-Sous-Bois, France

and

Laboratory MASI, University Paris 6, Tower 65

4 Place Jussieu, 75252 Paris Cedex 05, France

ABSTRACT The aim of this paper is to provide a hierarchical design method, refinement by replacing place-bordered subnets, with a hierarchical analysis method based on equivalence and preorder. We consider nets with distinguised places (interface places) and distinguished states (stable states), called open interface nets (OI-nets); OI-systems are OI-nets such that the stable state set is a home space. Two equivalence notions are defined: $\equiv_{SF}$ on OI-systems and $\equiv_{SST}$ on OI-nets. We show that if $N_1 \equiv_{SST} N_2$ and N_2 is robust (robust OI-nets are a subclass of OI-nets) then $N\,[N_1 \leftarrow N_2] \equiv_{SF} N$. Since an equivalence is too restrictive in hierarchical design and it is only possible to replace subnets of N whose border is a subset of the interface of N, an interface expansion operation is defined giving rise to a preorder $\preceq_{SF}$ such that $\preceq_{SF} \cap \preceq_{SF}^{-1} = \equiv_{SF}$.

KEYWORDS Place-Transition Nets, Hierarchical Design and Analysis, Open Interface Nets and Systems, Stable State Transformation Equivalence and Preorder, Replacement, Expansion, Robust Open Interface Nets

Contents

*This work is part of BULL's contribution to DEMON (ESPRIT BRA 3148)

1 Introduction

Refinement and abstraction are complementary methods in system design and analysis. Within hierarchical design, one starts with an abstract model and refines it stepwise by replacing some parts of the model by more detailed submodels. The inverse operation (abstraction) is useful when we want to analyse and understand an implemented system by building an abstract model of its behavior. Such hierarchical design method must be supported by a hierarchical analysis method: if $\mathcal{M}$ is transformed by a well defined operation *op*, the properties of $op(\mathcal{M})$ should be deduced from those of $\mathcal{M}$ and *op*.

The operation considered in this paper is the replacement of a place-bordered subnet (open subnet) with a net: if the replacement net is more detailed than the subnet it is a refinement otherwise it is an abstraction. If $N\,[N_1 \leftarrow N_2]$ is the net obtained by replacing the subnet N_1 with the subnet N_2 in N, we want to deduce $N\,[N_1 \leftarrow N_2] \equiv N$ from $N_1 \equiv' N_2$, for some equivalence relations $\equiv$ and $\equiv'$.

These equivalences are not based on labelling transitions and comparing the behaviors of nets expressed in terms of observable events. We adopt the dual point of view: the state transformation equivalences. Therefore, we label places and we distinguish "observable" states: two systems Σ_1 and Σ_2 are equivalent if there exists a correspondence between their observable states, and any transformation from an observable state to another one in Σ_1 is possible between the corresponding states in Σ_2. But we call these states "stable" rather than observable because they are not recognizable by an external observer (cf. the introductory example in the next section); the "observable" places are called interface places. So, the notions defined in this paper are not observational but they have to be considered a hierarchical analysis and proof method of net-based hierarchical design.

Open subnets naturally appear when a distributed system is modelled as a set of actors communicating through buffers by message passing. For instance, this analysis method may be applied to HOOD Nets [7] which have a place interface, or to the hierarchical design method based on "abstract actors" [8] where an abstract server is a net having a place interface and refinements are done by replacing such nets.

An open subnet is generated by a subset of transitions while a closed subnet (transition bordered) is generated by a subset of places. Replacement of closed subnets and composing nets by merging transitions have been widely studied by means of labelled-transition-based equivalences ([1, 2, 3, 16, 18] and see [11] for an overview of such equivalence notions). These notions are most of the time inspired from algebraic models like CCS and CSP, have elegant mathematical properties and are nicely handled; while replacing open subnets and composing nets by merging places are a bit more tricky and are not free operations since restrictions are necessary to obtain closure properties or to ensure the existence of some mathematical constructs [23] (when you compose two nets by merging transitions, the behavior of the whole net can be deduced from those of the two nets; this is not the case when composing nets by merging places).

Refinement of transition is a particular case of replacement of open subnet: you replace the subnet generated by this transition. This operation has been studied by [15, 14, 19, 9] either considering property preservation or considering equivalence notions which are congruences for such refinements. We are not looking for an equivalence notion which is preserved by such refinements but for an equivalence between a net and its refinement. In [17] a subnet generated by one transition is replaced with particular nets called "modules": we consider a more general replacement operation, and the equivalence notion of [17] is inspired from [1] and then based on labelling transitions. In [4] we have studied the subnet replacement from a more practical viewpoint: we have defined a restricted class of colored nets—reentrant nets—and an equivalence notion—OH-equivalence—with transition and place labelling to compare a net N with $N[N_1 \leftarrow N_2]$, where N_1 and N_2 are equivalent reentrant nets; but now we give up transition labelling and we reconsider the whole problem more generally and more theoretically.

This paper is organized as follows. In the second section, we give the basic definitions and an introductory example to motivate the notions studied in the paper. The point is that we do not consider plain PT-nets, but nets with a distinguished place subset called interface places, and a given set of "inner place" markings called stable states: these objects are called open interface nets (OI-nets). These OI-nets have not enough behavioral properties, so we define open interface systems (OI-systems) to be OI-nets with an interface marking such that the stable state set be a home space.

In the third section, we define two state transformation equivalence notions: when you refine actions you change the level of abstraction of events, and if you are seeking an equivalence between a net and its refinement, it is more relevant to compare the state transformations performed by the action with those performed by its refinement than comparing their behaviors expressed in terms of observable transitions (which is suitable when refining states and replacing closed subnets). Thus you are led to label places and study state transformation equivalences [13]. Stable functionality equivalence (SF-eq) is defined on OI-systems, and the preservation in a restricted sense of deadlock and home space property is shown. SF-equivalence being insufficient to do replacements, a stronger equivalence notion, stable state transformation equivalence (SST-eq), is defined on OI-nets. These two equivalences are bisimulations relating only stable states.

Actually, these equivalences follow the research line investigated by [5] where Exhibited Functionality equivalence (EF-eq) is defined on "S-observable systems", and by [12] where state transformation preorder and equivalence are defined. The stable states are a generalization of the observable markings. A similar result to the one aimed at in this paper was established for 1-safe superposed automata nets and EF-equivalence [6] (functional refinement of 1-safe superposed automata nets is a particular case of replacing an open subnet). The main difference between SST-equivalence and EF-equivalence is how the simulation of a state transformation is done (cf.Definition 8); and EF-equivalence is defined by means of an isomorphism between algebras (generated by the observable markings) while SST-equivalence is defined by means of a bisimulation.

In the fourth section, the replacement operation is defined on OI-nets and OI-systems: $rep(N)$ indicates the resulting object after replacing a subnet of N by an SST-equivalent net. For an OI-net OIN, $rep(OIN) \equiv_{SST} OIN$, but the set of OI-systems is not closed by rep. A restricted operation—robust replacement (rep_r)—is defined such that the set of OI-systems is closed by rep_r and $rep_r(OIS) \equiv_{SF} OIS$ if OIS is an OI-system. In the fifth section, an interface expansion operation is defined on OI-systems, giving rise to the definition of a preorder associated to SST-equivalence; property preservations are established. In the sixth section, we give an example of using these notions in hierarchical design.

2 Open Interface Nets

2.1 Preliminary Definitions

Throughout this paper we consider place-transition nets (PT-nets) with weighted arcs and unbounded capacities. First we recall the basic definitions about PT-nets, and the notations used. Some symbols are overloaded but this should not be confusing.

Definition 1 *Here are the basic definitions and notations.*

PT-nets *A place-transition net is a tuple $N = (P,T;W)$ where P and T are finite sets (set of places and set of transitons), $P \cap T = \emptyset$ and $W : (P \times T) \cup (T \times P) \rightarrow \mathbf{N}$ is the weight function. The incidence matrix is $C : P \times T \rightarrow \mathbf{N}$ defined by $C(p,t) = W(t,p) - W(p,t)$. W and C are extended to $(P \times T^*) \cup (T^* \times P)$ and $P \times T^*$ in the usual way; $\sigma \in T^*$, $t \in T$ and λ is the empty word:*

$$C(p,\lambda) = 0 \bigwedge C(p,\sigma t) = C(p,\sigma) + C(p,t)$$

$$W(p,\lambda) = 0 \bigwedge W(p,\sigma t) = \max(W(p,\sigma), W(p,t) - C(p,\sigma))$$

$$W(\lambda,p) = 0 \bigwedge W(\sigma,p) = C(p,\sigma) + W(p,\sigma)$$

The preset (resp. postset) of a set of nodes X is denoted ${}^\bullet X$ (resp. $X^\bullet$), and ${}^\bullet X^\bullet = {}^\bullet X \cup X^\bullet$. We assume there exist two sets $\mathcal{P}$ and $\mathcal{T}$ such that $\mathcal{P} \cap \mathcal{T} = \emptyset$, and all the PT-nets considered in this paper satisfy $P \subseteq \mathcal{P}$ and $T \subseteq \mathcal{T}$: then we can speak of the set of PT-nets satisfying some property.

PT-systems *A marked PT-net or a PT-system is a pair $(N;M_0)$ where $M_0 \in \mathbf{N}^P$ (the initial marking). We adopt the weak sequential firing rule:*

$$M \xrightarrow{\sigma} M' \text{ iff } \forall p \in P, M(p) \geq W(p,\sigma) \text{ and } M'(p) = M(p) + C(p,\sigma)$$

The reachability set is:

$$R(N;M_0) = \{M \in \mathbf{N}^P : \exists \sigma \in T^*, M_0 \xrightarrow{\sigma} M\}$$

Sum of markings *If $M_i \in \mathbf{N}^{P_i}$ for $i = 1,2$ then $M = M_1 + M_2$ is such that $M \in \mathbf{N}^{P_1 \cup P_2}$, $M(p) = M_i(p)$ if $p \in P_i \setminus P_j$ and $M(p) = M_1(p) + M_2(p)$ if $p \in P_1 \cap P_2$.*

Restriction and Extension *If $M \in \mathbf{N}^P$ and $P' \subseteq P$ then $M{\downarrow}_{P'}$ is the restriction of M to P'. A is a set, and $Q \subseteq \mathbf{N}^A$. The restriction of Q to $B \subseteq A$ is*

$$Q{\downarrow}_B = \{M \in \mathbf{N}^B : \exists M' \in Q, M = M'{\downarrow}_B\}$$

and the extension of Q to $B \supseteq A$ is

$$Q{\uparrow}^B = \{M \in \mathbf{N}^B : M{\downarrow}_A \in Q\}$$

If $\sigma \in T^*$ and $T' \subseteq T$, $\sigma{\downarrow}_{T'}$ is the sequence formed from σ by omitting all $t \notin T'$.

Subnet *If N is a PT-net and $T_1 \subseteq T$, then the T_1-generated subnet of N is a PT-net defined by $N(T_1) = (P_1, T_1, W_1)$ where $P_1 = {}^\bullet T_1{}^\bullet$, and $W_1 = W{\downarrow}_{((P_1 \times T_1) \cup (T_1 \times P_1))}$. If N_1 is a subnet of N, the border of N_1 in N is $bd_N(N_1) = P_1 \cap P_2$ where $P_2 = {}^\bullet(T \setminus T_1)^\bullet$.*

Replacement *Let $N = (P, T; W)$, and $N(T') = (P', T'; W')$ the T'-generated subnet of N. $N'' = (P'', T''; W'')$ is such that $T'' \cap T = \emptyset$ and $P'' \cap P = P'' \cap P' = bd_N(N(T'))$; then the replacement of $N(T')$ by N'' yields a PT-net defined by*

$$N\,[N(T') \leftarrow N''] = ((P \setminus P') \cup P''; (T \setminus T') \cup T''; (W \setminus W') \cup W'')$$

(consider the weight functions multirelations)

Deletion of Places *If $P' \subseteq P$, then $N \setminus P' = (P'', T; W'')$ where $P'' = P \setminus P'$ and $W'' = W{\downarrow}_{((P'' \times T) \cup (T \times P''))}$.*

Binary Relations *A binary relation $\mathcal{R}$ from a set A to a set B is a subset of $A \times B$. $(x, y) \in \mathcal{R}$ is written $x\mathcal{R}y$. The domain of $\mathcal{R}$ is $dom(\mathcal{R}) = \{x \in A : \exists y \in B, x\mathcal{R}y\}$, and the codomain $cod(\mathcal{R}) = \{y \in B : \exists x \in A, x\mathcal{R}y\}$. If $\mathcal{R}_1 \subseteq A \times B$ and $\mathcal{R}_2 \subseteq B \times C$, the composition of $\mathcal{R}_1$ and $\mathcal{R}_2$ is $\mathcal{R} = \mathcal{R}_1 \circ \mathcal{R}_2$ such that $\mathcal{R} \subseteq A \times C$ and $x\mathcal{R}z$ iff there exists $y \in B$, $x\mathcal{R}_1 y \wedge y\mathcal{R}_2 z$.*

2.2 Introductory Example

Consider the following basic client-server model (Figure 1): an idle client (CI) sends a request (R) and waits (CW) for the acknowledgement (A); there are n clients in the system. On receiving a request the idle server (SI) executes the request (SX); then he sends an ack to the client and becomes idle again. When the client receives the ack he becomes idle.

We want to add a buffer to receive the requests when the server is busy and only in this case: we obtain net $N2$ of Figure 2. BB is the number of buffered requests and FB the number of free positions. The server cheks the buffer (SC) before going back in the idle state.

If we confine ourselves to transition-labelled Petri nets and closed subnets, we are led to regard $N2$ as obtained by replacing the subnet $N3$ generated by the places SX and SI (Figure 3) with net $N4$ (transitions rr and pb have the same label rr).

In $N4$ the sequence $rr.rr$ is firable while it is not in $N3$ (the same holds resp. for $N1$ and $N2$); but all event-based equivalences at least require language equality: so $N3$

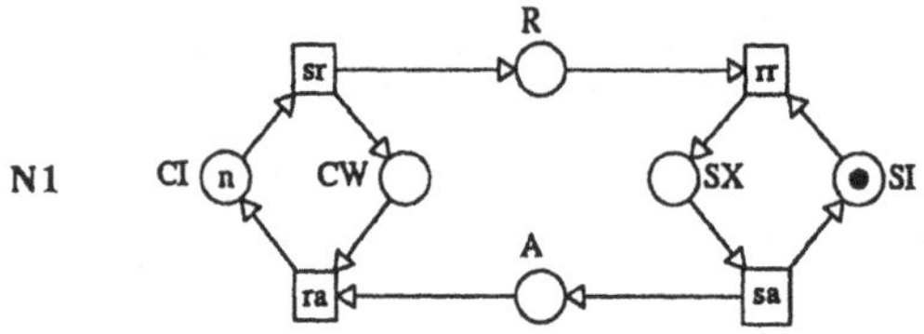

Figure 1: Client-Server Model

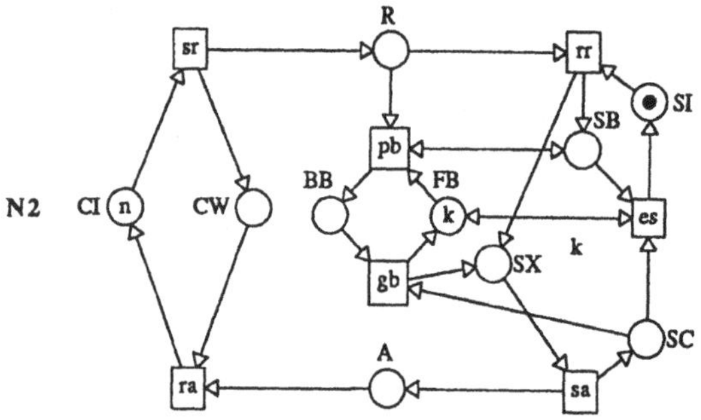

Figure 2: Addition of a buffer

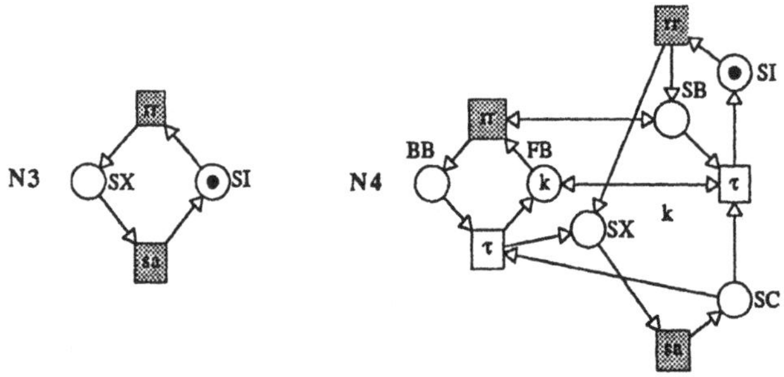

Figure 3: Replacement of a closed subnet

and $N4$ (resp $N1$ and $N2$) are not equivalent for any of these equivalence notions. This argument does not hold if we include the transition sr in the replaced net: but we do not want to include a transition of the client when replacing the server. Therefore we define state transformation based equivalence and regard this net transformation as the replacement of $N5$, the subnet generated by $\{rr, sa\}$, with $N6$ (Figure 4), because these two nets perform the same state transformation on $\{R, A\}$: a request got from R is transformed into an ack put in A.

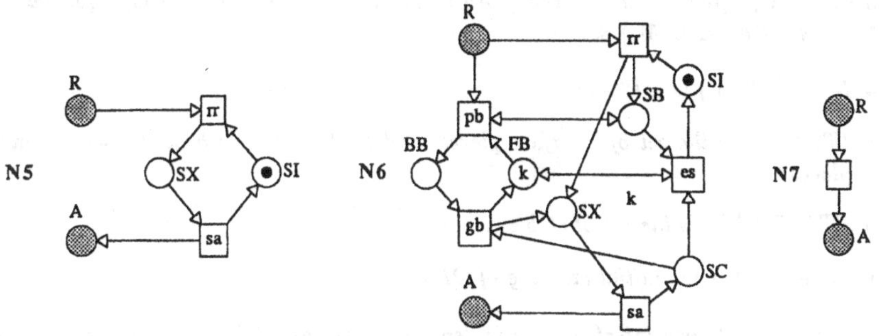

Figure 4: Replacement of an open subnet

By duality with the paradigm of event-labelling and event sequence observation one would think to label places and observes the evolution of the markings of observables places, and demands that the replacement net shows the same marking evolution than the subnet replaced. In our example the observable places—which we call interface places—are R and A.

This observational paradigm is too restrictive: the net $N7$ (Figure 4) is an abstraction of $N5$ and it seems reasonable to want to replace $N5$ by $N7$. But these two nets do not show the same marking evolution on $\{R, A\}$: in $N5$, from the state $M(R) = 1, M(A) = 0$, the state $M(R) = M(A) = 0$ is reachable and this is not possible in $N7$ because of the difference of atomicity between these two nets. Yet, if we only consider the states of $N5$ satisfying $M(SX) = 0$ then we observe the same state transformations on $\{R, A\}$: we call such states stable states; in $N2$ the stable states are those satisfying $M(SI) = 1, M(SC) = M(SX) = M(BB) = 0, M(FB) = k$.

The stable states are the only ones where the state of the interface is significant: they correspond to internal states where no "observable action" (ie, which modifies the interface value) is in progress.

There exists an infinite sequence of $N2$ which never drives the system in a stable state but it is always possible to reach such a state . Therefore, the comparison of two nets wrt their stable states is not an observational notion since it cannot be done by an external observer: the equivalence we define, based on stable state transformation(SST-eq), has to be considered a hierarchical analysis and proof method of net-based hierarchical design and not an observational notion.

2.3 OI-nets

We have given the intuition that has led to define a class of nets with a distinguished subset of places—the interface places, and a distinguished subset of states—the stable states. Thus the basic objects we deal with are not plain PT-nets but objets from this net class called open interface nets. Notice that this "interface" is either the border of a subnet or the "observable" places of a whole system.

Definition 2 (Open Interface Net) *An* open interface net *(OI-net) is a quadruplet* $OIN = (N; ITF; STB; M_0)$ *where*

- $N = (P, T; W)$ *is a PT-net*
- $ITF \subseteq P$ *is the set of interface places, and* $INR = P \setminus ITF$ *is the set of inner places*
- $STB \subseteq \mathbb{N}^{INR}$ *is the set of stable states*
- $M_0 \in STB$ *is the initial marking of* OIN

The domain of open interface nets is denoted $\mathcal{OIN}$, *and* $\mathcal{OIN}_{ITF}$ *is the domain of OI-nets whose interface set is* ITF.

An open interface net is a structure without any particular behavioral property of the stable states: the interface places are not marked and the stable states are an arbitrary set of inner states. So we define open interface systems which are open interface nets with an interface marking and a behavioral property of the stable states. This will allow us to separate what is structural from what is behavioral in the equivalence definition and replacement operation.

Definition 3 (Home Space) *Let* $\Sigma = (P, T; W; M_0)$ *be a PT-system. A set of markings* $H \subseteq \mathbb{N}^P$ *is a* home space *of* Σ *iff* $\forall M \in R(\Sigma), \exists \sigma \in T^*, M \xrightarrow{\sigma} M' \in H$. *If* $\{M\}$ *is a home space then* M *is called a home state.*

Definition 4 (Open Interface System) *An* open interface system *(OI-system) is a pair* $OIS = (OIN; m_0)$ *where*

- $OIN = (N; ITF; STB; M_0) \in \mathcal{OIN}$
- $m_0 \in \mathbb{N}^{ITF}$
- $STB\uparrow^P$ *is a home space of* $(N; M_0 + m_0)$

$\mathcal{OIS}$ *denotes the domain of open interface systems, and* $\mathcal{OIS}_{ITF}$ *the domain of OI-systems whose interface places are* ITF.

Definition 5 (Reachable Stable States) *Let* $OIS = (OIN; m_0)$ *be an OI-system. The* reachable stable state set *of* OIS *is*

$$RSS(OIS) = \{M \in R(N; M_0 + m_0); M\downarrow_{INR} \in STB\}$$

In an OI-system there is always a reachable stable state, and then it will be meaningful to compare OI-systems wrt their stable states. The need for stable states to be a home space will appear in the next section after the definition of SF-equivalence.

Figure 5 shows the difference between an OI-net and an OI-system. OIN_1 and OIN_2 are in $\mathcal{OIN}$ (the interface places are the shaded ones), and for every interface marking m_0, $(OIN_1; m_0)$ is in $\mathcal{OIS}$; but $(OIN_2; m_0)$ is an OI-system only if $m_0(p_1) \leq m_0(p_2)$ ($STB_2 = \{M : M(p_5) = 0\}$: if t_2 is fired from m_0 such that $m_0(p_1) = 1$ and $m_0(p_2) = 0$, it is impossible to reach a stable state.)

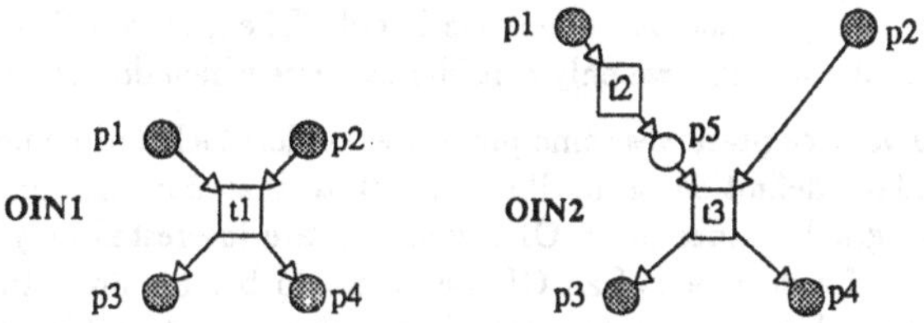

Figure 5: Difference between an OI-net and an OI-system

3 Stable State Transformation Equivalence

In this section, two equivalence notions are defined: stable functionality equivalence (SF-eq) on OI-systems and stable state transformation equivalence (SST-eq) on OI-nets. Replacements will be considered in the next section.

3.1 SF-Equivalence

The behavior of an OI-system is characterized by its stable states and the transition relation between these states: that is what we call its stable functionality. Then the equivalence of two OI-systems is defined by means of a bisimulation (stable functionality bisimulation) that is a correspondence between their respective stable states, such that, related stable states have the same interface marking, and allow transitions to equivalent stable states.

Definition 6 (SF-Equivalence on $\mathcal{OIS}$) *Let $OIS_i \in \mathcal{OIS}_{ITF}$, $i = 1, 2$. Then $\mathcal{R}_{SF} \subseteq RSS_1 \times RSS_2$ (RSS is defined in Definition 4) is a* stable functionality bisimulation *(SF-bisimulation) iff:*

1. $M_{01} + m_{01} \mathcal{R}_{SF} M_{02} + m_{02}$

2. $M_1 \mathcal{R}_{SF} M_2 \Rightarrow$

   a) $M_1{\downarrow}_{ITF} = M_2{\downarrow}_{ITF}$

   b) $M_1 \xrightarrow{\sigma_1} M_1' \in RSS_1 \Rightarrow \exists \sigma_2,\ M_2 \xrightarrow{\sigma_2} M_2' \in RSS_2$, *and* $M_1' \mathcal{R}_{SF} M_2'$

   c) *as b) but with the roles of 1 and 2 reversed.*

OIS_1 and OIS_2 are said SF-equivalent, written $OIS_1 \equiv_{SF} OIS_2$, iff there exists an SF-bisimulation from OIS_1 to OIS_2.

$\mathcal{R}_{SF}$ is not unique in general, but necessarily, $dom(\mathcal{R}_{SF}) = RSS_1$ and $cod(\mathcal{R}_{SF}) = RSS_2$.

It is easier now to see why the stable states have to be a home space. We will say that a system can "diverge" if there exists a sequence which cannot be completed to reach a stable state (that is, a system can diverge if the stable states are not a home space). Since SF-equivalence only considers transformations from a stable state to another one, if the stable states were not a home space, two OI-systems could be SF-equivalent while one of them is divergent and the other one is not. Then, since SF-equivalence cannot take divergence into account, we only consider systems which do not diverge.

The SF-equivalence preserves some properties of deadlock and home space.

In the standard definition, a deadlock is a state that does not have a successor in the reachability graph. Since in an OI-system, we are interested only in stable states, a first definition of a deadlock of an OI-system would be: a stable state from which it is impossible to reach another stable state; but with such a definition, we do not obtain deadlock preservation by SF-equivalence (see the below example).

Therefore we define an I-deadlock (I for interface) as being a stable state from which it is impossible to reach a stable state with a different interface marking.

Then an I-deadlock of an OI-system may be a "livelock": there may be firable sequences that modify the interface marking or lead to a different stable state but with the same interface marking, but there is no sequence leading to a stable state with a different interface marking. (It is a property of "dead-interface" stable marking.)

Definition 7 (I-deadlock of OI-systems) *An $OIS \in \mathcal{OIS}$ can I-deadlock iff*

$$\exists M \in RSS(OIS), \forall \sigma \in T^*, M \xrightarrow{\sigma} M' \in RSS(OIS) \Rightarrow M{\downarrow}_{ITF} = M'{\downarrow}_{ITF}$$

M is called an I-deadlock of OIS.

In Figure 6, OIS_1 and OIS_2 are SF-eq, where $ITF = \{p_0, p_1\}$ and $STB_2 = \{M : M(p_2) = 0\}$: p_1 is an I-deadlock of both of them.

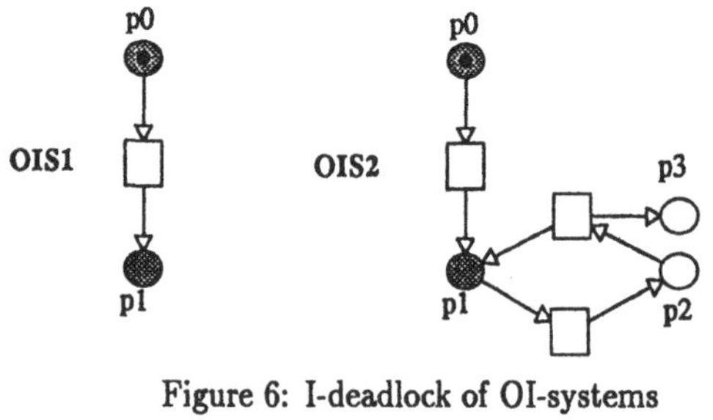

Figure 6: I-deadlock of OI-systems

The following propositions are direct consequences of the definitions of I-deadlock, home space and SF-equivalence.

Proposition 1 (I-deadlock Preservation by SF-Equivalence)

$$OIS_1 \equiv_{SF} OIS_2 \Rightarrow (OIS_1 \textit{ has an I-deadlock} \Leftrightarrow OIS_2 \textit{ has an I-deadlock})$$

Proposition 2 (Home Space Preservation by SF-Equivalence)
If $OIS_1 \equiv_{SF} OIS_2$ *and* $H_1 \subseteq RSS_1$ *is a home space of* OIS_1*, then* $H_2 = \{M_2 \in RSS_2 : \exists M_1 \in H_1 \wedge M_1 \mathcal{R}_{SF} M_2\}$ *is a home space of* OIS_2.

There is no "strict" preservation of home space: first it must be a *stable* home space and to a home state may correspond a home space: but if M_1 is a stable home state, then the corresponding home space H_2 satisfies $H_2{\downarrow}_{ITF} = \{M_1{\downarrow}_{ITF}\}$.

The SF-equivalence is sufficient to compare two OI-systems, not to do replacements: if we replace an OI-subsystem by an SF-equivalent system, we do not obtain an OI-system SF-equivalent to the original one. For SF-equivalence does not take into account the possible interactions of the subnet with its environment, which may occur during a transition from a stable state to another one.

The following two examples (Figures 7 and 8) show how the replacement problem have led us to a stronger equivalence notion. In the example comments, $\times$ denotes the composition of nets by merging places, and $a_1p_1 + \cdots + a_np_n$ denotes the marking M such that $M(p_i) = a_i$.

OIS_1 and OIS_2 in Figure 7 are SF-equivalent. $ITF = \{p_0, p_2, p_3, p_4\}$, $STB_1 = \{M : M(p_1) = 0\}$ and $STB_2 = \{M : M(p_1') = 0\}$. If they are composed with the environment N, in $OIS_2 \times N$, $t_4t_8t_5t_7$ is firable from $M(p_0) = 1$ and $p_3 + p_5 + p_6$ is reached, while this marking is not reachable in $OIS_1 \times N$.

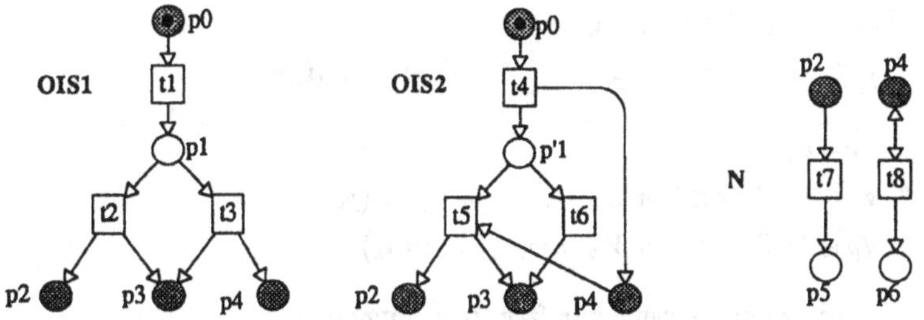

Figure 7: SF-eq is not strong enough to do replacement

Figure 8 gives the second counter example. In OIS_1, $STB_1 = \{M : M(p_1) = 0\}$, and in OIS_2, $STB_2 = \{M : M(p_1') = 0\}$; OIS_1 and OIS_2 are SF-equivalent. If they are composed with N, in $OIS_1 \times N$, $2p_0 \xrightarrow{\sigma_1} p_4$, where $\sigma_1 = t_1t_2t_7t_3$; but there is no sequence σ_2 in $OIS_2 \times N$ such that $2p_0 \xrightarrow{\sigma_2} p_4$.

3.2 SST-Equivalence

We define a stronger equivalence notion on OI-nets, independent of the initial marking: stable state transformation equivalence (SST-eq).

While SF-equivalence identifies systems having the same transformations from a stable state to another one and completely ignores the intermediate states during such a

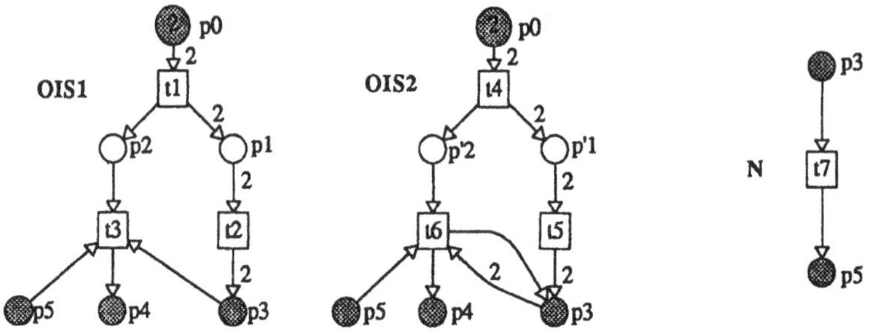

Figure 8: SF-eq is not strong enough to do replacement

transformation, SST-equivalence considers interface transformations *during* a transition from a stable state to another one: both nets may have different levels of atomicity and interact with their environment during the transformation, producing tokens in ITF and consuming tokens from it.

It is no longer enough that the sequences perform the same stable state transformation, it is also necessary that, to each sequence in a net corresponds a sequence in the other one which allows the same interactions with *any* environment. This leads to the definition of a sequence simulation denoted $\leq_{ITF}$.

Definition 8 (Sequence Simulation) *Let* $OIN_i \in \mathcal{OIN}_{ITF}$ *for* $i = 1,2$, *and* $\sigma_i \in T_i^*$. *Then we say that* σ_2 simulates σ_1 *(wrt* ITF*), written* $\sigma_1 \leq_{ITF} \sigma_2$ *iff*

(i) $\forall p \in ITF, C_2(p, \sigma_2) = C_1(p, \sigma_1)$

(ii) $(\sigma_1 = t_1 \dots t_n, t_k \in T_1) \Rightarrow (\exists (w_i)_{i=1,n} \in (T_2^*)^n)$ *such that*

1. $\sigma_2 = w_1 \dots w_n$
2. $\forall p \in ITF, \forall k \in 1..n, C_2(p, w_1 \dots w_k) \geq C_1(p, t_1 \dots t_k)$
3. $\forall p \in ITF, \forall k \in 1..n, W_2(p, w_k) \leq W_1(p, t_k)$

(i) σ_1 and σ_2 carry out the same interface transformation.
(ii) expresses the difference of atomicity and the interaction with the environment during the transformation: there is a decomposition of σ_2 such that after the kth step it has produced at least as much as σ_1, and for each step it consumes at most as much as σ_1. Notice that w_i may be the empty word.

The stable state transformation equivalence is defined analogously to the SF-eq by means of a bisimulation relating stable states, but the corresponding sequences (which perform equivalent stable state transformations) satisfy the simulation relation.

Definition 9 (Stable State Transformation Equivalence on $\mathcal{OIN}$)
Let $OIN_i \in \mathcal{OIN}_{ITF}$ *for* $i = 1,2$, *and let* $\longrightarrow_{i'}$ *denote firing in* $(N_i \setminus ITF; M_{0i})$. *Then* $\mathcal{R}_{SST} \subseteq STB_1 \times STB_2$ *is a* stable state transformation bisimulation *(SST-bisimulation) iff:*

1. $M_{01} \mathcal{R}_{SST} M_{02}$

2. $M_1 \mathcal{R}_{SST} M_2 \Rightarrow$

   a) $M_1 \xrightarrow{\sigma_1}_{1'} M_1' \in STB_1 \Rightarrow \exists \sigma_2,\ M_2 \xrightarrow{\sigma_2}_{2'} M_2' \in STB_2,\ \sigma_1 \leq_{ITF} \sigma_2$ *and* $M_1' \mathcal{R}_{SST} M_2'$

   b) *as a) but with the roles of 1 and 2 reversed.*

OIN_1 *and* OIN_2 *are* **stable state transformation equivalent** *(SST-eq), written* $OIN_1 \equiv_{SST} OIN_2$ *iff there exists an SST-bisimulation from* OIN_1 *to* OIN_2.

It is an equivalence because $\leq_{ITF}$ is transitive on $\mathcal{T}^*$. Only sequences leading from a stable state to another one are considered. Notice that we remove the interface places of OI-nets to define SST-equivalence on $\mathcal{OIN}$ but ITF is present through $\leq_{ITF}$: this implies that two SST-equivalent OI-nets behave the same in any environment.

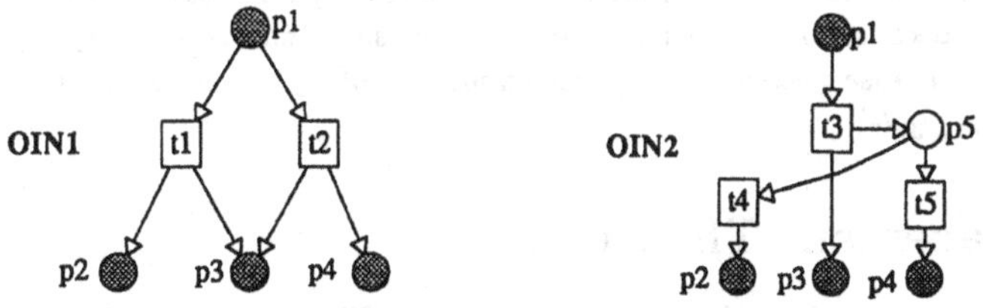

Figure 9: Two SST-equivalent OI-nets

OIN_1 and OIN_2 (Figure 9) are SST-equivalent: $ITF = \{p_1, p_2, p_3, p_4\}$, $STB_1 = \mathbb{N}^{\emptyset}$ and $STB_2 = \{M : M(p_5) = 0\}$. To $\sigma_1 = t_1$ corresponds $\sigma_2 = t_3 t_4$ and vice versa, the decomposition of σ_1 is $t_1 \lambda$.

It is easy to see that SST-equivalence is stronger than SF-equivalence: two OI-systems whose underlying OI-nets are SST-equivalent and have the same interface marking, are SF-equivalent.

Proposition 3 (SST-equivalence and SF-equivalence) *Let* $OIS_i \in \mathcal{OIS}_{ITF}$, $i = 1, 2$.

$$OIN_1 \equiv_{SST} OIN_2 \bigwedge m_{01} = m_{02} \Rightarrow OIS_1 \equiv_{SF} OIS_2$$

The following lemma shows that if σ_2 simulates σ_1, then σ_2 comsumes less tokens than σ_1 from the interface places.

Lemma 1 *If* $\sigma_1 \leq_{ITF} \sigma_2$ *then* $\forall p \in ITF$, $W_2(p, \sigma_2) \leq W_1(p, \sigma_1)$

Proof It is easy to see that Definition 8(ii) implies $W_2(p, \sigma_2) \leq W_1(p, \sigma_1)$ for all $p \in ITF$: you prove $W_2(p, w_1 \dots w_k) \leq W_1(p, t_1 \dots t_k)$ by induction on k using definition of W. □

Proof of Proposition 3 In order to lighten notations, $\longrightarrow$ will indicate firing in all nets, with or without their interface places.

$\mathcal{R}_{SST}$ is an SST-bisimulation from OIN_1 to OIN_2 (cf. Definition 9). Define $\mathcal{R}_{SF}$ by $M_1 \mathcal{R}_{SF} M_2$ iff $M_1{\downarrow}_{ITF} = M_2{\downarrow}_{ITF}$ and $M_1{\downarrow}_{INR_1} \mathcal{R}_{SST} M_2{\downarrow}_{INR_2}$.

If $M_1 \xrightarrow{\sigma_1} M_1' \in RSS_1$, then $M_1{\downarrow}_{INR_1} \xrightarrow{\sigma_1} M_1'{\downarrow}_{INR_1} \in STB_1$. By applying the definition of $\mathcal{R}_{SST}$ we get $\exists \sigma_2, M_2{\downarrow}_{INR_2} \xrightarrow{\sigma_2} M_2'' \in STB_2$, $\sigma_1 \leq_{ITF} \sigma_2$, and $M_1'{\downarrow}_{INR_1} \mathcal{R}_{SST} M_2''$.

By Lemma 1, $W_2(p,\sigma_2) \leq W_1(p,\sigma_1)$ for all $p \in ITF$; then $M_2 \xrightarrow{\sigma_2} M_2'$ such that $M_2'{\downarrow}_{INR_2} = M_2''$, and $M_2'{\downarrow}_{ITF} = M_1'{\downarrow}_{ITF}$ because of Definition 8(i). □

We have seen that the nets of figures 7 and 8 are SF-equivalent but not interchangeable. Now, we will show that they are not SST-equivalent, and thus explain the role of the definition of sequence simulation (Definition 8).

OIN_1 and OIN_2 of Figure 7 are not SST-equivalent (OIN_i is the underlying OI-net of OIS_i). For $\sigma_2 = t_4t_5$ there is no σ_1 such that $\sigma_2 \leq_{ITF} \sigma_1$: the only eligible candidate is $\sigma_1 = t_1t_2$, but there is no decomposition of $\sigma_1 = w_1w_2$ such that $C_1(p_4, w_1) \geq C_2(p_4, t_4)$. Actually, the aim of requirement Definition 8(ii)2 is to prevent such OI-nets from being equivalent.

The counter example of Figure 8 justifies Definition 8(ii)3. These two OI-nets are not SST-equivalent because for $\sigma_1 = t_1t_2t_3$, there is no σ_2 such that $\sigma_1 \leq_{ITF} \sigma_2$. $\sigma_2 = t_4t_5t_6$ is not suitable because necessarily any decomposition of σ_2 will associate t_6 to t_3 but $W_2(p_3, t_6) > W_1(p_3, t_3)$.

4 Replacement Theorems

In this section we define the replacement operations on $\mathcal{OIN}$ and $\mathcal{OIS}$. The replacement of a OI-subnet by an SST-equivalent OI-net does not pose any problem; but the result of the replacement of an OI-subnet by an SST-equivalent OI-net in an OI-system is not in general an OI-system. A restricted class of replacement on $\mathcal{OIS}$ is defined in order to obtain the closure property.

4.1 Replacements on $\mathcal{OIN}$

First, we give the definitions related to the "structural" part: what is an OI-subnet and what is a replacement of such a subnet. Graphically, an OI-subnet is an open subnet whose border (resp. inner place set) is a subset of the interface (resp. inner place set) of the original OI-net; its stable state set is then defined by restriction. The set of inner places of the original net is denoted INR, that of the subnet is denoted INR_1 and $INR_0 = INR \setminus INR_1$: any combination of two stable states on INR_0 and INR_1 must be a stable state on INR (cf. justification below).

Definition 10 (Open Interface Subnet) *If $OIN = (N; ITF; STB; M_0)$ and $T_1 \subseteq T$ such that $bd_N(N(T_1)) \subseteq ITF$, then the T_1-generated subnet of OIN is an open interface net defined by $OIN(T_1) = (N_1; ITF_1; STB_1; M_{01})$ such that:*

- $N_1 = N(T_1)$
- $ITF_1 = ITF \cap P_1$ *and* $INR_1 = P_1 \setminus ITF_1$
- $STB_1 = STB{\downarrow}_{INR_1}$

- $M_{01} = M_0{\downarrow}_{INR_1}$
- $STB = ((STB{\downarrow}_{INR_0}){\uparrow}^{INR}) \cap (STB_1{\uparrow}^{INR})$

The set of such subnets of OIN is denoted $\mathcal{SN}(OIN)$

Definition 11 (Replacement of OI-Subnet on $\mathcal{OIN}$) *Let* $OIN \in \mathcal{OIN}$, $OIN_1 \in \mathcal{SN}(OIN)$ *and* $OIN_2 \in \mathcal{OIN}$ *such that* $N[N_1 \leftarrow N_2]$ *is defined. Then the replacement of* OIN_1 *by* OIN_2 *in OIN yields an open interface net defined by:*

$$OIN' = OIN[OIN_1 \leftarrow OIN_2] = (N'; ITF'; STB'; M_0')$$

where

- $N' = N[N_1 \leftarrow N_2]$
- $ITF' = ITF$ *(and* $INR' = INR_0 \cup INR_2$ *where* $INR_0 = INR \setminus INR_1$*)*
- $STB' = ((STB{\downarrow}_{INR_0}){\uparrow}^{INR'}) \cap (STB_2{\uparrow}^{INR'})$
- $M_0'(p) = \begin{cases} M_0(p) & \text{if } p \in INR_0 \\ M_{02}(p) & \text{if } p \in INR_2 \end{cases}$

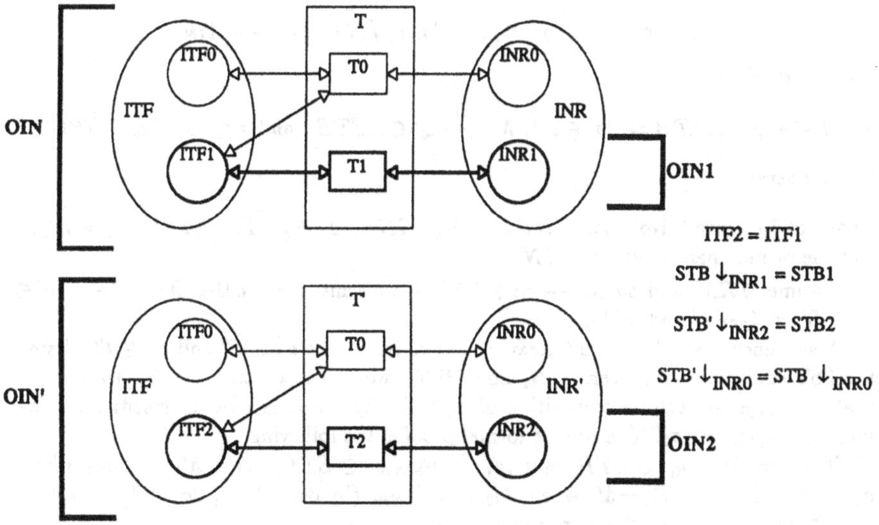

Figure 10: Replacement of OIN_1 with OIN_2

Figure 10 schematically summarizes the replacement operation and recalls the notations used throughout this paper. The ellipses represent *sets* of places, the boxes *sets* of transitions and an arrow from a set A to a set B means that an arrow *may* connect a node in A to a node in B.

OIN_1 is an OI-subnet of OIN generated by T_1. Its internal places (INR_1) are only connected to transitions in T_1. Its interface (ITF_1) is its border as a subnet (there may exist arrows between ITF_1 and T_0) and has to be a subset of ITF, the interface of OIN.

Due to the requirement on the stable states in Definition 10, replacing an OI-subnet by itself preserves the stable states of the original OI-net.

The following theorem is the fundamental result of this paper: replacing in OIN an OI-subnet by an SST-equivalent OI-net gives an OI-net SST-equivalent to OIN.

Theorem 1 (Replacement on $\mathcal{OIN}$ and Equivalence)

$$OIN_2 \equiv_{SST} OIN_1 \Rightarrow OIN\,[OIN_1 \leftarrow OIN_2] \equiv_{SST} OIN$$

To prove the above theorem, we have to construct an SST-bisimulation from OIN to $OIN' = OIN\,[OIN_1 \leftarrow OIN_2]$ (cf. Definition 9). The following lemma establishes a technical result whose interpretation is a bit tricky: there is a bisimulation relating states of OIN and OIN', whose restrictions resp. to INR_1 and INR_2 are resp. in STB_1 and STB_2. The stable states of resp. OIN and OIN' satisfy this restriction property.

Lemma 2 *If $OIN_2 \equiv_{SST} OIN_1$, $OIN' = OIN\,[OIN_1 \leftarrow OIN_2]$, $\mathcal{R}_{SST} \subseteq STB_1 \times STB_2$ is an SST-bisimulation from OIN_1 to OIN_2.*
We denote $XSTB = STB_1{\uparrow}^{INR}$ and $XSTB' = STB_2{\uparrow}^{INR'}$.
We define $\mathcal{R} \subseteq XSTB \times XSTB'$ by:

$$M\mathcal{R}M' \overset{\text{def}}{\Longleftrightarrow} M{\downarrow}_{INR_1}\, \mathcal{R}_{SST} M'{\downarrow}_{INR_2} \bigwedge M{\downarrow}_{INR_0} = M'{\downarrow}_{INR_0}$$

Then $M\mathcal{R}M' \Rightarrow$

a) $M \xrightarrow{\sigma} Q \in XSTB \Rightarrow \exists \sigma' \in T'^{*},\ M' \xrightarrow{\sigma'} Q' \in XSTB'$*, and* $\sigma \leq_{ITF} \sigma'$ *and* $Q\mathcal{R}Q'$

b) *vice versa*

Proof of Lemma 2 Notation: $INR_0 = INR \setminus INR_1$, $ITF_0 = ITF \setminus ITF_1$, $T_0 = T \setminus T_1$ and the primed names refer to OIN'.

Assume $M\mathcal{R}M'$ and $\exists \sigma, M \xrightarrow{\sigma} m \in XSTB$: we want to prove that $\exists \sigma', M' \xrightarrow{\sigma'} m' \in XSTB'$, $\sigma \leq_{ITF} \sigma'$ and $m\mathcal{R}m'$.

A sequence $\sigma \in T^*$ is an interleaving of two sequences $\sigma_0 \in T_0^*$ and $\sigma_1 \in T_1^*$. Using the SST-equivalence between OIN_1 and OIN_2, we can associate $\sigma_2 \in T_2^*$ to σ_1 such that $\sigma_1 \leq_{ITF_1} \sigma_2$; the decomposition of σ_2 given by $\leq_{ITF_1}$ is used to construct σ' by interleaving σ_0 and σ_2. The precise formal proof is the following.

If $M_1 = M{\downarrow}_{INR_1} \in STB_1$ and $m_1 = m{\downarrow}_{INR_1} \in STB_1$, then $M_1 \xrightarrow{\sigma_1} m_1$ where $\sigma_1 = \sigma{\downarrow}_{T_1}$. Since $M_1 \mathcal{R}_{SST} M_2$ where $M_2 = M'{\downarrow}_{INR_2}$ (by def. of $\mathcal{R}$), $\exists \sigma_2 \in T_2^*$ such that $M_2 \xrightarrow{\sigma_2} m_2 \in STB_2$, $\sigma_1 \leq_{ITF_1} \sigma_2$ and $m_1 \mathcal{R}_{SST} m_2$.

The sequence σ of $OIN \setminus ITF$ can be written $\sigma = (x_i y_i)_{i=1,n}, x_i \in T_0^* \wedge y_i \in T_1^*$. Then σ' is defined by $\sigma' = (x_i y_i')_{i=1,n}$ where $\sigma_2 = (y_i')_{i=1,n}$ and $y_i' = w_k \ldots w_l \in T_2^*$ if $y_i = t_k \ldots t_l$ (notations of Definition 8: remember that $\sigma_1 = (y_i)_{i=1,n}$ and $\sigma_1 \leq_{ITF_1} \sigma_2$).

Now we will show that $M' \xrightarrow{\sigma'} m' \in XSTB'$, $\sigma \leq_{ITF} \sigma'$ and $m\mathcal{R}m'$. $M' \xrightarrow{\sigma'} m' \in XSTB'$ and $m\mathcal{R}m'$ are easy to verify because when the interface places are removed, the surroundings of T_0 and T_1 (resp. T_2) do not share any place: thus $M' \xrightarrow{\sigma'} m'$

follows from $M{\downarrow}_{INR_0} \xrightarrow{\sigma'{\downarrow}_{T_0}}$ and $M{\downarrow}_{INR_2} \xrightarrow{\sigma'{\downarrow}_{T_2}}$; and m' satisfies $m'{\downarrow}_{INR_0} = m{\downarrow}_{INR_0}$ and $m{\downarrow}_{INR_1} = m_1 \mathcal{R}_{SST} m_2 = m'{\downarrow}_{INR_0}$.

It remains to verify $\sigma \leq_{ITF} \sigma'$. That $\forall p \in ITF, C'(p,\sigma') = C(p,\sigma)$ is obvious. First, we give the decomposition of σ': if $\sigma = t_1 \ldots t_q$ then $\sigma' = u_1 \ldots u_q$ where $u_i = t_i$ if $t_i \in T_0$, and $u_i = w_i$ (defined above) if $t_i \in T_1$. Finally the conditions of Definition 8 are easily verified by using the definitions of C and W. □

Proof of Theorem 1 We have to show there exists an SST-bisimulation $\mathcal{R}'_{SST} \subseteq STB \times STB'$ from OIN to $OIN' = OIN\,[OIN_1 \leftarrow OIN_2]$. Using notations of the previous lemma, we notice that $STB \subseteq XSTB$ and $STB' \subseteq XSTB'$. If $M\mathcal{R}M'$ and $M \in STB$ then $M' \in STB'$ (cf. Definition 11). Then define $\mathcal{R}'_{SST}$ by: $M\mathcal{R}'_{SST}M'$ iff $M\mathcal{R}M'$ and $M \in STB$: it follows from the lemma that $\mathcal{R}'_{SST}$ is a bisimulation. □

4.2 Replacements on $\mathcal{OIS}$

The next step is to define the replacement operation for OI-systems: it is a replacement performed on the underlying OI-net.

Definition 12 (Replacement on $\mathcal{OIS}$) *Let $OIS = (OIN; m_0) \in \mathcal{OIS}$, and let $(OIN_i)_{i=1,2} \in \mathcal{OIN}^2$ such that $OIN_1 \in \mathcal{SN}(OIN)$ and $OIN\,[OIN_1 \leftarrow OIN_2]$ is defined. Then the result of the replacement of OIN_1 by OIN_2 in OIS is the pair defined by*

$$OIS\,[OIN_1 \leftarrow OIN_2] = (OIN\,[OIN_1 \leftarrow OIN_2]\,; m_0)$$

Unfortunately, $\mathcal{OIS}$ is not closed under this operation: $OIS\,[OIN_1 \leftarrow OIN_2]$ is not in $\mathcal{OIS}$ in general, because the home space property is not preserved by replacement (cf. the below example). But we can state the following corollary that is implied by Proposition 3 and Theorem 1.

Corollary 1 (Replacement on $\mathcal{OIS}$ and Equivalence)

$$(OIN_2 \equiv_{SST} OIN_1) \wedge (OIS\,[OIN_1 \leftarrow OIN_2] \in \mathcal{OIS})$$
$$\Downarrow$$
$$OIS\,[OIN_1 \leftarrow OIN_2] \equiv_{SF} OIS$$

The OI-nets of Figure 11 are SST-equivalent, for $ITF = \{p_1, p_2\}$, and $STB_1 = \{M : M(p_3) = 1 \wedge M(p_4) = 0\}$, $STB_2 = \{M : M(p_5) = 1 \wedge M(p_6) = 0 \wedge M(p_7) = 0\}$. When they are composed with the environment N, $(OIN_1 \times N; p_1)$ is an OI-system, but $(OIN_2 \times N; p_1)$ is not: after firing t_5 it is not possible to reach a stable state; to do that, it is necessary to fire $t_5 \in ITF^\bullet$.(Notice that to t_2t_1, corresponds t_4t_3 and we do not have to consider t_5; but to $t_5t_5t_6$ corresponds $t_2t_1\lambda$.)

This leads to consider a restricted class of replacement nets to obtain closure for replacement in $\mathcal{OIS}$. The retrictions will be on the transitions fired to reach a stable state: the set of stable states is a $(T \setminus ITF^\bullet)$-home space.

Definition 13 (T'-Home Space) *H is a T'-home space of $(N; M_0)$ where $T' \subseteq T$ iff it is a home space reachable by only firing transitions in T', i.e.,*

$$\forall M \in R(N; M_0), \exists w \in T'^*, M \xrightarrow{w} M' \in H$$

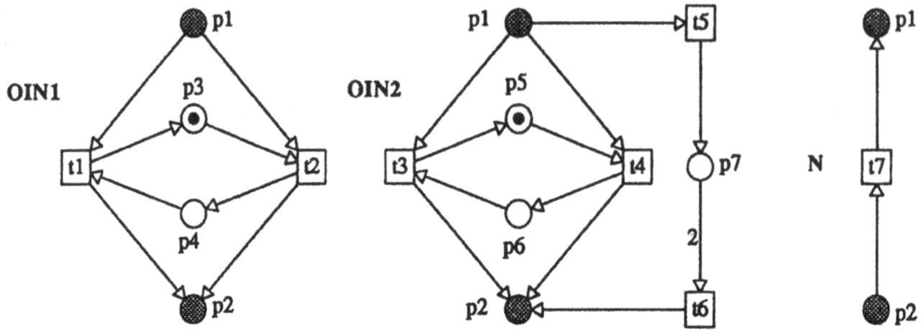

Figure 11: $\mathcal{OIS}$ is not closed by replacement

Definition 14 (Robust OI-Nets) *An OI-net is* robust *iff* $\forall m_0 \in \mathbb{N}^{ITF}$, $STB\!\uparrow^P$ *is a* $(T \setminus ITF^\bullet)$*-home space of* $(N; M_0 + m_0)$.

In a robust OI-net, for any initial marking of ITF, it is always *possible* to reach a stable state by a sequence not containing a transition in the postset of ITF, but the existence of other sequences is not excluded. Note that it is equivalent to say that STB is a $(T \setminus ITF^\bullet)$-home space of $(N \setminus ITF; M_0)$. All the examples of this paper are robust OI-nets except for OIN_2 of Figure 5 and OIN_2 of Figure 11. Reentrant Nets defined in [4] are a particular class of robust OI-nets.

Definition 15 (Robust Replacement) *A replacement of* OIN_1 *by* OIN_2 *is a* robust replacement *iff* OIN_2 *is a robust open interface net and* $OIN_2 \equiv_{SST} OIN_1$. *This operation is denoted* $OIS[OIN_1 \leftarrow OIN_2]_r$.

Theorem 2 (Closure for Robust Replacement)

$$OIS[OIN_1 \leftarrow OIN_2]_r \in \mathcal{OIS} \text{ and then } OIS[OIN_1 \leftarrow OIN_2]_r \equiv_{SF} OIS$$

Lemma 3 *If* $OIN_1 \equiv_{SST} OIN_2$ *and* $STB_2\!\uparrow^{P'}$ *is a home space of* $OIS' = OIS\,[OIN_1 \leftarrow OIN_2]$, *then* $OIS' \in \mathcal{OIS}$.

Proof We use the notations of Lemma 2. We want to show the home space property of an OI-system: if $M_0' + m_0' \xrightarrow{\sigma'} Q'$, there exists $\sigma'' \in T'^*$ such that $Q' \xrightarrow{\sigma''} Q'' \in STB'$.

Since $STB_2\!\uparrow^{P'}$ is a home space of OIS', there exists $u_2 \in T'^*$ such that $Q' \xrightarrow{u_2} X'$ and $X'\!\downarrow_{INR_2} \in STB_2$.

So if $v' = \sigma' u_2$, $M_0' + m_0' \xrightarrow{v'} X'$ and $X'\!\downarrow_{INR_2} \in STB_2$. By applying Lemma 2, there exists $v \in T^*$ such that $M_0 + m_0 \xrightarrow{v} X$ and $X\!\downarrow_{INR} \mathcal{R} X'\!\downarrow_{INR'}$ ($m_0 = m_0'$, cf. Definition 12). But $OIS \in \mathcal{OIS}$ implies that there exists $z \in T^*$ such that $X \xrightarrow{z} Y$ and $Y\!\downarrow_{INR} \in STB$: it follows from Lemma 2 that there exists $z' \in T'^*$ such that $X' \xrightarrow{z'} Y'$ and $Y\!\downarrow_{INR} \mathcal{R} Y'\!\downarrow_{INR'}$; then $Y'\!\downarrow_{INR'} \in STB'$. Hence $\sigma'' = u_2 z'$. □

Proof of Theorem 2 We will show that $STB_2\!\uparrow^{P'}$ is a home space of OIS', ie, if $M_0' + m_0' \xrightarrow{\sigma'} Q'$, there exists $\sigma'' \in T'^*$ such that $Q' \xrightarrow{\sigma''} Q'' \in STB_2\!\uparrow^{P'}$.

Define $\sigma_2 = \sigma'\downarrow_{T_2}$ and $m_{02} \in \mathbb{N}^{ITF_2}$ by $m_{02}(p) = \sum_{t\in T_0} \bar{\sigma}'(t)W(t,p)$ where $\bar{\sigma}'(t)$ is the number of appearances of t in σ'. Then in OIN_2, $M_{02} + m_{02} \xrightarrow{\sigma_2} Q_2$, $Q_2\downarrow_{INR_2} = Q'\downarrow_{INR_2}$ and $Q_2\downarrow_{ITF_2} \geq Q'\downarrow_{ITF_2}$.

Since OIN_2 is a robust OI-net, there exists $u_2 \in (T_2 \setminus ITF_2^\bullet)^*$ such that $Q_2 \xrightarrow{u_2} X_2$ and $X_2\downarrow_{INR_2} \in STB_2$. Hence $\sigma'' = u_2$. □

5 Expansion and Preorder

In this section we define the expansion of an OI-system which gives rise to the definition of a preorder. This preorder turns out to be associated with SF-equivalence and preserves I-deadlock-freeness and home space property.

The result obtained in the previous section is too restrictive for hierarchical design: a net and its refinement are equivalent. Particularly, this implies that they have the same interface places; but it is only possible to replace subnets whose border is a subset of the interface of the original net. In addition to the replacement operation, another useful refinement of an OI-system is to expand its interface: thus, hidden parts become visible and can be replaced.

Definition 16 (Expansion of OI-systems) *Let* $(OIS_i)_{i=1,2} \in \mathcal{OIS}^2$. OIS_2 *is an* expansion *of* OIS_1 *to* $ITF_2 \supseteq ITF_1$, *written* $OIS_2 = OIS_1\uparrow^{ITF_2}$, *iff*

- $N_1 = N_2$
- $ITF_1 \subseteq ITF_2$ *(then* $ITF_2 \setminus ITF_1 = INR_1 \setminus INR_2$*)*
- $STB_2 = STB_1\downarrow_{INR_2}$
- $M_{02} = M_{01}\downarrow_{INR_2}$
- $m_{02}(p) = \begin{cases} m_{01}(p) & \text{if } p \in ITF_1 \\ M_{01}(p) & \text{if } p \in ITF_2 \setminus ITF_1 \end{cases}$

It is easy to verify that this operation is well defined and $OIS_1\uparrow^{ITF_2}$ is actually in $\mathcal{OIS}$. Since the underlying PT-system does not change and $RSS_2 \supseteq RSS_1$, the home space property remains true.

Definition 17 (SF-Preorder) *Let* $(OIS_i)_{i=1,2} \in \mathcal{OIS}^2$. *Then* OIS_1 is less than OIS_2 wrt stable functionality, *written* $OIS_1 \preceq_{SF} OIS_2$, *iff there exists* $(OIS'_i)_{i=1,2}$ *such that* $OIS_i \equiv_{SF} OIS'_i$ *and* $OIS'_2 = OIS'_1\uparrow^{ITF_2}$.

The SF-preorder is based on expansion and equivalence: if OIS_1 is less than OIS_2, then OIS_2 has a larger interface and shows more "things" than OIS_1 but they are SF-equivalent on a "common part." If we have first defined SF-preorder by means of an SF-simulation and then SF-equivalence as its associated equivalence, we would not have obtained this equivalence on the common part which implies the preservation of some properties. But fortunately, SF-equivalence is compatible with SF-preorder, as shown by the following proposition.

Proposition 4 (SF-Equivalence is associated to SF-Preorder)

$$OIS_1 \preceq_{SF} OIS_2 \bigwedge OIS_2 \preceq_{SF} OIS_1 \Leftrightarrow OIS_1 \equiv_{SF} OIS_2$$

Proof
$\Rightarrow$) if $OIS_1 \preceq_{SF} OIS_2 \wedge OIS_2 \preceq_{SF} OIS_1$ than $ITF_1 = ITF_2$ and this implies $OIS'_1 = OIS'_2$ (notation of Definition 17).
$\Leftarrow$) consider $OIS'_1 = OIS'_2 = OIS_2$ □

Proposition 5 (Functionality Preservation by SF-Preorder) *If $OIS_1 \preceq_{SF} OIS_2$ then there exists a* stable functionality simulation *from OIS_1 to OIS_2, that is, a relation $\mathcal{S}_{SF} \subseteq RSS_1 \times RSS_2$ satisfying:*

1. $M_{01} + m_{01}\mathcal{S}_{SF}M_{02} + m_{02}$
2. $M_1\mathcal{S}_{SF}M_2 \Rightarrow$
   a) $M_1{\downarrow}_{ITF_1} = M_2{\downarrow}_{ITF_1}$
   b) $M_1 \xrightarrow{\sigma_1} M'_1 \in RSS_1 \Rightarrow \exists\sigma_2,\ M_2 \xrightarrow{\sigma_2} M'_2 \in RSS_2,$ *and* $M'_1\mathcal{S}_{SF}M'_2$

Moreover, $cod(\mathcal{S}_{SF})$ is a home space of OIS_2.

Proof We keep the notation of Definition 17. Let $\mathcal{R}^1_{SF} \subseteq RSS_1 \times RSS'_1$ be an SF-bisimulation from OIS_1 to OIS'_1 and let $\mathcal{R}^2_{SF} \subseteq RSS'_2 \times RSS_2$ be an SF-bisimulation from OIS'_2 to OIS_2. Thus $\mathcal{S}_{SF}$ is defined by $\mathcal{S}_{SF} = \mathcal{R}^1_{SF} \circ \mathcal{R}^2_{SF}$: this is well defined since $RSS'_1 \subseteq RSS'_2$.

The home space property is proved by using Corollary 2 and the fact that RSS'_1 is a home space of OIS'_2. □

It must be pointed out that the two following corollaries are especially due to the fact that $cod(\mathcal{S}_{SF})$ is a home space of OIS_2.

Since a lock may be a "livelock", when you expand the interface unobservable changes become visible: so SF-preorder preserves I-deadlock freeness in one way. Figure 6 shows a counter example: when $ITF_1 = ITF_2 = \{p_0, p_1\}$, OIS_1 and OIS_2 are SF-equivalent and they both I-deadlock in p_1. But if $ITF_2 = \{p_0, p_1, p_2\}$, then $OIS_1 \preceq_{SF} OIS_2$, and OIS_2 no longer I-deadlocks.

Corollary 2 (Deadlock-Freeness Preservation by SF-Preorder)

$$OIS_1 \preceq_{SF} OIS_2 \Rightarrow (OIS_1 \textit{ is I-deadlock-free } \Rightarrow OIS_2 \textit{ is I-deadlock-free })$$

Corollary 3 (Home Space Preservation by SF-Preorder) *If $OIS_1 \preceq_{SF} OIS_2$ and $H_1 \subseteq RSS_1$ is a home space of OIS_1, then $H_2 = \{M_2 \in RSS_2 : \exists M_1 \in H_1 \wedge M_1\mathcal{S}_{SF}M_2\}$ is a home space of OIS_2.*

6 Using Equivalence and Preorder in System Design and Analysis

The notions defined in the previous sections provide a hierarchical design method with a hierarchical analysis method. You model the real system with an OI-system, starting with an abstract model and then refining it stepwise. Two refinement operations are available: the replacement of an OI-subnet by an SST-equivalent OI-net or the expanding of the interface. If $ref(OIS)$ is the refinement of OIS, then in the former case, $ref(OIS) \equiv_{SF} OIS$, and in the latter case, $OIS \preceq_{SF} ref(OIS)$. So, if OIS_0 is the first abstract model and OIS_n the model obtained after n refinements, $OIS_0 \preceq_{SF} OIS_n$.

The client-server model presented in the introduction will serve as example. We start with the basic model OIS_0 (Figure 12): the interface places are the shaded ones, and $STB_0 = \{M : M(SX) = 0, M(SI) = 1\}$.

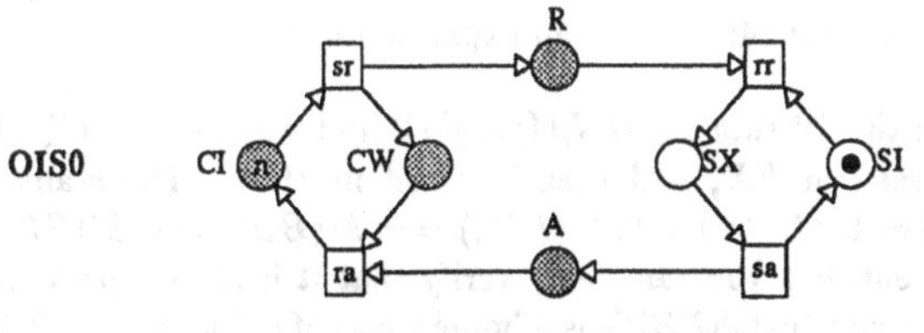

Figure 12: Basic model

The first refinement is the addition of the buffer: the OI-subnet $OIN_0(\{rr, sa\})$ is replaced resulting in OIS_1 (Figure 13), where $ITF = \{CI, CW, R, A\}$, $STB_0 = \{M : M(SX) = 0 \wedge M(SI) = 1\}$ and $STB_1 = \{M : M(BB) = 0, M(FB) = k, M(SB) = M(SX) = M(SC) = 0, M(SI) = 1\}$. It can be verified that it is a robust replacement (you have to check that, the replaced subnet and the replacement net are SST-equivalent, and in the replacement net, it is always possible to reach a stable state without firing rr or pb: this can be done using the invariant method of[10]); hence $OIS_0 \equiv_{SF} OIS_1$.

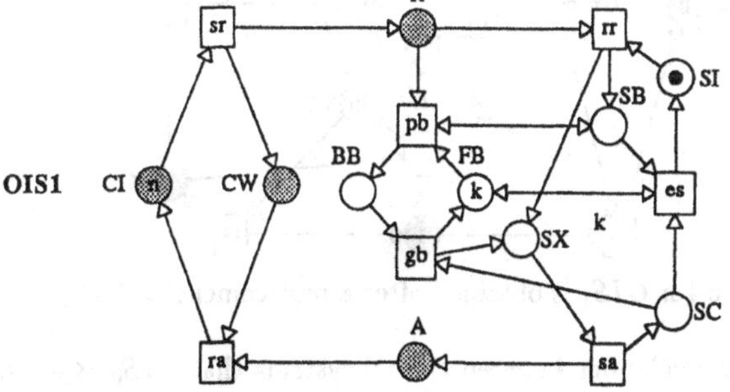

Figure 13: OIS_1 is obtained after a replacement on OIS_0

Actually, the buffer is not a passive storage component but the request is preprocessed before it is buffered in a x-position buffer: we want to replace the OI-subnet

$OIN_1(\{pb, gb\})$. But the border of this subnet is not a subset of the interface of OIS_1: therefore we expand this interface and we obtain OIS_2 (Figure 14): $OIS_2 = OIS_1 \uparrow^{ITF_2}$, where $ITF_2 = \{CI, CW, R, A, FB, SB, SX, SC\}$, and then $OIS_0 \preceq_{SF} OIS_2$.

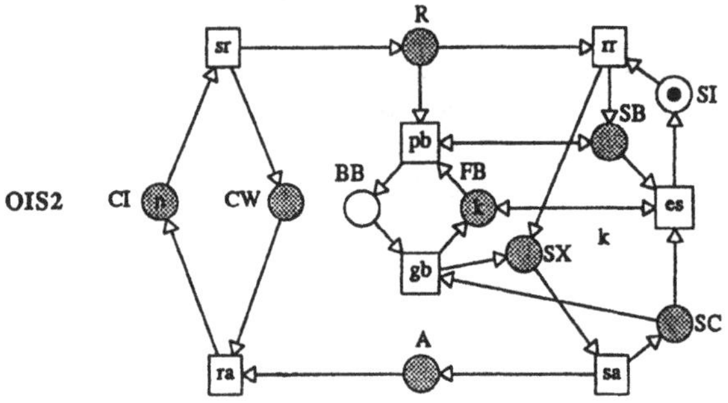

Figure 14: OIS_2 is an expansion of OIS_1

Finally, we replace the OI-subnet $OIN_2(\{pb, gb\})$, and we obtain OIS_3 (Figure 15): a request is preprocessed in PX, and then buffered in $BB2$. The stable states are $STB_3 = \{M : M(PI) = 1, M(PX) = 0, M(FB2) = x, M(BB2) = 0, M(SI) = 1\}$. It is not a robust replacement, but you can easily verify that it is always possible to empty PX and $BB2$, which means that $STB\uparrow^{P_3}$ is a home space of OIS_3 (where P_3 is the set of place of OIS_3 and $STB = \{M : M(PX) = M(BB2) = 0, M(PI) = 1, M(FB2) = x\}$). By applying Lemma 3 we have $OIS_3 \in \mathcal{OIS}$, and then $OIS_2 \equiv_{SF} OIS_3$.

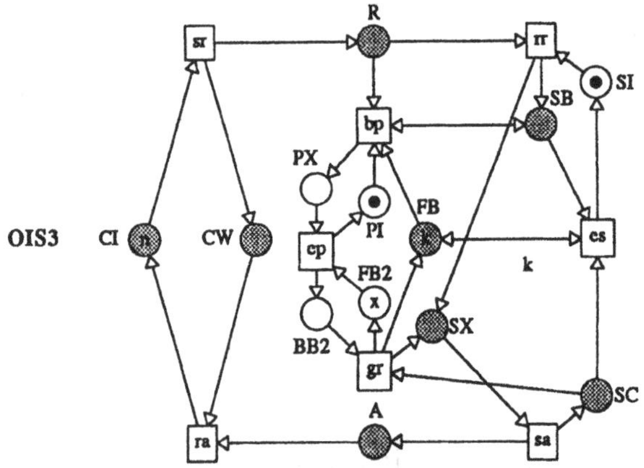

Figure 15: OIS_3 is obtained after a replacement on OIS_2

It follows from the relations between the OI-systems that $OIS_0 \preceq_{SF} OIS_3$. Then OIS_3 is I-deadlock-free since OIS_0 is I-deadlock-free; moreover, M_{00}, the initial state of OIS_0, is a home state and then $H_3 = \{M \in RSS_3 : M\downarrow_{ITF_0} = M_{00}\downarrow_{ITF_0}\}$ is a home space of OIS_3: but from the linear S-invariant of this net, it follows that $H_3 = \{M_{03}, M_3\}$, where M_{03} is the initial marking of OIS_3, and M_3 is the marking such that M_3 is equal to M_{03} on $P_3 \setminus \{SB, SC, SI\}$ and $M_3(SC) = M_3(SB) = 1 \wedge M_3(SI) = 0$. Hence M_{03} is a home state of OIS_3 since $M_3 \xrightarrow{es} M_{03}$.

This example shows how to alternate replacements and expansions in a hierarchical design an analysis process.

When the replacement is robust, the analysis is really "modular" since it suffices to verify that the replaced subnet and the replacement net are SST-equivalent, and the replacement net is robust.

But when the replacement net is not robust, in addition to the equivalence verification, one has to check a home space property on the whole net obtained after the replacement (and not only on the replacement net).

Besides, the linear-invariant analysis completes this method in allowing to narrow the home spaces obtained after a replacement: we have reduced H_3 to M_{03} using the linear place-invariants.

7 Conclusion

In order to associate a hierarchical analysis method to hierarchical design methods where refinement or abstraction consist in replacing a place-bordered subnet, we have defined classes of nets—open interface nets ($\mathcal{OIN}$) and open interface systems($\mathcal{OIS}$), and two equivalence notions: stable functionality equivalence on OI-systems and stable state transformation equivalence on OI-nets. If you replace an open subnet by an equivalent net you obtain an equivalent net to the original one; but $\mathcal{OIS}$ is not closed by the replacement operation and restricted replacements must be considered. An equivalence being too restrictive in hierarchical design, an SF-preorder was defined allowing the expansion of systems.

We have set out to study the replacement operation in a very general setting which can be used as a basis for particular cases. Indeed, the verification of SST-eq is practically too complex: you have to find a bisimulation ant to verify $\leq_{ITF}$. For practical issues, we must consider subclasses of OI-nets and OI-systems suited to some application area, and for which SST-equivalence can be verified efficiently. The proof that two reentrant nets [4] are SST-eq iff they have the same interface is in progress.

On the other hand, this equivalence is too fine, because two OI-nets are SST-equivalent only if they are interchangeable in any environment. This reduces its practicality and future work should consider an equivalence wrt a given environment.

ACKNOWLEDGEMENTS I wish to thank Claude GIRAULT and Serge HADDAD for their suggestions. The comments of five anonymous referees were very helpful in preparing the previous version of this paper that appeared under the same title in the Proceedings of the Twelfth International Conference on Petri Nets, 1991.

Concerning the present version, an error in the main result found by Walter VOGLER, has been corrected, and the comments of three anonymous referees have helped me to clarify some ambiguous notions.

References

[1] C. André. *Use of the Behavior Equivalence in Place-Transition Net Analysis.* Applications and Theory of Petri Nets, IF 52, Springer Verlag, 1982, pp 241-250.

[2] B. Baumgarten. *On Internal and External Characterizations of PT-nets Building Block Behavior.* Advances in Petri Nets 88, LNCS 340, pp 44-61.

[3] A. Bourguet-Rouget. *External Behavior Equivalence between two Petri Nets.* Concurrency 88, LNCS 335, pp 237-256

[4] G. Chehaibar. *Use of Reentrant Nets in Modular Analysis of Colored Nets.* Advances in Petri Nets 1991, LNCS, to appear.

[5] F. De Cindio, G. De Michelis, L. Pomello, C. Simone. *A State Transformation Equivalence for Concurrent Systems: Exibited Functionality Equivalence.* Concurrency 88, LNCS 335, pp 222-236.

[6] F. De Cindio, G. De Michelis, C. Simone. *GAMERU: A Language for the Analysis and Design of Human Communication Pragmatics within Organizational Systems.* Advances in Petri Nets 87, LNCS 266, pp 21-44.

[7] R. Di Giovanni. *Petri Nets and Software Engineering: HOOD Nets.* Eleventh International Conference on Application and Theory of Petri Nets, Paris, June 1990.

[8] C. Girault. *Petri Net Methods for Design and Analysis of Distributed Systems.* Invited Talk, Eleventh International Conference on Application and Theory of Petri Nets, Paris, June 1990.

[9] R. van Glabbeek, U. Goltz. *Equivalence Notions for Concurrent Systems and Refinement of Actions.* MFCS 89, LNCS 379, pp 237-248.

[10] G. Memmi and J. Vautherin. *Analysing Nets by the Invariant Method.* Petri Nets: Central Models and their Properties, LNCS 254, Springer Verlag, 1986, pp 300-337

[11] L. Pomello. *Some Equivalence Notions for Concurrent Systems: An Overview.* Advances in Petri Nets 85, LNCS 222, pp 381-400

[12] L. Pomello, C. Simone. *A State Transformation Preorder over a Class of EN-Systems.* Tenth International Conference on Application and Theory of Petri nets, Bonn, June 1989.

[13] L. Pomello. *Refinement of Concurrent Systems Based on Local State Transformations.* Stepwise Refinement of Distributed Systems, LNCS 430, pp 641-668.

[14] I. Suzuki, T. Murata. *A Method for Stepwise Refinement and Abstraction of Petri Nets.* JCSS 27, 1983, pp 51-76.

[15] R. Valette. *Analysis of Petri Nets by Stepwise Refinements.* JCSS 18, 1979, pp 35-46.

[16] A. Valmari. *Compositional State Space Generation.* Eleventh International Conference on Application and Theory of Petri Nets, Paris, June 1990.

[17] W. Vogler. *Behavior Preserving Refinements of Petri Nets.* Graph-Theoretic Concepts in Computer Science 86, LNCS 246, pp 82-93.

[18] W. Vogler. *Failures Semantics and Deadlocking of Modular Petri Nets.* Acta Informatica 26, pp 333-348, 1989.

[19] W. Vogler. *Failures Semantics Based on Interval Semiwords is a Congruence for Refinement.* Distributed Computing 4, pp 139-162, 1991.

[20] W. Vogler. *Failures Semantics of Petri Nets and the Refinement of Places and Transitions.* TUM 350, Janvier 1990.

[21] W. Vogler. *Asynchronous Communication of Petri Nets and the Refinement of Transitions.* TUM 342/7/91 A, 1991.

[22] K. Voss. *Interface as a Basic Concept for System Specification and Verification.* Concurrency and Nets, Springer Verlag 1987, pp 585-604.

[23] G. Winskel. *Petri Nets, Morphisms and Compositionality.* Advances in Petri Nets 85, LNCS 222, pp 453-477.

Bounded Self-Stabilizing Petri Nets

Ludmila Cherkasova
Hewlett-Packard Laboratories
1501 Page Mill Road, Bldg. 1U-14
P.O. Box 10490
Palo Alto, CA 94303, USA

Rodney R. Howell
Dept. of Computing and Information Sciences
Kansas State University
Manhattan, KS 66506, USA

Louis E. Rosier[†]
Dept. of Computer Sciences
The University of Texas at Austin
Austin, TX 78712, USA

ABSTRACT: We investigate the property of self-stabilization in bounded Petri nets. We give characterizations for both self-stabilizing bounded ordinary Petri nets (i.e., Petri nets without multiple arcs) and self-stabilizing bounded general Petri nets (i.e., Petri nets with multiple arcs). These characterizations allow us to determine the complexity of deciding self-stabilization for each of these classes. In particular, we show the self-stabilization problem to be PTIME-complete for bounded ordinary Petri nets and PSPACE-complete for bounded general Petri nets.

Keywords: Self-stabilization, bounded Petri nets, computational complexity.

[†]Louis Rosier passed away on May 6, 1991, before the final version of this paper was complete.

CONTENTS

0 Introduction

A system is said to be self-stabilizing if starting from any configuration the system is guaranteed to reach a "legal" configuration. The motivation behind this concept is that if, due to some unpredictable error, the system were to reach an "illegal" configuration, it would eventually correct itself, returning to some "legal" configuration. Thus, self-stabilizing systems are in some sense more robust than those that are not self-stabilizing, due to their inherent fault-tolerant nature. Self-stabilization has gained much attention in computer science research, particularly in the area of fault-tolerant distributed computing; see, e.g., [Dij73, Dij74, Lam86, BYC88, BP89, BGW89, Mul89, Gou90, GHR90].

In [GHR90], a number of curious properties were shown regarding simulations of self-stabilizing systems. For example, it was shown that there can be no self-stabilization-preserving simulation of vector addition systems with states (VASSs) by Petri nets.[1] This result is quite surprising, since most properties, such as deadlock freedom, liveness, and fair nontermination, can be preserved by simulations in either direction (see, e.g., [HP79]). The proof of this result relies on a rather interesting property of self-stabilizing Petri nets also shown in [GHR90]: if a self-stabilizing Petri net has an infinite computation, then all places are simultaneously unbounded.

The fact that any unbounded self-stabilizing Petri net must be unbounded in all places simultaneously suggests that unbounded self-stabilizing Petri nets have rather unusual properties. Indeed,

[1] We should point out that the definition of self-stabilization used in [GHR90] is a somewhat restricted definition in which the "legal" states are defined to be those reachable from the initial marking. It is often the case in self-stabilizing systems that the set of legal states is exactly the set of reachable states; see, e.g., [Dij73]. In order to avoid problems in specifying the set of legal states, we adopt this definition in this paper. See [GHR90] for a more detailed discussion.

we are as yet unable to give a good characterization of unbounded self-stabilizing Petri nets. In fact, the best bounds we have been able to derive for deciding whether an arbitrary Petri net is self-stabilizing are an upper bound of Π_2 (the second level of the arithmetic hierarchy) and a lower bound of exponential space. As a contrast, it is not too difficult to show that the same problem for Turing machines with empty input is complete for Π_2. Such a wide disparity between the known upper and lower bounds suggests that there is much to be learned concerning the properties of self-stabilizing Petri nets.

In this paper, we restrict our attention to self-stabilizing bounded Petri nets. We also consider separately a proper subclass: self-stabilizing bounded ordinary Petri nets (self-stabilizing bounded Petri nets in which no multiple arcs are allowed). Normally, not much distinction is made between ordinary Petri nets and general Petri nets, since there is a straightforward simulation of general Petri nets by ordinary Petri nets; however, this simulation does not preserve self-stabilization. In fact, we show in this paper that self-stabilizing bounded ordinary Petri nets have a much simpler characterization and are much easier to recognize than self-stabilizing bounded general Petri nets. Specifically, we give for each of these classes a characterization that allows us to determine the complexity of deciding self-stabilization. Furthermore, our algorithms for deciding self-stabilization are such that they reject all unbounded Petri nets (along with those that are not self-stabilizing), so boundedness does not need to be decided first. This last fact is important, since the boundedness problem for Petri nets requires exponential space [Lip76, Rac78].

The characterization we give for self-stabilizing bounded ordinary Petri nets is a structural characterization; i.e., it is independent of the initial marking. Thus, self-stabilization is a structural property of bounded ordinary Petri nets. This fact is important because Petri nets that can be characterized in terms of structure are typically easier to analyze than those that cannot (see, e.g., [JLL77, HRY87, HR88, HRY89, HJR91]). Furthermore, our characterization gives a close relationship between self-stabilizing bounded ordinary Petri nets and structurally bounded Petri nets — a class that has already been studied extensively (see, e.g., [Sil85, Mur89]). We use our characterization to give a polynomial time algorithm for determining self-stabilization, then show the problem to be PTIME-complete with respect to logspace many-one reductions.

For bounded general Petri nets, we show that self-stabilization is not a structural property; i.e., it is dependent upon the initial marking. Thus, a structural characterization is clearly impossible for this class. Therefore, let us consider what type of characterization would be more useful than the definition. Somewhat informally, the definition of self-stabilization states that every firing sequence occurring from each marking must eventually reach some marking reachable from the initial marking. Notice that this definition involves a universal quantifier over an infinite set. On the other hand, we give a characterization consisting of two properties, one of which is structural (i.e., independent of the initial marking), and the other of which gives a finite set of markings that must be reachable. This characterization is clearly more useful than the definition; however, reachability analyses are typically very costly. In particular, even for bounded Petri nets, the reachability problem requires at least exponential space [Lip76]; furthermore no primitive recursive algorithm is known (cf. [May84, Kos82, Lam88]). To overcome this obstacle, we show that for Petri nets satisfying the structural part of our characterization, reachability can be decided in PSPACE. Using this fact, we show the problem of determining self-stabilization for bounded general Petri nets to be PSPACE-complete.

The remainder of this paper is organized as follows. In Section 2, we give the basic definitions and notation to be used throughout the paper. In Section 3, we present some elementary properties of self-stabilizing Petri nets. In Section 4, we give a characterization of self-stabilizing bounded ordinary Petri nets and show the problem of deciding whether a given bounded ordinary Petri net is self-stabilizing to be PTIME-complete. In Section 5, we give a characterization of self-stabilizing bounded general Petri nets and show that the problem of deciding self-stabilization for this class is PSPACE-complete. We conclude in Section 6 with a discussion of possible extensions to this work.

1 Basic definitions and notation

A net is a tuple: $N = (P, T, F, W)$, where

- P is a finite set of places,
- T is a finite set of transitions,
- $F \subseteq (P \times T) \cup (T \times P)$ is an incidence relation, and
- $W : F \to \mathbb{N} \backslash \{0\} = \{1, 2, 3, \ldots\}$ is an arc weight function.

Graphically, the places are represented by circles, the transitions by boxes or bars, the incidence relation F by arcs connecting places with transitions and transitions with places, and the arc weight function by the multiplicity of the arcs. A Petri net is a pair (N, M_0) where

- $N = (P, T, F, W)$ is a net, and
- $M_0 : P \to \mathbb{N} = \{0, 1, 2, \ldots\}$ is an initial marking.

$\mathbf{0}$ will denote the zero marking; i.e., $\mathbf{0}(p) = 0$ for all $p \in P$. Graphically, the initial marking is represented by tokens (dots) inside the circles. A Petri net with multiplicity of arcs all equal to 1 is called an ordinary Petri net. We will use the term general Petri net to explicitly indicate that multiple arcs are allowed.

On the basis of incidence relation F and weight function W, we define an incidence function $F : (P \times T) \cup (T \times P) \rightarrow \mathbf{N}$ as follows:

$$F(x,y) = \begin{cases} n & \text{if } xFy \wedge (W(x,y) = n) \\ 0 & \text{if } \neg(xFy). \end{cases}$$

For any net element x ($x \in P \cup T$) we will denote:

- ${}^{\bullet}x = \{y \mid yFx\}$ — the set of its input elements,
- $x^{\bullet} = \{y \mid xFy\}$ — the set of its output elements.

A transition t is enabled in the net N at marking M (written as $M[t\rangle$) iff $\forall p \in {}^{\bullet}t : M(p) \geq F(p,t)$. For ordinary Petri nets this condition means that each input place of transition t has at least one token inside, i.e., a non-zero marking. If a transition t is enabled at M, then t may occur (or can fire), changing the marking M to the marking M' by the following rule:

$$\forall p \in P : M'(p) = M(p) - F(p,t) + F(t,p);$$

we then write: $M[t\rangle M'$. A marking M' is reachable from the marking M in the net N iff there exists a sequence of transitions (firing sequence) $\tau = t_1 t_2 \ldots t_k$ and a sequence of markings $M_1, \ldots, M_{k-1}$ such that

$$M[t_1\rangle M_1[t_2\rangle M_2 \ldots [t_k\rangle M'.$$

In this case, we will write: $M[\tau\rangle M'$, or $M[\ \rangle M'$ if τ is not essential. To simply indicate that τ can fire from M, we will write $M[\tau\rangle$. If $\tau = t_1 t_2 ...$ is an infinite firing sequence and there exists an infinite sequence of markings $M_1, M_2, ...$ such that

$$M[t_1\rangle M_1[t_2\rangle M_2 ...,$$

then we also write $M[\tau\rangle$. The reachability set of (N, M_0), denoted $R(N, M_0)$, is the set $\{M \mid M_0[\ \rangle M\}$, or the set of all its reachable markings. For a Petri net (N, M_0) we define the reachability tree $Tr(N, M_0)$ as follows. The root of the tree is labeled M_0. Let v be any node of the tree, and let the label of v be some marking M. Suppose k different transitions are enabled at M. Then v has k children, one for each transition enabled at M, and each child is labeled by the marking resulting from the firing of the respective transition at M. For the Petri net (N_1, M_{01}) shown in Figure 1, its reachability tree is represented in Figure 2.

A marking M is called a dead marking for a net N iff there are no enabled transitions in (N, M). We will denote by $R_d(N)$ the set of all dead markings for a net N, and by $R_d(N, M_0)$ the set of all dead markings in $R(N, M_0)$. For example, the markings $M_d^1 = (2,0,0,1,0), M_d^3 = (1,0,0,1,1)$ and $M_d^5 = (0,0,0,1,2)$ (see reachability tree in Figure 2) are dead markings for the net (N_1, M_{01})

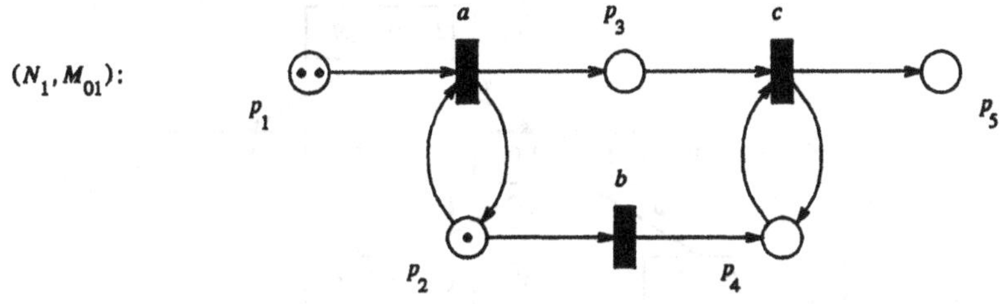

Figure 1.

shown in Figure 1. Moreover, $R_d(N_1, M_{01}) = \{M_d^1, M_d^3, M_d^5\}$. The set of all dead markings (i.e., independent of the initial marking) for the net N_1 shown in Figure 1 is given by:

$$R_d(N_1) = \{(k_1, 0, 0, k_2, k_3) \mid k_1, k_2, k_3 \geq 0\} \cup \{(k_1, 0, k_2, 0, k_3) \mid k_1, k_2, k_3 \geq 0\}.$$

Let τ be a firing sequence, and let $|\tau|$ denote its length. If τ is infinite then $|\tau| = \infty$. Let us consider the markings which are reachable in the net (N, M_0) via firing sequences τ with $|\tau| = k$ together with dead markings reachable with $|\tau| \leq k$. More precisely, let

$$\begin{aligned} R^k(N, M_0) &= \{M \mid (M_0[\tau\rangle M) \wedge (|\tau| = k)\} \cup \\ &\quad \{M \mid (M_0[\tau\rangle M) \wedge (M \in R_d(N, M_0)) \wedge (|\tau| \leq k)\} \end{aligned}$$

We will call $R^k(N, M_0)$ the reachability set of level k for (N, M_0). The utility of this definition will become apparent when we introduce self-stabilizing Petri nets.

In graphical representation, the markings from $R^k(N, M_0)$ are exactly the nodes in the reachability tree for (N, M_0) at level k (i.e., nodes which are reachable by paths with length equal to k), plus all leaves above level k (i.e., dead markings which are reachable by paths with length no more than k). For example, for Petri net (N_1, M_{01}) shown in Figure 1 with reachability tree shown in Figure 2 its reachability sets of levels 2 and 4 are the following:

$$R^2(N_1, M_{01}) = \{M_1^2, M_2^2, M_d^1\}, \qquad R^4(N_1, M_{01}) = \{M_1^4, M_d^3, M_d^1\}.$$

Let us define $R^{\geq k}(N, M_0) = \{M' \mid (M[\tau\rangle M') \wedge (M \in R^k(N, M_0))\}$. In graphical representation, the markings from $R^{\geq k}(N, M_0)$ are the nodes in the reachability tree for (N, M_0) at or below level k (i.e., the nodes reachable from the root by paths with length $\geq k$; the root is considered to be the topmost node), plus all leaves. For example, for Petri net (N_1, M_{01}) in Figure 1 with reachability tree in Figure 2, its reachability trees of level 2 and 4 are presented in Figure 3a, b. Let us denote by $R^{<k}(N, M_0) = \{M \mid (M_0[\tau\rangle M) \wedge (M \notin R_d(N, M_0)) \wedge |\tau| < k\}$; i.e., the markings

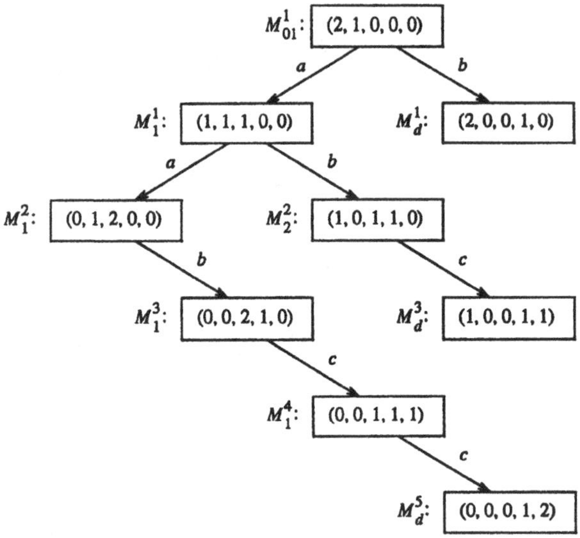

Figure 2.

of $R^{<k}(N, M_0)$ belonging to the reachability tree strictly above level k, minus all leaves. It is clear that $R(N, M_0) = R^{<k}(N, M_0) \cup R^{\geq k}(N, M_0)$.

Petri net (N_1, M_{01}) shown in Figure 1 has a finite set of finite firing sequences (i.e., it defines finite behavior). As a result, the reachability set and reachability tree are finite. For Petri net (N_2, M_{02}) shown in Figure 4a the reachability set $R(N_2, M_{02})$ is finite: $R(N_2, M_{02}) = \{(1,0),(0,1)\}$, but its reachability tree (shown in Figure 4b) is infinite (because of the infinite firing sequence $\tau = aa\ldots a\ldots$). For Petri net (N_3, M_{03}) shown in Figure 5a, both the reachability set and the reachability tree (shown in Figure 5b) are infinite due to the fact that place p_3 is unbounded (i.e., can get arbitrarily many tokens as a marking). A place $p \in P$ in Petri net (N, M_0) is bounded iff $(\exists k \in \mathbf{N})(\forall M \in R(N, M_0)): \quad M(p) \leq k$. Otherwise, place p is called unbounded. A Petri net is bounded iff all its places are bounded.

It is clear that a bounded Petri net has a finite reachability set, and conversely, if a Petri net is unbounded, then its reachability set is infinite. It is well-known that the boundedness problem for Petri nets is decidable [KM69]; in fact, the problem is complete for DSPACE($2^{poly(n)}$) with respect to logspace many-one reductions [Lip76, Rac78] (see also [HR87]).

The set $\mathcal{L}(N, M_0) = \{\tau \in T^* \mid M_0[\tau\rangle\}$ is called the free language of Petri net (N, M_0), or the set of all its firing sequences.

a) $R^{\geq 2}(N_1, M_{01})$

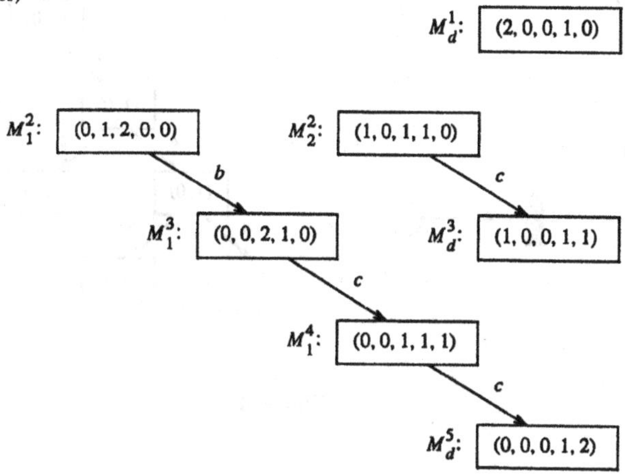

b) $R^{\geq 4}(N_1, M_{01})$

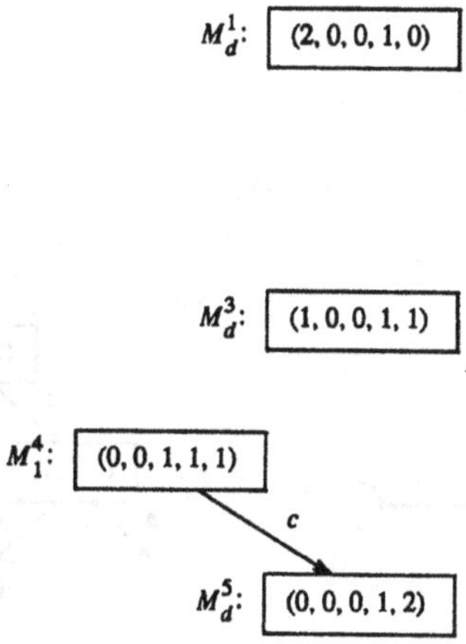

Figure 3.

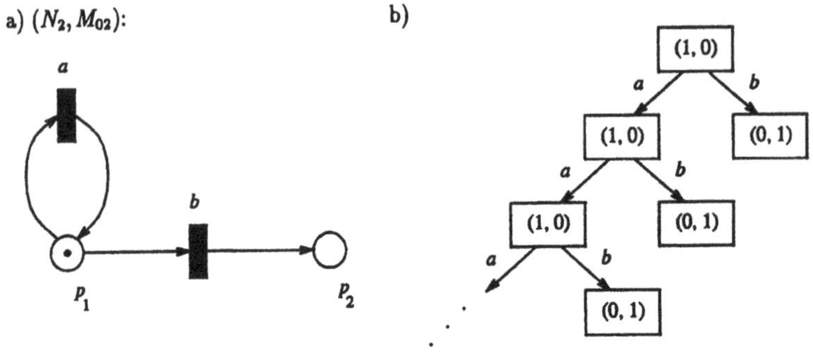

Figure 4.

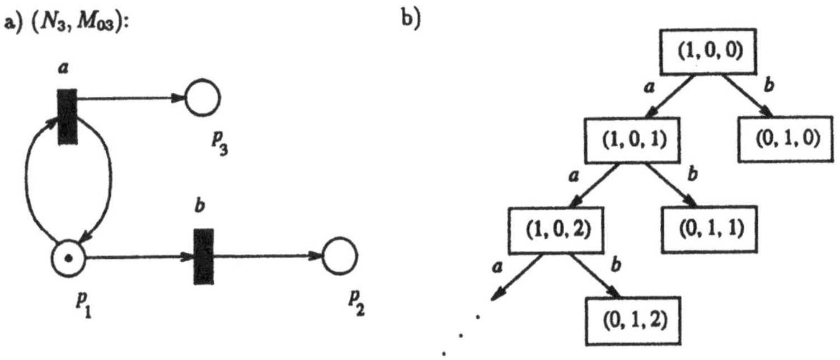

Figure 5.

2 Self-stabilizing Petri nets: definition and elementary properties

In this section, we introduce self-stabilizing Petri nets and give some of their elementary properties. We then use these properties to motivate the study of self-stabilizing bounded Petri nets.

A Petri net (N, M_0) is self-stabilizing (abbreviation: *ss*) iff $\forall M \exists k : R^k(N, M) \subseteq R(N, M_0)$. This definition is equivalent to the following: $\forall M\ \exists k : R^{\geq k}(N, M) \subseteq R(N, M_0)$. Thus, if we consider the net N with an arbitrary initial marking M, then sooner or later all the firing sequences of the net N will reach a marking in the reachability set of (N, M_0). In this sense, the behavior of the net N under an arbitrary initial marking will always stabilize to the behavior of the net N with initial marking M_0. The self-stabilization problem is to determine, for a given Petri net (N, M_0), whether (N, M_0) is self-stabilizing. The Petri nets shown in Figure 6a, b are self-stabilizing, whereas the Petri nets in Figures 1, 4a, 5a are not *ss*. The following lemma holds for self-stabilizing systems in general.

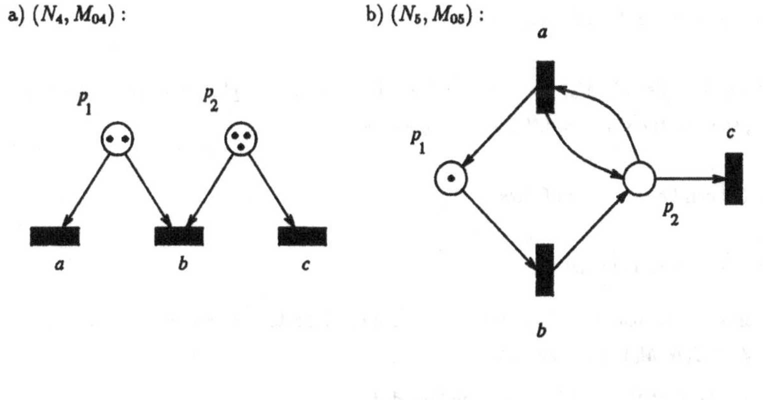

Figure 6.

Lemma 3.1 (from [GHR90]): If (N, M_0) is a *ss* Petri net then $R_d(N) \subseteq R(N, M_0)$; i.e., all dead markings for N are reachable in (N, M_0).

Proof. Since (N, M_0) is a *ss* Petri net, then $\forall M \exists k : R^{\geq k}(N, M) \subseteq R(N, M_0)$. By definition, $R^{\geq k}(N, M) = \{M' \mid (M[\tau\rangle M') \wedge |\tau| \geq k\} \cup R_d(N, M)$. Hence, $\forall M : R_d(N, M) \subseteq R(N, M_0)$. Thus $R_d(N) \subseteq R(N, M_0)$. ■

The following lemma gives an interesting property of self-stabilizing Petri nets with infinite firing sequences.

Lemma 3.2 (from [GHR90]): Let (N, M_0) be a *ss* Petri net. If there exists an infinite sequence τ in (N, M_0) (i.e., $\tau \in \mathcal{L}(N, M_0)$) then all places of the net (N, M_0) are unbounded.

Proof. Let us suppose, to the contrary, that some place p in (N, M_0) is bounded. By definition, $\exists k \in \mathrm{N}(\forall M \in R(N, M_0) : M(p) < k)$. Let us consider the same net N with the following initial marking $M_0 + K$, where

$$K(p_i) = \begin{cases} k & \text{if } p_i = p \\ 0 & \text{otherwise.} \end{cases}$$

Now let us compare the markings reachable in (N, M_0) and $(N, M_0 + K)$ through the same infinite firing sequence $\tau = t_1 t_2 t_3 \ldots t_n \ldots$. (By the monotonicity property of Petri nets, if $\tau \in \mathcal{L}(N, M_0)$, then $\forall M \geq M_0 : \tau \in \mathcal{L}(N, M)$). So, if $M_0[t_1\rangle M_1[t_2\rangle M_2 \ldots [t_n\rangle M_n \ldots$, then $(M_0 + K)[t_1\rangle(M_1 + K)[t_2\rangle(M_2 + K)\ldots[t_n\rangle(M_n + K)\ldots$. For any marking $M_i + K$ in $(N, M_0 + K)$, place p has at least k tokens. However, $\forall M \in R(N, M_0) : M(p) < k$. Hence $\neg\exists n : R^n(N, M_0 + K) \subseteq R(N, M_0)$. This contradicts the lemma condition that (N, M_0) is a *ss* Petri net; hence the initial assumption is false, and all the places of the net (N, M_0) are unbounded. ■

Since the existence of one unbounded place immediately implies the existence of an infinite firing sequence, we have the following corollary.

Corollary 3.3: Let (N, M_0) be a *ss* Petri net. If there exists a place p in (N, M_0) which is unbounded, then all the places of (N, M_0) are unbounded.

Lemma 3.2 can be restated as follows:

If (N, M_0) is a *ss* Petri net then

(1) either all its places are bounded and there are no infinite firing sequences in it, i.e., $\forall \tau \in \mathcal{L}(N, M_0) : |\tau| < \infty$, or

(2) all places of the net (N, M_0) are unbounded.

The remainder of the paper is devoted to investigation of the first case: *ss* bounded Petri nets. We will consider separately the properties of *ss* bounded ordinary Petri nets and *ss* bounded general Petri nets. First, however, we give an important result that holds for all *ss* bounded Petri nets.

Lemma 3.4: Let (N, M_0) be a *ss* bounded Petri net. Then for arbitrary marking M,

(1) (N, M) is bounded, and

(2) $\forall \tau \in \mathcal{L}(N, M) : |\tau| < \infty$.

Proof. Since (N, M_0) is a bounded Petri net, the reachability set $R(N, M_0)$ is finite. Since (N, M_0) is a *ss* Petri net, $\forall M \exists k : R^{\geq k}(N, M) \subseteq R(N, M_0)$. Hence for arbitrary marking M the reachability set $R(N, M)$ is finite. Therefore for arbitrary marking M the net (N, M) is bounded. By using an argument similar to the proof of Lemma 3.2, we can now conclude that $\forall \tau \in \mathcal{L}(N, M) : |\tau| < \infty$. ■

Part (1) of Lemma 3.4 states that any *ss* bounded Petri net is structurally bounded (see, e.g., [Sil85, Mur89]). Part (2) gives a stronger property, which is important enough to give a name. We say that a net N is structurally terminating if for every marking M, $\forall \tau \in \mathcal{L}(N, M) : |\tau| < \infty$. Thus, every *ss* bounded Petri net is structurally terminating.

3 A characterization of self-stabilizing bounded ordinary Petri nets

In this section, we examine self-stabilizing bounded ordinary Petri nets. We first characterize the set by showing that a bounded ordinary Petri net is *ss* iff it is structurally terminating and for every place there is a transition whose set of input places is exactly that place. Thus, we show self-stabilization to be a structural property of bounded ordinary Petri nets, independent of their initial marking (recall from Lemma 3.4 that bounded *ss* Petri nets must be structurally bounded). We then use our characterization to give a polynomial-time algorithm for deciding self-stabilization for bounded ordinary Petri nets. We conclude the section by showing this problem to be PTIME-complete with respect to logspace many-one reductions.

Lemma 4.1: Let (N, M_0) be a *ss* bounded ordinary Petri net. Then $R_d(N) = R_d(N, M_0) = \{0\}$.

Proof. First, let us notice that if $M \in R_d(N)$ then $\forall \tilde{M} : \tilde{M} \leq M$ we have $\tilde{M} \in R_d(N)$. Since (N, M_0) is a *ss* bounded Petri net, there are no infinite firing sequences in it (see Lemma 3.2). Hence, the reachability tree for (N, M_0) is finite, and the set of dead markings for (N, M_0) is not empty. Therefore, $0 \in R_d(N)$. Let us suppose that there exists a dead marking M of N which is not 0; i.e., $M \in R_d(N)$ and $\exists \tilde{p} \in P : M(\tilde{p}) = k > 0$. Since (N, M_0) is bounded, the place $\tilde{p}$ is bounded, and $\exists \tilde{k} \forall \tilde{M} \in R(N, M_0) : \tilde{M}(\tilde{p}) < \tilde{k}$. Let us consider the net N with the following marking $M + \tilde{K}$, where

$$\tilde{K}(p_i) = \begin{cases} \tilde{k} \text{ if } p_i = \tilde{p}, \\ 0 \text{ otherwise.} \end{cases}$$

Note that for each place p_i, $M(p_i) = 0$ iff $(M + \tilde{K})(p_i) = 0$, so since (N, M_0) is an ordinary Petri net, any transition enabled at $M + \tilde{K}$ is also enabled at M. Hence, $M + \tilde{K}$ is also a dead marking for N. But $M + \tilde{K} \notin R(N, M_0)$. Then by Lemma 3.1, (N, M_0) is not a *ss* Petri net — a contradiction.

Hence, $R_d(N) = R_d(N, M_0) = \{\mathbf{0}\}$. ∎

Corollary 4.2: Let (N, M_0) be a bounded ordinary Petri net. (N, M_0) is *ss* iff

(1) N is structurally terminating; and

(2) $R_d(N) = \{\mathbf{0}\}$.

Proof.

$\Rightarrow$

Immediately follows from Lemma 3.4 and Lemma 4.1.

$\Leftarrow$

Since for any marking M there are no infinite firing sequences in (N, M), i.e., $\forall \tau \in \mathcal{L}(N, M) : |\tau| < \infty$, it means that reachability tree for any (N, M) is finite. Since $R_d(N) = \{\mathbf{0}\}$, $\forall M : R_d(N, M) = \{\mathbf{0}\}$; i.e., all the leaves in the reachability tree for any (N, M) are the $\mathbf{0}$ marking. Thus, at least at the last level all the reachability trees are the same. Hence, (N, M_0) is a *ss* Petri net. ∎

Since the conditions of Corollary 4.2 are both independent of the initial marking, we also have the following corollary.

Corollary 4.3: Let (N, M_0) be a *ss* bounded ordinary Petri net. Then for any marking M the net (N, M) is *ss*.

In what follows, we will show how to test the conditions of Corollary 4.2 in polynomial time. Condition (1) can be tested by determining the existence of an integer solution to a system of homogeneous linear inequalities, which may be done using (rational) linear programming techniques. In order to give an efficient means of testing condition (2), we now show that if condition (1) holds, then condition (2) is equivalent to a simple syntactic property of the net.

Lemma 4.4: Let N be a structurally terminating ordinary net. Then $R_d(N) = \{\mathbf{0}\}$ iff for each net place p there exists a transition t such that ${}^{\bullet}t = \{p\}$.

Proof.

$\Leftarrow$

Since N is structurally terminating, there cannot be any transition enabled at $\mathbf{0}$. On the other hand, if some place p has a nonzero marking, then the transition t such that ${}^{\bullet}t = \{p\}$ is enabled. Therefore, $R_d(N) = \{\mathbf{0}\}$.

$\Rightarrow$

Suppose, to the contrary, that $R_d(N) = \{0\}$ and for some place $\tilde{p}$ there is no transition t such that ${}^{\cdot}t = \{\tilde{p}\}$; i.e., $(\forall t \in \tilde{p}^{\cdot})(\exists p \neq \tilde{p}) : p \in {}^{\cdot}t$. Let us consider the following marking $\tilde{M}$:

$$\tilde{M}(p_i) = \begin{cases} 1 & \text{if } p_i = \tilde{p} \\ 0 & \text{if } p_i \neq \tilde{p} \end{cases}$$

The marking $\tilde{M}$ is a dead marking for the net N, i.e., $\tilde{M} \in R_d(N)$. However, $\tilde{M} \neq 0$ — a contradiction. ∎

The following theorem now follows immediately from Corollary 4.2 and Lemma 4.4.

Theorem 4.5: Let (N, M_0) be a bounded ordinary Petri net. (N, M_0) is *ss* iff

(1) N is structurally terminating, and

(2) $\forall p \in P \exists t \in T : {}^{\cdot}t = \{p\}$.

We can use Theorem 4.5 to show that the self-stabilization problem for bounded ordinary Petri nets is solvable in polynomial time. First, we need to introduce some notation. Let $N = (P, T, F, W)$ be a net. The incidence matrix C for the net N is defined as $C(p,t) = F(t,p) - F(p,t)$. For example, the net N_5 in Figure 6b is characterized by the following incidence matrix:

p \ t	a	b	c
p_1	1	−1	0
p_2	0	1	−1

Theorem 4.6: The self-stabilization problem for bounded ordinary Petri nets is solvable in polynomial time.

Proof. We will show that conditions (1) and (2) from Theorem 4.5 can be verified in polynomial time. Clearly, (2) can be verified in polynomial time. We verify (1) as follows. Let N be an arbitrary bounded ordinary net, and let C be the incidence matrix of N. It is easily seen that N is structurally terminating iff there is no nonnegative, nonzero integer solution to the inequality $Cx \geq 0$. We first note that any rational solution to this inequality can be transformed into an integer solution by multiplying by a common denominator of the components of the solution vector. By using either Khachian's algorithm [Kha79] or Karmarkar's algorithm [Kar84] to determine whether there is a nonnegative, nonzero solution to the above inequality, we can therefore decide self-stabilization in polynomial time. ∎

Note that if the algorithm in the above proof is given an unbounded ordinary Petri net, it will be rejected because it is not structurally terminating; thus, given any ordinary Petri net, the algorithm will determine, in polynomial time, whether the Petri net is both bounded and self-stabilizing. We also note that as an alternative algorithm, we could first convert the net N into a net N' that is structurally bounded iff N is structurally terminating; Silva [Sil85] gives a polynomial-time algorithm for deciding whether a net is structurally bounded.

We conclude this section by showing the self-stabilization problem for bounded ordinary Petri nets to be PTIME-complete. In order to show this problem to be PTIME-hard, we use a reduction from the complement of the path system problem, which is known to be PTIME-complete [JL77]. A path system is a 4-tuple $P = (X, R, S, T)$, where X is a finite set of nodes, $S(\subseteq X)$ is the set of starting nodes, $T(\subseteq X)$ is the set of terminal nodes, and $R(\subseteq X \times X \times X)$ is the set of rules. A sequence of rules ρ is said to be a path if

(1) $\rho = \epsilon$; or

(2) $\rho = \rho'(x, y, z)$, where ρ' is a path such that for every $w \in \{y, z\} \backslash T$, some rule (w, y', z') occurs in ρ'.

ρ is said to admit $x \in X$ if either $x \in T$ or x occurs in some rule in ρ. A node x is said to be admissible if there is some path admitting x. We say that P has a solution if there is an admissible node in S.

Theorem 4.7: The self-stabilization problem for bounded ordinary Petri nets is complete for PTIME with respect to logspace many-one reductions.

Proof. We will show that the complement of the path system problem logspace reduces to the self-stabilization problem for bounded ordinary Petri nets; the theorem will then follow from Theorem 4.6. Let $P = (X, R, S, T)$ be an arbitrary path system. Without loss of generality, we assume $S \cap T = \emptyset$. We will construct a structurally bounded net N such that conditions (1) and (2) of Theorem 4.5 hold iff P does not have a solution. (More precisely, condition (2) will always hold, and condition (1) will hold iff P does not have a solution). Let $X = \{x_1, x_2, ..., x_n\}$. We will construct N to consist of n "levels," each of which will contain places representing the nodes in X. A somewhat informal flow of control for N is shown in Figure 7a. Intuitively, when a new node is admitted, control passes to the next level. Once a node in S is admitted, control will be allowed to return to Level 1. Thus, N will have a structural loop iff P has a solution.

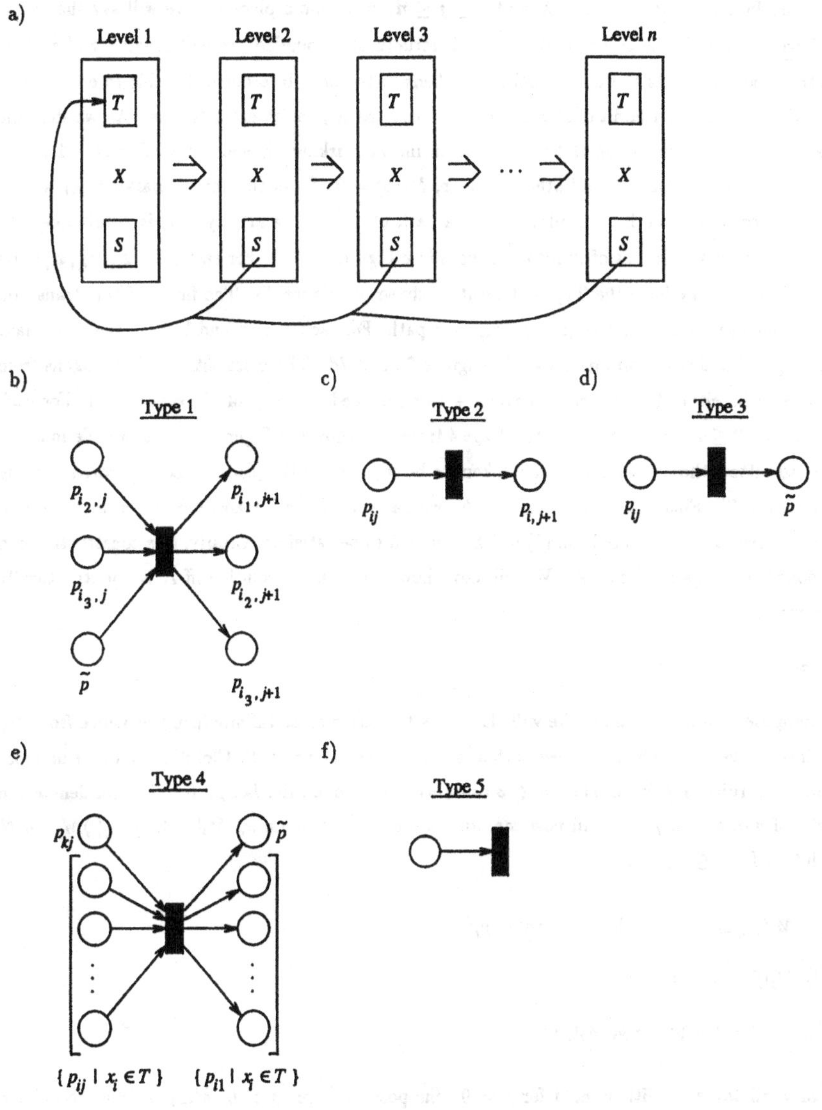
a)
Level 1
Level 2
Level 3
Level n
T
X
S
b)
Type 1
$p_{i_2,j}$
$p_{i_3,j}$
$\tilde{p}$
$p_{i_1,j+1}$
$p_{i_2,j+1}$
$p_{i_3,j+1}$
c)
Type 2
p_{ij}
$p_{i,j+1}$
d)
Type 3
p_{ij}
$\tilde{p}$
e)
Type 4
p_{kj}
$\tilde{p}$
$\{p_{ij} \mid x_i \in T\}$
$\{p_{i1} \mid x_i \in T\}$
f)
Type 5

Figure 7.

More formally, for each $x_i \in X$ and $1 \leq j \leq n$, we define a place p_{ij}; we will say that p_{ij} is at Level j. In order to assure that the net is structurally bounded, we will construct N so that no transition increases the total number of tokens in the net. In order to be able to enforce this behavior, we need an additional place $\tilde{p}$ to be used as a pool of extra tokens. As we describe the transitions, it will be helpful to imagine an initial marking M_0 such that $M_0(p_{i1}) = 1$ for all $x_i \in T$, $M_0(\tilde{p}) = n$, and for all other places p, $M_0(p) = 0$. From this initial marking, p_{ij} will be able to receive a token if x_i is admitted by a path of length j, and only if x_i is admissible. We will classify the transitions of N into five types (see Figures 7b–7f). For each rule $(x_{i_1}, x_{i_2}, x_{i_3})$ and $1 \leq j \leq n-1$, we have the Type 1 transition shown in Figure 7b. The firing of this transition corresponds to the inclusion of $(x_{i_1}, x_{i_2}, x_{i_3})$ in a path. For each $x_i \in X$ and $1 \leq j \leq n-1$, we have the Types 2 and 3 transitions shown in Figures 7c and 7d. These transitions allow tokens from Level j to be either transferred to Level $j+1$ or returned to the pool of extra tokens. For each $x_k \in S$ and $2 \leq j \leq n-1$, we have the Type 4 transition shown in Figure 7e. Once a node in S has been admitted, these transitions allow tokens to be returned to the places in Level 1 corresponding to nodes in T. Finally, for each place in N, we have the Type 5 transition shown in Figure 7f. These transitions allow condition (2) of Theorem 4.5 to be satisfied. Clearly, this construction can be done using logarithmic space. We will now show that P has a solution iff N is not structurally terminating.

$\Rightarrow$

Suppose P has a solution. We will show how to construct an infinite firing sequence from M_0 (defined above). Let ρ be a shortest path admitting some node $x_k \in S$. Clearly, ρ contains no more than $n-1$ rules, and since $S \cap T = \emptyset$, ρ contains at least one rule. Let ρ_j, $0 \leq j \leq |\rho|$, denote the prefix of ρ of length j. We will now construct a sequence of markings $M_0[\ \rangle M_1[\ \rangle \cdots [\ \rangle M_{|\rho|}$ of N such that for $0 \leq j \leq |\rho|$:

(1) $M_j(p_{i,j+1}) = 1$ if x_i is admitted by ρ_j;

(2) $M_j(\tilde{p}) = n - j$; and

(3) for all other places p, $M_j(p) = 0$.

Clearly, all three conditions hold for $j = 0$. Suppose for some $j > 0$, M_{j-1} satisfies the above conditions. Let $(x_{i_1}, x_{i_2}, x_{i_3})$ be the jth rule in ρ. Then x_{i_2} and x_{i_3} are admitted by ρ_{j-1}. Therefore, from condition (1), $M_{j-1}(p_{i_2,j}) = M_{j-1}(p_{i_3,j}) = 1$. We can therefore fire a Type 1 transition removing the tokens from these places and placing tokens on $p_{i_1,j+1}$, $p_{i_2,j+1}$, and $p_{i_3,j+1}$. Note that this firing leaves $n-j$ tokens on $\tilde{p}$, and the places that now need tokens (to produce M_j) are exactly those place $p_{i,j+1}$ such that p_{ij} has a token. Therefore, by firing Type 2 transitions, we can reach M_j. Proceeding thus, we eventually arrive at $M_{|\rho|}$. In $M_{|\rho|}$, from condition (1), there is a token on $p_{k,|\rho|+1}$. Therefore, we may fire Types 3 and 4 transitions to return to M_0. We therefore have $M_0[\tau\rangle M_0$ for a nonempty firing sequence τ, so N is not structurally terminating.

$\Leftarrow$

Suppose N is not structurally terminating; i.e., there is a marking at which an infinite firing sequence can fire. From [KM69], there must exist markings M_1 and M_2 and a nonempty firing sequence τ such that $M_1[\tau\rangle M_2$ and $M_1 \leq M_2$. Since no transition in N increases the number of tokens in the net, $M_1 = M_2$, and there can be no Type 5 transitions in τ. Since $M_1 = M_2$, for every transition $t \in \tau$ and every place p, if $p \in {}^{\cdot}t$, there must be a transition $t' \in \tau$ with $p \in t'^{\cdot}$. Notice that all transitions of Types 1–4 have at least one input place other than $\tilde{p}$. Let j_0 be the lowest level such that some transition in τ has an input place in Level j_0. Then in τ, only Type 4 transitions can have output places Level j_0 (i.e., $j_0 = 1$). We conclude that τ must contain a Type 4 transition. This transition has as an input place p_{kj}, where $x_k \in S$. We will now show by induction on j that there is a transition in τ with p_{ij} as an input place only if x_i is admissible; it will then follow that x_k is admissible, and, hence, P has a solution. For $j = 1$, the only places p_{ij} that are output places are those such that $x_i \in T$; therefore, if a transition in τ has p_{i1} as an input place, x_i is admissible. We now inductively assume that for some $j > 1$, if there is a transition in τ with $p_{i,j-1}$ as an input place, then x_i is admissible. Suppose there is some transition t_1 in τ with $p_{ij} \in {}^{\cdot}t_1$. Then there must be some transition t_2 in τ with $p_{ij} \in t_2^{\cdot}$. Since $j > 1$, t_2 must be either of Type 1 or Type 2. Suppose t_2 is of Type 2. Then $p_{i,j-1} \in {}^{\cdot}t_2$, and from the induction hypothesis, x_i is admissible. On the other hand, suppose t_2 is of Type 1. Then $\{p_{i_2,j-1}, p_{i_3,j-1}\} \subseteq {}^{\cdot}t_2$, and $\{p_{i_1,j}, p_{i_2,j}, p_{i_3,j}\} = t_2^{\cdot}$, where $(x_{i_1}, x_{i_2}, x_{i_3}) \in R$ and $x_i \in \{x_{i_1}, x_{i_2}, x_{i_3}\}$. From the induction hypothesis, both x_{i_2} and x_{i_3} are admissible, so x_{i_1} is also admissible. Therefore, x_i is admissible. This completes the induction and the proof that P has a solution.

We have shown that P has a solution iff N is not structurally terminating. From Theorem 4.5, we now conclude that $(N, \mathbf{0})$ is *ss* iff P does not have a solution. ∎

4 A characterization of self-stabilizing bounded general Petri nets

In this section, we examine self-stabilizing bounded general Petri nets. We first demonstrate that the characterization given for bounded ordinary Petri nets no longer holds, and that self-stabilization is not even a structural property when we allow multiple arcs. We then characterize this more general class by showing that a bounded Petri net is *ss* iff it is structurally terminating and every dead marking is reachable. We conclude by showing the self-stabilization problem for bounded general Petri nets to be PSPACE-complete; thus, allowing multiple arcs increases the complexity of the problem from PTIME to PSPACE, assuming these two complexity classes are not identical.

If we consider bounded general Petri nets, then Lemma 4.1, Corollary 4.2, and Theorem 4.5 no longer hold. For example, the net (N_7, M_{07}) in Figure 8a is *ss*, but $R_d(N_7) = R_d(N_7, M_{07}) = \{\mathbf{0}, (0,1), (0,2)\} \neq \{\mathbf{0}\}$. For the net (N_7, M'_{07}) in Figure 8b, the conditions of Theorem 4.5 hold, but (N_7, M'_{07}) is not *ss*. In particular, $R_d(N_7, M'_{07}) = \{\mathbf{0}, (0,1)\} \not\supseteq R_d(N_7)$; i.e., not all dead markings for N_7 are reachable in (N_7, M'_{07}). Thus, we can see that the conditions of Theorem 4.5 are not sufficient to guarantee self-stabilization for bounded general Petri nets; however, as we show in the lemma and theorem below, both conditions are still necessary. Furthermore, Figure 8 illustrates that self-stabilization for bounded general Petri nets is not a structural property; rather, it depends on the initial marking.

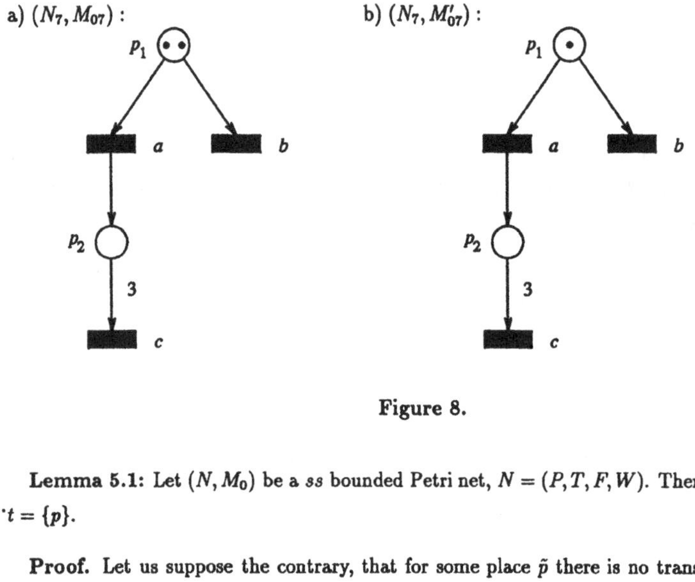

Figure 8.

Lemma 5.1: Let (N, M_0) be a *ss* bounded Petri net, $N = (P, T, F, W)$. Then $\forall p \in P\ \exists t \in T :$ ${}^\bullet t = \{p\}$.

Proof. Let us suppose the contrary, that for some place $\tilde{p}$ there is no transition t such that ${}^\bullet t = \{\tilde{p}\}$, i.e., $\forall t \in \tilde{p}^\bullet\ \exists p \neq \tilde{p} : p \in {}^\bullet t$. Let k be such that $\forall M \in R(N, M_0) :\ \ M(\tilde{p}) < k$. Let us consider the following marking $\tilde{M}$.

$$\tilde{M}(p_i) = \begin{cases} k & \text{if } p_i = \tilde{p} \\ 0 & \text{if } p_i \neq \tilde{p} \end{cases}$$

The marking $\tilde{M}$ is a dead marking for the net N, i.e., $\tilde{M} \in R_d(N)$. However, $\tilde{M} \notin R(N, M_0)$; this contradicts Lemma 3.1. ∎

We now give a characterization for *ss* bounded general Petri nets.

Theorem 5.2: Let (N, M_0) be a bounded Petri net. (N, M_0) is *ss* iff

(1) N is structurally terminating, and

(2) $R_d(N) \subseteq R_d(N, M_0)$.

Proof.

$\Rightarrow$

Immediately follows from Lemma 3.1 and Lemma 3.4.

$\Leftarrow$

Let M be an arbitrary marking of N. Since N is structurally terminating, the Petri net (N, M) has no infinite firing sequences. Hence, the reachability tree for (N, M) is finite. The leaves in this tree are dead markings for the net N. But by condition (2), $R_d(N) \subseteq R_d(N, M_0)$. Hence, to satisfy the *ss* property:

$$\forall M \exists k \ : \ R^k(N, M) \subseteq R(N, M_0)$$

we can choose k which defines the last level in the reachability tree. ■

Condition (1) of Theorem 5.2 may be tested in polynomial time as in Theorem 4.6 (that algorithm works for arbitrary nets). However, condition (2) appears to require a reachability analysis, and therefore seems to be much more difficult to decide. Recall that even for bounded Petri nets, the reachability problem requires at least exponential space [Lip76]; in fact, there is no primitive recursive algorithm known for the problem (cf. [May84, Kos82, Lam88]). On the other hand, from Theorem 5.2, we may restrict our attention to structurally terminating Petri nets. In what follows, we will show that if the necessary condition given in Lemma 5.1 holds, then each dead marking can be generated in PSPACE, and that if the Petri net is structurally terminating, reachability can be decided in PSPACE. From these two facts, we conclude that the self-stabilization problem for bounded Petri nets is in PSPACE. We then give strong evidence that this bound cannot be tightened: we show the problem to be PSPACE-complete.

Lemma 5.3: Let $N = (P, T, F, W)$ be a net such that $\forall p \in P \ \exists t \in T : {}^{\cdot}t = \{p\}$. Then $R_d(N) \subseteq \{M \mid M \leq M'\}$, where $M'(p) = \min\{W(p, t) \mid {}^{\cdot}t = \{p\}\} - 1$.

Proof. Let M_1 be any marking in $R_d(N)$. Suppose that for some place p, $M_1(p) > M'(p)$. Then there is a transition t such that ${}^{\cdot}t = \{p\}$ and $W(p, t) \leq M_1(p)$. Then t can fire at M_1 — a contradiction. ■

Corollary 5.4: Let $N = (P, T, F, W)$ be a net such that $\forall p \in P \ \exists t \in T : {}^{\cdot}t = \{p\}$. Then each marking in $R_d(N)$ can be generated and written down in turn using only a polynomial amount of space.

It was shown in [How91] that the reachability problem for structurally bounded Petri nets is PSPACE-complete. Since any structurally terminating net is clearly structurally bounded, the following lemma is immediate.

Lemma 5.5: Let (N, M_0) be a structurally terminating Petri net, and let M be a marking of N. It can be decided in PSPACE whether $M \in R(N, M_0)$.

From Corollary 5.4 and Lemma 5.5, we can test condition (2) of Theorem 5.2 in PSPACE. We therefore have the following Theorem.

Theorem 5.6: The self-stabilization problem for bounded Petri nets is in PSPACE.

Again, as in the previous section, if we are given an arbitrary Petri net without knowing whether it is bounded, we can decide in PSPACE whether it is both bounded and self-stabilizing: any unbounded Petri net will be rejected because it is not structurally terminating.

We conclude by showing the self-stabilization problem for bounded Petri nets to be PSPACE-complete.

Theorem 5.7: The self-stabilization problem for bounded Petri nets is PSPACE-complete with respect to logspace many-one reductions.

Proof. We will show that the LBA acceptance problem (see [Kar72]) logspace reduces to the self-stabilization problem for bounded general Petri nets; the theorem will then follow from Theorem 5.6. Let L be an arbitrary linearly bounded automaton (LBA), and w an arbitrary input. Jones, Landweber, and Lien [JLL77] show how to construct, using logarithmic space, a Petri net that simulates L on w. It is a straightforward matter to modify this construction such that the resulting Petri net (N_1, M_1) can reach some marking in which a designated place p_f has no tokens iff L accepts w. Furthermore, (N_1, M_1) can be constructed such that each move of L is simulated by the firing of one transition. Thus, if (N_1, M_1) can set the place p_f to 0, it can do so via a firing sequence of length at most $p(|L|)^{|w|} = 2^{|w|\lg(p(|L|))}$, where p is some polynomial independent of L and w, and lg denotes the base-2 logarithm. Using $|w|\lg(p(|L|)) + 1$ places and $|w|\lg(p(|L|))$ transitions, we can construct a Petri net (N_2, M_2), as shown in Figure 9, that can generate $2^{|w|\lg(p(|L|))}$ tokens. We then couple the two Petri nets as shown in Figure 9 so that the net is structurally terminating, and p_f can still be emptied iff L accepts w. Finally, we add additional transitions so that from any marking, all places except p_f can be emptied, and p_f may always be reduced to at most one token (see Figure 9). The resulting net (N, M_0) has two dead markings — $\mathbf{0}$ and the marking in which all places are 0 except p_f, which is 1. The latter of these markings is clearly in $R_d(N, M_0)$, and $\mathbf{0} \in R_d(N, M_0)$ iff p_f can be emptied iff L accepts w. Thus, from Theorem 5.2, (N, M_0) is self-stabilizing iff L accepts w. ■

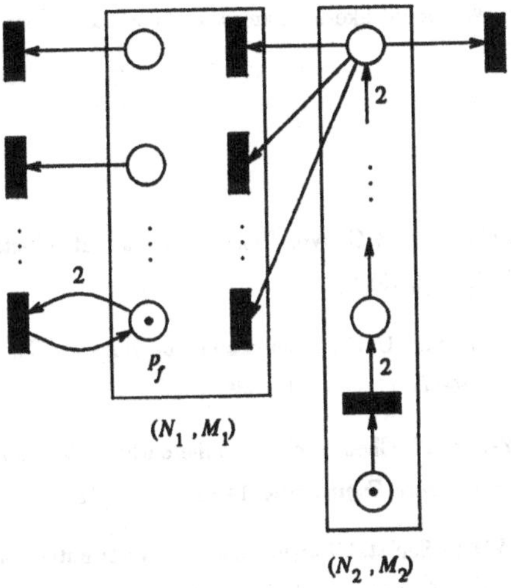

Figure 9.

Note that the above reduction also shows that the reachability problem for structurally terminating Petri nets is PSPACE-hard. Thus, from Lemma 5.5 and Theorem 5.7, we have the following corollary.

Corollary 5.8: The reachability problem for structurally terminating Petri nets is PSPACE-complete with respect to logspace many-one reductions.

5 Conclusion

We have given characterizations for self-stabilizing bounded Petri nets, both for ordinary Petri nets (no multiple arcs) and general Petri nets (multiple arcs allowed). Our characterizations have enabled us to give completeness results for the problems of determining whether a bounded ordinary Petri net is self-stabilizing and whether a bounded general Petri net is self-stabilizing. The complexities of these two problems were shown to be PTIME-complete and PSPACE-complete, respectively.

The precise complexities of the above problems for potentially unbounded Petri nets are unknown at this time; in fact, it is not currently known whether these problems are decidable, or even recursively enumerable. The best bounds we can achieve at the present time are an upper bound of Π_2 (the second level of the arithmetic hierarchy) and a lower bound of exponential space. Hence, we do not yet have as helpful a characterization for unbounded self-stabilizing Petri nets as we do for bounded self-stabilizing Petri nets.

Acknowledgments. We would like to thank the three anonymous referees for their helpful comments.

References

[BGW89] G. Brown, M. Gouda, and C. Wu. Token systems that self-stabilize. *IEEE Trans. on Computers*, 38:845–852, 1989.

[BP89] J. Burns and J. Pachl. Uniform self-stabilizing rings. *ACM Trans. on Programming Languages and Systems*, 11:330–344, 1989.

[BYC88] F. Bastani, I. Yen, and I. Chen. A class of inherently fault tolerant distributed programs. *IEEE Trans. on Software Engineering*, 14:1432–1442, 1988.

[Dij73] E. Dijkstra. EWD391 Self-stabilization in spite of distributed control, 1973. Reprinted in *Selected Writings on Computing: A Personal Perspective*, Springer-Verlag, Berlin, 1982, pp. 41-46.

[Dij74] E. Dijkstra. Self stabilizing systems in spite of distributed control. *Communications of the ACM*, 17:643–644, 1974.

[GHR90] M. Gouda, R. Howell, and L. Rosier. The instability of self-stabilization. *Acta Informatica*, 27:697–724, 1990.

[Gou90] M. Gouda. The stabilizing philosopher: Asymmetry by memory and by action, 1990. To appear in *Science of Computer Programming*.

[HJR91] R. Howell, P. Jančar, and L. Rosier. Single-path Petri nets. In *Proceedings of the 16 International Symposium on Mathematical Foundations of Computer Science*, pages 202–210, 1991. LNCS 520. To appear in *Information and Computation*.

[How91] R. Howell. The complexity of problems concerning structurally bounded and conservative Petri nets. *Information Processing Letters*, 39:309–315, 1991.

[HP79] J. Hopcroft and J. Pansiot. On the reachability problem for 5-dimensional vector addition systems. *Theoret. Comput. Sci.*, 8:135–159, 1979.

[HR87] R. Howell and L. Rosier. Recent results on the complexity of problems related to petri nets. In G. Rozenberg, editor, *Advances in Petri Nets 1987*, pages 45–72. Springer, 1987. LNCS 266.

[HR88] R. Howell and L. Rosier. Completeness results for conflict-free vector replacement systems. *J. Comput. System Sci.*, 37:349–366, 1988.

[HRY87] R. Howell, L. Rosier, and H. Yen. An $O(n^{1.5})$ algorithm to decide boundedness for conflict-free vector replacement systems. *Inform. Process. Lett.*, 25:27–33, 1987.

[HRY89] R. Howell, L. Rosier, and H. Yen. Normal and sinkless Petri nets. In *Proceedings, 7th International Conference on Fundamentals of Computation Theory*, pages 234–243, 1989. LNCS 380. To appear in *J. Comput. System Sci.*

[JL77] N. Jones and W. Laaser. Complete problems for deterministic polynomial time. *Theoret. Comp. Sci.*, 3:105–117, 1977.

[JLL77] N. Jones, L. Landweber, and Y. Lien. Complexity of some problems in Petri nets. *Theoret. Comput. Sci.*, 4:277–299, 1977.

[Kar72] R. Karp. Reducibility among combinatorial problems. In R. Miller and J. Thatcher, editors, *Complexity of Computer Computations*, pages 85–103. Plenum Press, 1972.

[Kar84] N. Karmarkar. A new polynomial-time algorithm for linear programming. *Combinatorica*, 4:373–395, 1984.

[Kha79] L. Khachian. A polynomial algorithm in linear programming. *Dokl. Akad. Nauk. SSSR*, 244:1093–1096, 1979. In Russian. English translation in *Soviet Math. Dokl.*, 20:191-194.

[KM69] R. Karp and R. Miller. Parallel program schemata. *J. Comput. System Sci.*, 3:147–195, 1969.

[Kos82] R. Kosaraju. Decidability of reachability in vector addition systems. In *Proceedings, 14th ACM Symposium on Theory of Computing*, pages 267–280, 1982.

[Lam86] L. Lamport. The mutual exclusion problem: Part II — Statement and solutions. *JACM*, 33:327–348, 1986.

[Lam88] J. Lambert. Consequences of the decidability of the reachability problem for Petri nets. In G. Rozenberg, editor, *Advances in Petri Nets 1988*, pages 266–282. Springer, Berlin, 1988. LNCS 340. An expanded version to appear in *Theoret. Comput. Sci.*

[Lip76] R. Lipton. The reachability problem requires exponential space. Technical Report 62, Yale University, Dept. of CS., Jan. 1976.

[May84] E. Mayr. An algorithm for the general Petri net reachability problem. *SIAM J. Comput.*, 13:441–460, 1984. A preliminary version of this paper was presented at the "13th ACM Symposium on Theory of Computing," 1981.

[Mul89] N. Multari. *Self-stabilizing Protocols.* PhD thesis, Dept. of Computer Sciences, University of Texas at Austin, 1989.

[Mur89] T. Murata. Petri nets: properties, analysis, and applications. *Proc. of the IEEE*, 77:541–580, 1989.

[Rac78] C. Rackoff. The covering and boundedness problems for vector addition systems. *Theoret. Comput. Sci.*, 6:223–231, 1978.

[Sil85] M. Silva. *Las Redes de Petri: en la Automatica y la Informatica.* Editorial AC, Madrid, 1985. ISBN 84 7288 045 1.

Generative families of positive invariants in Coloured nets sub-classes

J.M. COUVREUR S. HADDAD J.F. PEYRE

Université Paris VI - C.N.R.S. MASI
4 Place Jussieu
75252 Paris Cedex 05
e.mail : peyre@masi.ibp.fr

Abstract

In Petri nets and high-level nets, positive flows provide additional informations to the ones given by the flows. For instance with the help of positive flows one decides the structural boundeness of the nets and one detects the structural implicit places. Up to now, no computation of positive flows has been developed for coloured nets. In this paper, we present a computation of positive flows for two basic families of coloured nets : unary regular nets and unary predicate/transition nets. At first we show that these two computations are reducible to the resolution of the parametrized equation $A.X_1 = \ldots = A.X_n$ where A is a matrix, X_i, the unknowns are vectors and n is the parameter. Then we present an algorithm to solve this equation. At last we show how the solutions of the parametrized equation can be used to solve the complete equations system for unary regular nets and unary predicate/transition nets.

KEYWORDS

Coloured nets, structural analysis, positive flows computation, Farkas' algorithm

Contents

1 Introduction

In Petri net theory, the computation of a set of integer vectors - called flows - or a set of non-negative integer vectors - called semi-flows or positive flows- is one of the key point for the analysis of systems [Mem83], [Jen81] [Gen83]. Indeed to each flow is associeted an invariant of the net providing informations on its behaviour. So, as abbreviations of Petri nets - coloured nets [Jen86] and predicate/transition nets [Gen81] - were introduced in order to model complex systems, many researchers have extended the main results of the Petri net theory and in particular the flow and positive flow calculi.

These researches have provided, for the flows computation, a general algorithm [Cou90] when the size of colour domains are fixed, and many algorithms [Vau84], [Had88] available on subclasses of coloured nets which allow to leave free the size of colour domains -parametrized algorithms-. Unfortunately the algebra technics on which these results are based can no more be applied in the case of positive flows calculus because Q^+ - instead of Q - is not a ring. Moreover only few heuristics have been proposed for the computation of positive flows [Vau84], [Trev86].

In this paper we present the parametrized computation of a generative family of positive flows for two categories of parametrized coloured nets : the unary regular nets (U-R nets)[Had87] and the unary predicate/transitions nets (U-Pr/T nets) [Vau84].

In section 1, we recall the definition of coloured nets and of these two sub classes. Two examples of modelling are providing.

In section 2, we recall the definition of positive flows and the definition of a generative family of such flows. Computing such invariants is equivalent to solve equations systems. So, we introduce the concept of a parametrized computation. Then we show how to reduce associated equations systems to the basic equation $A.X_1 = \ldots = A.X_n$.

In section 3 we solve this last equation; i.e we show that the set of solutions - for all $n \geq 2$ - can be generated by a finite and calculable set of integer vectors.

In section 4 we use this result to compute a generative family of positive flows for unary regular nets and unary predicate/transitions nets.

At last we apply our algorithm on the examples given in the first part in order to emphasize the usefulness of positive flows in coloured nets.

2 Subclasses of coloured nets

The purpose of this section is to briefly review the most basic definitions of coloured net (e.g. muti-set, linear application, coloured net, incidence matrix, firing rule, unfolded net ...) and the definition of two subclasses of coloured net: unary regular nets and unary predicate/transitions nets. For more details about these definitions please refer to the original papers [Jen86], [Had86], [Gen81].

2.1 Coloured nets

Definition 2.1 *A multi-set, over a finite non-empty set A, is a mapping from A to* N *where* N *denotes the set of non-negative integers.*

Informaly, a multi-set is a set which may include multiple occurrences of the same item. Each multi-set a over A is represented as a formal sum : $a = \sum a(x).x$ for all x in A, and where the non-negative integer $a(x)$ denotes the number of occurrences of the element x in the multi-set a. We denote by $Bag(A)$ the set of multi-set over A. The order on Bag(A) is a natural extension of the order on N as defined below :

Definition 2.2 *Let be* $a = \sum a(x).x$ *and* $b = \sum b(x)$ *two items of* $Bag(A)$*. Then* a *is greater or equal than* b*, denoted* $a \geq b$*, iff :* $\forall x \in A, a(x) \geq b(x)$.

Definition 2.3 *The sum of two items* a,b *of* $Bag(A)$ *is defined by :*

$$a + b = \sum_{x \in A}(a(x) + b(x)).x$$

Definition 2.4 *The product of an item* a *of* $Bag(A)$ *by an integer* λ *is defined by :*

$$\lambda.a = \sum_{x \in A}(\lambda.a(x)).x$$

Definition 2.5 *A mapping* f *from* $Bag(A)$ *to* $Bag(B)$ *is a linear application iff :*
$\forall a, a' \in Bag(A), f(a + a') = f(a) + f(a')$ *and* $\forall \lambda \in \mathbb{N}, f(\lambda.a) = \lambda.f(a)$.

A linear application can be defined as the unique linear extension of a mapping from A to Bag(B). We could also define the $B \times A$ matrix of the linear application.

Coloured nets allows the modelling of more complex systems than ordinary ones because of the abreviation providing by this model. In a coloured net, a place contains coloured tokens instead of neutral tokens in Petri nets, and a transition may be fired in a multiple ways. So to each place and each transition is attached a colour domain. An arc from a transition to a place (resp. from a place to a transition) is labelled by a linear function called colour function. This function determines the colours to be added (resp. removed from) to the place upon firing the transition with the respect of a colour.

These different concepts are formalized by the following definitions.

Definition 2.6 *A coloured net is a 6-tuple* $N = \langle P, T, C, W^+, W^-, M_0 \rangle$ *where :*

- P *is the non-empty set of places.*
- T *is the non-empty set of transitions with* $P \cap T = \emptyset$.
- C *is the colour function from* $P \bigcup T$ *to* Ω*, where* Ω *is a set of finite non empty sets. An item of* $C(s)$ *is called a colour of* s *and* $C(s)$ *is called the colour domain of* s.
- $W^+(W^-)$ *is the forward (backward) incidence matrix of* $P \times T$.
  $W^+(p,t)$ *and* $W^-(p,t)$ *are linear applications from* $Bag(C(t))$ *to* $Bag((C(p))$.
- M_0 *the initial marking of the net is a vector of* P *where* $M_0(p)$ *is an item of* $Bag(C(p))$.

Definition 2.7 *The incidence matrix* W *of a coloured net is defined by :* $W = W^+ - W^-$.

Definition 2.8 *The firing rule of a coloured net is defined by :*

- *A transition* t *is enabled for a marking* M *and a colour* $c_t \in C(t)$ if and only if :
  $\forall p \in P, M(p) \geq W^-(p,t)(c_t)$.
- *The firing of a transition* t *for a marking* M *and a colour* $c_t \in C(t)$ *gives a new marking* M' *defined by :*
  $\forall p \in P, M'(p) = M(p) + W(p,t)(c_t)$.

In fact a coloured net is an abbreviation of a Petri net with the same behaviour. The next definition explains how to unfold a coloured net net in its corresponding ordinary one.

Definition 2.9 *Let N be a coloured net. Then $N_d =< P_d, T_d, W_d{}^+, W_d{}^-, M_{d0} >$ the unfolded Petri net of N is defined by :*

- $P_d = \bigcup_{p \in P, c \in C(p)} (p, c)$, *the set of places*
- $T_d = \bigcup_{t \in T, c \in C(t)} (t, c)$, *the set of transitions*
- $W^+(W^-)$ *the forward (backward) incidence matrix of $(P \times C) \times (T \times C)$ defined by :*
  $W_d{}^+(p,c)(t,c') = W^+(p,t)(c)(c')$ *and* $W_d{}^-(p,c)(t,c') = W^-(p,t)(c)(c')$
- M_{d0} *the initial marking defined by :*
  $M_{d0}(p,c) = M_0(p)(c)$

Unary regular nets [Had87] and unary predicate/transition nets [Gen81] are obtained by a restriction of colour domains and colour functions.

2.2 Unary regular nets

To each unary regular net is associated a single colour domain denoted Cl. The size of this domain is the parameter of the model. Colour functions are build by linear sums of two basic functions X et S. X denotes the identity function of Bag(Cl) and allows to express the free evolution of an objet. S denotes the constant sum of all the colours and allows to express global synchronizations and broadcasts.

Definition 2.10 *A coloured net N is an unary regular net* if and only if *:*

- *There is some set* $Cl = \{c_1, \ldots, c_n\}$, *such that :*
  $\forall s \in P \bigcup T, C(s) = Cl.$
- $\forall p \in P, \forall t \in T, W^-(p,t)$ *and* $W^+(p,t)$ *are linear sums :*
  $W^-(p,t) = d^-_{p,t}.X + b^-_{p,t}.S,\ \ W^+(p,t) = d^+_{p,t}.X + b^+_{p,t}.S$, *with*
  $b^-_{p,t},\ b^+_{p,t},\ d^-_{p,t} + b^-_{p,t},\ d^+_{p,t} + b^+_{p,t}$ *positive integers,*
  S and X defined by : $S(c) = \sum_{c' \in Cl}(c')$ *and* $X(c) = c$

Example 1 ([Had87, page 23-26]) *A data base management with multiple copies.*

In order to modify the data base, a site must get a grant from all the sites modelled by the multiset S in the place Mutex. Then the site sends messages with the updates to all the others sites. It releases all the grants after having received acknowledgments from all the others sites.

The unique colour class is the sites, and initially there is a token of each site colour in the place Idle and in the place Mutex.

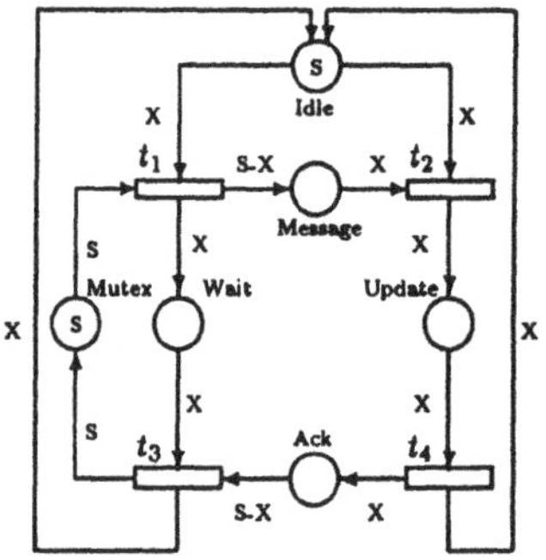

Figure 1

2.3 Unary predicate/transitions nets

We introduce predicate/transition nets as a subclass of coloured nets. The original definition can be found in [Vau84].

All the colour domains are built from a basic domain also denoted Cl. This domain is composed by some distinguished colours, called constants in a fixed number q, and other standard colours. The number of these standard colours is the parameter of the model noted n.

The colour domain of any place is Cl, while the colour domain of any transition is Cl^k which means that the firing of a transition involves k variables colours of Cl. In the colours functions these k variables are denoted by $Y_1, \ldots, Y_k$.

Definition 2.11 *A coloured net N is an unary predicate/transition net* if and only if *:*

- *There is some set $Cl = \{a_1, \ldots, a_q, c_1, \ldots, c_n\}$, such that :*
  $\forall p \in P, C(p) = Cl$ *and* $\forall t \in T, C(t) = Cl^k$ *where k is a positive integer*

  $a_1, \ldots, a_q$ are called the constants of the net.
- $\forall p \in P, \forall t \in T, W^-(p,t)$ *and* $W^+(p,t)$ *are linear sums :*

$$W^+(p,t) = \sum_{i=1}^{k} {\alpha^+}^i_{p,t}.Y_i + \sum_{i=1}^{q} {\beta^+}^i_{p,t}.a_i,\ W^-(p,t) = \sum_{i=1}^{k} {\alpha^-}^i_{p,t}.Y_i + \sum_{i=1}^{q} {\beta^-}^i_{p,t}.a_i$$

where ${\alpha^+}^i_{p,t}$, ${\beta^+}^i_{p,t}$, ${\alpha^-}^i_{p,t}$, ${\beta^-}^i_{p,t}$ *belong to* N.

Forall i in $[1..k]$, *Y_i is a linear application from $Bag(Cl^k)$ to $Bag(Cl)$ defined by :*

$\forall (e_1, \ldots, e_i, \ldots, e_k) \in Cl^k,\ Y_i(e_1, \ldots, e_i, \ldots, e_k) = e_i$

We give now an example of unary predicate/transition net. This model is only proposed to illustrate the positive flow computation in this kind of coloured nets.

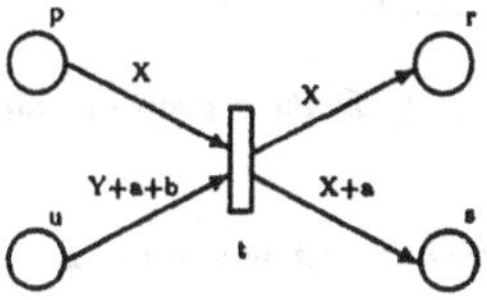

Figure 2

3 Positive Flows in coloured nets

Positive-flows computation is much more important in coloured nets than in ordinary Petri nets. It enables to verify behavioural properties without developing all or a part of the reachability graph which for a coloured net has usually a huge size. It gives also informations on the evolution of the tokens. At last, other proof methods (like, for instance, the reduction theory) require this computation.

Many kinds of positive flows have been introduced in [Gen83], [Vau84], but the authors who looked for the flows calculus algorithms [Col89], [Had88], [Cou90] have taken the most appropriate definition : a positive flow of a coloured net is a set of positive flows in the unfolded Petri net.

Thus, given a coloured net, a solution for computing its positive flows should be to unfold this net and then to compute these flows with the help of classical methods. However, such a solution is expansive in time and in space - because of the unfolded net size - and provides invariants whose meaning is not always clear. Furthermore, when the size of domains is let variable, it becomes impossible to unfold the net. Thus, it is necessary to find alternative methods.

3.1 Preliminaries

3.1.1 Notations

Let p be the size of the set P of places. Semi-flows of a Petri net are vectors of $(Q^+)^p$,where Q^+ denotes the non-negative rationals, and positive flows of a unary regular net or of a U-Pr/T net are vectors of $((Q^+)^p)^n$, where n is an integer greater than 1 representing the parameter of the model.

We introduce the following notations:

- Q^+ denotes the set of non-negative rationals
- We note $E = (Q^+)^p$, and $E^n = ((Q^+)^p)^n$ $p, t \in$ N or alternatively $E^n = \oplus E_i$, $\forall i \in [1..n]$ where each E_i is isomorphic to E (i.e E^n is the direct sum of n copies of E).
- The image of a vector e of E by the canonical bijection from E to E_i is noted $e(i)$
- A vector e of E^n has a unique decomposition $e = \sum e_i(i)$ or $e =< e_1, e_2, \ldots, e_n >$ with e_i in E
- $\mathcal{P}(E)$ denotes the powerset of E.
- "$\subset$" denotes the stong inclusion and "$\subseteq$" the weak inclusion.
  $a \subset b \Rightarrow a \neq b$, and $a \subseteq b$ iff $a = b$ or $a \subset b$.
- If W is a matrix then W^T is the matrix defined by $W^T[i, j] = W[j, i]$.

3.1.2 Definitions

We recall now some basic definitions relative to positive flows in Petri nets.

Definition 3.1 *Let N be a Petri net and W its incidence matrix. A vector f in E is a positive flow* if and only if *f is a solution of the equation* $W^T.f = 0$.

Definition 3.2 *Let f be a vector indexed by E, the support of f noted Supp(f) or* $\|f\|$ *is the subset of E defined by* $\|f\| = \{e \in E / f_e \neq 0\}$.

Definition 3.3 *Let F be a set of vectors of E. A vector g of F is minimal in F - with support notion -* if and only if *:* $\forall f \in F \setminus g, \|f\| \not\subset \|g\|$

Example 2 *Let* $F = \{f_0 = (2,0,0,3), f_1 = (1,1,0,2), f_2 = (1,1,3,0)\}$ *a set of vector of* Q^4*; then* $\|f_0\|$ *can be view as the vector* $(1,0,0,1)$, $\|f_1\|$ *as the vector* $(1,1,0,1)$ *and* $\|f_2\|$ *as the vector* $(1,1,1,0)$. *Also,* f_0 *and* f_2 *are of minimal support in F.*

Definition 3.4 *Let W be the incidence matrix of a Petri net R. A set* $\{f_1, ..., f_k\}$ *of vectors of E is a generative family of positive flows of R* if and only if *:*

- $\forall i, W^T.f_i = 0$
- $\forall f \in E, f \neq 0$ *with* $W^T.f = 0$, $\exists \lambda_1, ..., \lambda_k \in Q^+$ *with* $f = \lambda_1.f_1 + \ldots + \lambda_k.f_k$

It is also possible to characterize a generative family with the help of the notion of support [Mem83], [Aba64].

Characterization 1 *Let W be the incidence matrix of a Petri net R. A set* $\{f_1, \ldots, f_k\}$ *of vectors of E is a generative family of positive flows of R* if and only if *:* $\forall f \in E, f \neq 0$ *with* $W^T.f = 0$, $\exists f_i \in F$ *such* $\|f\| \supseteq \|f_i\|$.

This characterization and the definition 3.4 provide the Farkas algorithm [Far02] which allows to compute a minimal generative family of positive flows of a Petri net. This algorithm is studied in [Mem83] or more recently in [Col89] where some heuristics provide an efficient programming of the Farkas algorithm.

3.2 Reduction of the equation system

In order to compute positive flows it is necessary to solve the equation $W^T.X = 0$, where W is the incidence matrix of the unfolded net. In unary regular net (resp. U-Pr/T net) this matrix has $p*n$ rows and $t*n$ columns (resp. $(p+q)*n$ and $(t+q)*n$), where p and t are respectively the places and transitions number of the net; n is the parameter corresponding to the size of the domain colours.

Also we have to solve a system parametrized in two different ways:

- the equations of this system are parametrized : solutions belong to E^n
- the number of equations depends on n : there is $t*n$ or $(t+q)*n$ equations

We shall see in the following sections that we can reduce our problem in the both cases - *U-Rr and U-Pr/T* - to a system with only two equations including the one : $D.X_1 = \ldots = D.X_n$, where D is a $P \times T$ matrix depending on the net.

3.2.1 Equation system for unary regular nets

Let be $R = < P, T, C, W^+, W^-, M_0 >$ a unary regular net. The incidence matrix of the unfolding net is defined by - *definitions 2.10, 2.9* - :

$$\forall p \in P, \forall t \in T, \forall c, c' \in [1..n]^2, W_d((p,c),(t,c')) = W(p,t)(c,c') = (d_{p,t}.X + b_{p,t}.S)(c,c')$$

So we have :

$$\forall p \in P, \forall t \in T, \forall c, c' \in [c_1..c_n] : \begin{cases} W_d((p,c),(t,c')) = d_{p,t} + b_{p,t} \;\; if\; c = c' \\ W_d((p,c),(t,c')) = b_{p,t} \;\; if\; c \neq c' \end{cases}$$

If we denote now by D the $P \times T$ matrix defined by $D(p,t) = d_{p,t}$ for all (p,t) in $P \times T$ and by B the $P \times T$ matrix defined by $B(p,t) = b_{p,t}$ for all (p,t) in $P \times T$, the transposition of the incidence matrix of the unfolded net can be written as :

$$\mathrm{W_{dn}} = \begin{array}{c} \\ T_{c_1} \\ T_{c_2} \\ \vdots \\ T_{c_n} \end{array} \begin{array}{c} \begin{array}{cccc} P_{c_1} & P_{c_2} & \ldots & P_{c_n} \end{array} \\ \begin{pmatrix} D+B & B & \ldots & B \\ B & D+B & \ldots & B \\ \ldots & \ldots & \ddots & \ldots \\ B & B & \ldots & D+B \end{pmatrix} \end{array}$$

where P_{c_i} and T_{c_i} denote respectively the set of unfolded places and unfolded transitions for the colour c_i i.e $P_{c_i} = \bigcup_{p \in P}(p, c_i)$ and $T_{c_i} = \bigcup_{t \in T}(t, c_i)$.

So a vector $X = < X_1, \ldots, X_n >$ in E^n - *with notations of part 3.1.1* - is a positive flow *if and only if* this vector fulfils the system :

$$\forall i \in [1..n], D.X_i + \sum_{j=1}^{n} B.X_j = 0 \qquad (1)$$

Let be now the system :

$$\begin{cases} (D + n.B).\sum_{j=1}^{n} X_j = 0 \\ D.X_1 = D.X_2 = \ldots = D.X_n \end{cases} \qquad (2)$$

We have the following proposition:

Proposition 1 *Systems 1 and 2 are equivalent.*

Proof: $1 \Longrightarrow 2)$

Let be $X = < X_1, \ldots, X_n >$ a solution of 1. Then

$\forall i,j \in [1.n]^2, (D.X_i + \sum_{k=1}^{n} B.X_k) - (D.X_j + \sum_{k=1}^{n} B.X_k) = 0$

so it comes :

$\forall i,j \in [1.n]^2, D.X_i = D.X_j$, which can also be written $D.X_1 = \ldots = D.X_n$

We have also :

$\sum_{i=1}^{n} (D.X_i + \sum_{k=1}^{n} B.X_k) = 0$ which is equivalent to :

$D.(\sum_{j=1}^{n} X_j) + n.B.(\sum_{j=1}^{n} X_j) = 0$

$2 \Longrightarrow 1)$

Let be $X = < X_1, \ldots, X_n >$ a solution of 2. Then

$(D + nB) \sum_{j=1}^{n} X_j = 0$ and $\forall i,j \in [1..n]^2, D.X_i = D.Xj$

so we have :

$\forall i \in [1,n], nD.X_i + nB. \sum_{j=1}^{n} X_j = 0.$

◇◇◇

For our example of U-R net, figure 1, we obtain the following matrices D and B.

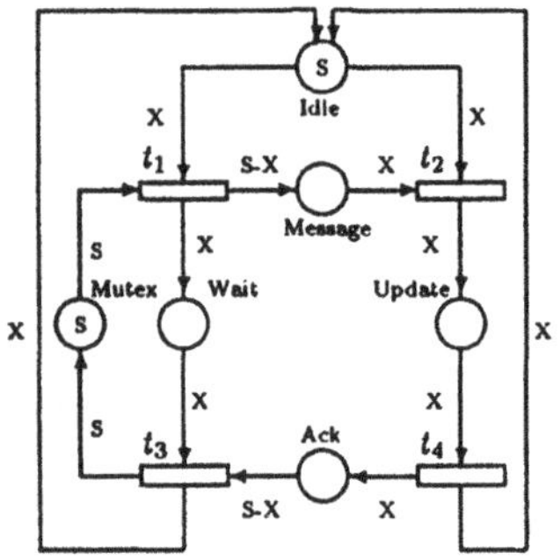

$$D = \begin{array}{c} \\ t_1 \\ t_2 \\ t_3 \\ t_4 \end{array} \begin{array}{c} \begin{array}{cccccc} Idle & Message & Wait & Update & Mutex & Ack \end{array} \\ \begin{pmatrix} -1 & -1 & 1 & 0 & 0 & 0 \\ -1 & -1 & 0 & 1 & 0 & 0 \\ 1 & 0 & -1 & 0 & 0 & 1 \\ 1 & 0 & 0 & -1 & 0 & 1 \end{pmatrix} \end{array}$$

$$B = \begin{array}{c} \\ t_1 \\ t_2 \\ t_3 \\ t_4 \end{array} \begin{array}{c} \begin{array}{cccccc} Idle & Message & Wait & Update & Mutex & Ack \end{array} \\ \begin{pmatrix} 0 & 1 & 0 & 0 & -1 & 0 \\ 0 & 0 & 0 & 0 & 0 & 0 \\ 0 & 0 & 0 & 0 & 1 & -1 \\ 0 & 0 & 0 & 0 & 0 & 0 \end{pmatrix} \end{array}$$

Figure 3

3.2.2 Equation system for unary predicate transition nets

Let N be a U-Pr/T net.

Items of the incidence matrix are noted $W(p,t) = \sum_{i=1}^{k} \alpha_{p,t}^{i}.Y_i + \sum_{i=1}^{q} \beta_{p,t}^{i}.a_i$, where k denoted the number of variables or linear applications of the net and q the number of constants.

We define now the following matrices:

- The matrix D defined by a column for each place of the net and a row for each transition and each variable with :

  $\forall p \in P, \forall (t,i) \in T \times [1,k], \; D(p,t_i) = \alpha_{p,t}^{i}$

- The matrix H_{i_0}, $i_0 \in [c_1, c_n]$, defined by a column for each place and a row for each transition with:

  $\forall p \in P, \forall t \in T, H_{i_0}(p,t) = \sum_{i=1}^{k} \alpha_{p,t}^{i}$

- The matrices H_{a_i}, $a_i \in \{a_1, \ldots, a_q\}$, defined by a column for each place and a row for each transition with :

  $\forall a_i \in \{a_1, \ldots, a_q\}, \forall p \in P, \forall t \in T, H_{a_i}(p,t) = \beta^i_{p,t}$

At last, let W'_{dn} be the block matrix defined by (i_0 is choosed equal to c_1 for more clarity) :

$$W'_{dn} = \begin{array}{c} \\ T_{a_1} \\ \vdots \\ T_{a_q} \\ T_{c_1} \\ \vdots \\ T_{c_n} \end{array} \begin{array}{c} \begin{array}{ccccccc} P_{a_1} & \ldots & P_{a_q} & P_{c_1} & \ldots & P_{c_n} \end{array} \\ \begin{pmatrix} -D & \ldots & 0 & D & \ldots & 0 \\ \ldots & \ddots & \ldots & \vdots & \ldots & \ldots \\ 0 & \ldots & -D & D & \ldots & 0 \\ H_{a_1} & \ldots & H_{a_q} & H_{i_0} & \ldots & 0 \\ \ldots & \ldots & \ldots & \vdots & \ddots & \ldots \\ 0 & \ldots & 0 & D & \ldots & -D \end{pmatrix} \end{array}$$

We have the following proposition :

Proposition 2 *For each n, W_{dn} and W'_{dn} are equivalent for the calculus of positive flows :*
e.g : $\forall n \geq 0, \forall X \in E^{n+q}, W^T_{d\ n}.X = 0$ if and only if $W'_{dn}.X = 0$

Proof: The main idea of this demonstration is to make gathering of equations in order to simplify these equations by linear combinations.

Let $X = < x^1_1, \ldots, x^1_P, \ldots, x^1_n, \ldots, x^n_P >$ be a solution of $W^T_{d\ n}.X = 0$. Then X fulfils :

$$\forall t \in T, \forall c_t \in Cl^k, \sum_{c \in Cl} \sum_{p \in P} W^T_{d\ n}(p,c)(t,c_t).x^c_p = 0$$

which is noted for more clarity of the following : $\forall t \in T, \forall c_t \in Cl^k$, $Sys(c_t) = 0$

Let be now $i_0 \in \{c_1, \ldots, c_n\}$. The previous system is also equivalent with a first grouping to :
$\forall t \in T, \forall i \in [1,k], \forall c_t \in Cl^k \ / \ \forall j < i, c_t(j) = i_0, \ \ Sys(c_t) = 0$

We make now a last grouping, and we obtain the equivalent system :

$$\forall t \in T, \forall i \in [1,k], \forall c_t, c'_t \in Cl^k \ / \left\{ \begin{array}{l} \forall j < i, c_t(j) = i_0 \\ \forall j \leq i, c'_t(j) = i_0 \end{array} \right. \text{ and } \forall j > i, c_t(j) = c'_t(j),$$

$sys(c_t) = 0$ and $sys(c'_t) = 0$

In the previous system, all equations, except those , appears twice. So it is equivalent to solve the system :

$$\forall t \in T, \forall i \in [1,k], \forall c_t, c'_t \in Cl^k \ / \left\{ \begin{array}{l} \forall j < i, c_t(j) = i_0 \\ \forall j \leq i, c'_t(j) = i_0 \end{array} \right. \text{ and } \forall j > i, c_t(j) = c'_t(j),$$

$sys(c_t) - sys(c'_t) = 0$ and $sys((i_0, \ldots, i_0)) = 0$

By definition,

$$W^T_{d\ n}(p,c)(t,c_t).x^c_p = \left\{ \begin{array}{ll} \sum_{i \in I} \alpha^i_{p,t} & if\ c \notin \{a_1, \ldots, a_q\} \\ \sum_{i \in I} \alpha^i_{p,t} + c & if\ c \in \{a_1, \ldots, a_q\} \end{array} \right. \quad with\ I = \{i \in [1,k] / c_t(i) = c\}$$

So for all (c_t, c'_t) defined as previousely we have :

$$W^T_{d\ n}(p,c)(t,c_t) - W^T_{d\ n}(p,c)(t,c'_t) = \alpha^i_{p,t} - \alpha^{i_0}_{p,t}$$

We have also

$$\begin{aligned} \sum_{c \in Cl} \sum_{p \in P} W^T_{d\ n}(p,c)(t,(i_0,\ldots,i_0)) &= \sum_{p \in P} \sum_{c \in Cl} W^T_{d\ n}(p,c)(t,(i_0,\ldots,i_0)) \\ &= \sum_{p \in P} [\sum_{c \in \{a_1,\ldots,a_q\}} W^T_{d\ n}(p,c)(t,(i_0,\ldots,i_0)) + \sum_{c \in \{c_1,\ldots,c_n\}} W^T_{d\ n}(p,c)(t,(i_0,\ldots,i_0))] \\ &= \sum_{p \in P} (\sum_{i=1}^{k} \alpha^i_{p,t}.x^{i_0}_p + \sum_{i=1}^{q} \beta^i_{p,t}.x^{a_i}_p) \end{aligned}$$

So, because of definitions of matrices D, H_{i_0}, H_{a_i}, X is solution of $W_{d\,n}^T.X = 0$ *if and only if* X is solution of $W'_{dn}.X = 0$.

◇◇◇

So we have translate the problem of computing positive flows of an U-Pr/T net into the problem of finding solutions of the equation $W'd_n.X = 0$ which can also be written :

$$\left[\begin{array}{l} H_{i_0}.X_{i_0} + H_{a_1}.X_{a_1} + \ldots + H_{a_q}.X_{a_q} = 0 \\ D.X_{a_1} = \ldots = D.X_{a_q} = D.X_1 = \ldots = D.X_{i_0} = \ldots = D.X_n \end{array}\right. \tag{3}$$

We find again in this system the equation $D.X_1 = \ldots = D.X_n$. The purpose of the next section is to solve it.

For our example of U-Pr/T net, fig. 2.3, we obtain the following matrices :

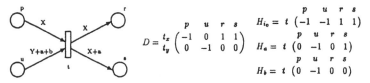

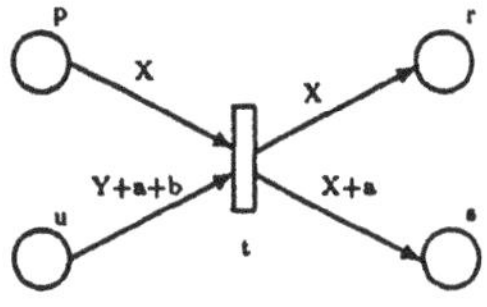

$$D = \begin{matrix} \\ t_x \\ t_y \end{matrix} \begin{matrix} p & u & r & s \\ \left(\begin{matrix} -1 \\ 0 \end{matrix}\right. & \begin{matrix} 0 \\ -1 \end{matrix} & \begin{matrix} 1 \\ 0 \end{matrix} & \left.\begin{matrix} 1 \\ 0 \end{matrix}\right) \end{matrix}$$

$$H_{i_0} = t \begin{pmatrix} -1 & -1 & 1 & 1 \end{pmatrix} \quad (p\ u\ r\ s)$$

$$H_a = t \begin{pmatrix} 0 & -1 & 0 & 1 \end{pmatrix} \quad (p\ u\ r\ s)$$

$$H_b = t \begin{pmatrix} 0 & -1 & 0 & 0 \end{pmatrix} \quad (p\ u\ r\ s)$$

Figure 4

4 Resolution of the parametrized equation $A.X_1 = \ldots = A.X_n$

Our purpose is now to provide an algorithm which computes a generative family of the equation $A.X_1 = \ldots = A.X_n$ for any finite matrix A. We first define the notion of pseudo-generative family. Then, in order to compare pseudo-generative families, we extend the support notion to families of vectors, and we give then the algorithm 4.

From up to now, we denote by A a matrix composed by t rows and p columns, by b a vector of Q^t and we note (i) the equation $A.X_1 = \ldots = A.X_n$.

Definition 4.1 *Let $F = \{V_1, \ldots, V_m\}$ be a vectors family of E solutions of the equation $A.X = b$. F is a pseudo-generative family of $A.X = b$* if and only if *:*

$\forall V \in E, V \neq 0$ *with* $A.V = b, \exists V_i \in F$ *with* $\|V_i\| \subseteq \|V\|$

We note $Sol(A, b)$ a pseudo-generative family of $A.X = b$.

Remark : According to characterization 1, $Sol(A, 0)$ is a generative family of the equation $A.X = 0$.

We propose now an algorithm which, given a matrix A and a vector b, computes a pseudo-generative family of $A.X = b$.

Algorithm 1 : $A.X = b$

1. Compute - *with Farkas* - a generative family $F = \{(X, \lambda) \in E \times N / [A \ \ -b].\begin{bmatrix} X \\ \lambda \end{bmatrix} = 0\}$.
2. Remove from this family the solutions such as the second component λ is null
3. For each solution divide the first component X by the second component λ to normalize the family; then eliminate the component λ.

Proposition 3 *The family F' of vectors of E obtained at the step 3 is a pseudo-generative family of the equation $A.X = b$.*

Proof: • Each item of the family satisfies $A.X = b$ by construction.

• Each solution V of $A.X = b$ gives a solution (V, λ) of $A.X = \lambda.b$; this solution is generated by the family obtained at the point (1). Because the λ component of (V, λ) is no null, the linear combination which generates this solution included at less one element V' of the family obtained at the second point. So the solution deduced from V' at the point (3) is of minimal support compared to V.

So F satisfies the definition 4.1 and is a pseudo-generative family of the equation $A.X = b$.

◇◇◇

Definition 4.1 *We note :*

- *If* $b \neq 0$, $Sol^n(A,b) = \{\sum_{i=1}^{n} V_i(i) \in E^n / \forall i, Vi \in Sol(A,b)\}$.
- *If* $b = 0$, $Sol^n(A,0) = \{< 0, \ldots, v_i, 0, \ldots, 0 > \in E^n / V_i \in Sol(A,0)\}$.

Example 3 *If* $Sol(A,b) = \{V_1, V_2\}$, *then :*

if $b \neq 0$, $Sol^3(A,b) = \{< V_1, V_1, V_1 >, < V_1, V_1, V_2 >, \ldots, < V_2, V_1, V_2 >, \ldots, < V_2, V_2, V_2 >\}$

if $b = 0, Sol^3(A,b) = \{< V_1, 0, 0 >, < V_2, 0, 0 >, < 0, V_1, 0 >, \ldots, < 0, 0, V_2 >\}$

If we remark now that, for any b, $Sol^n(A,b)$ gives a set of solution of the equation (i), one can think is sufficient to solve (i) for $n = 2$, e.g to solve $A.X = A.Y$. We are going to see on an example, that a generative family of $A.X = A.Y$ doe not give a generative family of (i) for all n.

The following algorithm computes a generative family of $A.X = A.Y$.

Algorithm 2 : $A.X = A.Y$

1. Compute - *with Farkas* - a generative family $Fg = \{(X,Y)/[A \ -A].\begin{bmatrix} X \\ Y \end{bmatrix} = 0\}$
2. Construct the set $S = \{b = A.X, b \neq 0 \ with \ (X,Y) \in Fg\}$
3. Construct the set $F = \bigcup_{b \in S \cup \{0\}} Sol^2(A,b)$

Proposition 4 *The set F built by the previous algorithm is a generative family of* $A.X = A.Y$.

Proof: It is clear that by construcion F contains a generative family of $A.X = A.Y$.

◇◇◇

Fact 1 *The family computed by the algorithm 4 does not provide a generative family of the equation* $A.X_1 = \ldots = A.X_n$ *for all* $n \geq 2$.

Let be A the matrix:

$$A = \begin{bmatrix} 1 & -1 & 1 & -1 & 1 & 1 & -1 \\ 1 & -1 & -1 & -1 & -1 & 1 & -1 \\ 1 & 1 & -1 & -1 & 1 & 1 & -1 \\ 1 & -1 & 1 & -1 & -1 & 1 & 1 \end{bmatrix}$$

The set of b_i compute by the algorithm 4 is (with on the right of each b_i the set $Sol(A, b_i)$).
- *((- 1 3 - - - -) denotes the vector (0 1 3 0 0 0 0))* -

$b_0 = (0\ -2\ 0\ 0)$	X = (- 1 1 - - - -)	$b_1 = (1\ -1\ -1\ 1)$	X = (- - 1 - - - -)
	X = (- - - - 1 - 1)		X = (1 - - - 1 1 2)
$b_2 = (1\ -1\ 1\ -1)$	X = (- - - - 1 - -)	$b_3 = (-1\ -1\ -1\ -1)$	X = (- - - 1 - - -)
	X = (1 2 1 - - 1 -)		X = (- 1 - - - 1 1)
$b_4 = (0\ -2\ 0\ -2)$	X = (- - - 1 1 - -)	$b_5 = (0\ -2\ -2\ 0)$	X = (- - 1 1 - - -)
	X = (- 1 - - 1 1 1)		X = (- - - - 1 1 2)
	X = (- 2 1 - - 1 -)		X = (- 1 1 - - 1 1)

Let be now the vector b_6 - *with* $\{X_1, X_2, X_3\} = Sol(A, b_6)$ - defined by :

$b_6 = (\ 1\ \text{-}3\ \text{-}1\ \text{-}1)$ X1 = (_ _ _ _ 2 1 2)
X2 = (_ _ 1 1 1 _ _)
X3 = (_ 2 2 _ _ 1 _)

This last vector is not computed by the algorithm 4 because none vector of $Sol^2(A, b_6)$ is minimal in support between the set $\{\bigcup Sol^2(A, b_i), b_i \in [b_0, ..., b_5]\}$. Nevertheless this vector b_6 gives for $n = 3$ the vector of $E^3X =< X_1, X_2, X_3 >$ which is minimal in the set $\{\bigcup Sol^3(A, b_i), b_i \in [b_0, ..., b_5]\}$. Also, because we want a generative family, we have to compute this vector.

It is thus necessary to iterate this calculus; we want to say that after solving $A.X_1 = A.X_2$ we have to solve $A.X_1 = A.X_2 = A.X_3$ and then $A.X_1 = A.X_2 = A.X_3 = A.X_4$ and so on. The key point is the termination of this iteration. In order to prove it, we extend the definition of supports to vectors famillies.

Definition 4.1 $Supp : \mathcal{P}(E) \longrightarrow \mathcal{P}((\mathcal{P}(P))$
such as $Supp(F) = \{Supp(V)/V \in F\}$ *; by extension we note* $\|F\| = Supp(F)$.

Definition 4.1 *Let F and F' two sets of vectors of E.*
We say that F is minimal in comparison with F' - noted $F \prec F'$ - if and only if :
$\exists f \in F$ *such* $\forall f' \in F', \|f'\| \not\subset \|f\|$

We have for the last example, $Sol(A, b_6) \prec Sol(A, b_i)$ for each b_i.

The following proposition prooves that it cannot exist an infinite suite of "minimal" sets.

Proposition 5 $\forall \{Fi\}_{i \in N}$ *with* $F_i \in \mathcal{P}(E)$, $\exists i_0 \in N$ *such as* $\forall j \geq i_0$, $F_{i_0} \prec F_j$.

Proof: Let be a series $\{Fi\}_{i \in N}$. This series takes its values in P((P(P)).
As P((P(P)) is a finite set, $\exists i, j$ with $i < j$ such as $\|Fi\| = \|Fj\|$. Also, by definition, we have $F_i \prec F_j$.

◇◇◇

We give now the algorithm which computes a generative family of the equation $A.X_1 = \ldots = A.X_n$.

Algorithm 3 : $A.X_1 = \ldots = A.X_n$

1. $S = \{b_0, \ldots, b_k\}$: result of the algorithm 4 on the matrix A ($A.X = A.Y$)
2. $IncS = \emptyset$
3. DO
   (a) K = Cardinal(S) : number of non nul elements of S
   (b) Compute - *with Farkas* - a smallest generative family F
   $$F = \{(X, \lambda_1, \ldots, \lambda_K) \in E \times (Q^+)^K / [-b_1 \ldots - b_k\ A].\begin{bmatrix} \lambda_1 \\ \vdots \\ \lambda_K \\ X \end{bmatrix} = 0\}$$
   (c) $IncS = \{b' = A.X / < X, \lambda_1, \ldots, \lambda_K > \in F, b' \neq 0$ and $\forall b \in S, Sol(A, b') \prec Sol(A, b)\}$
   (d) S = $S \bigcup IncS$

   WHILE $IncS \neq \emptyset$
4. $S = S \bigcup \{0\}$

Proposition 6 *The set S computed by the last algorithm provides a generative family of the equation* $A.X_1 = \ldots = A.X_n$ *for all* $n \geq 2$.

i.e $\bigcup_{b \in S} Sol^n(A, b)$ *is a generative family for all* $n \geq 2$.

Proof: **Ending :** If this algorithm doesn't end, it constructs with the instruction 3d a infinite set $\{b_i\}$ indexed by their insertion order in S. If we consider the family $\{Sol(A, b_i)\}$, the instruction 3c implies that this family does not satisfy the proposition 3.6. So here is a contradiction.

Correctness : We don't give the proof because of its technical nature but the reader might refer to [CHP90].

◇◇◇

5 Application to the positive flows computation in coloured nets

The purpose of this section is to see how we can use results developed in the last part to compute a generative family of positive flows in two kinds of coloured nets.

5.1 Computation of positive flows for unary predicate/transition nets

Computing a generative family of positive flows in a U-Pr/T net is equivalent to compute a generative family of the system 3 - *where $D, H_0, H_{a_1}, ..., H_{a_q}$ are the matrices defined on part 3.2.2* -

$$\left[\begin{array}{l} H_{i_0}.X_{i_0} + H_{a_1}.X_{a_1} + \ldots + H_{a_q}.X_{a_q} = 0 \\ D.X_{a_1} = \ldots = D.X_{a_q} = D.X_1 = \ldots = D.X_{i_0} = \ldots = D.X_n \end{array}\right.$$

So we propose the following algorithm which computes a generative family of positive flows in a U-Pr/T net. The principle is to solve the second equation by the algorithm developed in part 4 and then to report the solutions in the first equation. As the size of this equation is not dependent on n, it is just necessary to develop the solutions computed on the first $q+1$ components and to keep the rest of the components as a formal sum.

We remind that the unique colour class Cl is noted $Cl = \{a_1, \ldots, a_q, c_1, \ldots, c_n\}$ where $a_1, \ldots, a_q$ are the q constants of the net.

Algorithm 4 : $A.X_1 = \ldots = A.X_n$

1. $S = \{b_0, \ldots, b_k\}$: result of the algorithm 4 on the matrix A $(A.X = A.Y)$
   We note m_j the size of the set $Sol(A, b_i)$ and $Sol(A, b_i) = \{V_1^{b_j}, \ldots, V_{m_j}^{b_j}\}$.
2. Express solutions of $D.X_1 = \ldots = D.X_n$ as a formal sum with only the first $q+1$ components developed - *for the constants and the particular colour i_0* -
   (a) for each $b_j \neq 0$ in S, for each application $\sigma_{j,k}$ from $[0, q]$ to $[1, m_{b_j}]$, *(0 for the colour i_0)* , form the symbolic vector $X_{j,k}$ in E^n :
   $$X_{j,k} = \sum_{c \in [1,q]} V^{b_j}_{\sigma_{j,k}(c)}(a_c) + V^{b_j}_{\sigma_{j,k}(0)}(i_0) + \sum_{i=1}^{m_{b_j}} \sum_{c \in C_i^{j,k}} V_i^{b_j}(c)$$
   with $C_i^{j,k}$ a partition of $[c_1, c_n] \setminus i_0$.
   (b) for each V_k^0 in $Sol(D, 0)$, for each colour c in $[1, q] \cup \{i0\}$ form the vector $X_{0,k}^c$ in E^n :
   $X_{0,k}^c = V_k^0(a_c)$ if $c \neq i_0$ and $X_{0,k}^c = V_k^0(i_0)$ if $c = i_0$
3. for each X constructed at the step 2 make the projection $P(X_{j,k})$ on the first equation
   $P(X_{j,k}) = H_{i_0}.X(i_0) + H_{a_1}.X(a_1) + \ldots + H_{a_q}.X(a_q)$ where $X(i)$ denotes the ith component of the vector X
4. solve by Farkas $\sum \mu_{j,k}.X_{j,k} = 0$ and construct the set $S^* = \{< \mu_{j,k} >\}$

The following proposition makes the link between the family computed by the last algorithm and the solutions of the equation 3 : e.g. the positive flows of the U-Pr/T net :

Proposition 7 *Let be F the family composed by the vectors :*

- $\forall i \geq q+1, \forall X \in Sol(D,0)$ *the vector* $X(i)$
- $\forall <\mu_{j,k}> \in S^*$, *the vector:* $Z = \sum \mu_{j,k}.X_{j,k}$

Then F is a generative family of positive flows.

Proof: The proof lies on the fact that the number of constant is finite - non depending on n - and that the Farkas algorithm computes a generative family. For a complete proof, please refer to [CHP90]. ◇◇◇

Remark : The family obtained is not necessary minimal.

Example :

We apply the algorithm on the net defined in section 2, figure 2 and 4.

The first step of the algorithm - *algorithm 4 on the matrix D* - computes the set S defined by :

$S = \{0 = (0,0), b_1 = (-1,0), b_2 = (0,-1), b_3 = (1,0)\}$ with :

- $Sol(D,0) = \{(p+r),(p+s)\}$
- $Sol(D,b_1) = \{(p)\}$
- $Sol(D,b_2) = \{(u)\}$
- $Sol(D,b_3) = \{(r),(s)\}$

We develop now the symbolic vectors associated to each b_i in S - *step 2* - :

- b_1 :

  Because there is only one vector in $Sol(D,b_1)$, there is only one partition of $[1,n]$ and one application σ from $[0,2]$ to $[1,1]$: $\sigma(0) = \sigma(1) = \sigma(2) = 1$.

  Also the vector b_1 gives only one symbolic vector $X_{1,1}$ with:

$$X_1 = \sum_{c\in[1,2]} p(a_c) + p(i_0) + \sum_{c\in[c_1,c_n]\setminus\{i_0\}} p(c) = p(a) + p(b) + p(i_0) + \sum_{c\in[c_1,c_n]\setminus\{i_0\}} p(c)$$

- b_2 :

  Because of the same raisons the vector $b_2$gives only one symbolic vector $X_{2,1}$ with:

$$X_2 = \sum_{c\in[1,2]} u(a_c) + u(i_0) + \sum_{c\in[c_1,c_n]\setminus\{i_0\}} u(c) = u(a) + u(b) + u(i_0) + \sum_{c\in[c_1,c_n]\setminus\{i_0\}} u(c)$$

- b_3 :

  There is two vectors in $Sol(A,b_3)$. Also the vector b_3 gives height symbolic vectors because there is height applications from $[0,2]$ to $[1,2]$.

  We note these vectors :

$$X_{3,rrr} = r(a) + r(b) + r(i_0) + \sum_{c\in C_1} r(c) + \sum_{c\in C_2} s(c) \text{ with } C_1 \oplus C_2 = [c_1,c_n] \setminus \{i_0\}$$

  to

$$X_{3,sss} = s(a) + s(b) + s(i_0) + \sum_{c\in C_1} r(c) + \sum_{c\in C_2} s(c) \text{ with } C_1 \oplus C_2 = [c_1,c_n] \setminus \{i_0\}$$

- $b_0 = 0$:

  The vector 0 gives the six vectors :

$$X^a_{0,1} = (\text{ p+r })(a) \quad X^a_{0,2} = (\text{ p+s })(a)$$
$$X^b_{0,1} = (\text{ p+r })(b) \quad X^b_{0,2} = (\text{ p+s })(b)$$
$$X^{i_0}_{0,1} = (\text{ p+r })(i_0) \quad X^{i_0}_{0,2} = (\text{ p+s })(i_0)$$

We have now to make the projection of these vectors on the first equation - *step 3* - : Compute the sum : $P(X_{j,k}) = H_{i_0}.X(i_0) + H_{a_1}.X(a_1) + \ldots + H_{a_q}.X(a_q)$

We obtain :

- $P(X_1) = -1$
- $P(X_2) = -3$
- $P(X_{3,rrr}) = P(X_{3,rrs}) = P(X_{3,rsr}) = P(X_{3,rss}) = 1$
- $P(X_{3,sss}) = P(X_{3,ssr}) = P(X_{3,srs}) = P(X_{3,srr}) = 2$
- $P(X^a_{0,1}) = P(X^b_{0,1}) = P(X^{io}_{0,1}) = 0$
- $P(X^b_{0,2}) = P(X^{io}_{0,2}) = 0$
- $P(X^a_{0,2}) = 1$

At this step we can use some equalities , $P(X_{3,sss}) = P(X_{3,ssr}) = P(X_{3,srs}) = P(X_{3,srr})$ for instance, to condense the information.

For example, because $P(X_{3,sss}) = \ldots = P(X_{3,srr})$, the four different vectors $X_{3,sss}, X_{3,ssr}, X_{3,srs}, X_{3,srr}$ can be view as the same one :

$X_3^{s(a)} = s(a) + \sum_{c \in C_1} r(c) + \sum_{c \in C_2} s(c)\ C_1 \oplus C_2 = [c_1, c_n] \bigcup \{b\}$.

If we use the others equalities we can make three others renomations :

- $X_{3,rrr}, X_{3,rrs}, X_{3,rsr}, X_{3,rss} \longrightarrow X_3^{r(a)} = r(a) + \sum_{c \in C_1} r(c) + \sum_{c \in C_2} s(c)\ C_1 \oplus C_2 = [c_1, c_n] \bigcup \{b\}$
- $X^a_{0,1}, X^b_{0,1}, X^{io}_{0,1} \longrightarrow X_{0,1} = (p + r)(c), c \in \{a, b, i_0\}$
- $X^b_{0,2}, X^{io}_{0,2} \longrightarrow X^{b,io}_{0,2} = (p + s)(c), c \in \{b, i_0\}$

We execute now the fourth step of the algorithm ... and we obtain the generative family :

$\{(\mu_{0,1}), (\mu^{b,io}_{0,2}), (\mu_1 + \mu_3^{r(a)}), (2.\mu_1 + \mu_3^{s(a)}), (\mu_1 + \mu^a_{0,2}), (\mu_2 + 3\mu_3^{r(a)}), (2\mu_2 + 3\mu_3^{s(a)}), (\mu_2 + 3\mu^a_{0,2})\}$

We just have now to develop these solutions with the help of proposition 7; we obtain the generative family F composed by the vectors :

- $Sol(D, 0) \longrightarrow$
  $(p + r)(c) \forall c \in Cl \setminus \{a, b\}$
  $(p + s)(c) \forall c \in Cl$
- $(\mu_{0,1}) \longrightarrow$
  $(p + r)(c) c \in \{a, b, i_0\} \forall i_0 \in [c_1, c_n]$
- $(\mu^{b,io}_{0,2}) \longrightarrow$
  $(p + s)(c) c \in \{b, i_0\} \forall i_0 \in [c_1, c_n]$
- $(\mu_1 + \mu_3^{r(a)}) \longrightarrow$
  $\sum_{c \in Cl} p(c) + \sum_{c_1 \in C_1} r(c_1) + \sum_{c_2 \in C_2} s(c_2)$ with $C_1 \oplus C_2 = Cl, a \in C_1$
- $(2.\mu_1 + \mu_3^{s(a)}) \longrightarrow$
  $\sum_{c \in Cl} 2.p(c) + \sum_{c_1 \in C_1} r(c_1) + \sum_{c_2 \in C_2} s(c_2)$ with $C_1 \oplus C_2 = Cl, a \in C_2$
- $(\mu_1 + \mu_2^a) \longrightarrow$
  $(p + s)(a) + \sum_{c \in Cl} p(c)$
- $(\mu_2 + 3.\mu_3^{r(a)}) \longrightarrow$
  $\sum_{c \in Cl} u(c) + \sum_{c_1 \in C_1} 3.r(c_1) + \sum_{c_2 \in C_2} 3.s(c_2)$ with $C_1 \oplus C_2 = Cl, a \in C_1$
- $(2.\mu_2 + 3.\mu_3^{s(a)}) \longrightarrow$
  $\sum_{c \in Cl} 2.u(c) + \sum_{c_1 \in C_1} 3.r(c_1) + \sum_{c_2 \in C_2} 3.s(c_2)$ with $C_1 \oplus C_2 = Cl, a \in C_2$
- $(\mu_2 + 3.\mu^a_{0,2}) \longrightarrow$
  $(3.p + 3.s)(a) + \sum_{c \in Cl} u(c)$

If we keep only the minimal solutions we obtain the generative family:

- $(p+r)(c), \forall c \in Cl$
- $(p+s)(c), \forall c \in Cl \setminus \{b\}$
- $(p+s)(a) + \sum_{c \in Cl} p(c)$
- $(3p+3s)(a) + \sum_{c \in Cl} u(c)$
- $\sum_{c \in Cl} u(c) + \sum_{c_1 \in C_1} 3.r(c_1) + \sum_{c_2 \in C_2} 3.s(c_2)$ with $C_1 \oplus C_2 = Cl, a \in C_1$
- $\sum_{c \in Cl} 2.u(c) + \sum_{c_1 \in C_1} 3.r(c_1) + \sum_{c_2 \in C_2} 3.s(c_2)$ with $C_1 \oplus C_2 = Cl, a \in C_2$

5.2 Computation of positive flows for unary regular nets

As we see in section 3.2.1, the computation of positive flows in unary regular net is equivalent to solve the system :

$$\left[\begin{array}{l} (D+n.B).\sum_{j=1}^{n} X_j = 0 \\ D.X_1 = D.X_2 = \ldots = D.X_n \end{array} \right.$$

Let us suppose that b_j is a vector obtained by the algorithm 4 on the matrix D and that $Sol(A, b_j)$ is the set $\{V_{j,k}\} = \{V_{j,1}, \ldots, V_{j,m_j}\}$. Each vector of $Sol^n(A, b_j)$ is a solution of $D.X_1 = \ldots = D.X_n$ and can be expressed as the formal sum:

$$X = \left\{ \begin{array}{l} \sum_{c \in C_{j,k}} V_{j,k}(c) \; with \; \oplus C_{j,K} = C \; if \; b_j \neq 0 \\ V_{0,k}(c_i) \; \forall i \in [1.n] \; if \; b_j = 0 \end{array} \right.$$

In order to solve the system 2 we have to report the solutions of the equation $D.X_1 = \ldots = D.X_n$ to the first one. So, the report of these vectors on the first equation gives for each $b_j \neq 0$ the formal vector :

$W_j = \sum k_{j,k}(D+nB).V_{j,k}$ with $k_{j,k} = Cardinal(C_{j,k})$ and $\sum k_{j,k} = n$

and for $b_j = 0$ we have for all $V_{0,k}$ in $Sol(D, 0)$ the formal vector :

$W_0^k = (D+nB).V_{0,k}$

So we have to solve the system :

$$\sum_{V_{0,k} \in Sol(D,0)} \mu_k^0.W_k^0 + \sum_{b_j \in S \setminus \{0\}} \mu_j.W_j = 0 \; where \; \{\mu_k^0, \mu_j\} \; are \; the \; unknowns$$

which corresponds to:

$$\sum_{V_{0,k} \in Sol(D,0)} \mu_k^0.(D+nB).V_{0,k} + \sum_{b_j \in S \setminus \{0\}} \mu_j. \left[\sum_{k=1}^{m_j} k_{j,k}(D+nB).V_{j,k} \right] = 0$$

As for each b_j and each vector $V_{j,k}$ of $Sol(D, b_j)$, $D.V_{j,k} = b_j$, it is equivalent to solve the system:

$$\sum_{V_{0,k} \in Sol(D,0)} \mu_k^0.(0 + nB.V_{0,k}) + \sum_{b_j \in S \setminus \{0\}} \mu_j. \left[n.b_j + \sum_{k=1}^{m_j} nk_{j,k}B.V_{j,k} \right] = 0$$

which is also equivalent to:

$$\sum_{V_{0,k} \in Sol(D,0)} \mu_k^0.B.V_{0,k} + \sum_{b_j \in S \setminus \{0\}} \mu_j. \left[b_j + \sum_{k=1}^{m_j} k_{j,k}B.V_{j,k} \right] = 0 \qquad (4)$$

So resolution of system 2 consists in solving first the equation (i) and then in solving in a formal way the equation 4. Because this formal resolution is not the purpose of this paper, we only give an example. The reader interests in this resolution may refer to [CHP90].

We consider the example given in part 2.2 (figure 1) and we prove that the place Idle is a structural implicit place.

In order to do that, we compute a generative family of positive flows on the net in which we have reversed the arcs adjoining to the place Idle.

Matrices D and B of this new net are defined by :

$$D = \begin{array}{c} \\ t_1 \\ t_2 \\ t_3 \\ t_4 \end{array} \begin{array}{c} \begin{array}{cccccc} Idle & Message & Wait & Update & Mutex & Ack \end{array} \\ \begin{pmatrix} 1 & -1 & 1 & 0 & 0 & 0 \\ 1 & -1 & 0 & 1 & 0 & 0 \\ -1 & 0 & -1 & 0 & 0 & 1 \\ -1 & 0 & 0 & -1 & 0 & 1 \end{pmatrix} \end{array}$$

$$B = \begin{array}{c} \\ t_1 \\ t_2 \\ t_3 \\ t_4 \end{array} \begin{array}{c} \begin{array}{cccccc} Idle & Message & Wait & Update & Mutex & Ack \end{array} \\ \begin{pmatrix} 0 & 1 & 0 & 0 & -1 & 0 \\ 0 & 0 & 0 & 0 & 0 & 0 \\ 0 & 0 & 0 & 0 & 1 & -1 \\ 0 & 0 & 0 & 0 & 0 & 0 \end{pmatrix} \end{array}$$

We first solve the equation $D.X_1 = \ldots = D.X_n$ and we obtain the family S :

$S = \{(0), b_1 = (0,1,0,-1), b_2 = (0,0,1,1), b_3 = (1,0,-1,0), b_4 = (-1,-1,0,0), b_5 = (1,1,-1,-1)\}$ with :

- $Sol(D,(0)) = \{(Mutex), (Message + Update + Wait + Ack), (Idle + Message + Ack)\}$
- $Sol(D,b_1) = \{(Update)\}$
- $Sol(D,b_2) = \{(Ack)\}$
- $Sol(D,b_3) = \{(Wait)\}$
- $Sol(D,b4) = \{(Message)\}$
- $Sol(D,b_5) = \{(Idle), (Update + Wait)\}$

Each b_i of S provides a symbolic vector solution of $D.X_1 = \ldots = D.X_n$. We have to make the report of these solutions on the second equation : $(D + nB).\sum X$. For each b_i we obtain :

- (0) gives the three vectors : $f_{0,1} = (-1,0,1,0), f_{0,2} = (1,0,-1,0), f_{0,3} = (1,0,-1,0)$
- b_1 gives the vector : $f_1 = (0,1,0,-1)$
- b_2 gives the vector : $f_2 = b_2 + k_1(0,0,-1,0)$ with $k_1 = n$ so $f_2 = (0,0,1-n,1)$
- b_3 gives the vector : $f_3 = (1,0,-1,0)$
- b_4 gives the vector : $f_4 = (n-1,-1,0,0)$
- b_5 gives the vector : $f_5 = b_5 + k_1(0,0,0,0) + k_2(0,0,0,0)$ with $k_1 + k_2 = n$, so $f_5 = (1,1,-1,-1)$

Also we have to solve the new system $U.X = 0$ where U is the matrix defined by :

$$U = \begin{array}{c} \\ t_1 \\ t_2 \\ t_3 \\ t_4 \end{array} \begin{array}{c} \begin{array}{cccccccc} f_{0,1} & f_{0,2} & f_{0,3} & f_1 & f_2 & f_3 & f_4 & f_5 \end{array} \\ \begin{pmatrix} -1 & 1 & 1 & 0 & 0 & 1 & n-1 & 1 \\ 0 & 0 & 0 & 1 & 0 & 0 & -1 & 1 \\ 1 & -1 & -1 & 0 & 1-n & -1 & 0 & -1 \\ 0 & 0 & 0 & -1 & 1 & 0 & 0 & -1 \end{pmatrix} \end{array}$$

We "nullify" the second and the fourth row of the previous matrix and we obtain :

$$U = \begin{array}{c} \begin{matrix} f_{0,1} & f_{0,2} & f_{0,3} & f_3 & f_1+f_2+f_4 & f_2+f_4+f_5 \end{matrix} \\ \begin{pmatrix} -1 & 1 & 1 & 1 & n-1 & n \\ 1 & -1 & -1 & -1 & 1-n & -n \end{pmatrix} \end{array}$$

The parameter n is greater or equal to 1. So we must have a discussion on the sign of the polynom $n-1$ which is null for $n=1$ and positive when $n>1$. So we decompose the vector $f_1+f_2+f_4$ in two vectors with constraints on the value of n :

$$f_1+f_2+f_4 \longrightarrow \begin{cases} (f_1+f_2+f_4)_{n=1} \\ (f_1+f_2+f_4)_{n>1} \end{cases}$$

So we have to solve the system $U'.X=0$ where U' is the matrix defined by :

$$U = \begin{array}{c} \begin{matrix} f_{0,1} & f_{0,2} & f_{0,3} & f_3 & (f_1+f_2+f_4)_{n=1} & (f_1+f_2+f_4)_{n>1} & f_2+f_4+f_5 \end{matrix} \\ \begin{pmatrix} -1 & 1 & 1 & 1 & 0 & n-1 & n \\ 1 & -1 & -1 & -1 & 0 & 1-n & -n \end{pmatrix} \end{array}$$

We obtain finally the solutions :

- $f_{0,1}+f_{0,2}$ provides the positive flow :
  $Mutex(c)+(Message+Update+Wait+Ack)(c'), \forall c,c' \in Cl$
- $f_{0,1}+f_{0,3}$ provides the positive flow :
  $Mutex(c)+(Idle+Message+Ack)(c'), \forall c,c' \in Cl$
- $f_{0,1}+f_3$ provides the positive flow :
  $Mutex(c)+\sum_{x\in Cl} Wait(x), \forall c \in Cl$
- $(n-1).f_{0,1}+(f_1+f_2+f_4)_{n>1}$ provides the positive flow :
  $(n-1).Mutex(c)+\sum_{x\in Cl}(Update+Ack+Message)(x), \forall c \in Cl$ and $n>1$
- $(f_1+f_2+f_4)_{n=1}$ provides the positive flow :
  $(Update+Ack+Message)(c)$ with $Cl=\{c\}$
- $n.f_{0,1}+f_2+f_4+f_5$ provides the positive flow :
  $n.Mutex(c)+\sum_{x\in Cl}(Ack+Message)(x)+\sum_{c_1\in C_1} Idle(c_1)+\sum_{c_2\in C_2}(Update+Wait)(c_2), \forall c \in Cl$ and $C_1 \oplus C_2 = Cl$

If we keep only the minimal vectors, we obtain a minimal generative family of positive flows composed by :

- $(Update+Ack+Message)(c)$ with $Cl=\{c\}$
- $Mutex(c)+(Message+Update+Wait+Ack)(c'), \forall c,c' \in Cl$
- $Mutex(c)+\sum_{x\in Cl} Wait(x), \forall c \in Cl$
- $Mutex(c)+(Idle+Message+Ack)(c'), \forall c,c' \in Cl$

This last flow, $Mutex(c)+(Idle+Message+Ack)(c')\forall c,c' \in Cl$, provides that Idle is a structural implicit place of the original net.

6 Conclusion

We have proposed two algorithms for the computation of a generative family of positive positive flows in two basic families of coloured nets. These two algorithms are based on the resolution of the parametrized equation $A.X_1 = \ldots = A.X_n$, where n is the parameter of the model, A a matrix and X_i the unknowns are vectors. We have also proposed an algorithm which solves this equation. The general idea of this algorithm is that the resolution of the system for some n_0 depending on the net provides the general form of a generative family for any n.

The perspective of this work is of course the computation of positive positive flows in more complex systems. There is two possible way : on one hand, similar systems but with multiple parameters - like regular nets or predicate/transition nets - and in the other hand, systems with more complex structure but with only one parameter - like ordered nets - An other perspective of this work can also be the computation of others linear invariants like deadlocks and traps.

Acknowledgements

We would like to thank each of the two anonymus referees for their comments, which were helpfull when it came to improving the presentation of this paper.

References

[Aba64] J.ABADIE
Méthode de Fourier et méthode duale pour les systèmes d'inéquations linéaires", communication invitée au "Mathematical Programming Symposium , Londres 64. Note E.D.F. N. HR 5.759/3, June 5 1964.

[Bra83] G.W. BRAMS
Réseaux de Petri. Théorie et pratique. Masson éditeur, Paris, 1983.

[CHP90] J.M. COUVREUR, S. HADDAD, J.F. PEYRE
Résolution paramétrée de familles de systèmes linéaires , RAIRO-Operations Research, vol. 26, n°2, AFCET-Gauthier-Villars, Paris 1992, p. 183-206.

[Col89] J.M. COLOM, M. SILVA
Improving the linearly based Characterization of P/T nets. Advances in Petri nets 1990. L.N.C.S. 483, G.Rozenberg (eds.). Springer-Verlag, pp. 113-145

[Col89] J.M. COLOM, M. SILVA
Convex geometry and semiflows in P/T nets. A comparative study of algorithms for computation of minimal P-semiflows. Advances in Petri nets 1990. L.N.C.S. 483, G.Rozenberg (eds.). Springer-Verlag, pp. 79-112

[Cou90] J.M. COUVREUR
The general computation of flows for coloured nets. Proceeding of the 11th International Conference on Application and Theory of Petri Nets. Paris. June 90. pp 204-223

[Far02] J.FARKAS
Theorie der einfachen Ungleichungen Journal fur die reine und andgewandte Mathematik, 124, pp. 1-27 1902 .

[Fou27] J.FOURIER
Histoire de l'Académie Royale des Sciences, Analyse des travaux pendant l'année 1824, Partie Mathématique, Paris 1827 pp. xlvij - lv.

[Gen81] H.J. GENRICH, K. LAUTENBACH
System modelling with high-level Petri nets,Theoretical Computer Science 13,1981,pp 103-136.

[Gen83] H.J. GENRICH, K. LAUTENBACH
S-Invariance in predicate transition nets. Informatik Fachberichte 66 : Application and Theory of Petri Nets. A.Pagnoni, G.Rozenberg (eds.). Springer-Verlag. pp. 98-111

[Had86] S. HADDAD, C. GIRAULT

Algebraic structure of flows of a regular net, Oxford England, june 1986, Advances in Petri nets, G.Rozenberg ed., L.N.C.S. N. 266, G.Rozenberg ed., Springer Verlag, 1987, pp 73-88.

[Had87] S. HADDAD

Une catégorie régulière de réseau de Petri de haut niveau: définition, propriétés et réductions. Application à la validation de systèmes distribués, Thèse de l'Université Pierre et Marie Curie, Paris, juin 1987.

[Had88] S. HADDAD, J.M. COUVREUR

Towards a general and powerful computation of flows for parametrized coloured nets. 9th European Workshop on Application and Theory of Petri Nets. Vol.II. Venice (Italy). June 1988.

[Jen81] K. JENSEN

Coloured Petri nets and the invariant method. Theorical Computer Science 14. North Holland Publ. Co.pp.317-336

[Jen86] K. JENSEN

Coloured Petri nets : Central models and their properties. Advances in Petri nets, G.Rozenberg ed.,L.N.C.S. N. 254, Springer-Verlag Part I. Bad Honnef, September 1986. pp 248-299.

[Mem80] G.MEMMI and G.ROUCAIROL

Linear algebra in net theory. Proc. of Advanced course on general Net Theory of Processes and Systems Hambourg 1979, L.N.C.S. 84, W.Brauer (Ed.), Springer Verlag (1980)

[Mem83] G. MEMMI

Méthodes d'analyse de réseaux de Petri, réseaux à files et applications aux systèmes temps réel, Thèse d'état,Université Pierre et Marie Curie, Paris, juin1983.

[Sil85] M. SILVA, J. MARTINEZ, P. LADET, H. ALLA

Generalized inverses and the calculation of symbolic invariants for coloured Petri nets, Technique et Science Informatiques, Vol.4 n1, 1985, pp 113-126.

[Trev86] N. TREVE

Le calcul d'invariants dans les réseaux à prédicats/transistions unaires. Thèse de l'universitée Paris Sud, Paris 1986.

[Vau84] J. VAUTHERIN, G. MEMMI

Computation of flows for unary predicates transitions nets, Advances in Petri nets, G.Rozenberg (eds.), L.N.C.S. 188 , Springer-Verlag 1984, pp. 455-467.

AUTONOMOUS AND TIMED CONTINUOUS PETRI NETS

René DAVID

Hassane ALLA

Laboratoire d'Automatique de Grenoble, ENSIEG,
Institut National Polytechnique de Grenoble -Unité de Recherche Associée au CNRS
BP 46, 38402 Saint-Martin-d'Hères, France -

ABSTRACT

Since an autonomous continuous Petri net is presented as a limit case of autonomous discrete Petri nets, this new model thus preserves most of the properties of classical Petri nets.

A timed continuous Petri net, with firing speeds associated with transitions, can be obtained from a timed discrete Petri net by means of an approximation. Two kinds of approximations are proposed, with constant firing speeds and variable firing speeds, respectively. These models are compared.

Keywords : Petri nets, continuous PN, discrete PN, real marking, quantity of firing, firing speed.

CONTENTS

0. INTRODUCTION

In a Petri net (PN), the marking of a place may correspond either to the boolean state of a device (for example a resource is available or not), or to a number (for example the number of parts in a buffer). When a PN contains a large number of marks, the number of reachable states explodes. This is a practical limitation to the use of Petri nets [1]. Continuous models for discrete systems may provide very good approximations [2], [3], this being the basic idea leading to the definition of continuous Petri nets [4].

A continuous PN is a model in which the markings of places are real numbers. This model was introduced taking into account that a transition was fired with fairly constant speed, provided that it is enabled [4]. This corresponds to a continuous counterpart of a timed PN. The main objective of this paper is to give a formal definition of Continuous Petri nets. An Autonomous Continuous Petri Net (ACPN) is defined as a limit case of an Autonomous Discrete Petri Net (ADPN) [5] *(no time is involved in this model)*. The basic properties of ACPNs are presented as counterparts of basic properties of ADPNs. Then a continuous PN can be obtained from a *timed* discrete PN. Since an approximation is necessary, two kinds of models can be considered : either with constant speeds, or with variable speeds.

1. AUTONOMOUS CONTINUOUS PETRI NETS

A Petri net is a quadruple R = <P, T, Pre, Post > which can be represented by a graph. An example is presented in Fig. 1.a. In this example $P = \{P_1, P_2\}$ is the set of places, $T = \{T_1, T_2\}$ is the set of transitions. Pre (P_i, T_j) and Post (P_i, T_j) defined the weights of arcs $P_i \rightarrow T_j$ and $T_j \rightarrow P_i$, respectively.

In the next section a marked Petri net is transformed into another net by splitting marks. In order to introduce a continuous model for a manufacturing system, a similar splitting (of parts) has been used in [6].

1.1. *Continuous Petri Nets as a limit case of discrete Petri nets*

1.1.1. *Reachable markings*

A marked Petri net is defined by a pair $<R, M_0>$ where M_0 denotes an initial marking. A marking is a vector* $M = (M(P_1), M(P_2), ...)$ such that $M(P_i)$ is the number of marks in place P_i. This number is an integer greater than or equal to 0 in the classical (discrete) Petri nets. In Fig. 1.b $M(P_1) = 2$ and $M(P_2) = 0$, then $M = (2, 0)$.

Usually the terms "mark" and "token" are synonymous. In this paper we consider the transformation such that a mark is split into k tokens (then mark and token are synonymous when k = 1). This transformation results in a new Petri net $<R, M'(k)>$ such that $M'(k) = (k\, M(P_1), k\, M(P_2), ...)$. The marking $M = (2, 0)$ in Fig. 1.b leads to the marking $M'(k) = (2k, 0)$ in Fig. 1.c.

The coverability graph for the Petri net $<R, M>$ in Fig. 1.b is shown in Fig. 1.d. When the marking is (2, 0) transition T_1 is enabled since there is at least one mark in the input place P_1. Firing of T_1 leads to marking (1, 1), for which both T_1 and T_2 are enabled and so on. The set of reachable markings is {(2, 0), (1, 1), (0, 2)}. Now for the Petri net $<R, M'(k)>$ in Fig. 1.c, firing of T_1 from marking (2k, 0) leads to (2k-1, 1) and so on, as illustrated in Fig. 1.e. As far as the marking of $<R, M'(k)>$ is expressed in tokens it corresponds to an integer number of tokens. However if we come back to the initial unit, the markings of the Perti net in Fig. 1.c are expressed by a rational number of "marks", as shown in Fig. 1.e.

Notation : In order to simplify, let us use the following notations :

$m_i = M(P_i)$: marking expressed in marks (initial or transformed PN)

$m'_i(k) = k\, M(P_i)$: marking expressed in tokens. Then $m_i = m'_i/k$

□

Figure 1.f shows the set of possible markings and the corresponding transition firings (i.e. the coverability graph) in the plane defined by m_1 and m_2. The possible markings are presented in Fig. 1.g for $<R, M'(4)>$. When $k \rightarrow \infty$, the set of markings becomes infinite. It can be represented by the segment of a line, as shown in Fig. 1.h.

Another example is presented in Fig. 2. The marked Petri net in Fig. 2.a has four reachable markings, namely $M_0 = (2, 0, 0)$, $M_1 = (1, 0, 1)$, $M_2 = (0, 0, 2)$ and $M_3 = (0, 3, 0)$. The coverability graph is illustrated in Fig. 2.c. When each mark is split into k = 2 tokens (Fig. 2.b), there are nine reachable states which are also illustrated in Fig. 2.c. When k tends towards infinity, the set of reachable markings corresponds to all points in the shaded triangle in Fig. 2.d.

---

* In order to simplify the notation, the transposed matrix is represented in parentheses i.e. $(a, b) = [a\ \ b]^T$

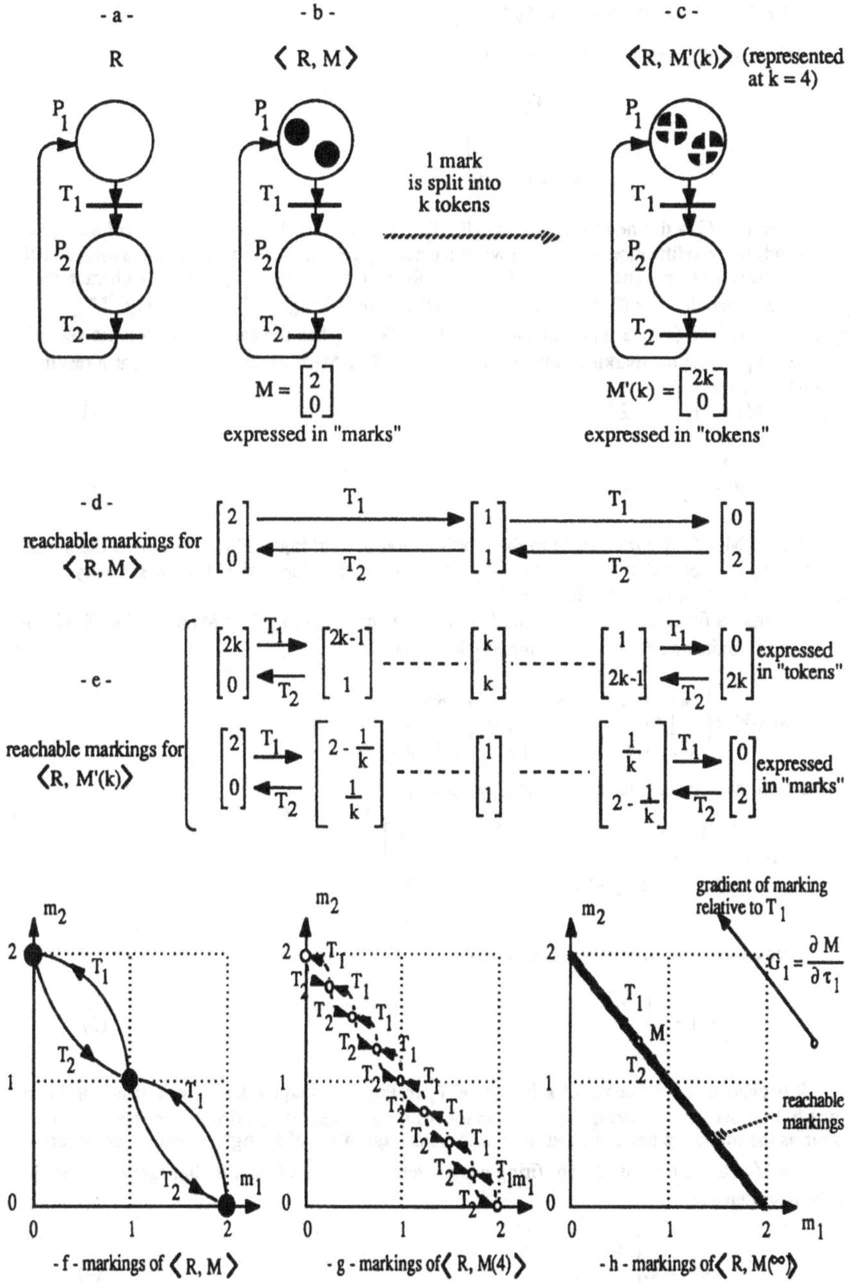

Fig. 1. From autonomous discrete Petri net to autonomous continuous Petri net.

1.1.2. *Gradient of marking and trajectory*

The incidence matrix of PN in Fig. 1.a is

$$C = \begin{array}{c} \\ P_1 \\ P_2 \end{array} \begin{array}{c} \begin{array}{cc} T_1 & T_2 \end{array} \\ \begin{bmatrix} -1 & +1 \\ +1 & -1 \end{bmatrix} \end{array}$$

A term in C is defined by c_{ij} = Post (P_i, T_j) - Pre (P_i, T_j). In other words a column of C corresponds to a modification of marking when the corresponding transition is fired in a marked PN.

The transition sequence $S = T_1T_1T_2$ can be obtained from M_0 in Fig. 1.b. The characteristic vector of S is denoted $\underline{S} = (2, 1)$. This means that there are 2 firings of T_1 and 1 firing of T_2 in the transition sequence (notice that transition sequence $T_1T_2T_1$ has the same characteristic vector).

Let M_1 denote the marking obtained after S, from M_0. M_1 is obtained from M_0 as a result of the fundamental equation :

$$M_1 = M_0 + C \,.\, \underline{S} \tag{1}$$

One can write

$$\Delta M = M_1 - M_0 = C \,.\, \underline{S} \tag{2}$$

Then $\Delta M = C.\, \underline{S}$ corresponds to the modification of marking due to S. Firing of the single transition T_1 is a particular sequence $S_1 = T_1$. The modification due to this firing is given by C. $\underline{S}_1$ which corresponds to the first column of C.

Consider a firing of T_1 from the marking of the Petri net in Fig. 1.c : $M'_0(k) = (2k, 0)$. Using the token as a unit, we obtain the marking $M'_2(k)$ defined by :

$$M'_2(k) = \begin{bmatrix} 2k \\ 0 \end{bmatrix} + \begin{bmatrix} -1 & 1 \\ 1 & -1 \end{bmatrix} \begin{bmatrix} 1 \\ 0 \end{bmatrix} = \begin{bmatrix} 2k-1 \\ 1 \end{bmatrix}$$

Now if we convert tokens into marks, we obtain :

$$M_2 = \begin{bmatrix} 2 \\ 0 \end{bmatrix} + \begin{bmatrix} -1 & 1 \\ 1 & -1 \end{bmatrix} \begin{bmatrix} 1/k \\ 0 \end{bmatrix} = \begin{bmatrix} 2-1/k \\ 1/k \end{bmatrix}$$

Then ΔM expressed in marks is given by

$$\Delta M = C \begin{bmatrix} 1/k \\ 0 \end{bmatrix} \tag{3}$$

It is clear that a sequence of k firings of T_1 in Fig. 1.c is equivalent to one firing of T_1 in Fig. 1.b. In other words a firing expressed in tokens is equivalent to 1/k firing expressed in marks. As far as the markings are expressed in marks, some **"quantity of firing"** 1/k can be considered. Let $d\tau_1 = 1/k$ denote this quantity of firing when k tends towards infinity. In that case equation (3) can be rewritten as :

$$dM = C \begin{bmatrix} d\tau_1 \\ 0 \end{bmatrix} \tag{4}$$

Consider now marking M in Fig. 1.h. For this marking, either T_1 or T_2 can be fired. Then the partial derivatives of M can be defined with respect to τ_1 and τ_2

$$G_1 = \frac{\partial M}{\partial \tau_1} = \begin{bmatrix} -1 \\ 1 \end{bmatrix}$$

$$G_2 = \frac{\partial M}{\partial \tau_2} = \begin{bmatrix} 1 \\ -1 \end{bmatrix}$$

Remark. The arrow labelled T_1 in Fig. 1.h is an illustration of G_1 at this point. However it is not represented in full size so as to obtain clearer figures (scale is about 1/4).

□

Consider now the examples in Fig.2. The incidence matrix of this generalized Petri net is :

$$C = \begin{matrix} & \begin{matrix} T_1 & T_2 & T_3 \end{matrix} \\ \begin{matrix} P_1 \\ P_2 \\ P_3 \end{matrix} & \begin{bmatrix} -1 & -1 & +1 \\ 0 & +3 & -3 \\ 1 & -1 & +1 \end{bmatrix} \end{matrix}$$

For some marking A (see Fig. 2.d) $G_1 = (-1, 0, 1)$, $G_2 = (-1, 3, -1)$, $G_3 = (1, -3, 1)$ are obtained. These gradients of markings are illustrated by the arrows labelled T_1, T_2 and T_3. Now when the marking corresponds to some bound of the domain of reachable markings some transitions cannot be fired. For marking B, T_2 cannot be fired since $m_3 = 0$. For marking C, T_3 cannot be fired since $m_2 = 0$. For marking D, neither T_1 nor T_2 can be fired since $m_1 = 0$. When the marking corresponds to a vertex, only the firings corresponding to both corresponding sides are possible. In particular for marking E one can observe that there is a deadlock since $m_1 = m_2 = 0$.

In a discrete PN, from a marking M, a *firing sequence* implies a string of successive markings. In a continuous PN, from a marking M, a firing sequence implies a **trajectory** (corresponding to a string of successive markings). For example, in Fig. 2. the firing sequence $S_1 = T_1T_2T_3$ from marking $M_0 = (2, 0, 0)$ leads to the marking $M_1 = (1, 0, 1)$ for the discrete PN. To reach M_1 from M_0, the following firing sequences are possible for the continuous PN :

$$S_2 = (T_1)^{0.5}(T_1)^{0.5}(T_2)^{0.5}(T_2)^{0.5}(T_3)^{0.5}(T_3)^{0.5} = ((T_1)^{0.5})^2((T_2)^{0.5})^2((T_3)^{0.5})^2,$$
$$S_3 = (T_1)^{0.5}(T_2)^{0.5}(T_1)^{0.5}(T_3)^{0.5}(T_2)^{0.5}(T_3)^{0.5},$$
$$S_4 = (T_1)^{0.7}(T_2)^{0.3}(T_3)^{0.1}(T_2)^{0.4}(T_1)^{0.3}(T_3)^{0.5}(T_2)^{0.3}(T_3)^{0.4},$$

since 1) the total quantity of firing is 1 for the 3 transitions in each of these sequences (for S_4 : $0.7 + 0.3 = 1$ for T_1, $0.3 + 0.4 + 0.3 = 1$ for T_2, and $0.1 + 0.5 + 0.4 = 1$ for T_3), and 2) at any time in these sequences the total quantity of firings $N(T_1)$, $N(T_2)$ and $N(T_3)$ are such that $N(T_2) \leq N(T_1)$, $N(T_3) \leq N(T_2)$ and $N(T_1) + N(T_2) \leq 2 + N(T_3)$ (which are implied by initial markings of P_3, P_2 and P_1, respectively).

The sequence S_2 may be generalized for any positive integer k :

$$S_5 = ((T_1)^{1/k})^k((T_2)^{1/k})^k((T_3)^{1/k})^k$$

When k tends towards infinity, the length of S_5 becomes infinite. Nevertheless, the sum of the exponents of each S_5 is always equal to 1 for the 3 transitions. More generally, any firing sequence of any length

$$S_6 = (T_1)^a(T_2)^b(T_3)^c \ldots\ldots.(T_2)^x(T_1)^y(T_3)^z,$$

is possible from M_0 as long as $N(T_2) \leq N(T_1)$, $N(T_3) \leq N(T_2)$ and $N(T_1) + N(T_2) \leq 2 + N(T_3)$, i.e. $a \leq 2$, $a - b \geq 0$ and $2 - a - b \geq 0$, $c \leq b$, ...(a, b, c...are non negative numbers which may be infinitelly small).

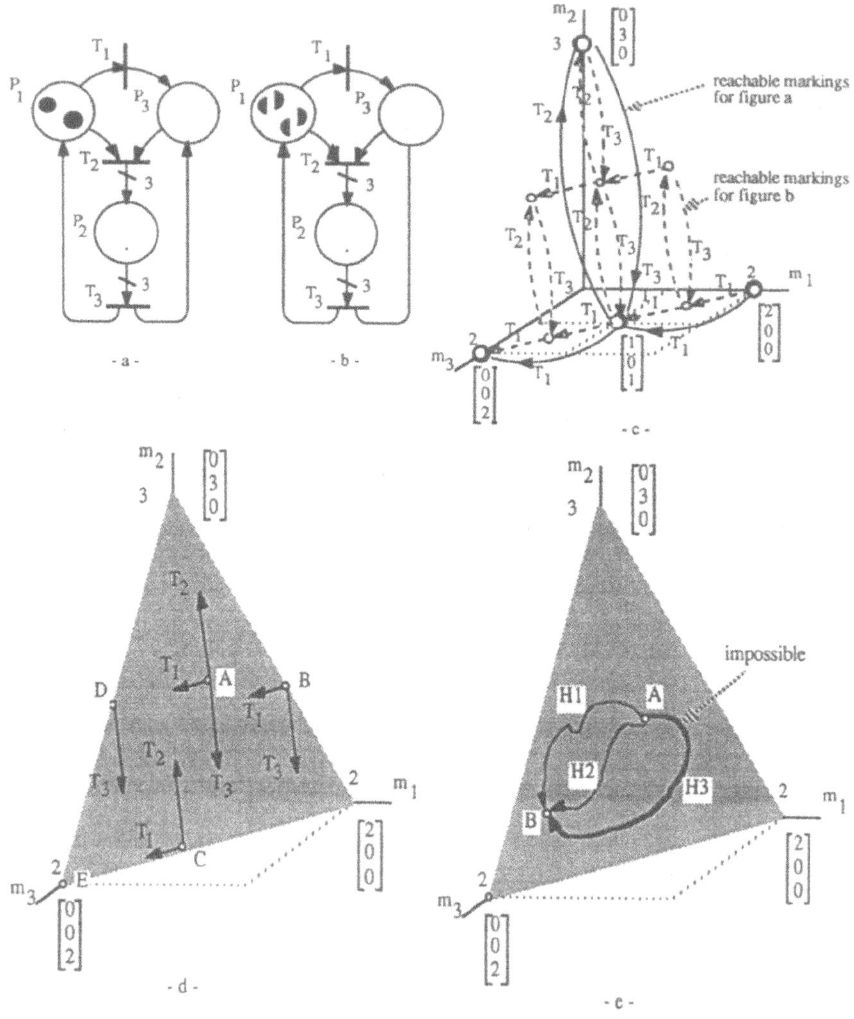

Fig. 2. Illustration of gradients of markings and trajectories.

However the sequences with infinite lenghts are not used in practical cases. The notion of trajectory is easier to use. The goal of the explanations given above is to show that firing sequences of continuous PNs are counterpart of firing sequences of discrete PNs.

Figure 2.e illustrates three trajectories from marking A to marking B. Trajectory H_1 may be obtained by a firing sequence S_1 such that

$$B = A + C \cdot \underline{S}_1$$

Similarly H_2 may be obtained by a firing sequence S_2 such that $C \cdot \underline{S}_1 = C \cdot \underline{S}_2$ (which does not imply that $\underline{S}_1 = \underline{S}_2$).

On the other hand, there is no firing sequence S_3 able to produce trajectory H_3 because at any point of the trajectory the gradient of marking must be a weighted sum with positive coefficients of G_1, G_2 and G_3. This is not possible according to Fig. 2.d.

1.2. *Similarities and differences between ACPN and ADPN.*

1.2.1. *Similarities*

A. Any structural property is true both for an ADPN and an ACPN. This is obviously true since a structural property is a property of a PN without marking.

Consider the Petri net R in Fig. 1.a. It is clear that all the properties of this PN are independent of the marking. Some examples of structural properties are given below :

1) A Petri net may be a state graph, an event graph, without conflict, free-choice, simple, pure...

2) Structurally bounded, structurally alive.

3) P-invariants, T-invariants. Consider for example Fig. 1.a. F = (1, 1) is a P-invariant since $F^T \cdot C = 0$. That means that the total number of marks in the set of places $\{P_1, P_2\}$ is constant. G = (1, 1) is a T-invariant since $C \cdot G = 0$. That means that any transition sequence from the initial marking which contains the same number of firings for T_1 and T_2, in an ADPN, and any trajectory containing the same quantity of firings for T_1 and T_2, in an ACPN, leads the net back to the initial marking.

B. Notions of boundedness, liveness, deadlock freeness can easily be generalized. The notions relative to **synchronic distance** between transitions can also be generalized.

C. Some abbreviations (places with bounded capacity, coloured PN, PN with predicates) and **some extensions** (with inhibitors arcs, with priorities) can be used for both ADPNs and ACPNs.

1.2.2. *Differences* (see Fig. 3)

Marking of a place is a real number instead of an integer. For example $m_1 = 2.1$ and $m_2 = 0.2$ in Fig. 3.a.

The weights of arcs i.e. Pre (P_i, T_j) and Post (P_i, T_j) may be real numbers instead of integers. For example Post $(P_2, T_2) = 3.4$ and Pre $(P_3, T_2) = 0.4$ in Fig. 3.

A transition is enabled if for any place P_i in ${}^{\circ}T_j$, $M(P_i) > 0$ (the classical notation ${}^{\circ}T_j$ defines the set of places P_i such that Pre $(P_i, T_j) > 0$). In fact this can be written $M(P_i)/\mathrm{Pre}(P_i, T_j) > 0$. This expression is the same as for discrete PNs. The only difference is that "> 0" means "≥ 1" for a discrete PN, while "> 0" corresponds to any positive real number for a continuous PN.

It now seems interesting to introduce the notion of q-enabling.

Definition. A transition T_j in a continuous Petri net is q-enabled if

$$q = \min_i (m_i/\mathrm{Pre}\,(P_i, T_j)) > 0 \quad , \quad P_i \in {}^{\circ}T_j$$

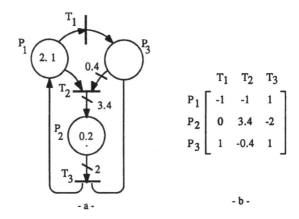

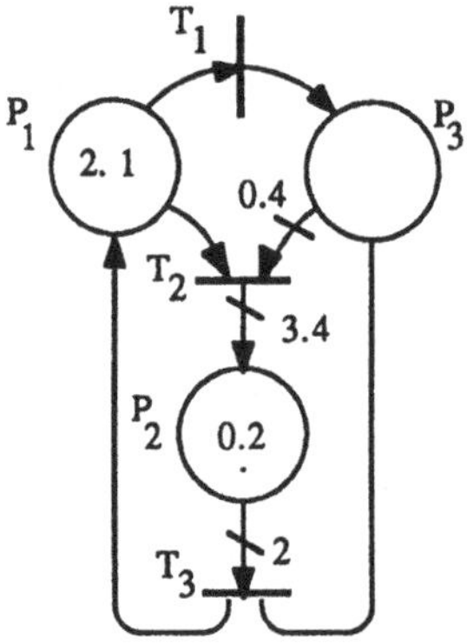

- a -

$$
\begin{array}{c} \\ P_1 \\ P_2 \\ P_3 \end{array}
\begin{array}{c}
\begin{array}{ccc} T_1 & T_2 & T_3 \end{array} \\
\begin{bmatrix} -1 & -1 & 1 \\ 0 & 3.4 & -2 \\ 1 & -0.4 & 1 \end{bmatrix}
\end{array}
$$

- b -

Fig. 3 An Autonomous continuous Petri net

That means that the maximum "quantity of firing" for T_j, assuming that no other transition is fired, is q. In Fig. 3.a, T_1 and T_3 are enabled. Transition T_3 is 0.1-enabled since $m_2/\text{Pre}(T_3, P_2) = 0.2/2 = 0.1$. Transition T_1 is 2.1-enabled.

When a transition is fired, the quantity of firing is r such that r is a real number, $r \leq q$. The quantity of marks taken from or added to the places is defined by the incidence matrix. In Fig. 3.a the quantity of firing of T_3 (before another transition is fired) is at the most 0.1. Assume it is 0.01, then 0.02 mark is taken out of P_2, while 0.01 mark is added to P_1 and 0.01 mark is added to P_3.

Now another difference is that there is an infinity of markings (if the initial marking is not a deadlock) which define a continuous domain of markings. It is sometimes easier to define such a domain than to define a finite but rather big number of discrete markings.

For an ADPN the coverability graph is made up of 1) a set of markings and 2) a set of transitions, labelled by names of transitions, between these markings. The counterpart for an ACPN is 1) a domain of markings and 2) gradients of markings, labelled by names of transitions, at every point in the domain.

For an ADPN, a firing sequence from a marking M_0 defines a sequence of successive markings. The counterpart of this sequence of markings is a continuous trajectory from M_0.

2. TIMED CONTINUOUS PETRI NETS

Timed Petri nets with constant times associated either with places or with transitions [7],[8], [9] are used in order to model various systems. Since these tools are widely admitted for modelling and performance evaluation, a question arises : is it possible to define timed continuous Petri nets as a limit case of timed discrete Petri nets ?

It is known that a Petri net with delays associated with transitions can be transformed into a Petri net (describing the same behaviour) with delays associated with places and vice-versa. For our purpose a Petri net with timed transition fits better.

2.1. *Example of a timed discrete PN*

In a transition timed discrete PN, the firing policy of an enabled transition is carried on according the following three-phase schema : 1) enabled transitions reserve tokens in zero time, 2) reserved tokens are kept still for a fixed amount of time, 3) tokens are removed from input places and deposited in ouput places in zero times upon expiration of the specified delay. In a timed PN, transitions may be simultaneously fired.

Consider the timed PN in Fig. 4.a. Times d_1 and d_2 are associated with transitions T_1 and T_2, respectively. The marking in Fig. 4.a corresponds to time t = 0. The timed PN is assumed to work at its maximum speed, i.e. a transition is fired as soon as it can be fired. In Fig. 4.a, only transition T_2 is enabled at t = 0 then a mark is reserved in P_2 and a mark is reserved in P_4 in order to fire this transition. At time $t = d_2$ transition T_2 is fired : this means that the reserved marks are taken away from P_2 and P_4 and no-reserved marks are put into P_1 and P_4 which are the output places of T_2. Then, at time $t = d_2$, both transitions T_1 and T_2 are enabled (enabling is due to no-reserved marks) : the marks necessary to fire these transitions are reserved. Transition T_1 will be fired at time $t = d_2 + d_1$ and T_2 will be fired at $t = d_2 + d_2$, and so on.

The corresponding behaviour is illustrated in Fig. 4.b for $d_1 = 3$ and $d_2 = 1$. The markings of P_1 and P_2 (i.e., m_1 and m_2) correspond to all the marks, reserved or not, in these places. The markings of places P_3 and P_4 remain constant.

It may be observed that, at any one time there is at the most one mark reserved in P_2, because there is only one mark in P_4. On the other hand when there are two marks in P_1, they can be reserved because there are two marks in P_3. This means that marks are reserved for two firings of T_1. Roughly speaking two "simultaneous firings" of T_1 may occur. Then places P_3 and P_4 correspond to **explicit limitations** to two firings and one firing respectively, at the same time. Notice that the concept of infinite server (classical in queueing networks) corresponds to an explicit limitation which is infinite.

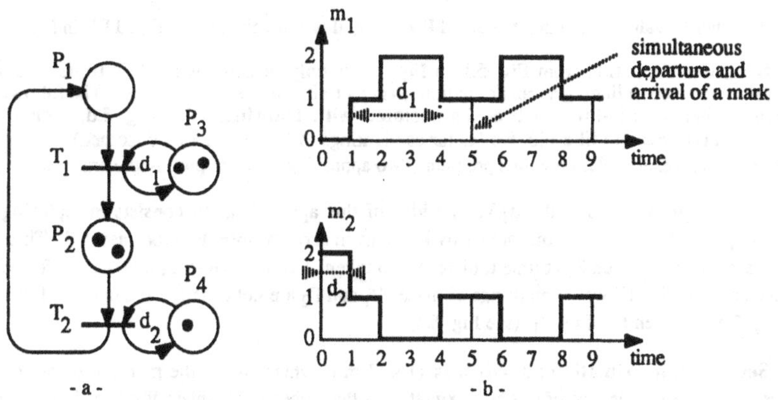

Fig. 4. -a- A timed Petri net -b- Behaviour for $d_1 = 3$ and $d_2 = 1$.

2.2. *From discrete timed PNs to continuous timed PNs*

For a simple presentation, consider a part of a timed PN containing a single transition T_1, whose explicit limitation is 1. See Fig. 5.a.

2.2.1. *Approximations with k finite*

Consider the (part of) timed PN in Fig. 5.a. It may be transformed into another timed PN in Fig. 5.b, by splitting each mark into k tokens. The behaviour of Fig. 5.b is exactly similar to the behaviour of Fig. 5.a, when 1 mark = k token is considered as a unit. As a matter of fact, 1 mark passes from P_1 to P_2 after time d_1 in Fig. 5.a, while k tokens pass from P_1 to P_2 after time d_1 in Fig. 5.b (k simultaneous firings). Now the timed PN in Fig. 5.c behaves exactly like the one in Fig. 5.b, as far as markings of P_1 and P_2 are concerned.

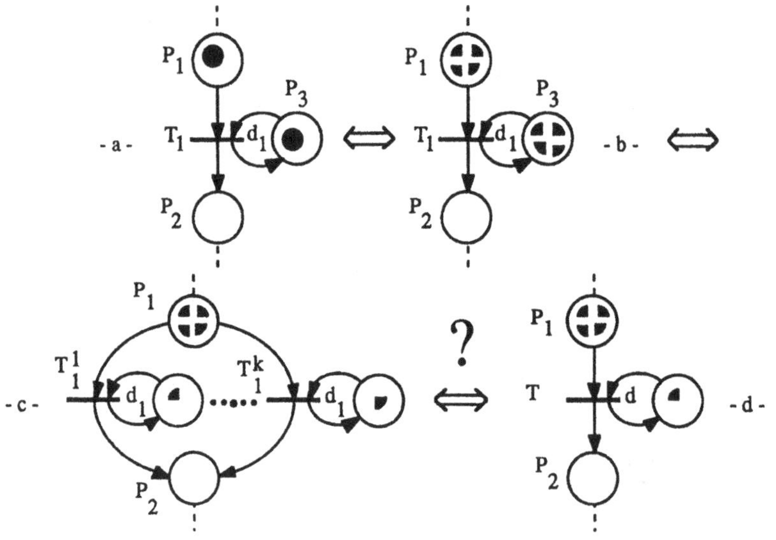

Fig. 5. Is there a value d such that the timed PN in Fig. d is equivalent to the timed PN in Fig. c ?

Now, transformation from Fig. 5.b to Fig. 5.c is only possible when k is finite. We are obviously interested in finding a transformation giving a finite number of transitions. The following problem is then set : **is-there a time d associated with transition T in Fig. 5.d, such that** Fig. 5.d **behaves exactly like** Fig. 5.c (as far as markings of P_1 and P_2 are concerned) ?

There is no exact solution to this problem. Two approximations are proposed, namely :

First approximation : $d = d_1/k$. The idea of this approximation consists in replacing k firings in parallel whose durations are d_1 by k firings in series whose durations are d_1/k. Then if there are k tokens in place P_1 at time t, there are no tokens left in place P_1 at time $t + d_1$, for both Fig. 5.c and Fig. 5.d. However markings of places P_1 and P_2 are not exactly the same for Fig. 5.c and Fig. 5.d, between t and $t + d_1$. (see Fig. 6.a).

Second approximation : $d = d_1 \max (1/k, 1/m'_1)$ where m'_1 is the marking of place P_1 expressed in tokens. The idea of this approximation is that, when the number of tokens in P_1 is less than k, k transitions of Fig. 5.c cannot be fired simultaneously. Assume there are $m'_1 < k$ tokens in P_1 (Fig.5.c). m'_1 transitions can be fired during time d_1. Then the average duration of firing per token is d_1/m'_1 (see Fig. 6.a).

□

These approximations are illustrated in Fig. 6 for k = 4. Fig. 6.a corresponds to marking of P_1 in Fig. 5.d. For the first approximation each firing lasts $d_1/4$, and the marking of P_1 is correct at time 0 and at time d_1. For the second approximation one has $d = d_1 \max (1/4, 1/m'_1)$. Initially $m'_1 = 4$, then the first firing lasts $d_1/4$. The following firings then last $d_1/3$, $d_1/2$ and d_1. For this approximation it can be shown that the area under graph C is exactly the same as the area under graph A. This means that the average number of tokens per time unit exactly corresponds with this approximation.

Fig. 6.b shows the behaviour assuming there are 3 marks (i.e., 12 tokens) in P_1 at time 0 (provided there is no other firing putting tokens into P_1). It can be seen that both approximations behave similarly as long as $m_1 \geq 1$.

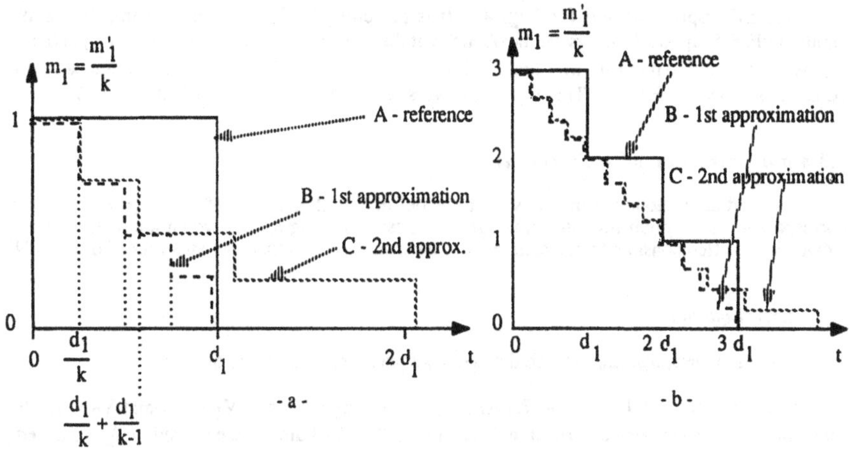

Fig. 6. Illustration of approximations for k = 4

2.2.2. *k infinite : timed-continuous PN*

For each approximation, a model of a timed continuous PN is obtained. As d_1/k and d_1/m'_1 tend towards 0. A measure can be employed which is more convenient for a continuous flow, namely the firing speed.

Let V_j denote the firing speed of transition T_j, i.e. the number of marks which can pass through T_j per time unit.

Then for the example in Fig. 5, one has

$V_1 = 1/d_1$, for the first approximation

$V_1 = (1/d_1) \min(1, m_1)$, for the second approximation

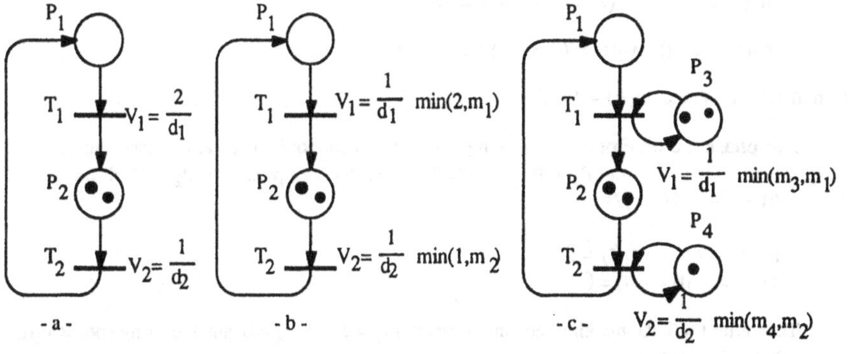

Fig. 7. Approximations for the timed PN in Fig. 4.a. -a- First approximation -b- Second approximation

Let us now come back to Fig. 4, and consider both approximations.

First approximation for Fig. 4.a. It is presented in Fig. 7.a. For T_2, $V_2 = 1/d_2$ is obtained. Since there are two marks in P_3, a transformation similar to the one in Fig. 5 leads to a set of 2 k transitions in parallel instead of k. We have obtained a model which is a **Constant speed Continuous Petri Net** (CCPN). This is the model which was initially defined and studied in [4].

Second approximation for Fig. 4.a. It is presented in Fig. 7.b. From a transformation similar to Fig. 5, up to 2 k firings can be obtained at the same time. In Fig. 7.b, min (2, m_1) and min (1, m_2) correspond to min (m_3, m_1) and min (m_4, m_2) respectively. The explicit limitation can then be used as shown in Fig. 7.c. This is a **Variable speed Continuous Petri Net** (VCPN).

2.3 *Main properties of both models*

A timed continuous PN may obviously be defined, with numbers of marks (even in places corresponding to implicit limitation), weights of arcs, and firing speeds which are real numbers. However, we often consider integers, in order to have an easier comparison with a timed discret PN.

2.3.1. *Equations*

In both models, markings can be defined by equations, as functions of time.

Consider the CCPN in Fig. 7.a with $d_1 = 3$ and $d_2 =1$. Then $V_1 = 2/3$ and $V_2 = 1$. The following analysis has been described in details in [4]. At initial time, since transition T_2 is enabled, the flow through T_2 is $V_2 = 1$, then marking of P_1 increases, and T_1 is fired at $V_1 = 2/3$ (since $V_1 < V_2$). Let $v_j(t)$ denote the instantaneous speed associated with transition T_j at time t.
$\dot{m}_i$ (t) denotes the time derivative of the marking of place P_i.

The functioning of a CCPN is decomposed into phases. Each one is characterized by a set of enabled transitions and a constant firing speeds vector. The evolution of the markings is obtained by computing the balance markings of each place. The changing of firing speeds vector occurs when the marking of a place becomes zero. The time evolution of a CCPN is then characterized by a finite number of phases. This number is very small compared with the number of reachable states of the corresponding discrete PN.

1st phase ($0 \leq t < 6$). $v_1(t) = V_1 = 2/3$, $v_2(t) = V_2 = 1$ are obtained. Then

$$\dot{m}_1(t) = v_2(t) - v_1(t) = (1 - 2/3)\, t = 1/3\, t$$

$$\dot{m}_2(t) = v_1(t) - v_2(t) = (2/3 - 1)\, t = - 1/3\, t$$

then $m_1(t) = 1/3\, t$ and $m_2(t) = 2 - 1/3\, t$.

2nd phase ($t \geq 6$). From time $t = 6$, $m_2 = 0$, then T_2 cannot be fired at the maximum speed. Only the marks passing from P_1 to P_2 through T_1 (speed V_1) can pass from P_2 to P_1 through T_2. Then $v_1(t) = v_2(t) = V_1 = 2/3$

$$\dot{m}_1(t) = v_2(t) - v_1(t) = 0$$
$$\dot{m}_2(t) = v_1(t) - v_2(t) = 0$$

Then after $t = 6$, the marking remains constant, $m_1 = 2$ and $m_2 = 0$, and the firing speeds $v_1(t)$ and $v_2(t)$ remain constant.

The corresponding behaviour is illustrated in Fig.8.a. This is a simple example. The way to analyse a CCPN has been presented in [4], in which two algorithms of computing the set of enabled transitions and the instantaneous firing speeds are given. The instantaneous firing speeds of transitions remain constant in a functioning interval. This interval defines a phase and, providing there is no conflict, the number of phases is finite and each phase (except the last one) lasts a finite time.

Consider the VCPN in Fig. 7.b or c, with $d_1= 3$ and $d_2 = 1$. The behaviour is illustrated in Fig. 8.b.

1st phase $(0 \leq t < t_1)$

$$v_1(t) = V_1 = \frac{1}{3}\min(2, m_1) = \frac{1}{3} m_1$$
$$v_2(t) = V_2 = 1 \min(1, m_2) = 1$$
$$\dot{m}_1(t) = v_2(t) - v_1(t) = 1 - \frac{1}{3} m_1$$
$$\dot{m}_2(t) = v_1(t) - v_2(t) = \frac{1}{3} m_1 - 1$$

then :

$$m_1(t) = 3\left(1 - e^{-\frac{t}{3}}\right)$$
$$m_2(t) = -1 + 3\, e^{-\frac{t}{3}}$$

this phase ends when $m_1 = m_2 = 1$, at $t_1 = 3 \ln 1.5 \sim 1.2$.

2nd phase $(t \geq t_1)$

$$v_1(t) = \frac{1}{3} m_1$$
$$v_2(t) = m_2$$
$$\dot{m}_1(t) = -\frac{1}{3} m_1 + m_2 = \frac{4}{3} m_2 - \frac{2}{3}$$
$$\dot{m}_2(t) = -\ m_2 + \frac{1}{3} m_1 = \frac{2}{3} - \frac{4}{3} m_2$$

then

$$m_1(t) = \frac{3}{2} - \frac{1}{2} e^{-\frac{4t}{3}}$$
$$m_2(t) = \frac{1}{2}\left(1 + e^{-\frac{4t}{3}}\right)$$

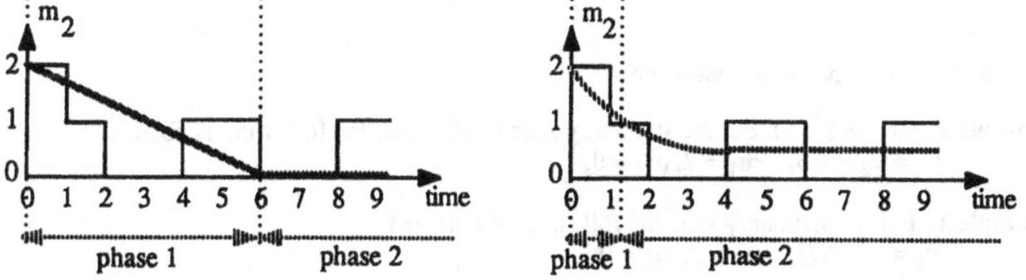

- a -　　　　　　　　- b -

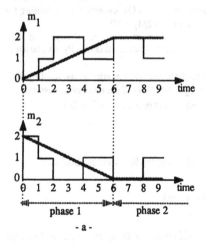

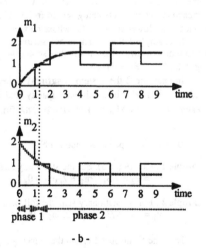

Fig. 8. Behaviour of a timed continuous PN, approximation of the timed discrete PN in Fig.4 (with $d_1 = 3$ and $d_2 = 1$), -a- Constant speed continuous PN -b- Variable speed continuous PN.

2.3.2. *Stationary state*

A - Timed discrete PNs

It appears clearly in Fig. 4.b that a periodic behaviour occurs after some time. This is true for any timed discrete PN, providing that the PN is bounded, there is no effective conflict, and delays are rational numbers. Firing frequencies associated with the stationary (periodical) state can be calculated [7] [9].

Let $\underline{m}_i$ be the average number of marks in P_i and F_j be the firing frequency of transition T_j for the stationary state.

Example 1 : Consider the timed discrete PN of Fig. 4.a. When transition T_1 is fired, that implies that a mark was reserved in P_1 for at least time d_1, then the average marking $\underline{m}_1$ is such that $\underline{m}_1 \geq F_1 d_1$. Similarly $\underline{m}_2 \geq F_2 d_2$, and so on. From the set of three P-invariants $m_1 + m_2 = 2$, $m_3 = 2$, $m_4 = 1$ one can obtain three inequations : $\underline{m}_1 + \underline{m}_2 = 2 \geq F_1 d_1 + F_2 d_2$, $\underline{m}_3 = 2 \geq F_1 d_1$, $\underline{m}_4 = 1 \geq F_2 d_2$. From the T-invariant $F_1 = F_2$ is obtained. Given $d_1 = 3$ and $d_2 = 1$, this set of four equations gives the solution $F_1 = F_2 = 0.5$ (in a functionning with maximum speed). From $\underline{m}_1 \geq F_1 d_1$, $\underline{m}_2 \geq F_2 d_2$, $\underline{m}_1 = 1.5$ and $\underline{m}_2 = 0.5$ are obtained (there is not always a unique solution for the average markings).

Example 2 : Similar to example 1, except that initial marking of P_2 is $m_2 = 3$. All equations are similar except that $\underline{m}_1 + \underline{m}_2 = 3 \geq F_1 d_1 + F_2 d_2$. The result $F_1 = F_2 = 2/3$, $\underline{m}_1 \geq 2$ and $\underline{m}_2 \geq 2/3$ is obtained. Then $2 \leq \underline{m}_1 \leq 7/3$ and $2/3 \leq \underline{m}_2 \leq 1$, with $\underline{m}_1 + \underline{m}_2 = 3$. The values $\underline{m}_1$ and $\underline{m}_2$ depend on the initial marking. There is no analytic method able to calculate these values. They can be obtained only from simulation.

□

Assume that timed PN in Fig. 4.a models a manufacturing system. Transition T_1 corresponds to a 2-server station Q_1 (2 marks in P_3). The service time is $d_1 = 3$ for each server. Transition T_2 corresponds to a single server station Q_2, whose service time is $d_2 = 1$. Marks in P_1 and P_2 correspond to customers being served (reserved marks) by Q_1 and Q_2 respectively, or waiting for service. The slower station is Q_2 whose maximum throughput is $2/d_1 = 2/3$.

In example 1 the system is **not saturated** since the slower station is not always used at its maximum capacity (that means that sometimes there are less than 2 marks in P_1, as shown in Fig. 4.b). Then $F_1 = F_2 < 2/3$.

In example 2 the system is **saturated** because there are more marks in the set $\{P_2, P_3\}$. Station Q_1 is used at its maximum capacity, and $F_1 = F_2 = 2/3$. Now, if the number of customers is greater, i.e. for any $M_0(P_1) + M_0(P_2) \geq 3$, the firing frequencies remain $F_1 = F_2 = 2/3$.

B - Constant speed continuous PN

Example 1 : (see Fig. 8.a). For the stationary state (2nd phase) the following is obtained :

$$v_1 = v_2 = 2/3, \quad m_1 = 2, m_2 = 0.$$

Example 2 : For the stationary state the following is obtained

$$v_1 = v_2 = 2/3, \quad m_1 = 3, m_2 = 0.$$

Now the firing speed v_j and the marking m_i of a CCPN can be compared respectively to the firing frequency F_j and to the average marking $\underline{m}_i$ of the timed discrete PN. This CCPN model emphasizes the accumulation of customers waiting for the slower station. For any $M_0(P_1) + M_0(P_2) > 0$ it gives the maximum speed ($v_1 = v_2 = 2/3$). This model, which is very easy to use is a **good model** for a **saturated system.** It is optimistic for a no-saturated model [10].

C - Variable speed continuous PN

In this model, the stationary state is generally reached asymptotically, i.e. for $t = \infty$.

Example 1 (see Fig. 8.b). For the stationary state $v_1 = v_2 = 0.5$, $m_1 = 1.5$ and $m_2 = 0.5$ are obtained. It can be observed that these values are similar to the values obtained for the discrete model ($v_j = F_j$ and $m_i = \underline{m}_i$).

Example 2. For the stationary state $v_1 = v_2 = 2/3$, $m_1 = 7/3$ and $m_2 = 2/3$ are obtained. These values are quite coherent with the timed discrete PN. Furthermore they are the actual values. Hence this model provides an analytic way to calculate the average markings in the stationary state of a timed discrete PN.

Then this VCPN model is a **good model** even for a **non-saturated** system.

2.3.3. *Conflicts*

A - Timed Discrete PN

In a timed discrete PN there is an effective conflict at a time t if, at that time : 1) a place P_i contains $m_i \geq 1$ marks; 2) there are more than m_i output transitions of P_i which are enabled.

Now let us see how this notion can be transposed for both models CCPN and VCPN. Roughly speaking, there is an effective conflict at time t, if there is a place P_i such that : 1) at least 2 output transitions of P_i can be fired ; and 2) all the output transitions of P_i cannot be fired at there maximum instantaneous speeds, due to marking of P_i.

B - Constant Speed Continuous PNs

Consider the example in Fig. 9.

a) When $m_1 > 0$, there is no effective conflict because both T_2 and T_3 can be fired at their maximum speed $v_2 = V_2$ and $v_3 = V_3$, respectively.

b) When $m_1 = 0$, and $v_1 = 0$ there is no conflict because neither T_2 nor T_3 can be fired.

c) When $m_1 = 0$, and $0 < v_1 < V_2 + V_3$, there is an effective conflict.

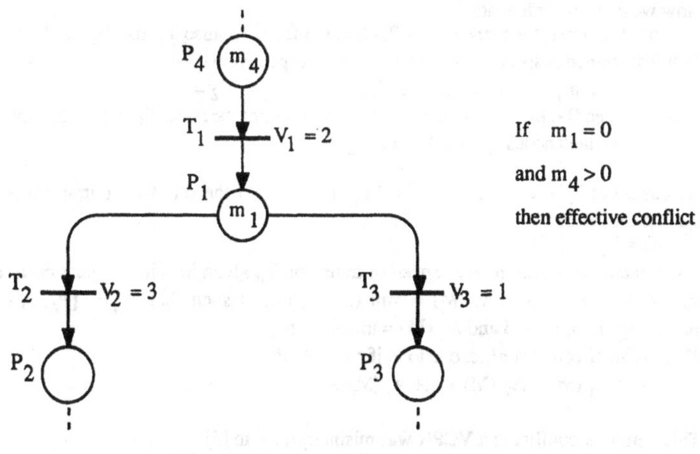

Fig. 9. Effective conflict in a CCPN

Consider Fig. 9, with $m_4 > 0$ and $m_1 = 0$. Since $m_4 > 0$, one has $v_1 = V_1 = 2$. Since P_1 is fed through transition T_1, transition T_2 and T_3 can be fired. However they cannot be fired at their maximum speeds because $v_1 < V_2 + V_3 = 4$, i.e. there is an effective conflict between both transitions. The actual speeds must be such that $v_2 + v_3 = v_1$. There is an infinite number of solutions. Such a conflict may be solved by adding some rule to the CCPN (priority or sharing). Here are some examples.

Hypothesis 1. Transition T_2 has priority over T_3. Since $v_1 < V_2$, $v_2 = v_1 = 2$, and $v_3 = 0$ are obtained.

Hypothesis 2. Transition T_3 has priority over T_2. Since $v_1 > V_3$, $v_3 = V_3 = 1$, and $v_2 = v_1 - v_3 = 1$.

Hypothesis 3. Sharing proportional to the maximum speeds, i.e. $v_2/v_3 = 3$. One obtains $v_2 = 1.5$, and $v_3 = 0.5$.

C - Variable Speed Continuous PNs

Fig. 10. Illustration for understanding the meaning of an effective conflict in a VCPN

The notion of conflict is not easy to understand for a VCPN. Let us first consider the example in Fig. 10.a. Is there a conflict between transitions T_1 and T_2 ? Of course if $m_1 = 0$ there is no effective conflict since no transition can be fired ($V_1 = V_2 = 0$). Now if m_1 is big enough there is no effective conflict because both transitions can be fired at their maximum instantaneous speeds, i.e. $v_1 = V_1$ and $v_2 = V_2$. Now what means "big enough" ? For example is there a conflict for $m_1 = 1.5$?

The VCPN in Fig. 10.a may be considered as a 2-server-station. Each server has a maximum firing speed which is 3. This VCPN is exactly equivalent, as far as the markings of P_1 and P_2 are concerned, to the VCPN in Fig. 10.b. It is clear in Fig. 10.b that the maximum speed of transition T_{12} is obtained only if $m_1 \geq 2$. Then this is also true in Fig. 10.a. This property can be verified using the same tranformation as from Fig. 5.a to 5.c. This transformation leads to 2k transitions in parallel for both Fig. 10.a and 10.b. The corresponding set of 2k transitions is saturated only if there are at least 2k tokens in place P_1, then only if $m_1 \geq 2$.

Consider again Fig. 10.a. The maximum speed of T_1 can be obtained if $m_1 \geq 1$. Similarly, the maximum speed if T_2 can be obtained if $m_1 \geq 1$. However the maximum speed of both transitions can be obtained only if $m_1 \geq 2$. Marking m_1 looks like a "potential of firing" which is shared between both transitions.

Now we can conclude that :

a) When $m_1 \geq 2$ there is no effective conflict, because T_1 and T_2 can be fired at their maximum instantaneous speeds $V_1 = 3$ and $V_2 = 3$, respectively.

b) When $m_1 = 0$ there is no conflict because $V_1 = V_2 = 0$.

c) When $0 < m_1 < 2$ there is an effective conflict, because T_1 and T_2 cannot be fired at their maximum instantaneous speeds V_1 and V_2.

General case. Let P_i be a place and $P_i° = \{T_1, T_2, \ldots, T_j, \ldots\}$ the set of the output transitions. Let M be the marking at time t.

$V_j(M) = U_j . A_j(M)$

denotes the *maximum instantaneous speed* of transition T_j, given M. The absolute *maximum speed* (constant value) is U_j, and $A_j(M) = \min(m_a, \ldots, m_i, \ldots)$ such that $°T_j = \{P_a, \ldots, P_i, \ldots\}$. For example, in Fig. 10.a, $U_1 = 3$ and $A_1(M) = \min(m_1, m_3)$.

There is an effective conflict due to P_i if and only if

$$m_i < A_1(M) + A_2(M) + \ldots + A_j(M) + \ldots$$

□

This notion of conflict in a VCPN was misinterpreted in [5].

Example. a timed continuous PN is presented in Fig. 11.a. The maximum speeds are noted as $U_1 = 2$ and $U_2 = 1$. This is a generic representation : if the CCPN model is used then $V_1 = 2$ and $V_2 = 1$; if the VCPN model is used then $V_1 = 2 \min(m_4, m_1)$ and $V_2 = \min(m_5, m_1)$.

Figure 11.b shows the behaviour of this continuous PN interpreted as a VCPN, with priority of transition T_1 over transition T_2.

There are three phases :

First phase. $m_1 \geq 2$. One has $A_1(M) = \min(1, m_1) = 1$ and $A_2(M) = \min(1, m_1) = 1$. Since $m_1 \geq A_1(M) + A_2(M) = 2$, there is no effective conflict, $v_1 = 2$ and $v_2 = 1$.

Second phase. $1 \leq m_1 \leq 2$. One has $A_1(M) = 1$ and $A_2(M) = 1$. Since $m_1 < A_1(M) + A_2(M) = 2$, there is an effective conflict. Since $m_1 \geq 1$, T_1 can be fired at the maximum speed because of the priority, then $v_1 = 2$ and $v_2 = m_1 - 1$.

Third phase. $m_1 < 1$. One has $A_1(M) = m_1$ and $A_2(M) = m_1$. Since $m_1 < A_1(M) + A_2(M) = 2$, there is an effective conflict. Due to priority $v_1 = 2\,m_1$ and $v_2 = 0$.

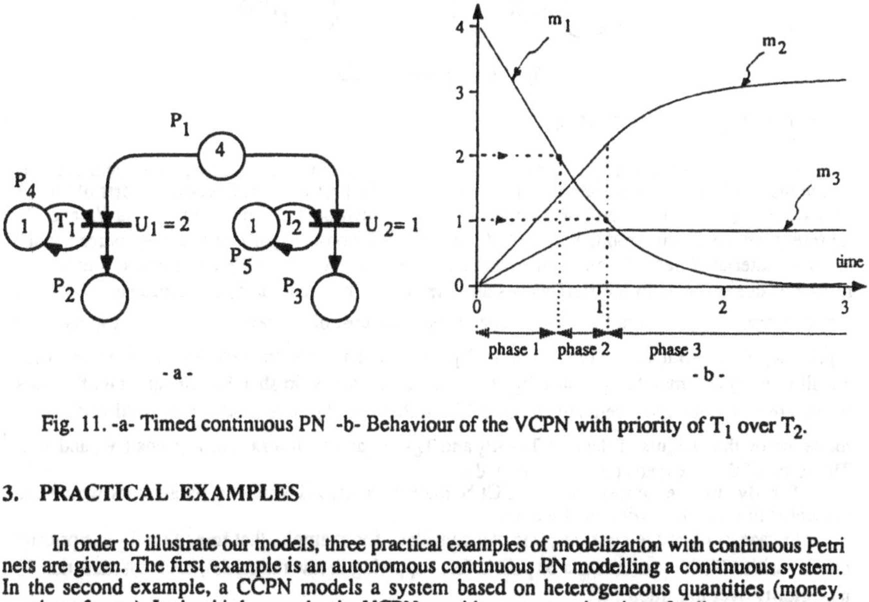

Fig. 11. -a- Timed continuous PN -b- Behaviour of the VCPN with priority of T_1 over T_2.

3. PRACTICAL EXAMPLES

In order to illustrate our models, three practical examples of modelization with continuous Petri nets are given. The first example is an autonomous continuous PN modelling a continuous system. In the second example, a CCPN models a system based on heterogeneous quantities (money, number of parts). In the third example, the VCPN provides an approximation of a discrete sytem.

A. *Chemical process*

This example corresponds to a continuous chemical process (Fig. 12). It shows how a continuous system containing concurrency and synchronization can be modelled by a continuous PN. This process describes what can be obtained from a solution containing 100 g of soda and 50 g of hydrochloric acid. 40 g of NaOH is decomposed in 23 g of ions Na^+ and 17 g of ions OH^-. Similarly HCl is decomposed in Cl^- and H^+. Now ions OH^- plus ions H^+ produce water H_2O, while ions Cl^- plus ions Na^+ produce sodium chloride, NaCl. The continuous PN in Fig. 12 is an autonomous one i.e., the reactions speeds are not considered. The function of water (solution, then evaporation to obtain NaCl) is not represented. Notice that the weights associated with arcs can be multiplied by any positive number for each arc. For example, if the weights of arcs $P_1 \rightarrow T_1$, $T_1 \rightarrow P_3$ and $T_1 \rightarrow P_4$, were 1, 23/40 and 17/40, respectively, the behaviour of the ACPN would be quite similar (if a firing speed V_1 was associated with transition T_1 in Fig. 12, it should be multiplied by 40 in order to have a similar behaviour).

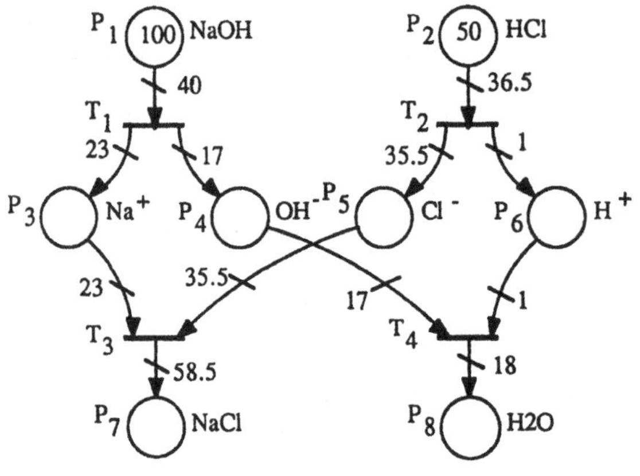

Fig. 12. A chemical process

B. Production/Management system

The CCPN given in Fig.13., models a production system composed by two manufacturing worshops. This system was presented in detail in [11].The first workshop produces parts of type A (transition T_3) and the second one parts of type B (transition T_4).The firing speeds V_3 and V_4 represent the maximum production rates of the two workshops.They use common resources which are raw materials (place P_2) and human and material resources (place P_3). The cost of the human resources corresponds to the staff wages and the cost of the material to the investissements and maintenance (weight of arc $P_1 \rightarrow T_2$ and speed V_2). The cost of the raw materials corresponds to a regular supplying with a price (weight of arc $P_1 \rightarrow T_1$) and a maximum speed V_1. All these expenses are allowed by common funds (place P_1). Each manufacturing workshop has an output buffer stock where are stored the produced parts (places P_4 and P_5). Finally these products are sold with prices modelled by the weights of the arcs $T_5 \rightarrow P_1$ and $T_6 \rightarrow P_1$ and with maximum speeds (V_5 and V_6). The result of the sale feeds the common funds.

The dynamic evolution of this CCPN may be analysed with the parameters which are presented in Fig. 13, or with other values.

In case of effective conflicts, one can consider , for example, that transition T_2 has priority over transition T_1 (the wages must be paid before supplying in raw materials), and that transition T_4 has priority over transition T_3.

C. *Manufacturing system*

Let us consider a simple manufacturing system composed by three stations. A station is composed by a machine and a buffer-stock. The parts are carried by pallets. At each end of production, the pallet is unloaded and loaded by a new part. The continuous PN in Fig.14.a models the evolution of the pallets, in the system. This number is constant (loading and unloading of parts is not modelled). In this model, places P_1, P_2, and P_3 represent the buffer-stocks and the transitions T_1, T_2 and T_3 are assocciated with the machines where the service times are $1/U_1$, $1/U_2$ and $1/U_3$ respectively. At the initial time 20 pallets are available in the buffer-stock of station 1.

The VCPN model is considered. That means that V_1 = 4 min (m_1, m_4), and so on. The evolution of the timed PN and the VCPN are compared in Fig. 14.b. This example shows that the continuous model gives a good approximation of the discrete model. As it has been emphasized in section 3.3.2, the VCPN provides an analytic way to calculate the average markings in the stationnary state. This is not possible with a discrete PN.

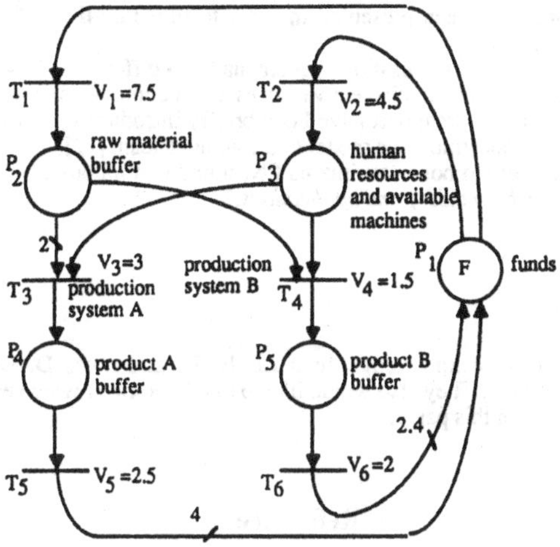

Fig. 13. A production/management system

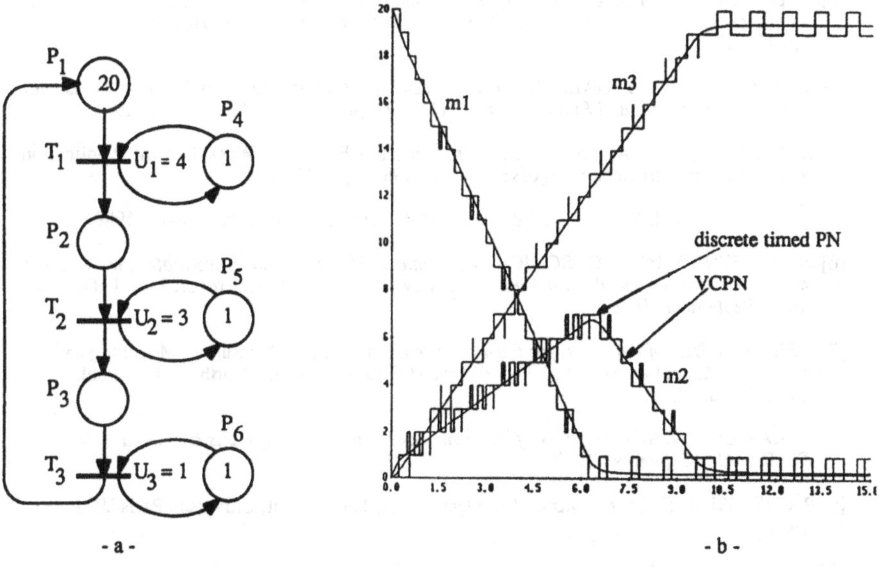

Fig. 14. A manufacturing system

4. CONCLUSION

Continuous Petri nets (autonomous and timed) have been defined as limit cases of discrete Petri nets. The objective of this paper was not to give in an exhaustive way properties of continuous PNs but to give a formal definition of this model.

Now, timed continuous PNs may have several applications. They provide an analytic approximation to discrete timed PN. Furthermore they allow modelling of continuous systems.

Three practical examples have been presented in order to illustrate the different possibilities of modelling by continuous PNs.

In a continuous PN, the synchronisation phenomena has a different form which is weaker than in a discrete PN. In order to associate discrete variables and a continuous model, Hybrid Petri nets with a continuous part and a discrete part have been briefly introduced [4], [5] ; some research is being currently carried out concerning this model in the authors' team [12].

These new models (autonomous continuous PN, timed continuous PN, hybrid PN) *require further research concerning both theory and applications.*

Acknowledgement

The authors gratefully acknowledge Jean LE BAIL and Yves DALLERY for fruitful discussions about this research. They also would like to thank the two reviewvers for their valuable suggestions and comments on this paper.

References

[1] M. K. MOLLOY, *Fast Bounds for Stochastic Petri Nets,* Intrenational Workshop on Timed Petri Nets, Torino (I), July 1985, pp. 244-249.

[2] D. DUBOIS, J.-P. FORESTIER, *Productivité et en-cours moyens d'un ensemble de deux machines séparées par un stock,* Revue RAIRO Automatique, vol. 16, n°2, 1982, pp. 105-132.

[3] R. DAVID, X. XIE, Y. DALLERY, *Properties of Continuous Models of Transfer Lines with Unreliable machines and Finite Buffers,* Technical report L.A.G. n° 88-50, May 1988.

[4] R. DAVID, H. ALLA, *Continuous Petri Nets,* 8th European Workshop on Application and Theory of Petri Nets, Saragosse (E), June 1987, pp. 275-294.

[5] R. DAVID, H. ALLA, *Du Grafcet aux réseaux de Petri,* Editions Hermès, Paris, 1989.

[6] S. B. GERSHWIN, I. C. SCHICK, *Continuous Model of an Unreliable Two - Stage Material Flow System With a Finite Interstage Buffer,* Technical report MIT LIDS - R - 1032, September 1980.

[7] J. SIFAKIS, *Use of Petri Nets for Performance Evaluation,* in "Measuring, Modelling and Evaluating Computer Systems", H. Beilner and E. Gelenbe (Eds), North-Holland Publ. Co, 1977, pp. 75-93.

[8] C. RAMCHANDANI, *Analysis of Asynchronous Concurrent Systems by Timed Petri Nets,* Ph. D., MIT, September 1973.

[9] P. CHRETIENNE, *Les réseaux de Petri temporisés,* Thèse d'Etat, Université Paris VI, June 1983.

[10] H. ALLA, R. DAVID, *Modelling of Production Systems by Continuous Petri Nets,* 3rd International Conference on CAD/CAM, CARS & FOF88, Detroit (USA), August 1988, pp. 344-348.

[11] H. ALLA, R. DAVID, *Modélisation de production / gestion par réseaux de Petri continus,* Congrès Afcet-Automatique, Grenoble, octobre 1988, pp. 106-115.

[12] J. LE BAIL, H. ALLA and R. DAVID, *Hybrid Petri Nets,* Note interne L.A.G. n° 89-53, Grenoble, juin 1989.

The Devnet: a Petri Net for Discrete Event Simulation

John B. EVANS
Department of Computer Science
University of Hong Kong
email: evans@csd.hku.hk

ABSTRACT *A relationship between Petri nets and discrete-event systems is outlined. Previous attempts at providing a diagrammatic description of discrete-event systems are critically reviewed. For a Petri-net design, the extent of detail to be provided, the representation of decisions and the precise interpretation of a state, all emerge as problematic. The type of Petri net proposed here, the Devnet, takes as its aim the description of the entity-flow logic of a general simulation program, involving a reinterpretation of transition enablement and firing. Facilities to incorporate the representation of higher system complexity, leading up to the concept of transitions with disjunctive sides, are described with examples. Particular difficulties, such as the representation of temporal expressions and modular decomposition are discussed. The special relationship between the Devnet and the control of activation in the implementation of the simulation language Simian is examined, especially in relation to the latter's circumspect approach to object advancement. Finally, some questions are posed and some speculation is indulged in as to where this approach may be useful in other fields.*

KEYWORDS Circumspect token, control structures, discrete-event simulation, engagement strategy, entity interaction, firing strategy, net implementation, object net, parallelism, processes, program activation, Simian language, simulation complexity, temporal expressions.

CONTENTS

1) Petri nets and discrete-event systems

A discrete-event system is a dynamic system which changes at certain points in time by means of the instantaneous movement of entities from one state to another. Such a system can be described in terms of entity interactions, any number of which may be simultaneously taking place in parallel. Fundamental to any discrete-event simulation (which is what we will denote by the term *simulation* from here onwards) is the perception, at least in the mind of the simulationist, of the object system as a discrete-event system: that is, that all change in the system is seen as being at discrete points in time (*events*). When an event occurs, various kinds of interactions between entities may be brought into being, or terminated. While at first sight the discreteness assumption may appear limiting for building dynamic models, the modeller is able to control the time granularity, or, where convenient, to define certain types of change as occurring between two events and thus possessing a duration. The perception, suitably interpreted, enables a considerable number of real systems, which inevitably possess a large degree of parallelism, to be simulated on a sequential computer by simply time-ordering the events. Simulation is thus a valuable means to assess a wide variety of existing or hypothetical designed systems (Evans, 1991).

1.1) Correspondence between the Petri net and the Devnet

Discrete-event systems, with their concern for parallel happenings and resource availability, are obvious candidates for some kind of Petri-net description which shares the basic paradigm of instantaneous state-changes. In the Devnet, we seek to make the following correspondences between Petri nets and discrete-event systems:

- *place* becomes the state in which the entity may reside for some non-negative duration of time. In simulation the concept of state is closely associated with that of *activity*– the idea being that an entity in a state is actually doing something productive. Thus Devnet places are usually named. We may maintain this association as long as we are prepared to accept that durations in which entities wait idly for resources, or for some condition to arise, are also counted as 'activities'.

- *transition* becomes a generic event which defines and controls the change from one state to another. Such events delimit activity durations, and initiate and terminate entity interactions.

- *token* becomes the individual entity, typed as a member of an entity class. The class definition may include attributes which themselves are typed. Equivalently, we may consider tokens as objects representing instances of their respective class (Sibertin-Blanc, 1985). The tokens are coloured according to their class (Peterson, 1980). The instantaneous marking of a Devnet corresponds to the overall configuration of the discrete-event system given by the totality of entities-in-state.

- *arcs* denote the connections between state and event, or between the activities and the events which start and terminate them. More particularly, arcs which are input to a transition indicate an enabling relationship, while arcs which are output from a transition indicate the possible routes of tokens dispersed by the transition's firing. Since arcs refer to the passage of tokens, they are coloured according to the class of entity they transport.

- *firing* then becomes a discrete-event occurrence, an activation of the transition where the controls and consequences defined in the event are made manifest on behalf of a specific entity, or collection of entities. Firing involves moving tokens from places input to the transition to places in its output set, and occurs at a discrete point in time.

Engagements between entities of different class have mixed colours. No entity can be involved in more than one activity at any particular time, but an activity can be simultaneously subject to more than one outcome; i.e. the terminating event of its activity can be determined in more than one way. Transition firing is accompanied by the execution of various actions, including alteration of the value of attributes of transiting entities. Places are largely passive receptacles for entities. The type of entity which can occupy a place is determined by the colour of the arcs input to that place.

Any number of transitions may fire at the same point in simulated time; normally there will be a logical sequence to the firings, which is determined by the passage of tokens along the arcs of the net. Sometimes synchronous firings occur due to pure chance, in which case a random choice is made, or due to the system being too loosely defined. In the latter case some influence can be exerted over the choice of firings by establishing a priority between eventual activities. Coincidences are monitored closely in the Simian system: a large number may indicate an under-defined system.

1.2) Uses of the Devnet in simulation

Armed with this correspondence, the simulationist can use the Devnet as an intermediate model (Overstreet and Nance, 1985) in the specification of a simulation program. A diagram has inherent advantages over a program especially in the representation of systems exhibiting large degrees of parallelism.The extra dimension made use of by a diagram enables the simulationist to draw parallel actions alongside one another, a feature denied to the writer of a sequential program.Using conventional algorithmic programming languages, programs can of course describe parallel phenomena but only in a way in which involves special syntactic constructs to denote operations like splitting from and re-merging into a particular sequence.

Naturally a diagram will indicate only generic dynamic phenomena of the various classes of entity. A marking of the Devnet will correspond to a static snapshot of the total system configuration of entities which pertains to any particular instant in time. To unfold the dynamic of a system, the dynamic of every current entity must be unfolded separately in the order of the sequence of event occurrences for the *whole system*, which is different from the sequence of events experienced by a single entity going through the system. The precise way in which this unfolding is achieved in a simulation program depends on the strategy adopted in the design of the simulation language (Evans, 1988, Chapter 4). One particular simulation language, Simian (Evans, 1992*a*), which pursues the engagement strategy, has an intimate relationship with the Devnet, as will be described later.

A Simian program is written in terms of entity clases, where each process describes what happens to a typical entity of that class. Interpretation, however, occurs at the level of the entity instances (=objects) and is made in terms of the current configuration (marking) of the system. In the implementation of a Simian program, a Devnet data structure is built to model the processes, to guide activations and to steer entity movements. The Devnet properties can be understood from two main viewpoints: that of the entity and that of the system as a whole. The semantic aspect is described in the specification of the net topology and firing characteristics, while the run-time performance and means of entity advancement comprises the pragmatic aspect, expressed through the Primate algorithm.

Once any diagrammatic means of representation is seen to be a useful and an enlightening tool in the methodological development of a simulation, one question naturally occurs: Why not use the diagram's conventions as a programming language and hide away the conventional simulation program under the cover of the "implementation"? This certainly seems possible and is consistent with current trends in the description of management information systems using CASE tools, etc. However, as we will demonstrate, there are a few difficulties and limitations in adopting this approach wholesale.

Nevertheless, there are certainly advantages in using diagrams as a step in the development of a simulation. The Devnet may be used to explicate a system's workings, with the tokens being moved from place to place in the manner of a board game. When this is skillfully done, it can go a long way to get the corresponding simulation program *accepted* as a representation of the real system dynamic, since people will more naturally appreciate the workings of a board game rather than the cryptic operations of compiler-generated code derived from a simulation program. Taking this idea a stage further, an *animated display* of token movement over the Devnet could be useful for demonstration purposes, extended by system-specific icons. Its generic nature means it can apply to any discrete-event system and provides a base on which to build any desired *customisation* of the animation. Further, the Devnet can act as a kind of *semantic domain* for discrete-event languages, at least at an informal level, and the various constructs of the simulation language can be said to "mean" particular movements of Devnet tokens under certain conditions pertaining to the current marking. It may also be useful as a *means of communication* between members of a project team, some of whom might find reading a program too daunting.

In the Simian project, the Devnet, in the form of an internal data structure, has a special role as the activation controller of the program. During run time, given a specific marking, all enablement possibilities and dispersal routes expressed by the Devnet are examined by the executive program (the Primate algorithm, (Evans, 1992*b*)) to ensure that no opportunity for event occurrence nor entity advancement is lost during the simulation run. The static analysis of the Devnet may reveal certain conflict properties of systems, properties usually ignored, or treated arbitrarily, in the implementation of many simulation languages and in Simian the user may supply resolution logic. Incorporating the Devnet into the simulation program in this way, gives a more coherent and intelligent interpretation of the system described, which in turn enables the design of the Simian language to be *declarative* at a high level (Evans, 1990).

2) Activity cycle diagrams, simulation networks

Naive approaches to simulation start out by writing what is essentially an event-driven program controlled by retrievals from a future-events set (FES). Each retrieval obtains the earliest event notice and advances the system time to its occurrence time. Associated with the notice is an indication of which event procedure is to be invoked. During the procedure call further event notices may be inserted into the FES. The system's dynamic structure is reduced to merely a set of procedures describing the state changes which make up the system, thus seeming to reduce any simulation to a simple program.

This approach is called the event-scheduling (ES) strategy, and, being relatively easy to understand, it is still rather popular. Despite its appeal, the ES strategy suffers from many pitfalls, being difficult to get right, to comprehend, to debug and to maintain. The major problem lies in the need for event modules to check conditions for the invocation of others (Evans, 1988). Needless to say, such a requirement rapidly leads to repetitious and complicated event procedures and a poor program structure, especially with greater system complexity. Some help is provided by the use of an event-graph (Schruben, 1983) which indicates the invocation pattern between event procedures and assists the programmer in keeping track of inter-event relationships.

2.1) Activity cycle diagrams and their derivatives

When simulation programs were first written it was soon realised that conventional design tools such as program flowcharts were inadequate since they can describe a only a single entity in its process. A better alternative was to describe the flow of entities as a sequence of activities through a set of cycles, rather in the manner of a jobshop model where jobs are sequenced through a set of machines. A description of the general entity flow is nearer to a representation of the real system, in that, unlike a flowchart, it contains many points (entities) at which there is a locus of activation. The cycles represent the usual busy-idle alternation of machines (resources) that one might find in industry, while the flow of entities is seen as as typifying the passage of a job through the workshop.

Tocher and Owen's (1960) wheel diagrams describe such a system by a set of intermeshing cogs, aptly describing the management's perennial dream of an industrial plant running like clockwork! Each machine cycle represents a busy-idle alternation, while some resources require a star-shaped description because their use is multi-purpose. Activities occur on the meeting of cycles and linear processes, the conjunction of jobs and machines. Out of this perspective there naturally arises two kinds of flow interaction: those denoting the joining of job-flow with machine cycles, which may involve waiting, and those denoting their separation, called C-activities and B-activities, respectively. The identification and grouping of these activities is the distinguishing factor in the methodology of the activity-scanning (AS) strategy.

The simulation language ECSL (Clementson, 1977) is arranged so that the kinds of activities strictly alternate along the job sequence, even to the extent of requiring the insertion of artificial activities to keep up the alternation. The CAPS package is a front-end for ECSL which offers a flexible form of system specification, by undertaking a dialogue with the user reading from one of these diagrams, called an *activity-cycle diagram*. Hocus (Poole and Szymankiewicz, 1977) follows a similar kind of diagram, using a data-driven specification of a system. Modern variants of these approaches are still widely used by simulationists. One reason for the continued commercial popularity of these packages is that being designed on the basis of an internal model, albeit relatively simple, they can have considerable checking power.

Birtwistle (1979), although being concerned with the process-interaction (PI) strategy language DEMOS, also recognises that a variant of the activity-cyle diagram is a valuable methodological aid. He gives the two types of resource entity considered in DEMOS their own symbols and allows arcs to be associated with an integer constant representing the number of resources required. Here one recurring uncertainty with diagrams emerges– whether to include the depth of detail such as the number of entities involved, or simply indicate the class of entities.

DRAFT (Tate, *et al.*, 1983) is an interactive program generator which accepts a description of a model in a 'life-cycle' form and produces an annotated Simula program. The input format closely follows the diagrammatic form of the activity-cycle diagram. Versions of DRAFT exist to produce simulation programs in Simon75, GASP, ACSL and Simscript II.5.

Activity-cycle diagrams, and their derivatives, are mostly associated with AS strategy languages. However, a close investigation reveals some uncertainty about exactly what an *activity* is: there are several contributing factors to this confusion. Firstly there is, as was first pointed out by Dahl (1968), an inversion of activity in a simulation program. That is to say, the time during which a simulation program is most active corresponds to just an instant of real time, while the productive durations of the real system are skipped over by the program. Inversion simply arises out of the need, in simulation, to concentrate attention on and to describe state-*changes*, and the consequent ignoring of real activity. One result of the confusion is the conventional use of the terms 'B-activity' and 'C-activity' for what are actually two kinds of events.

Secondly, there has long been a tendency to consider the time duration necessary for the acquisition of resources of an activity along with the activity itself. A similar definition of 'activity' is used in critical path analysis (Wiest and Levy, 1977). This conflation is reinforced when using the AS strategy since the so-called C-activity modules contain both the conditions for starting (i.e. the necessary acquisitions) alongside the determination of the duration of resource usage. Although it may seem quite natural to lump these two contiguous durations together, it does not properly express the usage pattern of the resources, since, if one is measuring resource utilisation, for instance, one would be ill-advised to include waiting time along with usage. The C-activity thus describes the waiting state, the usage state, and the condition from going from one to the other, altogether in one module.

2.2) Simulation networks

Quite apart from AS-inspired diagrams, there have been other diagram designs put forward as aids in simulation methodology. Roughly contemporarily with Tocher's wheel charts, the GPSS language (Gordon, 1975) was being devised along with its own block diagrams, which are claimed to be an alternative way of programming with easier and a more natural syntax (Gordon, 1978). The main entity (transaction) flow is described, while storage and facility cycles being are regarded as subsidiary, thereby hampering the modelling of any but the simplest resource dynamics. The 51 types of blocks have many different functions. We have blocks for assignments, making measurements, setting up tabulations, as well as for describing the transaction's process through the system. The system dynamic can be difficult to identify within such a mass of detail. In fact, the block diagram of GPSS is in a one-to-one relationship with the GPSS program, a relationship which is claimed to make programming easier, but, if the diagram is nothing but a program in symbolic form, the language description could in principle do without it.

The SLAM II network (Pritsker *et al.*, 1989) consists of branches which represent activities and nodes to model decision points or queues. The language incorporates PERT techniques for critical path analysis. Entities, which may have attributes, flow through the network directed by routeing conditions placed on activities. There are 24 network symbols, with 20 node types, with each node being capable of carrying values.

SIMAN (Hoover and Perry, 1989, App. B) takes a similar approach to the blocks of GPSS, but reduces the number of block types to ten, expressing up to forty operations. Some of the blocks have a specialised nature since the language is biassed towards describing systems with material handling. RESQ (MacNair and Sauer, 1985) is another specialist simulation language, being focussed towards computer networks and systems. There are symbols for queues, service centres, passive centres and various specialities, like a half-duplex line. As with GPSS, only the main entities figure in the diagram. In all there are about 20 nodes, some special ones being concerned with allocation, others for splitting and merging.

SIMNET (Taha, 1988) reduces the node types even further to four main kinds, expressing source, queue, facility and auxiliary functions. Each node contains compartments in which to write pertinent data. There seven types of arc representing different routeing mechanisms, alongside which conditions and assignment statements may be written.

For many simulation networks, it may be said that they are difficult to read. For a few, there is quite a lot of symbolism to learn, there being too many types of nodes. The modeller is tempted to put too much detail into a diagram, rendering it cluttered, overwhelming the natural structural simplicity of a diagram. It seems that these problems may stem from some uncertainty on the part of the designers as to whether they are representing the real system or the eventual program.

2.3) Petri nets for simulation

The recognition that activity-cycle diagrams, simulation networks and Petri nets have something in common did not dawn on the simulation community until simulation graphs, and later simulation nets, were described by Törn (1981, 1985). He proposed the use of an extended Petri net for modelling as a methodological tool for writing a simulation program. The main extension is a feature to represent the elapse of time. When a transition is enabled, its firing may be extended over a duration of time. Other extensions, including inhibitor arcs, test arcs, queues and entities as coloured tokens were added. He identified the time-delay as the most significant omission from the Petri formalism, if it were to be of value for discrete-event simulation.

Also noticed by Törn (1988) is the problem of transition conflicts. If any place is an input place for two or more transitions, then there is the possibility that it may enable both of them simultaneously. In this case the rule is made that the system decides between the transitions arbitrarily, but control can be exercised by the user introducing appropriate inhibitor arcs.

It is interesting to look at the various ways in which the time-delay mechanism has been introduced into Petri nets. Prompted by the need to express time elapse in computer performance evaluation studies, the concept of *Timed Petri Nets* (Ramchandani, 1974) emerged. With these nets, when a transition is enabled, a firing is initiated by removing the required number of tokens from each of the transitions's input places. These tokens remain 'in the transition' for the firing time, after which the firing terminates by adding the required number of tokens to the transition's output places. During firing, other firings of the same transition may be initiated. On the other hand, Sifakis (1977) preferred instead to associate delays with places. In the latter case the instantaneous firing feature of the basic Petri net model is maintained.

A different approach to give a time-delay mechanism is the concept of *Time Petri Nets* (Merlin and Farber, 1976), in which every transition has an associated pair of non-negative real numbers (*fmin*, *fmax*). The first value indicates the shortest time the transaction should be enabled before firing; the second is the longest time that it will remain continuously enabled. Thus a continuously enabled transition will fire by *fmax* in any case; if it ceases to be enabled at time *e*, then its firing is inhibited until *e* + *fmin* and must occur by *e* + *fmax* unless it is disabled before that time by the movement of tokens brought about by the firing of another transition. This approach is of interest since it attempts to give a solution to the problem of representing time-outs, important in the simulation of computer systems. The Devnet solution is given Fig. 4(d), which is derived from a Simian temporal expression using the || operator.

Another Petri-net formalism which includes the notion of time is the generalised stochastic Petri net (GSPN) which has been used for the analysis of manufacturing and computer systems (Molloy, 1982). According to the GSPN approach, transitions can belong to two classes: immediate and timed. When timed transitions fire, the time between enablement and actual firing is an exponentially distributed random variable, rendering the net amenable to mathematical analysis.

By simply allowing the token to be differentiated into classes and having attributes, it becomes an object. The relationship between object Petri nets (Sibertin-Blanc, 1985) and the coloured Petri nets of Jensen (1981) has been investigated and applied by Ben Ahmed, *et al.* (1991), in the search for net invariants. Although not explicitly dealing with time, the objects may evolve along with the net by being affected by assignments carried out when a transition fires. Baldassari and Bruno (1988) present a form of Timed Petri net with tokens as objects. However their nets are limited in the expression of decision and the splitting and merging of tokens.

A recent, and more complete, description and discussion of many kinds of simulation diagrams is given by Pooley (1991). Evidently, there are many questions which beset a designer of a new kind of net. What should be the role of net construction in the programming methodology and what level of detail should be included? How should time elapse be incorporated? For our purposes, the answer to these design questions will also be affected by the relationship to a simulation language. Let us move on to see how these questions are tackled in the Devnet.

3) The Devnet design philosophy

As we shall explain more fully in section six, the purpose of the Devnet is primarily to act as an activator for a simulation program. By its nature, it will be quite abstract, generalising away all particular circumstances and conditions into its own features. An early formulation of the Devnet was introduced, as 'an augmented Petri net', in Evans (1988, Chapter 8, section 3), followed by Evans (1989). During this development, there have been three major design decisions which have determined its properties:

- to concentrate on the portrayal of the entity-flow topology;
- to describe the various types of entity-interaction inaugurated at transition firing;
- to avoid numerical details in the pictorial representation.

The entity-flow topology is the set of routes followed by entities of different types through the system, determining what activity may follow what, for each type of entity. The existence of an arc of a particular colour indicates that entities of corresponding type may proceed along the arc. Such topologies are better described by diagrams, while programs excel at describing more specific aspects of a discrete-event system, such as the rules for the selection of entities.

In the course of devising a template against which the many simulation languages could be compared, a characterisation of discrete-event system *complexity* was put forward (Evans, 1986). The capabilities of any simulation language could then be measured off against the template. Complexity thus identifies the different types of entity-interaction phenomena, and the features of the Devnet are designed to reflect the complexity characterisation, as fully as possible and in keeping with clarity.

The conditions for firing transitions of the Devnet may be arbitrarily complicated and dependent on the attribute values of the entities in the enabling states. For this reason, we make no implication in the diagram about the precise conditions under which particular entities will traverse transitions, nor how they will be dispersed after transition firing. Inclusion of such information in a diagram would be confusing. What can be definitely told is that if there is no connection between a place and a particular transition, then there can be no enablement relationship. Arcs thus represent a route by which entities may proceed; the conditions under which they do so are specified elsewhere in the associated Simian program– this is the reason for designing the language simultaneously with the net.

For further simplicity, the Devnet is described in terms of the entity classes, each with its particular colour for tokens and arcs. The places and transitions linked by arcs of a particular colour serve as a map of the *process* of that particular entity class. This decision avoids complications in dealing with individual entities, such as expressing the number of resources needed alongside an arc. Of course, the individual entities may be represented by coloured tokens in a marked Devnet, but we gain a further abstraction in that the same (unmarked) net will apply no matter what *quantity* of entities are involved.

In summary, the Devnet should be fairly close to the overall process structure of the simulation program. While it is a considerable distance from the pure Petri net, it still retains the latter's instantaneous firing concept. Methodologically it is an aid, displaying in broad brush strokes the system interconnections, but without being cluttered by too much detail or by having too many node types. Its marking will give important information about the imminent unfolding of the system dynamic. Given any unmarked Devnet, we can tell which transitions may be in mutual conflict. For any marked Devnet we can tell which transitions are not enabled, and thus the set of transitions whose enablement status should be further investigated. The precise workings of how a Devnet may drive a simulation program is defined by the Primate algorithm, which is briefly described in sections 8-10 below.

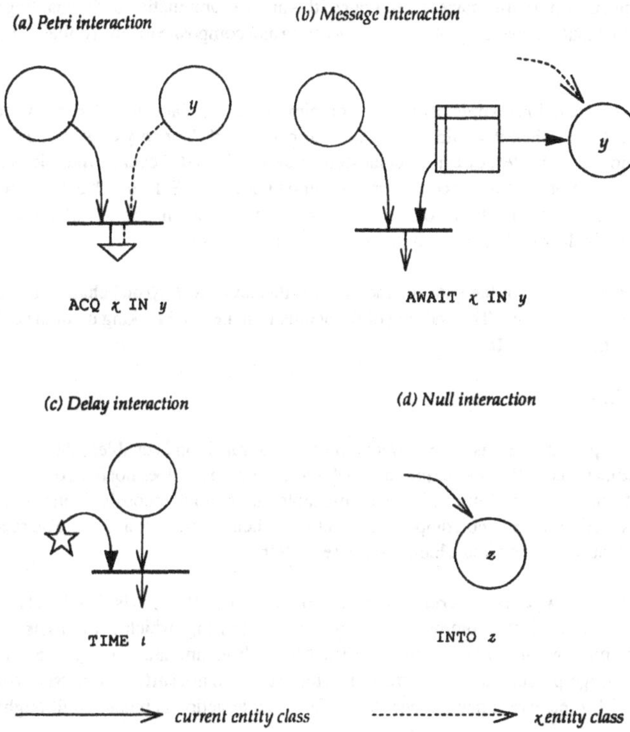

Fig. 1: Devnet of basic entity interactions.

Basically, the Devnet aims at representing a system in its current configuration by having tokens-in-place corresponding to entities-in-state. Not only the static configuration, but the future potentialities are indicated by the output transitions from a place. The pattern of arcs input to a transition show the types of interaction between entities, the four basic kinds of which are shown in Fig. 1.

The Devnet is perhaps best regarded as analogous to an underground-railway map, which eschews particular detail, such as the position of trains, their time between stations and how a train might be selected for alternative routes. It offers instead an instantaneous grasp of the interconnections and routeing possibilities of the total system. The Devnet's corresponding Simian program contains the full details of timings, route choices, etc., like a railway timetable, whose usefulness is enhanced by being used in conjunction with a map. Considered together they should provide an accessible and complete description of the system and its dynamic.

3.1) Petri interaction

This interaction is referred to as *resource* complexity in Evans (1988). It defines a basic condition for the transition to fire, namely that there are tokens in both input places. Whether or not an enabled transaction will actually fire may be dependent on other factors, in particular the properties of the enabling tokens. What the Devnet does *not* show is the number or means of selecting individual tokens for advancement. However once an enabling set of tokens has been obtained, the transition fires, the selected tokens are removed from the enabling places and the output arc from the transition is taken, with a token being put into the output place. The colour of this arc is a combination of the enabling arc colours, reflecting the fact that the enabling tokens are now acting as a composite token, a collaboration between entity types.

One category of simulation complexity (*select* complexity) has no place in the Devnet since it does not take any time: if it did then it would already be a component of the entity dynamic. The entities are assumed to know their routes, or can instantaneously derive them. Of course, the selection logic and information must be present in the corresponding Simian program. Selection has the power to derive a subset of tokens from the enabling tokens and to fire the transition on their behalf. Selection can also inhibit a firing which would be enabled in the pure Petri-net sense.

The Simian representation of the Petri interaction uses the keyword `ACQ` on behalf of one of the entity processes acquiring the other. The undoing of the acquisition, i.e. the breaking up of the collaboration, is achieved by the use of `REL`.

3.2) Message interaction

The interaction specified here is informational in nature; a transition is enabled, through a *fact* which contains a predicate (i.e. a Boolean expression) which either holds or does not hold over a set of places. The same fact can affect a multitude of transition-enablements simultaneously. Notice that, as distinct from Petri interaction there is no composing of entities when the transition fires. The fact concept is adapted from that of Genrich and Thieler-Mevissen (1976).

This interaction is known as *configurational* complexity in Evans (1988). It is closely related to the idea of process instances (objects) communicating by message passing, which is the basis of the object-oriented programming paradigm (Wegner, 1990). Although in simulation we deal extensively with objects, the message-passing kind of interaction is too weak and not sufficient in itself to describe the whole range of discrete-event phenomena. In Simian the interaction is modelled through the `AWAIT` keyword.

Without this type of interaction, all entity-entity interaction would be of an exclusive type, and this is not really suitable in all cases (see example Fig. 4(b)). There are many situations where the presence or absence of an entity in a state can have an excitatory or an inhibitory effect elsewhere, and this is aptly demonstated by the message interaction. The concept can be extended to an interaction in which information other than a Boolean-valued predicate is passed. By such means, the precise effect of control information may be modelled. There is also evidence that the use of message interactions would be more useful than Petri interactions in the modelling and maintenance of dynamic belief systems (Drummond, 1986).

3.3) Delay interaction

This type of interaction is called *temporal* complexity in Evans (1988). It is denoted by the transition having a star connected to its upside. One can imagine that the event occurrence momentarily fills the star "place" with a special "enabling" entity on behalf of a token in the input place. Once the enablement has been affected, the special entity disappears.

The delay interaction is the *sine qua non* of discrete-event simulation since it expresses the idea of an event occurring (i.e. a transition firing) at a particular value of time. Looked at from the pure Petri-net point of view, delay interactions considerably reduce the non-determinism of a situation where a set of transitions are simultaneously enabled, the timing of the event occurrences forming a *firing strategy* for the net.

When the event occurs, it does so at a particular value of time, on the behalf of a specific entity in the enabling place and causes the firing of a specific (starred) transition. As we have already noted, the transition fires instantaneously, which means that at any given time during a simulation any token (entity) can be unequivocally associated with a place (state), a situation which is consistent with the fundamental discrete-event paradigm.

In Simian the delay interaction is usually denoted by a statement involving the `TIME` keyword, which is followed by an expression (typically involving the call of a random-sampling procedure) to calculate the future event time, relative to the current time. An absolute event time is generated by using the `AT` statement. Another possible source of events is the attainment of an event threshold in a concurrent continuous simulation.

In the modelling of the elapse of a specific duration of time in a Petri net, two broad approaches seem to have been tried. Either the transition fires immediately it is enabled, but continues in a firing mode for the duration, or the enablement is witheld for the duration with the enabling entities being kept in their places, only being allowed to transit at the end of the duration. For most applications, it seems that the first approach is preferred, but if we represent entities being in an activity by place occupancy, then it seems, at the outset, we must be committed to the event which is to complete the activity. As we will see in connection with the implementation of Simian's || operator, such a commitment may curtail the expressive power of the language.

Also, the question as to what activity or state the entities are now in might be ambiguous if they were currently involved in a firing. The Devnet joins with the activity-cycle diagram in the natural assumption that time is consumed while an entity is in an activity. In this way the entities always can be considered unambiguously to be in a particular place and the firings take place instantaneously. From this description of the handling of time, it should be clear that the Devnet has followed the advice of Petri (1987) insofar as tokens spend almost all of their time in places. The only times when they are not emplaced is during those instants of measure zero when firing occurs. In the time-evolution of a Devnet, we should imagine token movement happening against a background of a real-valued clock which determines the firing instants of starred transitions. Regretfully, we are not able to follow Petri's advice in dispensing with Newtonian absolute time.

3.4) Null interaction

The most trivial kind of interaction is no interaction at all, i.e., the entity just passes into a place and stays there for an undetermined duration of time. This does not necessarily indicate a dead-end in the entity's process, but that the eventual interaction is to be determined elsewhere by another process. In Simian the `WAIT` or `INTO` keyword is used to specify the null interaction. Typically, the *idle* state of a simple resource, in which resources simply wait to be `ACQ`uired, is modelled in this way.

3.5) Engagements and firing

The three-way association of entity-event-time (or, in net terms, token-transition-time) is taken as fundamental, forming the *engagement* data-structure, which is the means by which all entity interactions are implemented in Simian. Also present in the data structure is the idea of entities coming together in *collaboration*, as specified in the Petri interaction, for the duration of particular activities. On transition firing, input tokens can be fused together for collaboration or separated for dispersal. The unfolding of the system dynamic is then seen as a series of making and breaking of engagements as time advances, as prompted by the Devnet structure.

In addition, creation and destruction of entities may happen on firing. Having tokens as objects means that in a Devnet firing, it is important that the right tokens are advanced. For the Petri interaction using

ACQ, the user may specify a particular number of entities to be acquired, or their necessary properties. If available, the transition will fire on the behalf of those particular tokens. In the case of the delay interaction, the token and the transition are already connected in the engagement data structure, retrieved from the FES in order that the transition may fire. Once again, the firing occurs on behalf of the specific token. Of course, for the message interaction using AWAIT, since the critical movement of tokens is not directly involved in the firing, the firing applies to *all* tokens in the input place(s).

4) The Devnet: Control structures

For any diagram representing flows of discrete items, there is a certain ambiguity when it comes to the convergence and divergence of arcs. In the case of the Petri net, it is assumed that when two arcs converge on, or diverge from a transition, *both* arcs are simultaneously transporting tokens; while for convergence on, or divergence from a place, only one arc need be transporting at any one time. The synchronising effect of transitions may be called *and*-parallelism, while the less demanding places are involved in *or*-parallelism. These assumptions carry over to the Devnet, but may be overridden by certain constructs in order to describe a different relationship.

As pointed out in the discussion on *route* complexity in Evans (1988), there is a large number of ways in which an entity may be guided along its route. We consider here three general classes of route: choice, iteration and parallel, corresponding to roughly similar features from the control structures of algorithmic programming languages. For the first two classes, a new feature is added to the Devnet, that of a transition which may have *disjunctive* sides. This feature allows the modelling of non-deterministic enablement and dispersal (see Fig. 2).

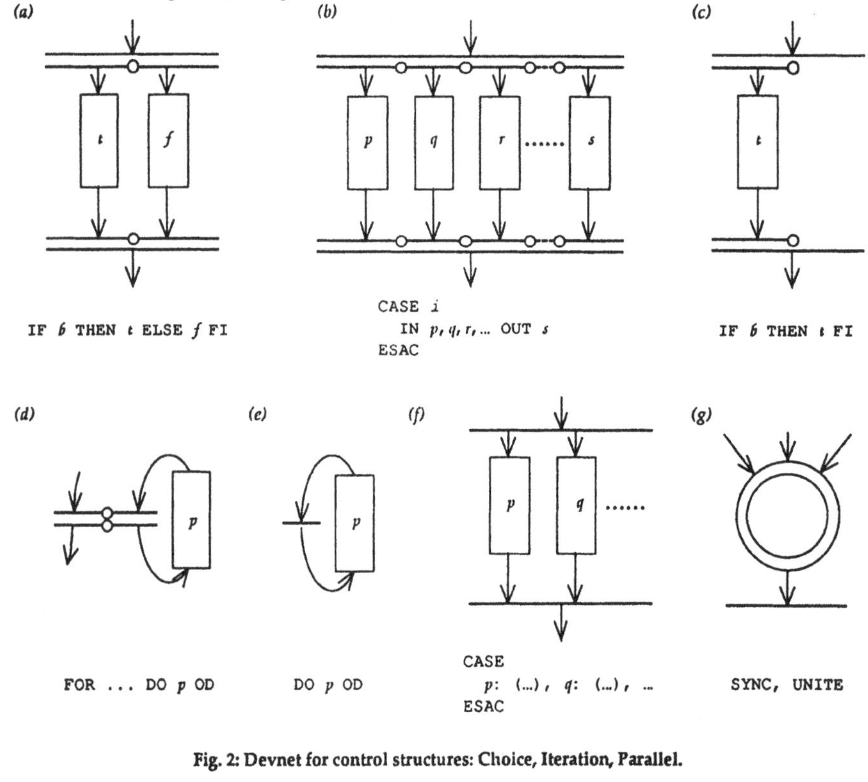

Fig. 2: Devnet for control structures: Choice, Iteration, Parallel.

Firstly, the input and output arcs are re-arranged so that all the input arcs join the transition on one side and the output arcs leave the transition on the other. (When dealing with entity-flows this is quite natural and common practice anyway). The separation into upside and downside enables the simulationist to consider the enablement and dispersal properties of the transition separately. Each side can then be broken into a number of segments which represent disjunctive alternatives to the functioning of the respective side. Nevertheless, the unity of the transition is not compromised when considered in terms of side segments. The essential actions of the transition (movement of tokens, making of measurements, assignment to attributes, etc.) is made irrespective of which upside is enabled or which downside is to be selected.

In the case of the *choice* structure, we have a subnet which is preceded by a transition with a disjunctive downside. This indicates that when the transition fires, a choice is made and one of the two output routes, and thus one of the subnets, is chosen. When either of the subnets is completed, this has the effect of firing of the closing transition which has a disjunctive upside, indicating that only one upside need be enabled for the transition to fire.

The first example in Fig. 2(a) corresponds to the

`IF - THEN - ELSE - FI`

structure where a choice is taken based on an evaluation of the Boolean expression immediately after the `IF`. The disjunctive downside corresponds to the `IF` and the disjunctive upside corresponds to the `FI`, while the subnets are constructed from the alternative paths specified after `THEN` and `ELSE`. Where the choice is required to be taken over more than two possibilities, we have the Devnet as in Fig. 2(b), corresponding to the

`CASE - IN ... OUT - ESAC`

structure where the ellipsis represents a finite set of alternatives, one of which is chosen based on the evaluation of an integer expression situated after the `CASE`. In other words, if the expression evaluates to an integer *n*, then the *n*th alternative after `IN` is chosen. If *n* lies outside the range of the alternatives, the one after `OUT` is taken.

It often happens that when encountering a choice one of the outcomes is "do nothing", corresponding to the structure `IF - THEN - FI`, as in Fig. 2(c), or a case structure without an `OUT` part. In this situation the upside of the initial transition should be united with the downside of the final transition, with nothing in between. This is rather confusing to show pictorially, so it has to be remembered that "empty" segments associate like brackets.

The second class of control structures deals with a commonly occurring situation in which an activity, or a series of activities, is repeated until a certain condition is met, corresponding to the algorithmic construction known as *iteration*. Let us consider the controlled DO-loop of Fig. 2(d). For convenience, we have labelled the upside segments `init` and `next` and the downside segments `exit` and `enter`.

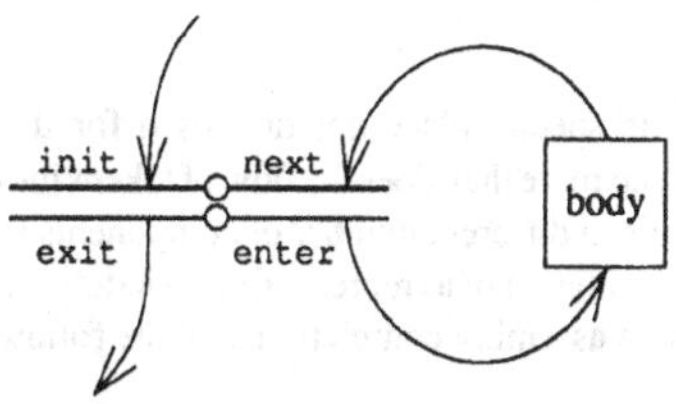

First of all we may notice that the whole loop body is suspended from what amounts to a single transition. Assuming `init` is enabled, tokens are removed from its input place(s). The actions associated with the transition will include the execution of an expression to decide whether or not the loop completion condition has been satisfied. If it has, then `exit` is chosen and the transiting entities are dispersed among its output place(s). The result could be that the partaking entities will have changed state without the loop body ever being entered.

However, when the loop completion condition evaluates to *false*, the entities follow the dispersal specified in `enter` and the loop body is entered. When a passage through the body is complete, `next` becomes enabled and the loop completion condition is re-evaluated. Thus controlled loops of the `FOR`, and `WHILE` varieties can be accomplished. If the logic should specify a loop corresponding to Pascal's `repeat ... until`, all that is required is a linear process with a decision like those of Fig. 2(a) or (c), and an arc going back to the place which is the head of the loop. The corresponding algorithmic structure is

```
DO - OD
```

preceded by an optional controlling condition. If the loop is infinite, then no disjunctive transition is necessary, as in Fig. 2(e).

The last class of control structures defines the *parallel* processing of component parts and the possibility of their later re-merging. A token denoting a single entity may be divided into separate streams (perhaps each stream is denoted by a different colour), so the effect of separate concurrent activities may be portrayed. In Fig. 2(f) we assume that an entity class can be broken into certain named subclasses and these require to be processed separately. In Simian this is expressed by using a statement like:

```
CASE p: (...), q: (...), ... ESAC
```

where *p, q* are the named components heading their respective processes. Another case involving parallel control, where the objects to be advanced are members of a set and they all carry out the same process in parallel, is represented by the Simian statement:

```
FOR ALL x IN y BY PARA DO ... OD
```

It has no special Devnet representation, because it is defined at the level of objects of the same class.

Often it is necessary when dealing with parallel processes to have the separate parts re-unite at some stage. This can be denoted in the Devnet by a special place (see Fig. 2(g)) which signifies the waiting of component parts until the specified whole is remade, at which point the following transition will fire. The effect is similar to a Petri interaction, if we allow the number of enabling places at the transition to be determined by the properties of the enabling entities. In the case where the components have come from an original whole or from being members of the same set, the recombination is denoted by the Simian keyword `SYNC` inside the `CASE - ESAC` or `DO - OD` brackets. Otherwise, for entities which do not share the same originating event, we can unite them with a similar place, denoted by the Simian keyword `UNITE`.

It should be emphasised that the special place notation used for this purpose does not serve to *synchronise* the inflow of tokens, no more than does the flow of tokens into any place. Different entities, even of the same class, may require a different number of components in order to be assembled into a complete whole. The place can be thought of as representing an indefinite number of Petri interactions. Instead, synchronisation occurs on assembly completion, and the following transition fires on behalf of the completed entity. There would be considerable pictorial awkwardness if such a state of affairs was to be denoted by a separate place for each type of waiting subcomponent, hence the special notation.

Notice that in the description of the control structures we have referred to subnets denoted by a box in the Devnet. This should be interpreted in a symbolic sense only, because, as we shall see later, there are certain difficulties in representing subnets of Devnets.

A Simian program, along with its Devnet, may be said to be highly structured. If ever the structures are found to be too constricting, there is a maverick statement `INTO`, analogous to the **goto**, which causes an entity to move directly to a specified place and thereby override the surrounding structures.

5) Devnet constructions

Any language, whether textual or pictorial, which is seeking to allow the expression of a large, possibly boundless, variety of circumstances must have the facility to compose its elements in some way, otherwise the language constructs themselves would have to be infinite! In this section we consider three ways of combining entity interactions, both basic interactions and control structures, each of which has its own Simian expression counterpart. In as far as it is possible, the simplest Devnets for these interactions are shown in Fig. 3.

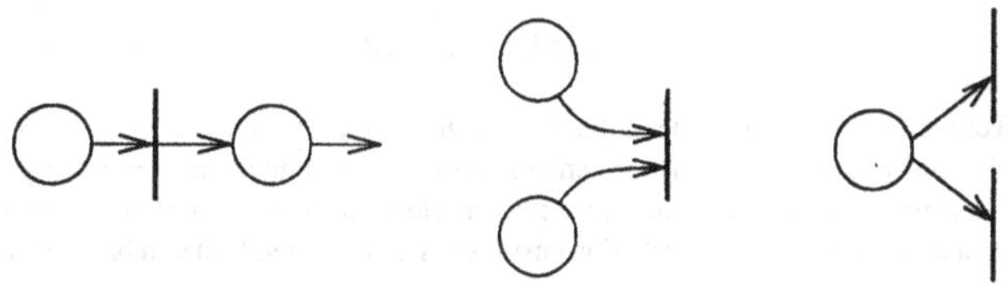

	a ; b	a | b	a || b
effective time:	**sum(a,b)**	**max(a,b)**	**min(a,b)**

Fig. 3 : Devnet constructions with corresponding Simian symbol.

The most obvious way of combining two interactions is to put them into a sequence, putting one after another. Assuming that certain constraints, such as continuity of arc colour, are respected, the operation is fairly straightforward. It corresponds to the Simian semicolon connector. Another useful extension is to extend the combining power of a transition by allowing extra arcs to be input to the same transition, or upside. This has the effect of increasing the conditions placed on the firing, since each input arc represents an extra enabling condition. In its simplest form, this Devnet looks exactly like that for the `ACQ` statement; in fact the advantages of the | operator are only clear when we consider a Simian statement corresponding to a situation where more than two synchronisations impinge on the same transition upside.

For instance, in Fig. 4(b) we have an example where the availability of tugs, berth and the presence of high tide must simultaneously hold before allowing a ship to enter harbour. In net terms, we can readily consider extra arcs affecting a transition's firing capability in a conjunctive manner; but for a sequential language we need an operator such as | to describe the effect. The programming of multi-resource acquisition has long been troublesome, since, with recourse only to the semicolon, the programmer is led to invent unrealistic states where some resources are held while still waiting for others. Such states can easily lead the program into deadlock. In Simian the interaction is effected by use of the single-stick | operator, combining the appropriate temporal expressions (Evans, 1992*a*).

The third kind of combination is a little more complicated, involving the interruption of a sequence of activities by another, a situation which is called *virtual* complexity in Evans (1988). Normally we expect that any entity in an activity is waiting for a single outcome to occur, defined by one of the entity interactions we have already discussed. Sometimes, however, we need to think of its waiting until the first of a number of outcomes happens. At the outset of the activity, it is not determinable which will occur first, and the conflict persists until the first occurrence.

The entity is then potentially subject to several virtual future behaviours, each one capable, at some point in its evolution, to maintain that it will take exclusive control over the entity and to banish the other possibilities to non-existence. Being a kind of interrupt, we must make sure that the system is not left with any dangling "futures", and ensure that any future events put into the FES by non-manifesting processes are automatically cancelled. As far as the Devnet is concerned, virtual complexity is indicated by a place with many possible output arcs. In Simian the virtual processes are separated by a double-stick || operator, and the exclusion points are indicated by the `EXCL` keyword (not indicated on the Devnet). Should any two transitions in a || relation to one another be simultaneously enabled, the situation is treated as a normal activity conflict. Normally, we would expect such an occurrence to be purely coincidental.

For example, consider the following temporal expression:

```
TIME a || TIME b;
```

This will complete when either one of the individual timed events occurs, in fact the earliest one. Very commonly, the argument of a `TIME` statement involves sampling from a probability density function, so it will in general not be ascertainable whether a is less than b or not, until the expression is activated under specific conditions. The expression ensures that that the duration will be the minimum of the two durations.

The classic example of virtual complexity is that of the impatient lift-user, first described by Vaucher (1973). The situation is also commonly encountered when dealing with so-called "time-out" situations, which occur in studies of computer networks and protocols. We give an example in Fig. 4(d) of a Devnet representation of a CSMA/CD bus protocol. Another example of virtual complexity is when tanks are being simultaneously filled and emptied at changeable rates, reminiscent of school algebra problems involving bathtubs and overflows. Generally speaking it cannot be foretold whether a 'tank full' or 'tank empty' event will occur next, the consequences of either being different; thus the need for alternative futures arises.

Elmaghraby (1977) makes a passing reference, in the context of precedence networks, to the need for a relationship between activity sequences such that one will commence when the *first* of its immediate precedents is complete. The situation can be modelled using the || operator. But it is not immediately apparent that the | and || operations are complementary. This can be seen if we consider the effects of the operators in merging separate entity histories. While the | operation merges different enabling conditions on to one transition/upside, the || operation can be regarded as a set of alternative routes stemming from a single merged place. The syntax for the | and || operations is directly analogous to that for Boolean **and** and **or** operations, giving a control specification language which is a little more highly structured than the bilogic precedence graphs of Nutt (1991).

6) Examples of the Devnet

Basic to Simian is the second paradigm which holds that discrete-event system programs can be divided into three separate flows of control: *engagements*, describing the pattern of flow; *allocations* which decide which entities are to move in response to which transition firings, and *data-probes* which are attachable to transitions in the engagement pattern for the purpose of making measurements. The main implication for language design is that the measurement and process specification can be separate from each other, giving a tidier structure. A Simian program thus has four divisions: SCHEMA (optional) for specifying entity data structures, DYNA for the entity processes, INIT for the system initialisation and RUN indicating the measurements to be made and the length of the run. The descriptive scope of Simian, and therefore the Devnet, extends to those discrete-event systems expressible by temporal expressions. As far as the Devnet is concerned, the engagement pattern is expressed in the net topology, while the allocation and data-probes correspond to modules invoked during entity advancement. These modules are invoked from the Primate algorithm, to be described later.

Let us turn to some example Devnets, shown in Fig. 4. Alongside is shown the corresponding Simian dynamics, so the interrelationship between net and program can be appreciated. A full description of Simian will be available in Evans (1993).

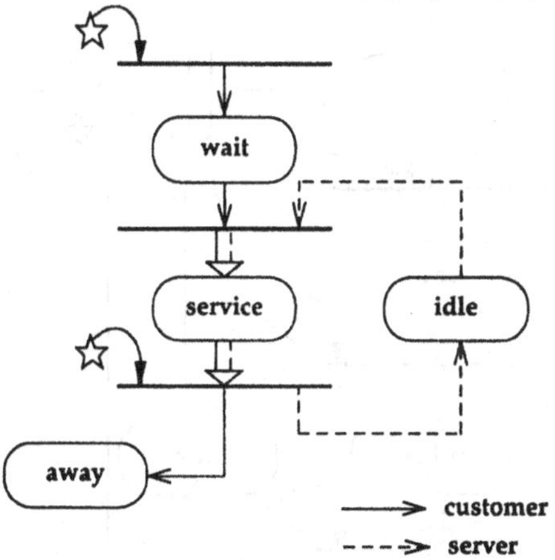

Fig. 4(a): Customer-server Devnet.

```
DYNA
customer:
    (   GEN customer EVERY inter_arrival NEG;

    wait:   ACQ server;
        TIME service;
        REL server;
        INTO away
    )
INIT
    SIZE server := 4;
    inter_arrival := expn (0.25);
    service := unif (0.9,1.1)
RUN
    REPORT wait, server : UNTIL 50 X customer IN away
END
```

Fig. 4(a) (cont'd): Customer-server Simian program.

The first example (Fig. 4a) is the basic customer-server interaction, the archetypal queueing-theory system. The two entity routes are distinguished by arc colour. The server entity has a busy-idle cycle process, while the customer process is a linear sequence of activities, starting with the arrival event. For the complete picture, we should perhaps incorporate the cycle of the fictitious entity, sometimes called the arrival machine, which causes the generation of each customer at events separated by the appropriate inter-arrival time, but since the entity is not strictly speaking a property of any customer itself, its cycle is conventionally omitted. While arrival and end-of-service events are temporal in nature, the commencement of the interaction at start-of-service is a Petri interaction. Notice that the whole server busy-idle cycle can be defined by default in Simian, taking advantage of the high-level viewpoint of PI languages.

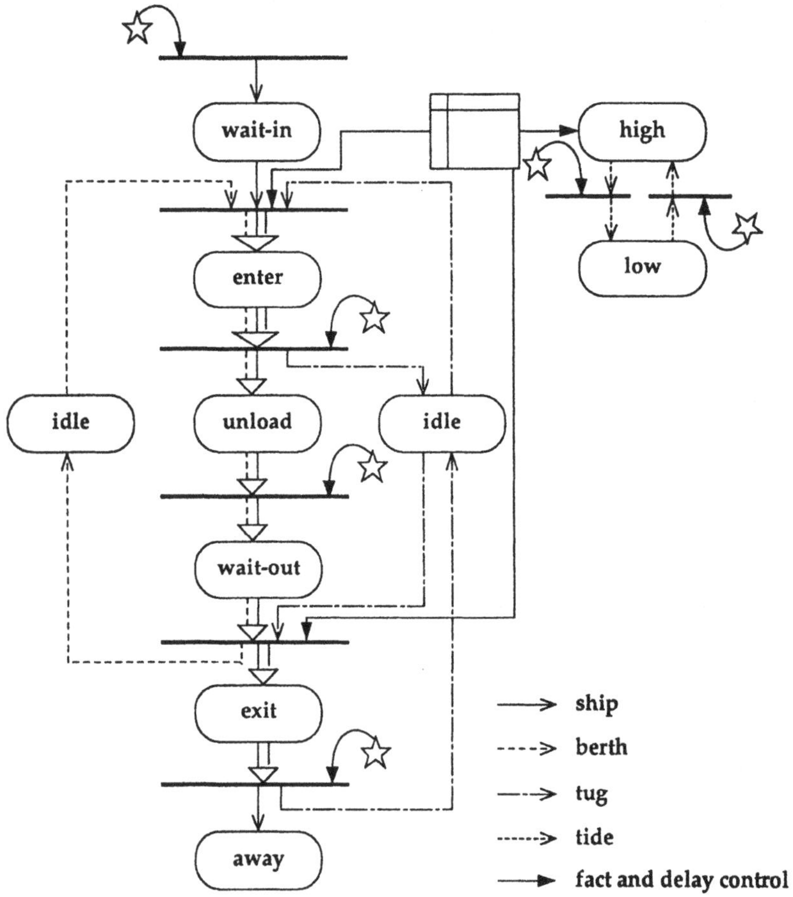

Fig. 4(b): Ship-and-harbour Devnet.

In the ship-and-harbour Devnet of Fig. 4b, we show a simple system with several interesting features. After approaching the harbour, the ship requires several entities to be available and a condition to be true, and that these preliminaries should be met simultaneously before proceeding. If any requirement is missing the ship stays outside and no resources are taken up. The ability to express such an all-or-nothing requirement, shared by Simian and the Devnet, reduces the problems of inadvertently involving deadlock into the system, Birtwistle (1979). Once again, the simple resource nature of both berth and tug entity types enables their processes to be defined by default. The `tide IS high` condition is required at two points of the ship process: before entering and exiting the harbour and the interaction with the tide entity is of message type.

We can also see how a simple Devnet property can warn the implementation, and the user, of an incompletely specified dynamic. From the Devnet it can be ascertained that there is the possibility of an activity conflict whenever a tug re-enters the *idle* state, since it is possible that there are simultaneously ships waiting to enter and ships waiting to leave. The user has the opportunity to define, using a `PRIO` statement, that the `exit` activity should take priority over the `enter` activity. If no such definition were given the Simian system would prompt the user for one.

```
DYNA
ship:(  GEN ship EVERY inter_arrival NEG;

wait_in:ACQ 2 X tug | ACQ berth | AWAIT (tide IS high);
        TIME enter;
        REL tug;
        TIME unload;

wait_out:   ACQ tug | AWAIT (tide IS high);
        REL berth;
        TIME exit;
        REL tug;
        INTO away
    ),

tide:   DO
      TIME high;
      TIME low
    OD
INIT
    PRIO exit > enter;
    inter_arrival := expn (180);
    enter := unif (28,33);
    unload := 60;
    high := 540;
    low := 240;
    exit := unif (25,28)
RUN
    REPORT ship, tug : UNTIL 100 X ship IN away
END
```

Fig. 4(b) (cont'd): Ship-and-harbour Simian program.

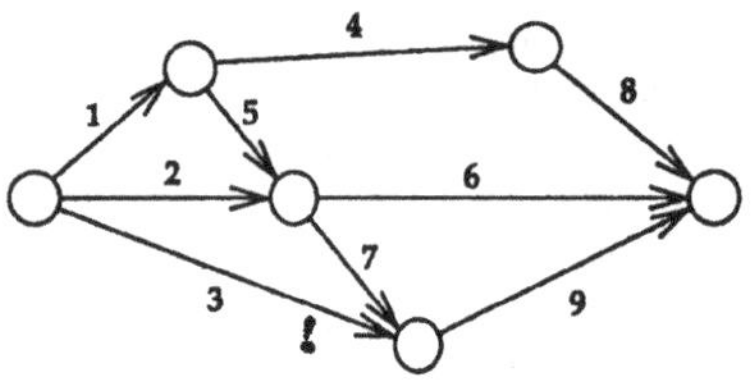

Fig. 4(c): A PERT network, based on an example from Pritsker, *et al.* (1989). Each arc represents an activity, the nodes indicating activity precedence.

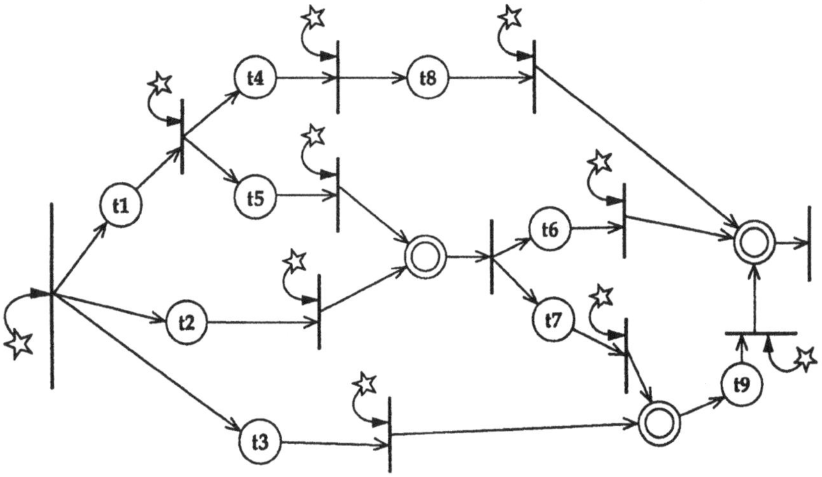

Fig 4(c): (cont'd): The PERT network's Devnet.

Fig. 4c shows a conventional PERT network with its Devnet and Simian program. While considerably more complex than the PERT net, a Devnet representation would however enable the effect of resource allocation to be included in the system, which might have a considerable inter-activity effect were resource limitation a significant problem. The `UNITE` symbol is used to denote that there is a dependency on more than one predecessor finishing. In the program, note the use of the `SYNC` to denote the unification of all routes within its enclosing `CASE` statement. For critical path analysis, a critical activity can be identified by being the *last* element of a unification to complete, thus enabling criticality estimations to be made on a project with stochastic components by repeated replications.

```
SCHEMA
    01 project
      02 one
        03 four
        03 five
          04 six
          04 seven
      02 two
      02 three
DYNA
  project:
  (  GEN project NEG;   /* the source */

    DIVIDE project INTO one & two & three;
    CASE
      one:
        ( TIME t1;
          DIVIDE one INTO four & five;
          CASE
            four: ( TIME t4; TIME t8),
            five: ( TIME t5;
                    UNITE five WITH two;
                    DIVIDE five INTO six & seven;
                    CASE
                      six:     TIME t6,
                      seven: ( TIME t7;
                               UNITE seven WITH three;
                               TIME t9)
                    ESAC
                    )
          SYNC        /* the sink */
          ESAC
        ),
      two:  TIME t2,
      three:TIME t3
    ESAC
  )
END
```

Fig. 4(c) (cont'd): A PERT network's Simian program.

While the discipline of critical path analysis has its own methods of work, the Simian approach opens the possibility of incorporating in one language a discrete-event system description containing aspects of operational research cultures previously considered distinct, through the medium of the Devnet. With the advent of constraint logic programming (van Hentenryck, 1989) and the concern of its advocates with so-called *disjunctive* problems (essentially resource-availability restrictions) we see this field as one in which a more general and unified approach might prove valuable.

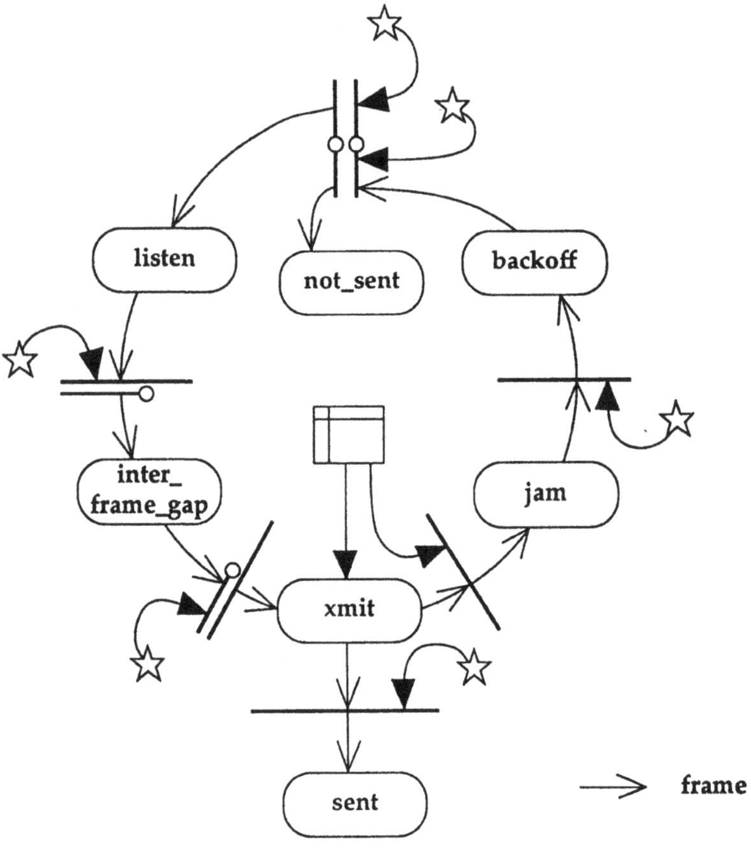

Fig. 4(d): CSMA/CD bus protocol.

```
DYNA
  frame: (GEN frame EVERY inter_frame NEG;

        FOR i TO attempts UNLESS (THIS frame IN sent)
        DO
          TIME listen;
          IF carrier_sense
          THEN
            TIME inter_frame_gap
          FI;

          (   TIME xmit;
              INTO sent
          )
          ||
          (   AWAIT (OTHER frame IN xmit);
                        /* collision detection */
              TIME jam;
              EXCL;           /* abort the xmit */
              TIME backoff (i)
          )
        OD;

        INTO not_sent
  )
```

Fig. 4(d) (cont'd): Simian program for the CSMA/CD bus protocol.

The final application (Fig. 4d) is in the area of communication networks, a CSMA/CD protocol, which shows the representative capabilities of the Devnet stretched to their limits. The basic process topology is a cycle, entered immediately after the generation of a frame. For a short period the carrier is sensed to detect whether any traffic is being communicated. If so, a duration corresponding to an inter-frame gap is consumed in waiting. If not, the Devnet rather awkwardly represents the omission of this wait by bracketing it between an empty downside and an empty upside. Then the frame is transmitted, which takes a certain duration. During this activity, the frame is subject to two virtual futures, depending on whether a collision is detected or not. If transmission duration elapses and no other sender is detected in the `xmit` state at the same time, the communication is successful and the frame enters the `sent` state. On the other hand, the transmission must be aborted, which requires the sending of a short jamming signal, after which the `xmit` activity is interrupted. So there is a very significant interruptive interaction between the transition following the `jam` activity and the `xmit` activity which is not shown in the Devnet. After interruption, the sender delays for a certain backoff duration, which is dependent upon the number of loop cycles completed, and, if the number of cycles has not exceeded its limit, the cycle is restarted.

It is interesting to compare different perspective of this broad-brush description with the more detailed nets given in Ajmone Marsan, *et al.* (1987), which uses deterministic and stochastic Petri nets (DSPN) with timed transitions and inhibitor arcs. Use of the || operator allows the expression of more general time-outs caused by non-time-delay interactions, like `ACQ` and `AWAIT`.

7) Concurrency, Conflict and Decision in the Devnet

In this section we take up some of the Devnet notions of parallel behaviour for which Petri nets make such a clear characterisation. In doing so, we are making use of the Devnet constructions as an informal explanation of Simian semantics. Potential difficulties of interpretation arise with the convergence and divergence of arcs, and some aspects have already been discussed along with the nets of Fig. 3. Here we consider the constructions in Figs. 5-8.

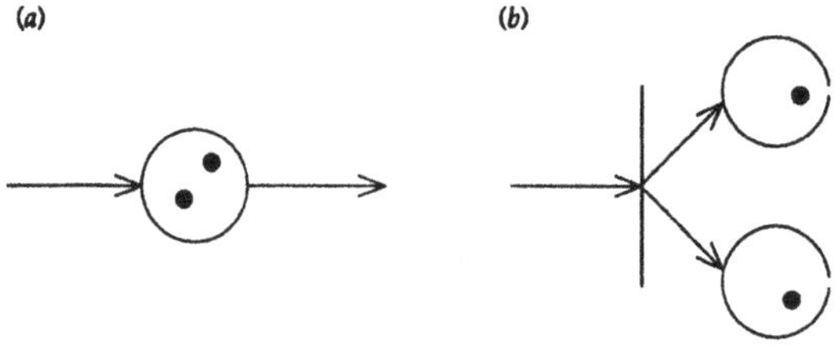

Fig. 5: Concurrency in the DEVNET.
(a) two entities undertaking the same activity;
(b) two concurrent activities are commenced simultaneously.

Entity concurrency: (Fig. 5a) This is the simplest kind of concurrency, and occurs when two or more entities happen to be involved in the same activity in overlapping durations of time. Naturally the entities will be of the same type.

Activity concurrency: (Fig. 5b) More than one activity may be started simultaneously by the firing of a single transition. In this case the incoming entity may represent an engagement of separable entities, so it may be of mixed type, or a single entity may be split into component parts. Of course activity concurrency is extremely commonplace, since, in a given marking, at a particular point in time, all occupied places represent activities being partaken concurrently by entities.

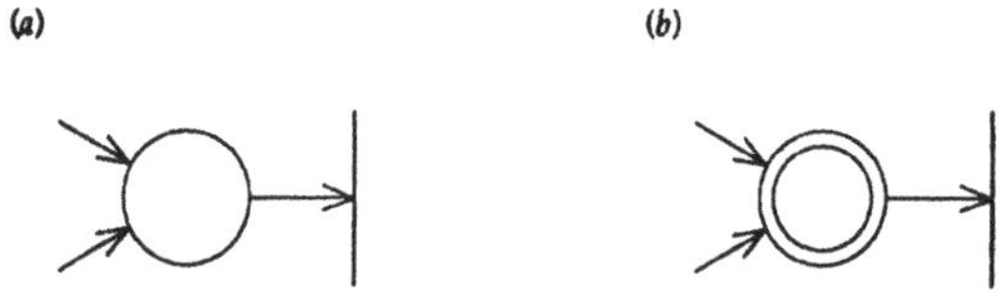

Fig. 6: Activity entry in the DEVNET.
(a) Entry by entities of the appropriate class into an activity is unrestricted except by the firing of a preceding transition.
In (b) as the entities enter, they assemble themselves into wholes. On the completion of an entity, the following transition is enabled.

"Don't care" activity entry: (Fig. 6a) Since the places are for the most part passive components in the evolution of the net, entry into an activity by an entity is a low-key affair and does not cause or require any synchronisation. Essentially the Devnet doesn't care how entities arrive in their states, apart from their movements originating in some transition firing. However, we have seen that the use of the fact, programmed by the `AWAIT` keyword, can cause the occupancy of a state to have an excitatory or inhibitory effect on a transition's firing, through a message interaction.

Assembly activity entry: (Fig.6b) Furthermore, where an activity is such that it involves the (re)assembly of components into a whole, as programmed by a `SYNC` or `UNITE` statement, then the subsequent transition will fire on behalf of the completed entity. These statements are similar in their assembling function, `SYNC` gathering entities which have been split in the closest binding `CASE` – `ESAC` or `DO` – `OD`, while `UNITE` assembles a specified set of entities regardless of their origin.

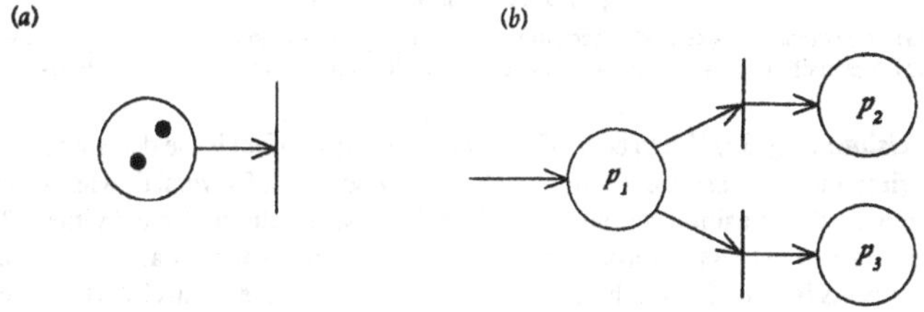

Fig. 7: Conflict in the DEVNET.
(a) Entity conflict. There may be a conflict as to which entity is the enabling one.
(b) Activity conflict. If two transitions are enabled simultaneously then extra rules may be required to resolve the conflict between activities p_2 and p_3.

Entity conflict: (Fig. 7a) Various types of conflict are also possible in discrete-event systems. The simplest is entity conflict, where a firing occurs and there is a choice as to which of many entity candidates should be advanced. This is a generalisation of the queueing discipline concept. By default, and in conformity with most simulation languages, Simian assumes a FIFO discipline, but LIFO, attribute-based priorities and attribute-matching between potential engagees are also possible.

Activity conflict: (Fig. 7b) In contrast to the ease with which an entity may enter an activity, if there is a choice of which arc to follow in exiting an activity, the situation can be much more complicated. With Murata (1989) we concur that any place with two or more output arcs is capable of being in conflict. Most current simulation languages pay scant regard to conflicts, naively assuming they can be resolved by consulting entity attributes. In Simian, the || operator can be used to program activity conflicts. The entity occupying the place is subject to more than one exiting event and, in general, it is not foreseeable which will happen first. The complexity of the situation is increased from the observation that each of the competing transitions may have interactions with other places and the choice of the firings will in general produce quite different future markings. Activity conflict also must be treated specially in the entity advancement phase controlled by the Primate algorithm. This is discussed in section 9.

On the other hand, if a token in the place *p1* satisfies the firing rules for both transitions simultaneously, then extra rules should be invoked to resolve the conflict. The situation is exemplified in the Devnet of Fig. 4(b) when we consider a tug entering the *idle* state. As was mentioned previously, a conflict between `enter` and `exit` activities may then ensue, which requires the application of the `PRIO` rule for resolution. Typically the output places *p2* and *p3* are prioritised with respect to one another. Alternatively a random choice may be made, to be exercised independently on behalf of each entity in conflict.

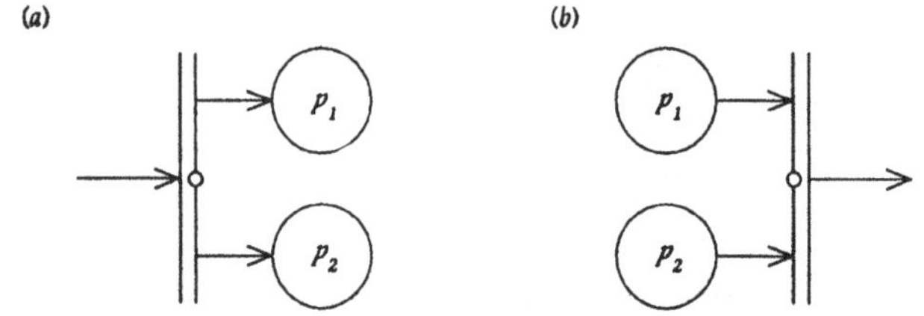

Fig. 8: Decision in the DEVNET.
(a) The transition fires and a decision is made to choose between alternative activities.
(b) A transition fires by means of one of many alternative enablement conditions.

Activity decision: (Fig. 8a) Not to be confused with activity conflict is the decision process, in which a transition fires and the consequent actions determine which one of several downside paths should be taken. Effectively the transition actions decide between a set of alternative activities. The decision is made by the spiritual expressions associated with the transition, while for activity conflict the choice of alternative paths is made by which transition fires first. This is the means by which the temporal `IF` and `CASE` statements are handled.

Common consequences: (Fig. 8b) When the end of the alternative paths is reached, a "don't care" transition firing may happen in which the same set of actions is carried out and the entities are subject to a common downside logic, no matter how the firing is caused. This kind of transition corresponds to a `FI` or `ESAC` keyword. Unlike the assembly activity entry, here we have a confluence of logical paths which occurs on an instantaneous firing.

8) Devnet activation

Overall, Devnet activation can be seen as an elaborated version of the three-phase executive as implemented for so-called activity-scanning (AS) simulation languages (Evans, 1988). After the Devnet has been built, the `INIT` stage specifies the initial system configuration, defining the starting occupancies of places, number of entities of each class, parameters of sampling distributions, etc. The `RUN` stage defines the measurements to be made and the terminating event for the execution. The Simian program is then executed by activating the Devnet according to a standard *executive program*, comprising:

- future-event retrieval,
- entity advancement,
- activity conflict resolution,

the last two parts being repeatedly carried out until no more advancement is possible.

Originally, future-event notices, which are the root cause of all event occurrences, are created either in the `INIT` stage, or during the execution of actions brought about by inserting tokens into places corresponding to `TIME` statements. Such notices are collected in a global set, the future-events set (FES). The record structure of a future event contains an engagement which identifies the essential triple of (token, upside, time) indicating that a specific token has been scheduled to enable the transition containing the upside, at a particular point in time. The next future event to be retrieved is determined by that notice in the FES which currently has the minimum occurrence time, i.e. it is the soonest to occur. The simulation clock is updated to the occurrence time of the impending event and retains this fixed value until the completion of the executive, during what is called a *time beat*. The next time beat is performed when repeating the executive for a new time value.

The notice identifies the firing of a particular starred transition, and all other token movements for the remainder of the time-beat can be seen as consequential to that firing. For entity advancement, the Primate algorithm is invoked, which seeks out and defines further transition firings, and implements the basic types of transition enablement and firing corresponding to `TIME`, `ACQ` and `AWAIT` statements. A complete desription of the Primate algorithm will be available shortly in Evans (1992*b*). To a large extent, the strictures laid down in a Simian program will provide additional conditions serving, in many cases, to disambiguate what would otherwise be conflicting firing strategy for a pure Petri net. Thus many of the decisions of the *token player* (Colom, *et al.*, 1986) are pre-ordained by the Simian text.

Once the initial firing of the time beat has been established, Primate peruses the Devnet for further enablement. During the entity advancement and conflict resolution stages, all other starred upsides can be ignored since their enablement must await a different time beat. To omit a large number of upsides from further consideration for the current time beat saves a great deal of effort; it resembles the partitioning of places into the *representing* and *synchronization* categories of Colom, *et al.* (1986), although Primate does not need to add extra places for this purpose. Throughout, Primate seeks out further advancement possibilities by following Devnet arcs for advancing tokens, and by detecting conflict possibilities for proper resolution.

When further advancement appears to have ceased, any conflicting enablements are resolved. If this gives rise to more enablements, the Primate algorithm is resumed. Eventually all the consequences of the initial firing for the current time beat will have subsided and further advancement can be awaited from the next retrieval from the FES, and the grand cycle repeats.

9) The Primate algorithm

Having an internal representation of the Devnet as a pathfinder for the Simian executive program enables entities to be advanced in a *circumspect* way, taking into account a system-wide perspective. Primate, by making use of the topological properties of the Devnet, can thereby take note of all the conflicts and reactivations which might otherwise be forgotten, ignored or swept under the carpet. Although represented as a data structure, the Devnet acts as a control structure for the evolution of the system, in common with the approach of Valette and Bako (1991). Moreover, any number of entities can be advanced simultaneously without giving any particular advantage or hindrance to any one of them, while maintaining respect of the conditions of priority and conflict resolution, etc. which the simulationist has stipulated.

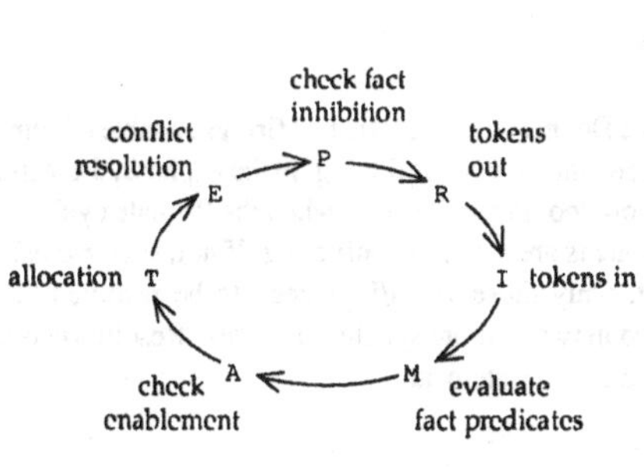

Fig. 9: The PRIMATE algorithm: an outline.

Primate consists of a cycle of seven phases (Fig. 9), which is invoked after the time-advance phase has determined the set of engagements which will be the subject of the next state-change. For ease of description, we will assume here that there is only one engagement, although the algorithm can handle an arbitrary number of coincident engagements, as might be occasioned by coincident occurrences. It is stored in a set called *Enab*, which identifies both the firing transition and the enabling token(s). The Primate cycle is invoked starting from phase P. This simply checks whether there is any inhibitory fact preventing the firing of the transition. If not, the enabling tokens are removed from the input places in the R-phase and re-associated before being relocated in the output places in the I-phase. Also new tokens can be created, and existing ones destroyed, in the R-phase.

The actual configuration of the system changes only through the movement of tokens between R and I. Specific tokens are identified in the input places and brought into transit, where the tokens may be added to or broken up, destroyed, or new tokens created, but what ever their fate, some token(s) are likely to emerge from the transition's actions. During their transit, tokens' attributes are updated and actions performed according to spiritual statements in the Simian text. According to the demands made in RUN, desired movements are logged and measurements made, through activation of the data-probes. When the I-phase assigns tokens to a new place, it may entail changing the value of a fact, or entering a future-event notice into the FES.

Synchronisations caused by ACQ are detected only by examining the consequences of token movements of previous firings in the time-beat. Places that are being watched by facts are also monitored. Any change in occupancy will cause the watching fact's predicate to be re-evaluated; if a *true* value results, the affected upsides are brought into consideration for firing.

The result of the I-phase is a new marking which must be examined to see whether any transition is still enabled. The places whose occupancy has changed are stored in a set *Place*, and any fact whose value might be affected is stored in the set *Fact*. In the M-phase, these facts are re-evaluated so they reflect the new system configuration, and the A-phase eliminates non-enabled transitions from further consideration. The T-phase allocates tokens from places input to the enabled transitions for firing, in accordance with the selection logic. If the transition corresponds to an ACQ, then the tokens of the input places may need to be searched for suitable firing candidates. Occasionally there can be a tie in the selection, resulting from an unresolved entity conflict, in which case the selection is made arbitrarily. Successful enablements are stored in the set *Enab*. In the E-phase a check is made that no enabling token is being used to enable more than one transition firing. Conflicting enablements are temporarily removed from the *Enab* set. While there remain enablements in *Enab*, the Primate cycle continues from the P-phase. If at any inter-phase juncture, the set which indicates the items of concern to the next phase is empty, the cycle is quit.

10) Conflict handling

Structural properties of the Devnet will reveal that all firings capable of being influenced by places with more than one output arc are potentially conflicting. In the E-phase, these *q-conflicts* are extracted from *Enab* and stored in *Q*. From looking at the *Q* set when the Primate cycle has been exhausted, it can be seen whether any enablements are actually conflicting. If not, such *r-conflicts* are put back into *Enab* for further advancement. Only those *s-conflicts* need to be resolved, in which the same token is simultaneously implicated in two or more synchronisations. Resolution is carried out according to the stipulation of the user in a PRIO statement.

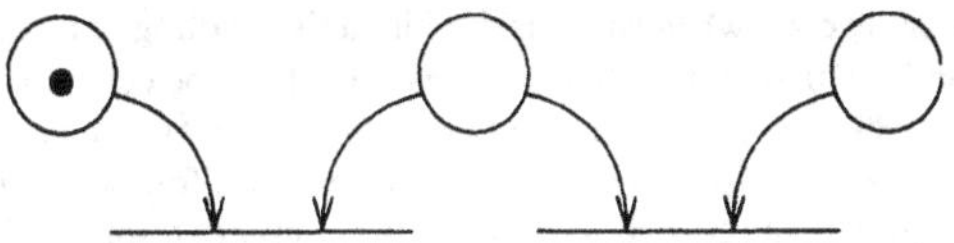

q-conflict, potentially an actual conflict

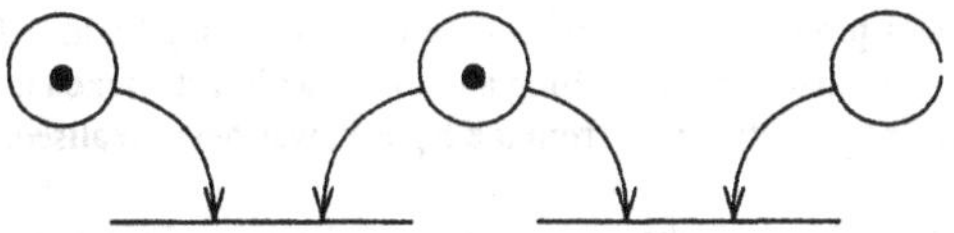

r-conflict, does not require resolution

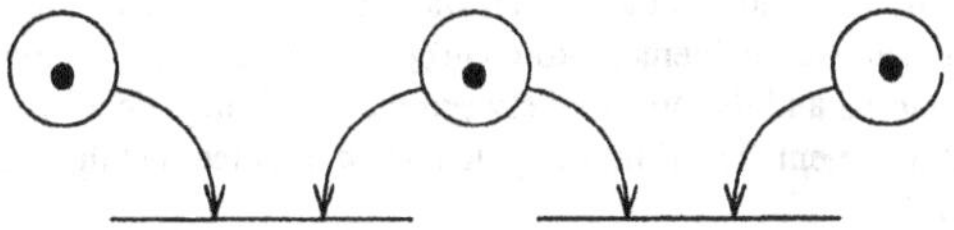

s-conflict, requires resolution

Simulation languages which adopt the process-interaction (PI) strategy have an executive program which puts the entity in the role of an *egoistical* token (Hartung, 1988). They reserve places selfishly. As such, the executive program of Simian is distinct from those object-based simulation languages such as Simula, in which an entity (i.e. an object) is forced along its path as far as possible without regard for the advancement of other entities. Object-based approaches thus suffer from a short-sightedness when a broader system-wide perspective needs to be adopted.

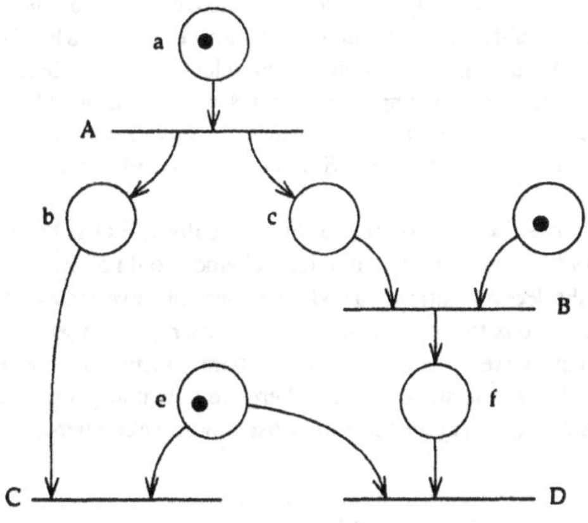

Fig. 10: A Devnet to compare the handling of conflicts.

The difference is especially clear when we consider Simian's handling of conflict between activities. Consider the Devnet in Fig. 10, which exhibits features of conflict and concurrency, called *asymmetric confusion* by Murata (1989). On purely structural grounds we could claim that there is a potential for conflict between the firing of transitions C and D. However if we follow a *selfish* token philosophy, detection of this possibility could be overlooked and the conflict "resolved" in an uncontrolled and unintended fashion.

Let us interpret the evolution of the net in such a manner, starting with the marking in the Figure. We may assume Petri firing rule since there are no facts, and starred transitions are ignored by Primate. The token in *a* enables *A* which produces tokens in *b* and *c*, thereby enabling *B* and *C*. There being no conflict between these two, both transitions fire, leaving a marking with just a token in *f*. In other words, the conflict evidenced by the two output arcs from the *e* place, was never realised.

We can contrast this evolution with the one taken by the Primate algorithm which instead adopts a *circumspect* token philosophy. Once again the token in *a* causes *A* to fire and tokens appear in *b* and *c*. In the E-phase, the enablement firing of *C* will be recognised as a q-conflict since one of its input places has more than one output arc. The enablement is added to the *Q* set. Meanwhile the enablement of *B* is recognised as conflict-free and fires in the normal way, resulting in a token in *f*. Now *D* is recognised as enabled but in conflict and its enablement stored in *Q*. The *Enab* set being empty, the activity conflict resolution section is entered and the priority between the two firings decided according to the user's indications in a `PRIO` statement. The Primate cycle is then re-entered at the P stage with the resolved set of enablements *Enab*.

The cycle repeats until the algorithm detects that no more activation can be performed. In this way we ensure that the full consequences of any movement of tokens is fully explored and the time-beat can be assumed complete. The time-advance procedure is then called upon again to deliver a new future-event notice and the Primate cycle is entered once more. Although it may seem quite complicated (indeed this brief description only skims the surface), the Primate algorithm aims at covering all possible avenues of reactivation and checking which can be derived from the Simian system description.

11) Limitations of nets

From the underground-train map analogy, it is clear that the Devnet is not intended to be a complete description from which one could derive a simulation program. To include a level of detail which would allow the full description of routeing decisions and token selection would obscure one of the principal attractions of the diagram: its essential simplicity. For this reason, a Devnet by itself will not contain sufficient information to act as a description from which to derive a simulation model, except in the broadest terms. Interpreted independently from Simian, the Devnet is clearly less informative.

If we were to extend its power, we can foresee further difficulties. As has been pointed out by many authors, e.g. Peterson (1980), a good methodological scheme should allow the aggregation of many parts into a whole and/or the decomposition of a node, whether a place or a transition, into separate parts, or functions. We have used a box to represent some Devnet operations in sections four and five, but it was stressed there that these were to be interpreted in a purely symbolic way. The subnet cannot be effectively regarded as a black box since inside it there are potentially a multitude of nodes, either transitions or places, where an arc may join. (There is a discussion of a counter-argument to this in Nolan, *et al.*,(1989)).

With introduction of disjunctive sides we are able to make more clear which arcs are involved with the current enablement or dispersal. However, if we look at the most general case, the usefulness of disjunctive sides also has its limitations. Consider, for instance, the case of an iteration immediately followed by a choice control. We are faced with the possibility of a series of disjunctions within disjunctions. Whichever way we choose to proceed, the resulting Devnet will be more complicated and its meaning more obscure.

When it comes to the modelling of interrupts, whether of the virtual or external kind, they are found to be difficult to represent on any diagram. We have already noted the difficulty of indicating the position of the EXCL statement in virtual complexity. A further kind of complexity arises when an entity is commandeered from outside, maybe in order to model a breakdown of normal behaviour. In fact an interaction involving any kind of interruption is difficult to show, unless we are going to impose a hierarchy of Devnets, with a higher net capable of displacing the tokens of a lower one; yet the added complication seems hardly worth while. But even such a net hierarchy is incapable of showing interruptions caused by time-elapse with respect to a particular token, as would be required, for example, in a model of breakdown based on the expiry of working life. Of course, these pictorial Devnet difficulties pose less of a problem for the internal data-structure implementation.

12) Conclusions and further work

Simian, by means of the Devnet, represents an attempt to make an intimate connection between different areas of informatics which have developed from quite separate origins. There remain some interesting questions. Currently, the Devnet is just a convenient means to formulate the implementation of the underlying dynamic semantics of a Simian program. Can the Devnet be sufficiently formalised to act as a semantic domain for general descriptions of discrete-event systems? The structural and behavioural properties and the role of invariants (Murata, 1989) in analysing the Devnet remain as yet unexplored. Also one may ask, does the Devnet have a role in the software development of a system description in the Simian language? Here, the work summarised in Huber, *et al.* (1991) is relevant. If so, can the actual programming be short-circuited so that the description is presented, more or less completely, in diagram form, in a similar manner to a CASE tool? Maybe it is at this level that the opportunity to apply AI tools (planning etc.) especially in respect of CIM applications (Silva and Valette, 1990)? Hopefully the link between theoretical mathematical studies of Petri nets and the practical world of simulation can be brought into a fruitful synergy.

We have tried to show that the Devnet diagram, as a qualitative expression of system properties, has some definite benefit as a portrayal of the outline of a system's dynamic, and has some methodological value as an intermediate model. But its primarily usefulness is in conjunction with the implementation of a simulation program. In the form of a data-structure serving as an activator for a Simian program it can serve:

- for detecting conflict possibilities;
- as an internal model of event interdependencies;
- to automatically reactivate entities;
- as a basis for driving a back-end animation.

Although simulation diagrams are mainly touted for their assistance in model development, we should remain suspicious of their imposing too much rigidity in methodology, while remaining aware that the amount of assistance required is perhaps a matter of the simulationist's subjective familiarity with the simulation language. All told, this author is generally lukewarm over the Devnet's methodological uses, beyond what has been said here, although it has been found very useful for educational purposes. Perhaps a mutually supportive methodology would be better, in which there is no strict before-and-after relation between the Devnet and its program. A more interactive relationship might best be appreciated through a hypertext display upon which a simulationist could view the overall flow properties, while examining the detailed transition effects in program form. This remains an unexplored avenue of development.

One of the prime reasons for using diagrams in simulation has been the obscureness of existing simulation languages. To some extent, by internalising the net, Simian offers a more declarative language, so this need is perhaps not so acute. Experience shows that when dealing with even moderately complex systems, especially those encountered outside the classroom, it is sometimes necessary to venture to write an outline program first. With familiarity, the Devnet stage can be skipped, especially when dealing with large systems, as any diagram can get unwieldy when it becomes too large.

Promising future work on the Devnet might extend its application into the area of the monitoring of a control system, and in the area of AI planning, both of which are areas with significant dynamic and decision components. Finally, giving the Devnet more descriptive power is inevitably balanced by a reduction in its evaluative power as regards finding net invariants, etc. On the theoretical side, some examination of the other work in Petri nets, looking at semantic properties and the role of invariants, might prove useful. At a practical level, a broader development of the possibilities of animation would be interesting.

Acknowledgements

I would like to acknowledge the assistance of Yuen Yik Kwong in the preparation of the Devnet figures and the comments of the two anonymous referees who have reviewed this paper.

References

Ajmone Marsan, M., Chiola, G. and Fumagalli, A. (1987) 'An Accurate Performance Model of CSMA/CD Bus LAN', in Rozenberg, G. (Ed.) *Advances in Petri Nets 1987*, Lecture Notes in Computer Science 266, Springer-Verlag, Berlin 146-161.

Baldassari, M. and Bruno, G. (1988) 'An Environment for Object-Oriented Conceptual Programming Based on PROT Nets', in Rozenberg, G. (Ed.) *Advances in Petri Nets 1988*, Lecture Notes in Computer Science 340, Springer-Verlag, Berlin, 1-19.

Ben Ahmed, S., Moalla, M., Courvoisier, M. and Valette, R. (1991) 'Flexible Manufacturing Production System Modelling Using Object Petri Nets and their Analysis', *IMACS-IFAC Symposium on Modelling and Control of Technological Systems*, Lille, May 7-10, Proceedings 1 553-560.

Birtwistle, G.M. (1979) *Discrete Event Modelling on Simula*, Macmillan, Basingstoke, UK.

Clementson, A.T. (1977) *Extended Control and Simulation Language – Computer Aided Programming System*, Lucas Institute for Engineering Production, University of Birmingham, UK.

Colom, J.M., Silva, M. and Villaroel, J.L. (1986) 'On Software Implementation of Petri Nets and Coloured Petri Nets Using High-Level Concurrent Languages', in *Seventh European Workshop on Application and Theory of Petri Nets*, Oxford, UK, 207-241.

Dahl, O.-J. (1968) 'Discrete Event Simulation Languages', in Genuys, F. (Ed.) *Programming Languages*, Academic Press, London, 349-395.

Drummond, M.E. (1986) *A Representation of Action and Belief for Automatic Planning Systems*, AIAI-TR-16, Artificial Intelligence Applications Institute, University of Edinburgh.

Elmaghraby, S.E. (1977) *Activity Networks*, Wiley, New York.

Evans, J.B. (1986) 'A Characterisation of Discrete-event Simulation Complexity', *Proceedings JSST Conference on Recent Advances in Simulation of Complex Systems*, July 15-17, 1986, Tokyo, 24-28.

Evans, J.B. (1988) *Structures of Discrete Event Simulation: An Introduction to the Engagement Strategy*, Ellis Horwood, Chichester, UK.

Evans, J.B. (1989) 'DEVNET: An Activation Net for Discrete Event Simulation', in Lasker, G.E. (Ed.) *Advances in Computer Science*, Windsor, Ontario, Canada; also Technical Report TR-88-03, Department of Computer Science, University of Hong Kong.

Evans, J.B. (1990) 'Towards a Declarative Simulation Language: SIMIAN', *International Conference on Systems Management '90*, Hong Kong, June 11-13, Proceedings 343-348.

Evans, J.B. (1991) 'Description of Designed Systems in SIMIAN', *IMACS-IFAC Symposium on Modelling and Control of Technological Systems*, Lille, May 7-10, Proceedings 1 669-674.

Evans, J.B. (1992*a*) 'The Temporal Expressions of SIMIAN', *ACM Transactions on Modeling and Simulation*, submitted; also Technical Report TR-91-04 of Department of Computer Science, University of Hong Kong.

Evans, J.B. (1992*b*) 'PRIMATE: An Executive Program for the Engagement Strategy', *ACM Transactions on Modeling and Computer Simulation* (in preparation).

Evans, J.B. (1993) *Temporal Programming in Simian*, to appear.

Genrich, H.J. and Thieler-Mevissen, G. (1976) 'The Calculus of Facts', in Marzurkiewicz, A. (Ed.) *Mathematical Foundations of Computer Science*, Proceedings of the Fifth Symposium, Gdansk, September 6-10, 1976, 588-595. *Lecture Notes in Computer Science* 45, Springer-Verlag, Berlin.

Gordon, G. (1975) *The Application of GPSS V to Discrete System Simulation*, Prentice-Hall, Englewood Cliffs, NJ.

Gordon, G. (1978) 'The Development of the General Purpose Simulation System (GPSS)', *ACM Sigplan Notices* **13** 8 183-198.

Hartung, G. (1988) 'Programming a Closely Coupled Multiprocessor System with High Level Petri Nets', in Rozenberg, G. (Ed.) *Advances in Petri Nets 1988*, Lecture Notes in Computer Science 340, Springer-Verlag, Berlin, 151-174.

van Hentenryck, P. (1989) *Constraint Handling in Logic Programming*, MIT Press, Cambridge, MA.

Hoover, S.V. and Perry, R.F. (1989) *Simulation: A Problem-Solving Approach*, Addison-Wesley, Reading, MA.

Huber, P., Jensen, K., and Shapiro, R.M. (1991) 'Hierarchies in Coloured Petri Nets', in Jensen, K. and Rozenberg, G. (Eds) *High-level Petri Nets: Theory and Application*, Springer-Verlag, Berlin, 215-243.

Jensen, K. (1981) 'Coloured Petri Nets and the Invariant Method', *Theoretical Computer Science* **14** 317-336.

MacNair, E.A. and Sauer, C.H. (1985) *Elements of Practical Performance Modeling*, Prentice-Hall, Englewood Cliffs, NJ.

Merlin, P.M. and Farber, D.J. (1976) 'Recoverability of Communication Protocols: Implications of a Theoretical Study', *IEEE Transactions on Communications* **COM-24** 9 1036-1043.

Molloy, M. K. (1982) 'Performance Analysis Using Stochastic Petri Nets', *IEEE Transactions on Computers* **C-31** 9 913-917.

Murata, T. (1989) 'Petri Nets: Properties, Analysis and Applications', *Proceedings of the IEEE*, **77** 4 541-580.

Nolan, P.J., Lane, G.M. and Fegan, J.M. (1989) 'A Lisp-based Stochastic Petri Net Simulation Environment', in Tzafestas, S., Eisinberg, A. and Carotenuto, L. (Eds) *System Modelling and Simulation*, Elsevier Science, New York, 287-296.

Nutt, G.R. (1991) 'A Simulation System Architecture for Graph Models', in Rozenberg, G. (Ed.) *Advances in Petri Nets 1991*, Lecture Notes in Computer Science 524, Springer-Verlag, Berlin, 417-435.

Overstreet, C.M. and Nance, R.E. (1985) 'A Specification Language to Assist in Analysis of Discrete Event Simulation Models', *Comm. ACM* **28** 2 190-201.

Peterson, J.L. (1980) 'A Note on Colored Petri Nets', *Information Processing Letters* **11** 1 40-43.

Petri, C.A. (1987) '"Forgotten Topics" of Net Theory', in Brauer, W., Reisig, W. and Rozenberg, G. (Eds) *Advances in Petri Nets 1986*, II *Petri Nets: Applications and Relationships to Other Models of Concurrency*, Lecture Notes in Computer Science 255, Springer-Verlag, Berlin, 500-514.

Poole, T.G. and Szymankiewicz, J.Z. (1977) *Using Simulation to Solve Problems*, McGraw-Hill, London.

Pooley, R.J. (1991) 'Towards a Standard for Hierachical Process Oriented Discrete Event Simulation Diagrams'; 'Part I: A Comparison of Existing Approaches', 'Part II The Suggested Approach to Flat Models', (with Hughes, P.H.) 'Part III: Aggregation and Hierarchical Modelling', *Transactions of the Society for Computer Simulation*, **8** 1 1-20, 21-31, 33-41.

Pritsker, A.A.B., Sigal, C.E. and Hammesfahr, R.D.J. (1989) *SLAM II: Network Models for Decision Support*, Prentice-Hall, Englewood Cliffs, NJ.

Ramchandani, C. (1974) *Analysis of Asynchronous Concurrent Systems by Timed Petri Nets*, Project MAC TR-120 Massachusetts Institute of Technology, Cambridge, MA.

Schruben, L. (1983) 'Simulation Modeling with Event Graphs', *Comm. ACM* **26** 11 957-963.

Sibertin-Blanc, C. (1985) 'High-level Petri Nets with Data-structures', *Sixth European Workshop on Application and Theory of Petri Nets*, Espoo, Finland.

Sifakis, J. (1977) 'Petri Nets for Performance Evaluation', in Beilner, H. and Gelenbe, E. (Eds) *Measuring, Modeling, and Evaluating Computer Systems*, Proceedings of the 3rd Symposium, IFIP Working Group 7.3, North-Holland, New York, 77-93.

Silva, M. and Valette, R. (1990) 'Petri Nets and Flexible Manufacturing', in Rozenberg, G. (Ed.) *Advances in Petri Nets 1989*, Lecture Notes in Computer Science 424, Springer-Verlag, Berlin, 374-417.

Taha, H.A. (1988) *Simulation Modeling and SIMNET*, Prentice-Hall, Englewood Cliffs, NJ.

Tate, A.R., Mathewson, S.C. and Downes, V.A. (1983) *An Interactive Program Generator for Simula*, Imperial College of Science and Technology, Department of Computing, Research Report DoC 83/23, London.

Tocher, K.D. and Owen, D.G. (1960) 'The Automatic Programming of Simulations', *Proc. IFORS Conference*, IEEE, New York.

Törn A.A. (1981) 'Simulation Graphs: A General Tool for Modeling Simulation Designs', *Simulation* **37** 6 187-194.

Törn A.A. (1985) 'Simulation Nets, a Simulation Modeling and Validation Tool', *Simulation* **45** 2 71-75.

Törn A.A. (1988) 'Systems Modelling and Analysis Using Simulation Nets', in Kulikowski, C.A., *et al.*, (Eds) *Artificial Intelligence and Expert Systems Languages in Modelling and Simulation*, Elsevier Science North-Holland, New York, 283-288.

Valette, R. and Bako, B. (1991) 'Software Implementation of Petri Nets and Compilation of Rule-Based Systems', in Rozenberg, G. (Ed.) *Advances in Petri Nets 1991*, Lecture Notes in Computer Science 524, Springer-Verlag, Berlin, 298-316.

Vaucher, J.G. (1973) 'A "Wait Until" Algorithm for General Purpose Simulation Languages', *Proc. of the Winter Computer Simulation Conference*, 77-83.

Wegner, P. (1990) 'Concepts and Paradigms of Object-Oriented Programming', *OOPS Messenger* **1** 1 8-87.

Wiest, J.D. and Levy, F.K. (1977) *A Management Guide to PERT/CPM*, Second Edition, Prentice-Hall, Englewood Cliffs, NJ.

A new technique for finding a generating family of siphons, traps and st-components. Application to colored Petri Nets

J. Ezpeleta

Dpto. Ingeniería Eléctrica e Informática.Universidad de Zaragoza
C/ María de Luna 3 50015-Zaragoza.Spain

J.M. Couvreur

Laboratoire MASI.Université Paris VI
4, Place Jussieu.75252-Paris Cedex 5.France

M. Silva

Dpto. Ingeniería Eléctrica e Informática.Universidad de Zaragoza
C/ María de Luna 3 50015-Zaragoza.Spain

Abstract: In this paper we propose a new solution to the problem of finding generating families of siphons (structural dead-locks in classical terminology), traps and st- components in Petri Nets. These families are obtained as solutions of some systems of linear inequalities. Their transformation into a system of linear equations allows to interpret the technique as follows: traps (siphons, st-components) of a net N are deduced from the support of p-semiflows of a transformed net N_Θ (N_Σ,$N_{\Sigma\Theta}$).

One of the basic advantages of the proposed technique is its direct applicability to colored nets, allowing the symbolic computation of traps (siphons, st-components), whose definitions are introduced in this work.

Keywords: Petri net, colored Petri net, siphon, trap, st-component, p-semiflow

CONTENTS

1. INTRODUCTION

Structural analysis techniques are indigenous to net models. They use *linear algebraic* representations (based on the incidence matrix) or the *underlying graph* (possibly inscribed with valuations in Place/Transition nets or, more generally, with expressions in high level nets). In both cases, behavioral properties of the net are related to the net structure. Among several others, traps, siphons and st-components provide necessary, sufficient or necessary and sufficient conditions for the analysis of behavioral properties such as liveness, deadlock freeness, reversibility.....

In ordinary nets (i.e., P/T with arc weights equal to 1), *traps* are sets of places which remain marked once they have gained ("trapped") at least one token, while (structural) *deadlocks* or, probably more appropriate, *siphons* (think in soda-siphons!) are sets of places that remain empty once they have lost all tokens.

An empty siphon leads to non-liveness. Moreover, when an ordinary net system reaches a (behavioral) deadlock (i.e., no transition is firable) the set of unmarked places forms a (structural) deadlock. To avoid confusion, siphon will be the term used in the sequel instead of (structural) deadlock.

The computation of *generating families* of traps, siphons and siphon/trap-components (st-components) has received some attention in the literature [Sifa 79,Toud 81,Silv 85,AlTo 85,Laut 87,EsSi 90]. All previous works can be classified into two groups of methods. The first one, Method 1, contains [Sifa 79,Toud 81,Silv 85,AlTo 85] and aims to compute a generating family of *all* components. The approach receives in [Sifa 79] a first statement: components were characterised as solutions of *booleans equations*. The transformation of the particular class of boolean equation systems which this approach generates into *linear inequalities* was done in [Silv 85], the obtained linear inequality system being equivalent to that directly proposed in [Toud 81,AlTo 85].

The addition of *slack variables* allows to transform a linear inequality system into an *homogeneous system of equations* with non-negative solutions. The interpretation of this system as a transformed net allows to see the computation of components (e.g. traps) as the computation of p-semiflows of this transformed net.

The second approach, Method 2 [Laut 87,EsSi 90] computes a generating family of unions of *strongly connected* components. This approach is based on obtaining p-semiflows of an expanded net, derived using some local transformation rules.

Other works related to siphons and traps, but not to the computation of generating families of them, treat different problems: in [BaLe 89] a characterisation of the minimal components based on graph theory is given; in [MiBa 88a] the satisfiability problem of Horn clauses is used to prove Commoner's property of nets in some cases (but not in all cases), and in [MiBa 88b] polynomial algorithms for finding component sub-sets are presented.

The approach presented in this work, Method 3, allows the computation of a generating family of all components (as for Method 1) in terms of the solutions of a system of inequalities, with a matrix "analogous" to the incidence matrix of the given net. Moreover, the inequality system can be transformed into an homogeneous system of linear equations and then, the approach admits an interpretation in terms of the computation of a generating family of p-semiflows of a transformed net. One of the advantages of this easy-to-use approach is that it can be applied to the symbolic computation of a generating family of components for *colored nets*, provided that the *symbolic* computation of a generating family of p-semiflows is feasible.

This work is structured as follows. In section 2 we recall some basic definitions about Petri nets and its underlying graph; in section 3 we introduce a linear algebraic characterisation of generating families of traps, siphons and st-components. A new method to find these families is developed here. A comparison between classical methods and the one developed here is also carried out. In section 4 we introduce the definitions of siphons, traps and st-component for Colored Nets, and we apply the new method to the symbolic computation of these components.

2. BASIC DEFINITIONS

Definition 2.1: A Place/Transition (P/T) net is a 4-tuple $N = \langle P,T,W^-,W^+\rangle$ where
- •P is a non-empty set, called set of places
- •T is a non-empty set, called set of transitions
- •$P \cap T = \emptyset$
- •W^- is the pre-incidence matrix representing a mapping from PxT into $\mathbb{N}$
- •W^+ is the post-incidence matrix representing a mapping from PxT into $\mathbb{N}$

A net can be redefined in terms of its *underlying graph* plus some arc inscriptions defining *arcs valuations* (i.e., arc weights)

Definition 2.2: The underlying graph of a P/T $N = \langle P,T,W^-,W^+\rangle$ is that whose nodes are $P \cup T$ and whose arcs are

$$\Gamma=\{ (p,t)\in PxT \mid W^-(p,t) \neq 0 \} \cup \{(t,p)\in TxP \mid W^+(p,t) \neq 0 \}$$

In words, the underlying graph of a P/T net is that graph obtained removing arc valuations. Therefore, nets can be alternatively defined as $N = \langle P,T,\Gamma,V\rangle$, where V is the *arc valuation* (i.e., a mapping from Γ into $\mathbb{N}^*$).

Being **x** a node of the underlying graph, we will denote the set of its input nodes by $^\bullet x$ and the set of its output nodes by $x^\bullet$ (i.e., the set of nodes x' such that $(x',x) \in \Gamma$ and $(x,x') \in \Gamma$, respectively).

Definition 2.3: [Bram 83] Let $E \subseteq P$ be a set of places of a net $N = \langle P,T,\Gamma,V\rangle$.

(a) E is a siphon iff $^\bullet E \subseteq E^\bullet$

(b) E is a trap iff

$$E^\bullet \subseteq {}^\bullet E \text{ and } \forall\ t \in E^\bullet,\ \exists p \in E \cap t^\bullet \text{ such that } p^\bullet = \emptyset \text{ or } V(t,p) \geq \min_{t' \in p^\bullet}\{V(p,t')\}$$

(c) E is a siphon/trap-component (st-component) iff E is a set of places being a siphon and a trap at the same time.

Nevertheless, the second condition in the trap definition is redundant in the case of non-blocking valuation nets [Bram 83], in which case, a set of places E is a trap if, and only if, $E^{\bullet} \subseteq {}^{\bullet}E$.

Definition 2.4: [Bram 83] Let N = <P,T,Γ,V> be a net. V is a *non-blocking valuation* iff $\forall\ t \in T$, $\forall\ p \in t^{\bullet}$, $V(t,p) \geq \min_{t' \in p^{\bullet}} \{V(p,t')\}$

In the sequel, we are interested in the computation of set of places verifying ${}^{\bullet}E \subseteq E^{\bullet}$ (siphons) or $E^{\bullet} \subseteq {}^{\bullet}E$ (traps of nets with a non-blocking valuation). Therefore, throughout the rest of the paper, when we refer to a net, we will suppose a net with a non-blocking valuation (it is important to notice that ordinary nets, i.e., nets with arc valuations in the set {0,1}, are particular cases of nets with non-blocking valuation).

Nevertheless, in the case of nets with a valuation that is not a non-blocking one, we can compute traps as sets of places verifying $E^{\bullet} \subseteq {}^{\bullet}E$ in the net obtained by deleting all arcs (t,p) that fulfil the following property: $p^{\bullet} \neq \emptyset$ and $V(t,p) < \min_{t' \in p^{\bullet}} \{V(p,t')\}$

3. HOW TO COMPUTE TRAPS, SIPHONS AND ST-COMPONENTS

In this section we are dealing with the computation of siphons, traps and st-components in Petri Nets. Therefore, sections 3.1 and 3.2 are devoted to the development of the new method for traps. In section 3.3 we present the way this method is applicable to the computation of siphons and st-components. Finally, in section 3.4 a comparison among three methods to obtain siphons of a net is carried out.

It is easy to prove that traps, siphons and st-components are stable structures under the union. Then, we can give the following definition:

Definition 3.1: Let $F = \{f_1, ..., f_k\}$ be a family of traps (siphons, st-components) of a P/T net N. F is called a *generating family* of traps (siphons, st-components) iff for any Θ trap (siphon, st-component) of N, $\Theta = \bigcup_{j \in J} f_j$, where J is a sub-set of {1,2,...,k}

It is clear that a *generating family* of traps includes the set of minimal traps (i.e., traps that do not contain other traps), but, in general, the set of minimal traps is not a generating family. We must do the same remark for siphons (as it will be seen using Figure 3.2) and st-components.

Let v be a vector indexed by P (places of a net), $\|v\|$ denotes the support of v , i.e., the subset of places for which $v(p) \neq 0$.

3.1. Linear algebraic characterisation of traps

Let $N = <P,T,W^-,W^+>$ be a PN and W its incidence matrix: $W=W^+-W^-$

Proposition 3.2: Let y be an integer non-negative solution of $y^T.W\geq 0$, and let $\|y\|=\Theta$ be the support of y. Then, Θ is a trap of N.

Proof: Let us assume that y is a solution of $y^T.W\geq 0$, and that $p\in\Theta$; then $\forall$ $t\in T$

$$\sum_{p\in\Theta} y(p).W(p,t) \geq 0$$

which is equivalent to say that $\forall$ $t\in T$

$$\sum_{p\in\Theta} y(p)\left(W^+(p,t) - W^-(p,t)\right) \geq 0$$

Let us suppose that $t\in\Theta^\bullet$; then, there exists $p\in\Theta$ such that $t\in p^\bullet$ and then $W^-(p,t)\neq 0$. The last inequality and the fact that $y\geq 0$, imply that there exists $p'\in\Theta$ for which $W^+(p',t)\neq 0 \Longrightarrow t\in {}^\bullet p' \Longrightarrow t\in {}^\bullet\Theta$

□

The converse of proposition 3.2 is not true, as shown in figure 3.1.

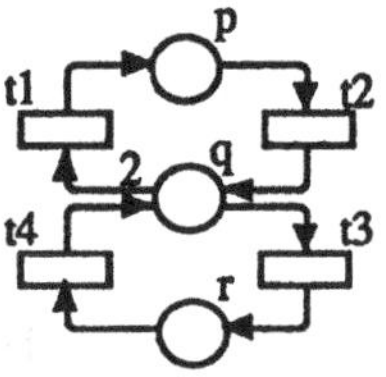

Figure 3.1. {p,q,r} is a trap, but there is no integer non-negative solution of yT.W≥ 0 whose support is {p,q,r}

The result in Proposition 3.2 can be stated not only for the incidence matrix W, but for many other incidence matrices of nets with identical underlying graphs.

Proposition 3.3: Let $N = <P,T,W^-,W^+>$ be a PN, let W_Θ^-, W_Θ^+ be two non negative PxT matrices such that $W_\Theta^+(p,t) = 0 \Leftrightarrow W^+(p,t) = 0$, $W_\Theta^-(p,t) = 0 \Leftrightarrow W^-(p,t) = 0$. And let $W_\Theta=W_\Theta^+-W_\Theta^-$.

If y is an integer non-negative solution of $y^T.W_\Theta\geq 0 \Longrightarrow \|y\|$ is a trap of N

Proof: Analogous to that in Proposition 3.2

□

The key result for the new method is stated in the next Proposition: some arc valuations on the underlying graph of the net being studied give full linear algebraic characterisation of traps. In particular the arc valuations in the pre-incidence matrix can be preserved. Thus, only the arc valuations in the post-incidence function should be partially changed.

Proposition 3.4: Let $N = <P,T,W^-,W^+>$ be a P/T net; let $\Theta \subseteq P$ be a set of places and let W^+_Θ and W^-_Θ be two integer non-negative PxT-matrices such that :

1- $W^+_\Theta(p,t) = 0 \Leftrightarrow W^+(p,t) = 0$

2- $W^-_\Theta(p,t) = 0 \Leftrightarrow W^-(p,t) = 0$.

3- $\forall\, t \in T, \forall\, p \in t^\bullet \;\; W^+_\Theta(p,t) \geq \sum_{p' \in {}^\bullet t} W^-_\Theta(p',t)$.

If $W_\Theta = W^+_\Theta - W^-_\Theta$, then Θ is a trap of the net N *iff* there exists an integer non-negative vector y solution of $y^T.W_\Theta \geq 0$ such that $\|y\| = \Theta$

Proof:

⇐=) It follows immediately from Proposition 3.3

==⇒) Let Θ be a trap and let $y \in \mathbf{N}^{|P|}$ be the characteristic vector of Θ:

If $p \in \Theta$ then $y(p)=1$ else $y(p)=0$;

$\forall\, t \in T$ we want to prove that $y^T.W_\Theta(t) = \sum_{p \in P} y(p)\big(W_\Theta(p,t)\big) \geq 0$

which is equivalent to prove that $\forall\, t \in T$

$$\sum_{p \in \Theta} W^+_\Theta(p,t) - \sum_{p \in \Theta} W^-_\Theta(p,t) \geq 0 \qquad (1)$$

If $\sum_{p \in \Theta} W^-_\Theta(p,t)=0$, the result follows immediately.

Let us suppose that there exists $p \in \Theta$ such that $W^-_\Theta(p,t) \neq 0$. From condition 2 being imposed to the matrix W^-_Θ, it follows that $W^-(p,t) \neq 0$, and then $t \in \Theta^\bullet$. As Θ is a trap of N, there exists $p' \in \Theta$ such that $t \in {}^\bullet p'$, and then $W^+(p',t) \neq 0$, which implies (condition 1) that $W^+_\Theta(p',t) \neq 0$.

Then, from condition 3 $$W^{+}_{\Theta}(p',t) \geq \sum_{p\in {}^{\bullet}t} W^{-}_{\Theta}(p,t) \geq \sum_{p\in\Theta} W^{-}_{\Theta}(p,t)$$

and (1) follows immediately

□

3.2. How to compute traps

Given a net N, in order to compute a generating family of traps we need to obtain a generating family of the set of integer non-negative solutions of a system of inequalities $y^T.W_\Theta \geq 0$, being W_Θ an integer matrix satisfying the conditions of Proposition 3.4. This matrix can be interpreted as the incidence matrix of a net N' of identical underlying graph Γ but with a different valuation V'.

A classical method, yet not the most efficient one, to solve this inequalitiy system consists in adding one *slack variable* for each column to matrix W_Θ and then in solving the system of equations

$$(y^T, z^T).\begin{pmatrix} W_\Theta \\ -I \end{pmatrix} = 0$$

where I is the (|T|x|T|)-identity matrix, by means of any variation of the Fourier-Motzkin [CoSi 89] algorithm.

The solutions of this equation system can be interpreted as the p-semiflows of a transformed net for which the incidence matrix is $W_\Theta' = \begin{pmatrix} W_\Theta \\ -I \end{pmatrix}$ where an input place p_t has been added to the net for every transition t, so that $W^{-}_{\Theta}(p_t,t)=1$ and $W^{+}_{\Theta}(p_t,t)=0$.

The family of projections of these solutions over its |P| first components is a generating family of solutions of $y^T.W_\Theta \geq 0$.

In the following we present two particular valuation transformations of a net $N = <P,T,W^-,W^+>$ that satisfy the conditions of Proposition 3.4 and which we will use later:

<u>Graph valuation:</u> only takes into account the underlying graph.

To compute traps of a net N, find the solutions of $y^T.W_\Theta \geq 0$, where $W_\Theta = W^{+}_{\Theta} - W^{-}_{\Theta}$

being

- $\forall\, t \in T,\ \forall\, p \in t^{\bullet}$ $\quad W^{+}_{\Theta}(p,t) = |{}^{\bullet}t|$
- $\forall\, t \in T,\ \forall\, p \in {}^{\bullet}t$ $\quad W^{-}_{\Theta}(p,t) = 1$

Linear valuations: These type of transformations take into account the arc valuations of the net. They will be used later for colored nets.

To compute traps of N, find the solutions of $y^T.W_\Theta \geq 0$, where $W_\Theta = W_\Theta^+ - W_\Theta^-$, being

$$- \forall t \in T, \forall p \in t^\bullet, \quad W_\Theta^+(p,t) = K_t * W^+(p,t) \text{ with } K_t \geq \sum_{p' \in {}^\bullet t} W^-(p',t)$$

$$- \forall t \in T, \forall p \in {}^\bullet t \quad W_\Theta^-(p,t) = W^-(p,t)$$

3.3. Computation of siphons and st-components

It is a classical result that traps and siphons are reverse concepts: a siphon of a net N is a trap of its reverse net N^{-1} (i.e., the net obtained by reversing all arcs). Therefore, the same method that compute traps may be used in order to compute siphons.

Let $N = \langle P,T,W^-,W^+\rangle$ be the net whose siphons we want to compute, and let $N^{-1} = \langle P,T,W'^-,W'^+\rangle$ be the reverse net ($W'^- = W^+$, $W'^+ = W^-$). Let W'_Θ be a transformed flow matrix in order to compute traps of N^{-1}. The computation of traps of this reversed transformed net requieres to solve the system of inequalities $y^T.W'_\Theta \geq 0$ (or, equivalently, $y^T.(-W'_\Theta) \leq 0$). We obtain a generating family of siphons of the net N from the family of integer non-negative solutions of the last inequality system.

Because a st-component is a set of places being a siphon and a trap at the same time, we obtain a generating family of st-components from the set of non-negative solutions y such that $y^T.W'_\Theta \geq 0$ and $y^T.W_\Theta \geq 0$ (being W'_Θ as above and W_Θ a transformed matrix in order to compute traps of the net N). From a technical point of view, certain inequalities in the previous systems can be removed because they are redundant: for instance, a transition with a unique input arc and a unique output arc, both with the same valuation, generates twice the same inequality (one due to the trap condition and another due to the siphon condition).

3.4. A comparison of the three methods

This paragraph is devoted to point out the main features of Methods 1, 2 and 3. We apply them in order to compute siphons in a particular example.

The first method and the one developed here lead to the solution of a system of linear inequalities. As we have already stated, to solve this system we can add some slack variables, which transform the inequality system into a system of equations. The matrix of this equation system may be regarded as the incidence matrix of a transformed net. The computation of a family of solutions of this system may be regarded as the computation of the set of p-semiflows of the transformed net. Siphons and traps are obtained as supports of these p-semiflows.

In general, for Method 1 [Toud 81,AlTo 85], the number of places is equal to that in the initial net plus the number of added slack variables, meanwhile the number of transitions has grown (e.g., to calculate siphons, a transition t has been "unfolded" in $|t^\bullet|$ transitions).

In the method developed here the number of places of the transformed net is the number of places of the initial net plus the number of slack variables added (one for each transition of the net), meanwhile the number of transitions of the initial and the transformed nets are the same.

Then, in general, the dimensions of the system generated by our method are lower than those of Method 1.

In Method 2 [Laut 87,EsSi 90], siphons and traps are computed as supports of p-semiflows of a transformed net, obtained by expansion of shared places (places for which $|{}^{\bullet}p| > 1$ or $|p^{\bullet}| > 1$) of the initial net and by addition of some constraints represented by means of new transitions. The set of siphons obtained is the one formed by unions of strongly connected siphons. A siphon S is strongly connected if and only if the subnet generated by S and the set of its input transitions is strongly connected (see references for further detail).

The following table shows the features of the three methods when applying in order to compute **siphons** of a net. To compare them, let us suppose that in Method 1 and Method 3 we transform the inequality system in a system of equations, for which we will compute p-semiflows; then, in the dimensions of the matrices we count the added slack variables. (Remark: from a computational point of view this may be not convenient, but the addition of this places has been done to better compare the three methods).

We call $n=|P|$, $m=|T|$, SP the set of Shared Places and NS=P-SP.

Method	Dimensions of the transformed matrix	Siphons obtained
Method 1	$(n + \sum_{t\in T}\lvert t^{\bullet}\rvert) \times \sum_{t\in T}\lvert t^{\bullet}\rvert$	A generating family
Method 2	$(\lvert NS\rvert + \sum_{p\in SP}(\lvert{}^{\bullet}p\rvert+\lvert p^{\bullet}\rvert)) \times (m + \sum_{p\in SP}\lvert{}^{\bullet}p\rvert)$	Unions of strongly connected siphons
Method 3	$(n+m) \times m$	A generating family

Table 1: Some features of the three methods when applied to compute siphons of a net

In the following, we apply the three methods in order to compute siphons of the net in Figure 3.2.a.

The application of Method 1 leads us to solve the system $\mathbf{y^T \cdot W_S^1 \leq 0}$, where the matrix W_S^1 is as follows:

$$W_S^1 = \begin{array}{c} \\ p \\ q \\ r \\ s \\ u \\ v \\ w \end{array} \begin{array}{c} \begin{array}{cccccccc} t1 & t2r & t2s & t3 & t4 & t5 & t6 & t7 \end{array} \\ \begin{bmatrix} -1 & -1 & -1 & & & & & 1 \\ 1 & & & & & & & -1 \\ & 1 & & -1 & & & & \\ & & 1 & & -1 & & & \\ & & & 1 & & -1 & & \\ & & & & 1 & & -1 & \\ & & & & & 1 & 1 & -1 \end{bmatrix} \end{array}$$

The solutions of this inequality system adding slack variables may be regarded as the calculation of p-semiflows of the transformed net in Figure 3.2.b (shadow places represent slack variables added).

{(p,q),(p,r,q),(p,s,q),(p,r,u,q),(p,s,v,q),(p,r,s,u,v,w)} is obtained as a generating family of siphons. Observe that only the first and the last siphons of the family are minimal.

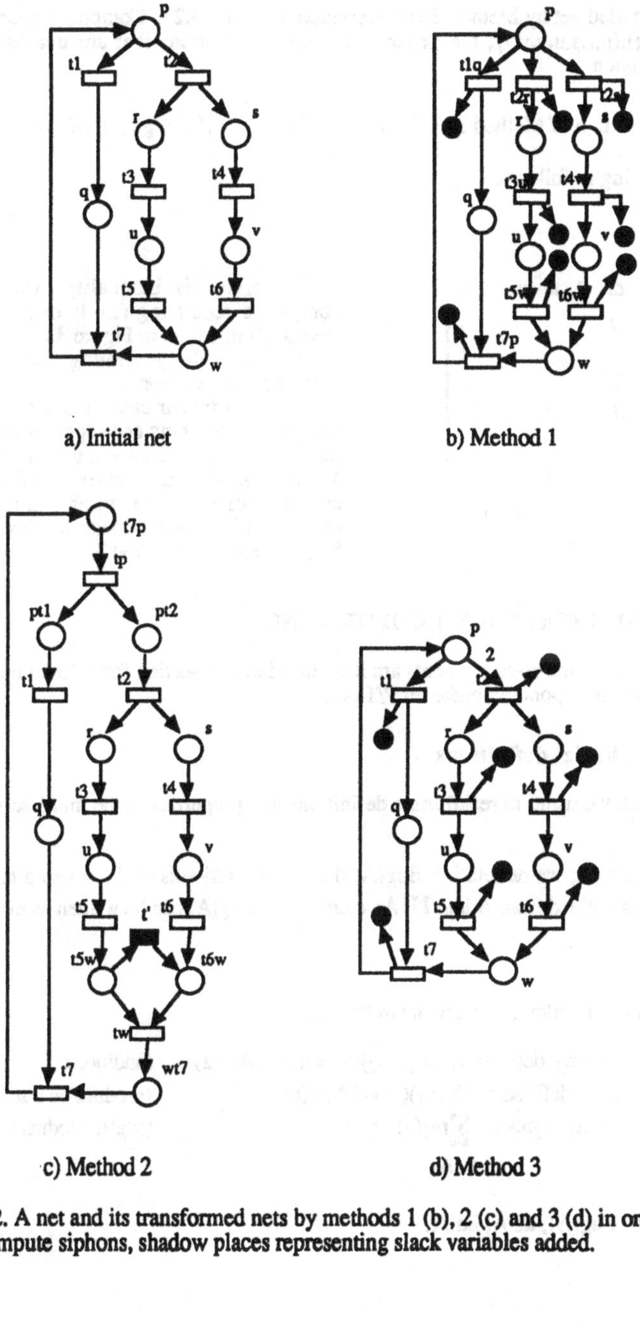

Figure 3.2. A net and its transformed nets by methods 1 (b), 2 (c) and 3 (d) in order to compute siphons, shadow places representing slack variables added.

The expanded net by Method 2 is represented in Figure 3.2.c. Computing p-semiflows we obtain {(p,q),(p,r,s,u,v,w)}, the generating family of siphons that are unions of strongly connected siphons.

The application of Method 3 leads to solve $y^T W_S^2 \leq \mathbf{0}$, if the graph valuation is used, the matrix W_S^2 being as follows:

$W_s^2 =$

	t1	t2	t3	t4	t5	t6	t7
p	-1	-2					1
q	1						-1
r		1	-1				
s		1		-1			
u			1		-1		
v				1		-1	
w					1	1	-1

To solve this inequality system, we can compute a generating family of p-semiflows of the transformed net in Figure 3.2.d.

We obtain the generating family of siphons obtained from Method 1.

In this particular case, it is easy to see that if we add the columns corresponding to the same transition in the initial net in the matrix of Method 1, we obtain the matrix of Method 3 corresponding to the graph valuation. Then, every solution obtained with Method 1 may also be obtained from Method 3.

4. APPLICATION TO COLORED NETS

Traps, siphons and st-components are introduced in this section for colored nets. They are defined on the corresponding unfolded P/T net.

4.1. Basic definitions

First of all, we want to recall some definitions and properties of the multi-sets of a given set:

- let A be a set; we denote by Bag(A) the set of multi-sets of A, where a multi-set is a mapping defined from A into $\mathbb{N}$. An element $m \in Bag(A)$ can be written as $m = \sum_{a \in A} m(a).a$

- we define the following operators in Bag(A) :

m_1+m_2 defined by $(m_1+m_2)(a) = m_1(a)+m_2(a)$	(addition)
$k \cdot m_1$ defined by $(k \cdot m_1)(a) = k * m_1(a)$	(product by a scalar)
$\langle\langle m_1,m_2 \rangle\rangle = \sum_{a \in A} m_1(a) * m_2(a)$	(scalar product)

$\forall m_1,m_2 \in Bag(A),\ a \in A,\ k \in \mathbb{N}$.

• $\forall m \in Bag(A)$ we define

$*$*support* of m as $supp(m) = \{a \in A \mid m(a) \neq 0\}$

$*$*length* of m as $|m| = \sum_{a \in A} m(a)$

Definition 4.1: A colored Petri Net (CN) is a 6-tuple $N = \langle P,T,\mathbf{C},\Omega,W^-,W^+\rangle$ where:

- •P is a non-empty set, called the set of colored places
- •T is a non-empty set, called the set of colored transitions
- •$P \cap T = \emptyset$
- •**C** is a mapping from $P \cup T$ into Ω, a set of finite non-empty sets, in which every element is called a color set
- •W^- , the pre-incidence matrix, represents a mapping from PxT into the set of linear mappings from $Bag(\mathbf{C}(t))$ into $Bag(\mathbf{C}(p))$
- •W^+ , the post-incidence matrix, represents a mapping from PxT into the set of linear mappings from $Bag(\mathbf{C}(t))$ into $Bag(\mathbf{C}(p))$

In a colored net, we call $\mathbf{P} = \{p(c_p) \mid p \in P, c_p \in \mathbf{C}(p)\}$ the set of unfolded places and $\mathbf{T} = \{t(c_t) \mid t \in T, c_t \in \mathbf{C}(t)\}$ the set of unfolded transitions.

Let $N = \langle P,T,\mathbf{C},\Omega,W^-,W^+\rangle$ be a colored net. The unfolded graph of N is the underlying graph of the unfolded net.:

Definition 4.2: The *unfolded graph* of a CN $N = \langle P,T,\mathbf{C},\Omega,W^+,W^-\rangle$ is the bipartite graph whose nodes are $\mathbf{P} \cup \mathbf{T}$ and whose arcs are:

$$\Gamma = \{ (p(c_p),t(c_t)) \mid c_p \in Supp(W^-(p,t)(c_t)) \} \cup \{ (t(c_t),p(c_p)) \mid c_p \in Supp(W^+(p,t)(c_t)) \}$$

Given N, an arc valuation for it is a mapping from Γ into $\mathbb{N}^*$. Matrices W^+,W^- induce an arc valuation, V, so that

$$V(p(c_p),t(c_t)) = W^-(p,t)(c_t)(c_p) \text{ and } V(t(c_t),p(c_p)) = W^+(p,t)(c_t)(c_p)$$

As in the case of Place/Transition nets, being **x** a node of the unfolded graph, we call $^\bullet\mathbf{x}$ and $\mathbf{x}^\bullet$ the sets of input and output nodes of **x** respectively. We will say that a CN has a *non-blocking* valuation iff the valuation induced by W^+,W^- is a non-blocking valuation in the unfolded net. In the sequel, we will assume that CN have non-blocking valuations.

Definition 4.3: Let $E \subseteq \mathbf{P}$ be a set of unfolded places of a net $N = \langle P,T,\mathbf{C},\Omega,W^+,W^-\rangle$:

(a) E is a colored trap iff $E^\bullet \subseteq {}^\bullet E$

(b) E is a colored siphon iff ${}^\bullet E \subseteq E^\bullet$

(c) E is a colored st-component iff $E^\bullet = {}^\bullet E$; i.e., E is a colored trap and a colored siphon at the same time.

4.2. How to compute colored traps (siphons and st-components)

In the following, we will apply a linear valuation transformation to a colored net in order to find a generating family of traps (siphons and st-components).

First of all, we need to find valuation transformations verifying conditions imposed by the linear algebraic characterisation of traps.

Let $N = \langle P,T,C,\Omega,W^-,W^+\rangle$ be a colored net and let W_Θ be a valuation transformation of N for which $\bullet W^+_\Theta(p,t)=K_t \, . \, W^+(p,t)$ with $K_t \geq \max_{c_t \in C(t)} \{ \sum_{p \in P} | W^-(p,t)(c_t) | \}$

$\bullet W^-_\Theta(p,t)=W^-(p,t)$

It is clear that this transformation satisfies the conditions of Proposition 3.4 for the unfolded net, and therefore, we can obtain a generating family of traps of N solving the system $y^T.W_\Theta \geq 0$.

It is important to notice here that the last inequality system is a symbolic system (the elements of W_Θ are linear functions from Bag(**C**(t)) into Bag(**C**(p)) and y is a P-indexed vector in which $y(p) \in (\mathbb{Q}^+)^{\mathbf{C}(p)}$, and that it will be convenient to solve it in a symbolic way.

Summarising, in order to compute traps for a colored net, the method proposed leads us to solve the inequality system $y^T.W_\Theta \geq 0$, that can be written as

$$\forall t \in T \qquad \sum_{p \in P} \langle\langle y(p), W_\Theta(p,t) \rangle\rangle \geq 0$$

By means of $\langle\langle y(p),W_\Theta(p,t)\rangle\rangle$ we represent the scalar product $\langle\langle y(p),W_\Theta(p,t)(c_t)\rangle\rangle$ for each $c_t \in \mathbf{C}(t)$.

A straightforward generalisation of the method applied to ordinary nets in order to compute a generating family of solutions of this inequality system would consist in adding a place p_t to every transition and associating the same color domain of the transition to it: $\mathbf{C}(p_t)=\mathbf{C}(t)$, $W^+_\Theta(p_t,t)=0$ and $W^-_\Theta(p_t,t)=I$, being I the identity function over **C**(t). We could, then, calculate the p-semiflows of this transformed net. However, it is necessary that this identity function belongs to the domain of color functions.

We have seen the computation of traps, siphons and st-components of a CN provided the symbolic computation of p-semiflows of a transformed CN is feasible. In [CoHP 91] this problem is solved for Unary Predicate/Transition systems [MeVa 87] and Unary Regular nets [Hadd 86]. The two following sections apply these results in order to compute traps in these two classes of colored nets.

4.3. Application to the Unary Regular nets

First of all we introduce the definition of this class of CN, and then, we apply the method in order to compute a generating family of traps to a "toy" example.

4.3.1. Unary Regular Colored nets

Definition 4.4: [Hadd 87] An *Unary Regular Net* $N = \langle P,T,\mathbf{C},\Omega,W^+,W^- \rangle$ is a colored net for which:

- $\Omega=\{C\}$, where C is the unique color class, of size n
- $\mathbf{C}(p) = \mathbf{C}(t) = C$ for all place p and transition t
- W^+ (W^-) is of the form $W^+(p,t) = a(p,t)X + b(p,t)S$ where

  * $X(c) = c$ is the identity function
  * $S(c) = \sum_{c' \in C} c'$ is the diffusion function
  * $a(p,t), b(p,t) \in \mathbb{Z}$, $a(p,t)+b(p,t) \geq 0$, $b(p,t) \geq 0$

It is easy to see that a valuation transformation such that $\forall\, t \in T$

- $W^+_\Theta(p,t) = K_t \,.\, W^+(p,t)$ with $K_t \geq \sum_{p \in {}^\bullet t} (b(p,t)*n + a(p,t))$
  being n the size of the color class C
- $W^-_\Theta(p,t) = W^-(p,t)$

verifies constraints imposed by linear algebraic characterisation of traps.

4.3.2. An example

Let us consider the little example shown in Figure 4.1-a, that corresponds to a Unary regular net.

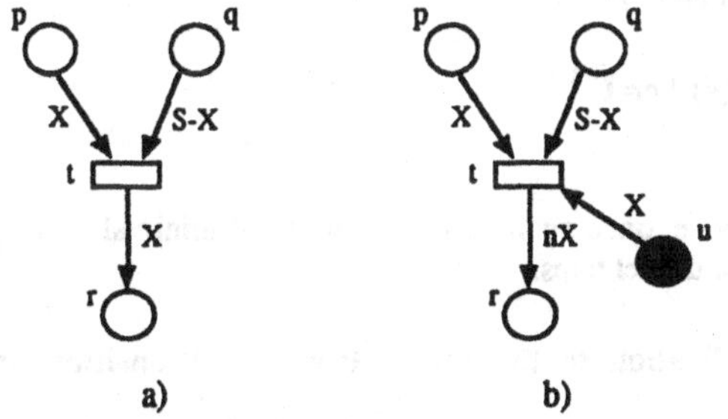

Figure 4.1: A Unary Regular net a), and its transformed in order to compute traps b)

The application of the previous transformation of valuation leads us to compute the solutions of the symbolic system of inequalities

$$(Y_p, Y_q, Y_r).\begin{pmatrix} -X \\ -(S-X) \\ nX \end{pmatrix} \geq 0$$

The transformation of this system of inequalities into a system of equations adding slack variables, leads us to the computation of the solutions of

$$(Y_p, Y_q, Y_r, Z_u).\begin{pmatrix} -X \\ -(S-X) \\ nX \\ -X \end{pmatrix} = 0$$

corresponding to the p-semiflows of the transformed net showed in Figure 4.1-b. Remember that Y_p, Y_q, Y_r and Z_u represent C-indexed vectors.

The computation of p-semiflows in this last net applying the method developed in [CoHP 91] gives us the generating family

1) $r(c) + n*u(c) \qquad c \in C$

2) $n*p(c) + r(c) \qquad c \in C$

3) $n*q(c) + \sum_{x \neq c} r(x) \qquad c \in C$

Therefore, taking the supports of this family, we obtain as a trap generating family the family formed by the following sets:

1) $\{r(c) \mid c \in C\}$

2) $\{p(c) \cup r(c) \mid c \in C\}$

3) $\{q(c) \cup \bigcup_{x \neq c} r(x) \mid c \in C\}$

We want to notice, once again, that the family of minimal traps $\{r(c) \mid c \in C\}$ is not a generating family of the net traps.

4.4. Application to the Unary Predicate/Transition Systems

In this section, we apply the developed method for the symbolic computation of generating families of traps and siphons in Unary Predicate/Transition systems.

4.4.1. Unary Predicate/Transition systems

Definition 4.5: [MeVa 87] An *Unary Predicate/Transition System* * (UPT system) $N = \langle P,T,C,\Omega,W^+,W^- \rangle$ is a colored net for which:

- C is the unique color class of, *size n*; and $\Omega=\{\{\bullet\},C,C^2,\ldots,C^n\}$
- $C(p)=C$ or $C(p)=\{\bullet\}$ $\forall p \in P$. If $C(p)=\{\bullet\}$, we call p an *ordinary* place.
- $C(t)=C^{n_t}$ $\forall t \in T$, $n_t \geq 0$. If $n_t=0$ then $C(t)=\{\bullet\}$ and we call t an *ordinary* transition.

- if p is an ordinary place then $W(p,t)=\alpha(p,t)$

  else $W(p,t)=\sum_{i=1}^{nt} \alpha_i(p,t)*X_i + \beta(p,t)$

  where $\alpha(p,t),\alpha_i(p,t)\in \mathbb{N}$, $\beta(p,t)\in Bag(C)$ and X_i is the mapping from $Bag(C^{n_t})$ into $Bag(C)$ defined as

$$X_i\Big(\sum_{(c_1,\ldots,c_{n_t})\in C^{n_t}} \lambda(c_1,\ldots,c_{n_t})*(c_1,\ldots,c_{n_t})\Big) = \sum_{(c_1,\ldots,c_{n_t})\in C^{n_t}} \lambda(c_1,\ldots,c_{n_t})*c_i$$

Then, to compute generating families of traps (siphons, st-components) for UPT systems we need to solve the inequality system

$$\forall t\in T \quad \sum_{p\in P} \langle\langle y(p), W_\Theta(p,t)\rangle\rangle \geq 0$$

where $W_\Theta(p,t)$ are unary functions.

If we apply the method used for the ordinary nets to transform the system $y^T.W_\Theta \geq 0$ into an equation system, the incidence matrix of this system contains identity functions of the type $\langle X_1,\ldots,X_{n_t}\rangle$ (Figure 4.1.b).

Nevertheless, the function $\langle X_1,\ldots,X_{n_t}\rangle$ with $n_t > 1$ is not a valid color function for UPT systems. Moreover, in the following theorem we prove that to solve the system $y^T.W_\Theta \geq 0$ for a UPT system is equivalent to solve a linear system of equations, where the elements of the matrix are in the color function domain for UPT systems (Figure 4.2.c), and then, we can apply the algorithm for finding p-semiflows in UPT systems [CoHP 91].

We show in theorem 4.6 that every non-negative solution of the system of inequalities $y^T.W_\Theta \geq 0$ may be obtained from the set of solutions of a system of equations, where every function appearing in this system is a valid function for UPT systems.

---

* This definition of Unary Predicate/Transition systems corresponds to an extension of the initial definition given in [MeVa 87], where ordinary places and transitions have been added.

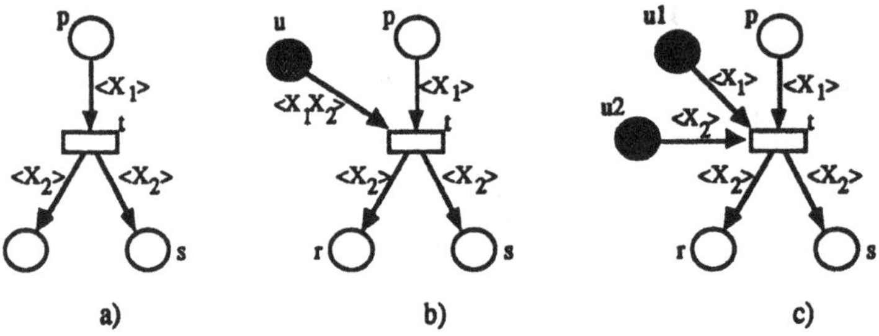

Figure 4.2. A UPT system and its direct (wrong) and indirect (correct) transformations in order to compute p-semiflows. $C(t)=C^2$, $C(r)=C(s)=C(p)=C(u1)=C(u2)=C$, $C(u)=C^2$

The form of the equivalent system of equations allows us to assure that a generating family of traps can be obtained from the set of p-semiflows of a transformed net, in which for every colored transition t ($n_t \neq 0$) we add an input place p_{t_i} for every variable X_i appearing around t; the color domain for every added place is C, and $W^+_\Theta(p_{t_i},t)=0$, $W^-_\Theta(p_{t_i},t)=\langle X_i \rangle$. If the transition is an ordinary one ($n_t=0$), we add an input ordinary place p_t such that $W^+_\Theta(p_t,t)=0$ and $W^-_\Theta(p_t,t)=1$.

Theorem 4.6.: Let $N = \langle P,T,C,\Omega,L^+,L^- \rangle$ be a UPT system, let $L = L^+ - L^-$ be the net incidence matrix of N and let V be a P-indexed vector for which $V(p) \in (\mathbb{Q}^+)^{C(p)}$. Then, $\forall\, t \in T$ the two following statements are equivalent:

1) V is a non-negative solution of the inequality $\sum_{p \in P} \langle\langle V(p),L(p,t)\rangle\rangle \geq 0$

2) There exists a family of multi-sets $U_i(t) \geq 0$, $i \in \{1,\dots,n_t\}$ if $n_t \neq 0$ or a scalar $U(t) \geq 0$ if $n_t=0$ so that V is a non-negative solution of the equation:

$$\text{if } n_t \neq 0 \quad \sum_{p \in P} \langle\langle V(p),L(p,t)\rangle\rangle + \sum_{i=1}^{n_t} \langle\langle U_i(t),-X_i\rangle\rangle = 0 \text{ with } U_i(t) \geq 0$$

$$\text{if } n_t = 0 \quad \sum_{p \in P} \langle\langle V(p),L(p,t)\rangle\rangle - U(t) = 0 \text{ with } U(t) \geq 0$$

Proof:

2) $\Rightarrow$1) Straightforward

1) $\Rightarrow$2) In the following, we will denote by P0 the set of ordinary places, and by P1 the set of colored places: $P = P0 \cup P1$ and $P0 \cap P1=\emptyset$

• if $n_t=0$, then the inequality 1) can be written as

$$\sum_{p\in P} \langle\langle V(p),L(p,t)\rangle\rangle = \sum_{p\in P1} \langle\langle V(p),\beta(p,t)\rangle\rangle + \sum_{p\in P0} V(p)*\alpha(p,t) \geq 0$$

where $\beta(p,t)$ is that in Definition 4.5.

Clearly, if we call $U(t)= \sum_{p\in P1} \langle\langle V(p),\beta(p,t)\rangle\rangle + \sum_{p\in P0} V(p)*\alpha(p,t)$ it is obvious that 2 is true.

• if $n_t\neq 0$: In the following, we will denote $T(t)= \sum_{p\in P} \langle\langle V(p),L(p,t)\rangle\rangle$. Then, being $T(t) \geq 0$, we must find a family $U_i(t)\geq 0$, $i\in \{1,\ldots,n_t\}$ so that $T(t)= \sum_{i=1}^{n_t} \langle\langle U_i(t),X_i\rangle\rangle$

Substituting L(p,t) by its value in Definition 4.5

$$T(t)= \sum_{p\in P1} \langle\langle V(p), \sum_{i=1}^{n_t} \alpha_i(p,t)*X_i + \beta(p,t)\rangle\rangle + \sum_{p\in P0} V(p)*\alpha(p,t)$$

By the properties of the scalar product, this equality can be written as

$$T(t)= \sum_{p\in P1} \sum_{i=1}^{n_t} \langle\langle V(p),\alpha_i(p,t).X_i\rangle\rangle + \beta(t)$$

where $\beta(t)$ is the constant integer $\beta(t) = \sum_{p\in P1} \langle\langle V(p),\beta(p,t)\rangle\rangle + \sum_{p\in P0} V(p)*\alpha(p,t)$

Exchanging the summations we can write

$$T(t)= \sum_{i=1}^{n_t} \langle\langle \sum_{p\in P1} \alpha_i(p,t).V(p),X_i) \rangle\rangle + \beta(t)$$

If we denote $U'_i(t)= \sum_{p\in P1} \alpha_i(p,t).V(p)$, the equality can be written as

$$T(t)= \sum_{i=1}^{n_t} \langle\langle U'_i(t),X_i\rangle\rangle + \beta(t)$$

Taking into account that the color set C is finite, for each $i=1..n_t$ we define

$$\rho_i(t)= \min_{x_c\in C}\{U'_i(t)(x_c)\}.$$

Then we can write $U'_i(t)=U''_i(t)+\rho_i(t).S$ where S is the C-indexed vector for which $S(x_c)=1\ \forall\ x_c\in C$ (S is the multi-set $\sum_{c\in C} 1*c$).

At this point it is important to remark two things:

* $U''_i(t) \geq 0 \quad i=1..n_t$
* for every multi-set $U''_i(t)$ there exists a particular color $c_i\in C$ such that $U''_i(t)(c_i)=0$ (i.e., the coefficient of the multi-set $U''_i(t)$ over the color c_i is 0)

Then, we can write the equation as

$$T(t)=\sum_{i=1}^{n_t} \langle\langle U''_i(t),X_i\rangle\rangle + \beta'(t) \qquad (*)$$

where $\beta'(t)=\sum_{i=1}^{n_t} \langle\langle \rho_i(t).S,X_i\rangle\rangle+\beta(t);$

Taking into account that $\langle\langle S,X_i\rangle\rangle = 1$, we have

$\beta'(t)= \sum_{i=1}^{n_t} \rho_i(t).\langle\langle S,X_i\rangle\rangle+\beta(t)=\sum_{i=1}^{n_t} \rho_i(t)+\beta(t)$ which is a constant integer.

Because $T(t)\geq 0$ for each color $(x_1,x_2,\ldots\ldots,x_{n_t}) \in C^{n_t}$, and, in particular, for the color $(c_1,c_2,\ldots\ldots,c_{n_t})$, and taking into account that $X_i\ (1*(c_1,c_2,\ldots\ldots,c_{n_t})) = 1*c_i$, the expression $\sum_{i=1}^{n_t} \langle\langle U''_i(t),X_i\rangle\rangle$ evaluated for this color gives $\sum_{i=1}^{n_t} U''_i(t)(c_i) = 0$ and therefore $\beta'(t) \geq 0$ (see formula (*)).

Finally, we define $U_i(t)$ as

$$U_1(t)=U''_1(t)+\beta'(t).S \text{ and } U_i(t)=U''_i(t) \text{ if } i\neq 1$$

After this last transformation we can write the equality

$$\sum_{p\in P} \langle\langle V(p),L(p,t)\rangle\rangle = \sum_{i=1}^{n_t} \langle\langle U_i(t),X_i\rangle\rangle$$

or, in an equivalent way,

$$\sum_{p\in P} \langle\langle V(p),L(p,t)\rangle\rangle + \sum_{i=1}^{n_t} \langle\langle U_i(t),-X_i\rangle\rangle = 0 \text{ where } U_i(t)\geq 0$$

and we have done. □

4.4.2. An example

In this paragraph we apply the method in order to compute a generating family of traps of the Unary Net in Figure 4.3-a

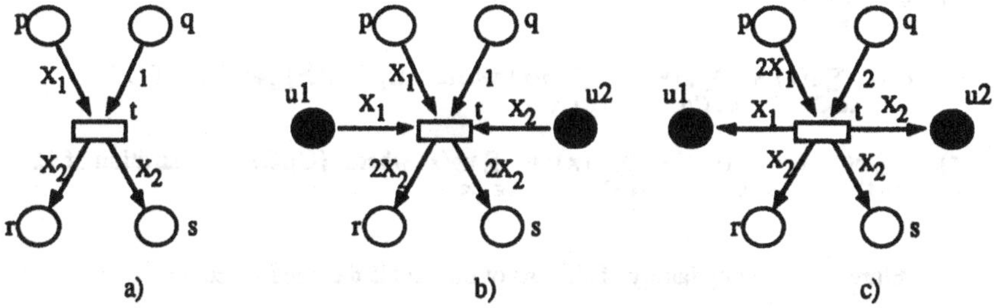

Figure 4.3: A Unary net and its transformed nets in order to calculate the traps and siphons. $C(t)=C^2$, $C(p)=C(r)=C(s)=C(u1)=C(u2)=C$, $C(q)=\{\bullet\}$

Computing traps of the net in Figure 4.2.a leads to the computation of p-semiflows of the net in Figure 4.2.b, from which we obtain the following generating family :

1) $r(x) + 2u_2(x) \quad x \in C$

2) $s(x) + 2u_2(x) \quad x \in C$

3) $2q + \sum_{x \in C_1} r(x) + \sum_{x \in C_2} s(x)$, where $\{C_1, C_2\}$ is a partition of class color C.

4) $2 \sum_{x \in C_1} p(x) + 2 \sum_{x \in C_2} u_1(x) + \sum_{x \in D_1} r(x) + \sum_{x \in D_2} s(x)$, where $\{C_1, C_2\}$ and $\{D_1, D_2\}$ are partitions of class color C.

Therefore, taking the supports of this family, we obtain as a trap generating family the one formed by the following sets:

1) $\{r(x) \mid x \in C\}$

2) $\{s(x) \mid x \in C\}$

3) $\{q \cup \bigcup_{x \in C_1} r(x) \cup \bigcup_{x \in C_2} s(x) \mid \{C_1, C_2\} \text{ partition of } C\}$

4) $\{(\bigcup_{x \in D} p(x) \mid D \subseteq C) \cup (\bigcup_{x \in C_1} r(x) \cup \bigcup_{x \in C_2} s(x) \mid \{C_1, C_2\} \text{ partition of } C)\}$

To compute a generating family of siphons of the net, we calculate a generating family of p-semiflows of the net in Figure 4.2.c, and we obtain the family

1) $p(c) + u_1(c) \quad c \in C$

2) $q + \sum_{x \in C} u_1(x)$

3) $q + \sum_{x \in C_1} r(x) + \sum_{x \in C_2} s(x) + \sum_{x \in C_3} u_2(x)$ where $\{C_1, C_2, C_3\}$ partition of C.

4) $\sum_{x \in C} p(x) + \sum_{x \in C_1} r(x) + \sum_{x \in C_2} s(x) + \sum_{x \in C_3} u_2(x)$ where $\{C_1, C_2, C_3\}$ partition of C.

Therefore, a generating family of siphons of this net is the one formed by

1) $\{p(c) \mid c \in C\}$

2) $\{q\}$

3) $\{q \cup \bigcup_{x \in C_1} r(x) \cup \bigcup_{x \in C_2} s(x) \mid C_1 \cap C_2 = \emptyset \text{ and } C_1 \cup C_2 \subseteq C\}$

4) $\{\{\bigcup_{x \in C} p(x)\} \cup \{\bigcup_{x \in C_1} r(x) \cup \bigcup_{x \in C_2} s(x) \mid C_1 \cap C_2 = \emptyset \text{ and } C_1 \cup C_2 \subseteq C\}\}$

5. CONCLUSIONS

This paper introduces a new technique for the computation of a generating family of traps, siphons and st-components. The technique is based on a new algebraic characterisation of components, and transforms the original problem into the computation of the solutions of linear inequality systems. The addition of slack variables transforming the linear inequality system into a system of equations leads to interpret the siphons (traps, st-components) in terms of p-semiflows of some associated nets.

The basic qualities of the proposed method are:

(a) A simple computation of a generating family of components.

(b) A direct generalisation to colored nets, transforming the problem of symbolic computation of components (traps, siphons and st-components) into that of the symbolic computation of p-semiflows (problem actually solved for two subclasses of Colored Nets: Unary Predicate/Transitions Nets and Unary Regular Nets).

ACKNOWLEDGEMENTS. This work was done while J. Ezpeleta was a researcher at the Laboratoire MASI under grant of the "Programa Nacional de becas de formación de Personal investigador en el Extranjero" of the Ministerio de Educación y Ciencia of Spain, and was partially supported by the DEMON Esprit Basic Research Action 3148 and the Spanish Research Project PRONTIC-0358/89

Authors want to thank to J.F. Peyre who helped us in the computation of colored p-semiflows, and to the 2 anonymous referees, whose remarks helped us to improve this paper.

REFERENCES

[AlTo 85] ALAIWAN H., TOUDIC J.F., Recherche des semi-flots, des verrous et des trappes dans les réseaux de Petri, *TSI,vol. 4, n. 1*, 1985, p. 103-112.

[BaLe 89] BARKAOUI K., LEMAIRE B., An effective characterization of minimal deadlocks and traps in Petri Nets based on graph theory *Proc. of the 10h. Petri Net Conference on Theory and Applications of Petri Nets*, Bonn,1989

[Bram 83] BRAMS G.W., *Réseaux de Petri. Theorie et Pratique* (2 vol.), Masson,Paris,1983

[CoHP 91] COUVREUR J.M.,HADDAD S.,PEYRE J.F., *Computation of Generative Families of Positive Semi-flows in Two Types of Colored Nets*, 12h. Petri Net Conference on Theory and Applications of Petri Nets, Gerjn (Denmark), June 1991.

[CoSi 89] COLOM J.M., SILVA M., Convex Geometry and Semiflows in P/T Nets. A comparative Study of Algorithms for Computation of Minimal p-Semiflows. *10th International Conference on Application and Theory of Petri Nets*, Bonn,1989.

[Espa 89] ESPARZA J.,*Structure theory of Free Choice Nets*, Ph. D. Thesis, Universidad de Zaragoza (Spain),1989

[EsSi 90] ESPARZA J.,SILVA M., A polynomial-time algorithm to decide liveness of bounded free choice nets, To appear in *Theoretical Computer Science*.

[EsSB 89] ESPARZA J., SILVA M.,BEST E., Minimal deadlocks in Free Choice Nets, *Hildesheimer Informatik Fachberichte 1/89*,1989

[Hadd 87] HADDAD S., *Une catégorie régulière de réseau de Petri de haut niveau: définition, propriétés et réductions*. Application á la validation de systèmes distribués, Thèse de l'Université Pierre et Marie Curie,Paris,1987

[Laut 87] LAUTENBACH K., *Linear Algebraic calculation of deadlocks and traps*, Concurrency and nets, Voss-Genrich-Rozenberg eds., Springer Verlag,1987.

[Memm 83] MEMMI G., *Methode d'analyse de réseaux de Petri, réseaux à files. et applications au temps réel*, Thèse de l'Université Pierre et Marie Curie,Paris,1983.

[MeVa 87] MEMMI G., VAUTHERIN J.,Analysing nets by the invariant method, *Advances in Petri Nets 1986*, L.N.C.S. 254,Springer-Verlag,1987.

[MiBa 88a] MINOUX M., BARKAOUI K., Polynomial time algorithms for proving or disproving Commoner's structural property in Petri Nets, *Proc. of the 9th. Petri Net Conference on Theory and Applications of Petri Nets*, Venice,1988

[MiBa 88b] MINOUX M., BARKAOUI K., Polynomial algorithms for finding deadlocks, traps and other substructures relevant to Petri net analysis, *Internal research report N. 212 of the Laboratoire MASI*, Univ. Paris 6, Paris, 1988

[Sifa 79] SIFAKIS J., *Contrôle des systèmes asynchrones: concepts, proprietés, analyse statique*, Thèse de l'Université Scientifique et Médical de Grenoble,1979.

[Silv 85] SILVA M., *Las redes de Petri en la Informática y la Automática*, Ed. AC, Madrid,1985.

[Toud 81] TOUDIC J.M., *Algorithmes d'analyse structurelle de réseaux de Petri*, Thèse de l'Université Pierre et Marie Curie,Paris,1981.

A Concept of Hierarchical Petri Nets with Building Blocks

Rainer Fehling*

Universität Dortmund, LS Informatik 1
Postfach 500 500, W - 4600 Dortmund 50
e-mail: fehling@jupiter.informatik.uni-dortmund.de

ABSTRACT: This paper introduces a formal concept of hierarchical Petri nets with building blocks. The hierarchy concept allows to handle the refinement of places *and* transitions even if they are adjacent. The building blocks are introduced as slightly restricted hierarchical Petri nets with hierarchically structured interfaces. The main purpose of the concept is to facilitate the modeling of large real-world systems, rather than using them for theoretical considerations. This will form the foundation of an editor-simulator-tool with a direct manipulation interface for this type of nets.

Keywords: Computer tools for nets, system design using nets

CONTENTS

---

* Authors current adress: STZ GmbH, Helenenbergweg 19, W-4600 Dortmund 50, e-mail: fehling@stzdo.de

1. Introduction

Modeling large real-world systems with Petri nets is feasible only when using powerful structuring mechanisms (cf. e.g. [Ditt89], [Reis85], [HuJS89]). One of these mechanisms is *hierarchical modeling*, which allows

- to inspect the modelled system at varying levels of detail,
- to visualize selected parts of the system (e.g. the "refinement" of one node),
- to facilitate the multiple (re-)use of parts of the model.

Good arguments for the usefulness of hierarchical modeling were given by Huber / Jensen / Shapiro in [HuJS89]; we repeat just one of them here:

> *From a theoretical point of view some kind of hierarchy may look like a graphical convenience that does not add any theoretical modeling power. However, it is necessary to have powerful structuring tools to cope with large models in practice.*

We add:

> For the development of tools which are able to cope with large models a sound *formal concept* of "hierarchy" is needed.

Even if it will be necessary at a later stage to study the reationship between the hierarchical structure of a net and its behaviour, devising a 'good' hierarchy is a first step which is not trivial and is necessary as a foundation of a powerful modeling technique and tool. This conviction originates in our experience in developing such tools and using them for modeling systems (cf. [BrBu90], [Ditt89], [LeWo89]).

Especially in large models we found it very helpful to have the places refined as well as the transitions, as otherwise the passive components have to be modelled in full detail from the beginning. Unfortunately, in the case of neighbouring refinements it is rather difficult to save the consistency of the model with all its level-crossing arcs; in particular when ***changing*** the model (for example by moving some nodes into another level of abstraction) the interfaces of the sub-diagrams may change in a way that is hard to maintain.

On the other hand, showing just the refinement of one node as a subnet in a window for its own is not the only way of visualizing "views" on the model. One may think of many other kinds of views which may e.g. consist of two or more adjacent refinements or parts of them, possibly from different levels of abstraction. From this the need arose to have a formal model of the hierarchy which is not based on the set of sub-diagrams and their interconnections but on the set of all nodes (refined and not refined) and the corresponding arcs (which partly can be computed from other arcs).

A graphical editor should distinguish between the logical model, views on this model and the graphical representation. In this paper we deal with the logical model but keep the views in mind. The kernel is the concept of the hierarchical ***net-structure*** dealing with nodes, arcs, and additional structure-information. "Semantic" information given by inscriptions or labels is not treated here.[1]

We consider the concept of net morphism (in particular: quotients) as a good starting-point. However, we do not want to visualize the complete net at all times (as e.g. shown in [Reis86]), but just

[1] It is not a major task to add "semantic" inscriptions because generally only the most detailed nets will be "executable".

parts of it, such as the subnet consisting of the refinement of one node (i.e. the pre-image of one node with respect to a given morphism) together with the "connections" to its environment.

These "connections" are easy to handle when either just places or transitions are refinable, as is the case with many tools. Other tools forbid the refinement of *adjacent* nodes, such as the CPN Palette tool package (see [HuJS89]). Again, no problems exist with respect to connections if fixed "levels of abstraction" are used, with every node being on the same level as all its neighbour nodes. This applies also, when a fixed order for the substitution of the refined nodes by their refinements is given, as in the hierarchy concept for arbitrary graphs of Lengauer / Wagner in [LeWa87] and in some graph grammar concepts. In all these cases the vicinity of refined nodes is *fixed*. Thus it is sufficient for the refining "subnet" to have a *fixed* set of "ports" showing each adjacent component at one level of abstraction only.

If, however, adjacent nodes are refined independently and arbitrarily[2], the connections have to be defined in a more sophisticated way. In this case the environment of the refinement of each node includes all adjacent nodes *and* the (adjacent) "border" of the *refinements* of the adjacent nodes (and the border of the refinement of the border and so on). **Chapter 2** will discuss this problem in detail (guided by an example). **Chapter 3** develops the term "hierarchical Petri net", gives a formal definition for it and shows that it incorporates all necessary information. In addition morphisms between hierarchical Petri nets are defined. While this concept mainly supports the *top-down* development of hierarchical nets, in **Chapter 4** "building blocks" are introduced, which facilitate the (re-)use of (parts of) a hierarchical Petri net, support the possibility of bottom-up development of parts of the model and lay the foundations for "dynamic invocation" (cf. "invocation transitions" in [HuJS89]) and "global objects" (cf. "fusion sets" in [HuJS89]).

Proofs have not been incorporated in the paper in order to keep it short, but they can be found in [Fehl91]. The same holds for many other details, especially regarding chap. 4.

2. The Problem

The following model of a simple process control system will illustrate the problems arising when adjacent nodes are refined. The net N_1 shows the system on the most abstract level.

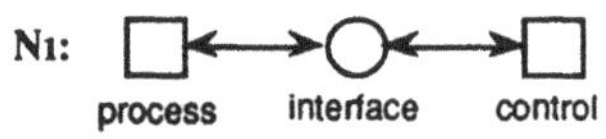

First we refine[3] the place called interface by the very simple net N_{2a}, consisting of two isolated places. This net has to be connected to the transitions process and control, because they are adjacent to the refined node. Both the nodes of the refinement are connected to the two adjacent nodes, yielding net N_2.

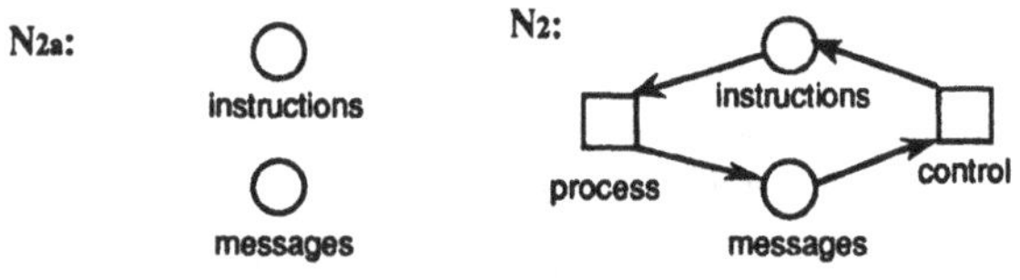

[2] Even the refinement of a node in the *"border" of the refinement* should be possible.

[3] For the definition of "refinement", "net-morphism" etc. see chapter 3.

How would a **tool** support this way of proceeding? The Petri net editor-simulator-tool *PetriLab* (cf. [BrBu90]) presents a drawing window which is empty except for the "ports" (process and control); these are just different representations of the corresponding nodes. The user subsequently draws the new (sub-)net and connects it to the ports. Note that the arcs on the abstract level only make sense when there exist corresponding arcs on the finer level; thus the ports *must* be connected to yield a complete refinement.

From a theoretic point of view each of the finer nets (N_{2a} and N_2) is a refinement of N_1 as there exist netmorphisms from N_{2a} and N_2 to N_1 [4]. Furthermore the morphism from N_2 to N_1 is a quotient, i.e. it is surjective and all (directed) arcs in N_1 have a pre-image in N_2. [5]

Second, we refine the transition process. Again we have to draw the refining net and connect it to the adjacent node(s) (here: interface). As we want to get a quotient again, we complete this net in a straight-forward manner such that the resulting morphism is the identical mapping on all nodes but the refined one (net N_{3a}). (Nodes which are identified by this morphism are not distinguished by different names.)

Up to this point the connections between the two refinements are missing. Now consider net N_2: The places instructions and messages are adjacent to the currently refined node process. Hence these two places have to be linked to the (sub-)net refining the node process. This is done as shown in net N_3.

N_{3a}:

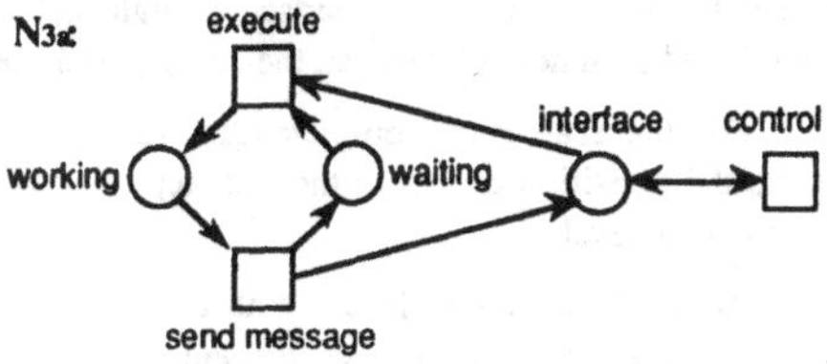

N_3:

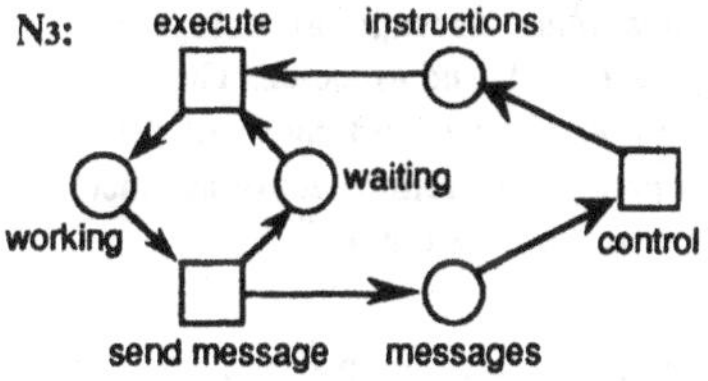

An **editor-tool** could support this process by offering both the places instructions and messages *and* the coarser place interface as ports.

The net N_3 may be imagined as the result of another way of proceeding: Starting from the most abstract net N_1, one refines the transition process as shown above; then one refines interface and connects the refinement to the new environment of interface, i.e. execute and send message. So, these nodes belong to the set of ports of the refinement of interface.

Note that again for all arcs in the nets that are more abstract there are corresponding arcs in the finer nets (and no others). N_{3a} and N_3 are constructed in such a way that there exist quotients from these nets to N_1; in addition we have quotients from N_3 to N_{3a} and N_2; hence N_3 is a refinement of N_1, N_2 and N_{3a}.

In a third step the transition execute is refined by two transitions, called execute1 and execute2, as shown in net N_4.

---

[4] If nothing else is specified, we mean the "natural" morphism, as suggested by the names of the nodes.

[5] In [Reis86] only this is a refinement.

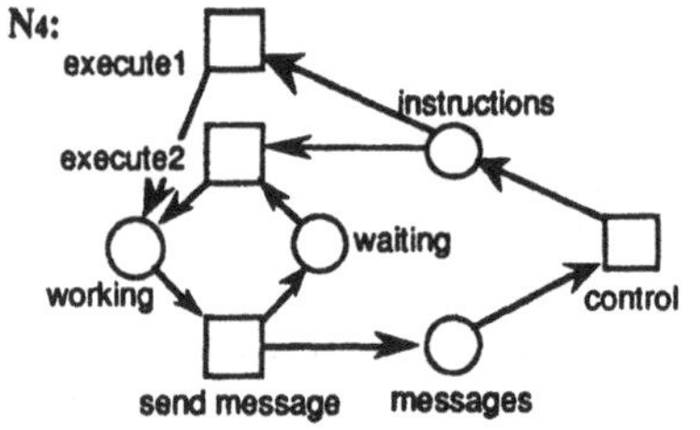

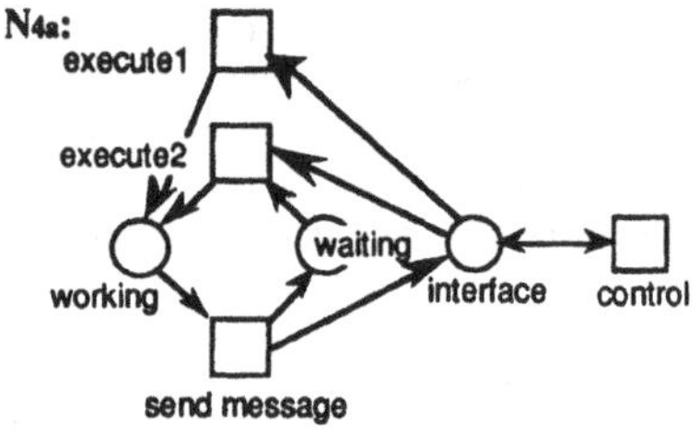

The new nodes are connected to the vicinity of execute in net N_3. *Implicitly* they are also adjacent to the "father" of instructions, interface, though such an arc is not explicitly contained in any of the nets constructed until now.[6] However, the net N_{4a} could be drawn without additional information.

For the reason of completeness we refine the transition control in the last step; net N_5 is the result.

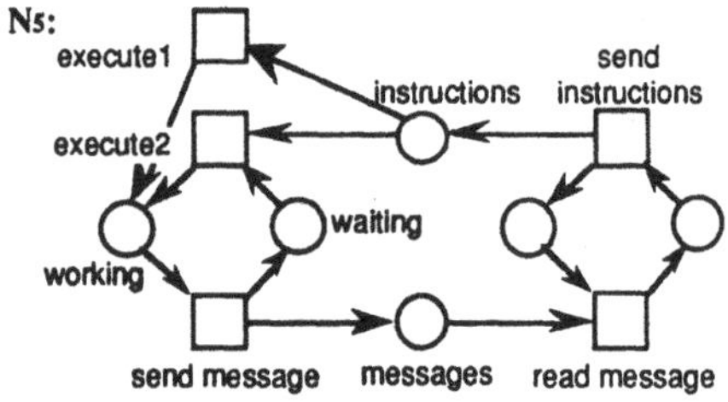

Across the different "levels of abstraction" the place interface is now adjacent to the transitions control, process, send instructions, read message, execute, send message, execute1, and execute2. The Petri net editor *PetriLab* would show all these nodes as ports of the refinement of interface (but not all at the same time).

The following diagram shows the relations between the nets, which are all quotients. Two facts are worth to be noticed:

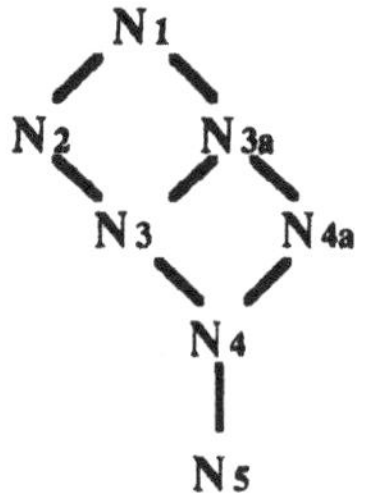

1.) The order of refinement of the nodes is not significant (first interface, then process ($N_1 \rightarrow N_2 \rightarrow N_3$) or first process, then interface ($N_1 \rightarrow N_{3a} \rightarrow N_3$) or any other order not mentioned here). The result, N_4, is always the same. For that reason the nets N_2, N_{3a} and N_{4a} may be ignored without loosing any information about the nodes and the relations between them (i.e. the arcs and the is-refinement-of relation).

2.) Even if N_2, N_{3a} and N_{4a} are skipped some redundant information remains:

- Some nodes exist two or more times (e.g. control or instructions)[7].

- All arcs connecting two nodes of which at least one is refined can be computed from the arcs between unrefined nodes (quotients!).

Based on this idea we will give the definition of "hierarchical Petri net" as given in the next chapter.

---

[6] These *implicit arcs* will prove to be central to the formal concept as developed in chapter 3.

[7] Properly speaking the "same" nodes in the different nets are not equal, but they are identified by the morphisms and have "the same meaning" with respect to the modelled system.

3. Hierarchical Petri Nets

In the following, the proofs of the lemmas and propositions are omitted; they are mainly evident from the step by step development of the concepts.

The following definitions are well known and included for reasons of completeness only.

Definitions 3.1

a) A triple $N = (S,T;F)$ is called a **net**, iff $S \cap T = \emptyset$, $S \cup T \neq \emptyset$ and $F \subseteq (S \times T) \cup (T \times S)$.

Notation: $X := S \cup T$.

b) Let N be a net and $X' \subseteq X$ a subset of the nodes of N. The **border** of X' (in N) is defined by $\underline{\mathbf{bd}}_N(X') := \{ x \in X' \mid \exists\, y \in X \setminus X' : (x,y) \in F \vee (y,x) \in F \}$.

The **environment** is the border of the rest: $\underline{\mathbf{env}}_N(X') := \underline{\mathbf{bd}}_N(X \setminus X')$.

c) Let $N_1 = (S_1,T_1;F_1)$, $N_2 = (S_2,T_2;F_2)$ be nets and $f: X_2 \rightarrow X_1$ a mapping.

(N_2,N_1,f) is called a **netmorphism**, iff

i) $f(F_2) \subseteq F_1 \cup id_{X_1}$ and

ii) $\forall\, t \in T_2\ \forall\, s \in {}^\bullet t \cup t^\bullet : f(t) = f(s) \vee (f(t) \in T_1 \wedge f(s) \in S_1)$

where $f((x,y)) := (f(x), f(y))$.

(i) saves the structure except for identification of nodes; ii) saves the kind of the nodes as far as necessary.)

Notation: N_2 is called a **refinement** of N_1; N_1 is an **abstraction** of N_2.

For $x \in X_1$ the subnet N' of N_2 with $X' = f^{-1}(x)$ and $F' = F_2 \cap X'^2$ is called (direct) **refinement of** x; x is the **predecessor** of N'.

In the sequel we use the following convention: Indices and primes used to denote a net N are carried over to all parts of N (i.e. S, T, F, X, ...).

d) A netmorphism (N_2,N_1,f) is called a **quotient**, iff f is "surjective" on both the nodes and the edges, that means iff

i) $f(X_2) = X_1$ ii) $F_1 \setminus f(F_2) = \emptyset$.

Remark 3.2: If (N_2,N_1,f) is a morphism between nets N_2 and N_1, and if $x \in S_1$ (resp. $x \in T_1$) is a refined place (transition), then the border of the refinement of x consists of places (transitions) only, i.e.:

$$\underline{\mathbf{bd}}_{N_2}(f^{-1}(x)) \subseteq S_2 \ (\subseteq T_2).$$

3.1 Sequences of Refinements

Now we will look at sequences of refinements. We assume that each node is refined in at most one way and that each node is contained in at most one refinement of any other node.[8]

Definition 3.3

Let (for $n \in \mathbb{N}$) $N_1,\dots,N_n$ be nets with disjoint sets of nodes and $f_1,\dots, f_{n-1}$ mappings such that (N_{i+1}, N_i, f_i), $i = 1,\dots, n-1$, are quotients.

Then $V = (N_1, f_1,\dots, f_{n-1}, N_n)$ is called a **sequence of refinements**.

Notation 3.4: $S_V := \bigcup_{i=1,\dots,n} S_i$ (disjoint union); T_V, X_V, etc. resp. .

Example 3.5

In the process control system of the preceding chapter the nets N_1, N_2, N_3, N_4, N_5 together with the morphisms defined implicitly form a sequence of refinements. The same holds if net N_2 is exchanged by N_{3a} or is omitted. N_4 may be omitted, too.

Now we enhance each such sequence of refinements by adding another net and a morphism f_0 from N_1 to the new net. The new net contains a single node, "⊥". Then the morphisms $f_0,\dots, f_{n-1}$ form a tree-structure on the set of nodes $X_V \cup \{\bot\}$ with ⊥ as the root. Fig. 3.1 shows the tree of the control system from chapter 2.

The tree-structure is a partial order on the sets of nodes.

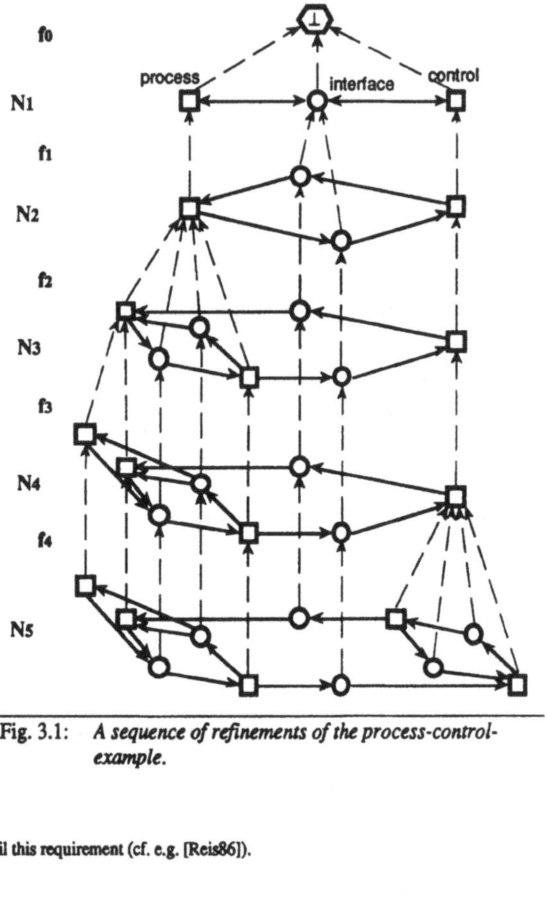

Fig. 3.1: *A sequence of refinements of the process-control-example.*

[8] Not all examples known from literature fulfil this requirement (cf. e.g. [Reis86]).

Notations 3.6

a) "<" denotes the partial order on the tree induced by the relation "is-predecessor-of", which is given by the morphisms $f_0, \ldots, f_{n-1}$ here and by a similar mapping later on. The root $\perp$ always is the *bottom* element with respect to $<$; the leaf-nodes of the tree are the *greatest* elements.

b) • $x \leq y \;:\Leftrightarrow\; x < y \;\vee\; x = y$.

• $x^+ := \{ z \mid x \leq z \}$ is the **set of successors** of x, that is the set of all nodes in the **subtree** of x.

• $x \;\underline{\mathbf{li}}\; y \;:\Leftrightarrow\; x < y \;\vee\; y < x \;\vee\; x = y$; $x \;\underline{\mathbf{co}}\; y \;:\Leftrightarrow\; \neg(x \;\underline{\mathbf{li}}\; y) \;\vee\; x = y$.

Nodes that are **co** describe distinct, not overlapping parts of the modelled system.

c) $\underline{\mathbf{leaf}}(x) := \{ y \in x^+ \mid y^+ = \{y\} \}$ is the set of leafs in the subtree with root x, i.e. the set of nodes of the finest refinement of x.

Remark 3.7: In the tree belonging to a sequence of refinements $V = (N_1, f_1, \ldots, f_{n-1}, N_n)$ all leaf-nodes are nodes from the finest net:

$$\forall x \in X_V \cup \{\perp\} : \underline{\mathbf{leaf}}(x) \subseteq X_n.$$

It is easily proved:

Proposition 3.8

Let $V = (N_1, f_1, \ldots, f_{n-1}, N_n)$ be a sequence of refinements and $x_0 \in S_V$ (resp. $x_0 \in T_V$) a place (transition), then the border of the finest refinement of x consists of places (transitions) only, i.e.:

$$\underline{\mathbf{bd}}_{N_n}(\underline{\mathbf{leaf}}(x_0)) \subseteq S_n \quad (\subseteq T_n).$$

3.2 Generated Nets

Now we show how the "implicit" arcs (see chapter 2) are generated by the arcs in the finest net:

Definition 3.9

Let $V = (N_1, f_1, \ldots, f_{n-1}, N_n)$ be a sequence of refinements and $X \subseteq X_V$ a subset of the nodes. Then the **net generated by X** is defined as:

$\underline{\mathbf{gn}}(X) := (S, T; F)$ with

$S := S_V \cap X,\; T := T_V \cap X,$

$F := \{ (x,y) \in X^2 \mid x \;\underline{\mathbf{co}}\; y \wedge x \neq y \wedge \exists x' \in \underline{\mathbf{leaf}}(x)\; \exists y' \in \underline{\mathbf{leaf}}(y) : (x',y') \in F_n \}.$

I.e.: Two nodes are linked by an arc iff no one is a predecessor of the other and their leaf-sets are connected by an arc in the same direction.

Remarks 3.10: a) For all $X \subseteq X_V$, $\underline{\mathbf{gn}}(X)$ is a net, as immediately follows from the preceding proposition.

b) Note that the definition is given by means of the tree-structure.

c) The nodes in X do not have to be **co** (though in most cases they will be).

The nets N_i of a sequence of refinements are examples of generated nets:

Proposition 3.11

Let $V = (N_1, f_1, \ldots, f_{n-1}, N_n)$ be a sequence of refinements. Then

$$\forall i \in \{1,\ldots,n\} : \underline{\mathbf{gn}}(X_i) = N_i ,$$

i.e. the nodes of the net N_i generate this net.

However, not all generated nets are nets or sub-nets in the underlying sequence of refinements. Let V be the sequence of refinements formed by the nets N_1, N_2, N_3, N_4, N_5 of the process-control-example. The nodes control, interface, execute1, execute2, working, send message, and waiting generate the net N_{4a} (cf. picture in chap. 2) being not a (sub-)net in V. By generating this net we added also some arcs. Note that these are the arcs we called "implicit" in chapter 2.

3.3 Equivalent Nodes

In the process-control-example above formally different nodes are identified by their labels, when the morphism between them is trivial. In other words: A node x and its predecessor y are identified, if x is the only successor of y, i.e. if y is not "really refined". Now we want to formalize this by the means of an equivalence relation. We start by defining the "really refined nodes":

Definition 3.12

Let $V = (N_1, f_1, \ldots, f_{n-1}, N_n)$ be a sequence of refinements. Then

$$VX_V := \bigcup_{i=1,\ldots,n-1} VX_i$$

with

$$VX_i := \{ x \in X_i \mid |f_i^{-1}(x)| > 1 \} , \quad i \in \{1,\ldots,n-1\}$$

is called the set of **really refined nodes.**[9] [10]

Now we need a new "is-predecessor-of" relation. Formally we replace the morphisms by a mapping that skips the nodes which are not really refined:

[9] Cf. "attachment" in [Reis86].

[10] One may think of other definitions of a "really refined node" (for instance by an additional predicate). However, they will result in a finer equivalence-relation, and all the following results will hold in this case as well.

Definition 3.13

Let $V = (N_1, f_1, \ldots, f_{n-1}, N_n)$ be a sequence of refinements and VX_V the set of really refined nodes of V. We define

$f_V : X_V \rightarrow VX_V \cup \{\perp\}$,

$$f_V(x) := \begin{cases} f_{i-1}(x), & \text{if } x \in X_i,\ i \in \{2,\ldots,n\} \wedge f_{i-1}(x) \in VX_V \\ f_V(f_{i-1}(x)), & \text{if } x \in X_i,\ i \in \{2,\ldots,n\} \wedge f_{i-1}(x) \notin VX_V \\ \perp, & \text{if } x \in X_1 . \end{cases}$$

$f_V(x)$ denotes the "real" predecessor of x.

The image of the mapping f_V is the complete set $VX_V \cup \{\perp\}$.

Fig. 3.2 shows the really refined nodes (dark) and the mapping f_V.

The equivalence relation "≡" will identify nodes "lying on one line" and having the same real predecessor:

Definition and Proposition 3.14

$\equiv\ \subseteq X_V \times X_V$,
defined as
$x \equiv y \Leftrightarrow$
$f_V(x) = f_V(y) \wedge x\ \underline{\mathbf{li}}\ y$,
is an equivalence relation.

Fig. 3.2 shows 7 of the 15 equivalence classes of the process-control-example.

The proof is omitted here. As a by-product, it shows that equivalent nodes are in the same predecessor-successor-relation to all nodes outside the equivalence class. In particular equivalent nodes have the same "finest refinements":

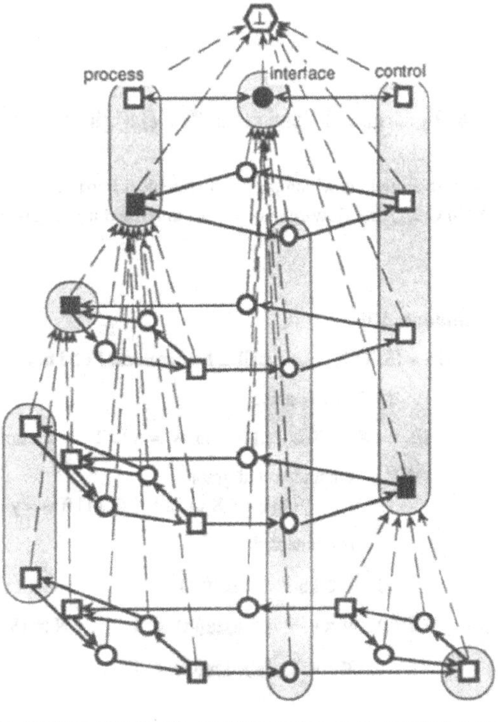

Fig. 3.2

$$\forall\, x,y \in X_V : x \equiv y \Rightarrow \underline{\mathbf{leaf}}(x) = \underline{\mathbf{leaf}}(y) .$$

Hence the tree-structure is not changed by comprising equivalent nodes into one class. The mapping f_V and the relations and operators concerning the partial order can be transferred to the equivalent classes by applying them to any element of the class.

As the tree-structure plays a major role in the definition of *generated nets*, it is easy to show that equivalent nodes have the same vicinity in any generated net. In particular:

Proposition 3.15

Nets generated by sets of equivalent nodes are isomorphic.

So we may identify every equivalence class with the greatest node contained; this is a really refined node or a leaf-node. By the definition of "$\equiv$" exactly one such node exists in every class.

3.4 Hierarchical Petri Nets: The Definition

Now it is obvious which parts a hierarchical Petri net has to consist of: A bipartite set of nodes (above: $VX_V \cup X_n$), the flow-relation on the unrefined nodes (above: F_n), and the predecessor-mapping (above: f_V).

Definition 3.16

$HN = (S, T; F, f, \perp)$ is called **hierarchical Petri net**, iff:

i) $(S, T; F)$ is a net

ii) $f: X \rightarrow X \cup \{\perp\}$ with $X := S \cup T$ is a mapping, such that:

(HN1) the undirected graph

$$G_{HN} = (X \cup \{\perp\}, \{ (x,y) \mid f(x) = y \vee f(y) = x \})$$

is connected,

(HN2) $F \subseteq \underline{\textbf{leaf}}(\perp) \times \underline{\textbf{leaf}}(\perp)$

(HN3) $\forall x \in S : \underline{\textbf{bd}}_N(\underline{\textbf{leaf}}(x)) \subseteq S$, $\quad (N := (S, T; F))$

$\forall x \in T : \underline{\textbf{bd}}_N(\underline{\textbf{leaf}}(x)) \subseteq T$.

(HN1) implies that f forms a tree-structure on the set of nodes $X \cup \{\perp\}$ with "$\perp$" as the root. (This holds because G_{HN} is connected and the number of arcs in G_{HN} equals the number of nodes less one). The appropriate relations ($\leq$, $\underline{\textbf{li}}$, $\underline{\textbf{co}}$) and operators (as $\underline{\textbf{leaf}}$) are defined on this structure again.

Fig. 3.3 gives an example.

Notation 3.17:

For simplification we define the operator **fn** to compute the finest net of a hierarchical Petri net HN:

fn(HN) := (S_f, T_f, F)

with S_f := S ∩ **leaf**(⊥)

and T_f := T ∩ **leaf**(⊥).

(S, T and F as given in HN.)

As the "generated net" **gn** is essentially based upon the tree structure and the finest net it is easily redefined on hierarchical nets.

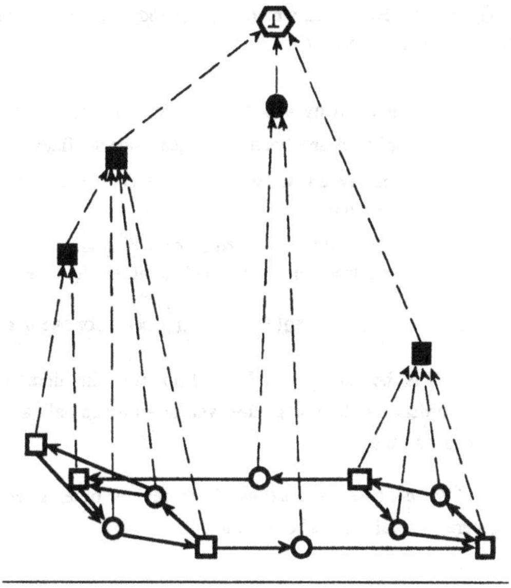

Fig. 3.3

3.5 Views on Hierarchical Petri Nets

The motivation for defining the term "hierarchical Petri net" was to visualize selected parts of hierarchically modelled systems at varying levels of abstraction. How can we extract such parts from a hierarchical Petri net? The answer is: Select a set of nodes such that none of them is a predecessor of another and compute the generated net. The corollary to the following lemma shows that these nets are proper descriptions of (parts of) the modelled system:

Lemma 3.18

Let HN = (S, T; F, f, ⊥) be a hierarchical Petri net and Z, Y ⊆ X sets of nodes, such that

- Y and Z are *cuts*
  (I.e.: any two nodes in Y (Z) are in the relation **co**, and Y (Z) is a greatest (not extendable) set with this condition.)
- $Z \leq Y$ with $Z \leq Y :\Leftrightarrow \forall y \in Y\ \forall z \in Z : z \leq y \vee z$ **co** y.

Then there is a mapping $g : Y \rightarrow Z$, such that (**gn**(Y), **gn**(Z), g) is a quotient.

Corollary 3.19

Let HN = (S, T; F, f, ⊥) be a hierarchical Petri net and $Y' \subseteq Y \subseteq X$ sets of nodes, such that Y is a cut.

i) Then there is a mapping $g : X_{\mathbf{fn}(HN)} \rightarrow Y$, such that (**fn**(HN), **gn**(Y), g) is a quotient.

ii) **gn**(Y') is a (induced) subnet of **gn**(Y).

(I.e.: if x, y ∈ Y' and (x,y) is an arc in **gn**(Y), then (x,y) is an arc in **gn**(Y'), too.)

This means: Every net, which is generated by a cut or a subset of a cut, is a homomorphic image of the finest net or a part of it.

One can imagine many ways to select nodes for generating nets:

- The set of unrefined nodes generates the finest net, **fn**(HN), by definition.
- Selecting all nodes having the root ⊥ as the only predecessor, yields the most abstract representation.
- In our **editor-tool** *PetriLab* each diagram consists of the refinement of one node together with the environment on all levels of abstraction, i.e.:

$$\mathbf{gn}(\, f^{-1}(x) \cup \mathbf{env}_N(x)\,) \quad \text{for one } x \in X_{HN} \cup \{\bot\}\,,$$

where N is the net generated by all nodes in the hierarchical net: $N := \mathbf{gn}(X_{HN})$. The nodes in the environment are the ports. However, at all times only a subset of the ports is visualized, where every two nodes are **co**.

We consider it worth-while to review other selections of nodes and to check whether they generate useful "views" of the modelled system.

Remark about a side-issue:

The set of all cuts of a given hierarchical Petri net together with the partial order "≤" as given in the lemma above is a *distributive, complete lattice* with the node-set of the finest net as *greatest element* and the node-set of the most abstract net as *least element.*

One can construct a lattice with the *subsets* of the cuts of a hierarchical Petri net as elements as well; however, there are several ways to expand "≤" to a partial order on the set of these subsets. Under the definition: $Z' \leq Y' \;:\Leftrightarrow\; \forall\, y \in Y' \;\exists\, z \in Z' : z \leq y$, where Y' and Z' are subsets of cuts, the set of all subsets of cuts is a *distributive, complete lattice* with the empty set as greatest element and the node-set of the most abstract net as least element. The given definition of "≤" makes sense, because for all $x,y \in X_{HN}$ it holds that $\{x\} \leq \{y\} \Leftrightarrow x \leq y$. The set of cuts is a sub-lattice of this lattice, and for each cut the set of subsets of this cut is a boolean sub-lattice.

3.6 Hierarchical Petri Nets and Sequences of Refinements

Now we demonstrate the relation between hierarchical Petri nets and sequences of refinements. Therefore we define the operator **hn** which constructs a hierarchical Petri net, given a sequence of refinements:

Definition 3.20

Let $V = (N_1, f_1,..., f_{n-1}, N_n)$ be a sequence of refinements and VX_V the set of really refined nodes of V. Then

$\underline{\mathbf{hn}}(V) := (SS_V, TT_V; F, f_V, \perp)$

where

- $SS_V := S_V \cap (VX_V \cup S_n)$, $TT_V := T_V \cap (VX_V \cup T_n)$, $F := F_n$,
- f_V is the predecessor-mapping as defined above,
- $\perp$ is a new node,

is the **hierarchical Petri net to V.**

Proposition 3.21

For each sequence of refinements V, $\underline{\mathbf{hn}}(V)$ is a hierarchical Petri net.

The hierarchical net $\underline{\mathbf{hn}}(V)$ contains all relevant information of V. As already shown, one can construct the nets N_1 and N_n and, given the node-set X_i, the net N_i for all i, $1<i<n$. Additionally, all "implicit" nets and arcs can be constructed.

In turn, we can compute a sequence of refinements from a given hierarchical net:

Lemma 3.22

For each hierarchical Petri net HN with $|f_{HN}^{-1}(x)| \neq 1$ for all $x \in X_{HN} \cup \{\perp\}$ one can construct a sequence of refinements V such that

$$\underline{\mathbf{hn}}(V) = HN.$$

The algorithm for the construction of V is non-deterministic. Thus there are many sequences linked in this way to the same hierarchical net. They differ by the order of the nodes´ refinements. However, all of them have the same meaning to the user:

- They all use the same set of nodes (except for equivalence),
- the nodes are in the same predecessor-/successor-relation,
- the most detailed description of the modelled system (i.e. the finest net) is the same.

3.7 HN-Morphisms

As in the non-hierarchical case (cf. [GeLT79]), it is possible to define *morphisms* on the class of hierarchical Petri nets. Such a concept of morphisms should respect both the net structure and the hierarchy structure and "cover" the netmorphisms. So, an HN-morphism is defined as a mapping on the set of nodes of a hierarchical Petri net:

Definition 3.23

Let $HN_1 = (S_1, T_1; F_1, f_1, \perp_1)$ and $HN_2 = (S_2, T_2; F_2, f_2, \perp_2)$ be hierarchical Petri nets and $g: X_2 \cup \{\perp_2\} \rightarrow X_1 \cup \{\perp_1\}$ a mapping. Then (HN_2, HN_1, g) is called a **HN-morphism**, iff:

i) $g(F_2) \subseteq F_{\underline{gn}1}(X_1) \cup id(X_1 \cup \{\perp_1\})$,

ii) $\forall t \in T_2\ \forall s \in {}^\bullet t \cup t^\bullet: g(t) = g(s) \vee (g(t) \in T_1 \wedge g(s) \in S_1)$,

iii) $g(\perp_2) = \perp_1$,

iv) $\forall x, y \in X_2 \cup \{\perp_2\}$: a) $x <_2 y \Rightarrow g(x) \leq_1 g(y)$

b) $x\ \underline{co}_2\ y \Rightarrow g(x)\ \underline{co}_1\ g(y)$.

$F_{\underline{gn}1}(X_1)$ is the set of *all* arcs in HN_1 (i.e. the "explicit" arcs from F_1 and all implicit arcs generated in HN_1). Hence, i) and ii) correspond to the conditions of netmorphisms. Only the explicit arcs of the hierarchical net on the left side of the morphism (i.e. those in F_2) are involved in the conditions i) and ii), but it is possible to show that the conditions hold for the implicit arcs as well.

iv) means: If one node from HN_2 is an element of the subtree of another node from HN_2, then the images of the nodes have to stand in the same relation; they may be mapped into the same node, however, (i.e. the morphism does not have to be injective on "lines") and new nodes may be injected between them (i.e. the morphism does not have to be surjective on "lines"). The same holds for nodes which are $\underline{co}$; remember that $\underline{co}$ is reflexive.

Figures 3.4 to 3.6 show examples.

Remark and Definition 3.24

a) The class of hierarchical Petri nets together with the HN-morphisms is a category.

b) This category is called <u>HNET</u>.

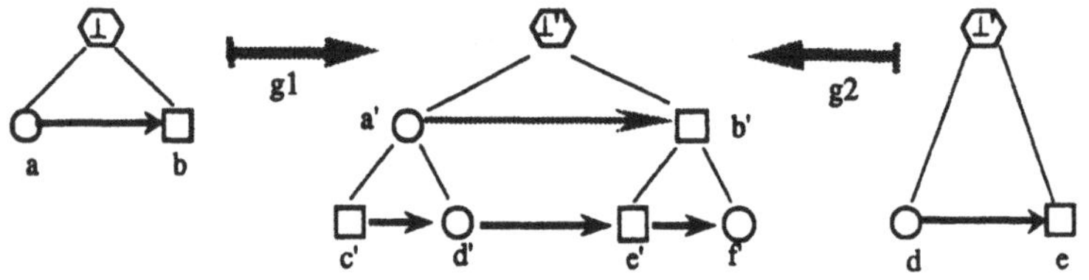

Fig. 3.4: *Two examples of HN-morphisms (here: monomorphisms). The mappings are given by the names of the nodes* (g1(a) = a' *etc.) The gray arrow in the target net is one of the implicit arcs.*

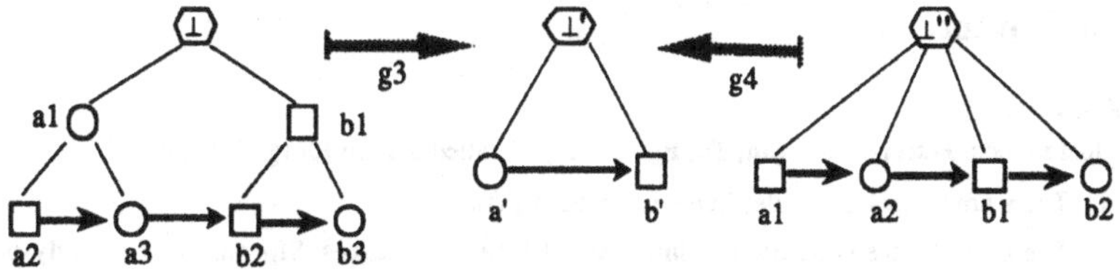

Fig. 3.5: *Two examples of HN-morphisms with "contractions". Again the mappings are given by the names of the nodes* (g3(a1) = g3(a2) = ... = a' *etc.). Even more,* g4 *is a mere netmorphism on the Petri net nodes (i.e. all nodes without the root).*

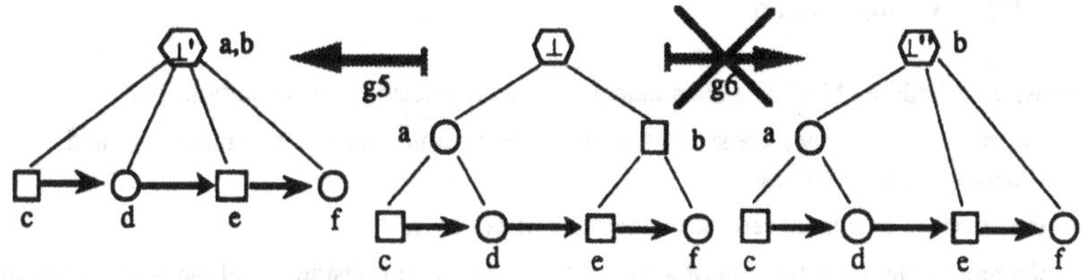

Fig. 3.6: *An example of a mapping not being an HN-morphism:* a <u>co</u> b , *but not* g6(a) <u>co</u> g6(b)..

4. Building Blocks

In this chapter we will give a short survey of our concept of building blocks, skipping most parts of the formalism.

Imagine a building block to be an already existing refinement of a single node, place or transition. One may use a building block for the purpose of

❶ - re-using nets
- multiple use of sub-nets

❷ - storing just one instance of a multiple used sub-net
- modifying just one instance

❸ - "dynamic calling" of sub-nets; using nets "recursively"
(this comprises e.g. the "invocation transitions" in [HuJS89][11]).

A building block should have an interface which encapsulates the body. The interface has to be passive if the building block is an aktive one (as e.g. a procedure) and has to be aktive if the building block is passive (like an object which is encapsulated by its methods). In our concept the interface is hierarchically arranged as well as the body.

[11] But note: In this paper we merely treat the <u>structure</u> of hierarchical nets and building blocks, whereas the "invocation transitions" are part of coloured nets with all the accompanying inscriptions which have to be respected, too.

4.1 The Structure

Definition 4.1

A hierarchical Petri net $B = (S_B, T_B; F_B, f_B, \bot_B)$ is called a **T-building block**, iff:

1) There are no isolated nodes in the finest net $\underline{\mathbf{fn}}(B)$.
2) The set of nodes is partitioned into a set of **interface-places** SI_B and a set of **body-places** SB_B:

$$S_B = SI_B \cup SB_B, \quad SI_B \cap SB_B = \emptyset,$$

3) There is a distinguished transition $r_B \in T_B$ (the **representative**), such that:

   (i) $\forall y \in SB_B \cup T_B : y \geq r_B$

   (ii) $\forall x \in SI_B : x \, \underline{\mathbf{co}} \, r_B$.

This means: A T-building block is a hierarchical Petri net restricted by the conditions that

- the most abstract net consists of a single transition (the representative r_B) and a set of (interface-)places "around" it,
- the interface-places are refined by interface-places only,
- the representative is the root of a sub-tree containing all transitions and the body-places in an arbitrary refinement hierarchy, thus forming the body of the building block.

Remarks 4.2: (1) $f_B(r_B) = \bot_B$, i.e. the representative belongs to the most abstract net.

(2) r_B, SI_B, and SB_B are unambiguously determined by f_B.

Fig. 4.1 shows an example with a simple hierarchy: The hierarchical net in the dashed triangle is a T-building block.

S-building blocks are defined completely dual to T-building blocks. For the sake of simplicity we treat T-building blocks only; however, all statements concerning the structure hold for S-building blocks correspondingly.

As the interface-nodes "know" their connections into the body of a building block, it is sufficient to have access to (a copy of) the **interface definition part** of the building block (that is the **head**, consisting of the *interface-nodes* and the *representative*) when putting the building block into use. So the ith "use" of a building block B (with $i \in I_B$, where I_B denotes all "uses" of B) consists of

- a node that shall become the father of the building block (denoted by $\mathbf{f_{B,i}}$), and
- an injective mapping (possibly partial) from the set of the unrefined interface-places to the set of the unrefined places in the underlying hierarchical net, called the **glueing-mapping** (denoted by $\mathbf{GF_{B,i}}$).

Such a "use" $(f_{B,i}, GF_{B,i})$ is **allowed**, iff

- the structure yielded by i) *insertion* of the (head of the) building block according to the given "use" and ii) *identifying* all pairs of glued nodes is a hierarchical Petri net,
- no glued node is the designated father $f_{B',j}$ of another building block.

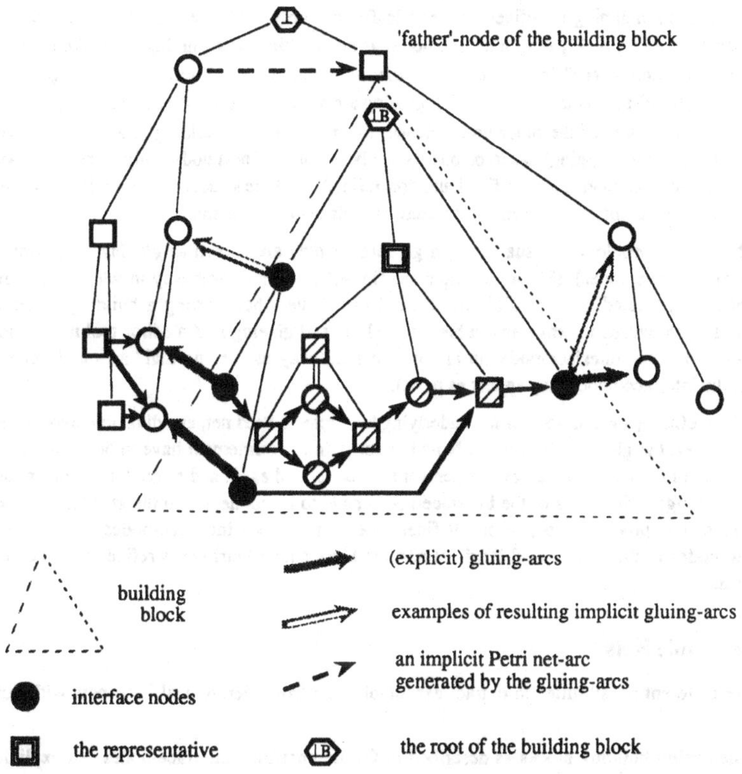

Fig. 4.1: *A hierarchical Petri net with a T-building block which is used only once.*

So we may define:

Definition 4.3

$HB = (HN, \mathcal{B}_T, \mathcal{B}_S, (I_B, (f_{B,i}, GF_{B,i})_{i \in I_B})_{B \in \mathcal{B}_T \cup \mathcal{B}_S})$, where

- HN is a hierarchical Petri net,
- $\mathcal{B}_T$, $\mathcal{B}_S$ are sets of T- resp. S-building blocks,
- I_B is a finite set, denoting the "uses" of the building block $B \in \mathcal{B}_T \cup \mathcal{B}_S$,
- $(f_{B,i}, GF_{B,i})$ is an allowed "use" for every $B \in \mathcal{B}_T \cup \mathcal{B}_S$ and every $i \in I_B$,

is called a **hierarchical Petri net with building blocks.**

It is easy to enhance this definition by the possibility of using building blocks *within* building blocks. As only the *head* of a building block is needed to establish a "use" it is even possible to use a block *in its own body*, thus yielding *recursion*.

The glueing mapping is defined between leaf-nodes only. However, if we treat a pair of nodes $(x, GF_{B,i}(x))$ (where $x \in SI_B$ is an interface node) as an *arc*, **"implicit glueing arcs"** are generated by this **"explicit glueing arc"** in just the same way as "implicit (Petri net) arcs" were generated by (explicit) arcs ($\in F$) in chapter 3. An implicit glueing arc says that a *part* of one of the nodes is "glued" (identified) with a *part* of the other node. Hence, the interface of a building block and its image (in respect to the glueing mapping) has to be one-to-one between the finest nodes only. A refined node may be glued with several other nodes (refined and non-refined), and the structure of the refinements of their images may differ significantly from the structure of their own refinements.

There is no problem to visualize such glueings if they are shown as *glueing arcs* (instead of visually glueing the nodes). (For an example see fig. 4.1.) - In the same way in which a hierarchical Petri net is constructed, it is possible to proceed ***top-down*** when putting a building block with a hierarchically structured interface into a hierarchical net and glueing it. An editor-tool may handle the glueing-arcs and the interface-nodes in almost the same way as the "normal" arcs and nodes. (For instance, the interface-nodes may appear as ports).

When refining a glued node of the underlying hierarchical Petri net, an editor-tool may present the interface-nodes it is glued with as ports. Now the nodes in the refinement have to be connected to the ports and one of the nodes in the new refinement may be refined again and so on. On the other hand the (already existing) refinements of the interface-nodes have to be connected to the glued node(s) and its refinements. The process stops, when all finest (i.e. not refined) interface-nodes are connected to unrefined nodes in the hierarchical Petri net and the hierarchical Petri net is refined to the extent the user wants.

4.2 Executable Nets

There are different possibilities to extract executable nets from hierarchical Petri nets with building blocks.

When using building blocks as described in ❶, the unrefined interface-nodes can explicitly be identified with the nodes they are glued with; the interface-nodes are no longer needed and may be removed; hence an ordinary hierarchical Petri net results which may be edited in any way and is executable by execution of the finest net.

When using building blocks as described in ❷, the identification of the interface-nodes with the glued nodes should be delayed until an executable net is needed (for instance for simulation of the net). This has two advantages:

- The information about the connections between the building block and the hierarchical net can be kept in the interface-nodes so that modifications in the body of the building block do not concern the hierarchical net.
- The interface is visualized during the process of editing the net.

The "invocation transitions" in [HuJS89] may suffice as an example for the use of (T-)building blocks in the sense of ❸ [12]. A more general concept of "dynamically called" nets is shown in [LeWo89]).

In ❷ it is possible to use a ***new copy*** of the building block at every insertion-place or to use ***a single instance*** for all insertions. Using a single instance of an S-building block consisting of one place

[12] Cf. footnote 11.

only (except for the interface) results in a "fusion set" (cf. [HuJS89]). We think it worth-while to investigate the usefulness of other cases as well.

5. Conclusion

In this paper we developed a formal definition for hierarchical Petri nets on the basis of netmorphisms with refinements of adjacent nodes. We showed it to be complete in the sense that it includes all necessary information. Any set of nodes fulfilling the condition of no node belonging to the refinement of another generates a net being a homomorphic image of the finest representation of the modelled system.

In the last chapter we gave an overview of the concept of building blocks in hierarchical Petri nets. The idea of *generated arcs* again proved to be useful to handle the connections between nodes on different "levels of abstraction".

Though we only treated the *static structure* of hierarchical Petri nets with building blocks, we think the concept is useful to understand the process of repeatedly refining nodes in a Petri net and the resulting structural object. A presentation of the *operations* to build up and change hierarchical Petri nets would have gained in an even deeper insight into this structure; but this would have exceeded the limits of this paper. A description of the operations as well as a more detailed version of almost all the other topics mentioned can be found in [Fehl91].

Further topics to work on are: Different "views" on the hierarchy, how to describe and to determine these views in an editor-tool, more than one hierarchy over a single finest net, and sensible ways of getting executable nets from building blocks.

Acknowledgements

We thank G. Dittrich, G. Szwillus and the three anonymous referees for their valuable comments.

References

BrBu90 Brodda, A. / Buttler, P.: PetriLab, ein Tool zur Modellierung und Simulation petrinetzbasierter Systembeschreibungen. Diplomarbeit am FB Informatik, Universität Dortmund, 1990

BrRR87 Brauer, W. / Reisig, W. / Rozenberg, G. (eds.): Petri Nets: Part I: Central Models and Their Properties.Part II: Applications and Relationships to Other Models of Concurrency. Advances in Petri Nets 1986. LNCS Vol. 254/255, Springer, 1987

Ditt89 Dittrich, G.: Specification with Nets. In: Pichler, F. (ed.): Advances in Computer Aided Systems Theory - EUROCAST'89, Springer, LNCS 410, 1990

Fehl91 Fehling, R.: Hierarchical Petri Nets: Contributions to Theory and Formal Basis of Appropriate Tools. *In German.* Verlag Dr. Kovac, Hamburg, 1992

GeLT79 Genrich, H.J. / Lautenbach, K. / Thiagarajan, P.S.: Elements of General Net Theory. In: Brauer, W. (ed.): Net Theorie and Applications. Procs. of the Advanced Course of General Net Theory of Processes and Systems. Hamburg 1979, LNCS Vol. 84, Springer, 1980

HuJS89 Huber, P. / Jensen, K. / Shapiro, R.M.: Hierarchies in Coloured Petri Nets. In: Procs. of 10th ICPN, Bonn, 1989

LeWa87 Lengauer, T. / Wagner, K.W.: The correlation between the complexities of the non-hierarchical and hierarchical version of graph problems. In: Brandenburg, F.J. / Vidal-Naquet, G. / Wirsing, M. (eds.): Procs. of STACS '87, LNCS 247, Springer, 1987

LeWo89 Leufke, A. / Wolberg, D.: Bausteine für Petrinetze - Konzepte und Einsatz. Diplomarbeit am FB Informatik, Universität Dortmund, 1989

Reis85 Reisig, W.: Systementwurf mit Netzen. Springer, 1985

Reis86 Reisig, W.: Petri Nets in Software Engineering. In: [BrRR87]

PETRI NET TOOL OVERVIEW 1992

Frits Feldbrugge
Rakkersveld 128
7327 GD Apeldoorn, The Netherlands

ABSTRACT

This paper provides an overview of the characteristics of all net based tools which are known to be currently available. It is a compilation of information provided by tool authors or contact persons.

KEYWORDS

Petri Nets, net theory, tools, computer aided design, simulation, system specification, system analysis, performance analysis, system validation.

INTRODUCTION

For drawing, analysis and simulation of various types of nets, representing real systems, the assistance of appropriate computer tooling is indispensable. This is reflected by a wide interest in such tools and an increasing industrial usage. Moreover, a Petri Net tool exhibition has become a standard part of the program of the yearly European Workshop on Applications and Theory of Petri Nets.

In comparison with the 1989 list [1] various tools have disappeared and other tools entered the scene. The total number of tools increased with about 50% to 23. This increase is partly due to new contributions from Eastern Europe (such as CPNA, GRAPH and PNANALYSER). Moreover some tools are strongly related or stem from the same root, for instance CPNA and PAN, FORSEE and PROMPT + TORAS + Design/CPN, PACE and SPECS. Also some tools have further evolved, even with respect to their names, such as DIOGENES (was MARS), EASE (includes TEBE), PAN (was probably Petri-Netz-Maschine), TORAS and PROMPT (evolved from PROTEAN).

The process of convergence, predicted and advocated in the previous List, has not yet been effectuated to a desirable degree. We see that Design/CPN is indeed a carrier for FORSEE, but this is one of the few concrete examples.

A questionnaire was sent to authors or contact persons of all known net based tools. The present overview is the result of a compilation of the responses. Only tools have been included which are generally available.

The author tried to reflect the responses as faithfully as possible; nevertheless he cannot accept any liability in whatever form for any errors or shortcomings.

In order to refresh this overview regularly, authors or contact persons of tools are invited to provide the author with update information or, in case of a new tool, to ask for a questionnaire.

[1] Feldbrugge, F.: "Petri Net Tool Overview 1989."
in: Rozenberg, G. (ed.):
"Advances in Petri Nets 1989."
Lecture Notes in Computer Science, Vol. 424.
Springer Verlag 1990; pp 151-178.

Name of tool: **AMI**

Version number: 1.2
Year of completion: 1990
Interface language: French, English
Documentation language: French

Environment:

System configuration: Server/workstation network.
Servers are SUN/3 and/or SUN/4 systems with SUN OS 4.0 or later.
Workstations are Apple Macintosh systems with Mac OS 6.0.2 or later.
Open/closed system: Open
Source program language: C
Extensibility: Interface library for new tools (C, ADA, PASCAL, LISP).

Availability:

Price: Educational institutions pay a nominal fee. The package has not yet been commercialized. User license to be negotiated.
Documentation: User Manual.
Maintenance: No guarantee; reported errors will be fixed in due time.
Contact person:
Name: Dr. Jean-Marc Bernard, or
Dr. Jean-Luc Mounier
Institute: University Pierre & Marie Curie
MASI Laboratory
Address: 4, Place Jussieu (Tour 56-66)
75252 Paris Cedex 05
France
Tel: (+33) 1 44 27 61 89
Fax: (+33) 1 44 27 62 86
E-mail: mars@masi.ibp.fr

Functionality:

AMI is a highly interactive software environment based on typed graphs with attributes. It is a sufficient general model to allow easy extensions to new kinds of graphs or Petri Nets.
The AMI workshop forms an interactive toolkit for creation, manipulation, transformation, analysis and verification of graphs. It has been designed with extension to other domains in mind.

A graphics editor, MACAO, allows multiple net entry and display of results on a dedicated workstation, either in connection with the workshop or alone.

An inference engine, MIAMI, based on constraints, has been integrated to allow logic programming into expert system rules.

AMI is an open workshop which allows easy integration of new applications. Currently it integrates several applications, most of which are Petri Net based: Combag [Trèves], Coverability Graphs [Finkel], Structural property algorithms from GreatSPN [Chiola], OCCAM prototyping [Bréant], ADA prototyping [Kordon].

Future plans:

- X-Windows version of the user interface.
- Hierarchical modelling techniques assisted by the graphical interface.
- Tools for Well Formed Nets.
- Performance evaluation tools from GreatSPN.
- Synchronous Timed Petri Nets.

References:

Bernard, J-M.; Mounier, J-L.; Beldiceanu, N.; Haddad, S.:
"AMI: an extensible Petri Net interactive workshop."
Proc. 9th European Workshop on Application and Theory of Petri Nets; Venice, Italy; June 1988; pp 101-117.

Beldiceanu, N.; Souissy, Y.:
"Deterministic systems of sequential processes: theory and tools."
Proc. Int. Conf. on Supercomputers; Hamburg, Germany; October 1988.

Bernard, J-M.; Mounier, J-L.:
"L'atelier logiciel AMI: un environnement multi-utilisateurs, multi-sessions pour une architecture distribuée."
Séminaire franco-Brésilien sur les systèmes informatiques répartis; Florianopolis, Brésil; Sept. 1989; pp 200-206.

Kordon, F.; Estraillier, P.; Card, R.:
"Rapid ADA prototyping: principles and examples of a complex application."
Proc. Int. Phoenix Conf. on Computer and Communications; April 1990.

Chiola, G.; Dutheillet, C.; Franceschinis, G.; Haddad, S.:
"On Well-Formed Coloured Nets and their symbolic reachability graph."
Proc. 11th Int. Conf. on Application and Theory of Petri Nets; Paris, France; June 1990; pp 387-410.

Bréant, F.:
"Tapioca: OCCAM rapid prototyping from Petri Nets."
Proc. Vth Jerusalem Conf. on Information Technology; Jerusalem, Israël; Oct. 1990.

Bernard, J-M.; Mounier, J-L.:
"Conception et Mise en Oeuvre d'un environnement système pour la modélisation, l'analyse et la réalisation de systèmes informatiques."
Thesis; Paris VI; 1991.

Other Remarks:

Name of tool: **COMDES Petri Net tools**

Version number: 1
Year of completion: 1989
Interface language: English
Documentation language: English

Environment:

System configuration: SUN/SPARC with UNIX 4.2
Open/closed system: Open
Source program language: C
Extensibility: User obtains object code.

Availability:

Price: DM 500 (universities DM 250).
Documentation: Description of the special class of Petri Nets and the software.
Maintenance: No guarantee; major errors will be fixed if reported.
Contact person:

Name: Prof. Dr. W. Damm
Institute: Universität Oldenburg
FB 10 - Abteilung Rechnerarchitektur
Address: Postfach 2503
D-2900 Oldenburg
Germany
Tel: (+49)-441-798 4502
Fax: (+49)-441-798 3000
Telex: 25 655 unol d
E-mail: UUCP: Werner.Damm@arbi.informatik.uni-oldenburg.de

Functionality:

The computer architecture design tools of the COMDES project use a special class of Petri Nets as intermediate language. These nets extend the usual 1-safe C/E-nets by a state space modified by transitions and special arcs connected with predicates over the state space [Damm, Döhmen, 89]. The package consists of two tools:

- The **simulation** tool compiles nets into C code for a fast interactive simulation of large nets. Moreover, functions for debugging etc. may be inserted in the code.
- The **verification tool** generates an extended case graph of a net for the verification of temporal logic formulae over nets by model checking [Josko, 87].

Future plans: -

References:

[Damm, Döhmen, 89]:
"AADL: a net based specification method for computer architecture design."
In: Bakker, J. de (ed.):
"Languages for parallel architectures: design, semantics and implementation models."
John Wiley and Sons (UK); to appear in 1989.

[Josko, 87]:
Josko, B.:
"Model checking of CTL formulae under liveness assumptions."
Proc. ICALP 87; Springer Lecture Notes in Computer Science 267; 1987; pp. 280-289.

Other remarks: -

Name of tool: **CPNA - Coloured Petri Net Analyzer**

Version number: 1.7
Year of completion: First shipped 1989
Interface language: English
Documentation language: German (English in preparation)

Environment:

System configuration:
- DEC-VAX workstation with VMS
- SUN workstation with UNIX
- IBM PC and compatibles with MS-DOS

Open/closed system: Open
Source program language: MODULA-2
Extensibility: Communication with the program and between its parts is done by ASCII-files; the user may interfere with own programs.

Availability:

Price: DM 15,000.- (VAX/SUN workstations)
DM 10,000.- (IBM PC)
Universities 50% discount
DM 1,000.- (PC-version for education only)
Documentation: User's Reference Guide
Maintenance: One year of maintenance free. Extensions to be negotiated. Consulting services available.

Contact person:
Name: Prof. Dr. P. Starke
Institute: Humboldt Universität
FB Informatik
Address: Postfach 1297
0-1086 Berlin
Germany
Tel: starke@hubinf.uucp
Fax: (+37)-2-20315366
Telex: (+37)-2-20315285
E-mail: starke@hubinf.uucp

Functionality:

CPNA supports the analysis of Coloured Petri Nets (CPN).

CPNA combines the following:
- a textual CPN editor
- a by-hand simulation part
- an analysis part to compute
  - structural information
  - place and transition invariants
  - reachability and coverability graphs

  which are then used to verify properties like boundedness, liveness, reversability, etc.

The editor is used to construct and modify CPNs. One can use any graphical editor too, if one knows the structure of its database file by writing a program which converts it to a CPNA file. Using the CPNA editor, editing the arc functions is supported by a lot of standards.

The by-hand simulation part allows you to fire forward/backward single transition colours or maximal steps, starting at a given marking. In this way parts of the reachability graph can be traversed.

Analysis can be carried out under different transition rules (normal, safe), with or without priorities or time restrictions (two types) and firing single transition colours or maximal sets of concurrently enabled transition colours.

The analysis part contains a small expert system which draws all consequences from the known properties of the net under consideration.

The structural information computed includes:
- conflicts (static, dynamic) and their structure (e.g. free-choice),
- deadlocks and traps (deadlock-trap property),
- state machine decomposition and covering.

For certain subclasses of CPN these properties can be used to deduce dynamic properties.

Invariant analysis can be done by computing generator sets of all P-/T-invariants and of all non-negative invariants. Vectors can be tested for invariant properties.

For checking boundedness and coverability, the coverability graph of the actual net can be computed and analysed. For bounded nets, the reachability graph can be computed and analysed for liveness, reversability, dynamic conflicts, realisable transition invariants, livelocks, etc. The symmetries of the actual net can be computed and used to reduce the size of the reachability graph. The reachability graph can be printed either as a tree or as an (adjacency) matrix. Many options help to avoid printing unnecessary information.

Except for the educational version, there are no restrictions on the size of the net other than the computer's RAM capacity. During a session, all commands and options are saved to a command file such that the session can be repeated automatically with a different net.

Future plans:

-

References:

-

Other remarks:

-

Name of tool: **Design/CPN**

Version number: 1.75 or later
Year of completion: First shipped 1989
Interface language: English
Documentation language: English

Environment:

System configuration:
- Apple Macintosh SE, II, IICX, IICI, IIFX (at least 8MB RAM) with Mac OS
- SUN/3, SUN/4, SPARC workstation (at least 16 MB RAM) with SunOS 4.0.3 or later + X-Windows version 11 release 4
- HP 9000 workstation (at least 16 MB RAM) with HPUX 7.0 + X-Windows version 11 release 4

Open/closed system: Open
Source program language: C and Standard ML.
Extensibility: The C part of Design/CPN is programmed by means of Design/OA (see separate description). The ML part uses Design/ML (ML interpreter with graphical interface, based on the University of Edinburgh's SML interpreter).

Availability:

Price: $24,000
Universities 50% discount.
Documentation: Users Reference Guide.
Maintenance: $4000 per year including product upgrades. Local maintenance also available from distributors. CPN modelling and consulting services available from Meta.
Contact person:
Name: Robert Seltzer
Institute: Meta Software Corporation
Address: 125 Cambridge Park Drive
Cambridge, MA 02140, U.S.A.
Tel: (+1)-617-576-6920
Fax: (+1)-617-661-2008
E-mail: seltzer@metasoft.com
Local distributors for
Denmark: Elektronikcentralen; John Mølgaard; tel. (+45)-4286-7722
France: IGL Technology; Philip Kelly; tel. (+33)-1-47731100
Germany: C.I.T. GmbH; Gert Scheschonk; tel. (+49)-30-434-6561
UK: Micromatch; Peter Yeomans; tel. (+44)-344-772794

Functionality:

Design/CPN is a tool package supporting Coloured Petri Nets (CP-net or CPN). Design/CPN combines the following:
- Coloured Petri Nets, with which the size of models is kept much smaller than with ordinary Petri Nets, while at the same time retaining their rigorous formality.
- Hierarchical models, with which it is possible to construct large, complex system models using a sound notion of hierarchy that is consistent with CPN simulation and formal analysis techniques.
- Computer Tool Support, with which it is possible to create an executable hierarchical CP-net, in a user-extensible environment that includes an evaluation engine for code segments associated with the CPN model.

- Open Architecture, with which it is possible to extend the system to handle several types of Petri Nets, provide new analysis tools, or interface with other modelling techniques.

Design/CPN allows the user to construct and edit hierarchical CP-nets: the CP-net may contain a set of subnets, which are formally related. Subnets are called "pages"; they can be related to each other in three different ways: substitution, invocation and fusion. Each of these relationships constitutes a powerful structuring method, and together they allow the user to construct large CP-nets which are modular and manageable. Hierarchical CP-nets are described in a paper presented at the 10th International Conference on Applications and Theory of Petri Nets, Bonn, 1989.

The user works directly with the CP-net graph, at a graphical workstation with a high-resolution screen and a mouse. Each editing operation is directly visible on the screen, which always contains an exact image of the current net (albeit at a lower resolution than the final laser printer output).

The Design/CPN Editor recognizes the structure of CP-nets. It will refuse meaningless operations on CP-nets, e.g. drawing an arc between two transitions. When the user moves or reshapes a place or transition, all corresponding arcs are automatically updated. When a place or transition is deleted, all its arcs will be deleted. With these facilities, CP-net editing can be performed much more quickly and smoothly than with ordinary drawing tools. The Editor also has a set of "power commands" for shaping and positioning arcs in a very precise, general and effective way.
The Design/CPN Editor contains a set of default attributes (size, form, shading, font, colour, etc.) for each of the different kinds of objects which can be contained in a CP-net (places, transitions, arcs, initial markings, colour sets, guards, arc expressions, etc.). The user can change all defaults and can overwrite them (i.e. set attributes for each individual object). The Editor also has a large number of optional syntax checks, comparable with type checking in a programming language. This means that the system can detect potentially unsafe situations and report them to the user.

The user can construct hierarchies top-down, by creating new pages (giving a more detailed description of existing nodes), or bottom-up, by moving existing subnets to new pages (replacing each subnet by a single node). Moreover, there is great freedom in the lay-out of the CP-net, and the user can apply all fancy forms of graphics that are available in modern drawing systems.

Design/CPN also allows the user to simulate hierarchical CP-nets. Each page in a hierarchical CP-net is shown in its own window. The enabled transitions are highlighted and the occurrence of a simulation step is animated, allowing the user to see input tokens moving along input arcs towards the transition. The Simulator contains a large number of options to perform and observe the simulation process in many different ways.
The simulation can be manual (each step defined by the user) or automatic (each step generated by the system, making random choices when necessary). In both cases the Simulator calculates the effects of simulation steps.
In manual mode, the user has complete control over the simulation steps (defining how the variables in arc expressions and guard are bound). It is however still possible to get a lot of help from the system; for example, the user can ask the Simulator to calculate all possible bindings for a given transition. Such system facilities allow the user to concentrate on the interpretation of the simulation instead of on the calculation of possible simulation steps.
In addition to manual and automatic simulation modes, a so-called super-automatic mode is also provided. In this mode there is no user-interaction (for the selection of bindings) and there is no feedback during the simulation. In this way the simulation runs much faster, since it is performed by ab SML program (which can be run as a stand-alone application independently from Design/CPN.

Standard ML (SML) is a functional programming language, developed at the University of Edinburgh. Design/CPN uses an extension of SML (called CPN ML) for the following purposes:

- The user specifies the inscriptions of a CP-net (colour sets, initial markings, arc expressions, guards) in CPN ML.
- The internal algorithms, for calculating enabling and occurrence of transitions, have been written in CPN ML.
- Each transition can have an attached code segment, which is executed each time the transition occurs. The user writes the code segments in CPN ML. In particular, code segments can calculate values for output tokens, but are often used for input/output and animation.

It is important to notice that the first two uses of CPN ML are entirely independent of the last one. This means that in later versions of Design/CPN the user will be able to write code segments in other programming languages and still use CPN ML for the first two purposes.

The Design/CPN Editor and Simulator are integrated into a single program which has an editing and a simulation mode. The user can hence easily switch between editing and simulation, e.g. to correct minor modelling errors discovered during simulation.

Design/CPN can also be used in conjunction with Design/IDEF (see separate tool description). Design/IDEF supports primarily the creation of SADT models. It is possible to automatically generate a CP-net from an SADT model for simulation and formal analysis (when available).

The routines of Design/OA for the manipulation of graphical objects are available to the user via an SML interface. In this way models built with Design/CPN can be animated with Design/OA routines in code segments attached to transitions. Stand-alone applications may also be generated automatically with sophisticated user interfaces.

Additional functions to Design/CPN may be built by the user in SML. For example, the user may write a program that parses a text file and generates a CPN diagram (SML equivalents of the UNIX tool LEX and YACC are also available). This approach is used to integrate Design/CPN with other tools via text interfaces (a textual specification language for hierarchical CPNs is provided). SML programs may be written also to implement CPN analysis tools.

Future plans:

Version 1.75, released in Sept. 1991, includes timed simulation. Version 1.9, to be released 1H92 will also support reporting facilities that will allow easier visualisation of the simulated results (e.g. bar and pie charts). This means that the same CPN model can be used to analyze both correctness and performance.
Later versions will support occurrence graph analysis and place invariants.

References:

A list of publications concerning Design/CPN can be obtained from the contact person.

Other remarks:

Meta Software has invested more than 60 man years over the past decade in developing and enhancing its software to support large hierarchical and executable graphic models.
Design/CPN is the product of a close cooperation with Kurt Jensen of Aarhus University (Denmark). Hartmann Genrich of GMD has also extensively influenced the development of Design/CPN.

Name of tool: **Design/IDEF**

Version number: 2.0
Year of completion: First shipped in 1987
Interface language: English
Documentation language: English

Environment:

System configuration:
- Apple Macintosh Plus, SE, II, IIX with Mac OS
- IBM PC-AT, 386, PS/2 and compatibles with MS-DOS + MS-Windows
- SUN workstation with UNIX + X-Windows
- HP-9000 workstation with UNIX + X-Windows

Open/closed system: Closed

Extensibility: Design/IDEF can be extended by writing programs in C using Meta's graphical application shell Design/OA (see separate tool description). Meta will provide Design/IDEF source code to Design/OA customers who want to extend or modify the application.

Availability:

Price: $3,995 (universities 50% discount).
Documentation: Users Reference Guide and Tutorial.
Maintenance: Maintenance contract $600 per year. Maintenance is also available from local distributors.
Contact person:
Name: Robert Seltzer
Institute: Meta Software Corporation
Address: 125 Cambridge Park Drive
Cambridge, MA 02140, U.S.A.
Tel: (+1)-617-576-6920
Fax: (+1)-617-661-2008
E-mail: seltzer@metasoft.com
Local distributors for:
Denmark: Elektronikcentralen; John Mølgaard; tel. (+45)-4286-7722
France: IGL Technology; Philip Kelly; tel. (+33)-1-47731100
Germany: C.I.T. GmbH; Gert Scheschonk; tel. (+49)-30-434-6561
UK: Micromatch; Peter Yeomans; tel. (+44)-344-772794

Functionality:

A structured graphics editor for SADT or IDEF0, supporting a widely used hierarchical system specification method. IDEF boxes represent activities and arrows represent data and control flow. Design/IDEF includes a facility which allows the user to create IDEF/CPN diagrams (see below) and translate these diagrams into equivalent hierarchical Coloured Petri Nets, which can then be analyzed by means of simulation using Design/CPN (see also the Design/CPN tool description).
IDEF/CPN is an IDEF dialect, which allows the user to specify behavioural models that are executable. This is achieved by demanding a more precise syntax for the arrow expressions in IDEF. Having done this, there is a nearly one to one correspondence between IDEF activities and CPN transitions, IDEF arrow structures and CPN places, IDEF arrow expressions and CPN arc expressions, and IDEF hierarchies and CPN hierarchies.

Other remarks:

Design/IDEF has been successfully used by hundreds of customers in Asia, Europe and U.S.A.

Name of tool:	**Design/OA**
Version number:	3.0 or later
Year of completion:	First shipped in 1986
Interface language:	English
Documentation language:	English

Environment:

System configuration:
- Apple Macintosh Plus, SE, II, IIX with Mac OS
- IBM PC-AT, 386, PS/2 and compatibles with MS-DOS + MS-Windows or OS/2 + Presentation Manager
- SUN workstation with UNIX + X-Windows
- HP-9000 workstation with UNIX + X-Windows

Open/closed system: Open

Source program language: C

Extensibility: Design/OA programs are written in C. The Design/ML prototyping system can be used in conjunction with Design/OA. Design/ML programs are written using the functional language Standard ML.

Availability:

Price:	$7,500 (Macintosh, IBM PC)
	$15,000 (SUN, HP)
	plus run-time fees if applicable.
	Universities 50% discount.
Documentation:	Users Reference Guide and Tutorial.
Maintenance:	Maintenance contract $1000 per year. Maintenance is also available from local distributors.
Contact person:	
Name:	Robert Seltzer
Institute:	Meta Software Corporation
Address:	125 Cambridge Park Drive
	Cambridge, MA 02140, U.S.A.
Tel:	(+1)-617-576-6920
Fax:	(+1)-617-661-2008
E-mail:	seltzer@metasoft.com
Local distributors for	
Denmark:	Elektronikcentralen; John Mølgaard; tel. (+45)-4286-7722
France:	IGL Technology; Philip Kelly; tel. (+33)-1-47731100
Germany:	C.I.T. GmbH; Gert Scheschonk; tel. (+49)-30-434-6561
UK:	Micromatch; Peter Yeomans; tel. (+44)-344-772794

Functionality:

Design/OA is a development system for building applications with a graphical interface. Its kernel functionality eliminates the burden of re-implementing many fundamental features such as basic drawing and editing capabilities. Design/OA's high level interface to the kernel frees the developer from a range of implementation concerns, from storage requirement to window management.

Applications created with Design/OA have three components:

- The Design/OA Kernel, the editor that each application extends and modifies.

- The Design/OA interface; a library of functions that support direct creation, manipulation and display of diagrams, menus and dialogue boxes.

- The developer's module; code written in C that makes calls to the interface (and optionally to the underlying low level environment, Microsoft Windows, the Macintosh Toolbox and the X Window System).

Design/OA's built-in editor constitutes a stable, well-supported kernel. With no developer's code, it is the stand-alone product MetaDesign (see separate tool description). Design/OA is the Open Architecture version of MetaDesign.

Design/OA offers portability at the level of data files as well as the level of application source code. This means that only resource files related to menu and dialogue management need to be generated for the platform of interest. Meta provides a utility for converting Macintosh resource files to and from Microsoft Windows resource files and those for the X-Windows system.

Future plans:

-

References:

-

Other remarks:

Meta Software has invested more than 60 man years over the past decade in developing and enhancing its software to support large hierarchical and executable graphic models. Design/OA is a product of this work and is currently used by Petri Net scientists in universities, research institutions and industry.

Name of tool:	**DIOGENES**
Version number:	5.0
Year of completion:	1991
Interface language:	English (some tools also German)
Documentation language:	English

Environment:

System configuration:	DEC-VAX with VMS, GKS (Graphical Kernel System) and suitable graphics display (VT-340, Tektronix, GPX, VAXstation, etc.). Graphics display may be used as secondary screen or shared with alpha-numeric dialogue. Print and plot facilities require MS-DOS machine, EPSON printer, Houston Instruments plotter.
Open/closed system:	Open.
Source program language:	Pascal (most program parts). Modula (text processors only). ADA (task communication; central user shell).
Extensibility:	Net inscription procedures may be extended to any level of detail. Questions about this and requests for new features can be addressed to the Contact Person.

Availability:

Price:	DM 20,000 to 50,000 depending on requested modules. Educational institutions 75% reduction without support. User obtains compiled programs, installation software, net examples and a brief description of the product.
Documentation:	On-line Help. Brief product description. Copies of publications (English and German).
Maintenance:	Consultations. Introduction courses. Correction of reported errors. Addition of requested extensions. Updates for reduced price or free.
Contact person:	
Name:	Prof. Jürgen Kaltwasser
Institute:	GSI Gesellschaft für Steuerungs- und Informations-systeme m.b.H.
Address:	Kurstrasse 33 O-1086 Berlin Germany
Tel:	East-Berlin 20372310
Fax:	East-Berlin 20372301
E-mail:	grfr@city.zki-berlin.adw.dbp.de

Functionality:

Construction, modification and execution of M-nets. M-nets are timed Petri Nets with finite/infinite place capacities, arc weights inhibitor arcs, token data records, partial firing rule, conflict resolution mechanisms, variable time consumption and data manipulation by firings. Additional features allow for modelling of interrupts.

No self-concurrency of transitions.

Graphical editor:

Syntax checking. Arbitrary net size. Arbitrary positions, individual colours and sizes of net components. Print and plot facilities.

Text processors for formulation of net inscriptions:
Definition of token data structure and of procedures that (during simulation) check for strong concession, select token individuals and their paths, compute firing times, etc. Without any of these inscriptions, an M-net acts as a Place/Transition Net with maximum firing rule.
Net Description Language compiler:
For models fully described by NDL text instead of being developed by the graphical editor.
Net Linker:
Includes in a main net all macro nets used; arbitrary hierarchy depth. Checks whether all formal places of each macro net instance correspond to suitable actual places of the caller.
Simulator:
Model execution based on the earliest firing rule and on the given procedural inscriptions. Conflicts unsolved by these procedures are reported but do not require user interaction.
Built-in debugging facilities: breakpoints, trace output, output scope restriction, graphical representation, animation with free selection of conditions for screen actualisation, interactive data modification. All these facilities are optional.
Collected data: performance parameters of net nodes, firing sequence, reached marking vectors, warnings, errors, additional net specific statistics.
Evaluators:
Graphical representation and statistical evaluation of collected data.
User shell:
Start of tools depending on given commands and on net development states.
Limitations of the net size only exist in the simulator and may be modified upon the customer's request.
Using procedural inscriptions, an M-net may be a mixed model containing process models as well as real software components.

Future plans: Application specific shell for transport simulation. Extension of net editor and built-in model procedures. User Manual.

References:

- Kaltwasser, J.; Friedrich, G.-R.; Leipner, P.; Müller, B.; Vieweg, Th.: "Dialog-orientiertes graphisches Petri-Netz-Entwicklungssystem (DIOGENES)." Akademie der Wissenschaften der DDR; ZKI-Informationen 4/87; Berlin; Dec. 1987.
- Müller, B.; Friedrich, G.-R.: "Using Petri Nets in a test environment for FMS control software." Proc. 7th Bilateral Workshop "Information in Manufacturing Automation" GDR-Italy with international participation; Berlin; Oct. 10 - Nov. 4, 1989; pp 187-200.
- Müller, B.: "Beschreibung, Modellierung und Simulation kooperierender Systeme mit höheren Petri-Netzen am Beispiel der Steuerung flexibeler Fertigungssysteme." Diss. A; Akademie der Wissenschaften; ZKI; Berlin; 1990.
- Müller, B.; Friedrich, G.-R.: "Die Bearbeitung höherer zeitbewerteter Petri-Netze mit DIOGENES." Material Summer School "Petri Netze: Systementwurf und Werkzeuge"; Univ. Hildesheim; Aug. 6-10, 1990.
- Kaltwasser, J.; Müller, B.; Friedrich, G.-R.; Fischer, H.; Bolemant, M.; Sadowski, H.: "Entwicklung und Anwendung eines Simulationsmodells für die Ermittlung der Leistungsfähigkeit und der Belegung des Fahrwegs." Study report of the project "Fahrwegnutzungsstrategie" (Strategy for railway utilisation) of the German Reichsbahn; Berlin; May 1991.

Other Remarks: DIOGENES
- is a successor of MARS, with extended model components, graphical net representation, service tools for model formulation, active debugging during model execution.
- has been applied within studies concerning analysis and design of manufacturing and welding systems, DMA control and distributed software.
- has been applied to the simulation of railway transport systems.
- has been demonstrated on the 12th Petri Net Conference in Arhus, Denmark.

Name of tool: EASE

Version number: 2
Year of completion: 1990
Interface language: Italian
Documentation language: Italian

Environment:

- System configuration: DEC MicroVAX with VMS 4.0
- Open/closed system: Open
- Source program language: Common LISP
- Extensibility: User can extend source code functions

Availability:

- Price: Free of charge
- Documentation: Thesis (see References)
- Maintenance: -
- Contact person:

Name: Fiorella De Cindio
Lucia Pomello
Institute: Dpt de Scienze dell'Informazione
Università degli Studi di Milano
Address: Via Comelico 39
20135 Milano, Italy
Tel: (+39)-2-55006 288/290
Fax: (+39)-2-55006 276
E-mail: decindio@hermes.mc.dsi.unimi.it
pomello@hermes.mc.dsi.unimi.it

Functionality:

EASE (Environment for Action and State based Equivalences) is a system consisting of three components:

TEBE (Tools for Exhibited Behaviour Equivalence (EBE)):
implements a rewriting system for Petri Nets, in particular a subclass of 1-safe nets. It takes as input a net and produces a reduced net of the same class, preserving EBE between input and output nets. Therefore this tool supports proving EBE, which is an equivalence notion close to but less restrictive than Milner's Observational Equivalence. The reduction process is based on the application of nine rules, each one preserving EBE.

TSTE (Tools for State Transformation Equivalence):
implements the construction of system state space as Local State Transformation Algebra (LSTA), from which the canonical representative of the equivalence class containing the original system is synthesised. The considered equivalence notion is State Transformation Equivalence that is the kernel of a preorder based on morphisms of LSTA. The equivalence is proved in an interactive way by confronting the related canonical representatives that are isomorphic when equivalent.

SDB (System Data Base):
is a set of functions checking the structure of the input net against the definition of 1-safe Superposed Automata (SA) Nets, and allowing the composition of and decomposition into (elementary) components starting from SA Nets. Moreover, SDB records the result of the equivalence verification of the stored nets, in the vein of facilitating the reuse of components in system design based on 1-safe (SA) nets.

The current package is a prototype, organised in about 80 functions to obtain highly modifiable code.

Net type:

1-Safe nets covered by monomarked S-invariants of which SA Nets are a subclass.
In TEBE, labels can be associated with input net transitions to distinguish between observable and non-observable transitions. More transitions may have the same label. In TSTE, a subset of the places are called observable while names of transitions are irrelevant.

User interface:

EASE has an alpha-numerical interface (English) in the style of functional programming. No graphics. The net is described by a list of places along with their input and output transitions and their labels (if any).

Net reductions in TEBE:

Full reduction of the input net in a single step. Application of reduction rules as many times as possible. Application of reduction rule to specific part of input net.

Net editing:

Editing, loading and saving of nets.
Printing of manipulated net, saved net or reduction process.

Future plans:

- Re-implementation of EASE in another environment provided with graphical facilities and standard algorithms for net analysis; in this respect Meta's Design packet is considered (see separate description).
- Integration of the various components in order to constitute a kernel of a homogeneous environment.

References:

Detailed description of TEBE:
Marcon, G.:
"TEBE, tools for Exhibited-Behaviour Equivalence."
Master thesis in Information Sciences; Univ. degli Studi di Milano; 1986.

Definition of Exhibited-Behaviour Equivalence:
Pomello, L.:
"Equivalence notion for concurrent systems."
in: Rozenberg, G. (ed.):
"Advances in Petri Nets 1985."
Springer; Lecture Notes in Computer Science 222; 1986.

First definition of the reduction rules:
De Cindio, F.; De Michelis, G.; Pomello, L.; Simone, C.:
"Exhibited-Behaviour Equivalence and organizational abstraction in concurrent system design."
Proc. 5th IEEE Conference on Distributed Computing Systems; Denver, CO, USA; 1985.

Definition of State Transformation Equivalence (1):
Pomello, L.; Simone, C.:
"A State Transformation Preorder over a class of EN Systems."
in: Rozenberg, G. (ed.):
"Advances in Petri Nets 1990."
Springer; Lecture Notes in Computer Science 483; 1991.

Definition of State Transformation Equivalence (2):
Pomello, L.; Simone, C.:
"An algebraic characterization of EN System (Observable) State Space."
To appear in Formal Aspects of Computing (1992).

Other Remarks: -

Name of tool: **ExSpect**

Version number: 3.0
Year of completion: 1991
Interface language: English
Documentation language: English

Environment:

- System configuration: SUN/3 or SUN/4 with SUN OS 4.1.1 or later + Sunview.
- Open/closed system: Open
- Source program language: C
- Extensibility: Simulator is extensible by means of user defined processes, for example coded in C.

Availability:

- Price: Educational institutions pay a nominal fee. The package has not yet been commercialized. User license to be negotiated.
- Documentation: User Manual.
- Maintenance: No guarantee; reported errors will be fixed in due time.
- Contact person:

  - Name: L. Somers
  - Institute: Eindhoven University, Dept. of Mathematics and Computer Science
  - Address: P.O. Box 513
    5600 MB Eindhoven
    The Netherlands
  - Tel: (+31) 40 472 733 or 805
  - Fax: (+31) 40 436 685
  - E-mail: wsinlou@win.tue.nl or wsinfsys@win.tue.nl

Functionality:

ExSpect is an acronym for Executable Specification Tool. It is a software tool for design and simulation of hierarchical Coloured Timed Petri Nets.
Once defined, subnets can be instantiated several times. The subnets can be parameterised which encourages the reuse of specifications. The colours are based on a typed functional language. Tokens may have time stamps denoting the earliest time they may be consumed.
The ExSpect package consists of the following parts:

- Shell controlling all other components.
- Graphical editor for designing a specification. The editor allows the user to build his nets and functions in a top-down manner by means of separate subnets.
- Type checker for checking the consistency of the instantiations and definitions of the subnets and the typing rules of the functions that describe the transitions.
- Simulator for interpreting the specification and simulating the dynamics of the specified system.
- Run-time user interface to interact with a running simulation (inspecting places, adding tokens, reading from and writing to files or other applications).
- Applications to analyze the results statistically, like an interactive bar graph.

Future plans:

Migration to X-Windows; integration with object oriented data modelling; time analysis methods independent of simulation; course development.

References:

A list of publications can be obtained from the contact person.

Other Remarks: -

Name of tool: **FORSEE**

Version number:	0.x
Year of completion:	Only prototype exists
Interface language:	English
Documentation language:	English

Environment:

System configuration:	SUN workstations with UNIX.
Open/closed system:	Open.
Source program language:	Eiffel, C.
Extensibility:	See the components TORAS and PROMPT (elsewhere in this Tool List).

Availability:

Price:	Currently only the PROMPT and Design/CPN (from Meta) components are available. For both components see elsewhere in this Tool List.
Documentation:	Idem.
Maintenance:	Idem.
Contact person:	
Name:	J. Billington and G. Wheeler
Institute:	Telecom Australia Research Laboratories
Address:	P.O. Box 249 Clayton Victoria 3168 Australia
Tel:	(+61) 3 541 6416 (+61) 3 541 6415
Fax:	(+61) 3 544 2362
E-mail:	j.billington@trl.oz.au g.wheeler@trl.oz.au

Functionality:

FORSEE is a formal systems engineering environment. It contains a collection of tools that provide computer-based assistance in the development of concurrent systems.

Currently the environment consists of three components:

- Design/CPN
- TORAS
- PROMPT.

For each of there components, see elsewhere in this Tool List.

Future plans:

Eventually it is hoped that FORSEE will include tools for specification, verification, performance analysis, simulation/animation, compilation and testing.

References:

-

Other Remarks:

-

Name of tool: **GRAPH**

Version number: 4.0
Year of completion: 1991
Interface language: English/Polish
Documentation language: English/Polish

Environment:

System configuration: IBM PC and compatibles with MS-DOS 3.x or higher
Open/closed system: Open
Source program language: Turbo Pascal 5.0
Extensibility: Extensions on source code level possible.

Availability:

Price: Please call.
Documentation: User Manual; on-line HELP facility.
Maintenance: No guarantee; reported bugs will be corrected.
Contact person:

Name: dr. Zbigniew Suraj
Institute: Pedagogical University
Computer Science Laboratory
Address: Rejtana Str. 16a
35-310 Rzeszów
Poland
Tel: (+48)-451-28-221 or
(+48)-451-28-321
Fax: 324-22
Telex: 063 33 43
E-mail:

Functionality:

A graphical editor and a fully integrated simulator for P/T nets, self-modifying nets, nets with inhibitor arcs and priority nets. GRAPH may be operated in interactive or automatic mode. The nets can be structured hierarchically to facilitate reading and understanding. Its facilities cover four main areas:

- Interactive/automatic net creation and manipulation.
- Interactive/automatic net simulation.
- Hierarchical techniques for development of large models.
- Structural analysis of a net graph.

Mouse interface and colour graphics are available.

Commands are entered with a hierarchy of pop-up menus or by keystrokes. GRAPH includes on-line help, accessible at any moment. The graphical editor can work directly with the textual representation of Petri Nets. It is also possible to automatically construct the graphical representation of a net from its textual representation. Net size is only limited by virtual memory space. Optionally, a net can be output to a graphical printer or plotter for obtaining a colour graphics hardcopy and much better typographical quality.

Main editor functions:

- Add/delete place/transition/arc.
- Edit marking/capacity of places.
- Rescale nodes.
- Undo deletions.
- Name places/transitions.
- Add/delete/reposition text comments.
- Associate text comment with places/transitions/arcs/net.
- Move/copy/delete/save/load subparts of the net.

- Rotate/symmetry subparts of the net.
- Rescale (sub)net.
- Merge subnets into single net.
- Refine net nodes.
- Create/modify/draw net layers.
- Name/select views of the net.
- Redraw the net.
- Produce output at different quality/speed.
- Use grid for aligning items.
- Save/load file to/from disk.

Any operation preserves the syntactical correctness of the net. For instance, deleting a place also deletes the adjacent arcs. The nets can be output in a terse text format, a verbose text format suitable for careful checking, and graphically. GRAPH can cooperate with other systems, e.g. the Petri-Netz-Maschine[1].

Simulation/animation:

The net may be executed interactively/automatically in single-step or multi-step mode.

In interactive single-step mode, GRAPH displays the enabled transitions and the user selects a transition to be fired. The firing sequence can be undone by firing backward.

In interactive multi-step mode, the user can select a set of enabled transitions to be fired simultaneously. At each stage of a simulation, the user may access details of the current marking. Various firing rules are possible.

In automatic single- or multi-step mode, transitions are selected by the system, normally by some random process. Historical results are produced.

A simulation of hierarchical nets is also possible.

<u>Future plans</u>:

GRAPH will be extended for other net types, for instance High-Level Petri Nets, Timed and Stochastic Petri Nets. Besides, the analysis of nets will be realised and these tools will be integrated in the PNTOOL system.

<u>References</u>:

Gasior, T.; Suraj, Z.: "A system for automatic drawing Petri Nets - AGRAPH."
Report of Researches in Departmental Problem RP I.09; Ped. University; Rzeszów; 1989.

Skudlarski, K.: "A software package for the analysis of Generalized Stochastic Petri Net models - GSPN." (in Polish). INFORMATYKA No. 5; 1991; p.3 (in Polish).

Starke, P.H.: "Petri-Netz-Maschine; a software tool for analysis and validation of Petri Nets."
Proc. of the 2nd Int. Symp. on Systems Analysis and Simulation; Berlin, 1985.
Oxford, Pergamon; pp. 474-475; 1985.

Suraj, Z.: "GRAPH: A graphical system for Petri Net design and simulation."
Petri Net Newsletter no. 35; 1990.

Suraj, Z.; Chrobak, R.; Stefaniak, R.: "A system for modification of concurrent programs - DEADLOCK." (in Polish). Zeszyty Naukowe Politechniki Rzeszowskiej Nr. 72; Seria: Elektrotechnika, z.9; Rzeszów; 1990.

<u>Other remarks</u>:

GRAPH designers are interested in collaboration with other research teams to further develop GRAPH and interface it with other tools.

---

[1] This is an old tool, which is no longer listed in this overview.

Name of tool: **GRASPIN**

Version number: 2.0
Year of completion: 1990
Interface language: English
Documentation language: English

Environment:

System configuration:
- Symbolics LM
- SUN with UX400 board
- MacII with Ivory board

all with the Genera operating system (version 7.2 or 8.0)

Open/closed system: Open
Source program language: COMMON LISP
Extensibility: User obtains source code. Menus can be changed. New net types and tools can be added.

Availability:

Price: Licence under reasonable conditions (cost of tape).
Documentation: User Guide, Reference Manuals.
Maintenance: None, but major errors will be fixed when reported.
Contact person:

Name: H. Nieters
Institute: Institut für Systemtechnik, Fachbereich Konstruktionstechnik
Address: Gesellschaft für Mathematik und Datenverarbeitung
Postfach 1240
5205 St. Augustin 1
Germany
Tel: (+49)-2241-14-2444
Fax: (+49)-2241-14-2618 or 2889
E-mail: nit@gmdzi.gmd.de

Functionality:

Interactive graphic design of diagrams, graphs, nets, including the usual lay-out operations (selection, alignment, adjustment and profile options, buffer and file operations).

Net classes: Pr/T systems are supported with P/T, Pr/E and E/N as subclasses.

The operations and variables used in inscriptions are defined in an algebraic specification language (SEGRAS), written with the host text editor (ZMACS).
SEGRAS specifications are checked for consistency, completeness and termination properties, as equations are transformed to rewrite rules which are then compiled into Common Lisp functions.

A simulator for flat (non-hierarchical) Pr/T systems with lots of options and a dedicated simulator for E/N systems are available. Analysis tools for graphs and E/N Systems. Coarsening and refinement. For presentation and other purposes during simulation, transitions may be associated with hand-coded Common-Lisp functions. They are executed after each transition firing.

Future plans: -

References:

A list of publications concerning GRASPIN can be obtained from the contact person.

Other remarks: -

Name of tool:	**MetaDesign**
Version number:	3.0 or later
Year of completion:	First shipped in 1986
Interface language:	English / German
Documentation language:	English / German

Environment:

System configuration:
- Apple Macintosh Plus, SE, II, IIX
- IBM PC AT, 386, PS/2 and compatibles with MS-DOS + MS-Windows or OS/2 + Presentation Manager
- SUN or HP-9000 Workstations with UNIX + X-Windows

Open/closed system: Closed, except for Apple Macintosh.

Extensibility: The Apple Macintosh version can be extended by C program modules ("Add-On"s) that extend MetaDesign's functionality. Two extra Meta modules, Simulator and Arrows, are included in version 2.3A. The Simulator supports C/E- and P/T-nets. Arrows supports the creation of entity-relationship type of arrowheads.

Availability:

Price:	$250 (Macintosh); $350 (IBM PC); $495 (SUN, HP)
	Universities special price upon request.
Documentation:	Users Reference Guide and Tutorial.
Maintenance:	Maintenance and service available from local distributors.
Contact person:	
Name:	Robert Seltzer
Institute:	Meta Software Corporation
Address:	125 Cambridge Park Drive
	Cambridge, MA 02140, U.S.A.
Tel:	(+1)-617-576-6920
Fax:	(+1)-617-661-2008
E-mail:	seltzer@metasoft.com
Local distributors for:	
Denmark:	Elektronikcentralen; John Mølgaard; tel. (+45)-4286-7722
France:	IGL Technology; Philip Kelly; tel. (+33)-1-47731100
Germany:	C.I.T. GmbH; Gert Scheschonk; tel. (+49)-30-434-6561
Holland:	PC Computing; Max Loos; tel. (+31)-29-68-94-694
Italy:	C.H. Ostfeld; Claude Ostfeld; tel. (+39)-28-37-83-41
Sweden:	InfoTool; Ake Nyberg; tel. (+46)-8-753-4968
Switzerland:	Noser AG; Rüdi Noser; tel. (+41)-52-28-43-21
UK:	Micromatch; Peter Yeomans; tel. (+44)-344-772794

Functionality:

A structured graphics editor for all types of Petri Nets and other types of diagrams consisting of graphics and text. Supports hierarchical descriptions based on net morphisms. Recognizes four types of relationships:

- Refinement between a node with its neighbourhood and a subpage with its port.
- Connection between two nodes.
- Substructure between a node, connector or its region, and its "subregion".
- Link between a position in a text block and another text block (hypertext).

Other remarks:

MetaDesign has been successfully used by thousands of customers in Asia, Europe and U.S.A.

Name of tool: PACE

Version number: 1.0.0
Year of completion: 1991
Interface language: English/German
Documentation language: English/German

Environment:

System configuration:	386- or 486-based PC with MS-DOS and MS-Windows; Apple Macintosh II; Atari; DECstation with Ultrix; SUN/3, Sun/4, SUN386i or SPARC workstation; Apollo series 2500, 3500, 4500; Hewlett-Packard HP-9000; IBM RISC System/6000; PCS Cadmus and Cadmus RCU
Open/closed system:	Open
Source program language:	Smalltalk-80
Extensibility:	Tool functionality extension; user interface customising.

Availability:

Price:	On request.
Documentation:	On-line. User Manual.
Maintenance:	Maintenance contract with update service available.
Contact person:	
Name:	Dr. R.E. Schöpflin
Institute:	Grossenbacher Elektronik AG
Address:	Spinnereistrasse 10, CH-9008 St. Gallen, Switzerland
Tel:	(+41)-71 26 31 51
Fax:	(+41)-71 24 04 06
Local distributors for:	
Austria:	CSE GmbH; A-1090 Wien; tel (+43)-222-486472
Germany:	CAD/CAM Service; D-W7500 Karlsruhe; tel. (+49)-721-85254
	GPP mbH; D-8024 Oberhaching; tel. (+49)-89-613041
Switzerland:	Zückle Engineering AG; CH-8952 Schlieren-Zürich; tel. (+41)-1-7336611
	Remutas AG; CH-8340 Hinwil; tel. (+41)-1-9380106

Functionality:

- Interactive user interface based on multiple windows, context sensitive menus, mouse, etc.
- Fully integrated graphical editor and interactive simulator/animator. Other functions include: statistical analysis for performance evaluation, automatic code generation for target system (several implementations available), document generation, on-line help, etc.
- Customization of user interface and dynamic animation through user defined icons for nodes and tokens. Icon editor and import/export for standard paint tools.
- High Level Petri Nets combined with object-oriented data modelling in Smalltalk. Smalltalk-80 standard classes available for token attributes.
- Hierarchical nets, refinement of T- and S-elements; Timed Petri Nets; Stochastic Petri Nets.
- Reusable subnet libraries.
- Interactive syntax consistency analysis.
- Automatic, step mode, background, forward and backward execution; debugging facilities.
- Animation of any selection of net behaviour and statistical diagrams.
- Automatic code generation for fast simulation or final target implementation.

Future plans: Improvement on all levels.

References: Application reports (in German) and list of selected installations available on request.

Other remarks: PACE is the successor of the tool SPECS, which has been developed at ETH Zürich. PACE incorporates facilities of the tool FACTS, developed by Grossenbacher Elektronik AG.

Name of tool:	**PAN (Petri Net Analyser)**
Version number:	1.7
Year of completion:	First shipped 1987
Interface language:	English
Documentation language:	German, English

Environment:

System configuration:	DEC-VAX workstation with VMS SUN workstation with UNIX IBM-PC and compatibles with MS-DOS
Open/closed system:	Open
Source program language:	Modula-2
Extensibility:	Communication with the program and between its parts is done by ASCII files; the user may interfere with own programs.

Availability:

Price:	DM 15,000.- (VAX) DM 10,000.- (SUN, IBM-PC) Universities 50% discount DM 1,000.- (PC-version for education only)
Documentation:	User's Reference Guide
Maintenance:	One year of maintenance free. Extensions to be negotiated. Consulting services available.

Contact person:

Name:	Prof. Dr. P. Starke
Institute:	Humboldt Universität FB Informatik
Address:	Postfach 1297 0-1086 Berlin Germany
Tel:	starke@hubinf.uucp
Fax:	(+37)-2-20315366
Telex:	(+37)-2-20315285
E-mail:	starke@hubinf.uucp

Functionality:

PAN is a tool package supporting the analysis of P/T nets.
The package combines the following:

- a textual editor for P/T nets.
- a by-hand simulation part
- a reduction part
- an analysis part to compute
  - structural information
  - P-invariants, T-invariants
  - reachability and coverability graphs

  which then are used to verify properties like boundedness, liveness, reversability, etc. Reachability graphs can also be computed for P/T-nets under time constraints.

The editor gives the possibility to construct and edit P/T-nets. One can use any graphical editor too, if one knows the structure of its database file by writing a program which converts it to a PAN file.

The by-hand simulation part allows starting at a given marking to fire forward or backward single transitions or maximal steps. In this way the user can traverse parts of the reachability graph.

The reduction part can be used to reduce the size of a net (and of its reachability graph) preserving liveness and boundedness.

Analysis can be carried out under different transition rules (normal, safe), with or without priorities or time restrictions (two types) and firing single transitions or maximal sets of concurrently enabled transitions.

The analysis part contains a small expert system which draws all the consequences from the known properties of the actual net.

The structural information computed includes:
- conflicts (static, dynamic) and their structure (e.g. free-choice),
- deadlocks and traps (deadlock-trap property),
- state machine decomposition and covering.

For certain subclasses of P/T-nets these properties can be used to deduce dynamic properties.

Invariant analysis can be done by computing generator sets of all P-/T-invariants and of all non-negative invariants. Vectors can be tested for invariant properties.

For checking boundedness and coverability, the coverability graph of the actual net can be computed and analysed. For bounded nets, the reachability graph can be computed and analysed for liveness, reversability, dynamic conflicts, realisable transition invariants, livelocks, etc. The symmetries of the actual net can be computed and used to reduce the size of the reachability graph. The reachability graph can be printed either as a tree or as an (adjacency) matrix. Many options help to avoid printing unnecessary information.

Except for the educational version, there are no restrictions on the size of the net other than the computer's RAM capacity. During a session, all commands and options are saved to a command file such that the session can be repeated automatically with a different net.

Future plans:

-

References:

-

Other Remarks:

-

Name of tool: **PAPETRI**

Version number: 1.3
Year of completion: 1991
Interface language: English
Documentation language: English and French

Environment:

System configuration:	SUN workstation with SunOS 3.5 or higher + X-Windows
Open/closed system:	Open
Source program language:	C, PASCAL
Extensibility:	User may obtain source code. New tools can be added.

Availability:

Price:	Free of charge for educational and non-profit institutions.
Documentation:	User's Guide.
Maintenance:	No guarantee; reported errors will be fixed in due time.
Contact person:	

Name:	Laure Petrucci Gérard Berthelot
Institute:	Institut d'Informatique d'Enterprise
Address:	18, Allée Jean Rostand B.P. 77 F-91002 Evry Cédex France
Tel:	(+33)-1-60 77 97 40
Fax:	(+33)-1-60 77 96 99
E-mail:	berthe@cnam.cnam.fr

Functionality:

PAPETRI is a highly interactive tool for construction, modification and validation of P/T nets, coloured nets (with explicitly described colours) and algebraic nets. Manipulation of algebraic nets uses ASSPEGIQUE, an environment for algebraic specification developed at LRI. P/T nets can also be validated using rewriting techniques by means of REVE software, developed by CRIN-Nancy and MIT.

The graphical editor is based on object manipulation with an Apple Macintosh style of interaction.

Model validation:

- Interactive token game (for P/T and algebraic nets).
- Composition of nets.
- Computation of invariants (for P/T and coloured nets).
- Minimal covering graph (for P/T and coloured nets).
- Check of classical properties using the covering graph:
  - (Un)boundedness of places.
  - (Non-)quasi-liveness of transitions.
  - (Non-)liveness of transitions.
  - Termination.
  - Firable sequence from initial state.

- Home states.
- Mutual exclusion.

- Analysis using rewriting techniques. The net is transformed into a set of oriented equations representing its behaviour. Knuth-Bendix's completion transforms these equations into a rewriting system. If the obtained rewriting system is convergent, then the following properties can be checked independently of the initial marking:
  - Invariants.
  - Quasi-liveness.
  - Reachability.
  - Termination.
- Validation of algebraic nets:
  - Syntax and type checking of nets with abstract data types.
  - Verification of P-invariants.
  - Reachability graph.
  - Transformations (reductions preserving properties).
  - Generation of skeleton (P/T net).
  - Generation of normed net, on which the following tools are available:
    = Termination checking.
    = Computation of P-invariants.

Future plans:

-

References:

Berthelot, G.; Johnen, C.; Petrucci, L.:
"PAPETRI: Environment for the analysis of Petri Nets."
Proc. 2nd Computer-Aided Verification Workshop; New Brunswick, USA.
ACM/AMS DIMACS series, Volume 3; 1991.

Choppy, C.:
"ASSPEGIQUE User's Manual."
LRI Research Report no. 452; Orsay; 1988.

Choppy, C.; Johnen, C.:
"PETRIREVE: Petri Net transformation and proofs with rewriting systems."
Proc. 6th European Workshop on Application and Theory of Petri Nets; Helsinki, Finland; 1985.

Forgaard, R.; Guttag, J.V.:
"REVE: a term rewriting system generator with failure resistant Knuth-Bendix."
Proc. of an NSF Workshop on the rewrite rule laboratory; 1983.

Other remarks:

-

Name of tool: PNANALYSER

Version number: 1.0
Year of completion: 1989
Interface language: Czechoslovakian (English in preparation)
Documentation language: Czechoslovakian (English in preparation)

Environment:

System configuration: IBM-PC/AT or compatibles with MS-DOS 3.3 or higher.
Open/closed system: ?
Source program language: MS Fortran 4.0
Extensibility: ?

Availability:

Price: ?
Documentation: ?
Maintenance: ?
Contact person:
Name: Dr.-Ing. Milan Gregor
Institute: University of Transport and Communications
VSDS-KPI
Address: Velky Diel
010 26 Zilina
Czechoslovakia
Tel/Fax/E-mail: ?

Functionality:

The package is based on Generalised --timed Petri Nets (GPN). It contains four different interactive program parts:

PNEDIT:
Construction and editing of GPN matrices.

PNMAIN:
Quantative analysis of Generalised t-timed Petri Nets (simulation). In this program a mathematical model for system description control has been implemented with GPN.

RETREE:
Qualitative analysis of GPN: reachability graph, basic net properties, etc. This program is based on a modified Floyd algorithm.

TEXT:
Preparation of text, which is used to describe the various system states during simulation.

Future plans:

Implementation of the abovementioned elements in Coloured Petri Nets.

References:

Gregor, M.: "Modelling of FMS by using of Petri Nets."
Dissertation, University of Communications; Zilina; 1989.

Gregor, M.; Kosturiak, J.: "Using of Petri Nets in the modelling of FMS."
Automatizace, 32, 1989, c.3, pp 81-84 (in Czechoslovakian).

Gregor, M.; Kosturiak, J.: "Enumerative analysis of Petri Net qualitative properties."
Automatizace, 32, 1989, c.6 (in Czechoslovakian).

Other Remarks: -

Name of tool: **PNTBLSIM**

Version number: 1.1 (P)
Year of completion: 1991
Interface language: English
Documentation language: English

Environment:

System configuration: IBM PC and compatibles with MS-DOS.
Open/closed system: Open
Source program language: PASCAL
Extensibility: Open-ended.

Availability:

Price: Free for academic users.
Documentation: User Manual.
Maintenance: No guarantee; reported bugs will be fixed.
Contact person:

Name: A. Lew
Institute: University of Hawaii
Dept. of Information & Computer Sciences
Address: 2565 The Mall
Honolulu
Hawaii 96822
USA
Tel: (+1)-808-956-8995
Fax: (+1)-808-956-3548
E-mail: lew@uhics.ics.hawaii.edu

Functionality:

PNTBLSIM is an acronym for Petri Net TaBLe-based SIMulator.

Net types: general high-level nets (Coloured Petri Nets, Timed Petri Nets, etc.).
PNTBLSIM will handle general assumptions on transitions, places and tokens, such as annotations, inhibitions, colouring of and restrictions on tokens, data flow and timing.

Editor: text interface (tabular format).
Petri Nets are represented in a tabular format as text files. They can be prepared using a programming-language line editor or a general-purpose word processor.

Analysis: reachability analysis.
PNTBLSIM includes limited facilities for reachability analysis, such as for the determination of the coverability tree.

Simulation: interactive and executable code.
PNTBLSIM can be used for interactive processing (i.e. playing the token game) or for statistical simulation.

The tool is open-ended (programmer extensible).
The basic system consists of a Processor which translates Petri Nets, expressed in a decision table format, into executable code, and a Library of Pascal procedures designed mainly to

perform reachability analysis and to gather simulation statistics. Given the source, the Processor can be modified and the Library extended by the user for special purposes.

Future plans:

A version in C [Version 1.1(C)] for a Macintosh which uses a spreadsheet for tabular text input has been under development and will be available soon.

Future versions will extend functionality with respect to:
- graphical interface,
- analysis.

References:

Using decision tables as a data structure for representing Petri Nets was first reported in:
Lew, A.:
"Petri Net processing using decision tables."
Univ. of Hawaii, technical report; 1985.

A general-purpose simulator for both continuous and discrete systems, which uses a decision table processor, is described in:
Lew, A.:
"DTSIM: a decision table simulation language."
Univ. of Hawaii, technical report; 1987.

A description of PNTBLSIM is given in:
Lew, A.:
"PNTBLSIM: a tool for the simulation of High-Level Petri Nets."
(publication forthcoming)

Other Remarks:

Version 1.1(P) has the advantages of simplicity, economy and generality. It will simulate Coloured and Timed Petri Nets on a minimal machine, e.g. a 256KB PC-XT without a graphical interface or special-purpose software.

Since the tool has been coded in Pascal, it can easily be ported to other Pascal systems (e.g. to the Macintosh). Moreover, translation to other languages (e.g. C) is also straightforward.

In some variations, which demonstrate the extensibility of the tool, PNTBLSIM has been used to generate executable code in conventional (serial) and parallel-processing programming languages.

Name of tool:	**PRODUKTNETZMASCHINE**
Version number:	1.0
Year of completion:	1990
Interface language:	German
Documentation language:	German

Environment:

System configuration:	Symbolics or Apple Macintosh with Ivory card and Genera 8.0 operating system (incl. LISP environment).
Open/closed system:	?
Source program language:	COMMON LISP
Extensibility:	?

Availability:

Price:	?
Documentation:	?
Maintenance:	?
Contact person:	
Name:	Dr. Peter Ochsenschläger
Institute:	GMD - Bereich Darmstadt
Address:	Rheinstrasse 75 D-6100 Darmstadt Germany
Tel:	(+49)-6151-869283
Fax/E-mail:	?

Functionality:

Net type: Product Nets (German: Produktnetze).
The package consists of the following parts:

Graphical/Text Editor:

- Input via graphics or text (in terms of LISP code).
- Add/remove place, transition, arc.
- Move place, transition.
- Snap arc.
- Move/copy part of net.
- (Re)name node.
- Label arc.
- Declare part of net as subnet.
- Grid for aiding in positioning.
- Rotate/mirror part of net.
- Mark places.
- Inscribe transitions.
- Inhibitor/removal arcs.
- Definition of functions and sets (data structures) for description of Product Nets in a proprietary language.

Analysis Editor:
Partial or full syntax check.
Check of arc structure.
Full reachability analysis.
Partial reachability analysis for projections.
Deadlock analysis for projections.
Path finding in reachability graphs.

Simulator:
Random or user controlled simulation.
Single and multi-step mode.

Future plans:

- Reduced reachability and deadlock analysis for module homomorphisms.
- Deadlock analysis for arbitrary firing sequence homomorphisms.
- Minimal automata.
- Translation from Product Nets to SDL.

References:

Ochsenschläger, P.:
"Projektnetze und reduzierte Erreichbarkeitsgraphen."
Arbeitspapiere der GMD, No. 349; St. Augustin; 1988.

Burkhardt, H.J.; Ochsenschläger, P.; Prinoth, R.:
"PRODUCT NETS - a formal description technique for cooperating systems."
GMD-Studie, No. 165; St. Augustin; 1989.

Ochsenschläger, P.:
"Modulhomomorphismen."
Arbeitspapiere der GMD; St. Augustin; 1990.

Other Remarks:

-

Name of tool:	**PROMPT**
Version number:	2.5 or later
Year of completion:	1990
Interface language:	English
Documentation language:	English

Environment:

System configuration:	• SUN workstation with UNIX + SunView. • SUN workstation with UNIX + X-Windows. • VAX/VMS + Curses and VT100 terminals. • Other UNIX systems with Curses and VT100 terminals. • IBM PC-AT, 386 and compatibles under MS-DOS (limited version).
Open/closed system:	Open
Source program language:	C
Extensibility:	Uses standard C; user-written C code can be incorporated.

Availability:

Price:	Negotiable on application. Research license available to universities.
Documentation:	User's Manual covering SunView, X-Windows and Curses differences. Reference Manual.
Maintenance:	One year maintenance included in purchase price. Support not guaranteed for research license. Consulting services available from Unico Computer Systems.
Contact person:	
Name:	Michael Palmer
Institute:	Unico Computer Systems Pty Ltd
Address:	15-17 Prospect Street Box Hill Victoria 3128 Australia
Tel:	(+61) 3 899 1101
Fax:	(+61) 3 899 1019
E-mail:	unico@trl.oz.au
or	
Name:	Ken Parker
Institute:	Telecom Research Laboratories
Address:	770 Blackburn Road Clayton Victoria 3168 Australia
Tel:	(+61) 3 541 6797
Fax:	(+61) 3 544 2362
E-mail:	k.parker@trl.oz.au

Functionality:

PROMPT is a tool for implementation of protocols and other applications from a high level Petri Net language into C code. It provides the following components:

- A compiler which translates nets which have been expressed in XNL, the eXtended Net Language, into C code. XNL caters for a rich set of data types as well as for the logic of nets. It describes a net as a set of variables, whose values define the current state of the net and a set of transitions which defines how states of the net may change. XNL allows enabling conditions and transition operations to be expressed easily. XNL also supports submodules, which appear to the calling net as a single transition, but which are in fact made up of multiple transitions at the lower level. The XNL compiler supports separate compilation of submodules, run-time error checking and a subset of the standard C preprocessor commands, allowing conditional compilation, include files and macro definition.
- XDB, a full screen symbolic debugger, which allows debugging to be performed on the protocol specification (expressed in XNL) rather than on the resultant C code. This allows the designer to concentrate on the protocol specification and not on C implementation considerations. Apart from the usual symbolic debugger features, XDB also allows the user to fire one transition at a time or to step through several transitions, to choose transition firing order, to set traces on transitions and variables and to change variable values dynamically.
- SCI (System Control Interface), an interface for studying and controlling net execution. It allows up to 16 nets to run as separate processes simultaneously. A user can load a new process or suspend, resume or abort existing processes. SCI displays on the screen various statistics on the processes as they run. It also provides control of a trace logger facility allowing the user to specify various logging details such as what types of events for each process are to be logged.
- LFA (Log File Analyzer), a stand-alone utility for reading and formatting log files created during SCI runs. The user may specify selection criteria on the records in the log files so that only records of interest are displayed. LFA performs some symbolic data translation so that, for example, transitions are printed out under their names rather than as numbers.
- A set of libraries which provide non-net functions as submodules. These functions provide support in the following areas:
  - timer and delays, including means to advance time in a controlled manner when debugging;
  - file, terminal, socket and queue input/output, with the data involved encoded in ASCII, ASN.1, the PROMPT system's own encoding scheme or a user-supplied encoding scheme.
- A capability for a user to incorporate his own C-coded non-net functions into an XNL net.
- Facilities for assisting a user to debug nets and to analyse running efficiency:
  - A monitoring facility, invoked by a compiler switch, to allow the logging of the start and finish of transitions independently of the System Control Interface.
  - A net profiling capability, also invoked by a compiler switch, to gather timing statistics on the running of the net.
  - A script driver testing facility, to provide a means of testing a net in a systematic manner by using a script of commands which controls the flow of data between two PROMPT processes.
- A collection of benchmark nets which exercise the PROMPT system in different ways to allow quantitative comparisons to be made between different machines running PROMPT and to test the efficacy of code improvements.

Future plans:

- Porting of PROMPT to X-Windows.
- Addition of a run-time error checking capability.
- Division of the documentation into a tutorial manual and a separate reference manual.
- Provision of a capability to allow a user to test a protocol specification under a variety of automatically generated situations.

References:

[1] Unico Computer Systems:
"PROMPT System User Manual."
Unico Computer Systems and Telecom Australia; Sept. 1991.

[2] Unico Computer Systems:
"PROMPT System Reference Manual."
Unico Computer Systems and Telecom Australia; Sept. 1991.

[3] Billington, J.; Wheeler, G.; Wilbur-Ham, M.:
"PROTEAN: A High Level Petri Net tool for the specification and verification of communication protocols."
IEEE Transactions on Software Engineering; Vol. 14, No. 3; March 1988; pp 301-316.

[4] Billington, J.; Kinny, D.:
"Computer Aided Protocol Engineering."
Proc. I.E. Aust. Conf. on New Business Applications of Information Technology; Melbourne, Australia; April 1989; pp 69-73.

[5] Illing, G.C.:
"Automatic Petri Net based protocol implementation."
IREECON International; Melbourne, Australia; Sept. 1989; pp 358-361.

[6] Parker, K.R.:
The PROMPT automatic implementation tool - Initial impressions."
Proc. 3rd Int. Conf. on Formal Description Techniques (FORTE '90); Madrid, Spain; Nov. 1990; pp 701-707.

Other Remarks:

PROMPT has evolved from the PROTEAN tool (see reference [2]), which includes the capability to analyze NPNs with interactive simulation by displaying enabled transitions at each marking and having the user select which is to fire next.

PROMPT is currently in use at a small number of commercial institutions and at a larger number of academic institutions. A major application of PROMPT was the development of level 3 of the Message Transfer Part of CCITT's Common Channel Signalling System No. 7 (described in reference [6]).

PROMPT has been developed by UNICO Computer Systems Pty Ltd under a contract from Telecom Australia Research Laboratories. It is jointly owned by Unico and Telecom Australia.

PROMPT is a component of the FORSEE systems engineering environment, under development at Telecom Australia Research Laboratories.

Name of tool: **PSItool NET**

Version number: 4.0
Year of completion: 1991
Interface language: English and German
Documentation language: English and German

Environment:

System configuration: VAX-GPX and VAXstations >= 2000 running VMS + UIS or Ultrix + X-Windows/Motif. Other UNIX platforms on request.
Open/closed system: Open: ASCII file interfaces to other programs.
Source program language: PASCAL (VMS version) C++ (UNIX version)
Extensibility: Tool is equipped with a feature which allows to include user-defined functions (Pascal or C) in the system.

Availability:

Price: Licences can be bought or rented. Price upon request. Special conditions for universities and research centres.
Documentation: User Manual; Primer; a guide to systematic modelling.
Maintenance: 6 months guarantee. Future updates free available within a maintenance contract.

Contact person:
Name: Frank Itter
Institute: PSI GmbH, Division of Simulation
Address: Kurfürstendamm 67
D-1000 Berlin 15
Germany
Tel: (+49)-30-88423-0
Fax: (+49)-30-8824256
E-mail: itter@psise.uucp

Functionality:

With NET the user may construct, analyze, execute and animate so-called NET nets. NET nets are a modified version of Pr/T nets. There are additional features which can be compared with Timed and Stochastic Petri Nets. NET nets can be constructed hierarchically to facilitate reading and understanding.

Aim of the NET net definitions is to have a tool for practical simulation purposes. It is the responsibility of the user to delimit some features while modelling in order to be able to apply theoretical analysis methods.

The NET system consists of four integrated components: an Editor, a Simulator, an Analyzer and an animation component.

The Editor combines syntax-sensitive editing and documentary functions and makes it possible to create hierarchical NET nets on a graphical and interactive basis.

For net analysis, features of the Petri-Netz-Maschine[2] have been integrated in the tool. They consider NET nets as P/T nets and therefore ignore node inscriptions. So the analysis result has to be interpreted in terms of inscribed NET nets.

During the execution of a series of firing events and markings are calculated by the Simulator. It can be used in on-line and off-line mode.

In on-line mode, a stepwise net execution is possible. Between steps the user may inspect

---

[2] This is an old tool, which is no longer listed in this overview.

or interactively intervene in the execution process by modifying current markings. On-line statistics and firing protocols and monitoring can be used to observe an execution process. Monitoring gives a graphic representation of the qualitative development of the modelled systems dynamics. Several predefined monitors, such as bar charts and line diagrams are available.

In off-line mode, the Simulator makes it possible to conduct simulations in batch mode. It also enables series of experiments to be carried out for simulation investigations. Therefore, all information which is necessary and desired to execute a NET net is stored in a simulation control file. It is thus possible to vary experiments without amending the net.

Simulation results are written into separate files in the form of result protocols and statistics for each simulation run. Statistical data about all markings and firings may be reported.

The animation component allows visualisation of the behaviour of the execution process in a net independent and application specific graphical form on the screen.

Nets of up to 5000 nodes have been edited and executed. Depending on the size of a net, the complexity of the inscriptions and the number of current tokens, about 1 second of CPU-time is consumed by up to 50 firings.

The NET system needs 15 MB disk space. There are about 50 installations in industrial and research environments. The application areas are mainly in the field of production system simulation.

Future plans:

There are plans to develop NET further. Presently, dedicated net-pattern libraries for various production systems are under construction and soon additional features for performance evaluation will be available. The Ultrix/Motif version, written in C++, will be ported to VMS/Motif in order to substitute the older VMS/UIS version.

References:

NET User's Manual and other internal reports available upon request. Published application reports in English are:

Itter, F.; Relewicz, C.:
"Computer supported design of Kanban controlled production - integrated systems analysis and simulation with higher order Petri Nets."
in: Rozenberg, G. (ed.):
"Advances in Petri Nets 1990."
Lecture Notes in Computer Science; Springer Verlag.

Itter, F.; Lang, M.:
"Simulation of a chemical production system using Petri Nets."
in: Eckermann, R. (ed.):
"European Symposium on Computer Application in the Chemical Industry."
Erlangen, Germany; Dechema; Vol. 116; 1989.

A description of the analysis features is found in:

Starke, P.H.:
"Validation of Petri Net models by Petri-Net-Machine."
in: Proc. of the 5th IFAC/IFIP/IMACS/IFORS Conf.; Oxford, England; April 1986.

Other remarks:

-

Name of tool: **SPECS**

Version number: 2.0
Year of completion: 1991
Interface language: English
Documentation language: English

Environment:

System configuration:
- Apple Macintosh II
- 386-based PC with MS-DOS + MS-Windows 3.0
- SUN workstation
- Other workstations with Objectworks 4.0 for Smalltalk-80
- Transputer board and compiler of the OCCAM-2 tool set D7205 from Inmos (needed for very fast simulation only)

At least 8 MB RAM and 25 MB free disk space is required.

Open/closed system: Open
Source program language: Smalltalk-80; OCCAM-2; C
Extensibility: Source code available.

Availability:

Price: Educational institutions: nominal fee (non-disclosure contract). Others: to be announced.
Documentation: User manual, advanced features, SpecsLingua report, annotated examples documentation, IO manual.
Maintenance: Reported errors will be fixed.
Contact person:

Name: Rob Esser
Ruedi Mattmann
Heinz Oswald
Institute: Corporate Research & Development - 4001
Landis & Gyr Betriebs Corp.
Address: CH-6301 Zug
Switzerland
Tel: (+41) 42 24 11 24
Fax: (+41) 42 24 46 93
E-mail: specs@lgbe.landis+gyr.ch
X.400: C=ch A=arcom P=landis+gyr O=lgbe S=specs

Functionality:

- High Level Petri Nets.
- Inscription language for transitions, places and arcs: SpecsLingua (Pascal-like functional language with strong type checking).
- Graphical editor for nets; textual editor for inscriptions.
- Integrated simulator/animator.
- Hierarchical structuring of nets.
- Net analysis: S- and T-invariants, conflicts.
- Subnet metrics for validating the net decomposition.
- Subnet libraries, extendible by user; any subnet can be made reusable.
- I/O elements for entering data and displaying results during simulation.

- Hypertext-like extensions for commenting nets.
- Transparent fast simulation on Transputer-based parallel computer system.
- Code generation for Transputer-based parallel computer system.
- C++ code generation.
- Generating documentation in PostScript format (including EPSF).
- Longtime saving and restoring of nets.
- Integrated tools (browsers) for:
  - accessing, naming and managing several nets and subnet libraries;
  - editing reusable text elements like constants, types and functions;
  - constructing I/O elements;
  - constructing icons replacing the standard form of net elements.

Future plans:

- Further analysis methods.
- Integrated time modelling.
- Generate and replay firing sequences for testing.

References:

Bütler, B.; Esser, R.; Mattmann, R.:
"A distributed simulator for High Order Petri Nets."
Proc. 10th Int. Conf. on Application and Theory of Petri Nets; Bonn; 1989.

Oswald, H.; Esser, R.; Mattmann, R.:
"An environment for specifying and executing Hierarchical Petri Nets."
Proc. IEEE 12th Int. Conf. on Software Engineering; Nice; 1990.

Bütler, B.; Esser, R.; Mattmann, R.:
"A distributed simulator for High Order Petri Nets."
in: Rozenberg, G. (ed.):
"Advances in Petri Nets 1990."
Lecture Notes in Computer Science; Springer Verlag.

Ebert, C.; Oswald, H.:
"Complexity measures for the analysis of specifications and designs of (reliability related) computer systems."
SAFECOMP '91; Trondheim; Oct. 30 - Nov. 1, 1991.

Esser, R.; Bütler, B.:
"SPECS: a programming environment for parallel computing."
SI-PAR, Parallel Systems in Switzerland; Lausanne; Oct. 1, 1991.

Other Remarks:

SPECS is the successor of the original SPECS tool which has been developed at ETH Zürich.

Name of tool:	**TORAS**

Version number:	0.x
Year of completion:	Not yet complete, but prototype exists.
Interface language:	English
Documentation language:	English

Environment:

System configuration:	SUN workstation with UNIX.
Open/closed system:	Open
Source program language:	C, Eiffel
Extensibility:	Designed such that code depending on the various formal description techniques (including various net types) can be easily interfaced to the reachability analysis code. Additional analysis software can also be added.

Availability:

Price:	Not yet available.
Documentation:	Idem.
Maintenance:	Idem.
Contact person:	

Name:	J. Billington and G. Wheeler
Institute:	Telecom Australia Research Laboratories
Address:	P.O. Box 249 Clayton Victoria 3168 Australia
Tel:	(+61) 3 541 6416 (+61) 3 541 6415
Fax:	(+61) 3 544 2362
E-mail:	j.billington@trl.oz.au g.wheeler@trl.oz.au

Functionality:

TORAS [1] is a component of the FORSEE systems engineering environment (see elsewhere in this Tool List).

TORAS is a tool for analyzing Petri Nets using reachability analysis. To combat the well-known state explosion problem faced by reachability analysis it uses the stubborn set method to remove redundant interleavings [2].

As well as a simple algorithm which generates the complete state space, three variations of the stubborn set method are available. The basic algorithm guarantees that deadlocks and fact occurrence are preserved in the reduced state space. The other variations will, in addition, preserve livelocks, traces, failures and testing equivalence.

Another available option is Holzmann's reachability analysis technique [3]. This technique, unlike the stubborn set method, does not guarantee preservation of deadlocks and other properties, but it can allow the exploration of more of a large state space than complete reachability analysis. It may be combined with the stubborn set algorithms under some circumstances.

Currently, TORAS accepts a text form of Place/Transition Nets as input to the analyzer.

Future plans:

- Interface to Coloured Petri Nets, P-nets [4] and possibly LOTOS.
- Addition of various other reachability analysis algorithm techniques to provide practical analysis of diverse systems.
- Graphical interface based on Design/CPN.
- Sophisticated pre- and post-generation analysis.

References:

[1] Wheeler, G.; Valmari, A.; Billington, J.:
"Baby TORAS eats philosophers but thinks about solitaire."
Proc. 5th Australian Software Engineering Conference; Sydney, 1990; pp 283-288.

[2] Valmari, A.:
"Stubborn Sets for reduced state space generation."
Proc. 10th Int. Conf. on Application and Theory of Petri Nets; Bonn, 1989; pp II/1-22.

[3] Holzmann, G.J.:
"An improved protocol reachability analysis technique."
Software Practice and Experience; Vol. 18, No. 2; Febr. 1988; pp 137-161.

[4] Billington, J.:
"Many-sorted High Level Nets."
Proc. 3rd Int. Workshop on Petri Nets and Performance Models; Kyoto, Dec. 1989 (IEEE CS Press).

[5] Billington, J.; Wheeler, G.; Wilbur-Ham, M.:
"PROTEAN: A High Level Petri Net tool for the specification and verification of communication protocols."
IEEE Transactions on Software Engineering; Vol. 14, No. 3; March 1988; pp 301-316.

Other Remarks:

TORAS is the successor of PROTEAN [5], which was also developed in Telecom Australia Research Laboratories.

TORAS is a component of the FORSEE systems engineering environment, which is still under development.

THE MINIMAL COVERABILITY GRAPH FOR PETRI NETS[1]

Alain FINKEL

ENS Cachan
Laboratoire d'Informatique Fondamentale et Appliquée de Cachan
61 avenue du Président Wilson 94235 Cedex Cachan, France
e.mail: finkel@enscachan.ens-cachan.fr

Abstract. We present the unique minimal coverability graph for Petri nets. When the reachability graph of a Petri net is infinite, the minimal coverability graph allows us to decide the same problems as the well-known Karp-Miller graph : the Finite Reachability Tree Problem, the Finite Reachability Set Problem, the Boundedness Problem, the Quasi-Liveness Problem and the Regularity Problem. The algorithm given for computing the minimal coverability graph is based on a new optimization of the Karp and Miller procedure.

Key words. Petri nets, decidability, Karp-Miller graph, minimal coverability graph, effective computation of the minimal coverability graph, verification of protocols.

Content.

---

[1] A short and partial version of this paper was presented at the 11th Conference on Petri Nets under the following title: A minimal coverability graph for Petri nets. This paper was completed and corrected during the years 1990 and 1991.

1. INTRODUCTION

A Petri net is a mathematical model used for the specification and the analysis of parallel processes [Petri 62], [Brams 83], [Reisig 85], [Brauer...86]. The relations between Petri nets and numerous other models of parallel computation like Vector Addition Systems are formalized in [Miller 73], [Peterson...74], [Kasai...82].

We are interested in algorithms which take a Petri net PN and a property π in input and answer automatically, after a finite delay, whether or not PN satisfies π.

What sort of problems are encountered ?
To analyse a Petri net, the first question is often to know whether or not the net is bounded. If it is bounded, the net is theoretically analyzable ; however the net may be unbounded and equivalent to a finite automaton, which nevertheless makes it analysable. Lastly, it can be unbounded and not equivalent to a finite automaton and yet partially analysable. The Karp-Miller graph allows us to decide the Boundedness Problem (BP) and the following four other problems : the Finite Reachability Tree Problem (FRTP), the Finite Reachability Set Problem (FRSP), the Quasi-Liveness Problem (QLP) or the equivalent problem called the Coverability Problem (CP) and the Regularity Problem (RP) [Karp...69], [Valk...81]. Here, we are not directly interested in the Accessibility Problem (often also called the Reachability Problem) or the Deadlock Problem because these two problems can not be decided, by just using the Karp-Miller graph [Mayr 84], [Kosaraju 82], [Lambert 87], [Reutenauer 88]. The Inclusion Problems for Petri net reachability sets and for Petri nets languages are in general undecidable [Baker 73], [Hack 76].

There are several kinds of algorithms for analyzing Petri nets [Jensen 86b]: let us mention for instance, the reductions [Berthelot 86], the rewritting systems [Johnen 87], the structural analysis of the bipartite graph for subclasses of Petri nets [Best 86], the algorithms based on the algebraic methods for computing invariants [Kruckeberg 87], [Lautenbach 86] (for example, the Farkas algorithm and the Gaussian Elimination) and those based on the reduced reachability graph [Karp...69]. Only two classes of algorithms currently allow us automatic verification for **general** Petri nets. The first class of algorithms, based on the algebraic methods for computing invariants, is of low complexity (polynomial for the Gaussian Elimination) but in general, it is difficult to interprete a large list of invariants, automatically. On the other hand, the second class of algorithms, based on the reduced reachability graph, allows us to decide on almost all the mentioned problems however the size of the reduced reachability graph is often too large to be computed.

Our aim then is to reduce the time and the space for computing (finite !) reduced infinite reachability graphs. What has already been done in this field ?
The Karp-Miller procedure [Karp...69] computes a finite (non unique) coverability tree which allows us to decide upon the five mentioned problems. Let us remark that the Karp-Miller graph is often called "the coverability graph" but we prefer to call it the Karp-Miller graph because we will use the term "coverability graph" in a more general sense. The size of the Karp-Miller graph is not bounded by any primitive recursive function of the size of the Petri net [Rackoff 78], [McAloon 84]. The cpu-time and the storage requirements for the computation of the Karp-Miller graph as well as the effort for its evaluation often exceed practical limits [Moreau 89]. Although the Karp-Miller graph ideally makes it possible to decide these five problems, in practice it soon becomes impossible to use Karp-Miller graph because of the memory and time taken.

One of our aims here is to define a graph which permits to decide upon these five problems while, at the same time, being faster to compute and taking less space than the Karp-Miller graph.

Until now, the notion of a coverability graph has not been completely determined independently of the algorithm which computes it. In [Karp...69] an algorithm is given which computes a tree whose properties one proves. Let us take, for example, one of the first attempt to dissociate the algorithm from the (coverability) set or from the (coverability) graph : E. Mayr [Mayr 84] is the first to define a maximum cover pseudomarking notion independently from an algorithm but he did not define the minimal coverability graph. One should add that his aim is to solve the Reachability Problem, not to reduce the Karp-Miller graph.

The persistence of the confusion between algorithm and graph is in our opinion, the main reason for which the minimal coverability graph and an efficient computing algorithm have not been discovered earlier. We propose the following approach. Start from the properties needed to decide the problems; then define the notion of coverability graph (and before that, that of coverability set); only then should one search an efficient algorithm to compute it, knowing exactly what result is expected. To do this, we shall define a more general notion of the coverability graph. We show that a coverability graph allows us to solve the five mentioned problems.

We will define the coverability graph from the coverability set. A **coverability set** (an almost equivalent definition can be found in [Mayr 84] with "maximum cover pseudomarking") is a set CS of markings such that: 1) it covers all the markings of the reachability set and 2) for each marking m' in CS but not in the reachability set, there is an infinite strictly increasing sequence of reachable markings $\{m_n\}$ converging (this notion will be defined in the sequel) to m'. A coverability set CS is **minimal** (this definition is new) if no proper subset of CS is a coverability set. The minimal coverability set is shown to be unique and finite. We prove that the FRSP, the BP and the CP are all decidable with the minimal coverability set (Corollary 3.6).

A **coverability graph** of a Petri net PN is a graph such that its set of labels is a coverability set and there is an arc labelled by the transition t between two nodes labelled by m and m' if and only if the transition t is fireable from m and we reach the marking m'. The **minimal coverability graph** of a Petri net is the **unique** coverability graph such that its set of nodes is the minimal coverability set. We will prove that the five problems (FRTP, FRSP, BP, QLP, RP) are all decidable with the minimal coverability graph (Corollary 3.17).

There are four basic ideas for constructing the minimal coverability graph.

- The first idea is **to develop the Karp-Miller tree until** we meet two markings m and m' such that **$m \geq m'$** (we replace the test, $m=m'$, for stopping in the Karp-Miller tree, by the new test $m \geq m'$).

- The second idea is to **compact** the previous reduced Karp-Miller tree during its development. To do it, we continue a marking m' if and only if m' is not comparable with any computed markings m (($m' < m$ or $m'=m$ or $m < m'$) is false). In this last case ($m < m'$), if there is a marking m such that m' is reachable from m and $m < m'$, then we compute a new marking m'' such that for every marking m, we have : for every place p, if $m'(p) > m(p)$ then $m''(p) := \omega$ else $m''(p) := m'(p)$. Let n be the first node labelled by $m < m'$; we label n by m'' and we remove the subtree whose root is n (we keep n).

- The third idea consists of **removing** every subtree whose root is labelled by a marking m such that $m < m''$.

The second and the third ideas have been used in the refine procedure which computes a coverability graph (not the minimal coverability graph) helping to decide the Reachability Problem in [Mayr 84].

- Finally, the fourth idea is first to identify two nodes which have the same label ; and mostly to **only keep** arcs (m,t,m') such that the transition t is fireable from m and we reach the marking m' exactly.

All these ideas are based upon a kind of **monotonic behaviour of nets.**

In Section 2, we describe results concerning the decidability of problems for Petri nets by using the procedure of Karp and Miller. In section 3, we present the basic definition of the minimal coverability graph. We show that the minimal coverability graph allows us to decide the five problems. In Section 4, we give an algorithm which computes the minimal coverability graph by using space economically. In the case of a bounded net, the minimal coverability graph is also more efficient than the Karp and Miller graph as it is often smaller (see remark 4.1). A comparison between the size of the Karp-Miller graph and the size of the minimal coverability graph is made on a Petri net which models the PNCSA communication protocol [PNCSA 88]. These practical results on PNCSA show a gain in time and space of the order 10^4.

2. DECIDABILITY RESULTS OBTAINED BY USING THE KARP-MILLER TREE

Notation and definition 2.1. We denote by N the set of non negative integers and by $N \cup \{\omega\}$ the classical completion of N; the addition and the subtraction are extended on $N \cup \{\omega\}$ so that for every integer $n \in N$, $n+\omega= \omega+\omega=\omega-n=\omega$ and $n<\omega$. A **word** $x \in X^*$ is a sequence (may be empty) of letters of X; X^+ denotes X^* except the empty word. We write $|x|$ for the length of x; we have $|x.x'| = |x| + |x'|$, for every pair of words $x,x' \in X^+$. A language is **regular** when it is recognized by a finite automaton. A **labelled directed graph** is a triple <N,L,A> where N is the set of nodes, L is the set of labels of nodes and A is the set of labelled arcs between nodes (A is a subset of NxLxN). An **elementary circuit** is a circuit whose nodes are $n_1,\ldots,n_k, n_1$ such that for all $i \neq j$, we have $n_i \neq n_j$.
A **tree** is an acyclic labelled directed graph such that (1) there is a unique node r, called the root, from which every node is reachable and moreover (2) there is a unique path from the root r to each node. An **ancestor** n' of a node n is a node such that there is a path from n' to n; the **direct ancestor** n' of a node n is the unique node such that there is an arc from n' to n . A tree is **finitely branching** if every node has only a finite number of direct successors; when a finitely branching tree is infinite, it contains at least one infinite path [Konig...36]. A quasi-ordering on X is a **well quasi-ordering** if from every infinite sequence of X, we can extract

an infinite increasing sequence. We use the **Dickson** well-known result stating that the usual quasi-ordering on N^k is a well quasi-ordering [Dickson 13]. ❑

Definition 2.2. A **Petri net** [Brauer...86] is a four-tuple, PN = < P,T,V,M_0>, where P is the finite set of places, T is the finite set of transitions, V is the function from PxT ∪ TxP to **N** and $M_0 \in N^P$ is the initial marking. A transition t is **fireable from a marking** m if, for every place p, m(p)≥V(p,t). (We use the notation m(p) for the ith component of m if p is the ith place of the net). The **new marking** m' reached in firing t is computed by m'(p)=m(p) - V(p,t) + V(t,p) for every place p ; we write **m(t>m'**. This relation is extended on finite sequences of transitions : $m(t_1...t_n>m'$ means $m(t_1>m_1$ and $m_1(t_2>m_2$, ..., and $m_{n-1}(t_n>m'$. The marking m' is said to be **reachable from m** by firing $t_1...t_n$. The transition function is naturally extended on infinite markings. ❑

Definition 2.3. A marking m is a **deadlock** when no transition is fireable. The **reachability set** of a Petri net PN is denoted by RS(PN) and it is equal to the set of reachable markings from the initial marking M_0. A place p is **bounded** if there exists an integer K≥0 such that for every marking m in the reachability set, we have m(p)≤K. A transition t is **quasi-live** if there exists a marking m in the reachability set such that t is fireable from m. Following the notation used in [Valk...81], we associate an integer denoted by D(p,x), representing the number of tokens the sequence x adds or subtracts in the place p : $D(p,x)=V(t_1,p) - V(p,t_1) + V(t_2,p) - V(p,t_2) +...+V(t_k,p) - V(p,t_k)$ to every sequence of transitions $x = t_1...t_k$ and to every place p∈P. We say that a sequence of markings $\{m_n\}$ **converges** to the marking m' when, for every place p, and for every integer n≥0, if m'(p) ≠ ω then $m_n(p) = m'(p)$ else $m_n(p) \geq n$ (we write $\lim m_n = m'$). ❑

The following example, dealt with in this paper, is taken from the original paper of Karp and Miller [Karp...69].

Example 2.4. Let $PN_1 = < P_1,T_1,V_1,M_{01}>$ where $P_1 = \{p_1, p_2, p_3, p_4, p_5\}$, $T_1 = \{t_1, t_2, t_3, t_4, t_5, t_6\}$, V_1 is the function from $P_1xT_1 \cup T_1xP_1$ to **N** defined by:

$V_1(p_1,t_1) = V_1(p_1,t_2) = V_1(p_3,t_4) = V_1(p_2,t_3) = V_1(p_4,t_5) = V_1(p_5,t_6) = 1$,
$V_1(t_1,p_2) = V_1(t_4,p_2) = V_1(t_2,p_4) = V_1(t_6,p_4) = 1$ and $V_1(t_5,p_5) = V_1(t_3,p_3) = 2$,
$V_1(t_1,p_1) = 0$, ...
and $M_{01} = (1,0,0,0,0)$ is the initial marking.

The reachability set of PN_1 is clearly infinite. Every transition of PN_1 is quasi-live because transitions t_1, t_2, t_3, t_4, t_5 and t_6 are fireable from a reachable marking. ❑

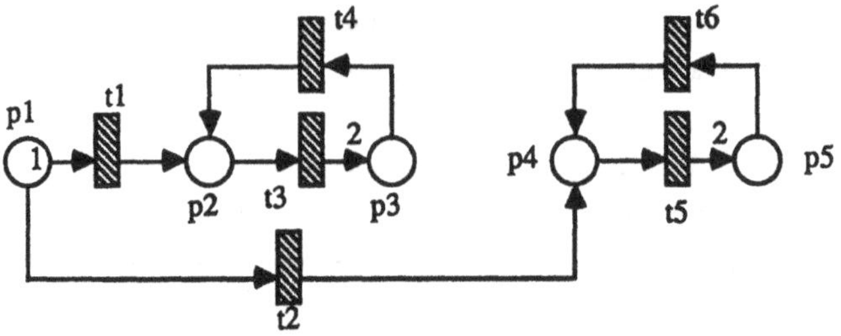

Figure 2.1: Petri net PN1.

The **reachability tree** of a Petri net PN is denoted by RT(PN). It is a rooted tree defined by the following procedure.

```
procedure reachability_tree(PN: Petri net; var RT: tree);          {* the result will be in RT *}
    begin
        unprocessednodes := {create_node(r,M0) };                  {* M0 is the marking of root r *}
        while unprocessednodes ≠ Ø do
            begin
                select some node n∈ unprocessednodes;
                unprocessednodes := unprocessednodes - {n};
                for every transition t such that m(t>m' do   {* m is the marking of node n *}
                    begin
                        create_node+arc((n,t,n'); RT);             {* m' is the marking of node n' *}
                        unprocessednodes := unprocessednodes + {n'};
                    end;
            end;
    end;
```

The procedure works in the following way: while there are unprocessed nodes (unprocessednodes≠Ø), one node n is selected and processed. The processing of a node starts with a loop in which one tests for every transition t : if there is m' such that m(t>m' then one creates a new arc (n,t,n') for all markings m' such that m(t>m'.

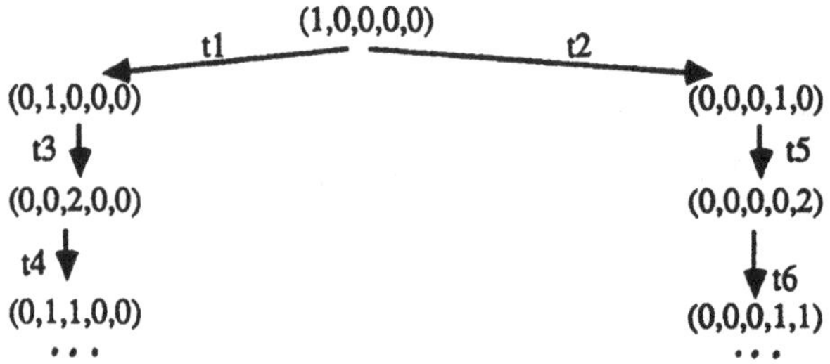

Figure 2.2: the beginning of the reachability tree of PN1

Example 2.5. The reachability tree of PN_1 is infinite (Figure 2.2.).

To have a more simplified figure, we have represented a node by its label. This abbreviation will be often used in the sequel whenever there is no ambiguity. ❑

Definition 2.6. The **reachability graph** RG(PN) is obtained by identifying nodes with the same label. The **language** L(PN) of a Petri net PN is the set of sequences of transitions which are fireable from the initial marking : $L(PN) = \{ x \in T^+ ; M_0(x\rangle \}$. ❑

Example 2.7. The language $L(PN_1)$ contains, for instance, the word t_1t_3 and the finite sequences of transitions $t_2(t_5t_6)^n$ for all integers $n \geq 0$. ❑

Let us briefly recall the definition of a Vector Addition System.

Definition 2.8. An **n-dimensional Vector Addition System** (V.A.S.) is a pair VAS = $\langle s_0, S\rangle$ where s_0 is an n-dimensional vector of non-negative integers, and $S = \{s_1, s_2, ..., s_k\}$ is a finite set of n-dimensional integer vectors. The **reachability set** of VAS is the set of all vectors of the form $s_0 + v_1 + v_2 + ... + v_q$ with $v_i \in S$ and $s_0 + v_1 + v_2 + ... + v_i \geq 0$ for every $i = 1, ..., q$.❑

It is well-known that Vector Addition Systems are equivalent to Petri nets [Kasai...82], [Miller 73], [Peterson...74]. We present an example taken from [Karp...69].

Example 2.9. [Karp...69, page 166] Let $VAS_1 = \langle s_{01}, S_1\rangle$ be the following Vector Addition System :

$s_{01} = (1,0,0,0,0)$ and $S_1 = \{ s_1 = (-1,1,0,0,0), s_2 = (-1,0,0,1,0), s_3 = (0,-1,2,0,0),$
$s_4 = (0,1,-1,0,0), s_5 = (0,0,0,-1,2), s_6 = (0,0,0,1,-1) \}$.
This Vector Addition System VAS_1 is equivalent to the Petri net PN_1. ❑

We are interested in verifying the following properties of a Petri net PN = $\langle P,T,V,M_0\rangle$.

Definition 2.10.

1. The **Finite Reachability Tree Problem (FRTP)** : Is the reachability tree RT(PN) finite ?
2. The **Finite Reachability Set Problem (FRSP)** : Is the reachability set RS(PN) finite ?
3. The **Boundedness Problem (BP)** : Given a place p, is p bounded ?
4. The **Quasi-Liveness Problem (QLP)** : Given a transition t, is t quasi-live ?

5. The **Regularity Problem (RP)** : Is the language L(PN) regular ? ❑

Remark 2.11. The FRSP is often confused with the BP; in general, the BP is more difficult than the FRSP (there are some models based on communicating finite automata for which only the FRSP is known to be decidable [Rosier...83]). For Petri nets, the **Coverability Problem (CP)** (given a marking m, is there a marking m', reachable from the initial marking, such that $m' \geq m$?) is reducible to the Quasi-Liveness Problem (QLP) : in fact, a transition t is quasi-live if and only if there is a reachable marking m such that $m(p) \geq V(p,t)$ for every place p; hence t is quasi-live iff there exists a reachable marking $m \geq (V(p_1,t),...,V(p_p,t))$. Conversely, the CP is also reducible to the QLP: a marking $m = (m_1,...,m_p)$ is covered in PN if and only if the associated transition t_m (t_m is defined by $V(p_i,t_m) = m_i$ and $V(t_m,p_i) = 0$) is quasi-live in the associated new Petri net "PN+$\{t_m\}$". ❑

We recall the algorithm of Karp and Miller and the main decidability results obtained by using the tree it computes. Our presentation of the Karp-Miller tree comes partly from [Jensen 86a]. The **Karp-Miller tree,** KMT(PN), of a Petri net PN = < P,T,V,M₀> is a tree constructed as follows.

```
procedure Karp_Miller_tree(PN: Petri net; var KMT: tree);      (* the result will be in KMT *)
  begin
    unprocessednodes := { create_node(r,M0) };                  (* M0 is the marking of root r *)
    while unprocessednodes ≠ Ø do
      begin
        select some node n∈ unprocessednodes;
        unprocessednodes := unprocessednodes - {n};
        case n : [1..3] of                   (* m is the marking of n and m1 is the marking of n1 *)
          1: there is a node n1 such that n1 is an ancestor of n and m = m1 : exit;   (* exit of case *)
          2: there is a node n1 such that n1 is an ancestor of n and m1<m :
            begin
              m2 := m;
              for all ancestors n1 of n such that m1<m do
                    for all places p such that m1(p)<m(p) do m2(p) := ω;
              m := m2;
              unprocessednodes := unprocessednodes + {n};
              exit;                                                          (* exit of case *)
            end;
          3: otherwise :
            begin
              for every transition t such that m(t>m'  do
                begin
                  create_node+arc((n,t,n'); KMT);   (* m' is the marking of the new node n' *)
                  unprocessednodes := unprocessednodes + {n'};
                end;
              exit;                                                          (* exit of case *)
            end;
      end;                                                                   (* end of while *)
  end;
```

The algorithm works in the following way: as long as there are unprocessed nodes (unprocessed nodes≠∅), one node n is selected and processed. The processing of a node n starts with a test on n : (case 1) if there is an ancestor n_1 of n such that m_1=m then the node n is a leaf and we stop the branch. If there is an ancestor n_1 of n with m_1<m (case 2), then we modify m in the following way : **for** all places p such that $m_1(p)<m(p)$ **do** $m_2(p):=\omega$; and then $m:=m_2$. In case 3, one creates a new node n', for all markings m' such that m(t>m', whose label is m', and a new arc (n,t,n').

Example 2.12. The Karp-Miller tree of PN_1 is shown in Figure 2.3. It has 21 nodes, i.e. more than in [Karp...69], but the "Karp-Miller tree" is not unique ! Another Karp-Miller tree can be obtained by changing the following line :

1: there is a node n_1 such that n_1 is an ancestor of n and m = m_1 : exit; (* exit of case *)

into the new line :

1: there is a node n_1 such that n_1 is not in unprocessednodes and m = m_1 : exit; (* exit of case *).

in procedure Karp-Miller tree. ❑

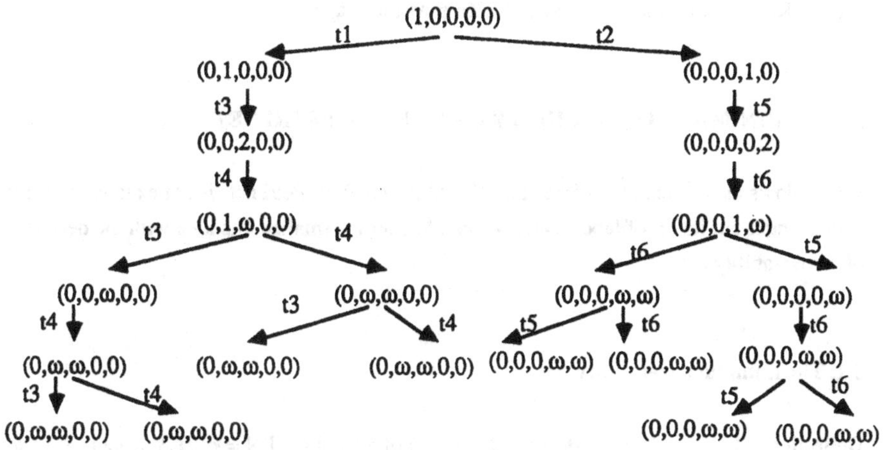

Figure 2.3: the Karp-Miller tree of PN1 (21nodes, 20 arcs)

The associated **Karp-Miller graph** of PN, KMG(PN), is obtained by identifying nodes with the same label.

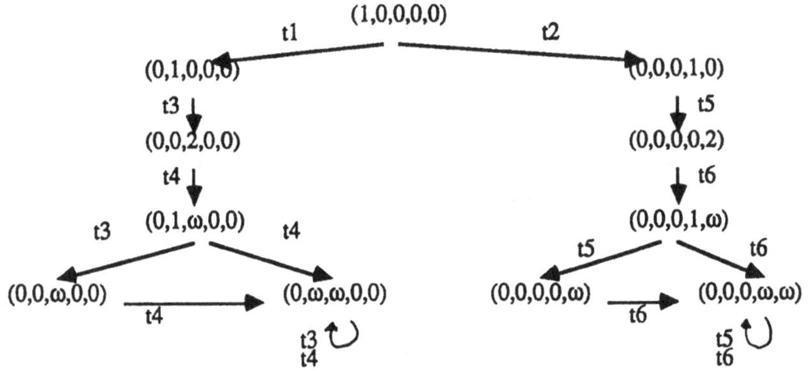

Figure 2.4: the Karp-Miller graph of PN1 (11 markings, 16 arcs)

The following results are well known.

Theorem 2.13.[Karp...69], [Valk...81] For Petri nets, the FRTP, the FRSP, the BP, the QLP and the RP are all decidable by using the Karp-Miller graph.

3. THE MINIMAL COVERABILITY GRAPH OF A PETRI NET

What allows us to decide the FRSP, the BP and the QLP for Petri nets is not exactly the Karp-Miller graph but its set of labels (=markings). We now formalize this idea with the definition of a coverability set.

3.1. The minimal coverability set

Definition 3.1. A **coverability set** CS(PN) of a Petri net PN = <P,T,V,M_0> is a subset of $(N\cup\{\omega\})^P$ such that the two following conditions hold :

1) for every reachable marking $m\in RS(PN)$, there is a marking $m'\in CS(PN)$ such that $m\leq m'$,

2) for every marking $m'\in CS(PN)-RS(PN)$, there is an infinite strictly increasing sequence of reachable markings $\{m_n\}$ converging to m'.

A coverability set CS(PN) is **minimal** iff no proper subset of CS(PN) is a coverability set of PN. ❑

Remark 3.2. A minimal coverability set does not contain two comparable markings. ❑

Proposition 3.3. Given any two coverability sets, their sets of maximal markings are the same and equal to the minimal coverability set.

Mayr has defined in [Mayr 84] a notion which is very close to that of a coverability set; but he does not give the definition of the minimal coverability set because it is out his scope (which is to decide the Reachability Problem but not to minimize coverability graphs).

Lemma 3.4. The minimal coverability set is finite and unique.

Proof. Show that the minimal coverability set is finite. Because the usual quasi-ordering on vectors of integers is a well quasi-ordering (which means that there is no infinite sequence of non-comparable vectors of integers), the minimal coverability set cannot be infinite. Suppose that the minimal coverability set MCS is infinite : hence, we can find two markings m and m' in MCS such that $m<m'$. This is in contradiction to the fact that MCS does not contain two comparable markings.

Let us prove now that the minimal coverability set is unique by assuming the contrary : that there are at least two minimal coverability sets $MCS \neq MCS'$; we decide, for instance, that there is a marking m such that $m \in MCS-MCS'$. There are two cases to consider.

1) m is in the reachability set RS, and, because MCS' is a coverability set, there is a marking $m' \in MCS'$ such that $m \leq m'$. Note that $m<m'$ because $(m=m')$ implies that $(m \in MCS')$ which is in contradiction to the hypothesis. There are still two cases.

1.1) $m' \in RS$, then there exists $m'' \in MCS$ such that $m''>m'>m$, hence m' is unnecessary and MCS is not minimal ! Contradiction.

1.2) $m' \notin RS$, then m' is the limit of a strictly increasing infinite sequence of reachable markings:

$m' = \lim m_n'$. Hence because $m \in RS$, there is an index p such that $m \leq m'_p$. This is in contradiction to the fact that MCS is a minimal coverability set.

2) m is not in the reachability set RS then m is the limit of a strictly increasing infinite sequence of reachable markings : $m=\lim m_n$. There is a marking $m' \in MCS'$ such that for every integer n, we have $m_n \leq m'$. Hence, $\lim m_n \leq m'$ then $m \leq m'$, hence $m<m'$. There are still two cases.

2.1) $m' \in RS$ is not possible because $m'>m$ and m' contains at least an ω.

2.2) $m' = \lim m_n'$. As every minimal coverability set is finite, we deduce that MCS is finite. Then, there exists $m'' \in MCS$ such that for every integer n, we have : $m_n' \leq m''$; hence the following inequality holds : $m' \leq m''$. Here is a contradiction because $m<m' \leq m''$, $m,m'' \in MCS$ and MCS is a minimal coverability set.

Hence there is a unique minimal coverability set. ❑

Theorem 3.5. Let MCS(PN) be the minimal coverability set of a Petri net PN. We have the following equivalences.

1) The reachability set of PN is infinite if and only if there is at least one marking $m \in MCS(PN)$ such that $m(p)=\omega$ for at least one place p.

2) A place p is not bounded if and only if there is at least one marking $m \in MCS(PN)$ such that $m(p)=\omega$.

3) A transition t is quasi-live if and only if there is at least one marking $m \in MCS(PN)$ such that for every place p, we have $m(p) \geq V(p,t)$.

From theorem 3.5., we can immediately deduce the following.

Corollary 3.6. To decide the FRSP, the BP and the QLP, it is sufficient only to compute the minimal coverability set.

Proof of Theorem 3.5. Let MCS(PN) be the minimal coverability set of a Petri net PN = $<P,T,V,M_0>$. Parts 1) and 2) can be deduced from the definition of a coverability set. Here, we only prove the third equivalence. Let m be equal to $m = (V(p_1,t),...,V(p_k,t))$.

3.1) If there is one reachable marking $m' \geq m$, then there is one marking $m'' \in MCS(PN)$ (because of condition 1) of Definition 3.1) such that $m'' \geq m'$. Hence, by transitivity of $\geq$, we obtain $m'' \geq m$.

3.2) If there is one marking $m'' \in MCS(PN)$ such that $m'' \geq m$, then there are two possibilities:

3.2.1) $m'' \in RS(PN)$ and then we can choose $m'=m''$,

3.2.2) $m'' \notin RS(PN)$, hence with the condition 2) of Definition 3.1, there is an infinite strictly increasing sequence of markings $\{m_n\}$ such that:

- $m_n(p)=m''(p)$ for every place p such that $m''(p) \neq \omega$, and,
- $m_n(p) \geq n$ for every place p such that $m''(p)=\omega$.

As $m'' \geq m$, there is one integer $k \geq 0$ such that $m_k \geq m$. One can choose $m'=m_k$. ❑

Example 3.7. The set of labels of the Karp-Miller graph of PN_1 (Figure 2.4.) is equal to $\{(1,0,0,0,0), (0,1,0,0,0), (0,0,2,0,0), (0,1,\omega,0,0), (0,0,\omega,0,0), (0,\omega,\omega,0,0), (0,0,0,1,0), (0,0,0,0,2), (0,0,0,1,\omega), (0,0,0,0,\omega), (0,0,0,\omega,\omega)\}$; this set is a coverability set of PN_1. The minimal coverability set of PN_1 is equal to $\{(1,0,0,0,0), (0,\omega,\omega,0,0), (0,0,0,\omega,\omega)\}$. ❑

The problem now is to construct the **minimal coverability set**. Although the reachability set is always a coverability set, it is not always finite. How to compute the finite minimal coverability set ?

Proposition 3.8. The set of labels of the Karp-Miller graph is a finite and computable coverability set. In general, the set of labels of the Karp-Miller graph is not the minimal coverability set.

Proof. The first part of Proposition 3.8. is proved without the formal definition of a coverability set in [Karp...69]. For the second part, see the set of labels of the Karp-Miller graph and the minimal coverability set of PN_1. ❑

3.2. The minimal coverability graph

We are therefore trying to find an algorithm which can efficiently compute the minimal coverability set. It should not be forgotten that we also wish to decide the FRTP and the RP. For the last two problems, we need to detect the circuits in the minimal coverability graph. Let us first define the minimal coverability graph.

Definition 3.9. A **coverability graph** of a Petri net PN = $<P,T,V,M_0>$ is a labelled directed graph <N,L,A> where the set of nodes N is a coverability set of PN, L=T and there is an arc (m,t,m')∈ A iff m(t>m'. The **minimal coverability graph** of a Petri net PN is the coverability graph such that its set of nodes is the minimal coverability set. ❑

The minimal coverability graph of PN_1 is shown in Figure 3.1.

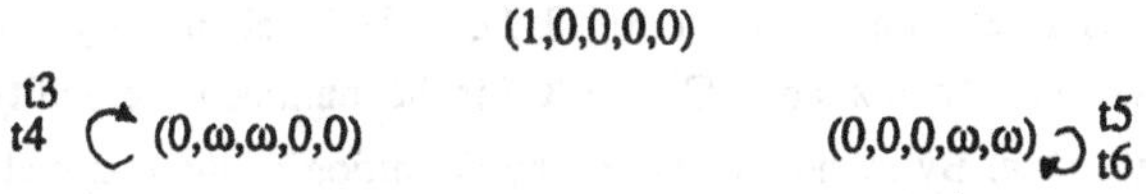

Figure 3.1: the minimal coverability graph of PN1 (3 markings, 4 arcs)

The minimal coverability graph is not necessary connected. In particular, there is no arc between two markings m,m'∈ MCS such that there is a place p such that m(p)<m'(p) = ω. ❑

Remark 3.10. The first definition of coverability graph given in [Finkel 90] specified the same set of nodes but a bigger set of arcs : arcs (m,t,m') such that not m(t>m' are in fact not useful. Let us note that our actual definition of "coverability graph" corresponds to the definition of "precoverability graph" given in [Finkel 89]. This "optimization" of the definition of coverability graphs has been triggered by a remark of R. Devillers about the fact that the algorithm given in [Finkel 90] does not compute the entire first minimal coverability graph : some (not useful) arcs were missing. ❑

Theorem 3.11. Let PN be a Petri net, MCG(PN) its minimal coverability graph and MCS(PN) its minimal coverability set.

1) The reachability tree RT(PN) is infinite if and only if there is at least one circuit in MCG(PN).

2) The reachability set RS(PN) is infinite if and only if there is at least one symbol ω in MCG(PN).

3) A place p is not bounded if and only if there is at least one marking $m \in$ MCS(PN) such that $m(p)=\omega$.

4) A transition t is quasi-live if and only if there is at least one marking $m \in$ MCS(PN) such that for every place p, $m(p) \geq V(p,t)$.

5) The language L(PN) is regular if and only if every elementary circuit of MCG(PN) containing an infinite marking is labelled by a sequence of transitions $x \in T^+$ such that $D(p,x) \geq 0$ for every place p.

The proof of this theorem requires two simple lemmas.

Lemma 3.12. There is at least one circuit in KMG iff there is at least one circuit in MCG.

Proof. As MCG is included in KMG, we only need to prove that if there is at least one circuit in KMG then there is at least one circuit in MCG. Let C be an elementary circuit of KMG such that m(x>m with $m \in C$ and x labels C. As MCS is the minimal coverability set, there is $m' \in$ MCS such that $m' \geq m$. By monotonicity and by definition of the minimal coverability graph, we have m'(x>m' ; hence there is a circuit (non necessary elementary) labelled by x in MCG. ❑

Lemma 3.13. Let MCG(PN) be the minimal coverability graph of PN and KMG(PN) be the Karp-Miller graph of PN. Let C be an elementary circuit in KMG(PN). We have :
If C contains at least one (maximal) marking of MCS(PN) then all markings of C are (maximal) markings in MCS(PN) and C also is an elementary circuit in MCG(PN).

Proof. Let C be an elementary circuit in KMG(PN) such that m(x>m where m is a (maximal) marking of MCS(PN). Suppose that there is one marking m_1 in C such that m_1 is not in MCS : $m(x_1>m_1(x_2>m$. Because the set of labels of MCG(PN) is a coverability set, there is at least one marking $m_1' \in$ MCS(PN) such that $m_1 \leq m_1'$ and $m_1(p)<m_1'(p)$ for a place p. By monotonicity, we have $m_1'(x_2>m_2'$ with $m_2'(p)= m_1'(p) + D(p,x_2) > m_1(p) + D(p,x_2) = m(p)$. Hence $m<m_2'$; this is in contradiction with the fact that m is maximal. Then all markings m_1 in C are maximal ; hence C is an elementary circuit of MCG(PN). ❑

Remark 3.14. The first version of this lemma said that every elementary circuit of KMG was an elementary circuit of MCG. We are indebted to Peter Starke who has shown, on an example, that this was wrong. We have then modified the lemma which still allows us to decide the RP. ❑

Proof of theorem 3.11. Parts 2,3 and 4 are trivial consequences from Theorem 3.5. Let us prove parts 1 and 5.
Let us show 1). From [Karp...69], [Valk...81], we know that the reachability tree is infinite if and only if there is at least one circuit in KMG(PN); by Lemma 3.12., we know that there is at least one circuit in KMG(PN) if and only if there is at least one circuit in MCG(PN). Therefore, we obtain that the reachability tree is infinite if and only if there is at least one circuit in MCG(PN); this is decidable.
We now show 5). From [Valk...81, Theorem 2.3, page 70], the language L(PN) is regular if and only if every elementary circuit C (containing at least one maximal marking) of KMG(PN) is labelled by a sequence of transitions $x \in T^+$ such that for all places p, we have $D(p,x) \geq 0$. By Lemma 3.13, we know that the set of elementary circuits C of KMG(PN) containing at least one maximal marking is exactly the set of elementary circuits C of MCG(PN). Hence, the language L(PN) is regular if and only if every elementary circuit of MCG(PN) is labelled by a sequence of transitions $x \in T^+$ such that for all places p, we have $D(p,x) \geq 0$; this last condition is decidable. ❑

Remark 3.15. To decide the five problems and more particularly the last two, it is sufficient to know if there is a circuit in MCG and to know the characteristic vectors of the words which label the elementary circuits of MCG containing at least one marking with an ω. ❑

Proposition 3.16. The minimal coverability graph is computable, finite and unique.

Proof. We know that the minimal coverability graph is computable (from the Karp-Miller graph, for instance). It is finite because the minimal coverability set and the set of transitions are finite. It is unique because the minimal coverability set is unique and because the definition of the arcs of a coverability graph is unambiguous. ❑

From Theorem 3.11 and Proposition 3.16., we can deduce the following result.

Corollary 3.17. The FRTP, the FRSP, the BP, the QLP and the RP are all decidable by using the minimal coverability graph.

The Karp-Miller graph is finite and is a computable coverability graph. In general, the Karp-Miller graph is not equal to the minimal coverability graph. Indeed, the set of labels of the Karp-Miller graph of PN_1 (Figure 2.4.) is not equal to the minimal coverability set $\{(1,0,0,0,0), (0,\omega,\omega,0,0), (0,0,0,\omega,\omega)\}$.

4. AN ALGORITHM TO COMPUTE THE MINIMAL COVERABILITY GRAPH OF A PETRI NET

4.1. Informal description of the algorithm

It is always possible to compute the minimal coverability graph by computing first the entire Karp-Miller graph, then by computing the subset of maximal markings and in keeping only useful arcs. Unfortunately, the Karp-Miller graph is often not feasible to build because its size is too large : the space **and** the time for building the Karp-Miller graph are in general both very large. Our aim is to obtain an algorithm which **directly** computes the minimal coverability graph **without** computing the whole Karp-Miller graph. We present an algorithm, which uses space economically, for the computation of the minimal coverability graph. This algorithm is based on a new optimization of the Karp-Miller procedure. This algorithm uses four ideas. Two of them appear in [Mayr 84] but they are not introduced to reduce the size of the KMG but rather to decide the Accessibility Problem

- The first idea consists in remarking that Petri nets are monotonic [Brams 83] which means that if $m \leq m_1$ then for every marking m' reached from m, there exists at least one marking m'_1 reached from m_1, such that $m' \leq m'_1$. This remark implies that it is possible (to obtain a coverability tree) to **stop** a branch of the Karp-Miller tree when we meet two markings m and m_1 such that m is reached from m_1 and $m \leq m_1$. We replace the following line in the procedure of Karp and Miller

```
1: there is a node n1 such that n1 is an ancestor of n and m = m1 : exit;   (* exit of case *)
```

with these new lines,

```
1: there is a node n1∈processednodes such that m = m1 :
 begin
         processednodes := processednodes + {n};
         exit;              (* exit of case *)
 end;
2: there is a node n1∈processednodes such that m<m1 :
 begin
         remove_node(n; MCT);
         (* the procedure "remove_node(n: node; var T: tree)" removes the node n and the arc from the ancestor of
         n to n, in the tree T *)
         exit;              (* exit of case *)
 end;
```

Remark 4.1. These new lines will also be interesting in the case of bounded Petri nets. For example, let PN be a Petri net with only one place and one transition such that there is an arc from the place to the transition. The initial marking of the place is 10^q. Therefore the Karp-Miller tree contains 10^q+1 nodes while the optimized Karp-Miller tree only contains a unique node ! ❑

- The second idea is to **compact** the previous reduced Karp-Miller tree during its development. To do it, we continue a marking m if and only if m is not comparable with any computed markings or if m is strictly superior to another computed marking m_1. In the last case, if there is a marking m_1 such that m is reachable from m_1 and $m_1<m$ then we label n by another marking m_2 such that for every place p, if $m(p)>m_1(p)$ then $m_2(p):=\omega$ else $m_2(p):=m(p)$. We also remove the subtree (except the root) whose root is n.

- The third idea is to **remove** every subtree whose root is labelled by a marking m_1 such that $m_1<m_2$ (m_2 is defined as above).

Remark 4.2. The first occurrence of the second and the third idea for constructing reduced Karp-Miller graphs occurs in [Mayr 84] where they are there embedded in another algorithm : E. Mayr points out that the second while-loop of his "refine procedure" in [Mayr 84, page 456] computes a coverability graph by using the compaction technique. J-L. Lambert also

noticed the second idea during an internal seminar about the Accessibility Problem at the University Paris 11 in 1985.
We rediscovered these two ideas in 1989 when we were thinking about an efficient computation of the minimal coverability set of a Petri net. ❑

- The fourth idea is the following : after identifying nodes with the same label, we **only keep** arcs (m,t,m') such that m(t>m'.

Remark 4.3. This last idea was not included in the algorithm exposed in [Finkel 90]. It allows us to exactly obtain the minimal coverability graph. ❑

4.2. The algorithm

We claim that the following procedure computes the minimal coverability graph MCG of a Petri net PN where the main procedure, "minimal_coverability_tree(PN; MCS; MCT)", computes a minimal coverability tree (not unique).

```
procedure minimal_coverability_graph(PN: Petri net; var MCS: set of markings; var MCG: graph);
(* the result will be in MCG *)
   begin
      minimal_coverability_tree(PN; MCS; MCT);
      identify_nodes_having_same_label(MCT; MCG);
      (* the procedure "identify_nodes_having_same_label(T: tree; G: graph)" transforms the tree T into a graph G
      such that two nodes in T having the same label are identified in G *)
      for every arc (m,t,m') of MCG do
      (* after having identify nodes with the same label, we confuse without ambiguity a node and its label *)
            if not ( m(t>m' ) then remove_arc((m,t,m'); MCG);
      (* the procedure "remove_arc((m,t,m'); var G))" only removes the arc (m,t,m') from G *)
   end;

procedure minimal_coverability_tree(PN: Petri net; var MCS: set of markings; var MCT: tree);
(* the result will be in MCT *)
   var unprocessednodes, processednodes: set of nodes; n, n', n1, n2: node; t: transition; ancestor: boolean;
   begin
      unprocessednodes := { create_node(r,M0) };                    (* M0 is the marking of root r *)
      processednodes := Ø;                  (* processednodes will be the minimal coverability set *)
      while unprocessednodes ≠ Ø do
         begin
            select some node n∈ unprocessednodes;
            unprocessednodes := unprocessednodes - {n};
            case n : [1..4] of             (* m is the marking of n and m1 is the marking of n1 *)
                1: there is a node n1∈processednodes such that m = m1 :
                     begin
                        processednodes := processednodes + {n};
                        exit;                                                       (* exit of case *)
                     end;
```

```
        2: there is a node n1∈processednodes such that m<m1 :
              begin
                remove_node(n; MCT);
                exit;                                                        {* exit of case *}
              end;
              {* the procedure "remove_node(n: node; var T: tree)" removes the node n and the arc from the
              direct ancestor of n to n, in the tree T *}
        3: there is a node n1∈processednodes such that m1<m :
            begin
              m2 := m; ancestor := false;
              for all ancestors n1 of n such that m1<m do
                    for all places p such that m1(p)<m(p) do m2(p) := ω;
              if there is an ancestor n1 of n such that m1<m2 then
                 begin
                   ancestor := true;
                   n1 := first node processed, on the path from the root to n such that m1<m2;
                   m1 := m2;
                   remove_tree(n1; MCT);
                   {* the procedure "remove_tree(n: node; var T: tree)" which removes the subtree
                   whose root is n in the tree T (note that we keep the root n) *}
                   remove from(processednodes+unprocessednodes) all nodes of tree(n1;MCT);
                   unprocessednodes := unprocessednodes + {n1};
                 end;
              for every n1∈processednodes such that m1<m2 do
                 begin
                   remove from(processednodes+unprocessednodes) all nodes of tree(n1;MCT);
                   remove_tree(n1; MCT);
                   remove_node(n1; MCT);
                 end;
              if ancestor = false then unprocessednodes := unprocessednodes + {n};
              exit;                                                          {* exit of case *}
            end;
        4: otherwise :
            begin
              for every transition t such that m(t>m' do
                 begin
                   create_node+arc((n,t,n'); MCT);   {* m' is the marking of the new node n' *}
                   {* the procedure "create_node+arc((n,t,n'); T)" creates a new node n' labelled by m'
                   and a new arc (n,t,n') in the tree T *}
                   unprocessednodes := unprocessednodes + {n'};
                 end;
              processednodes := processednodes + {n};
              exit;                                                          {* exit of case *}
            end;
    end;                                                                     {* end of case *}
    unprocessednodes := maximal(unprocessednodes);
    {* the function "maximal(S : set) : set" computes the set of nodes n such that every label(n) is maximal *}
    MCS := {label(n) ; n∈processednodes };
  end;                                                                       {* end of while *}
end;                                                                         {* end of procedure *}
```

Figures 4.1 (a) - (e) explain the construction of the minimal coverability graph in using our algorithm.

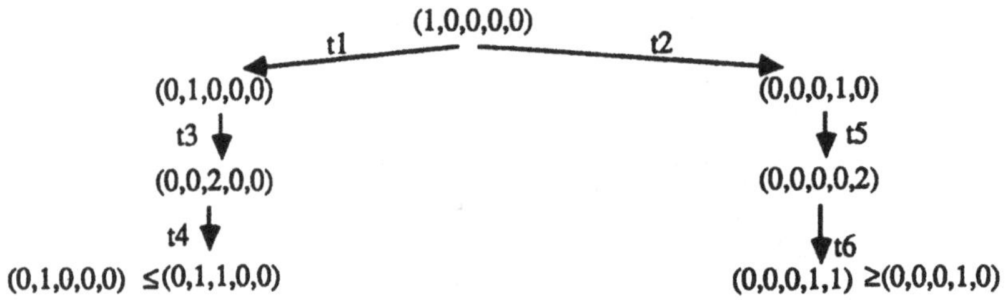

Figure 4.1.(a). We stop because we have reached m'≥m with m-*->m'.

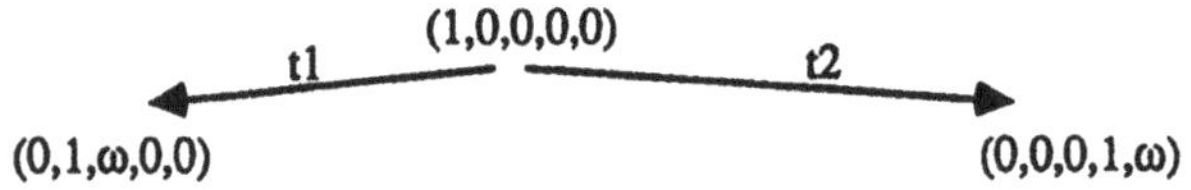

Figure 4.1.(b). We have contracted the two paths.

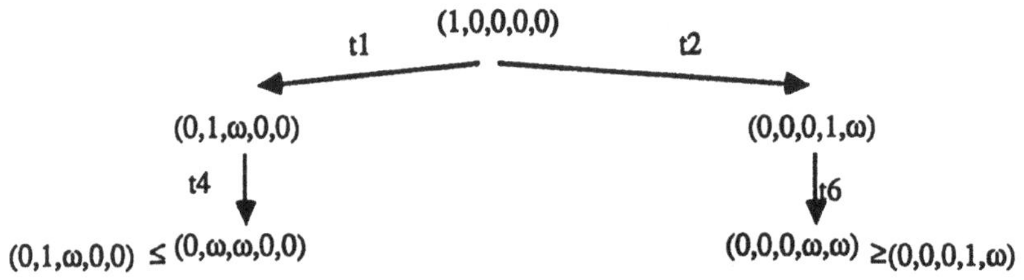

Figure 4.1.(c). We stop because we have reached m'≥m with m-*->m'.

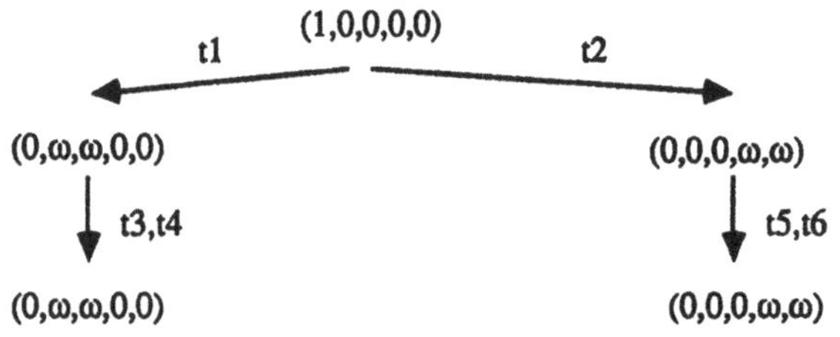

Figure 4.1.(d). The final MCT. We stop because m=m' with m-*->m'.

Figure 4.1.(e). MCG. We have identified nodes having the same label and removed useless arcs.

In case 1, the selected node n is removed from unprocessednodes, included into processednodes and therefore no longer processed. In case 2, the selected node is destroyed. The treatement of a node n begins with a test on n : if there is a node n_1 in processednodes such that $m_1=m$ (case 1) or $m_1>m$ (case 2), then the node n is a leaf (case 1) or we remove node n and the arc going on n (case 2) ; then we leave the case. If there is an ancestor n_1 such that $m_1<m$ (case 3), then we change the label of the first node n1 satisfying $m_1<m$ by m_2 (computed as indicated) ; after which, we remove the subtree whose root is n_1 (we keep the root). After then, we remove (including the root) every subtree whose root is n_1 such that $m_1<m_2$. Else (case 4) for every transition t which is fireable from m, we construct a new node n' labelled by the marking m' and a new arc (n,t,n') such that m(t>m'. After the while-instruction, if there are two nodes n,n' in unprocessednodes such that label(n)=m<m'=label(n') then we remove node n. ❑

4.3. Proof that the algorithm computes the minimal coverability graph

Theorem 4.4. The minimal_coverability_graph procedure computes the minimal coverability graph of a Petri net.

Proof. Let MCT be the tree computed by the minimal_coverability_tree procedure and MCS be the associated set of labels of MCT : one has, at the end of the procedure, MCS=processednodes. Let RS and RT be the reachability set and the reachability tree of PN=(P,T,V,M_0). To verify that the procedure minimal_coverability_graph computes exactly the minimal coverability graph, it is sufficient to prove that the set MCS and the tree MCT computed by the minimal_coverability_tree procedure satisfies the following properties :

1) The set MCS is a **coverability set** :

1.1) For every reachable marking $m\in RS$, there is at least one marking $m'\in MCS$ such that $m\leq m'$.

1.2) For each marking $m'\in MCS-RS$, there is an infinite strictly increasing sequence of reachable markings $\{m_n\}$, $m_n\in RS$, converging to m'.

2) The set MCS is the **minimal** coverability set : it does not contain two different comparable markings.

3) For two markings m, m' of MCS and for a transition t, if we have m(t>m' then there is an arc (n,t,n') in MCT with label(n)=m and label(n')=m'.

4) The minimal_coverability_tree procedure terminates.

Let us prove 1). Property 1.1) can be shown by induction on the length of a path labelled by $x\in T^{*}$ in the reachability tree RT of PN from the root r (label(r)=M_0) to a node n (label(n)=m), then on the length |x|. Let us prove that, for every $x\in T^{*}$, if r-x->m is a path of RT then r'-x'->s' is a path of MCT and label(s)≤label(s').

--> $|x| = 0$.

Then either the root r' of MCT is also labelled by M_0 and then label(r)=$M_0 \leq$label(r')=M_0 or either, by definition of MCT (in the unique case in which we remove the label of the root r', the new label is then strictly superior to the old), r' is labelled by a new marking M'_0 such that label(r')=$M'_0 > M_0$=label(r).

--> Suppose it is true for $|x|=k$. Let us denote $|xt|=k+1$, $|x|=k$ and $t \in T$, and,

r -x-> s_1 -t-> s_2 is a path of RT, and $M_0(x>m_1(t>m_2$.

Then, by the induction hypothesis, there is a path in MCT, labelled by a sequence x', from r' to s'_1 such that $m_1 \leq m'_1$.

r' -x'-> s'_1 is a path of MCT

By monotonicity, the transition t is fireable from m'_1 and we have :

m'_1 (t> m'_2.

There are two cases:

- s'_1 -t-> s'_2 is a path of MCT then label(s'_2)=m'_2 is maximal and $m'_2 \geq m_2$.
- s'_1 -t-> s'_2, with label(s'_2)=m'_2, is not a path of MCT then m'_2 is not maximal. By definition of MCT, there is m''_2 in MCT such that $m''_2 > m'_2$; by transitivity of $\leq$ and because $m'_2 \geq m_2$, we obtain $m''_2 > m_2$.

1.2) We want to show that for every marking m in MCS such that $m \notin RS$, there is an infinite strictly increasing sequence of reachable markings $m_n \in RS$ such that m=lim m_n. This is equivalent to the following formulation: for every node n of MCT such that label(n)=$m \notin RS$, there is an infinite strictly increasing sequence of reachable markings $m_n \in RS$ such that m=lim m_n. We are going to prove 1.2) by induction on the number k of nodes (=markings) containing at least one symbol ω, between the root r' labelled by M_0' (with 1.1.) we have $M_0' \geq M_0$) and a node n' labelled by m' (n' is not counted in k).

--> k=0.

We first deduce that r=r'. This means that every node between r' and s is in the reachability tree RT of PN.

r' -*-> s is a path of RT, and,

r' -*-> s --> n' is a path of MCT.

Then, because of the definition of the algorithm computing MCT and because $m' \notin RS$, we are sure that m' has been computed through case 3. Hence, there are p+1 nodes n_1, n_2,..., n_p, n in the reachability tree RT such that :

r -*-> s --> n_1 -*> n_2 -*-> ... -*-> n_p -*-> n is a path of the reachability tree RT, and,

$m_1 < m$, ..., $m_p < m$. Let us denote by m_i (x_i >m and label(n_i)=m_i; hence, by monotonicity, we have, for every i : m(x_i >.

m_n has only a finite number of components (=places), one deduces that there is a contradiction. Hence the hypothesis is false and the procedure terminates. **End of proof of theorem 4.4.** ❑

The algorithm which computes the minimal coverability graph constructs a **finite** sequence of **finite trees** MCT(k) that only contains **non-comparable** and **maximal markings** (except nodes which can be labelled by equal markings).

4.4. Comparison between the Karp-Miller graph and the minimal coverability graph

We are now interested in comparing the sizes of the Karp-Miller graph (KMG) and of the minimal coverability graph (MCG). The size of a graph is defined by (m,a) where m is the number of markings and a is the number of arcs. The following table shows the sizes of the Karp-Miller graph and of the minimal coverability graph for the Petri net PN_1.

SPACE (markings, arcs)

M_0	(1,0,0,0,0)	(1,1,0,0,0)	(1,1,1,0,0)	(1,1,1,1,0)	(1,1,1,1,1)	(2,2,2,2,2)
KMG	(11,16)	(55,147)	(74,207)	(305,1004)	(417,1401)	>15800
MCG	(3,4)	(2,6)	(2,6)	(1,4)	(1,4)	(1,4)

Table 4.2.

The following table shows the times of the Karp-Miller graph and of the minimal coverability graph for the Petri net PN_1.

TIME

M_0	(1,0,0,0,0)	(1,1,0,0,0)	(1,1,1,0,0)	(1,1,1,1,0)	(1,1,1,1,1)	(2,2,2,2,2)
KMG	0",09	1",61	3",03	57",27	122",97	>44h23'
MCG	0",05	0",15	0",17	0",49	0",49	0",83

Table 4.3.

For a marking (2,2,2,2,2), we have stopped the computation of the Karp-Miller graph after 44 hours and 23 minutes; the non-complete Karp-Miller graph already contained 15.800 nodes. The minimal coverability graph has been computed in 0,83 secondes and it only contains 1 node and 4 arcs. These first practical results show a large diminution for both time and space in comparison with the Karp and Miller graph.

For every integer i,
$UP(i) = \{ label(unprocessednodes(i)) \}$ and $P(i) = \{ label(processednodes(i)) \}$.
We have, for every integer i,

- $UP(i)\neq\emptyset$, finite and maximal, and,
- $P(i)\neq\emptyset$, finite and maximal,
- for every $x\in P(i)$ there is an $y\in P(i+1)$ such that $x\leq y$. We denote it by $P(i)\leq P(i+1)$.

We will prove the following lemmas :

Lemma 4.5. If the procedure does not terminate then there is an infinite sequence of computed markings $\{m_n\}$ such that :
- for every integer $n\geq 1$, we have $m_n<m_{n+1}$,
- we have detected, in a $MCT(k_n)$, a path m_n -*-> m_{n+1} which has been computed and removed.

Proof. Prove that if the procedure does not terminate then there is an infinite sequence of integer i such that $P(i)\neq P(i+1)$. Suppose the contrary. Hence, there is an integer i_0 such that for every $i>i_0$, we have $P(i)=P(i+1)$. Therefore from the step i_0, we never go through cases 3 and 4. Then there is an integer $j>i_0$ such that $UP(j)=\emptyset$ and then the procedure terminates. Contradiction. Hence, there is an infinite sequence $\{P(i_n)\}$ such that $P(i_n)\neq P(i_{n+1})$. For every integer n, we choose a marking $m_{i_n}\in P(i_n)$ such that $m_{i_n}\neq m_{i_1},\ldots, m_{i_{n-1}}$.
From the infinite sequence $\{m_{i_n}\}$ and because $\leq$ is a well-ordering on $(N\cup\{\omega\})^{card(P)}$ and because every considered partial tree is finitely branching, we may extract another infinite sequence of markings $\{m_{j_n}\}$ such that, for every integer $n\geq 1$, we have :

- $m_{j_n}<m_{j_{n+1}}$, and,
- m_{j_n} -*-> $m_{j_{n+1}}$ is a path computed and removed in a $MCT(k_n)$. ❑

Lemma 4.6. If $m<m'$ and there is an integer k such that the path m -*-> m' has been computed and removed in a MCT(k) then there is at least a place p such that $m(p)<m'(p)=\omega$.

Proof. By application of the treatment of case 3 in the procedure. ❑

From Lemma 4.5., we deduce that there is an infinite sequence m_n such that for every integer n, $m_n<m_{n+1}$ and we have detected, in a $MCT(k_n)$, a path m_n -*-> m_{n+1} which has been then removed.
But, if $m_n <m_{n+1}$ and m_n, m_{n+1} are in a partial minimal coverability tree $MCT(k_n)$ then (by Lemma 4.6.) there is at least one place p such that $m_n(p)<m_{n+1}(p)=\omega$; because every marking

For every integer $n \geq 1$, let us denote by $m_1((x_1x_2...x_p)^n > u_n$. Hence, $\{u_n\}$ is an infinite strictly increasing sequence of reachable markings such that :

$$(\forall n \geq 1) \quad u_n\, (x_1x_2...x_p > u_{n+1} \text{ and } \lim u_n = m'.$$

--> Suppose that it works for k=q and let us show it for k=q+1.

Let n' be a node of MCT such that there are q+1 nodes $n_1, n_2, \ldots, n_{q+1}$ from the root r' to n' such that for all i, $m_i(p)=\omega$ for at least one place p.

$$r' \text{ -*-> } s \text{ --> } n_1 \text{ -> } n_2 \text{ --> } \ldots \text{ --> } n_{q+1} \text{ -t-> } n' \text{ is a path of MCT.}$$

By the induction hypothesis, we know that there is an infinite strictly increasing sequence $\{u_n\}$, $u_n \in (N \cup \{\omega\})^{card(P)}$, (card(P) is the number of places of PN), such that $\lim u_n = m_{q+1}$ with $label(n_{q+1})=m_{q+1}$. Two cases are possible.

1.2.1.) t is fireable from m_{q+1} and we reach the marking m' : $m_{q+1}(t > m'$.

Then, there is an integer n_0 such that for every integer $n \geq n_0$, $u_n(t > v_n$ and $v_n \in RS$.

We obtain $m' = \lim v_n$.

1.2.2.) t is fireable from m_{q+1} and we reach the marking $h_1 \neq m'$; let us denote $m_{q+1}(t > h_1$. We have $h_1 \notin RS$. There were p+1 nodes $g_1, g_2, \ldots, g_p$, g in a previous partial version of MCT such that for every i, $label(g_i) < label(g)$ and which contains the following path :

$$r' \text{ -*-> } s \text{ --> } n_1 \text{ -> } n_2 \text{ --> } \ldots \text{ --> } n_{q+1} \text{ -t-> } g_1 \text{ -*-> } g_2 \text{ -*->} \ldots, \text{ -*-> } g_p \text{ -*-> } g.$$

Let us denote h = label(g) and for every i, $h_i = label(g_i)$ and $h_i(x_i > h$. By monotonicity, we have, for every integer n, $h_1((x_1...x_p)^n > v_n$; hence, there is an infinite strictly increasing sequence of markings $\{v_n\}$ such that : $(\forall n \geq 1) \quad v_n(x_1x_2...x_p > v_{n+1}$.

By applying the algorithm, we contract the previous path in the following one :

$$r' \text{ -*-> } s \text{ --> } n_1 \text{ -> } n_2 \text{ --> } \ldots \text{ --> } n_{q+1} \text{ -t-> } g_1,$$

where g_1 is now labelled by $\lim v_n$. Don't forget that in fact $n' = g_1$; hence $m' = \lim v_n$. We have not completely finished because every marking v_n is not a reachable marking: $v_n \notin RS$. But, for every integer j, there is an integer n(j) such that $u_{n(j)}(t.(x_1...x_p)^j > w_{j,n(j)}$. We obtain $m' = \lim w_{j,n(j)}$ and $\{w_{j,n(j)}\}$ is an infinite strictly increasing sequence of reachable markings.

2) By construction, it is clear that two different markings of MCS are not comparable. Therefore, with part 1), the set MCS is the minimal coverability set.

3) By construction.

4) Let us show that the procedure terminates. Let us suppose the contrary; there is an infinite number of rounds in the while-loop. Let us denote by unprocessednodes(i) (processednodes(i), resp.) the value of the set unprocessednodes (processednodes, resp.) after the i-th passage in the while-loop; MCT(i) is the partial tree computed after the i-th passage in the while-loop.

Example 4.7. The communication protocol PNCSA (Standard Protocol for Connection to the Authorisation System) [PNCSA 88], developed by SLIGOS, is used by the GIE Carte Bleue and VISA for their authorisations of electronic payment. It has been partially verified in [Moreau 89]. The following Petri net (Figure 4.4) describes a part of this protocol. We have verified this protocol with the minimal coverability graph, but the verification has not been possible with the Karp-Miller graph, it has not been computed because of its large size and time of computation (see Table 4.5).

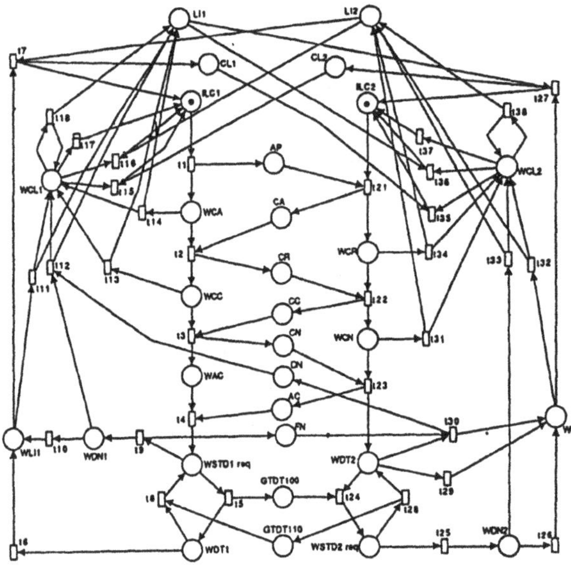

Figure 4.4. The initial marking M_0 is defined as a token in each place I.LC.

M_0	SPACE	TIME
KMG	>7000 markings	>16 hours
MCG	**81 markings**	**62 secondes**

Table 4.5.

The time for computing KMG is very large because, for every marking m, one needs to compare m with all previously computed markings. Let us note that we have not used hashing methods for KMG and MCG. Hence, these two times are mainly interesting because they give an indication about the efficiency of MCG compared to KMG.

Verification of the net : the places AP,CA,CC,CL,CR,FN,DN,LI,GTDT100 and GTDT110 are not bounded; the net is quasi-live.

The computations of the sizes of the Karp-Miller graph and of the minimal coverability graph come from the implementations realized principally by Jean-Marie Moreau, Colette Johnen and Laure Petrucci.

5. CONCLUSIONS AND FUTURE WORK

Let us recall that we have exhibited the minimal coverability graph for Petri nets which allows us to decide the five problems. The practical results on PNCSA show a **large gain**, both in time and space. The results are presented for the Petri nets model but they also apply for several formalisms which are in some sense equivalent [Kasai...82] to it. These formalisms include, (finite) Coloured Petri nets [Jensen 86a], Vector Replacement Systems, Vector Addition Systems and Vector Addition Systems with States [Karp...69].

The loss of information by computing the minimal coverability graph instead of the Karp-Miller graph only concerns us when we are interested in detecting deadlocks. Indeed, it is possible that deadlocks being in the Karp-Miller graph are not in the minimal coverability graph. But the Karp-Miller graph does not detect **every** deadlock and cannot allow us to decide whether there is a deadlock or not. Therefore, we do not lose important information by computing the minimal coverability graph instead of the Karp-Miller graph.

The minimal coverability graph defined in this paper (which corresponds to the minimal precoverability graph defined in [Finkel 89]) seems to be the minimal structure for solving the five mentioned problems.

The minimal coverability graph is always smaller than, or equal to, the Karp-Miller graph. We think that a theoretical study of the (upper/lower) **complexity** of the algorithm given here will give the same general results as those obtained by Lipton, Rackoff, Howell and Rosier. For the Coverability Problem, a lower bound of $O(2^{c*m})$ space was shown in [Lipton 76] for a constant c, where m represents the number of bits necessary to describe the Petri net. An upper bound for the Coverability Problem and the Finite Reachability Set Problem (this last problem is called the Boundedness Problem in [Rackoff 78]) was given by Rackoff who presented an algorithm requiring at most $O(2^{c*m*\log m})$ space. This upper bound has been refined in [Howell...87] by decomposing the parameter m into three other parameters. Our opinion is that for certain subclasses of Petri nets, the complexity of the procedure which computes the minimal coverability graph is smaller than that of the procedure of Karp and Miller.

Valk and Jantzen have proved in [Valk...85] that the Karp-Miller procedure can be used for associating a labelled Petri net PN' to every Petri net PN, such that the set of finite sequences of transitions of PN which can be infinitely continued is exactly that of PN' (modulo a projection). Moreover, there is no finite sequence of transitions that cannot be continued in PN'. The algorithm computing the minimal coverability graph can be used (instead of the Karp-Miller graph) to quickly construct the Petri net PN'.

K. Jensen et al. have shown how equivalences between markings can be used to reduce the size of the Karp-Miller tree [Jensen 86a]. Their idea is as follows: when one meets a marking m which is equivalent to another computed marking m' on a branch of the Karp-Miller tree, one does not develop the branch from m. We propose to integrate this idea in our algorithm which will compute a minimal coverability graph (depending on an equivalence relation) for Coloured Petri nets with equivalences on markings. Laure Petrucci has already proposed two possible algorithms integrating this idea [Petrucci 91].

Our construction of the minimal coverability graph can be generalized to a more powerful model than Petri nets, called the well-structured labelled transition systems model [Finkel 90]. In particular, certain classes of Communicating Finite State Machines which represent communication protocols [Finkel 88] are well-structured. This extension will be presented in another paper.

An implementation of the minimal coverability graph for Petri nets has been realized by J-M. Moreau at the University Paris 11 and at the SLIGOS. The implementation runs in C language on a SUN 3/50 (4 Mbyte, 68020 CPU). It is integrated to the tools PAPE (CEDRIC-CNAM Evry, LIFAC-ENS Cachan, LRI-University Paris 11), AMI (MASI-University Paris 6) and MACAO (SLIGOS).

ACKNOWLEDGEMENTS

The idea to compute directly the minimal coverability graph without computing the whole Karp-Miller graph arose during a discussion about Petri nets at the University of Toulouse with Pierre Azema, Jean-Pierre Courtiat and Michel Diaz.

The main results of this paper have been presented at seminars at the Universities of Paris 6, Paris 7, Paris 11 and the University of Amiens during the first semester of 1989. They were also presented at "the Journées Firtech 1990" and at the 11th International Conference on Application and Theory of Petri Nets. The author is very grateful for the many helpful suggestions to improve the presentation by the participants of seminaries and by anonymous referees of the Petri Net Conference and of the Advances in Petri Nets. In particular, Remark 3.2 and Proposition 3.3 have been included following the remarks from one of the referees.

Raymond Devillers pointed that the algorithm given in [Finkel 90] does not exactly compute the complete minimal coverability graph. From the algorithm described in [Finkel 90], we have constructed the minimal coverability graph by removing some unuseful arcs.

I also wish to thank Peter Starke for his attentive reading of the algorithm given in [Finkel 90]; he detects, on a counterexample, that a sequence which labels an elementary circuit in KMG does not necessarily labels an elementary circuit in MCG. From this remark, we show, in Lemma 3.13, that every elementary circuit of KMG, such that at least one marking is maximal, is also an elementary circuit of MCG; this is sufficient to decide the Regularity Problem.

I would like to thank the two anonymous referees whose comments and suggestions helped me in improving the final version of the paper.

At last, Colette Johnen and Laure Petrucci have spent quite a few hours discussions with me about different versions of this algorithm. Many thanks. I also wish to thank Ruxandra Ispas, Deirdre Lemass and Michel Petit for their careful reading of the second version of this paper.

6. REFERENCES

- Baker H. (1973) "Rabin's Proof of the Undecidability of the Reachability Set Inclusion Problem of Vector Addition Systems", MIT Project MAC CSGM 79, Cambridge, MA.

- Berthelot G. (1986) "Transformations and decompositions of nets" in Advances in Petri nets 1986, Part 1, in the Proceedings of an Advanced Course at Bad Honnef, in Lecture Notes in Computer Science No. 254, pp. 359-376, Springer Verlag.
- Best E. (1986) "Structure theory of Petri nets: the free choice hiatus", in Advances in Petri nets 1986, Part 1, in the Proceedings of an Advanced Course at Bad Honnef, in Lecture Notes in Computer Science No. 254, pp. 168-206, Springer Verlag.
- Brams (1983) "Réseaux de Petri: théorie et pratique", Masson.
- Brauer W., Reisig W. and Rosenberg G. (1986) (Eds) "Petri nets: central models and their properties", Advances in Petri nets 1986, Part 1, in the Proceedings of an Advanced Course at Bad Honnef, in Lecture Notes in Computer Science No. 254, Springer Verlag.
- Dickson L.E. (1913) "Finiteness of the odd perfect and primitive abundant numbers with n distinct prime factors", in Amer. J. Math. 35 pp. 413-422.
- Finkel A. (1987) "A generalization of the procedure of Karp and Miller to well structured transition systems ", in the 14th International Colloquium Automata Languages Programming, Karlsruhe, F.R.G., in Lecture Notes in Computer Science No. 267, pp. 499-508. A complete version is published in Information and Computation under the tittle "Reduction and covering of infinite reachability trees", Vol. 89, No. 2, pp. 144-179, (1990).
- Finkel A. (1988) "A new class of analyzable CFSMs with unbounded FIFO channels", in the 8th International Symposium on Protocol Specification, Testing, and Verification, Atlantic City.
- Finkel A. (1989) "A minimal coverability graph for Petri nets", Rapport interne de l'Université Paris 11, L.R.I., No. 501.
- Finkel A. (1990) "A minimal coverability graph for Petri nets", (another version of the previous one which does not contain the precoverability graph definition) in the proceedings of the 11th International Conference on Application and Theory of Petri Nets.
- Finkel A. and Johnen C. (1991) "Construction efficace du graphe de couverture minimal : applications à l'analyse de protocole", Rapport interne de l'Université Paris 11, L.R.I. Submitted.
- Gouda M. (1984) "Proving liveness for networks of communicating finite state machines", in Proceedings 3rd. Annual ACM Symposium on Principles of distributed Computing.
- Hack M. (1976) "The Equality Problem for Vector Addition Systems is undecidable", in Theoretical Computer Science 2, pp. 77-95.
- Howell R. and Rosier L. "Recent results on the complexity of problems related to Petri nets", Advances in Petri nets 1987, in Lecture Notes in Computer Science No. 266, pp. 45-72.
- Jensen K. (1986a) "Coloured Petri nets", in "Petri nets: Central models and their properties", Advances in Petri nets 1986, Part 1, Lecture Notes in Computer Science No. 254, pp. 248-299.

- Jensen K. (1986b) "Computer tools for construction, modification and analysis of Petri nets", in "Petri nets: Applications and Relationships to other models of concurrency", Advances in Petri nets 1986, Part 2, Lecture Notes in Computer Science No. 255, pp. 4-19.

- Johnen C. (1987) "Analyse algorithmique des réseaux de Petri: vérification d'espace d'accueil, systèmes de réécriture", Thèse de Doctorat, Université Paris 11 (Orsay).

- Karp R.M. and Miller R.E. (1969) "Parallel program schemata", in Journal of Computing S.S. (4) pp. 147-195.

- Kasai T. and Miller R.E. (1982) "Homomorphisms between models of parallel computation", in J.C.S.S. 25 pp. 285-331.

- König D. (1936) "Theorie der Endlichen und Unendlichen Graphen", in Akademische Verlags-gesellschaft, Leipzig.

- Kosaraju S.R. (1982) "Decidability of reachability in vector addition systems", in the Proceedings of the 14th Annual ACM STOC, pp. 267-281.

- Kruckeberg (1987) "Mathematical methods for calculating invariants in Petri nets", Advances in Petri nets 1987, in Lecture Notes in Computer Science No. 266, pp. 104-131.

- Lambert J.-L. (1987) "Le problème de l'accessibilité dans les réseaux de Petri", Thèse de Doctorat, Université Paris 11 (Orsay).

- Lautenbach K. (1986) "Linear algebraic techniques for Place/Transition nets" in "Petri nets: Central models and their properties", Advances in Petri nets 1986, Part 1, Lecture Notes in Computer Science No. 254, pp. 142-167.

- Lipton R. (1976) "The reachability problem requires exponential space", Yale University, Dept. of CS., in Report No. 62.

- McAloon K. (1984) "Petri nets and large finite sets", in Theoretical Computer Science 32, pp. 173-183.

- Mayr E.W. (1984) "An algorithm for the general Petri net reachability problem", in SIAM J. Computing, Vol. 13, No. 3.

- Miller R.E. (1973) "A comparison of some theoretical models of parallel computation", in IEEE Trans. Comput. C-22, pp. 710-717.

- Moreau J-M. (1989) "Graphe de couverture minimal dans les réseaux de Petri", mémoire de DEA, Université d'Orléans.

- Peterson and Bredt (1974) "A comparison of models of parallel computation", in Proc. IFIP Congress 74, North Holland, Amsterdam, pp. 466-470.

- Petri C. A. (1962) "Kommunikation mit Automaten", Institut fur instrumentelle Mathematik (Bonn), Schriften des IMM Nr. 2.

- Petrucci L. (1991) "Techniques d'analyse des réseaux de Petri algébriques", Thèse de Doctorat de l'Université Paris 6.

- PNCSA (1988) GIE CB: "Protocole normalisé de connexion au système d'autorisation: spécifications PNCSA Version 2", document C "Communication OSI".
- Rackoff C. (1978) "The covering and boundedness problems for vector addition systems", in Theoretical Computer Science 6, pp. 223-231, North Holland.
- Reisig W. (1985) "Petri nets", in EATCS Monographs on Theoretical Computer Science, Springer Verlag.
- Reutenauer C. (1988) "Aspects mathématiques des réseaux de Petri", Masson.
- Rosier L.E. and Gouda M.G. (1983) "Deciding progress for a class of communicating finite state machines", internal report of the University of Texas at Austin, TR-83-22.
- Valk R. and Vidal-Naquet G. (1981) "Petri nets and regular languages", in J.C.S.S. 23 (3) pp. 229-325.
- Valk R. and Jantzen M. (1985) "The residue of vector sets with applications to decidability problems for Petri nets", in Acta Informatica 21, pp. 643-674.

7. ANNEX: a formal definition of A coverability tree and of THE minimal coverability forest

To fix a coherent terminology, we define a coverability tree as follows.

Definition 7.1. A **coverability tree** CT(PN) of a Petri net PN = <P,T,V,M0> is a labelled directed tree <N,L,A> where the set of nodes N is a coverability set of PN, L=T and arcs (n,t,n') of A (with label(n)=m and label(n')=m') are of types (1) or (2) :

(1) if m(t>m' then there is an arc (n,t,n')∈ A;

(2) if m(t> and if (not (m(t>m')) then there is an infinite sequence of finite sequences of transitions $\{tx_n\}$ such that for every n≥0, the sequence of transitions tx_n is fireable from m, we reach a marking m_n and the sequence $\{m_n\}$ converges to m' : m(tx_n>m_n and $\lim m_n = m'$.❑

Definition 7.2. A **minimal coverability tree** of a Petri net PN, MCT(PN), is a coverability tree such that its set of nodes is the minimal coverability set. The **unique minimal coverability forest** of a Petri net PN, MCF(PN), is obtained from a minimal coverability tree by removing all arcs of type (2). ❑

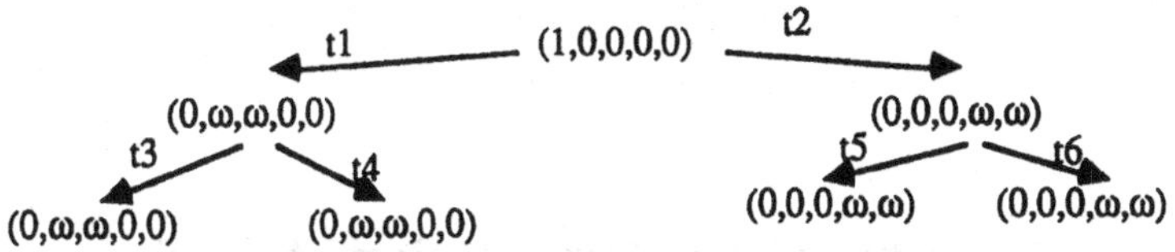

Figure 7.1: a minimal coverability tree of PN1
(7 nodes, 6 arcs)

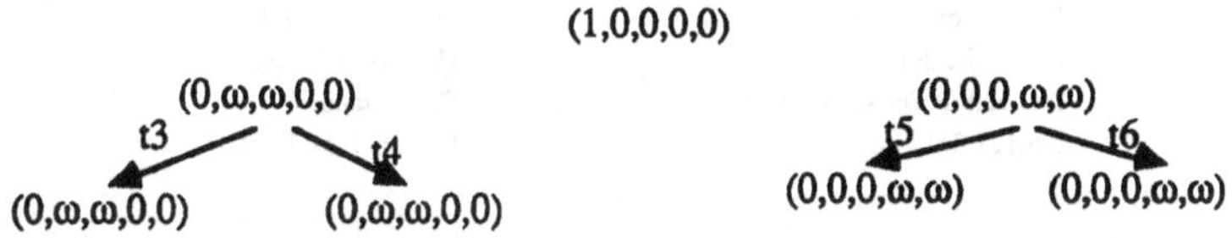

Figure 7.2: the minimal coverability forest of PN1
(7 nodes, 4 arcs)

Proposition 7.3.

1) There is not a unique minimal coverability tree.

2) There is a unique minimal coverability forest.

3) The minimal_coverability_tree procedure computes a minimal coverability tree.

Proof. Parts 1) and 2) are easy consequences of Definition 7.2. Part 3) follows from the proof of Theorem 4.4. ❑

Distributed Implementation of CCS

Roberto GORRIERI

Dipartimento di Matematica,
Università di Bologna,
Piazza di Porta S. Donato 5,
I-40127 Bologna ITALY

Ugo MONTANARI

Dipartimento di Informatica,
Università di Pisa,
Corso Italia 40,
I-56125 Pisa, ITALY

ABSTRACT. A distributed semantics for CCS is given by implementing Milner's Calculus of Communicating Systems onto a simpler calculus of Place/Transition Petri Nets. The net calculus, called SCONE$^+$, is an extension of SCONE [GM90], which has the finer grained operation of local nondeterministic choice, with some operations for modelling restriction and relabelling. In this way, full CCS can be given a net implementation in a purely algebraic way. The complex CCS operation of global nondeterminism is implemented by means of a suitable mapping, which makes explicit the fact that certain CCS transitions are implemented as SCONE$^+$ computations to be executed atomically. To this aim, CCS and SCONE$^+$ are given an operational semantics in algebraic form. In this way, the mapping from CCS transitions to SCONE$^+$ computations becomes simply an algebraic morphism, which can be interpreted as a denotational semantics for CCS having SCONE$^+$ as interpretation domain. The semantics of CCS obtained by quotienting the CCS transition system w.r.t. the implementation mapping is equivalent to the concurrent semantics by "permutation of transitions", as proposed in [BC90, FM90].

Keywords: Place/Transition Petri nets, concurrent calculi, net calculi, operational semantics, denotational semantics, atomicity, implementation morphism.

CONTENTS

Research partially supported by Esprit BRA n. 3011, project CEDISYS, and by Progetto Finalizzato Informatica e Calcolo Parallelo, Obiettivo LAMBRUSCO.

The first author did most of the work when he was with the Dipartimento di Informatica of Pisa University.

0. Introduction

In the last decade there has been a long fruitful debate between the advocates of the so-called "interleaving" approach and those of the "true-concurrent" one, whose arguments ranged from theoretical suitability to practical utility. The main merit of the "interleaving" approach is its well-established theory; unfortunately, there is a serious drawback because it relies on the well-known idea of describing system behaviours as sequences of transitions, perhaps too simplistic a view in many practical cases, when information about distribution in space, about causal dependency or about fairness must be provided. On the other side, in the "true-concurrent" approach, which started from the pioneering work of Petri [Pet62] with his net theory, this kind of information can be easily given, but net theory has not yet reached a completely satisfactory theoretical treatment compared with the assessed results coming from the interleaving side, at least when describing concurrent languages. Rephrasing and extending the ideas developed for the interleaving approach to the "true concurrent" case could be considered one of the main goals in concurrency theory. The present paper aims at giving a contribution in this direction.

Recently, several attempts have been done towards a unifying approach to concurrency. In particular, the work developed in Pisa is mainly concerned with the definition of a uniform algebraic framework in which specifications based both on transition systems and on Petri nets fit rather naturally [CFM90]. This investigation started with [MM88, MM90], where the basic model of Place/Transition Petri Nets has received an immediate categorical description by showing that a P/T net can be *statically* described as an ordinary directed graph equipped with a commutative monoidal operation ⊕ on nodes, and *dynamically* as a graph with also two operations on transitions (⊗ of parallel composition and ; of sequential composition), together with suitable axioms for identifying computations. In [DMM89] *firing* and *step sequences* as well as *concatenable processes* (a slight variant of *nonsequential* processes [GR83]) and Best/Devillers processes [BD87] (also called *commutative* processes) are given an intuitive algebraic axiomatization on the algebra of net computations.

By observing that transition systems are nothing but ordinary directed graphs with labelled transitions, we discover that the notion of graph is a possible unifying mathematical tool for investigating the relationship between the two approaches. Moreover, it can be easily shown that an SOS specification [Plo81], i.e. the interleaving operational definition of a language, can be described in algebraic form: the transition system is a two-sorted algebra with states and transitions as sorts [MY89, FM90, GM90]. Therefore, the other common link between the two approaches is the algebraic structure for nodes and transitions. Indeed, SOS specifications and Petri Nets are both specializations of the graph concept obtained by adding algebraic structure on nodes and transitions: thus, graphs defined as two-sorted algebras represent the uniform framework we were looking for.

A calculus for nets can be introduced by defining an algebra for the nodes of the graph possessing also the commutative monoidal operator ⊕. In [GM90], as a case study, we have introduced a Simple Calculus Of NEts (SCONE), whose combinators are the local choice operator and, similarly to CCS, (a family of) the prefix operator(s), the synchronization one and the recursive definition construct. Moreover, we showed how RCCS — the subset of CCS without restriction and relabelling — can be implemented in SCONE, by means of a suitable mapping from its transition system to the Petri Net of SCONE. RCCS agents are mapped to SCONE markings by considering prefixed (μ.E) and nondeterministically composed (E+E') agents as places and by interpreting parallel composition as multiset union of places. The implementation of RCCS transitions is less immediate and has been greatly influenced by the categorical formulation of Petri Nets proposed in [MM90], which provides a flexible tool for relating system descriptions at different levels of abstraction by means of morphisms, called *implementation* morphisms, in the category of net computations: a net transition can be mapped to an entire net computation. As a matter of fact, the combinators of SCONE are sometimes more elementary than those of RCCS, so that a RCCS transition may be mapped to a SCONE computation. Thus, the morphism maps basic operators of RCCS to derived operators of SCONE, as well as net transitions to net computations. The relevance of the result presented in [GM90] is that this mapping can be seen as a method for implementing concurrent languages (also in interleaving form) into others (possibly distributed). We want to stress that even if the implementation mapping details the description level, it does not affect the granularity of the execution: since an RCCS transition is executed atomically, the execution of the SCONE computation implementing it must be atomic as well. This is a natural consequence of our algebraic approach.

Furthermore, the SCONE Place/Transition net implementing an RCCS agent has been proved to be always finite (but not safe). Relevant related works on RCCS distributed implementation are [Gol88a, Gol88b, Tau89]. The semantics obtained by quotienting RCCS computations with respect to the implementation mapping turned out to be "sound and complete" with respect to the semantics defined directly on the transition system by the so-called "permutation of transitions" technique [BC89, FM90], which moreover is equivalent [FM90 BC90] to Winskel's event structure denotational semantics [Win82].

The present paper comes in pair with [GM90] and represents another example of application of the methodology for giving a uniform treatment to interleaving and true concurrency. Indeed, here we extend to the case of full CCS the results presented there; in particular, the technique of implementing a language into a simpler and distributed one. To this aim, we define a new calculus for nets, called SCONE$^+$ (extending SCONE with restriction and relabelling) as the target machine through which we give a distributed implementation of CCS.

There are some major differences when considering full CCS. First of all, we have to cope with the complexity of other operations; restriction, in particular, is a rather difficult operator to be modelled in a net. Following the idea behind [DDM85, DDM88], restriction is modelled by means of a syntactic construction which leads, as side effect, to a 1-safe P/T net representation of the reachable subnet implementing a CCS agent. The basic idea is that parallel composition is no more modelled by multiset union, rather by disjoint union of places (see Section 2 and the final remark for more details). Therefore, the net implementation of RCCS agents according to the present construction is rather different from the one in [GM90] whenever parallel composition is present. In particular, if in the body of a recursion construct a variable occurs within a parallel context (like in rec x. nil|β.x), then the resulting net associated to this RCCS agent is infinite. Nonetheless, for the RCCS agents not in this class, it may be proved that the net representation is finite. Moreover, for the RCCS subcalculus without parallel composition, the two net implementations coincide syntactically.

From the other hand, just because the resulting net is 1-safe, we can exploit the simpler algebra of commutative processes [BD87, MM90] because we know that for 1-safe nets concatenable and commutative processes coincide (thus causal dependencies are carefully represented also by commutative processes). In this way, the rather complex treatment of token exchanges, which is typical of concatenable processes [DMM89], can be completely removed in favour of a more accessible semantics which assumes commutative the operation of parallel composition of processes.

We will prove that the semantics we give to CCS agents as factorization of their computations with respect to the implementation mapping is *exactly* the same semantics proposed by [BC89, FM90, BC90] which is called "permutation of transitions".

The paper is organized as follows. A brief account of the algebraic formulation of Petri nets and the axiomatization of its commutative processes is presented in Section 1, where also the SOS specification of CCS in algebraic form is given. In Section 2 the proposed calculus of nets SCONE$^+$ is introduced, while in Section 3 we describe the implementation mappings from CCS to SCONE$^+$ and some considerations about the induced semantics are reported in Section 4. Finally, in Section 5, some comments on the relation between P/T nets and the chemical abstract machine [BB90, CG89] are presented.

1. Background

1.1 Safe Nets and Commutative Processes

Here we recall from [MM90] the definition of Petri (Place/Transition) Nets and the $\mathcal{T}[N]$ construction, giving an algebraic definition of Best/Devillers (commutative) processes [BD87].

Definition 1.1. *(Graph)*
A graph G is a quadruple $N = (V, T, \partial_0, \partial_1)$, where V is the set of nodes (or states), T is the set of arcs (or transitions), and ∂_0, ∂_1 are two functions, called source and target respectively: $\partial_0, \partial_1: T \rightarrow V$. A graph morphism from G to G' is a pair of functions <f,g>, $f: T \rightarrow T'$ and $g: V \rightarrow V'$ which preserve the source and the target functions: $g \cdot \partial_0 = \partial_0' \cdot f$ and $g \cdot \partial_1 = \partial_1' \cdot f$. This, with the obvious componentwise composition, defines the category Graph. ♦

Definition 1.2. *(Petri Nets)*
A *Place/Transition Petri Net* (a net, in short), is a graph $N = (S^{\oplus}, T, \partial_0, \partial_1)$, where $S^{\oplus}$ is a free commutative monoid of nodes over a set of *places* S. The elements of $S^{\oplus}$, called also the *markings* of the net N, are represented as formal sums $n_1a_1 \oplus \ldots \oplus n_ka_k$ ($a_i \in S$, n_i a natural number) with the order of the summands being immaterial, where addition is defined by $(\oplus_i\, n_ia_i) \oplus (\oplus_i\, m_ia_i) = (\oplus_i\, (n_i+m_i)a_i)$ and 0 is its neutral element.
A *Petri Net morphism* from N to N' is a graph morphism – i.e. a pair of functions $\langle f, g\rangle$, $f: T \rightarrow T'$ and $g: S^{\oplus} \rightarrow S'^{\oplus}$, preserving source and target – where g is a monoid morphism (i.e. leaving 0 fixed and respecting the monoid operation $\oplus$). With this definition of morphism, nets form a category, called Petri, equipped with products and coproducts. ♦

In other words, a Petri Net is an ordinary graph where the nodes are defined as an *algebra* with S as generators and $\oplus$ as the only operation which is monoidal and commutative. Notice that, in the finite case, multisets over a set S coincide with the elements of the free commutative monoid having S as set of generators.

We would like to stress that the notion of net we are talking about is rather concrete: places and transitions are actual objects of suitable sets; in other words, nets are *not* defined *up to isomorphism*. Indeed, if this is not the case, it would be impossible to define the implementation morphism correctly.

Definition 1.3. *(From a Net to the Category of its Computations)*
Given a net $N = (S^{\oplus}, T, \partial_0, \partial_1)$, the category $\mathcal{T}[N]$ is the strictly symmetric strict monoidal[1] category freely generated by N. The objects of $\mathcal{T}[N]$ are the nodes of N, i.e. $S^{\oplus}$. The arrows of $\mathcal{T}[N]$ are obtained from the transitions T of N by adding for every object u an identity morphism (denoted by $id(u)$) and by closing freely with respect to the operations _⊗_ of *parallel composition* and _;_ of *sequential composition*.
The resulting category is made into a strictly symmetric (strict) monoidal category by imposing functoriality and strict commutativity axioms on ⊗. In detail, the category $\mathcal{T}[N]$ is defined by the following rules of inference

$$\frac{t: u \rightarrow v \text{ in } N}{t: u \rightarrow v \text{ in } \mathcal{T}[N]} \qquad\qquad \frac{u \text{ in } S^{\oplus}}{id(u): u \rightarrow u \text{ in } \mathcal{T}[N]}$$

[1] For a precise definition of this notion, see [MacL71]. Intuitively, there is a binary operation, defined both on the objects and on the morphisms, that is functorial and satisfies the axioms of a monoid up to a natural isomorphism. If the monoid operation is commutative (again, up to a natural isomorphism), the monoidal category is called *symmetric*. If the natural isomorphisms are identities, then we get a *strict* version of the notion.

$$\frac{\alpha:u\to v \quad \alpha':u'\to v' \text{ in } \mathcal{T}[N]}{\alpha\otimes\alpha':u\oplus u'\to v\oplus v' \text{ in } \mathcal{T}[N]} \qquad \frac{\alpha:u\to v \quad \beta:v\to w \text{ in } \mathcal{T}[N]}{\alpha;\beta:u\to w \text{ in } \mathcal{T}[N]}$$

and axioms expressing the fact that the arrows form a commutative monoid:

$$(\alpha \otimes \beta) \otimes \delta = \alpha \otimes (\beta \otimes \delta) \qquad \alpha \otimes \beta = \beta \otimes \alpha \qquad \alpha \otimes 0 = \alpha$$

the fact that $\mathcal{T}[N]$ is a category:

$$\alpha \,;\, id(\partial_1(\alpha)) = id(\partial_0(\alpha)) \,;\, \alpha = \alpha \qquad (\alpha \,;\, \beta) \,;\, \delta = \alpha \,;\, (\beta \,;\, \delta)$$

and the functoriality of $\otimes$:

$$(\alpha \otimes \alpha') \,;\, (\beta \otimes \beta') = (\alpha \,;\, \beta) \otimes (\alpha' \,;\, \beta') \qquad id(u)\otimes id(v) = id(u\oplus v)$$ ♦

The intuitive meaning of the monoidal operation _⊗_ is parallel composition of arrows, and of course the meaning of the categorical operation _;_ is sequential composition of arrows. Since the generators of the arrows of $\mathcal{T}[N]$ are the transitions of N and the identities, the inference rules above amount to closing the transitions of N with respect to parallel and sequential composition, giving origin to a generalized notion of net computation. In other words, $\mathcal{T}[N]$ is a *two-sorted algebra* whose objects are defined by the algebra of the nodes of N (i.e., $S^{\oplus}$) and the arrows by the algebra having T and the identities as generators and _⊗_ , _;_ as operations satisfying the axioms above.

Furthermore, the axioms above define the arrows of $\mathcal{T}[N]$ as equivalence classes of net computations, called *commutative processes*, which can be proved to coincide with Best and Devillers processes [BD87]. In other words, an arrow α in the category represents the *observation* out of any computation in the equivalence class of α. In [DMM89] it is shown that also other interesting quotients can be defined axiomatically on net computations, giving rise to other well-known notions of observation on net computations, such as *firing* or *step sequences* (sequences of steps each with *one* or *at least one* firing transition) and *concatenable processes*, a slight variant of *nonsequential* processes [GR83].

Category $\mathcal{T}[N]$ is a *Petri category*[2], according to the terminology in [MM90]. Given two Petri categories C and D, a Petri category morphism $\langle f, g\rangle$: C → D is a Petri Net morphism such that, additionally, f is a monoid homomorphism, $f(\alpha;\beta)=f(\alpha);f(\beta)$, and $f(id(u))=id(g(u))$, i.e. an identity transition is mapped via f to the identity transition of the state mapped via g. This determines a category called CatPetri. In a categorical perspective, there is an obvious forgetful functor from CatPetri to Petri, which forgets about the structure of monoid on transitions and of category due to sequential composition. Conversely, construction $\mathcal{T}$[_] can be seen as the left adjoint from Petri to CatPetri, i.e. as the free generation of a Petri category from a Petri net. A morphism $\mathcal{T}[N] \to \mathcal{T}[N']$ in CatPetri, which is a functor between the two categories, provides a flexible way of relating system description at different levels of abstraction since a transition t in N can be mapped to an entire computation α in $\mathcal{T}[N']$.

1.2 An Algebraic View of CCS Operational Semantics

Now we recall the operational definition of CCS [Mil89] in terms of a graph "with algebraic structure" $N_{CCS} = (V_{CCS}, T_{CCS}, \partial_0, \partial_1)$ and with labelled transitions, as exemplified in [MY89, FM90, GM90].

Definition 1.4. *(The Algebra of CCS States)*
The CCS terms are generated by the following syntax:

$$E ::= nil \mid x \mid \mu.E \mid E{+}E \mid E\backslash\alpha \mid E[\Phi] \mid E|E \mid rec\ x.E$$

[2] A Petri category is a Petri Net where the set of transitions is a commutative monoid enriched with the partial function _;_ of composition of arrows in such a way that the Petri net becomes a category.

where $\Phi: M \rightarrow M$ is a permutation leaving τ fixed and respecting the involutive bijection $^-$. The algebra is quotiented by the following axiom which captures the essence of recursion, i.e., that of "unfolding":

$$\text{rec } x.E = E[^{\text{rec } x.E}/_x]$$

Only a subset of the terms, however, is relevant for the operational semantics: the closed, guarded terms, usually called ***agents***, which are the states of Milner's transition system[3]. These well-formed terms are ranged over by *u*, *v*, *w*, possibly indexed. ♦

The set of states V_{CCS} is composed of all the terms, freely generated by the syntax modulo the recursion axiom, which are closed and guarded. As usual, the final nil's are omitted, e.g., μ simply stands for μ.nil.

The transitions of an SOS specification, having the format $v{-}\mu{\rightarrow}v'$, are defined by a set of axioms and inference rules, i.e. by a deductive system. Here, instead, we characterize the set of transitions as an algebra: the axioms represent the set of the generators and the inference rules are the operations. In this way, the terms of the algebra T_{CCS} denote the *proofs* of the transitions in the corresponding SOS specification. Furthermore, every element of T_{CCS} has associated a source and a target state ($\partial_0(t)$ and $\partial_1(t)$, respectively), and also is labelled with an action in $\Lambda \cup \{\tau\}$. To help intuition, a transition is represented in the familiar format:

$$t: v{-}\mu{\rightarrow}v' \qquad \text{where } \partial_0(t) = v \text{ and } \partial_1(t) = v'.$$

In this respect, it is easy to see that there are (proofs of) transitions which have the same source and target but a different labelling (e.g., $[\alpha,\text{nil}\rangle <\!+\ \beta$ and $\alpha +\!> [\beta,\text{nil}\rangle$), as well as different (proofs of) transitions which have the same SOS triple (e.g., $[\alpha,\text{nil}\rangle <\!+\ \alpha$ and $\alpha +\!> [\alpha,\text{nil}\rangle$).

Definition 1.5. *(Algebra of Transitions)*

T_{CCS} is the free algebra generated by the following constant and operations, where $t: v_1{-}\mu{\rightarrow}v_2$ and $t': v'_1{-}\mu'{\rightarrow}v'_2$ range over transitions and v over V_{CCS}.

Act)	$[\mu,v\rangle : \mu.v{-}\mu{\rightarrow}v$	for any $\mu \in \Lambda \cup \{\tau\}$
Sum<)	$t <\!+\ v : v_1{+}v{-}\mu{\rightarrow}v_2$	
Sum>)	$v +\!> t : v{+}v_1{-}\mu{\rightarrow}v_2$	
Res)	$t\backslash\alpha : v_1\backslash\alpha{-}\mu'{\rightarrow}v_2\backslash\alpha$	**with** $\mu' :=$ if $\mu \notin \{\alpha,\alpha^-\}$ then μ else $*$
Rel)	$t[\Phi] : v_1[\Phi]{-}\Phi(\mu){\rightarrow}v_2[\Phi]$	
Com-⌋)	$t \rfloor v : v_1 \vert v{-}\mu{\rightarrow}v_2 \vert v$	
Com-⌊)	$v \lfloor t : v \vert v_1{-}\mu{\rightarrow}v \vert v_2$	
Sync)	$t \mid t' : v_1 \vert v'_1{-}\mu''{\rightarrow}v_2 \vert v'_2$	**with** $\mu'' :=$ if $\mu' = \mu^-$ then τ else $*$

where $*$ is a special symbol denoting error due to an impossible synchronization, or to restriction. Indeed, we focus our attention to transitions which are not $*$-labelled only. ♦

2. SCONE⁺: A Calculus of Nets

In this section we introduce our enriched Simple Calculus Of NEts, following as much as possible the algebraic formulation of Plotkin's paradigm, exemplified in the previous section.

[3] In a sense, we could say that our algebra is partial, or better that it is total but that we restrict our attention only to those terms which are well-typed, i.e., closed and guarded. Recently, *typed algebras* and *equational type logic* have been proposed to this aim [MSS90]; therefore, we could more rigorously redefine the algebra in this setting, which however gives rise sometimes to rather boring definitions when non trivial examples are taken into account. The same considerations apply for the algebra of transitions (Definition 2.5), where we should exploit typed algebras for dealing with the inherently partial operation of synchronization. For simplicity sake in the exposition, we prefer to work with an explicit representation of the error element.

Since the definition of sensible SCONE$^+$ operations depends on the possibility of mapping correctly CCS onto the SCONE$^+$ net, we want to explain through an example why, in our opinion, some auxiliary operators (with respect to those included in SCONE) are needed to this aim. The example is concerned with the troublesome interplay between parallelism and restriction. To be more concrete, let us consider the CCS agent $(\alpha \mid \alpha^-)\backslash\alpha$ which cannot perform asynchronously the two actions α and α^-, but only the communication step, labelled by τ. The mapping for the restriction operator should be defined by function g from CCS states to SCONE$^+$ markings as follows:

$$g(v\backslash\alpha) = g(v)\backslash\alpha$$

Thus, the SCONE$^+$ marking associated to the CCS agent $(\alpha \mid \alpha^-)\backslash\alpha$ might become

$$g((\alpha \mid \alpha^-)\backslash\alpha) = g(\alpha \mid \alpha^-)\backslash\alpha = (\alpha \oplus \alpha^-)\backslash\alpha.$$

On the other side, SCONE$^+$ must have a distributive axiom for restriction,

$$(v \oplus v')\backslash\alpha = v\backslash\alpha \oplus v'\backslash\alpha$$

because otherwise $(v \oplus v')\backslash\alpha$ would represent a single place, in contrast with the intuition that actions performed by v and v' are neither causally dependent, nor in conflict; indeed, whenever a parallel composition "|" is present, we should get a multiset union of places from the two components. However, the distributive axiom induces equalities which are not true at all, e.g. $(\alpha \mid \alpha^-)\backslash\alpha = \alpha\backslash\alpha \mid \alpha^-\backslash\alpha$, where the latter is a completely deadlocked agent. Thus, our interpretation of | as multiset union is too simplistic in this case. Disjoint union is the answer to our problem. We can introduce two new unary operators for both nodes and transitions, id|_ and _|id (called *right* and *left context*), with the intuition that v|id makes v the left part of a larger system. The mapping becomes:

$$g(v \mid v') = g(v)|\mathrm{id} \oplus \mathrm{id}|g(v')$$

and now distributivity of restriction w.r.t. multiset union preserves the intended semantics. In our example, we get $g((\alpha \mid \alpha^-)\backslash\alpha) = (\alpha|\mathrm{id})\backslash\alpha \oplus (\mathrm{id}|\alpha^-)\backslash\alpha$, which represents two places, each one independently stuck but able to cooperate for synchronization. The idea of using this auxiliary context operators for correctly dealing with the interplay between restriction and parallel composition dates back to [DDM85] and has been used by other authors [Old87, Old89, Tau89].

Definition 2.1. *(The algebra of SCONE$^+$ markings)*
The SCONE$^+$ terms are generated by the following syntax:

$$M ::= 0 \mid nil \mid x \mid \mu.M \mid M{+}M \mid M\backslash\alpha \mid M[\Phi] \mid M|\mathrm{id} \mid \mathrm{id}|M \mid M \oplus M \mid rec\ x.M$$

The algebra is quotiented by the following axioms

$M \oplus M' = M' \oplus M$	$M \oplus (M' \oplus M'') = (M \oplus M') \oplus M''$	$M \oplus 0 = M$	
$(M \oplus M')\backslash\alpha = M\backslash\alpha \oplus M'\backslash\alpha$	$(M \oplus M')[\Phi] = M[\Phi] \oplus M'[\Phi]$	$0\backslash\alpha = 0$	$0[\Phi] = 0$
$(M \oplus M')|\mathrm{id} = M|\mathrm{id} \oplus M'|\mathrm{id}$	$\mathrm{id}|(M \oplus M') = \mathrm{id}|M \oplus \mathrm{id}|M'$	$0|\mathrm{id} = 0$	$\mathrm{id}|0 = 0$
$rec\ x.M = M[rec\ x.M/x]$			

Only a subset of the terms, however, is relevant for the operational semantics: the closed, guarded terms, which are the *markings*. These well-formed terms are ranged over by u, v, w, with abuse of notation. ♦

The set of nodes V_{SCONE^+} is composed of all the terms, freely generated by the syntax modulo the axioms, which are closed and guarded. Let S_{SCONE^+} be the set of the terms in V_{SCONE^+} generated by the following syntax:

$$N ::= nil \mid \mu.M \mid M{+}M \mid N\backslash\alpha \mid N[\Phi] \mid N|\mathrm{id} \mid \mathrm{id}|N$$

Thus, $V_{SCONE^+} = (S_{SCONE^+})^{\oplus}$, i.e., V_{SCONE^+} is the free commutative monoid of nodes over a set of *places* S_{SCONE^+}, with 0 as neutral element. Hence, V_{SCONE^+} has, on nodes, the algebraic structure of a net.

Intuitively, $\mu.\nu$ is the place from which a transition labelled by μ can be performed reaching marking ν, $\nu+\nu'$ is a place from which two *pure choice* transitions reaching ν and ν', respectively, can be performed; $\nu\backslash\alpha$ may perform any transition of ν, provided that it is not labelled α or α^-; $\nu[\Phi]$ performs the transitions of ν, where moreover the label has been relabelled by Φ; ν|id can execute exactly the same transitions of ν, and represents the fact that ν is part of a larger system connected with it on its own right, and symmetrically for id|ν; this fact is made explicit by the synchronization operator on transitions; $\nu\oplus\nu'$ is multiset union of the two markings ν and ν'.

Definition 2.2. *(Algebra of SCONE⁺ Transitions)*
Let $\Gamma = M\cup\{\varepsilon\}$, ranged over by γ, where ε is a special unobservable and unrestricted action preserved by any relabelling function Φ. The transitions in T_{SCONE^+} are generated by the following constants (determined by *act*, *sum-<*, *sum->*) and operations (determined by *res*, *rel*, */id*, *id/*, *sync*), where t : $\nu_1-\gamma\rightarrow\nu_2$ and t' : $\nu'_1-\gamma'\rightarrow\nu'_2$ range over transitions and ν over V_{SCONE^+}.

act)	$[\mu,\nu\rangle$	: $\mu.\nu -\mu\rightarrow \nu$	for any $\mu\in\Lambda\cup\{\tau\}$
sum-<)	ν «+ ν'	: $\nu+\nu'-\varepsilon\rightarrow\nu$	
sum->)	ν' +» ν	: $\nu'+\nu-\varepsilon\rightarrow\nu$	
res)	$t\backslash\alpha$	: $\nu_1\backslash\alpha-\gamma''\rightarrow\nu_2\backslash\alpha$	with $\gamma'' := \text{if } \gamma\notin\{\alpha,\alpha^-\} \text{ then } \gamma \text{ else } *$
rel)	$t[\Phi]$	: $\nu_1[\Phi]-\Phi(\gamma)\rightarrow\nu_2[\Phi]$	
/id)	t|id	: ν_1|id$-\gamma\rightarrow\nu_2$|id	
id/)	id|t	: id|$\nu_1-\gamma\rightarrow$id|ν_2	
sync)	t|t'	: ν_1|id$\oplus$id|ν'_1 $-\gamma''\rightarrow\nu_2$|id$\oplus$id|$\nu'_2$	with $\gamma'' := \text{if } \gamma' = \gamma^- \text{ then } \tau \text{ else } *$

where * is the error symbol. Again, we will consider only transitions which are not *-labelled. ♦

SCONE⁺ is a P/T net $N_{SCONE^+} = (V_{SCONE^+}, T_{SCONE^+}, \partial_0, \partial_1)$ because V_{SCONE^+} is the free commutative monoid over the set of places S_{SCONE^+}.

The generators of the algebra are of two kinds: action prefixing ($[\mu,\nu\rangle : \mu.\nu -\mu\rightarrow\nu$) and local internal choice transitions (ν «+ $\nu' : \nu+\nu'-\varepsilon\rightarrow\nu$ and ν' +» $\nu : \nu'+\nu-\varepsilon\rightarrow\nu$). The operations for restriction, relabelling and left-, right-context are trivial. The intuition behind $t_1 \mid t_2$ is that it is a new transition, whose source and target are the *disjoint* (because of tags "id|" and "|id") *multiset union* (because of $\oplus$) of the two and whose label is the synchronization of the two, according to the fixed synchronization algebra.

Being SCONE⁺ a net, we can apply the algebraic construction of Definition 2.3 to gain the strictly symmetric strict monoidal category $\mathcal{T}[N_{SCONE^+}]$ of its computations observed as commutative processes.

Example 2.3.
The reachable sub-net for the marking $(\alpha+\beta)$|id $\oplus$ id|$(\alpha^-+\delta)$ is depicted in Figure 1. This marking will correspond to the CCS agent $(\alpha+\beta)|(\alpha^-+\delta)$. Of course, when describing graphically a net, we abandon the presentation of a net as a graph with algebraic structure for a more traditional representation as bipartite graph. ♦

Example 2.4.
Figure 2 represents the sub-nets reachable from the marking corresponding to the CCS term

$$E = (((\text{rec } x.\alpha x+\beta x) \mid \text{rec } x.\alpha x+\gamma x) \mid \text{rec } x.\alpha^- x)\backslash\alpha$$

The initial marking corresponding to the CCS agent is composed of three places:

$((\nu$|id)|id$)\backslash\alpha$	where $\nu = \text{rec } x.\alpha x+\beta x$
((id|w)|id$)\backslash\alpha$	where $w = \text{rec } x.\alpha x+\gamma x$
(id|$u)\backslash\alpha$	where $u = \text{rec } x.\alpha^- x$

♦

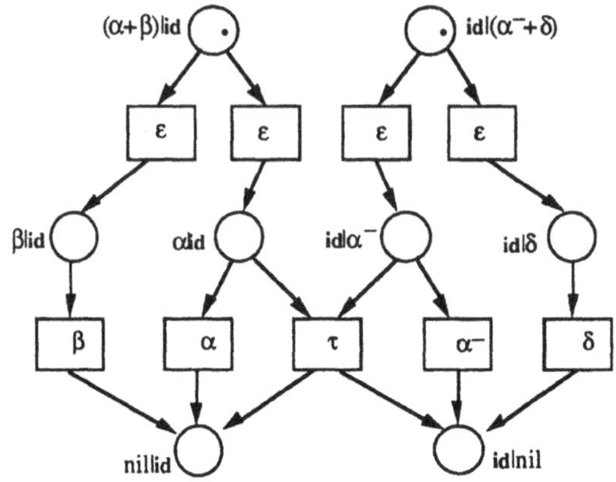

Figure 1. The relevant SCONE$^+$ sub-net for the marking $(\alpha+\beta)|\mathrm{id} \oplus \mathrm{id}|(\alpha^-+\delta)$.

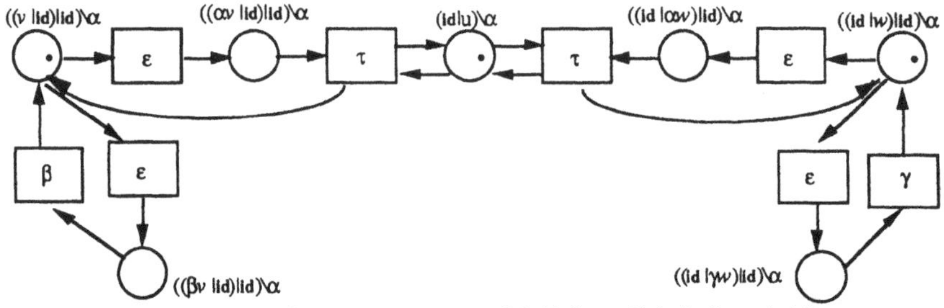

Figure 2. The SCONE$^+$ sub-net for the marking $((\nu|\mathrm{id})|\mathrm{id})\backslash\alpha \oplus ((\mathrm{id}|w)|\mathrm{id})\backslash\alpha \oplus (\mathrm{id}|u)\backslash\alpha$, where $\nu = \mathrm{rec}\ x.\alpha x+\beta x$, $w = \mathrm{rec}\ x.\alpha x+\gamma x$ and $u = \mathrm{rec}\ x.\alpha^- x$.

3. Distributed Implementation of CCS

Relating different languages whose operational semantics has been defined in terms of graphs with algebraic structure is now an easy task: we have simply to give a denotational semantics of the first in terms of the second, i.e., we have to define a morphism between the two graphs. In this way, not only the terms of the language (the nodes of the graph) are mapped, but also their operational behaviour is pointwise translated. Furthermore, if the target language is a Petri net language, then we get a distributed implementation for the language. This idea is related to the notion of implementation morphism introduced in [MM88, MM90]. The analogy is expressed by the fact that a denotational semantics maps basic operators to derived operators as well as an implementation morphism maps transitions to net computations. Here, we implement CCS in SCONE$^+$, thus providing it with a distributed implementation. This mapping can be seen as an evaluation function for CCS having SCONE$^+$ as semantic domain.

3.1. Implementing States

Definition 3.1. *(From CCS states to SCONE$^+$ markings)*
Let $g : V_{CCS} \rightarrow V_{SCONE^+}$ be defined as follows:

- $g(\mathrm{nil}) = \mathrm{nil}$
- $g(v{+}v') = g(v){+}g(v')$
- $g(v[\Phi]) = g(v)[\Phi]$
- $g(\mathrm{x}) = \mathrm{x}$
- $g(\mu.v) = \mu.g(v)$
- $g(v\backslash\alpha) = g(v)\backslash\alpha$
- $g(v \mid v') = g(v)\mathbf{|id} \oplus \mathbf{id|}g(v')$
- $g(\mathrm{rec\ x}.v) = \mathrm{rec\ x}.g(v)$ ♦

Mapping g is injective and invertible; any place in $g(v)$ occurs at most once, and from the set of places composing $g(v)$ it is possible to recover the original CCS agents v by means of a sort of unification procedure, where the various occurrences of **id** should be intended as different variables. Indeed, g is a sort of decomposition function which keeps track of the additional topological structure about sub-system interconnections *via* the auxiliary operators_**|id** and **id|**_. The markings which are target of some CCS states (thus guarded and closed) are called *complete*, see, e.g., [DDM88, DDM89]. Complete markings enjoy a nice property: the markings reachable from a complete marking v are, in turn, complete. Therefore, since complete markings are obviously 1-safe, the reachable sub-net is 1-safe.

Definition 3.2.
A SCONE$^+$ marking w is *complete* if there exists a CCS term v such that $g(v) = w$. ♦

Property 3.3.
i) A complete marking is composed of a *set* of places (i.e., it is a 1-safe marking).
ii) Function g defines a bijection between CCS terms and complete markings of SCONE$^+$.
Proof. Straightforward induction. ♦

Theorem 3.4.
Given a complete marking v and a computation $\xi{:}v{\to}u$ in $\mathcal{T}[N_{SCONE^+}]$, then u is a complete marking.
Proof. Straightforward induction on the structure of ξ. ♦

Corollary 3.5.
The SCONE$^+$ sub-net reachable starting from a complete marking v is 1-safe. ♦

3.2. Implementing Transitions

Let us try to define the mapping from CCS transitions to the arrows of $\mathcal{T}[N_{SCONE^+}]$, i.e. to SCONE$^+$ computations. We start with a couple of examples, just to point out some technical problems. Formally, the mapping has to be defined in a purely syntax-driven way. However, some CCS transitions have no obvious counterpart in SCONE$^+$. As an example, consider the CCS agent $(\alpha \mid \beta)\backslash\alpha$. Its sole transition is $(\alpha \lfloor\ [\beta,\mathrm{nil}\rangle)\backslash\alpha$; let us try to map it to a SCONE$^+$ computation:

$$f(\ [\beta,\mathrm{nil}\rangle) = \ [\beta,\mathrm{nil}\rangle$$

$$f(\alpha \lfloor\ [\beta,\mathrm{nil}\rangle) = id(\alpha)\mathbf{|id} \otimes \mathbf{id|}f(\ [\beta,\mathrm{nil}\rangle) = id(\alpha)\mathbf{|id} \otimes \mathbf{id|}\ [\beta,\mathrm{nil}\rangle$$

which is not a transition, rather a computation (parallel composition of a net transition with an identity), and thus restriction must be extended to computations[4]:

$$f(\alpha \lfloor\ [\beta,\mathrm{nil}\rangle\backslash\alpha) = (\alpha\mathbf{|id} \otimes \mathbf{id|}\ [\beta,\mathrm{nil}\rangle)\backslash\alpha$$

Indeed, restriction is not defined in $\mathcal{T}[N_{SCONE^+}]$. Similar arguments also hold for relabelling and for the two unary context operators. Thus, we should define an algebra $\mathfrak{a}_{NSCONE^+}$ obtained enriching the algebra of category $\mathcal{T}[N_{SCONE^+}]$ with the auxiliary **id|**_ and _**|id**, restriction and relabelling, and expressing which net computations the terms $\mathbf{id|}f(\mathrm{t})$, $f(\mathrm{t})\mathbf{|id}$, $f(\mathrm{t})\backslash\alpha$ and $f(\mathrm{t})[\Phi]$ should represent. For these operators, the solution is immediate: it is enough to add a distributive axiom, e.g., $(\mathrm{t}_1 \otimes \mathrm{t}_2)\backslash\alpha = \mathrm{t}_1\backslash\alpha \otimes \mathrm{t}_2\backslash\alpha$,

4 In the following, for the sake of simplicity, we use the coercion "state for its identity", i.e., u for $id(u)$.

stating that the restriction of a parallel execution of two transitions is the parallel execution of the restricted transitions. Back to our example:

$$f(\alpha \lfloor\ [\beta,nil>\backslash\alpha) = (\alpha|id \otimes id|\ [\beta,nil>)\backslash\alpha = (\alpha|id)\backslash\alpha \otimes (id|\ [\beta,nil>)\backslash\alpha$$

which is the parallel composition of a net transition and of an identity (note that $(\alpha|id)\backslash\alpha$ is a place which can stay idle or interact only, but cannot proceed alone).

The next problem is concerned with nondeterminism. The operator for nondeterministic choice is mapped to a derived operator, i.e. to a suitable combination of local choice and sequential composition, in such a way that a global choice CCS transition is implemented as a sequence of (at least) two transitions, the first of which is a local choice, resulting in a many step computation of SCONE$^+$. Indeed, any global choice can be seen as composed of, at least, two steps: the choice of the sub-components and the execution of an action from the selected components. As an example:

$$f(\ [\alpha,nil> <+\ \beta) = \alpha \ll+\ \beta\ ; f(\ [\alpha,nil>) = \ \alpha \ll+\ \beta\ ;\ [\alpha,nil>$$

The further example presents a harder problem. Let us consider the CCS agent $(\alpha+\beta) \mid (\alpha^-+\delta)$ which is mapped to the SCONE$^+$ marking $(\alpha+\beta)|id \oplus id|(\alpha^-+\delta)$ (see Example 2.3). The CCS transition

$$(\ [\alpha,nil> <+\ \beta) \mid (\ [\alpha^-,nil> <+\ \delta)$$

which represents the synchronization of α and α^- (thus an elementary step in Milner's transition system), should be mapped to the net computation (thus to a *derived* operator)

$$((\alpha \ll+\ \beta)|id \otimes id|(\alpha^- \ll+\ \delta))\ ;\ (\ [\alpha,nil> \mid\ [\alpha^-,nil>)$$

where first the local choices are executed in parallel and then the synchronization is performed. As expected, the mapping is

$$f((\ [\alpha,nil> <+\ \beta) \mid (\ [\alpha^-,nil> <+\ \delta)) \ = f(\ [\alpha,nil> <+\ \beta) \mid f(\ [\alpha^-,nil> <+\ \delta).$$

where unfortunately $f(\ [\alpha,nil>\ <+\ \beta) \mid f(\ [\ \alpha^-,nil>\ <+\ \delta)$ is not defined in $\mathcal{T}[N_{SCONE^+}]$, since the operator of synchronization is not defined *for computations*, but only for net transitions! Therefore, the algebra $\mathfrak{a}_{NSCONE^+}$ should be further enriched with the synchronization operation, and should express which net computation the term $f(t_1 \mid t_2)$ should represent.

Defining an operator of synchronization for commutative processes is a difficult task, because the operation seems to be intrinsically nondeterministic. Luckily, in the present case, only a restricted family of commutative processes is interesting for synchronization: the processes in $\mathcal{T}[N_{SCONE^+}]$ which are the image of CCS transitions according to function f. For this family, it turns out that a *deterministic* operation of synchronization can be defined which exactly reflects our intuition about CCS synchronization. Therefore, first we characterize the class of the relevant processes, we call *transactions*; then we define an operation of synchronization on them. Hence, we add to the term algebra $\mathcal{T}[N_{SCONE^+}]$ a corresponding operation together with an axiom expressing algebraically the effect of the synchronization. Finally, we show that $f(t)$ always evaluates to a particular kind of transaction, called *CCS transaction*.

Definition 3.6. *(Net Transactions and CCS Transactions)*
Let N be a 1-safe net. A *net transaction* for N is a commutative process, i.e. a labelled occurrence net, such that there is a (unique) net transition which is larger than all the others in the partial ordering. Such a transition is called the *commit* transition.
Let N be the SCONE$^+$ subnet reachable from a complete marking. A *CCS transaction* is a net transaction for N where, additionally, all the transitions are labelled by ε, with the exception of the commit transition which is labelled by a μ action. A CCS transaction with the commit transition labelled by μ is also called a μ-transaction. ♦

As an example, let us consider the SCONE$^+$ subnet reachable from $\gamma\ +\ (\alpha\,|id \oplus id|\beta)$, depicted in the figure below. Each one of its three CCS transactions is surrounded by a curve line. The algebraic representation of the three CCS transactions is given as follows:

$(\gamma$ «+ $(\alpha$lid $\oplus$ id$|\beta))$; $[\gamma$,nil$\rangle$, (the commit is $[\gamma$,nil$\rangle$)
$(\gamma$ +» $(\alpha$lid $\oplus$ id$|\beta))$; ($[\alpha$,nil$\rangle$lid $\otimes$ id$|\beta)$, (the commit is $[\alpha$,nil$\rangle$lid)
$(\gamma$ +» $(\alpha$lid $\oplus$ id$|\beta))$; $(\alpha$lid $\otimes$ id$|$ $[\beta$,nil$\rangle)$. (the commit is id$|$ $[\beta$,nil$\rangle$)

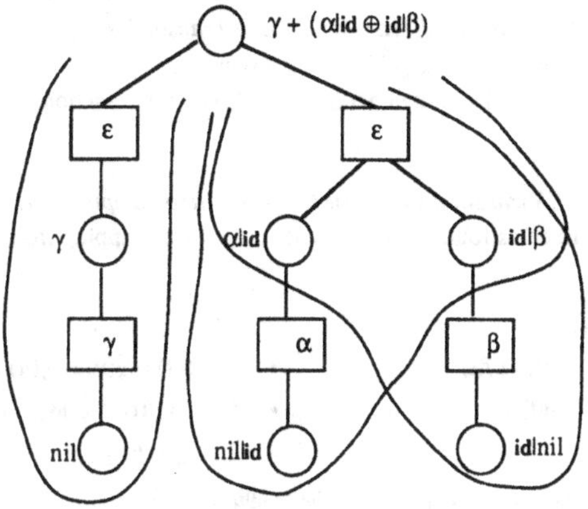

It is immediate to observe that any net computation ξ in $\mathcal{T}[N_{SCONE^+}]$ which evaluates to a transaction can be algebraically represented in the format $\eta;(u\otimes t)$ where η is a computation, t is the commit and u an identity (but also a net computation which is not a transaction, can have the same form). Indeed, it can be easily shown that ξ can be always reduced to the format $(u_1\otimes t_1);\ldots;(u_n\otimes t_n)$ by applying functoriality of $\otimes$. The commit transition, being caused by all the others, will always be the last.

With this notion in mind, a natural deterministic definition of synchronization between two transactions consists of putting in parallel the two processes but synchronizing the two commit transitions to become the commit for the resulting process. In the following definitions we introduce a new algebra by enriching $\mathcal{T}[N_{SCONE^+}]$ with some derived operations (in other words, by extending these operations to net computations). Among them, the most important is the operator [] of synchronization, expressing the intuitive fact that the synchronization of two transactions is again a transaction. In this way, a generalized notion of computation is defined.

Definition 3.7. *(from $\mathcal{T}[N_{SCONE^+}]$ to $\mathcal{A}_{NSCONE^+}$)*
$\mathcal{A}_{NSCONE^+} = (V_{SCONE^+}, \mathfrak{T}, \partial_0, \partial_1)$ is the same graph[5] as $\mathcal{T}[N_{SCONE^+}]$ with the extra operations $\_\backslash\alpha$, $\_[\Phi]$, _lid, id|_ and the (partial) operation _ [] _ on transactions. These operations are subject to the following axioms, which define them as derived operators inside the algebra of $\mathcal{T}[N_{SCONE^+}]$.

$(\xi\otimes\xi')\backslash\alpha = \xi\backslash\alpha\otimes\xi'\backslash\alpha$	$(\xi;\xi')\backslash\alpha = \xi\backslash\alpha;\xi'\backslash\alpha$
$(\xi\otimes\xi')[\Phi] = \xi[\Phi]\otimes\xi'[\Phi]$	$(\xi;\xi')[\Phi] = \xi[\Phi];\xi'[\Phi]$
$(\xi\otimes\xi')$lid $= \xi$lid $\otimes\xi'$lid	$(\xi;\xi')$lid $= \xi$lid ; ξ'lid
id$|(\xi\otimes\xi') =$ id$|\xi\otimes$ id$|\xi'$	id$|(\xi;\xi') =$ id$|\xi$; id$|\xi'$
$id(v)\backslash\alpha = id(v\backslash\alpha)$	$id(v)[\Phi] = id(v[\Phi])$
$id(v)$lid $= id(v$lid$)$	id$|id(v) = id($id$|v)$

Let $\xi = \eta;(u\otimes t)$ and $\xi' = \eta';(u'\otimes t')$ be two transactions, then

$$\xi\,[]\,\xi' = (\eta\,\text{lid}\otimes\text{id}|\eta');(u\text{lid}\otimes\text{id}|u'\otimes t\,|\,t')$$ ♦

[5] To be more rigorous, we should say that the two algebras are different but induce the same underlying graph.

The axioms above represent a kind of composition of transactions where the two last net transitions are synchronized. This is one of the few deterministic ways of synchronizing two net computations, and certainly the only one meaningful for CCS transactions.

Proposition 3.8. *(Synchronizations of Transactions are Transactions)*

i) Given two transactions ξ and ξ', $\xi \,\square\, \xi'$ is a transaction.

ii) Given a λ-transaction ξ and a λ^{-}-transaction ξ', $\xi \,\square\, \xi'$ is a τ-transaction.

Proof. Immediate. ♦

Definition 3.9. *(From CCS transitions to SCONE⁺ generalized computations)*

Let $f: T_{CCS} \rightarrow \mathfrak{T}$ be defined as follows, where function g is the mapping from CCS agents to SCONE$^+$ markings:

- $f([\mu,\nu\rangle) = [\mu,g(\nu)\rangle$
- $f(t <\!+\ \nu) = g(u) \ll\!+\ g(\nu)\ ; f(t)$
- $f(\nu +\!> t) = g(\nu) +\!\gg g(u)\ ; f(t)$
- $f(\nu \lfloor t) = g(\nu)|\mathbf{id} \otimes \mathbf{id}|f(t)$
- $f(t \rfloor \nu) = f(t)|\mathbf{id} \otimes \mathbf{id}|g(\nu)$
- $f(t\backslash\alpha) = f(t)\backslash\alpha$
- $f(t[\Phi]) = f(t)[\Phi]$
- $f(t_1 \mid t_2) = f(t_1) \,\square\, f(t_2) = (\eta_1|\mathbf{id} \otimes \mathbf{id}|\eta_2)\ ;\ (u_1|\mathbf{id} \otimes \mathbf{id}|u_2 \otimes t \mid t')$

where $f(t_1) = \eta_1;(u_1 \otimes t)$ and $f(t_2) = \eta_2;(u_2 \otimes t')$ ♦

Proposition 3.10.

For each CCS transition t, $f(t)$ is always a CCS transaction.

Proof. By structural induction.

- $f([\mu,\nu\rangle) = [\mu,g(\nu)\rangle$ This is the base of the induction. The net computation is simply a net transition, which is of course a CCS transaction.
- $f(t <\!+\ \nu) = g(u) \ll\!+\ g(\nu)\ ; f(t)$ Supposing by induction that the thesis holds for transition t, we have to prove that it holds also for $t <\!+\ \nu$. In fact, the ε-transition $g(u) \ll\!+\ g(\nu)$ causes all the transitions of $f(t)$, and in particular its commit. The symmetric case is omitted.
- $f(t\backslash\alpha) = f(t)\backslash\alpha$ By induction $f(t)$ is a μ-transaction. If $t\backslash\alpha$ is not $*$-labelled, then t is not labelled α (or α^{-}). Therefore, also $f(t)\backslash\alpha$ is a μ-transaction. Indeed, since restriction distributes w.r.t. monoidal composition, the process is, *structurally*, left unchanged.
- $f(t[\Phi]) = f(t)[\Phi]$ Similarly, as before.
- $f(t \rfloor \nu) = f(t)|\mathbf{id} \otimes \mathbf{id}|g(\nu)$ By inductive hypothesis, $f(t)$ is a CCS transaction, thus $f(t)|\mathbf{id} \otimes \mathbf{id}|g(\nu)$ is so, by definition, since $\mathbf{id}|g(\nu)$ does not generate any transition in the process associated to the transaction. The symmetric case is omitted.
- $f(t_1 \mid t_2) = f(t_1) \,\square\, f(t_2)$ By inductive hypothesis and Proposition 3.8. ♦

Of course, also the reverse is true, i.e. any CCS transaction is the image of a (not *-labelled) CCS transition.

Proposition 3.11.

The pair $\langle f, g\rangle : N_{CCS} \rightarrow \mathfrak{G}_{NSCONE^+}$ is a graph morphism, i.e., $g \bullet \partial_{iCCS} = \partial_{iSCONE^+} \bullet f$, $i = 0, 1$.

Proof. By structural induction where the first case is the base of the induction. For the sake of simplicity, ∂_{iSCONE^+} is shortened to ∂_{iS^+}.

- $\langle \partial_{0S^+}(f([\mu,\nu\rangle)), \partial_{1S^+}(f([\mu,\nu\rangle))\rangle = \langle \partial_{0S^+}([\mu,g(\nu)\rangle), \partial_{1S^+}([\mu,g(\nu)\rangle)\rangle =$
  $= \langle \mu.g(\nu), g(\nu)\rangle = \langle g(\mu.\nu), g(\nu)\rangle = \langle g(\partial_{0CCS}([\mu,\nu\rangle)), g(\partial_{1CCS}([\mu,\nu\rangle))\rangle,$
- $\langle \partial_{0S^+}(f(t <\!+\, \nu)), \partial_{1S^+}(f(t <\!+\, \nu)\rangle =$
  $= \langle \partial_{0S^+}(g(u) \ll\!+\, g(\nu) ; f(t)), \partial_{1S^+}(g(u) \ll\!+\, g(\nu) ; f(t))\rangle =$
  $= \langle \partial_{0S^+}(g(u) \ll\!+\, g(\nu)), \partial_{1S^+}(f(t))\rangle = \langle g(u) + g(\nu), g(\partial_{1CCS}(t))\rangle =$
  $= \langle g(u+\nu), g(\partial_{1CCS}(t))\rangle = \langle g(\partial_{0CCS}(t) + \nu), g(\partial_{1CCS}(t <\!+ \nu))\rangle =$
  $= \langle g(\partial_{0CCS}(t <\!+\, \nu)), g(\partial_{1CCS}(t <\!+\, \nu))\rangle,$ (the symmetric case is omitted).
- $\langle \partial_{0S^+}(f(t\backslash\alpha)), \partial_{1S^+}(f(t\backslash\alpha)\rangle = \langle \partial_{0S^+}(f(t)\backslash\alpha), \partial_{1S^+}(f(t)\backslash\alpha)\rangle =$
  $= \langle \partial_{0S^+}(f(t))\backslash\alpha, \partial_{1S^+}(f(t))\backslash\alpha\rangle = \langle g(\partial_{0CCS}(t))\backslash\alpha, g(\partial_{1CCS}(t))\backslash\alpha\rangle =$
  $= \langle g(\partial_{0CCS}(t)\backslash\alpha), g(\partial_{1CCS}(t)\backslash\alpha)\rangle = \langle g(\partial_{0CCS}(t\backslash\alpha)), g(\partial_{1CCS}(t\backslash\alpha))\rangle$
- $\langle \partial_{0S^+}(f(t[\Phi])), \partial_{1S^+}(f(t[\Phi])\rangle = \langle \partial_{0S^+}(f(t)[\Phi]), \partial_{1S^+}(f(t)[\Phi])\rangle =$
  $= \langle \partial_{0S^+}(f(t))[\Phi], \partial_{1S^+}(f(t))[\Phi]\rangle = \langle g(\partial_{0CCS}(t))[\Phi], g(\partial_{1CCS}(t))[\Phi]\rangle =$
  $= \langle g(\partial_{0CCS}(t)[\Phi]), g(\partial_{1CCS}(t)[\Phi])\rangle = \langle g(\partial_{0CCS}(t[\Phi])), g(\partial_{1CCS}(t[\Phi]))\rangle$
- $\langle \partial_{0S^+}(f(t \rfloor \nu)), \partial_{1S^+}(f(t \rfloor \nu))\rangle = \langle \partial_{0S^+}(f(t)|\mathbf{id} \otimes \mathbf{id}|g(\nu)), \partial_{1S^+}(f(t)|\mathbf{id} \otimes \mathbf{id}|g(\nu))\rangle$
  $= \langle \partial_{0S^+}(f(t))|\mathbf{id} \oplus \mathbf{id}|\partial_{0S^+}(g(\nu)), \partial_{1S^+}(f(t))|\mathbf{id} \oplus \mathbf{id}|\partial_{1S^+}(g(\nu))\rangle =$
  $= \langle g(\partial_{0CCS}(t))|\mathbf{id} \oplus \mathbf{id}|g(\nu), g(\partial_{1CCS}(t))|\mathbf{id} \oplus \mathbf{id}|g(\nu)\rangle = \langle g(\partial_{0CCS}(t) \mid \nu), g(\partial_{1CCS}(t) \mid \nu)\rangle$
  $= \langle g(\partial_{0CCS}(t \rfloor \nu)), g(\partial_{1CCS}(t \rfloor \nu))\rangle,$ (the symmetric case is omitted)
- $\langle \partial_{0S^+}(f(t_1 \mid t_2)), \partial_{1S^+}(f(t_1 \mid t_2))\rangle = \langle \partial_{0S^+}(f(t_1) [\,] f(t_2)), \partial 1_{0S^+}(f(t_1) [\,] f(t_2))\rangle =$
  $= \langle \partial_{0S^+}(f(t_1))|\mathbf{id} \oplus \mathbf{id}|\partial_{0S^+}(f(t_2)), \partial_{1S^+}(f(t_1))|\mathbf{id} \oplus \mathbf{id}|\partial_{1S^+}(f(t_2))\rangle =$
  $= \langle g(\partial_{0CCS}(t_1))|\mathbf{id} \oplus \mathbf{id}|g(\partial_{0CCS}(t_2)), g(\partial_{1CCS}(t_1))|\mathbf{id} \oplus \mathbf{id}|g(\partial_{1CCS}(t_2))\rangle =$
  $= \langle g(\partial_{0CCS}(t_1 \mid t_2)), g(\partial_{1CCS}(t_1 \mid t_2))\rangle.$ ♦

Example 3.12.

Let us consider again the CCS agent $E = (\alpha+\beta) \mid (\alpha^-+\delta)$ and the SCONE⁺ sub-net in Figure 1. The initial marking of the sub-net we are interested in is exactly $g(E) = (\alpha+\beta)|\mathbf{id} \oplus \mathbf{id}|(\alpha^-+\delta)$. Transitions are mapped to computations as follows.

- $f([\sigma,nil\rangle) = [\sigma,nil\rangle$ for $\sigma \in \{\alpha, \beta, \alpha^-, \delta\}$
- $f([\alpha,nil\rangle <\!+\, \beta) = \alpha \ll\!+\, \beta ; f([\alpha,nil\rangle) = \alpha \ll\!+\, \beta ; [\alpha,nil\rangle$ and similarly for the other choices
- $f(([\alpha,nil\rangle <\!+\, \beta) \rfloor (\alpha^-+\delta)) = f([\alpha,nil\rangle <\!+\, \beta)|\mathbf{id} \otimes \mathbf{id}|g(\alpha^-+\delta) =$
  $= (\alpha \ll\!+\, \beta ; [\alpha,nil\rangle)|\mathbf{id} \otimes \mathbf{id}|(\alpha^-+\delta)$
  $= ((\alpha \ll\!+\, \beta)|\mathbf{id} ; ([\alpha,nil\rangle)|\mathbf{id}) \otimes \mathbf{id}|(\alpha^-+\delta)$ and similarly for other asynchronous moves,
- $f(([\alpha,nil\rangle <\!+\, \beta) \mid ([\alpha^-,nil\rangle <\!+\, \delta)) = f([\alpha,nil\rangle <\!+\, \beta) [\,] f([\alpha^-,nil\rangle <\!+\, \delta) =$
  $= (\alpha \ll\!+\beta ; [\alpha,nil\rangle) [\,] (\alpha^- \ll\!+\, \delta ; [\alpha^-,nil\rangle) = ((\alpha \ll\!+\, \beta)|\mathbf{id} \otimes \mathbf{id}|(\alpha^- \ll\!+\, \delta)) ; ([\alpha,nil\rangle \mid [\alpha^-,nil\rangle)$

Summing up, $f([\alpha,nil\rangle <\!+\, \beta \mid [\alpha^-,nil\rangle <\!+\, \delta) = ((\alpha \ll\!+\, \beta)|\mathbf{id} \otimes \mathbf{id}|(\alpha^- \ll\!+\, \delta)) ; ([\alpha,nil\rangle \mid [\alpha^-,nil\rangle)$, i.e., the choices are executed in parallel and then the synchronization is performed. Of course, the choices can also be done in any order; it is easy to prove the following identifications:

$((\alpha \ll\!+\, \beta)|\mathbf{id} \otimes \mathbf{id}|(\alpha^-+ \delta)) ; (\alpha|\mathbf{id} \otimes \mathbf{id}|(\alpha^- \ll\!+\, \delta)) ; ([\alpha,nil\rangle \mid [\alpha^-,nil\rangle)$

$= (((\alpha \ll\!+\, \beta)|\mathbf{id};\alpha|\mathbf{id}) \otimes (\mathbf{id}|(\alpha^-+ \delta);\mathbf{id}|(\alpha^- \ll\!+\, \delta))) ; ([\alpha,nil\rangle \mid [\alpha^-,nil\rangle)$ (applying functoriality)

$= ((\alpha \ll\!+\, \beta)|\mathbf{id} \otimes \mathbf{id}|(\alpha^- \ll\!+\, \delta)) ; ([\alpha,nil\rangle \mid [\alpha^-,nil\rangle)$ (cancelling identities)

$= (((\alpha + \beta)|\mathbf{id};(\alpha \ll\!+\, \beta)|\mathbf{id}) \otimes (\mathbf{id}|(\alpha^- \ll\!+\, \delta);\mathbf{id}|\alpha^-)) ; ([\alpha,nil\rangle \mid [\alpha^-,nil\rangle)$ (introducing identities)

$= ((\alpha+\beta)|\mathbf{id} \otimes \mathbf{id}|(\alpha^- \ll\!+\, \delta)) ; ((\alpha \ll\!+\beta)|\mathbf{id} \otimes \mathbf{id}|\alpha^-) ; ([\alpha,nil\rangle \mid [\alpha^-,nil\rangle)$ (applying functoriality)

♦

4. Distributed Semantics of CCS

CCS semantics is investigated by exploiting the implementation mapping $\langle f,g\rangle: N_{CCS} \rightarrow \mathcal{G}_{N_{SCONE^+}}$. Function g is injective and thus no different CCS agents are mapped to the same marking. Also CCS transitions are not identified, since mapping f is injective, too. Therefore, the quotient of N_{CCS} w.r.t. $\langle f,g\rangle$ is again N_{CCS}.

Nonetheless, the mapping will equate those computations obtained by permuting transitions generating independent events. To prove this fact, we can homomorphically extend the implementation morphism $\langle f,g\rangle$ also to CCS computations, and then observe what kind of identifications are made on them. The graph N_{CCS} can be made transitively closed *via* the partial operation _ ; _ on transitions such that $f(t_1 \,;\, t_2) = f(t_1) \,;\, f(t_2)$. What we would like to show is that whenever two CCS computations are different only for the ordering of two transitions which are causally independent, they are identified; and also the converse. First, we will show this on some examples; then, we formally prove our statement.

Example 4.1.
Let us consider the CCS term $(\alpha+\beta)|(\alpha^-+\delta)$ and the net in Figure 1. The CCS computation

$$((\,[\alpha,\mathrm{nil}\rangle <\!+\, \beta)\,\rfloor(\alpha^-+\delta))\,;\,(\mathrm{nil}\,\lfloor(\,[\alpha^-,\, \mathrm{nil}\rangle\ <\!+\,\delta))$$

denotes the execution of an α followed by an α^-. It is mapped to the SCONE$^+$ computation

$$((\alpha \ll\!+\, \beta)\,;\,[\alpha,\mathrm{nil}\rangle)|\mathrm{id} \otimes \mathrm{id}|(\alpha^-+\delta)\ ;\ (\mathrm{nil}|\mathrm{id}\otimes\mathrm{id}|((\alpha^-\ll\!+\,\delta)\,;\,[\alpha^-,\mathrm{nil}\rangle)),$$

which, by distributing the auxiliary operators w.r.t. sequential composition, becomes

$$((\alpha\ll\!+\,\beta)|\mathrm{id}\,;\,[\alpha,\mathrm{nil}\rangle|\mathrm{id})\otimes\mathrm{id}|(\alpha^-+\delta)\ ;\ \mathrm{nil}|\mathrm{id}\otimes(\mathrm{id}|(\alpha^-\ll\!+\,\delta)\,;\,\mathrm{id}|\,[\alpha^-,\mathrm{nil}\rangle),$$

and, by functoriality and cancelling identities, is equivalent to the parallel execution of the two computations

$$((\alpha\ll\!+\,\beta)|\mathrm{id}\,;\,[\alpha,\mathrm{nil}\rangle|\mathrm{id})\ \otimes\ (\mathrm{id}|(\alpha^-\ll\!+\,\delta)\,;\,\mathrm{id}|\,[\alpha^-,\mathrm{nil}\rangle),$$

which, by introducing identities and applying functoriality, becomes

$$(\alpha+\beta)|\mathrm{id}\otimes(\mathrm{id}|(\alpha^-\ll\!+\,\delta)\,;\,\mathrm{id}|\,[\alpha^-,\mathrm{nil}\rangle)\ ;\ ((\alpha\ll\!+\,\beta)|\mathrm{id}\,;\,[\alpha,\mathrm{nil}\rangle|\mathrm{id})\otimes\mathrm{id}|\mathrm{nil},$$

where the transitions are performed in reverse order. Furthermore, by collecting the auxiliary operators w.r.t. sequential composition, it becomes

$$(\alpha+\beta)|\mathrm{id}\otimes\mathrm{id}|((\alpha^-\ll\!+\,\delta)\,;\,[\alpha^-,\mathrm{nil}\rangle)\ ;\ ((\alpha\ll\!+\,\beta)\,;\,[\alpha,\mathrm{nil}\rangle)|\mathrm{id}\otimes\mathrm{id}|\mathrm{nil},$$

which is the image of the CCS computation

$$((\alpha+\beta)\lfloor(\,[\alpha^-,\mathrm{nil}\rangle<\!+\,\delta))\,;\,((\,[\alpha,\mathrm{nil}\rangle\ <\!+\,\beta)\rfloor\mathrm{nil})$$

thus inducing an identification between the former and the latter CCS computations. ♦

Example 4.2.
An interesting test to measure the reliability of a true concurrent semantics is certainly represented by the CCS agent $E = \gamma + (\alpha|\beta)$, where an interweaving of nondeterministic and parallel operators may cause the possible loss of causal independency between the two concurrent actions α and β (see [DDM89, DDM90] for a discussion about this problem).
The place $\gamma + (\alpha|\mathrm{id} \oplus \mathrm{id}|\beta)$ is the image of E, and the two CCS transitions

$$\gamma +\!> (\,[\alpha,\mathrm{nil}\rangle \rfloor\beta)\ :\ \gamma + (\alpha|\beta) -\alpha\rightarrow \mathrm{nil}|\beta$$

$$\gamma +\!> (\alpha\lfloor\,[\beta,\mathrm{nil}\rangle)\ :\ \gamma + (\alpha|\beta) -\beta\rightarrow \alpha|\mathrm{nil}$$

are mapped to the following two net computations, respectively:

$$(\gamma \gg\!\!+ (\alpha|\mathrm{id} \oplus \mathrm{id}|\beta))\,;\,(\,[\alpha,\mathrm{nil}\rangle|\mathrm{id} \otimes \mathrm{id}|\beta)$$

$$(\gamma \gg\!\!+ (\alpha|\mathrm{id} \oplus \mathrm{id}|\beta))\,;\,(\alpha|\mathrm{id} \otimes \mathrm{id}|\,[\beta,\mathrm{nil}\rangle)$$

Note that the implementation of a CCS transition, which is an atomic activity, must be atomic according to our algebraic construction; hence, the intermediate state $\alpha|\mathrm{id} \oplus \mathrm{id}|\beta$ must be not testable by an external

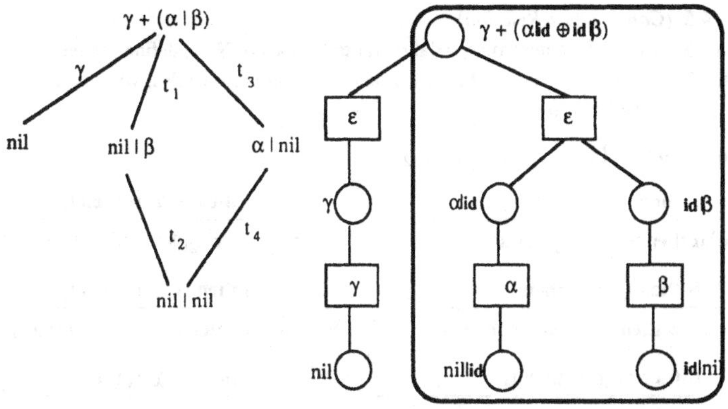

Figure 3. The transition system and the net for the agent $\gamma + \alpha \mid \beta$. Notice that both $t_1 ; t_2$ and $t_3 ; t_4$ are mapped to the same process, enclosed in the box.

observer. In other words, even if we describe the behaviour of a CCS transition more detailedly as a net computation, we do not alter the granularity of the observation.
The image of the CCS computation $(\gamma +> ([\alpha,nil> \rfloor\beta)) ; (nil \lfloor [\beta,nil>)$ is the net computation

$$(\gamma +\!\!> (\alpha|id \oplus id|\beta)) ; ([\alpha,nil>|id \otimes id|\beta) ; (nil|id \otimes id| [\beta,nil>),$$

where actions α and β are in fact causally independent. This net computation is equivalent to

$$(\gamma +\!\!> (\alpha|id \oplus id|\beta)) ; (\alpha|id \otimes id| [\beta,nil>) ; ([\alpha,nil>|id \otimes id|nil),$$

which is the image of the computation $(\gamma +> (\alpha \lfloor [\beta,nil>)) ; ([\alpha,nil> \rfloor nil)$ of CCS. Therefore, the two CCS computations are equivalent. ♦

Definition 4.3. *(Category of CCS Computations)*
Let $\mathbf{Cat}(N_{CCS})$ denote the category obtained by adding an identity arc to each node of N_{CCS} and closing freely w.r.t. the (partial) operation _ ; _ of sequential composition of its transitions, adding the usual categorical axioms (where $t{:}u \to v$)

$$t ; (t' ; t'') = (t ; t') ; t'' \qquad u ; t = t = t ; v$$ ♦

Note that the algebraic structure of CCS has not been extended to computations. The arrows of category $\mathbf{Cat}(N_{CCS})$ are only computations composed of N_{CCS} transitions. The mapping $\langle f,g\rangle : N_{CCS} \to \mathfrak{a}_{NSCONE^+}$ can be extended homomorphically to become a mapping from $\mathbf{Cat}(N_{CCS})$ to $\mathfrak{a}_{NSCONE^+}$ by further adding the equation $f(t_1 ; t_2) = f(t_1) ; f(t_2)$. In this way we obtain a quotient of CCS computations as exemplified in the previous examples.

Definition 4.4.
Category $\mathbf{Con}_{CCS}$ is the category obtained from $\mathbf{Cat}(N_{CCS})$ via the quotient map induced by $\langle f,g\rangle$. ♦

Now we want to prove that the identifications on CCS computations due to the implementation mapping are exactly the same obtained *via* a set of axioms proposed in [FM90], which defines in a self-evident way the truly concurrent semantics for CCS. A relation χ between computations of length two, called *concurrency relation*, relates computations differing just for "permuting" the order of independent transitions. This relation rephrases in our algebraic framework a previous proposal by Boudol and Castellani [BC89, BC90].

Definition 4.5. *(Concurrency Relation)*
Let _ **then** _ χ _ **then** _ be a quaternary relation on transitions of N_{CCS} defined as the least 1,2↔3,4 commutative[6] relation satisfying the following axiom and inference rules, with $\partial_0(t_i) = u_i$, $\partial_1(t_i) = v_i$, i = 1,..., 4, and $\partial_0(t) = u$, $\partial_1(t) = v$.

- $t_1 \rfloor u_2$ **then** $v_1 \lfloor t_2 \ \chi\ u_1 \lfloor t_2$ **then** $t_1 \rfloor v_2$

- $$\frac{t_1 \textbf{ then } t_2 \ \chi\ t_3 \textbf{ then } t_4}{t_1\backslash\alpha \textbf{ then } t_2\backslash\alpha \ \chi\ t_3\backslash\alpha \textbf{ then } t_4\backslash\alpha}$$

- $$\frac{t_1 \textbf{ then } t_2 \ \chi\ t_3 \textbf{ then } t_4}{t_1[\Phi] \textbf{ then } t_2[\Phi] \ \chi\ t_3[\Phi] \textbf{ then } t_4[\Phi]}$$

- $$\frac{t_1 \textbf{ then } t_2 \ \chi\ t_3 \textbf{ then } t_4}{t_1 \mathrm{<+}w \textbf{ then } t_2 \ \chi\ t_3 \mathrm{<+}w \textbf{ then } t_4}$$

- $$\frac{t_1 \textbf{ then } t_2 \ \chi\ t_3 \textbf{ then } t_4}{w \mathrm{+>} t_1 \textbf{ then } t_2 \ \chi\ w \mathrm{+>} t_3 \textbf{ then } t_4}$$

- $$\frac{t_1 \textbf{ then } t_2 \ \chi\ t_3 \textbf{ then } t_4}{t_1 \rfloor w \textbf{ then } t_2 \rfloor w \ \chi\ t_3 \rfloor w \textbf{ then } t_4 \rfloor w}$$

- $$\frac{t_1 \textbf{ then } t_2 \ \chi\ t_3 \textbf{ then } t_4}{w \lfloor t_1 \textbf{ then } w \lfloor t_2 \ \chi\ w \lfloor t_3 \textbf{ then } w \lfloor t_4}$$

- $$\frac{t_1 \textbf{ then } t_2 \ \chi\ t_3 \textbf{ then } t_4}{t_1 \mid t \textbf{ then } t_2 \rfloor v \ \chi\ t_3 \rfloor u \textbf{ then } t_4 \mid t}$$

- $$\frac{t_1 \textbf{ then } t_2 \ \chi\ t_3 \textbf{ then } t_4}{t \mid t_1 \textbf{ then } v \lfloor t_2 \ \chi\ u \lfloor t_3 \textbf{ then } t \mid t_4}$$

- $$\frac{t_1 \textbf{ then } t_2 \ \chi\ t_3 \textbf{ then } t_4 \ \text{ and }\ t'_1 \textbf{ then } t'_2 \ \chi\ t'_3 \textbf{ then } t'_4}{t_1 \mid t'_1 \textbf{ then } t_2 \mid t'_2 \ \chi\ t_3 \mid t'_3 \textbf{ then } t_4 \mid t'_4}$$ ♦

Proposition 4.6.
Given four transitions t_1, t_2, t_3 and t_4 in N_{CCS} such that t_1 **then** $t_2 \ \chi\ t_3$ **then** t_4, the following hold:
i) $t_1 ; t_2$ and $t_3 ; t_4$ are defined;
ii) $\partial_0(t_1) = \partial_0(t_3)$ and $\partial_1(t_2) = \partial_1(t_4)$;
iii) t_1 and t_4 (t_2 and t_3) have the same label.
Proof. Immediate by induction on the proof of t_1 **then** $t_2 \ \chi\ t_3$ **then** t_4. ♦

The concurrency relation singles out a "diamond" in the transition system N_{CCS} which is due to the different order of execution of independent transitions (for example, see Figure 3). The axiom algebraically singles out the basic diamonds, and the other rules reproduces the diamonds in all the other possible contexts.

Theorem 4.7. *(Consistency w.r.t. the truly concurrent semantics of CCS)*
Given four basic transitions of $\mathbf{Con}_{CCS}$, i.e., t_1, t_2, t_3 and t_4 in N_{CCS}, then we have

$$t_1 \textbf{ then } t_2 \ \chi\ t_3 \textbf{ then } t_4 \quad \text{implies} \quad t_1 ; t_2 = t_3 ; t_4$$

Proof. The proof is by induction on the proof of t_1 **then** $t_2 \ \chi\ t_3$ **then** t_4. Actually, in order to be able to prove the theorem in a completely syntactical manner, we prove a stronger result:

t_1 **then** $t_2 \ \chi\ t_3$ **then** t_4 *implies*

$$f(t_1)=(\xi; (t'\otimes u''))\otimes w,\ f(t_2)=(v'\otimes t'')\otimes w,\ f(t_3)=(\xi ; (u'\otimes t''))\otimes w \text{ and } f(t_4)=(t'\otimes v'')\otimes w,$$

where w and ξ are optional (i.e., if w is present in one of the $f(t_i)$, then it is present in all the other ones). Sequentially composing the two processes, we obtain $f(t_1 ; t_2) = (\xi ; (t'\otimes u'');(v'\otimes t''))\otimes w = (\xi ; (t'\otimes t''))\otimes w = (\xi ; (u'\otimes t'');(t'\otimes v''))\otimes w = f(t_3 ; t_4)$. This means that, apart from a possible initial common segment and some idle tokens, $t_1 ; t_2$ generates two independent events which are generated in reverse order by $t_3 ; t_4$. The order exchange is expressed by functoriality.
The "commutativity" condition holds because equality is a commutative relation.

[6] Namely, t_1 **then** $t_2 \ \chi\ t_3$ **then** t_4 *iff* t_3 **then** $t_4 \ \chi\ t_1$ **then** t_2.

The base case is the axiom: we have to prove that $f(t_1 \rfloor u_2 \,;\, v_1 \lfloor t_2) = f(u_1 \lfloor t_2 \,;\, t_1 \rfloor v_2)$.

$$f(t_1 \rfloor u_2 \,;\, v_1 \lfloor t_2) =$$
$$= (f(t_1)|id \otimes id|g(u_2))\,;\,(g(v_1)|id \otimes id|f(t_2)) = (f(t_1)|id ; g(v_1)|id) \otimes (id|g(u_2)\,;\,id|f(t_2)) =$$
$$= (f(t_1)\,;\,g(v_1))|id \otimes id|(g(u_2)\,;\,(f(t_2)) = f(t_1)|id \otimes id|f(t_2) =$$
$$= (g(u_1)\,;\,(f(t_1))|id \otimes id|(f(t_2)\,;\,g(v_2)) = (g(u_1)|id\,;\,f(t_1)|id) \otimes (id|f(t_2)\,;\,id|g(v_2)) =$$
$$= (g(u_1)|id \otimes id|f(t_2))\,;\,(f(t_1)|id \otimes id|g(v_2)) =$$
$$= f(u_1 \lfloor t_2 \,;\, t_1 \rfloor v_2).$$

For restriction, we have to prove that $f(t_1 \backslash \alpha \,;\, t_2 \backslash \alpha) = f(t_3 \backslash \alpha \,;\, t_4 \backslash \alpha)$, knowing that $f(t_1 \,;\, t_2) = f(t_3 \,;\, t_4)$ by inductive hypothesis. The similar case of relabelling is omitted.

$$f(t_1 \backslash \alpha \,;\, t_2 \backslash \alpha) =$$
$$= f(t_1 \backslash \alpha)\,;\,f(t_2 \backslash \alpha) = f(t_1) \backslash \alpha \,;\, f(t_2) \backslash \alpha = (f(t_1)\,;\,f(t_2)) \backslash \alpha = f(t_1 \,;\, t_2) \backslash \alpha = f(t_3 \,;\, t_4) \backslash \alpha =$$
$$= (f(t_3)\,;\,f(t_4)) \backslash \alpha = f(t_3) \backslash \alpha \,;\, f(t_4) \backslash \alpha = f(t_3 \backslash \alpha)\,;\,f(t_4 \backslash \alpha) =$$
$$= f(t_3 \backslash \alpha \,;\, t_4 \backslash \alpha)$$

In the case of the rule for nondeterminism, we have to prove that $f(w{+}{>}t_1 \,;\, t_2) = f(w{+}{>}t_3 \,;\, t_4)$, knowing that $f(t_1 \,;\, t_2) = f(t_3 \,;\, t_4)$ by inductive hypothesis. The proof for the symmetric rule is omitted.

$$f(w{+}{>}t_1 \,;\, t_2) =$$
$$= ((g(w) {+}{\gg} g(u_1))\,;\,f(t_1))\,;\,f(t_2) = (g(w) {+}{\gg} g(u_1))\,;\,(f(t_1)\,;\,f(t_2)) =$$
$$= (g(w) {+}{\gg} g(u_1))\,;\,f(t_1;t_2) = (g(w) {+}{\gg} g(u_3))\,;\,f(t_3;t_4) = (g(w) {+}{\gg} g(u_3))\,;\,(f(t_3)\,;\,f(t_4)) =$$
$$= ((g(w) {+}{\gg} g(u_3))\,;\,f(t_3))\,;\,f(t_4) = f(w{+}{>}t_3 \,;\, t_4).$$

In the case of asynchrony, we have to prove that $f(w \lfloor t_1 \,;\, w \lfloor t_2) = f(w \lfloor t_3 \,;\, w \lfloor t_4)$. The proof of the symmetric rule is omitted.

$$f(w \lfloor t_1 \,;\, w \lfloor t_2) =$$
$$= (g(w)|id \otimes id|f(t_1))\,;\,(g(w)|id \otimes id|f(t_2)) = (g(w);g(w))|id \otimes id|(f(t_1);f(t_2)) =$$
$$= g(w)|id \otimes id|f(t_1;t_2) = g(w)|id \otimes id|f(t_3;t_4) = (g(w);g(w))|id \otimes id|(f(t_3);f(t_4)) =$$
$$= (g(w)|id;g(w)|id) \otimes (id|f(t_3);id|f(t_4)) = (g(w)|id \otimes id|f(t_3));(g(w)|id \otimes id|f(t_4)) =$$
$$= f(w \lfloor t_3 ; w \lfloor t_4)$$

In the subsequent case, we have to prove that $f(t_1 \,|\, t \,;\, t_2 \rfloor v) = f(t_3 \rfloor u \,;\, t_4 \,|\, t)$. To this aim, we need the full power of the inductive hypothesis which guarantee the existence of two independent net transitions which are executed in reverse order by $f(t_1 \,;\, t_2)$ and $f(t_3 \,;\, t_4)$. We know that $f(t_1) = (\xi; (t' \otimes u'')) \otimes w$, $f(t_2) = (v' \otimes t'') \otimes w$, $f(t_3) = (\xi \,;\, (u' \otimes t'')) \otimes w$ and $f(t_4) = (t' \otimes v'') \otimes w$. Moreover, assume that $f(t) = \eta;(t \otimes z)$ and $\partial_0(f(t)) = g(\partial_0(t)) = u$, $\partial_1(f(t)) = g(\partial_1(t)) = v$. Finally, let $\partial_1(\xi) = u' \oplus u''$ and $\partial_1(\eta) = u_\eta$

$$f(t_1) \,\square\, f(t) = ((\xi \,;\, (t' \otimes u'')) \otimes w) \,\square\, (\eta;(t \otimes z)) = ((\xi \otimes w);(t' \otimes u'' \otimes w)) \,\square\, (\eta \,;(t \otimes z)) =$$
$$= (w \otimes \xi);(w \otimes u'' \otimes t') \,\square\, (\eta \,;(t \otimes z)) = [((w \otimes \xi);(w \otimes u' \otimes u''))|id \otimes id|\eta]\,;\,[(w \otimes u'')|id \otimes t'|t \otimes id|z]$$
$$= [(w \otimes \xi)|id \otimes id|\eta]\,;\,[(w \otimes u'')|id \otimes t' \,|\, t \otimes id|z]$$

Thus, we have that

$$f(t_1 \,|\, t \,;\, t_2 \rfloor v) = (f(t_1) \,\square\, f(t))\,;\,(f(t_2)|id \otimes id|v) =$$
$$= [(w \otimes \xi)|id \otimes id|\eta]\,;\,[(w \otimes u'')|id \otimes t'|t \otimes id|z]\,;\,[(w \otimes t'' \otimes v')|id \otimes id|v] =$$
$$= [(w \otimes \xi)|id \otimes id|\eta]\,;\,[w|id \otimes u''|id \otimes t'|t \otimes id|z]\,;\,[w|id \otimes t''|id \otimes v'|id \otimes id|v] =$$
$$= [(w \otimes \xi)|id \otimes id|\eta]\,;\,[w|id \otimes t''|id \otimes t'|t \otimes id|z] =$$

$= [(w\otimes\xi)|\mathrm{id}\otimes\mathrm{id}|\eta]\ ;\ [w|\mathrm{id}\otimes t''|\mathrm{id}\otimes u'|\mathrm{id}\otimes\mathrm{id}|u_\eta]\ ;\ [w|\mathrm{id}\otimes v''|\mathrm{id}\otimes t'\ |\ t\otimes\mathrm{id}|z] =$

$= [(w\otimes\xi)|\mathrm{id}\otimes\mathrm{id}|\eta]\ ;\ [(w\otimes t''\otimes u')|\mathrm{id}\otimes\mathrm{id}|u_\eta]\ ;\ [(w\otimes v'')|\mathrm{id}\otimes t'|t\otimes\mathrm{id}|z] =$

$= [((w\otimes\xi);(w\otimes u'\otimes t''))|\mathrm{id}\otimes\mathrm{id}|\eta]\ ;\ [(w\otimes v'')|\mathrm{id}\otimes t'|t\otimes\mathrm{id}|z] =$

$= [((\xi\ ;\ (u'\otimes t''))\otimes w)|\mathrm{id}\otimes\mathrm{id}|u]\ ;\ [(w\otimes v''\otimes u')|\mathrm{id}\otimes\mathrm{id}|\eta]\ ;\ [(w\otimes v'')|\mathrm{id}\otimes t'|t\otimes\mathrm{id}|z] =$

$= (f(t_3)|\mathrm{id}\otimes\mathrm{id}|u)\ ;\ [(w\otimes v''\otimes u')|\mathrm{id}\otimes\mathrm{id}|\eta]\ ;\ [(w\otimes v'')|\mathrm{id}\otimes t'|t\otimes\mathrm{id}|z] =$

$= (f(t_3)|\mathrm{id}\otimes\mathrm{id}|u)\ ;\ [(w\otimes v''\otimes t')\ []\ \eta\ ;\ (t\otimes z) = (f(t_3\rfloor u)\ ;\ (f(t_4)\ []\ f(t)) = f(t_3\rfloor u\ ;\ t_4\ |\ t).$

The proof of the symmetric rule is omitted.

Finally, in case of synchronization, we have to prove that $f(t_1\ |\ t'_1\ ;\ t_2\ |\ t'_2) = f(t_3\ |\ t'_3\ ;\ t_4\ |\ t'_4)$. By inductive hypothesis, we know that $f(t_1) = (\xi;\ (t_1\otimes u_2))\otimes w$, $f(t_2) = (v_1\otimes t_2)\otimes w$, $f(t_3) = (\xi\ ;\ (u_1\otimes t_2))\otimes w$, $f(t_4) = (t_1\otimes v_2)\otimes w$, $f(t'_1) = (\xi';\ (t'_1\otimes u'_2))\otimes w'$, $f(t'_2) = (v'_1\otimes t'_2)\otimes w'$, $f(t'_3) = (\xi'\ ;\ (u'_1\otimes t'_2))\otimes w'$ and $f(t'_4) = (t'_1\otimes v'_2)\otimes w'$.

$$f(t_1)\ []\ f(t'_1) = ((\xi;\ (t_1\otimes u_2))\otimes w)\ []\ ((\xi';\ (t'_1\otimes u'_2))\otimes w') =$$
$$= ((\xi\otimes w);\ (t_1\otimes u_2\otimes w))\ []\ ((\xi'\otimes w');\ (t'_1\otimes u'_2\otimes w')) =$$
$$= [(\xi\otimes w)|\mathrm{id}\otimes\mathrm{id}|(\xi'\otimes w')]\ ;\ [(u_2\otimes w)|\mathrm{id}\otimes t_1|t'_1\otimes\mathrm{id}|(u'_2\otimes w')]$$

$$f(t_2)\ []\ f(t'_2) = ((v_1\otimes t_2)\otimes w)\ []\ ((v'_1\otimes t'_2)\otimes w') = [(v_1\otimes w)|\mathrm{id}\otimes t_2|t'_2\otimes\mathrm{id}|(v'_1\otimes w')]$$

Let us abbreviate $\vartheta = [(\xi\otimes w)|\mathrm{id}\otimes\mathrm{id}|(\xi'\otimes w')]$.

$$f(t_1\ |\ t'_1\ ;\ t_2\ |\ t'_2) = (f(t_1)\ []\ f(t'_1))\ ;\ (f(t_2)\ []\ f(t'_2)) =$$
$$= \vartheta\ ;\ [(u_2\otimes w)|\mathrm{id}\otimes t_1|t'_1\otimes\mathrm{id}|(u'_2\otimes w')]\ ;\ [(v_1\otimes w)|\mathrm{id}\otimes t_2|t'_2\otimes\mathrm{id}|(v'_1\otimes w')] =$$
$$= \vartheta\ ;\ [u_2|\mathrm{id}\otimes w|\mathrm{id}\otimes t_1|t'_1\otimes\mathrm{id}|u'_2\otimes\mathrm{id}|w']\ ;\ [v_1|\mathrm{id}\otimes w|\mathrm{id}\otimes t_2|t'_2\otimes\mathrm{id}|v'_1\otimes\mathrm{id}|w'] =$$
$$= \vartheta\ ;\ [w|\mathrm{id}\otimes t_1|t'_1\otimes t_2|t'_2\otimes\mathrm{id}|w']$$

$$f(t_3)\ []\ f(t'_3) = ((\xi;\ (u_1\otimes t_2))\otimes w)\ []\ ((\xi';\ (u'_1\otimes t'_2))\otimes w') =$$
$$= ((\xi\otimes w);\ (u_1\otimes t_2\otimes w))\ []\ ((\xi'\otimes w');\ (u'_1\otimes t'_2\otimes w')) =$$
$$= [(\xi\otimes w)|\mathrm{id}\otimes\mathrm{id}|(\xi'\otimes w')]\ ;\ [(u_1\otimes w)|\mathrm{id}\otimes t_2|t'_2\otimes\mathrm{id}|(u'_1\otimes w')]$$
$$= \vartheta\ ;\ [(u_1\otimes w)|\mathrm{id}\otimes t_2|t'_2\otimes\mathrm{id}|(u'_1\otimes w')]$$

$$f(t_4)\ []\ f(t'_4) = ((t_1\otimes v_2)\otimes w)\ []\ ((t'_1\otimes v'_2)\otimes w') = [(v_2\otimes w)|\mathrm{id}\otimes t_1|t'_1\otimes\mathrm{id}|(v'_2\otimes w')]$$

$$f(t_3\ |\ t'_3\ ;\ t_4\ |\ t'_4) = (f(t_3)\ []\ f(t'_3))\ ;\ (f(t_4)\ []\ f(t'_4)) =$$
$$= \vartheta\ ;\ [(u_1\otimes w)|\mathrm{id}\otimes t_2|t'_2\otimes\mathrm{id}|(u'_1\otimes w')]\ ;\ [(v_2\otimes w)|\mathrm{id}\otimes t_1|t'_1\otimes\mathrm{id}|(v'_2\otimes w')] =$$
$$= \vartheta\ ;\ [u_1|\mathrm{id}\otimes w|\mathrm{id}\otimes t_2|t'_2\otimes\mathrm{id}|u'_1\otimes\mathrm{id}|w']\ ;\ [v_2|\mathrm{id}\otimes w|\mathrm{id}\otimes t_1|t'_1\otimes\mathrm{id}|v'_2\otimes\mathrm{id}|w'] =$$
$$= \vartheta\ ;\ [w|\mathrm{id}\otimes t_2|t'_2\otimes t_1|t'_1\otimes\mathrm{id}|w'].$$
♦

Theorem 4.8. *(Completeness w.r.t the truly concurrent semantics for CCS)*
Given four different basic transitions of Con_{CCS}, i.e., t_1, t_2, t_3 and t_4 in N_{CCS}, then we have

$$t_1\ ;\ t_2 = t_3\ ;\ t_4 \quad \text{implies} \quad t_1\ \textbf{then}\ t_2\ \chi\ t_3\ \textbf{then}\ t_4$$

Proof. We know that $t_1\ ;\ t_2 = t_3\ ;\ t_4$ if and only if the two computations are mapped to the same commutative process. Moreover, since we are assuming that the four transitions are different, we can prove that the commutative process comprises only two events labelled by some actions in M, and these two events are causally independent.
The proof of this fact is by induction on the structure of t_1 (and thus t_3).

- $t_1 = [\mu,v\rangle$
  In this case there is no transition t_3, different from t_1, starting from $\mu.v$, and thus the premise of the thesis is not satisfied.

- $t_1 = t <+ v'_1$, where $t : v_1 -\mu\rightarrow v_2$
  In this case there can be several candidate transitions t_3.
  - $t_3 = v_1 +> t'$, where $t' : v'_1 -\mu\rightarrow v'_2$
    Impossible, because they generate different concatenable processes (alternative choices).
  - $t_3 = t'' <+ v'_1$, where $t'' : v''_1 -\mu\rightarrow v''_2$
    The problem is then reduced to the simpler case
    $t ; t_2 = t'' ; t_4$ implies t **then** $t_2 \ \chi \ t''$ **then** t_4
    which by inductive hypothesis can be solved.
- $t_1 = v'_1 +> t$, where $t : v_1 -\mu\rightarrow v_2$
  Symmetrically.
- $t_1 = t^1 \backslash \alpha$.
  In this case, all the other involved transitions must have a similar format, $t_i = t^i \backslash \alpha$, and thus the problem is reduced to the simpler
  $t^1 ; t^2 = t^3 ; t^4$ implies t^1 **then** $t^2 \ \chi \ t^3$ **then** t^4.
- $t_1 = t^1[\Phi]$.
  Analogously to the previous case.
- $t_1 = t \rfloor u_1$, where $t : v_1 -\mu\rightarrow v_2$
  In this case there can be several candidate transitions t_3.
  - $t_3 = v_1 \llcorner t'$, where $t' : u_1 -\mu\rightarrow u_2$
    In order to have $t_1 ; t_2 = t_3 ; t_4$, it is necessary that t_2 produces the same event generated by t_3 and t_4 the same by t_1. This univocally forces the following assignements:
    $t_2 = v_2 \llcorner t'$ $\qquad$ $t_4 = t \rfloor u_2$.
    It is patent that this correspond to the axiom in Definition 5.5.
  - $t_3 = t'' \rfloor u_1$, where $t'' : v_1 -\mu\rightarrow v''_2$
    In order to be able to generate the same process, both t_2 and t_4 have $\rfloor$ as principal operator. Therefore, the problem is reduced to the simpler check on the left (sub)transitions.
  - $t_3 = t'' \mid t'$
    Again, the same concatenable can be generated only if t_2 produces the same event generated by t_3, and t_4 the same by t_1. This forces the definition of the two transitions; moreover, this means that we need an inductive check on the left sub-transitions.
- $t_1 = u_1 \llcorner t$, where $t : v_1 -\mu\rightarrow v_2$
  Analogously to the previous case.
- $t_1 = t \mid t'$
  There are three cases. Two of them (t_3 is an asynchronous move) are already covered by the previous two cases. The last is when $t_3 = t'' \mid t^*$. Again, by generating the same concatenable process, t_2 and t_4 have a fixed definition; moreover, we need two checks on both the right and the left sub-transitions. ♦

Corollary 4.9.
Given four different basic transitions of $\mathbf{Con}_{CCS}$, i.e., t_1, t_2, t_3 and t_4 in N_{CCS}, then we have

$t_1 ; t_2 = t_3 ; t_4$ if and only if t_1 **then** $t_2 \ \chi \ t_3$ **then** t_4

Proof. Obvious from Theorem 4.7 and 4.8. ♦

5. Concluding Remark

There has been a recent deep interest in finding inherently "truly concurrent" abstract machines which resulted in a series of proposals [BL86, CM88, CG89] ending with the *Chemical Abstract Machine* by

Berry and Boudol [BB90]. The basic paradigm of all these proposals can be called "programming by multiset transformation", where the sequential components of a system are organized in a multiset, each of which can autonomously proceed or interact. Anyway, Petri Nets *are* abstract machines which do work by multiset transformation: indeed, the *reaction law* of the Chemical Abstract Machine just corresponds to the definition of net transitions and the *chemical law* is simply another way of saying that the token game can be played in parallel. More abstractly, as Meseguer pointed out in [Mes90], all these models are rewriting systems where the application of the rewriting rules may be truly concurrent.

If we consider SCONE and its net semantics, we can observe that it can be seen as an algebraic (thus structural) representation of the basic features of the Chemical Abstract Machine, namely concurrency and communication. Indeed, the *parallel* rule is multiset union, *reaction* corresponds to the operation of communication, and *inaction cleanup* accounts for 0 as neutral element in multiset union. When considering SCONE$^+$, a relevant difference arises concerning the treatment of restriction. The Chemical Abstract Machine introduces to this aim two new concepts, namely *membranes* and *airlocks*, which allow to give an environment-like structure to the system. These two concepts do not have any correspondent concept in the classical net theory. Indeed, Degano, De Nicola and Montanari were forced to find an alternative solution, which we have followed here: parallel composition is modelled as disjoint union *via* the auxiliary unary operators of context _|id and id|_. It may be debatable which of the two solutions is more amenable. From one hand, the notion of membrane and airlock is appealing because it more faithfully describes the structure of restriction at the machine level. On the other hand, the mechanism is rather heavy (a lot of rewritings are needed in order to create an ion in a solution ready to reaction) if compared with the direct definition of transitions for communication we give also in presence of restriction.

A brief comment on comparing the permutation semantics of Boudol and Castellani and our implementation semantics is mandatory. In our view, the main merit of the former is its simplicity and generality which gives it a pivotal role in comparing different truly concurrent semantic for CCS (see [BC90]). Nonetheless, the permutation semantics is not appealing from an operational viewpoint because transitions can be executed one at a time. According to the terminology above, the transition system of [BC89] is a rewriting system where the application of the rewriting rules cannot be made in parallel. On the contrary, we feel that this operational aspect is definitely captured by the SCONE$^+$ sub-net implementing CCS.

The problem of implementing sequential specifications into truly concurrent specifications has been pursued, in a rather different framework, also by [Pro90, JM90]; however, we think that our approach better reveals the algebraic nature of process and net languages, and the relationship between them.

Acknowledgements

We would like to thank the three anonymous referees for their sharp comments.

6. References

[BB90] G. Berry, G. Boudol, "The Chemical Abstract Machine", in Proc. 17th Annual ACM Symposium on Principles of Programming Languages, San Francisco, 81-94, January 1990.

[BC89] G. Boudol, I. Castellani, "Permutation of Transitions: An Event Structure Semantics for CCS and SCCS", in Proc. REX School/Workshop on Linear Time, Branching Time and Partial Order in Logics and Models for Concurrency, Noordwijkerhout, LNCS 354, Springer-Verlag, 411-437, 1989

[BC90] G. Boudol, I. Castellani, "Three Equivalent Semantics for CCS", in Proc. 18th Ecole de Printemps sur la Semantique de Parallelism, La Roche-Posay, LNCS 469, 96-141, 1990.

[BD87] E. Best, R. Devillers, "Sequential and Concurrent Behaviour of Petri Net Theory", Theoretical Computer Science 55 (1), 87-136, 1987.

[BL86] J.P. Banâtre, D. Le Matayer, "A New Computational Model and its Discipline of Programming", Tech-Rep. INRIA n. 566, 1986.

[CFM90] A. Corradini, G.L. Ferrari, U. Montanari, "Transition Systems with Algebraic Structure as Models of Computation", in Proc. 18th *Ecole de Primtemps sur la Semantique de Parallelism*, La Roche-Posay, LNCS 469, Springer-Verlag, 185-222, 1990.

[CG89] N. Carriero, D. Gelerntner, "Linda in Context", Communications of the ACM 32 (4), 444-458, 1989.

[CM88] M. Chandy, J. Misra, Parallel Program Design, Addison-Wesley, 1988.

[DDM85] P. Degano, R. De Nicola, U. Montanari, "Partial Ordering Derivations for CCS", in Proc. FCT'85, LNCS 199, 520-533, 1985.

[DDM88] P. Degano, R. De Nicola, U. Montanari, "A Distributed Operational Semantics for CCS based on Condition/Event Systems", Acta Informatica, 26, 59-91, 1988.

[DDM89] P. Degano, R. De Nicola, U. Montanari, "Partial Ordering Description of Nondeterministic Concurrent Systems", in Proc. REX School/Workshop on Linear Time, Branching Time and Partial Order in Logics and Models for Concurrency, Noordwijkerhout, LNCS 354, Springer-Verlag, 438-466, 1989

[DDM90] P. Degano, R. De Nicola, U. Montanari, "Partial Ordering Semantics for CCS", Theoretical Computer Science 75, 223-262, 1990.

[DMM89] P. Degano, J. Meseguer, U. Montanari, "Axiomatizing Net Computations and Processes", in Proc. 4th Annual Symp. on Logic in Computer Science LICS, Asilomar, CA, IEEE Computer Society Press, 175-185, 1989.

[FM90] G.L. Ferrari, U. Montanari, "Towards a Unification of Models for Concurrency", in Proc. Coll. on Trees in Algebra and Programming (CAAP'90), LNCS 431, 162-176, 1990.

[Gol88a] U. Goltz, *Über die Darstellung von CCS-Programmen durch Petrinetze*, Ph.D. Thesis, RWTH Aachen, 1988.

[Gol88b] U. Goltz, "On Representing CCS Programs by Finite Petri Nets", Proc. MFCS'88, LNCS 324, 339-350, 1988.

[GM90] R. Gorrieri, U. Montanari, "SCONE: A Simple Calculus of Nets", in Proc. CONCUR'90 Conference, Amsterdam, LNCS 458, 2-30, 1990.

[GR83] U. Goltz, W. Reisig, "The Non-sequential Behaviour of Petri Nets", *Information and Computation* **57**, 125-147, 1983.

[JM90] R. Janicki, T. Müldner, "Transformations of Sequential Specificationsinto Concurrent Specifications by Synchronization Guards", *Theoretical Computer Science* 77, 97-129, 1990.

[Mes90] J. Meseguer, "Rewriting as a Unified Model of Concurrency", in Proc. CONCUR'90 Conference, Amsterdam, LNCS 458, 384-400, 1990.

[Mil89] R. Milner, *Communication and Concurrency*, Prentice Hall, 1989.

[MM88] J. Meseguer, U. Montanari, "Petri Nets are Monoids: A New Algebraic Foundation for Net Theory", in Proc. 3rd Annual Symp. on Logic in Computer Science LICS, Edinburgh, IEEE Computer Society Press, 155-164, 1988.

[MM90] J. Meseguer, U. Montanari, "Petri Nets are Monoids", Information and Computation 88 (2), 105-155, 1990.

[MSS90] V. Manca, A. Salibra, G. Scollo, "Equational Type Logic", Theoretical Computer Science 77, 1-29, 1990.

[MY89] U. Montanari, D. Yankelevich, "An Algebraic View of Interleaving and Distributed Operational Semantics for CCS", Proc. *3rd Conf. on Category Theory in Comp. Scie.*, LNCS 389, 5-20, 1989.

[Old87] E.-R. Olderog, "Operational Petri Net Semantics for CCSP", in Advances in Petri Nets 1987, LNCS 266, Springer-Verlag, 196-223, 1987.

[Old89] E.-R. Olderog, "Strong Bisimilarity on Nets", in Proc. REX School/Workshop on Linear Time, Branching Time and Partial Order in Logics and Models for Concurrency, Noordwijkerhout, LNCS 354, Springer-Verlag, 549-573, 1989.

[Pet62] C.A. Petri, "Kommunikation mit Automaten", Schriften des Institutes für Instrumentelle Mathematik, Bonn, 1962.

[Plo81] G. Plotkin, "A Structural Approach to Operational Semantics", Technical Report DAIMI FN-19, Aarhus University, Department of Computer Science, Aarhus, 1981.

[Pro90] P.W.Prószynski, "The Core Concurrency", Proc. of ICCI'90, LNCS 468, 1990.

[Tau89] D. Taubner, Finite Representation of CCS and TCSP Programs by Automata and Petri Nets, LNCS 369, 1989.

[Win82] G. Winskel, "Event Structures for CCS and Related Languages", in Proc. 9th ICALP, LNCS 140, Springer-Verlag, 561-576, 1982.

SATURATION CONDITIONS FOR STOCHASTIC PETRI NETS

R. GOUET
Departamento de Ingeniería Matemática
Universidad de Chile, Casilla 170, Correo 3
SANTIAGO - CHILE

F. PLO , M. SAN MIGUEL
Departamento de Métodos Estadísticos
Universidad de Zaragoza, Plaza San Francisco
50009 ZARAGOZA - SPAIN

B. YCART
Laboratoire de Mathématiques Appliquées, U.A. CNRS 1204
Faculté des Sciences, Av. de l'Université
64000 PAU - FRANCE

ABSTRACT : We give a necessary condition and a sufficient one for the saturation of a Markovian Stochastic Petri Net. These conditions can be explicitly checked in practical situations. As a particular case, we show that our conditions are equivalent to the classical condition of saturation for Jackson Queuing Networks. The applicability of the method is demonstrated also on examples of OSQN and OMS networks.

KEY WORDS : Stochastic Petri Nets, Conditions of saturation.

CONTENTS

0. INTRODUCTION

In the past ten years, the theoretical modelling of computer systems, particularly in the perspective of performance evaluation, has experienced a wide development. In this area, the notion of Petri Net has proved to be a very adequate tool by generalizing the notion of queuing system and allowing synchronization of tasks (cf. Peterson (1981) or Silva (1985) for general references). At first, Petri Nets were considered in a deterministic setting, but very soon stochastic versions of the theory were proposed (cf. Molloy (1982), Ajmone-Marsan et al. (1984), Florin and Natkin (1986)).

We consider a Petri Net as being composed of a finite set of places numbered from 1 to L, and a finite set of transitions numbered from 1 to T. Each place can contain an integer number of 'tokens'. An L-tuple of integers $m = (m^1,\ldots,m^L)$ will be called a 'marking' and m^i will be interpreted as the number of tokens in place i. The evolution of the marking is determined by the firing of transitions. We denote by c_{ij} the integer number (positive, null or negative) of tokens added to place i when transition j is fired. The matrix

$$C = (c_{ij}) \quad i = 1,\ldots,L \;, \quad j = 1,\ldots,T \;,$$

is called the incidence matrix of the net. A general Stochastic Petri Net (SPN) can be seen as a Jump Process $(M_t \;, t\geq 0)$ on $\mathbb{N}^L$, where the jumps go from state m to the states $m+C_j$ (when they still belong to $\mathbb{N}^L$) with C_j denoting the j-th column of some fixed incidence matrix C. Most practical situations can be modelled considering that $(M_t \;, t\geq 0)$ is a Jump <u>Markov</u> Process with rates of transition $\lambda_j(m)$ between states m and $m+C_j$.

Our aim is to study the evolution of M_t when t goes to infinity. We say that a Stochastic Petri Net 'saturates' if at least one linear combination with non negative coefficients of the coordinates of the vector M_t goes to infinity almost surely when t goes to infinity (definition 1.1). In the markovian case this definition is equivalent to that of transience of the embedded Markov chain. The main results of this note are Theorems 1.5 and 1.6 which give respectively a sufficient and a necessary condition for the saturation of a Markov Petri Net, in terms of the incidence matrix C and the transition rates $\lambda_j(m)$. These results are obtained as a consequence of a comparison result, valid for any Stochastic Petri Net (Proposition 1.4). The main tool is a classical theorem of Martingale theory (Proposition 1.3).

In the markovian case, our results are closely related to already known conditions of ergodicity and transience for Markov chains on a denumerable space of states, such as those obtained by Pakes (1969) and Szpankowski (1988). The difference between our conditions and other existing results lies in the martingale technique that allows us to give precise rates of convergence to infinity in the transient case.

Very little is known in general on the saturation conditions of a SPN . Apart from the classical case of Jackson networks, general saturation conditions have been proved so far for the two following types of synchronized networks : the Open Synchronized Queuing Networks (OSQN), studied by Florin and Natkin (1989), and the Open Markovian Systems (OMS) or 'Totally Open Systems of Markovian Sequential Processes', studied by Campos and Silva (1990). The latter model comes from Petri Nets called 'Deterministic Systems of Sequential Processes' (cf. Reisig (1982) or Souissi and Beldiceanu (1988)). In both cases, the saturation conditions are obtained as a consequence of theorem 6.5 p. 378 of Florin and Natkin (1989). The conditions that we prove in this paper may seem less complete than those of Florin and Natkin. However, they are obtained without any limiting hypothesis on the process { M_t , $t \geq 0$ }. Therefore, they can be applied to practical situations, whatever the number of unbounded places. We believe that our conditions may be a useful tool in providing a rapid insight into the properties of a given network, without much calculation. They should be used in our view as a first approach to the exact equilibrium conditions of the network. In general they are not equivalent, but they may be not so far from the necessary and sufficient condition. In order to illustrate the applicability of our results, we treat in section 3 three examples. For Jackson Queuing Networks we show that our conditions are actually equivalent to the classical necessary and sufficient condition of equilibrium (Theorem 2.1). We then study two more examples, one OSQN from Florin and Natkin (1989) and a particular case of OMS .

1. SATURATION CONDITIONS

The notations are those of the previous section. For our purposes, it will be sufficient to consider only the successive jumps of the process { M_t , $t \geq 0$ }.

We denote by M_0 the initial state and by $M_n = (M_n^i)$, $i = 1,\dots,L$, the state reached immediately after the n-th jump. Our definition of saturation is expressed in terms of the sequence { M_n , $n \geq 0$ }. In what follows ${}^tq$ denotes the transpose of a unicolumn vector q .

Definition 1.1 : The Stochastic Petri Net $\{ M_t \,,\, t\geq 0 \}$ *saturates iff*
$\exists\, q = (q_i)\ i = 1,\dots,L \,,\ q_i \geq 0\ \forall\, i$ *s.t.*
${}^t q\, M_n = \sum_{i=0}^{L} q_i\, M_n^i$ *goes to infinity a.s. when n goes to infinity.*

It is immediate to check that this definition is equivalent to the following one :

Definition 1.2 : The Stochastic Petri Net $\{ M_t \,,\, t \geq 0 \}$ *saturates iff*
$\forall\, q = (q_i)\ i = 1,\dots,L \,,\ q_i > 0\ \forall\, i$,
${}^t q\, M_n$ *goes to infinity a.s. when n goes to infinity.*

The linear combinations ${}^t q\, M_n$ can be interpreted as linear monotone state functions. For $q_i=1\ \forall i$, ${}^t q\, M_n$ is simply the total number of tokens in the system after the n-th firing of transition. But many more state functions may be of interest, as we shall see in section 2 .

We remark that under our general hypotheses a Stochastic Petri Net may saturate according to our definition although none of its coordinates go to infinity a.s. (compare with theorem 6.2.1. of Florin and Natkin (1989)). In the particular case where $\{ M_t \,,\, t\geq 0 \}$ is a Jump Markov Process, then $\{ M_n \,,\, n\geq 0 \}$ is a Markov Chain and it is a classical result that Definitions 1.1 and 1.2 are equivalent to that of transience of this Markov chain if it is irreducible (cf. Billingsley (1979), p. 99).

Let $\{ M_t \,,\, t\geq 0 \}$ be a general Stochastic Petri Net and $\{ M_n \,,\, n\geq 0 \}$ the corresponding sequence of states. We denote by $\chi_n = (\chi_n^j)\ j = 1,\dots,T$, the indicator vector of the n-th firing :

$$\chi_n^j = 1 \text{ if the n-th firing is that of transition j}$$
$$= 0 \text{ if not .}$$

The random vectors M_n and χ_n are related through the incidence matrix C as follows :

$$M_n - M_{n-1} = C\, \chi_n \qquad \forall\, n \geq 1 \tag{1}$$

$$M_n - M_0 = \sum_{k=1}^{n} C\, \chi_k \quad \forall\, n \geq 1 . \tag{2}$$

Let $\mathcal{F}_n$ be the σ-algebra generated by $\{ M_0 ,\ldots, M_n \}$, and let q be a vector in $\mathbb{R}^L$. Our idea is to compare ${}^t q(M_n - M_0)$ to the sum :

$$S_n = \sum_{k=1}^{n} {}^t q\, C\, E\,[\, \chi_k \mid \mathcal{F}_{k-1} \,] .$$

In order to interpret this sum, notice that the i-th coordinate of the vector $C\,E[\, \chi_k \mid \mathcal{F}_{k-1} \,]$ can be seen as the expected number of tokens that will be added to place i , when the k-th firing of transition occurs. The sequence $\{ S_n , n \geq 0 \}$ is usually referred to as 'compensating process'. It is immediate to check that the sequence (Y_n) , $n \in \mathbb{N}$ of random variables defined by :

$$Y_n = {}^t q\, (M_n - M_0) - S_n \qquad \forall\, n \geq 1 ,$$

is a square-integrable $(\mathcal{F}_n)$-martingale with uniformly bounded increments. We shall apply to this martingale the following result.

Proposition 1.3 : Let $(Y_n , \mathcal{F}_n)$ be a square-integrable martingale and (A_n) , $n \geq 1$, an increasing predictable sequence such that $A_1 \geq 1$ and $\lim_{n\to\infty} A_n = \infty$ a.s. .

If $\sum_{n=1}^{\infty} E\,[\, (Y_n - Y_{n-1})^2 \mid \mathcal{F}_{n-1} \,] \,/\, A_n^2 < \infty$ a.s. ,

then $\lim_{n\to\infty} Y_n / A_n = 0$ a.s. .

This is Theorem 4 , chap. VII.5 of Shiryayev (1984) . We apply this result to $A_n = n^{1/2+\varepsilon}$ to get the following proposition.

Proposition 1.4 : For any vector q in $\mathbb{R}^L$ and any $\varepsilon > 0$ one has :

$$\lim_{n\to\infty} Y_n \,/\, n^{1/2 + \varepsilon} = 0 , \text{ a.s.}$$

Proof : We just have to prove that

$$\sum_{n=1}^{\infty} E\,[\, (Y_n - Y_{n-1})^2 \mid \mathcal{F}_{n-1} \,] \,/\, n^{1+2\varepsilon} < \infty .$$

It is enough to check that $E\,[\, (Y_n - Y_{n-1})^2 \mid \mathcal{F}_{n-1} \,]$ remains bounded. But as we already remarked the martingale Y_n has uniformly bounded increments, hence the result.

Proposition 1.4 is a comparison result for the evolution of $\{ M_n , n\geq 0 \}$ in terms of the sequence $\{ S_n , n\geq 0 \}$. This gives a useful insight when $\{ S_n , n\geq 0 \}$ has a tractable form. Fortunately this happens in the Markovian case which is of main practical interest. Assume that $\{ M_t , t\geq 0 \}$ is a Markov Petri Net. Let us denote by $\mathcal{R}$ the set of all markings in $\mathbb{N}^L$ that can be reached from the initial state through a finite number of transitions (reachable markings). For all m in $\mathcal{R}$, $\lambda_j(m)$ denotes the rate of firing of transition j when the marking is m. The n-th firing of transition will be that of transition j with probability

$$p_j(m) = \lambda_j(m) \Big/ \sum_{h=1}^{T} \lambda_h(m) .$$

Let P(m) be the vector of the $p_j(m)$'s :

$$P(m) = E [\chi_n \mid M_{n-1} = m] .$$

Due to the Markov property one has :

$$S_n = \sum_{k=1}^{n} {}^t q \, C \, P(M_{k-1}) .$$

Proposition 1.4 leads to the following conditions of saturation :

Theorem 1.5 : If there exists $q = (q_i) \; i=1,\dots,L \quad q_i \geq 0 \; \forall i$ s.t.

$$\mathrm{Min} \{ {}^t q \, C \, P(m) , \; m \in \mathcal{R} \} > 0$$

then the Markov Petri Net saturates and :

$$\lim_{n\to\infty} {}^t q \, M_n / n^\alpha = \infty , \text{ a.s. } , \forall \alpha < 1 .$$

Theorem 1.6 : If there exist $\varepsilon > 0$ and some vector q_0 with non negative coordinates such that

$$\lim_{n\to\infty} {}^t q_0 M_n / n^{1/2 + \varepsilon} = \infty , \text{ a.s.}$$

then :

$$\forall q = (q_i) \; i=1,\dots,L \quad q_i > 0 \quad \text{and} \quad \forall N > 0$$

$$\mathrm{Max} \{ {}^t q \, C \, P(m) , \; m \in \mathcal{R} \text{ and } {}^t q_0 \, m > N \} > 0$$

Proofs : Due to proposition 1.4 , if $S_n / n^{1/2+\varepsilon}$ tends to infinity for some ε , then so does ${}^tq(M_n - M_0) / n^{1/2+\varepsilon}$. But under the condition of theorem 1.5 , this is obviously the case for any $\varepsilon < 1/2$. Hence the sufficiency of this condition. For theorem 1.6, notice first that if the hypothesis is true for some vector q_0 with non negative coordinates, then it is also true for any vector q with positive coordinates. Thus from proposition 1.4 , $S_n / n^{1/2+\varepsilon}$ goes to infinity for all q with positive coordinates. Thus the terms ${}^tq\ C\ P(M_n)$ have to be positive infinitely often. But the hypothesis is :

$$\forall N > 0 \quad \exists n_0 \text{ s.t. } \forall n > n_0 \quad {}^tq_0\ M_n > N \quad \text{a.s.}\ .$$

Hence the result.

<u>Remark 1.7</u> : Proposition 1.3 can be obtained as a consequence of proposition VII-2-4 of Neveu (1975). Using this latter result theorem 1.6 can be slightly improved by replacing the hypothesis on ${}^tq_0\ M_n$ by the following one, which is weaker :

$$\lim_{n\to\infty} {}^tq_0\ M_n / n^{1/2}(\log n)^{\alpha} = \infty \quad \text{a.s.}\ , \text{ for some } \alpha > 1/2\ .$$

In practical situations it is generally considered (cf. Florin and Natkin (1989)), that a given transition may be enabled (and will be fired after an exponential time with fixed parameter) or disabled (and cannot be fired). So that our functions $\lambda_j(m)$ may assume only two values, 0 and λ_j . With that simplification, the functions ${}^tq\ C\ P(m)$ may assume only a finite number of different values and the conditions we propose can always be checked by hand or at least algorithmically.

These conditions may seem rather rough. However, we believe that in a lot of practical situations, they provide an easy insight into the properties of the net, and may be very close to the 'true' (and unknown for the general case) necessary and sufficient condition of saturation for a Petri Net.

In section 2 we shall illustrate these two points with the classical case of Jackson queuing networks, one example of OSQN from Florin and Natkin (1989) and an example of OMS .

2. EXAMPLES OF APPLICATIONS

We shall consider first Open Jackson Networks with constant rates of service (cf. Jackson (1963) or Gelenbe and Pujolle (1982)). Such a network can be written in terms of a Markov Petri Net in the following way (our notations are coherent with those of Gelenbe and Pujolle (1982)).

The L places are interpreted as queues. There are as many transitions as there are connecting arcs in the queuing network model. The effect of the transitions can be described as follows.

- With rate $\lambda\ p_{0,i}$ a token is added to place i .

- With rate $\mu_i(m)\ p_{i,j}$ a token is taken from place i and added to place j .

- With rate $\mu_i(m)\ p_{i,L+1}$ a token is taken from place i and removed from the system.

The different rates satisfy :

$$\lambda > 0 \ , \quad p_{i,j} \geq 0 \quad \forall\ i = 0,\ldots,L \ , \ \forall\ j = 1,\ldots,L+1 \ ,$$

$$\sum_{i=1}^{L} p_{0,i} = 1 \ , \quad \sum_{j=1}^{L+1} p_{i,j} = 1 \quad \forall\ i \ ,$$

and
$$\mu_i(m) = \mu_i > 0 \quad \text{if } m^i > 0$$
$$= 0 \quad \text{if } m^i = 0 \ .$$

The necessary and sufficient condition for an open Jackson network to saturate (transient case) can be stated as follows (cf. Gelenbe and Pujolle (1982) , Theorem 2.6.1, p. 67).

Theorem 2.1 : The Jackson network saturates iff

$$\exists\ i \text{ s.t. } \quad \lambda\ e_i > \mu_i \ ,$$

where $(e_i)\ i = 1,\ldots,L$ *is the solution of*

$$e_i = p_{0,i} + \sum_{j=1}^{L} p_{j,i}\ e_j \quad \forall\ i = 1,\ldots,L \qquad (3)$$

We will show first that in this case, the sufficient condition of Theorem 1.5 is also necessary, by proving that it is a consequence of the condition of Theorem 2.1 .

Firstly, we need to evaluate the coordinates of the vector C P(m) for any marking m . Its i-th coordinate is :

$$[\ \lambda\ p_{0,i} - \mu_i(m) + \sum_{j=1}^{L} p_{j,i}\ \mu_j(m)\ ]\ /\ [\ \lambda + \sum_{i=1}^{L} \mu_i(m)\ ] \ .$$

Using relation (3) , one can rewrite this as :

$$[\ \lambda\ e_i - \mu_i(m) - \sum_{j=1}^{L} p_{j,i}\ (\ \lambda\ e_j - \mu_j(m)\ )\ ]\ /\ [\ \lambda + \sum_{i=1}^{L} \mu_i(m)\ ] \ .$$

So that for $q = (q_i)$, $i = 1,\dots,L$ one has :

$$^{t}q\ C\ P(m)$$

$$= [\lambda + \sum_{i=1}^{L} \mu_i(m)]^{-1} \sum_{i=1}^{L} q_i [\lambda e_i - \mu_i(m) - \sum_{j=1}^{L} p_{j,i}(\lambda e_j - \mu_j(m))]$$

$$= [\lambda + \sum_{i=1}^{L} \mu_i(m)]^{-1} \sum_{i=1}^{L} [\lambda e_i - \mu_i(m)] [q_i - \sum_{j=1}^{L} p_{i,j} q_j] .$$

Now if we denote by π the matrix of the $p_{i,j}$'s , the last bracket in the above relation is the i-th coordinate of $(I - \pi)q$. But $(I - \pi)^{-1}$ is a matrix with non negative coefficients. Hence for any $i = 1,\dots,L$ there exists a vector $q(i)$ with non negative coefficients such that :

$$^{t}q(i)\ C\ P(m) = [\lambda + \sum_{j=1}^{L} \mu_j(m)]^{-1} [\lambda e_i - \mu_i(m)]$$

Thus , if $\lambda e_i - \mu_i > 0$, $^{t}q(i)\ C\ P(m)$ is positive for all markings m . Since $^{t}q(i)\ C\ P(m)$ can assume only a finite number of different values, the result follows.

Let us now prove that the necessary condition of theorem 1.6 is also sufficient. We may assume with no loss of generality that the matrix π is irreducible, in which case the matrix $(I - \pi)^{-1}$, hence all the vectors $q(i)$ defined above, have positive coefficients. But the necessary condition of theorem 1.6 implies that all the quantities $^{t}q(i)\ C\ P(m)$ have to be positive if $^{t}q_0\ m$ is big enough, for some q_0 with non negative coefficients. But if $^{t}q_0\ m > N$, then at least one coordinate of the vector m is positive , say $m^k > 0$. But then $\mu_k(m)$ is equal to μ_k and $(\lambda e_k - \mu_k)$ is positive, hence the result.

The next example is the 'mutual exclusion OSQN', that appears in Florin and Natkin (1989), p. 371. It is represented below, with the usual conventions (bars for transitions, circles for places). When they are enabled, the transitions fire after exponential times, with rates λ_j's , as indicated below.

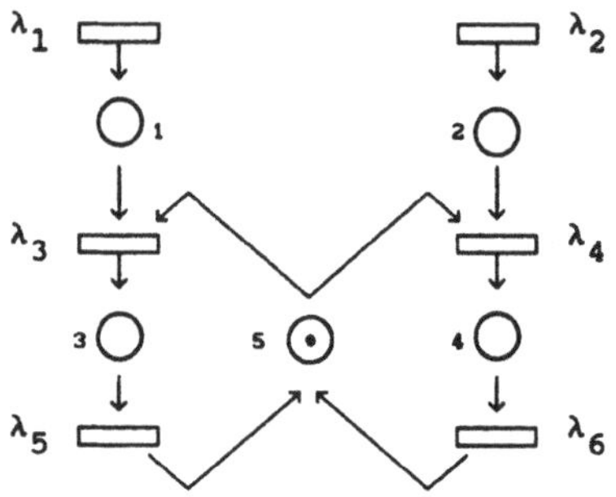

For this particular model, the following sufficient conditions of transience can be obtained, using Theorem 6.5 of Florin and Natkin (1989) (cf. pp. 371 and 378).

$$\lambda_2\lambda_5 > \lambda_4\lambda_6(\lambda_5-\lambda_1)/(\lambda_4 + \lambda_6) \quad \text{or} \quad \lambda_1\lambda_6 > \lambda_3\lambda_5(\lambda_6-\lambda_2)/(\lambda_3 + \lambda_5) .$$

These conditions may be rewriten as :

$$\lambda_1/\lambda_3 + \lambda_1/\lambda_5 + \lambda_2/\lambda_6 > 1 \quad \text{or} \quad \lambda_2/\lambda_4 + \lambda_2/\lambda_6 + \lambda_1/\lambda_5 > 1 . \qquad (4)$$

Let us apply Theorem 1.5 . The rates $\lambda_j(m)$ are now $\lambda_j(m) = \lambda_j$, j=1,2 and $\lambda_j(m) = 0$ or λ_j , for j = 3,4,5,6. So that the sum of all $\lambda_j(m)$'s is always positive. For our purposes, it will be clearer to replace the vector P(m) by the vector $\Lambda(m) = (\lambda_j(m))$, j=1,...,T . This does not change the saturation conditions. The product of the incidence matrix C by the vector $\Lambda(m)$ is the following vector (the numbering of the places is indicated on the figure)

$$C\,\Lambda(m) = {}^t(\lambda_1-\lambda_3(m) , \lambda_2-\lambda_4(m) , \lambda_3(m)-\lambda_5(m) , \lambda_4(m)-\lambda_6(m) , \lambda_5(m)+\lambda_6(m)-\lambda_3(m)-\lambda_4(m)) .$$

According to Theorem 1.5 , for any vector q with non negative coordinates, $\text{Min}\,\{{}^tq\,C\,\Lambda(m)\} > 0$ is a sufficient condition of saturation for the network. For trivial values of q , one gets immediately the 'obvious' saturation conditions. For instance, the choices ${}^tq = (1,0,0,0,0)$, $(0,1,0,0,0)$, $(1,0,1,0,0)$ and $(0,1,0,1,0)$ yield respectively the sufficient conditions $\lambda_1>\lambda_3$, $\lambda_2>\lambda_4$, $\lambda_1>\lambda_5$ and $\lambda_2>\lambda_6$. But with less trivial values of q one obtains exactly the conditions (4). Consider the following choice :

$$^{t}q = (\lambda_3\lambda_6+\lambda_5\lambda_6 , \lambda_3\lambda_5 , \lambda_3\lambda_6 , \lambda_3\lambda_5 , 0) .$$

Then

$$^{t}q \; C \; \Lambda(m) = (\lambda_1-\lambda_3(m))\lambda_5\lambda_6 + (\lambda_1-\lambda_5(m))\lambda_3\lambda_6 + (\lambda_2-\lambda_6(m))\lambda_3\lambda_5 .$$

Now observe that among the transitions 3 , 5 and 6 at most one can be enabled at a time. So that for any reachable marking m at most one of the terms $\lambda_3(m)$, $\lambda_5(m)$, $\lambda_6(m)$ can be non null. The saturation condition Min $\{^{t}q \; C \; \Lambda(m)\} > 0$ is equivalent to :

$$\lambda_1\lambda_3\lambda_6 + \lambda_1\lambda_5\lambda_6 + \lambda_2\lambda_3\lambda_5 - \lambda_3\lambda_5\lambda_6 > 0$$

or else :

$$\lambda_1/\lambda_3 + \lambda_1/\lambda_5 + \lambda_2/\lambda_6 > 1 .$$

A symmetric argument leads to :

$$\lambda_2/\lambda_4 + \lambda_2/\lambda_6 + \lambda_1/\lambda_5 > 1 .$$

Thus, with very little calculation, one obtains the same saturation conditions as by Florin and Natkin's technique.

The last example that we shall consider is the following OMS.

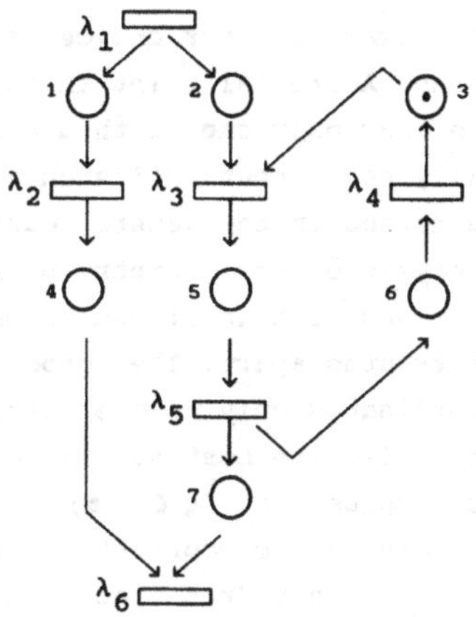

The following saturation condition can be obtained using Florin and Natkin's technique (cf. Campos and Silva (1990)).

$$\text{Max } \{ \lambda_1/\lambda_2 , \lambda_1/\lambda_6 , \lambda_1/\lambda_3 + \lambda_1/\lambda_4 + \lambda_1/\lambda_5 \} > 1 \qquad (5)$$

Proceeding as in the previous example, we first write the vector C $\Lambda(m)$.

$$C \; \Lambda(m) = {}^{t}(\lambda_1-\lambda_2(m) , \lambda_1-\lambda_3(m) , \lambda_4(m)-\lambda_3(m) , \lambda_2(m)-\lambda_6(m) ,$$
$$\lambda_3(m)-\lambda_5(m) , \lambda_5(m)-\lambda_4(m) , \lambda_5(m)-\lambda_6(m)) .$$

Among other possibilities, the trivial choices ${}^{t}q$ = (1,0,0,0,0,0,0) and (1,0,0,1,0,0,0) lead to the obvious conditions $\lambda_1>\lambda_2$ and $\lambda_1>\lambda_6$. Consider now the following choice :

$$ {}^{t}q = (0 , \lambda_4\lambda_5+\lambda_3\lambda_5+\lambda_3\lambda_4 , 0 , 0 , \lambda_3\lambda_5+\lambda_3\lambda_4 , \lambda_3\lambda_5 , 0) . $$

Then

$$ {}^{t}q\ C\ \Lambda(m) = (\lambda_1-\lambda_3(m))\lambda_4\lambda_5 + (\lambda_1-\lambda_4(m))\lambda_3\lambda_5 + (\lambda_1-\lambda_5(m))\lambda_3\lambda_4 . $$

Observe that among the transitions 3 , 4 and 5 at most one can be enabled at a time. So that for any reachable marking m at most one of the terms $\lambda_3(m)$, $\lambda_4(m)$, $\lambda_5(m)$ can be non null. The saturation condition Min $\{{}^{t}q\ C\ \Lambda(m)\} > 0$ is equivalent to :

$$ \lambda_1\lambda_4\lambda_5 + \lambda_1\lambda_3\lambda_5 + \lambda_1\lambda_3\lambda_4 - \lambda_3\lambda_4\lambda_5 > 0 $$

or else :

$$ \lambda_1/\lambda_3 + \lambda_1/\lambda_4 + \lambda_1/\lambda_5 > 1 . $$

Thus the saturation condition (5) has been obtained very simply using our method.

In the last two examples, our choices for the vectors q were guided by known conditions. A crucial point in both cases was to use sets of transitions such that only one of them could be enabled at a time. Let us call 'totally non concurrent' such a set. This notion is a guide-line to apply the method in the general case. A Petri Net being given, a preliminary analysis of its geometry permits to identify the totally non concurrent groups of transitions. Each of them corresponds to a subnet that can be treated apart. The 'good' vectors q for a given subnet have positive coordinates only on the places of the subnet (the other coordinated being null). The best saturation conditions will be obtained when, in the expression ${}^{t}q\ C\ \Lambda(m)$, all the terms $\lambda_j(m)$ corresponding to the totally non concurrent transitions appear with negative coefficients. Notice that from Theorem 1.5 the conditions on one subnet obtained as indicated above imply the saturation of that same subnet. Thus they are an indication on the local behavior of the net.

Acknowledgements : The first author wishes to acknowledge support from FONDECYT under grants 0550/88, 0876/89 and from the 'French-Chilean cooperation program'. The work of the second and the third authors has been supported by project PA86-0028 of the Spanish 'Comisión Interministerial de Ciencia y Tecnología' (CICYT). All authors wish to thank the two referees for helpful comments.

REFERENCES

M. AJMONE-MARSAN, G. BALBO, G. CONTE (1984) A class of generalized Stochastic Petri Nets for the performance evaluation of multiprocessor systems.
A.C.M. Transactions on Computer System, Vol. 2 , 2 , pp. 93-122.

P. BILLINGSLEY (1979) *Probability and measure*
Wiley, New York.

J. CAMPOS, M. SILVA (1990) Steady state performance evaluation of Totally Open Systems of Markovian Sequential Processes. *in 'Decentralized Systems', M. Cosnard, C. Girault eds., pp. 427-438, North-Holland, Amsterdam.*

G. FLORIN, S. NATKIN (1986) One-Place Unbounded Stochastic Petri Nets : Ergodic Criteria and Steady-State Solutions.
J. Syst. Software, Vol. 1 pp. 103-115.

G. FLORIN, S. NATKIN (1989) Necessary and sufficient ergodicity condition for open synchronized queuing networks.
IEEE Trans. on Software Engineering Vol. 15 , 4 , pp. 367-380.

E. GELENBE, G. PUJOLLE (1982) *Introduction aux réseaux de files d'attente.* Eyrolles , Paris.

J. R. JACKSON (1963) Jobshop-like queuing systems
Management Science Vol. 10, pp. 131-142.

M. K. MOLLOY (1982) Performance analysis using stochastic Petri nets
IEEE Transactions on Computers Vol. C-31, 9 , pp. 913-917.

J. NEVEU (1975) *Discrete-Parameter Martingales.*
North-Holland, Amsterdam.

A. G. PAKES (1969) Some conditions for Ergodicity and Recurrence of Markov Chains. *Opns. Res. Vol. 17 , pp. 1058-1061.*

J. L. PETERSON (1981) *Petri Net Theory and the modelling of systems*
Prentice Hall, New-Jersey.

W. REISIG (1982) Deterministic buffer synchronization of sequential processes. *Acta Inf., 18, pp. 117-134.*

A.N. SHIRYAYEV (1984) *Probability* Springer, New-York.

M. SILVA (1985) *Las redes de Petri en la automática y la informática* Editorial AC, Madrid.

Y. SOUISSI, N. BELDICEANU (1988) Deterministic systems of sequential processes : theory and tools. *in 'Concurrency 88', F.H. Vogt ed., pp. 380-400. Lecture Notes in Comp. Sci. 335 , Springer, New York.*

W. SZPANKOWSKI (1988) Stability Conditions for Multidimensional Queuing Systems with Computer Applications. *Opns. Res. Vol. 36 pp. 944-957.*

MARKING OPTIMIZATION IN TIMED EVENT GRAPHS

LAFTIT S., PROTH J.M., and XIE X.L.

INRIA-Lorraine
Technopôle Metz 2000
4, rue Marconi
57070 METZ
FRANCE

ABSTRACT:

This paper addresses the marking optimization problem in a strongly connected timed event graph. It consists in finding an initial marking such that the cycle time is smaller than a given value and that an invariant linear criterion is minimized. This linear criterion is based on a p-invariant of the strongly connected event graph under consideration. We prove some properties of the optimal solution and provide a heuristic algorithm which gives near optimal solution to the problem. Applications of the results to the work-in-process optimization of job-shops and Kanban systems are proposed.

KEY WORDS :

Petri Nets, Timed Event Graphs, Cycle Time, Marking, Job-shop, Kanban Systems, Modeling, Evaluation.

1. INTRODUCTION

Petri nets are well-known as efficient tools for modelling discrete event systems, and particularly manufacturing systems. In particular, Petri nets are able to represent synchronous events, asynchronous concurrent processes. An excellent survey on the subject can be found in MURATA [5] and the related references.

Timed Petri nets have been introduced to model duration of activities and, as a consequence, to represent the dynamic behaviour of discrete systems. Timed event graphs, a special type of Petri nets, have been proven to be adequate for modelling job-shops and assembly systems when the production is periodic (see for instance HILLION and PROTH [3] and HILLION et al. [4]).

The properties of the timed event graphs have been extensively studied by RAMCHANDANI [6], SIFAKIS [8], RAMAMOORTHY and HO [7] and CHRETIENNE [1].

All the previous works are related to deterministic event graphs, i.e. to event graphs in which the times assigned to the transitions are deterministic. This work makes the same assumption.

A challenging problem arising in this context is to reach a cycle time smaller than a given value while minimizing an invariant linear criterion. Such a criterion is a linear combination of the number of tokens in the places at the initial time. Its value remains constant by transition firings (assuming that tokens remain in the places preceding the transitions fired until the transition firing terminates).

In this paper, we assume that the basics of timed event graphs are known from the part of the reader as presented in HILLION and PROTH [3].

Section 2 introduces the problem at hand. In section 3, we discuss the properties of the optimal solutions. A heuristic algorithm which leads to a near optimal solution to the problem is given in section 4. Finally, applications in the field of work-in-process of manufacturing systems are presented in section 5.

2. PROBLEM DESCRIPTION

2.1. Preliminary assessment

Let N = (P,T,F) be the strongly connected event graph considered. P is the set of places, T is the set of transitions and $F \subset (P \times T) \cup (T \times P)$ the set of directed arcs. We denote by M_0 the initial marking of N. For every $t \in T$, τ_t is the transition firing time of t (τ_t is a positive rational number). We assume that a transition cannot be fired by more than one token at any time. In other words, a transition in a firing execution is not enabled for a new firing. This restriction can be explicitly modelled by adding a self loop with one token to each transition of the net as shown in figure 1.

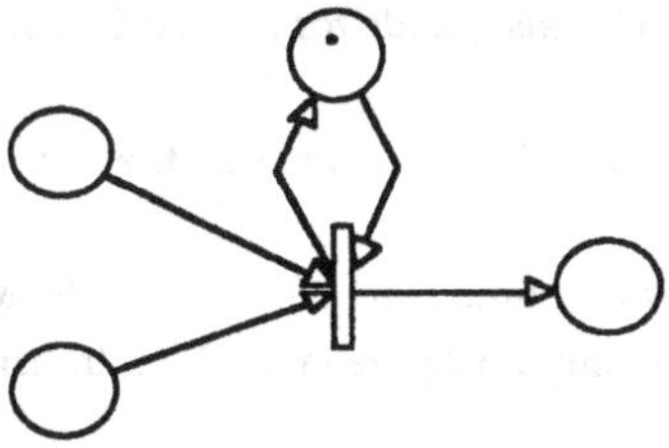

Figure 1: A transition with self loop

Let Γ be the set of elementary circuits of N which include the set of self loops. For each $\gamma \in \Gamma$, $C(\gamma) = \mu(\gamma) / M_0(\gamma)$, is the cycle time of γ. In this formula, $\mu(\gamma) = \sum_{t \in \gamma} \tau_t$ and $M_0(\gamma)$ is the number of tokens in γ. The cycle times of elementary circuits are invariant by transition firing. Of course, we assume that $M_0(\gamma) > 0$. If $M_0(\gamma) = 0$ for at least one elementary circuit, then a deadlock state is reached after a finite time.

If $\gamma^* \in \Gamma$ is such that $C(\gamma^*) = \max_{\gamma \in \Gamma} C(\gamma)$, then γ^* is a critical circuit and $C(\gamma^*) = C^*$ is the cycle time of N.

CHRETIENNE [1] has shown that, under an operational mode for which transitions fire as soon as they are enabled (called EOM -earliest operational mode- hereafter), the functioning becomes K-periodic after a finite time. More precisely, there exists one integer n_0 such that:

$$S_t(n + K) = S_t(n) + K\,C^*, \forall\, n \geq n_0, \forall\, t \in T \qquad (1)$$

where $S_t(m)$ is the instant of the m-th firing initiation of transition t.

We now consider a periodic firing policy. Such a policy is defined when the cycle time C and $S_t(1)$, $\forall\, t \in T$, are known.

For such an operational mode (called POM for periodic operational mode hereafter), the following relations hold:

$$S_t(n) = S_t(1) + (n - 1)\,C, \forall\, t \in T \text{ and } n \in N^+ \qquad (2)$$

A POM is feasible if and only if conditions (3) hold:

$$S_{^op}(1) + \tau_{^op} \leq S_{p^o}(1) + C\,M_0(p), \forall\, p \in P \qquad (3)$$

where:

^op is the input transition of p

p^o is the output transition of p

$M_0(p)$ is the initial marking of p (i.e. the initial number of tokens in p).

If we add the left-hand sides and the right-hand sides of inequalities (3) written for all the places belonging to an elementary circuit γ, we obtain:

$$\mu(\gamma) \leq C\,M_0(\gamma)$$

or:

$$C \geq \mu(\gamma) / M_0(\gamma) = C(\gamma)$$

and, because this inequality also holds for a critical elementary circuit γ^*:

$$C \geq C(\gamma^*) = C^*$$

RAMAMOORTHY and HO [7] have proven that for any $C \geq C^*$, there exists a feasible POM.

We also know that the cycle time reached under an EOM can also be reached under a POM if one is willing to temporarily delay enabled transitions from firing.

2.2. Invariant linear criteria

As mentioned in the introduction, we are interested in minimizing invariant linear criteria. The goal of this sub-section is to define these criteria and to present their properties. Let $P = \{p_1, p_2, ..., p_r\}$ be the set of places and $T = \{t_1, t_2, ..., t_n\}$ the set of transitions of the strongly connected event graph at hand. Such an event graph is defined as soon as the incidence matrix $A = [a_{i,j}]$, $i = 1, 2, ..., r$, $j = 1, 2, ..., n$, is known. The incidence matrix of an event graph is given by:

$$a_{i,j} = \begin{cases} 1 \text{ if } t_j \in {}^o p_i \\ -1 \text{ if } t_j \in p_i^o \\ 0 \text{ otherwise} \end{cases}$$

Let M_0 be an initial marking and M a marking reachable starting from M_0 by a sequence σ of transition firings. The following relation holds:

$$M = M_0 + A\, V_\sigma \qquad (4)$$

where $V_\sigma = (v_1, v_2, ..., v_n)^T$, v_i $(i = 1, 2, ..., n)$ being the number of occurrences of transition t_i in the sequence σ. The vector V_σ is called characteristic vector of σ.

Let $U = (u_1, u_2, ..., u_r)^T$ be a vector of non-negative integers such that:

$$U^T A = 0 \qquad (5)$$

U is p-invariant (also called P-semi flow) and the following properties hold:

Property 1

Let M_0 be an initial marking and M a marking reachable starting from M_0 by the sequence of transition firings σ (we say that $M \in R(M_0)$). Then:

$$U^T . M_0 = U^T . M \qquad (6)$$

Property 2

Let M_1 and M_2 be two markings. If $M_2 \geq M_1$ (i.e. if $M_2(p) \geq M_1(p)$, $\forall p \in P$), then $f_U(M_2) \geq f_U(M_1)$.

From now on, we denote

$$f_U(M_0) = U^T . M_0$$

and $f_U(M_0)$ is the criterion to minimize.

2.3. Problem formulation

Given a positive real value α, we call an initial marking M_0 a **feasible marking** for α if the cycle time C (M_0), obtained from M_0 by applying a POM is less than or equal to α.

According to sub-section 2.1., the following propositions are equivalent in a POM context:

(a) M_0 is a feasible marking for α

(b) $M_0(\gamma) \geq \mu(\gamma) / \alpha, \forall \gamma \in \Gamma$

(c) There exists a POM such that the following inequalities hold (see relation (3)):

$$S_{op}(1) + \tau_{op} \leq S_{po}(1) + \alpha \cdot M_0(p), \forall p \in P \quad (7)$$

E being the set of feasible markings (i.e. the set of markings verifying (b) or (c)), the problem to be solved when using a POM, denoted by $\mathcal{P}(\alpha,POM)$, can be formulated as follows:

Find $M^*_0 \in E$ and $S_t(1) \in \mathbb{R}$ for all $t \in T$ such that the relations (7)-c hold and

$$f_U(M^*_0) = \underset{M0 \in E}{\mathcal{Min}} f_U(M_0) \quad (8)$$

$\mathcal{P}(\alpha,EOM)$ denotes the previous problem when applying an EOM. In that case, the set E of feasible markings is only defined by (7)-b relations, (7)-c being worthless when applying an EOM.

The goal of this paper is to find a fast algorithm which leads to a near-optimal solution to $\mathcal{P}(\alpha,EOM)$.

Note that the optimal solution to $\mathcal{P}(\alpha,POM)$ is a marking and the set of the instants of the first firing initiations of the transitions while the optimal solution to $\mathcal{P}(\alpha,EOM)$ is only a marking.

3. PROPERTIES OF THE OPTIMAL SOLUTIONS

In this section, we provide some properties of optimal solutions to $\mathcal{P}(\alpha,POM)$. These properties will be used in the next section to solve the problem at hand.

Property 3

For any $\alpha \geq \mathcal{Max}\ \{\tau_t, t \in T\}$, the marking $M_0 = (1, 1, ..., 1)$, which consists in putting one token in each place, is a feasible marking for α.

Proof:

Let us initiate the first firing of all transitions at time 0. Proposition (c) in (7) becomes $\tau_{\circ p} \leq \alpha$ and thus M_0 is a feasible marking for α.

Q.E.D.

Since the transition firings are non preemptive, α cannot be less than $\mathcal{Max}\ \{\tau_t, t \in T\}$. Thus, according to property 3, $\alpha \geq \mathcal{Max}\ \{\tau_t, t \in T\}$ is a necessary and sufficient condition for the existence of a feasible marking.

Property 4

A marking M_0^* of an optimal solution to problem $\mathcal{P}(\alpha,POM)$ is an optimal solution to problem $\mathcal{P}(\alpha,EOM)$.

Proof:

Assume that an optimal solution M_0^{**} to $\mathcal{P}(\alpha,EOM)$ is such that $f_U\,(M_0^{**}) < f_U\,(M_0^*)$ and let $C^{**} \leq \alpha$ the cycle time obtained from M_0^{**} by applying the EOM. We know that C^{**} can also be reached from M_0^{**} by applying a POM obtained by temporarily delaying the enabled transitions from firing. Thus M_0^* would not be a solution to problem $\mathcal{P}(\alpha,POM)$, and this conclusion is contradictory to the hypothesis of property 4.

Q.E.D.

As a consequence of property 4, an optimal solution to problem $\mathcal{P}(\alpha,EOM)$ can be found by solving the problem $\mathcal{P}(\alpha,POM)$ which can be stated as follows:

Find M_0^* and a set of instants of first firing initiation of the transitions (denoted by $S_{{}^\circ p}$ (1) or S_{p° (1)) which minimize $f_U(M_0)$ and such that:

$$S_{{}^\circ p}(1) + \tau_{{}^\circ p} \leq S_{p^\circ}(1) + \alpha\, M^*_0(p),\ \forall p \in P \tag{9}$$

The following properties of this solution will result in a further simplification of problem $\mathcal{P}(\alpha,POM)$.

Property 5

There exists an optimal solution $\{M^*_0, S_t(1)\ \forall t \in T\}$ to problem $\mathcal{P}(\alpha,POM)$ such that:

(i) $-\tau_t < S_t(1) \leq \alpha - \tau_t,\ \forall\, t \in T$

(ii) $M^*_0(p) \leq 2,\ \forall\, p \in P$

Proof:

The property is trivially true if for any feasible POM, there exists another feasible POM which has smaller criterion value and for which relations (i) and (ii) hold. Hereunder, we prove in two steps that it is true.

(i) We first show that for any feasible POM $\{M_0, S_t(1)\ \forall t \in T\}$, there exists another feasible POM $\{M'_0, S'_t(1)\ \forall t \in T\}$ of same criterion value (i.e. $f_U(M'_0) = f_U(M_0)$) for which relations (i) hold. For this purpose, a cycle $]\, r, r+\alpha]$ in the steady state of this POM (i.e. $r \geq Max\{S'_t(1)\ \forall t \in T\}$) is considered.

Let M_r be the marking at instant r. Assume that no transition is being initiated at instant r and that when a transition is being fired, tokens stay in its input places. As a result, $f_U(M_0) = f_U(M_r)$.

According to the definition of the POM, one and only one firing of each transition is terminated in this cycle. Let this firing be the $n_t(r)$-th firing of transition t. Since the POM is feasible, it holds that for all $p \in P$,

$$S_{\circ p}(n_{\circ p}(r)) + \tau_{\circ p} \leq S_{p\circ}(n_{p\circ}(r) + M_r(p))$$

which implies that

$$S_{\circ p}(n_{\circ p}(r)) + \tau_{\circ p} \leq S_{p\circ}(n_{p\circ}(r)) + \alpha\, M_r(p) \tag{10}$$

Consider now a new POM $\{M'_0, S'_t(1)\ \forall t \in T\}$ with $M'_0 = M_r$ and $S'_t(1) = S_t(n_t(r)) - r$ $\forall t \in T$. From (10),

$$S'_{\circ p}(1) + \tau_{\circ p} \leq S'_{p\circ}(1) + \alpha\, M'_0(p) \tag{11}$$

which implies that the new POM is feasible.

Since $r < S_t(n_t(r)) + \tau_t \leq r+\alpha$,

$$-\tau_t < S'_t(1) \leq \alpha - \tau_t,\ \forall t \in T \tag{12}$$

(ii) We finally show that there exists a feasible POM $\{M''_0, S''_t(1)\ \forall t \in T\}$ for which relations (i) and (ii) hold and which has lower criterion value, i.e. $f_U(M''_0) \leq f_U(M_0)$.

From (10), it holds that for all $p \in P$,

$$S'_{op}(1) - S'_{po}(1) \leq (\alpha - \tau_{op}) - (-\tau_{po})$$

or:

$$S'_{op}(1) + \tau_{op} \leq S'_{po}(1) + \alpha + \tau_{op} \leq S'_{po}(1) + 2\alpha \tag{13}$$

From (11) and (13),

$$S'_{\circ p}(1) + \tau_{\circ p} \leq S'_{p\circ}(1) + \alpha\, .\, Min\{M'_0(p), 2\}\quad \forall p \in P \tag{14}$$

Relations (14) imply the feasibility of the POM $\{M''_0, S''_t(1)\ \forall t \in T\}$ with $M''_0(p) = Min\{M'_0(p), 2\}\ \forall p \in P$ and $S''_t(1) = S'_t(1)\ \forall t \in T$. This new POM satisfies the relations (i) and (ii), and from Property 2,

$$f_U(M''_0) \leq f_U(M'_0) = f_U(M_0)$$

Q.E.D.

At this point of the explanation, we know that there exists an optimal solution $\{M^*_0, S_{po}(1), \forall p \in P\}$ to the problem $\mathbf{P}(\alpha,POM)$ such that $M^*_0(p) \leq 2, \forall p \in P$. But, it is always possible to extend a strongly connected event graph in the way shown in figure 2, where the time assigned to t' is zero.

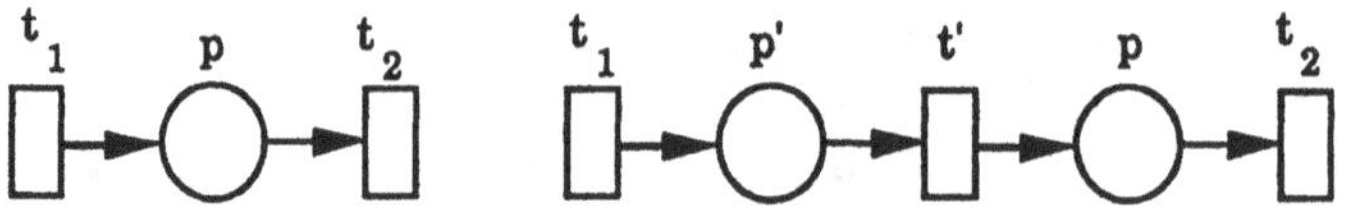

Initial situation — Extended situation

Fig. 2: Extension of the event graph

In that case, it is possible to put one token in place p and one token in place p' instead of putting two tokens in p.

Thus, taking into account part (ii) of property 5, the following property holds:

Property 6

The problem at hand can always be reduced to a problem whose optimal solution $\{M^*_0, S_t(1)\ \forall t \in T\}$ is such that $M^*_0(p) \le 1, \forall\, p \in P$.

This property shows that the marking optimization problem can be reduced to a 0-1 linear programming problem. We now introduce a necessary condition for a marking to be locally optimal for the problem at hand. This condition will be used in the first heuristic approach proposed hereafter.

A marking M belongs to a feasible solution to problem $\mathcal{P}(\alpha,POM)$ if and only if $\mu(\gamma) / M(\gamma) \le \alpha$ for any elementary circuit γ, as shown in section 2.1. The previous inequality can be rewritten as: $M(\gamma) - \mu(\gamma) / \alpha \ge 0$

Let us now define

$$\omega(M, p, \alpha) = \mathcal{M}in_{\gamma \in \Gamma_p} [M(\gamma) - \mu(\gamma) / \alpha]$$

where Γ_p is the set of the elementary circuits containing p. Thus the previous necessary condition can be rewritten as:

M belongs to a feasible solution to problem $\mathcal{P}(\alpha,POM)$ only if $\omega(M, p, \alpha) \ge 0$ for any $p \in P$.

The following properties hold:

Property 7

Let $\mathcal{M}(\alpha)$ be the set of markings M such that $\omega(M, p, \alpha) \in [0,1[$, $\forall\, p \in P$. According to the previous necessary condition, any $M \in \mathcal{M}(\alpha)$ is feasible.

(i) Let $M \in \mathcal{M}(\alpha)$ and M_1 such that $M_1 \le M$ and $M_1 \ne M$ (i.e. $M_1(p) \le M(p), \forall\, p \in P$ and there exists at least one $p^* \in P$ such that $M_1(p^*) < M(p)$). Then, M_1 is not feasible and thus cannot be part of an optimal solution to problem $\mathcal{P}(\alpha,POM)$.

(ii) $\mathcal{M}(\alpha)$ contains at least a marking belonging to an optimal solution to problem $\mathcal{P}(\alpha,POM)$.

Proof:

(i) $\omega(M_1, p^*, \alpha) = \mathcal{M}in_{\gamma \in \Gamma_{p^*}} [M_1(\gamma) - \mu(\gamma)/\alpha]$

$$= \mathcal{M}in_{\gamma \in \Gamma_{p^*}} [M_1(p^*) + \sum_{p \in \gamma,\, p \neq p^*} M_1(p) - \mu(\gamma)/\alpha]$$

And, because $M_1(p^*) < M(p)$ and $M_1(p) \leq M(p), \forall p \in P, p \neq p^*$

$$\omega(M_1, p^*, \alpha) \leq \mathcal{M}in_{\gamma \in \Gamma_{p^*}} [M(p^*) - 1 + \sum_{p \in \gamma,\, p \neq p^*} M(p) - \mu(\gamma)/\alpha]$$

Thus:

$\omega(M_1, p^*, \alpha) \leq \omega(M, p^*, \alpha) - 1 < 0$

and M_1 does not belong to a feasible solution to problem $\mathcal{P}(\alpha, POM)$.

(ii) Let M be a marking of an optimal solution to problem $\mathcal{P}(\alpha, POM)$ and assume that $M \notin \mathcal{M}(\alpha)$. Then, $\omega(M, p, \alpha) \geq 0, \forall p \in P$ and there exists at least one $p^* \in P$ such that $\omega(M, p^*, \alpha) \geq 1$.

Since a strongly connected event graph is alive, there exists M^* derived from M by transition firings ($M^* \in R(M)$) such that $M^*(p^*) \geq 1$. Furthermore, $\omega(M, p^*, \alpha) = \omega(M^*, p^*, \alpha)$ because the number of tokens in any elementary circuit remains the same by any transition firing.

We consider M^* and remove one token from p^*. Let us denote the new marking by M_1^*, i.e.:

$M_1^*(p^*) = M^*(p^*) - 1$

$M_1^*(p) = M^*(p), \forall p \in P, p \neq p^*$

Consequently:

$$\omega(M_1^*, p^*, \alpha) = \omega(M^*, p^*, \alpha) - 1 \geq 0 \tag{12}$$

and, for $p \neq p^*$:

$$\omega(M_1^*, p, \alpha) = \mathcal{M}in_{\gamma \in \Gamma_p} [M_1^*(\gamma) - \mu(\gamma)/\alpha]$$

$$= \mathcal{M}in\{\mathcal{M}in_{\gamma \in \Gamma_{p,p^*}} [M_1^*(\gamma) - \mu(\gamma)/\alpha], \mathcal{M}in_{\gamma \in \Gamma_{p,\bar{p}^*}} [M_1^*(\gamma) - \mu(\gamma)/\alpha]\} \tag{13}$$

where Γ_{p,p^*} is the set of elementary circuits containing both p and p^* and $\Gamma_{p,\bar{p}^*}$ is the set of elementary circuits containing p but not p^*.

But:

$$\mathcal{M}in_{\gamma \in \Gamma_{p,p^*}} [M_1^*(\gamma) - \mu(\gamma)/\alpha] = \mathcal{M}in_{\gamma \in \Gamma_{p,p^*}} [M^*(\gamma) - \mu(\gamma)/\alpha] - 1 \geq \omega(M_1^*, p^*, \alpha) \geq 0 \tag{14}$$

and:

$$\mathcal{M}in_{\gamma\in\Gamma_{p,\bar{p}^*}} [M_1^*(\gamma) - \mu(\gamma) / \alpha] = \mathcal{M}in_{\gamma\in\Gamma_{p,\bar{p}^*}} [M^*(\gamma) - \mu(\gamma) / \alpha] \geq 0 \quad (15)$$

Then, from (13), (14) and (15):

$$0 \leq \omega(M_1^*, p, \alpha) \leq \omega(M^*, p, \alpha) \quad (16)$$

From (12) and (16), it turns out that M_1^* is a feasible marking. Moreover, $\omega(M_1^*, p, \alpha) \leq \omega(M, p, \alpha)$, $\forall p \in P$ and that $\omega(M_1^*, p^*, \alpha) < \omega(M^*, p^*, \alpha)$. If $\omega(M_1^*, p, \alpha) \in [0,1[$, $\forall p \in P$, then $M_1^* \in \mathcal{M}(\alpha)$ and property (ii) is proved. Otherwise, we derive M_2^* from M_1^* as M_1^* has been built starting from M, and so on until we reach M_n^* such that $\omega(M_n^*, p, \alpha) \in [0,1[$.

Q.E.D.

As one can see, the computation of $\omega(M, p, \alpha)$ requires apparently the computation of all the elementary circuits containing p for any $p \in P$. But it is possible to turn this problem into the computation of a shortest path in a directed graph G = (T, V, d) where T, set of the transitions in the strongly connected event graph, is the set of nodes, $V \subset TxT$ is the set of directed arcs and $d: V \rightarrow R$ represents the length of the arcs. The length of the arcs are defined as follows:

$$d(t_i, t_j) = \begin{cases} M(p) - \tau_{{}^o p} / \alpha & \text{if p is the only place on the directed path joining } t_i \text{ and } t_j \\ & (\text{i.e. } t_i = {}^o p \text{ and } t_j = p^o) \\ +\infty & \text{otherwise} \end{cases}$$

G does not contain circuits with negative length for any feasible marking M. Thus the shortest distance between any pair of transitions exists and:

$\omega(M, p, \alpha) = d({}^o p, p^o) + z(p^o, {}^o p)$,

where $z(p^o, {}^o p)$ is the length of the shortest path joining p^o and ${}^o p$.

This approach will be used in the first algorithm presented in the next section.

4. AN HEURISTIC ALGORITHM

This algorithm proposed hereafter is mainly based on property 7. We call it the *token adjustment heuristic algorithm* in the following.

It starts with a feasible marking and removes iteratively tokens from places until a solution belonging to $\mathcal{M}(\alpha)$ is reached. The initial feasible marking can be the one suggested by property 3 (i.e. one token in each place), but it can also be any other feasible solution, for instance at least one token in each place.

At each iteration, the heuristic removes one token from a place as long as $\omega(M, p, \alpha) \geq 1$ for at least one $p \in P$. According to property 7, it is possible to remove

$\lfloor \omega(M, p, \alpha) \rfloor$ tokens from place p ($\lfloor \bullet \rfloor$ is the greater integer value less than or equal to •). We thus can remove one token from p if $\omega(M, p, \alpha) \geq 1$ and $M(p) \geq 1$. If $M(p) = 0$, we know that there exists $M^1 \in R(M)$ such that $M^1(p) \geq 1$. Thus, we compute M^1 and then remove one token from p.

If several $p \in P$ are such that $\omega(M, p, \alpha) \geq 1$, the choice of the place from which one token will be removed is made as explained hereafter.

Note that $\omega(M, p, \alpha)$ is, in some sense, a degree of freedom associated to place p as far as the problem at hand is to remove tokens from the system under the constraint that the marking remains feasible. Furthermore, removing a token from p may modify the $\omega(M, q, \alpha)$ values for other places $q \in P$ (these places, if any, belong necessarily to elementary circuits which contain p). Thus, we introduced a secondary criterion denoted by $g_U(M)$ and defined as follows:

$$g_U(M) = \sum_{p \in P} \omega(M, p, \alpha)$$

Let M_p^1 be the marking obtained by removing one token from M and $\Delta_p = [g_U(M) - g_U(M_p^1)] / u_p$, assuming that $\omega(M, p, \alpha) \geq 1$.

We choose the place p such that:

$$\Delta_p = \mathcal{M}in_{q \in F} \Delta_q \qquad (17)$$

where $F = \{ q \,/\, q \in P \text{ and } \omega(M, q, \alpha) \geq 1 \}$

The idea behind this strategy is to remove tokens with higher criterion coefficient which reduce as few as possible the degree of freedom of the system, i.e. which preserve further token removing and, as a consequence, increase the chance to reach a marking very close to the optimal one.

Note that the computation of the Δ_p values is simple: the amount of computation is proportional to the number of places.

The adjustment heuristic algorithm can be formalized as follows:

Step 1: Generate a feasible marking M

Step 2: If $\omega(M, p, \alpha) < 1$ for any $p \in P$, then stop the computation and keep M as the solution to problem

Step 3: If $\omega(M, p, \alpha) \geq 1$ for at least $p \in P$, compute p^* such that:

$$\Delta_{p^*} = \mathcal{M}in_{p \in F} \Delta_p \text{ (see relation (17))}$$

Step 4: If $M(p^*) \geq 1$, set:

$$\begin{cases} M(p) = M(p), \forall p \in P, p \neq p^* \\ M(p^*) = M(p^*) - 1 \end{cases}$$

Otherwise, compute a marking M^1 reachable from M and such that $M^1(p^*) \geq 1$ and set:

$M(p) = M^1(p), \forall p \in P, p \neq p^*$

$M(p^*) = M^1(p^*) - 1$

Step 5: Go to step 2.

Note:

The marking M obtained as a result of the adjustment heuristic algorithm is a near-optimal solution to problem $\mathcal{P}(\alpha,EOM)$. It is possible to complete this solution to obtain a near optimal solution to problem $\mathcal{P}(\alpha,POM)$ by solving the following system derived from (7)-c:

$$S_{op}(1) + \tau_{op} - S_{po}(1) = \alpha M(p), \forall p \in P$$

5. APPLICATIONS

In this section, we apply the previous algorithms to the optimization of the operations of a job-shop and of a Kanban system.

5.1. Optimization of job-shop operations

5.1.1. The problem: definition and modeling

The problem consists in maximizing the productivity of a job-shop with a minimal work-in-process (WIP) level, assuming a cyclic manufacturing of the parts. This problem has been studied by HILLION and PROTH [3]. It has been shown that the solution to this problem is the solution to an integer linear programming problem derived from the elementary circuits of the event graph model. For more information, we refer the reader to reference 3.

We use the same model in this section. It is illustrated by the following simple example. We consider a job-shop composed of four machines M_1, M_2, M_3 and M_4, which can manufacture three types of parts denoted by R_1, R_2 and R_3. The production mix is 25%, 25% and 50% for R_1, R_2 and R_3 respectively.

The production processes of the part types are respectively:

R_1: M_1 (1), M_2 (1), M_3 (3), M_4 (3)

R_2: M_1 (1), M_4 (1), M_3 (2)

R_3: M_1 (1), M_2 (2), M_4 (1)

The part types which need a same machine for operations are produced in a predetermined sequence. If $\sigma(M_i)$ (i = 1, 2, 3, 4) denotes the fixed sequencing of the part types on machine M_i, we choose:

$\sigma(M_1) = (R_1, R_2, R_3, R_3)$; $\sigma(M_2) = (R_1, R_3, R_3)$; $\sigma(M_3) = (R_1, R_2)$;

$\sigma(M_1) = (R_1, R_2, R_3, R_3)$

According to HILLION and PROTH [3], the model related to this problem is given in figure 3. The transition firing times are given in table 1.

Table 1: Transition firing times of the job-shop model

t1	t2	t3	t4	t5	t6	t7	t8	t9	t10	t11	t12	t13
1	1	3	3	1	1	2	1	2	1	1	2	1

This model is a strongly connected event graph. In such an event graph, an elementary p-invariant is a vector having as many components as places in the event graph and where 1-values are assigned to the elements related to the places belonging to one of the elementary circuit and 0-values are assigned to the other elements. Thus, there are as many elementary p-invariants as elementary circuits.

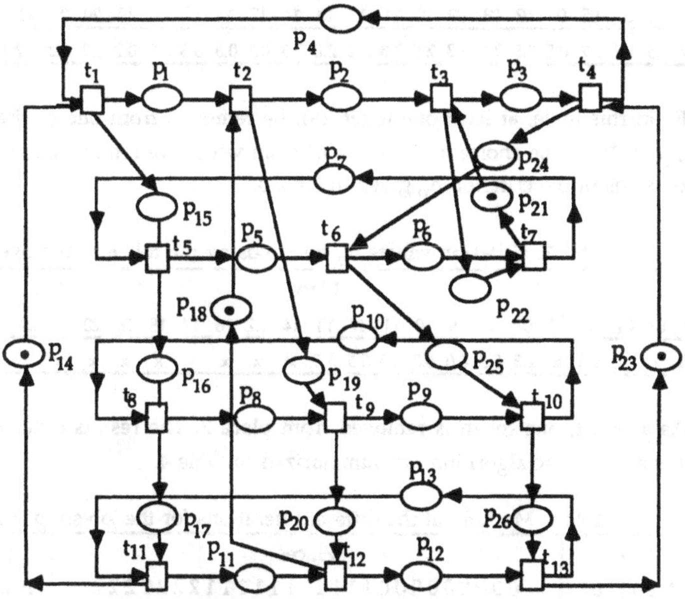

Fig. 3: Event graph model of the job-shop

For the problem at hand, we consider the p-invariant U which is the sum of all the elementary p-invariants, except those related to the command circuits. In other words, f_U is a linear function where all the coefficients are equal to 1 and whose variables represent the number of tokens in the places (except the places belonging to the command circuits).

For the model presented in figure 3, $f_U(M_0) = \sum_{i=1}^{13} M_0(p_i)$.

5.1.2. *Applying the adjustment heuristic algorithm*

The tokens in the places of the command circuits are assigned as shown in figure 3. Furthermore, $\alpha = 6$ (greatest cycle time among the cycle times of the command circuits).

We start with one token in each place, i.e. $M_0(p_i) = 1$ for $i = 1, 2, ..., 13$. The degrees of freedom associated to the places $\omega(M_0, p, \alpha)$ are given in table 2.

Table 2: Degrees of freedom associated to the places

Place																									
01	02	03	04	05	06	07	08	09	10	11	12	13	14	15	16	17	18	19	20	21	22	23	24	25	26
2.3	2.7	0.5	1.7	1.7	0.5	2.3	2.2	2.3	2.0	2.3	2.2	2.0	0.3	0.3	0.3	0.3	0.2	0.2	0.2	0.2	0.2	0.0	0.0	0.0	0.0

From this table, at least one token can be removed from one of the places with $\omega(M_0, p, \alpha) \geq 1$. The choice of the place p^* from which we remove one token is based on the values of the criterion Δ_p given in table 3.

Table 3: Criterion values Δ_p for choosing the token to remove

Place																									
01	02	03	04	05	06	07	08	09	10	11	12	13	14	15	16	17	18	19	20	21	22	23	24	25	26
2.7	2.5	x	7.0	4.0	x	2.3	5.3	4.0	6.3	4.3	5.5	5.5	x	x	x	x	x	x	x	x	x	x	x	x	x

As a result, one token is removed from place 7. The results obtained using the adjustment heuristic algorithm are summarized in table 4.

Table 4: Marking at the different iterations for the job-shop problem

Step	p*	Places 0000000001111-1111112222222 1234567890123-4567890123456	Total number of tokens
0		1111111111111-1000100101000	17
1	7	1111110111111-1000100101000	16
2	1	0111110111111-1000100101000	15
3	11	0111110111011-1000100101000	14
4	8	0111110011011-1000100101000	13
5	5	0111010011011-1000100101000	12
6	1	0110001011011-0100100101000	11
7	11	0101100110010-1000100010100	10

Note that we had to define the marking of the places belonging to the command circuits before applying the adjustment heuristic algorithm. It means that we have to completely define the sequencing of part types on machines. The total number of tokens in the final marking is ten while the total WIP (i.e. the number of tokens in places p_1 to p_{13}) is 6.

5.2. Optimization of Kanban system operations

5.2.1. The problem: definition and modeling

As shown by DI MASCOLO et al. [2], an event graph can be used to model a Kanban system. In figure 4, we show how to model the i-th stage of such a system.

Transition w_i represents the operation performed at stage i, p_i contains as many tokens as free Kanbans, $q_{i,1}$ contains as many tokens as parts waiting for being manufactured, and $q_{i,2}$ contains as many tokens as parts ready for the next operation. These parts will be transfered to the next operation if some Kanban are available (i.e. if there are some tokens in p_{i+1}).

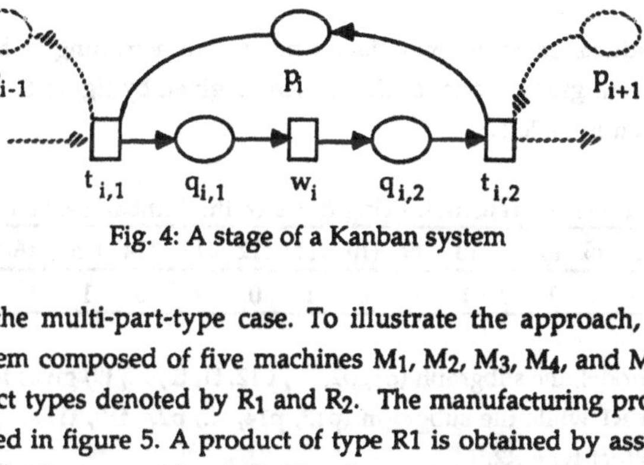

Fig. 4: A stage of a Kanban system

We consider the multi-part-type case. To illustrate the approach, we study a manufacturing system composed of five machines M_1, M_2, M_3, M_4, and M_5 which can produce two product types denoted by R_1 and R_2. The manufacturing processes of R1 and R2 are illustrated in figure 5. A product of type R1 is obtained by assembling two components C1 and C2 on machine M4. The first component C1 is manufactured successively by machines M1 and M2 while the second component C2 is manufatured by machine M3. A product of type R2 is obtained by assembling two components C5 and C6 on machine M3. The second component C6 is manufactured by machine M5. The component C5 is obtained by assembling two components C3 and C4 on machine M4 and this operation is also called sub-assembly operation. The two components C3 and C4 are obtained by operations on machine M1 and M2 respectively. All operations need one time unit.

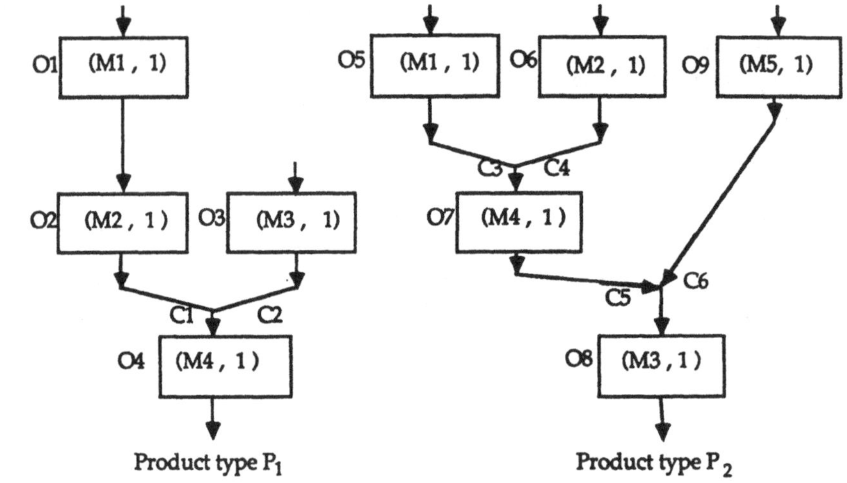

Fig. 5: Two types of product

The products enter the manufacturing system according to sequence R_1, R_2, R_1, R_2, ... The event graph model of this system is given by figure 6. The transition firing times are given in table 5.

Table 5: Transition firing times of the Kanban system model

t1	t2	t3	t4	t5	t6	t7	t8	t9	t10	t11	t12	t13	t14	t15	t16	t17	t18	t19	t20
0	1	0	1	0	1	0	1	0	0	1	0	1	0	1	0	1	0	1	0

In this model, the subgraph (p1, p2, ..., p12, t1, t2, ..., t9) gives the Kanban model of product type R1 while the subgraph (p13, p14, ..., p27, t10, t11, ..., t20) is the Kanban model of product type R2.

The elementary circuits (p_{28}, t_2, p_{29}, t_{11}), (p_{30}, t_4, p_{31}, t_{13}), (p_{32}, t_6, p_{33}, t_{19}), and (p_{34}, t_8, p_{35}, t_{15}) are command circuits. A command circuit is an elementary circuit which contains transitions corresponding to operations on a same machine. It is introduced to model the entrance sequence of products at each machine. Each command circuit contains exactly one token, which implies that a machine can perform at most one operation at a time.

We aim at producing a pair of parts of types R_1 and R_2 every 2 units of times with a minimal number of Kanban in the system.

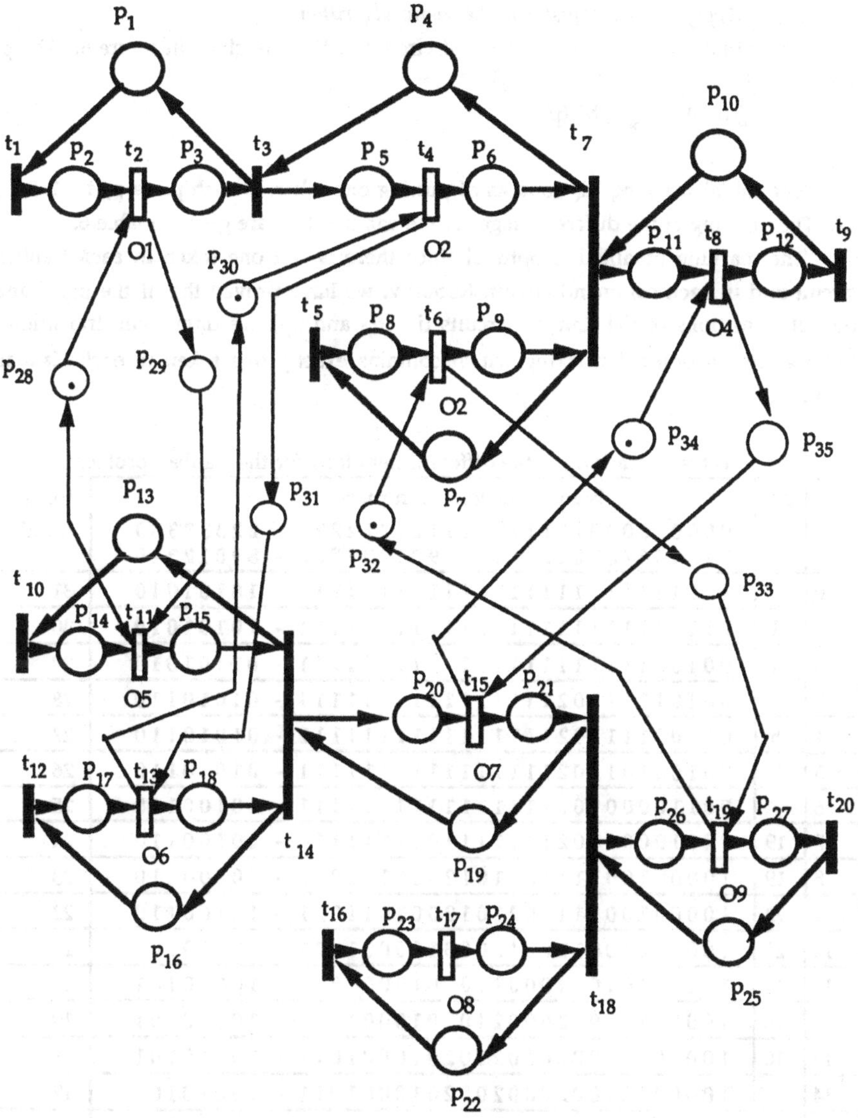

Fig. 6: Model of a Kanban system with 5 machines and 2 product types

5.2.2. Applying the adjustment heuristic algorithm

The initial marking of the command circuits is the one given in figure 6. The p-invariant U considered is $(1, 1, \ldots, 1)^T$. Thus:

$$f_U(M_0) = \Sigma_{p \in P} M_0(p)$$

and $\alpha = 2$.

The initial marking M_0 consists of putting one token in each place p_i, i = 1, 2, ..., 27. The marking at the different stages of the computation are given in table 6.

The marking obtained is optimal since there is just one token in each Kanban circuit and in each command circuit. Recently, we have proved that if the input and output transitions of the Kanban circuits (i.e. $t_{i,1}$ and $t_{i,2}$) are immediate transitions, there exists an optimal marking which contains exactly one token in each Kanban circuit.

Table 6: Marking at the different iterations for the Kanban problem

step	p*	Number of tokens in place 000000000111111111122222222 - 22333333 123456789012345678901234567 - 89012345	token number
0		111111111111111111111111111 - 10101010	31
1	1	011111111111111111111111111 - 10101010	30
2	1	001021111111111111111111111 - 01101010	29
3	4	001011111021111111111111111 - 01010110	28
4	5	001001111021111111111111111 - 01010110	27
5	7	001001011021111111111111111 - 01010110	26
6	7	001100001021111111111111111 - 10100110	25
7	19	001100001021111111011111111 - 10100110	24
8	19	100001001111021012001111021 - 10100110	23
9	22	100001001111021012001011021 - 10100110	22
10	22	100100100120012003100001021 - 10100101	21
11	13	100001010120002102010001021 - 10010101	20
12	26	100001010120002102010001011 - 10010101	19
13	10	100001010020002102010001011 - 10010101	18
14	16	100001010020002002010001011 - 10010101	17
15	13	001100100020001101010100101 - 01011001	16
16	26	100010001020001002100100001 - 01100110	15
17	10	010001001010001002100100001 - 01010101	14
18	16	010001001010100001010100001 - 01010101	13

6. CONCLUSION

This paper addresses the minimization of invariant criteria in strongly connected event graphs, assuming that the performance of the system is greater than a given value (i.e. that the cycle time of the system is less than a given value). It has been proven that a marking belonging to the optimal solution under a periodic operational mode (POM) is an optimal solution under an earliest operational mode (EOM). Thus we studied the POM.

We proposed an heuristic approach (the adjustment algorithm) based on property 7 which provides a limited set of feasible solutions containing at least one optimal solution. The heuristic adjustment algorithm provided near-optimal solutions in each of the applications we have made so far.

The work presented in this paper is of great interest for evaluating manufacturing systems assuming a cyclic manufacturing of the parts, since it has been shown that not only job-shops and Kanban systems, but also assembly systems, can be modelled using event graphs.

Work is in progress for finding an exact algorithm based on property 5 saying that there exists on optimal solution with at most two tokens per place. This algorithm, called convex optimization algorithm, needs more computation than the previous one but leads to an optimal solution in a reasonable amount of time.

REFERENCES

[1] P. CHRETIENNE, "Les Réseaux de Petri Temporisés," Univ. Paris VI, Paris, France, Thèse d'Etat, 1983.

[2] M. DI MASCOLO, Y. FREIN, Y. DALLERY and R. DAVID, "A Unified Modeling of Kanban Systems Using Petri Nets," Technical Report No 89-06, LAG. Genoble, France, September, 1989.

[3] H. HILLION and J.M. PROTH, "Performance Evaluation of Job-Shop Systems Using Timed Event-Graphs," IEEE Trans. Automat. Contr., vol. 34, No 1, pp. 3-9, January 1989.

[4] H.P. Hillion, J.M. Proth and X.L. Xie, "A Heuristic Algorithm for the Periodic Scheduling and Sequencing Job-shop Problem," Proc. 26th IEEE Conference on Decision and Control, Los Angeles, CA, Dec. 1987

[5] T. MURATA, "Petri Nets: Properties, Analysis and Applications," Proceedings of the IEEE, vol. 77, No 4, pp. 541-580, April 1989.

[6] C. RAMCHANDANI, "Analysis of Asynchronous Concurrent Systems by Timed Petri Nets," Lab. Comput. Sci., Mass. Inst. Technol. Cambridge, MA, Tech. Rep. 120, 1974.

[7] C.V. RAMAMOORTHY and G.S. HO, "Performance Evaluation of Asynchronous Concurrent Systems using Petri Nets," IEEE Trans. Software Eng., vol. SE-6, No 5, pp. 440-449, 1980.
[8] J. SIFAKIS, "A Unified Approach for Studying the properties of Transition Systems," Theoret. Comput. Sci. vol. 18, pp. 227-258, 1982.

Parameterized Reachability Trees for Predicate/Transition nets

MARKUS LINDQVIST

Nokia Telecommunications
P.O.Box 33, SF-02601 Espoo, Finland
e-mail:lindqvis@tele.nokia.fi

ABSTRACT Elaboration of reachability analysis in the context of Predicate/Transition nets is studied. For this purpose, parameters are introduced into the markings of Predicate/Transition nets. These parameters represent any fixed individual values potentially appearing in the marking. The formalism for dealing with parameterized markings is developed and the dynamics of Predicate/Transition nets are augmented to cope with parameters. These are used to define parameterized reachability trees and an algorithm for generating them is presented. They are shown to be significantly smaller than ordinary reachability trees and to contain the corresponding information: from one parameterized reachability tree several instances of ordinary reachability trees can be derived.

Keywords Petri nets, high level nets, Predicate/Transition nets, reachability analysis.

CONTENTS

Introduction

The main area of application of nets is to provide adequate means for modelling the behavior of systems featuring concurrency. As a result of such modelling an opportunity to analyse the behaviour of these systems becomes available. In this analysis the machinery offered by the modelling formalism, nets, may be exploited.

Several different techniques for the analysis of nets have been suggested over the years. The most prominent of these remain the *s-invariant method* [5], [9], [11] and *the generation of a reachability tree* or exhaustive search [11]. Here we will concentrate on the latter.

Reachability tree generation consists of generating the full state space of a system which in the case of nets means generating all reachable markings. Equivalently this means that a state machine describing the global states of a system and transitions between these states is produced. At present reachability analysis is undoubtly the most versatile analysis method for nets. Its most severe drawback is probably its inability to express true concurrency. This is due to the fact that the generation of a reachability tree is based on interleaving semantics [12]. Another drawback is that this method of analysis is quite arduous. Therefore only systems expressable by a net of reasonably small size are analysable at all. To be able to analyse larger problems as well one would need to be able to reduce the size of the reachability tree. But reducing the size of a reachability tree so that no relevant information is lost is a very difficult problem and usually possible only under special circumstances.

In the literature two approaches to elaborate reachability analysis have been presented. The first one uses P/T-systems and reduces the reachability tree by discarding certain transition sequences which all begin from and end in the same same global state [13]. As a result some markings are not generated. This discarding preserves the information of the reachability tree when it comes to certain properties concerning the analysed system. The other approach is developed for Coloured Petri nets and does not work with net formalisms like P/T- or C/E-systems [7], [8]. With it the generation of the reachability tree is done in the ordinary way, but certain parts of the tree can be omitted without loss of information. The use of this method can sometimes lead to drastic reductions in the size of the generated tree.

The latter method mentioned above relies on the existence of internal symmetries in the net and they are a prerequisite for the method to be effective. In other words, this imposes restrictions on the nets for which the method works well. In [4] and [3] the method has been elaborated further to avoid the need of heuristics in finding out the symmetries. They also introduce a level of symbolic treatment of markings under conditions where these symmetries hold. Nevertheless, the symmetries are still crucial and may be sometimes extremely hard to derive.

In relating these different reduction methods it should be clear that nothing is gained for free: there obviously is an unsurmountable trade off between the restrictions put on a net in order to make a reduction method work and of the expressiveness of the resulting reachability tree. If restrictions put on the net are loosened the expressiveness of the tree can be reduced either by

1. letting the size of it grow, i.e. letting the number of markings in it increase or
2. making it more of intermediate nature when it comes to proving properties of the net it was derived from.[1]

The method that will be introduced here for reducing the size of a reachability tree is based on the latter item in the above list. This trade off is made in order to allow the application of the method without having to introduce any restrictions on nets thus analyzed. In that respect it differs rather drastically from the reduction methods based on the symmetry concept.

So, our aim here is to reduce the size of the reachability tree produced by reachability analysis. We would not like to lose any information because of this reduction. We would also like to produce directly a reachability tree such that it is reduced. The means for trying to accomplish this task will be to use some kind of folding following the line of ideas applied in Predicate/Transition nets, or PrT-nets for short. In PrT-nets a folding is accomplished by introducing, among other things, individuals and variables into the net. This way the number of s- and t-elements can be decreased. But the marking of one s-element being a part of a node in a reachability tree is, however, not folded in a PrT-net in any way. To accomplish this something more is needed.

In PrT-nets variables on arcs may stand for anything since they are not bounded at all. The tuples representing markings on s-elements consist of individuals and are therefore totally bounded. Thus what is needed is something to allow some amount of freedom in the s-elements. The objects in the

[1] Actually, the net itself can be perceived as the most compact representation of a reachability tree.

s-elements should represent, not just anything, but *any* marking from the *set of possible* markings. Therefore, these objects should not consist of totally unbounded variables, but rather of something which is bounded to some extent. For this purpose we will introduce *parameters* into nets – or to put it better – into markings.

The paper starts with a definition of the Predicate/Transition nets involved in Section 1.1. In Section 2 the formalism as well as the notation for dealing with parameterized markings is developed. In Section 3 the formalism is applied to parameterization of the dynamics of PrT-nets. This leads to the central results: the parameterized transition rule and parameterized reachability trees. Before conclusions are drawn potentials in the use of parameterized reachability trees are briefly discussed. Because of the limitations on the length of this paper only an introduction to the central points of the formalism can be provided. For a thorough and detailed treatment of the matter we refer to [10].

1 Predicate/Transition nets

To make the paper self contained we start with a brief introduction into PrT-nets following the line of [6]. Defining PrT-nets starts with considering a structure $\mathcal{R}$ with a domain D of individuals. The set D is assumed always to be finite. Further, we have a first order language $\mathbf{L}$ whose non-logical alphabet consist of a set Π predicate symbols, a set Ω of operator symbols and a set V of individual variable symbols. By $\mathcal{M} = (D, \mathcal{W})$ we denote a model for $\mathbf{L}$ in the usual way [1], where D is the set of individuals as above and $\mathcal{W}$ the interpretation function. Used also is the set Ψ of variable predicates, the meaning of which is defined in the following definition:

Definition 1.1 *Let $\psi^n \in \Psi$, where n is the arity of Ψ, be a variable predicate annotating the S-element $s \in S$ of a net $N = (S, T; F)$. We say that ψ^n is true in marking M under the assignment $\alpha = [v_1 \leftarrow d_1, \ldots, v_n \leftarrow d_n]$, $d_i \in D, v_i \in V$ assigning individuals to the variables of ψ^n, iff $\langle d_1, \ldots, d_n \rangle \in M(s)$. A model $\mathcal{M}$ for Ψ in marking M is defined by: $\mathcal{M} \models \psi[d_1, \ldots, d_n]$ iff $\langle d_1, \ldots, d_n \rangle \in M(s)$ such that s is annotated by ψ.*

Predicate/Transition net is then defined as a directed net whose elements are annotated with expressions of the language $\mathbf{L}$ as follows [6]:

Definition 1.2 *Let D be the set of individuals, $\mathbf{L}$ a language built from Ω, Π, Ψ, V, and the logical alphabet, where V is the set of variables of $\mathbf{L}$ and $X = D \cup V$. Let $\mathcal{M} = (D, \mathcal{W})$ a model.*

Predicate/Transition nets (PrT-nets) are marked annotated nets $MN = (N, A, M_0)$, where N is the underlying net, A its annotation and M_0 the initial marking.

1. *N is a net, $N = (S, T; F)$.*
2. *A is the annotation of N, $A = (A_S, A_T, A_F)$, where:*
   (a) *A_S is an injective mapping of S into the set of variable predicates Ψ.*
   (b) *A_T is a mapping of T into the set of selectors which are syntactically correct formulae of $\mathbf{L}$ not involving elements of Ψ.*
   (c) *A_F is a mapping of F into the set of non-empty sets of tuples τ of individuals and variables, $\mathcal{P}(\langle X^* \rangle) - \{\emptyset\}$, such that if $(x, y) \in F$ is an arc connected to an s-element s (i. e. $x = s$ or $y = s$) and n is the index of the variable predicate annotating s then the tuples annotating (x, y) are of length n, $\emptyset \neq A_F(x, y) \subseteq \langle X \rangle^n$.*
3. *M_0 is a marking of N, i. e. a mapping from S into $\mathcal{P}(\langle D^* \rangle)$, that assigns to each place $s \in S$ a set $M_0(s)$ of tuples τ of individuals such that if $\psi^{(n)} \in \Psi$ is the variable predicate annotating s then the model $\mathcal{M}_0$ for M_0: $\mathcal{M}_0 \models \psi^{(n)} d_1, \ldots, d_n$ iff $\tau = \langle d_1, \ldots, d_n \rangle \in M_0(s)$.*

To define the dynamics of PrT-nets we present the transition rule in which the notions of feasibility and permissibility are used. The feasibility condition is concerned with, so to speak, static requirements which are not dependent of the marking. The permissibility condition deals then with more dynamic aspects and depends on the marking in question.

Definition 1.3 *Let $MN = (N, A, M_0)$ be a PrT-net, t a transition of MN and φ the selector formula annotating t. Let α be an assignment that replaces all variables that occur in the tuples $\tau \in A_F(s,t) \cup A_F(t,s)$, $s \in S$, or in the formula φ. The assignment α is called feasible for t at marking M iff*

1. *α satisfies the selector φ of t.*
2. *α does not generate an impurity; if $(s,t) \in F$ and $(t,s) \in F$ then for any two tuples $\tau_1 \in A_F(s,t), \tau_2 \in A_F(t,s), \tau_1\alpha \neq \tau_2\alpha$.*
3. *α does not create a multiple arc; if $\tau_1, \tau_2 \in A_F(s,t)$ (or $A_F(t,s)$) and $\tau_1 \neq \tau_2$ then $\tau_1\alpha \neq \tau_2\alpha$.*

Definition 1.4 *Let $MN = (N, A, M_0)$ be a PrT-net and t a transition of MN. Let α be an assignment that replaces all variables that occur in the tuples $\tau \in A_F(s,t) \cup A_F(t,s)$, $s \in S$ and $\mathcal{M}$ the model corresponding with a marking M. The assignment α is called permissible for t at M iff*

1. *For all arcs (s,t) leading to $t, \mathcal{M} \models \psi(\tau\alpha)$ if $\tau \in A_F(s,t)$.*
2. *For all arcs (t,s) leading to s, $\mathcal{M} \not\models \psi(\tau\alpha)$ if $\tau \in A_F(t,s)$.*

Using the feasibility and permissibility conditions we can now express the transition rule rather concisely:

Definition 1.5 *Let $MN = (N, A, M_0)$ be a PrT-net. Let M and M' be markings of MN and $\mathcal{M}$ and $\mathcal{M}'$ the corresponding models, t a transition and α as in Definition 1.3. Let α' be an assignment that replaces the variables in the index of a variable predicate $\psi \in \Psi$. Then the α-occurrence of t at M leading to M' is designated as $M\ [t\alpha\rangle\ M'$ and defined by: $M\ [t\alpha\rangle\ M'$ iff:*

1. *α is a feasible assignment for t at M.*
2. *α is a permissible assignment for t at M.*
3. *The follower marking $M'(s)$, such that $A_S(s) = \psi \in \Psi$, is the following:*
   (a) *For all places $s \in S$ such that $(s,t) \notin F$ and $(t,s) \notin F$, $\mathcal{M}' \models \psi\alpha'$ iff $\mathcal{M} \models \psi\alpha'$.*
   (b) *For all places $s \in S$ such that $(s,t) \in F$ and $\tau \in A_F(s,t)$, $\mathcal{M}' \not\models \psi(\tau\alpha)$ and $\mathcal{M}' \models \psi(\tau\alpha')$ iff $\mathcal{M} \models \psi(\tau\alpha')$ for $\tau\alpha' \neq \tau\alpha$.*
   (c) *For all places $s \in S$ such that $(t,s) \in F$ and $\tau \in A_F(t,s)$, $\mathcal{M}' \models \psi(\tau\alpha)$ and $\mathcal{M}' \models \psi(\tau\alpha')$ iff $\mathcal{M} \models \psi(\tau\alpha')$ for $\tau\alpha' \neq \tau\alpha$.*

We say that t is α enabled in M iff $M[t\alpha\rangle M'$.

As the reader may notice PrT-nets have been defined here according to the strict interpretation [6] limiting the marking to being sets of tokens rather than multisets. In this paper we will stick to the strict interpretation. The weak one has been briefly discussed in [10].

Having now the transition rule for PrT-nets we may speak of reachable markings and reachability trees of Predicate/Transition nets. The following sections will introduce parameters both to PrT-nets and to their dynamics. This will allow us to define finally parameterized reachability trees that will be significantly smaller than ordinary ones. Before going into the formal introduction of the method some notation and an informal outline of the most basic ideas is given in the following.

2 Parameterized markings

To start with the introduction of parameterized markings some basic notation is needed as stated in the following. The convention to be followed througout this presentation is that all expressions dealing with parameters consist of symbols with the *hat* symbol ^ over them:

Notation 2.1 *The set of individuals is denoted by D, the set of variables by V and the set of parameters by $\hat{V}$. Further $X = D \cup V$ and $\hat{X} = D \cup \hat{V}$. Then we have:*

1. *$d \in D$ is an individual.*
2. *$v \in V$ is a (local) variable.*
3. *$\hat{v} \in \hat{V}$ is a (global) parameter.*
4. *$\hat{x} \in \hat{X}$ is a parameter or an individual.*
5. *$\tau \in X^*$ is a tuple of individuals and variables appearing on the arcs of a PrT-net.*
6. *$\hat{\tau} \in \hat{X}^*$ is a tuple of individuals and parameters appearing as tokens in parameterized markings of s-elements of a PrT-net, also called a parameterized token.*
7. *M and $\widehat{M}$ are a marking and a parameterized marking of a PrT-net, respectively.*
8. *$\hat{X}(\widehat{M}) = \hat{V}(\widehat{M}) \cup D(\widehat{M})$ ($\hat{X}(\hat{\tau})$) denote the set of parameters and individuals in a parameterized marking $\widehat{M}$ (parameterized token $\hat{\tau}$).*
9. *$|M(s)|$ and $|\widehat{M}(s)|$ denote the cardinality, i.e. the number of tokens of a marking $M(s)$ and a parameterized marking $\widehat{M}(s)$, respectively.*
10. *$\widehat{M}[\hat{\tau}]$ denote the number of tokens $\hat{\tau}$ in $\widehat{M}$.*
11. *$\hat{\tau}(i)$ denote the i:th component of the token $\hat{\tau}$, i.e. if $\hat{\tau} = \langle \hat{x}_1, \ldots, \hat{x}_i, \ldots, \hat{x}_n \rangle$ then $\hat{\tau}(i) = \hat{x}_i$.*
12. *$\alpha, \hat{\alpha}, \beta$ and $\hat{\beta}$ are the following mappings:*
    (a) $\alpha : V \to D$ is called an assignment,
    (b) $\hat{\alpha} : V \to \hat{X}$ is called a parameterized assignment,
    (c) $\beta : \hat{V} \to D$ is called a fixing and
    (d) $\hat{\beta} : \hat{V} \to \hat{X}$ is called a substitution, in some cases a unifier.

In a parameterized marking $\widehat{M}$ we will have, in addition to individuals, parameters from the set $\hat{V}$ as well. Only after these parameters have been *fixed* to some particular individuals do we get an actual marking M. We say that M is a marking represented by $\widehat{M}$. Let us have, for example, the following three different markings on s-element s of a PrT-net:

$$M_1(s) = \{\langle a_1 \rangle, \langle b_1 \rangle\}, M_2(s) = \{\langle a_2 \rangle, \langle b_2 \rangle\}, M_3(s) = \{\langle a_3 \rangle, \langle b_3 \rangle\}.$$

These can all be expressed by using parameters instead of individuals with the following parameterized marking:

$$\widehat{M}(s) = \{\langle \hat{x}_1 \rangle, \langle \hat{x}_2 \rangle\}.$$

Suppose a transition t occurs in such a way that one of the two tuples in M_1, M_2 or M_3 is removed. How should this be reflected in the parameterized marking ? Suppose that the other parameter, say $\hat{x}_2$, is simply removed and we get the parameterized marking $\widehat{M}' = \{\langle \hat{x}_1 \rangle\}$. This leads, however, to problems. Let us consider the marking $M(s) = M_1(s) = \{\langle a_1 \rangle, \langle b_1 \rangle\}$. This is represented by the parameterized marking $\widehat{M} = \{\langle \hat{x}_1\rangle, \langle \hat{x}_2\rangle\}$ from which we get M by fixing the parameters, say, $\hat{x}_1 \leftarrow a_1, \hat{x}_2 \leftarrow b_1$. Transition t now occurs so that a_1 is removed and we get $M' = \{\langle b_1\rangle\}$ which should now be represented by $\widehat{M}' = \{\langle \hat{x}_1\rangle\}$ as we agreed above. The problem, however, is that $\hat{x}_1$ has already been fixed to a_1 and from this it follows that $\widehat{M}'$ can no longer represent M'. We should have guessed better and removed $\hat{x}_1$ from $\widehat{M}$ instead.

The solution to the above problem is to introduce a new parameter $\hat{x}_3$ which is fixed to either $\hat{x}_1$ or $\hat{x}_2$ and removed from $\widehat{M}$. To do this the parameterized marking $\widehat{M}'$ has to be divided into two parameterized markings $\widehat{M}'^{+}$ and $\widehat{M}'^{-}$ so that

$$\widehat{M}' = \widehat{M}'^{+} - \widehat{M}'^{-} = \{\langle \hat{x}_1\rangle, \langle \hat{x}_2\rangle\} - \{\langle \hat{x}_3\rangle\}.$$

There are also some other requirements a parameterized marking should fulfill and they will be returned to shortly. For now, however, we have enough material to present the definition of a parameterized marking:

Definition 2.2 Parameterized marking:

Let $MN = (N, A, M_0)$ be a PrT-net with $N = (S, T; F)$ and k, m integers such that $k \geq 1, m < 2k$. A non-empty parameterized marking $\widehat{M}$ of MN is for all $s \in S$ of the form:

$$\widehat{M}(s) = \{\nu_1\hat{\tau}_1, \ldots, \nu_k\hat{\tau}_k\} - \{\nu_{k+1}\hat{\tau}_{k+1}, \ldots, \nu_m\hat{\tau}_m\},$$

where $\nu_i \in \mathbf{N}^+$, $\hat{\tau}_i$ is a parameterized token such that $\hat{\tau}_i \in (\hat{V} \cup D)^n, i = 1, \ldots, m$, and n is the index of the predicate $\psi \in \Psi$ annotating s. By $\widehat{M}^+(s)$ we denote $\{\nu_1\hat{\tau}_1, \ldots, \nu_k\hat{\tau}_k\}$ and by $\widehat{M}^-(s)$ correspondingly $\{\nu_{k+1}\hat{\tau}_{k+1}, \ldots, \nu_m\hat{\tau}_m\}$.

2.1 Denotation of parameterized markings

So far we have defined a syntactical object called a parameterized marking but have not yet presented its exact meaning or semantics. It is, however, quite clear from the introduction that a parameterized marking represents a set of markings derived by replacing the parameters with individuals from the set D or by *fixing* the parameters.

Definition 2.3 *Let $\hat{o}$ be a parameterized object, marking or a token, with $\hat{V}(\hat{o}) = \{\hat{v}_1, \ldots, \hat{v}_n\}$. Let β be a mapping $\beta : \hat{V}(\hat{o}) \rightarrow D$ or $\beta = [\hat{v}_1 \leftarrow d_1, \ldots, \hat{v}_n \leftarrow d_n]$, where $d_i \in D, i = 1, \ldots, n$. Then β is called a fixing of the parameters of $\hat{o}$ and $\hat{o}\beta$ denotes the object obtained by substituting each occurrence of $\hat{v}_i$ in $\hat{o}$ with $d_i, i = 1, \ldots, n$ and it is called an unfolding of $\hat{o}$.*

After having defined the fixing of parameters we may now formally present what a parameterized marking denotes. In the language used to talk about parameterized objects we have adopted the convention that such objects are denoted by symbols with ^ over them. The denotation of these objects is then the set of objects they represent and it is obtained by fixing the parameters to individuals or by unfolding the parameterized object in a certain way.

Definition 2.4 *Let $\widehat{M}$ be a parameterized marking of a PrT-net $N = (S, T; F)$ with $\hat{V}(\widehat{M}) = \{\hat{v}_1, \ldots, \hat{v}_n\}$. Then*

$$\mathcal{V}(\widehat{M}) = \{M \mid M = \widehat{M}\beta \wedge M(s) \text{ is a set } \forall s \in S\}$$

is the denotation of the parameterized marking $\widehat{M}$ according to the strict denotation, where β is a fixing of the parameters in $\hat{V}(\widehat{M})$.[2]

[2]As already mentioned, we deal here only with the strict interpretation, for the weak one the denotation consists of positive multisets rather than of sets.

It is clear that such constraints which apply to parameterized markings are absent when parameterized tokens are considered. The denotation of a parameterized token is then the set of tokens resulting from all possible fixings replacing the parameters with individuals.

We now have the means to talk about parameterized markings and tokens, and also a meaning for expressions involving them. Therefore, we may now build the machinery needed for applying parameterized markings to constructing reachability trees. Here we will develop the parts of this machinery necessary to be able to present the parameterization of the dynamics of PrT-nets and of reachability trees. For a detailed presentation we refer to [10].

2.2 Unification and matching

Consider two non-identical parameterized markings $\widehat{M}$ and $\widehat{M}'$. Based on this information, what can be said about $\mathcal{V}(\widehat{M})$ and $\mathcal{V}(\widehat{M}')$: Are they disjoint, are they identical, or do they just have some markings in common? To decide this we have to compare the denotations of the parameterized tokens appearing in the markings and try to decide how they relate to each other. This process of comparing and deciding is very closely related to *unification* of expressions which is one of the main tools used in mechanical theorem proving, [2, pages 74 – 80].

The intuition behind the concept of matching to be defined here is that two parameterized tokens match exactly when there exist a fixing β such that $\hat{o}_1\beta$ and $\hat{o}_2\beta$ are the same. It is not, however, usually necessary to go as far as to find such a fixing to be able to decide whether the two tokens match. It is enough to find a substitution, or a unifier, replacing parameters with other parameters and individuals in such a way that the tokens become the same. After finding a unifier it is easy to find any fixing equating the two tokens since any fixing will thereafter be such a one. Consider, for example, the following two parameterized tokens:

$$\hat{\tau}_1 = \langle \hat{v}_1, a, \hat{v}_3, b, \hat{v}_5 \rangle, \hat{\tau}_2 = \langle \hat{v}_1, \hat{v}_2, \hat{v}_3, \hat{v}_4, \hat{v}_6 \rangle.$$

Then they become the same with the following substitutions: $[\hat{v}_2 \leftarrow a, \hat{v}_4 \leftarrow b, \hat{v}_6 \leftarrow \hat{v}_5]$. Only the parameters which had to be fixed or bound in some way were considered. The rest were still left open and one can freely choose the fixing of $\hat{v}_1, \hat{v}_3$ and $\hat{v}_5$ and still keep the unfolding of the two tokens the same. Therefore, we are interested in something which is the most general way of unifying parameterized tokens.

Definition 2.5 *Let $\hat{o}_1$ and $\hat{o}_2$ be two parameterized objects, markings or tokens and $\hat{\beta} : \hat{\mathcal{V}}(\hat{o}_1) \cup \hat{\mathcal{V}}(\hat{o}_2) \to \hat{\mathcal{X}}(\hat{o}_1) \cup \hat{\mathcal{X}}(\hat{o}_2)$. Then $\hat{\beta}$ is called a unifier iff $\hat{o}_1\hat{\beta} = \hat{o}_2\hat{\beta}$.*

Further, $\hat{\beta}$ is called the most general unifier iff for each unifier $\hat{\beta}'$ there exists a substitution $\hat{\beta}''$ such that $\hat{\beta}' = \hat{\beta}\hat{\beta}''$.

Now we may formalise the concept of matching with the help of a unifier in the following way:

Definition 2.6 *Let $\hat{o}_1, \hat{o}_2$ be two parameterized objects, tokens or markings. Then we say that $\hat{o}_1$ matches $\hat{o}_2$ or $\hat{o}_1 \simeq \hat{o}_2$ iff*

$$\exists \text{ a unifier } \hat{\beta} : \hat{\mathcal{V}}(\hat{o}_1) \cup \hat{\mathcal{V}}(\hat{o}_2) \to \hat{\mathcal{X}}(\hat{o}_1) \cup \hat{\mathcal{X}}(\hat{o}_2) \text{ such that } \hat{o}_1\hat{\beta} = \hat{o}_2\hat{\beta}.$$

Corollary 2.7 *Let $\hat{o}_1, \hat{o}_2$ be two parameterized objects such that $\hat{o}_1 \simeq \hat{o}_2$. Then clearly $\hat{o}_2 \simeq \hat{o}_1$.*

Corollary 2.8 *Let $\hat{o}_1, \hat{o}_2$ be two parameterized objects such that $\hat{o}_2 \simeq \hat{o}_1$. Then*

$$\mathcal{V}(\hat{o}_1) \cap \mathcal{V}(\hat{o}_2) \neq \emptyset.$$

The concept of matching is of paramount importance in reasoning about parameterized markings. It is not, however, suitable if the denotation has to be considered in order to be able to say whether an object matches another one or not. Of course there is always the trial-and-error method or exhaustive search as a means of trying to locate a unifying fixing[3] but its use is not that attractive. Especially if the set D of individuals is large there might be a vast number of possible fixings. It is, however, rather straightforward to find a unifier $\hat{\beta}$, especially when two tokens are considered. The same principle can also be extended to sets of tokens providing us with the possibility to compare parameterized markings with each other. For details and a description of the unification algorithms needed we again refer to [10].

Let us now consider two parameterized markings $\widehat{M}$ and $\widehat{M}'$ and their denotations in particular. How do these denotations relate to each other under all possible global fixings of their parameters ? We can have the following four cases:

1. The denotations of the two markings are disjoint,
2. the denotations have a common intersection,
3. the denotation of $\widehat{M}$ is included in the denotation of $\widehat{M}'$ or
4. the denotation of $\widehat{M}'$ is included in the denotation of $\widehat{M}$.

The cases which are of primary interest are 3 and 4 of the above list. If we know that $\widehat{M}$ includes, so to speak, $\widehat{M}'$ then all the markings that can be reached from $\widehat{M}'$ can also be deduced from $\widehat{M}$. This immediately points to the possibility of using this idea for defining a covering relation for parameterized markings. How including markings are actually used is postponed until Section 3.1. For now we will return to formalising the concept and to telling how including markings can be detected.

Definition 2.9 *Let $\widehat{M}$ and $\widehat{M}'$ be two parameterized markings of a PrT-net. Then we say that $\widehat{M}'$ includes $\widehat{M}$ denoted by $\widehat{M} \subseteq \widehat{M}'$ iff*

$$\mathcal{V}(\widehat{M}\beta) \subseteq \mathcal{V}(\widehat{M}'\beta)$$

for all fixings $\beta : \hat{\mathcal{V}}(\widehat{M}) \cap \hat{\mathcal{V}}(\widehat{M}') \rightarrow D$ of their common parameters.

In the above definition we have only considered those parts of the denotations of the two markings that are obtained through global fixings, i.e. fixings where each parameter is fixed only once. The reasoning for this is that when parameterized reachability trees are considered, only global fixings make sense whereas fixings local to a marking are useless.

When a parameterized marking $\widehat{M}'$ includes another one $\widehat{M}$ it is clear that any fixing possible for $\widehat{M}$ is also possible for $\widehat{M}'$ as stated in the following:

Theorem 2.10 *Let $\widehat{M}$ and $\widehat{M}'$ be two parameterized markings such that $\widehat{M} \subseteq \widehat{M}'$ and D the set of individuals. Then for all fixings $\beta : \hat{\mathcal{V}}(\widehat{M}) \rightarrow D$ such that $\widehat{M}\beta \in \mathcal{V}(\widehat{M})$ there exists a fixing β' such that $\widehat{M}'\beta' = \widehat{M}\beta$.*

Proof:

Follows directly from Definitions 2.4 and 2.9.

In order to detect such a pair of markings where the one includes the other we should concentrate on the possible fixings of the markings. But in this case we would, as before, not like to consider the denotation of the markings in order decide whether one includes the other. This, however, is not necessary. Again, we may use unification of sets of parameterized tokens and find a unifier which unifies the two markings [10, pages 66–67]. However, when constructing the unifier one must take care that it does not change the denotation of the marking which we hope will be included in the other one:

[3] Note that we are still dealing only with a finite D resulting in a finite number of different possible fixings β.

Theorem 2.11 *Let $\widehat{M}$ and $\widehat{M}'$ be parameterized markings of a PrT-net MN with $N = (S, T; F)$ such that they are of the same cardinality and $\forall s \in S : |\widehat{M}'^{+}(s)| \geq |\widehat{M}^{+}(s)|$. Then*

$$\widehat{M} \subseteq \widehat{M}' \Leftrightarrow \exists\hat{\beta} : \hat{\mathcal{V}}(\widehat{M}') - \hat{\mathcal{V}}(\widehat{M}) \rightarrow \hat{\mathcal{X}}(\widehat{M}) \cup \hat{\mathcal{X}}(\widehat{M}') \text{ such that } \widehat{M}'\hat{\beta} = \widehat{M}\hat{\beta} = \widehat{M}.$$

Proof:

See Theorem 3.28 of [10].

We have now rather briefly introduced the concept of parameterized markings. We have also shown the central points of how parameterized markings can be dealt with. For those interested in the details we refer to [10]. The purpose of introducing parameters into markings was to be able to fold markings in a manner similar to the one which is used to fold s- and t-elements in PrT-nets. How this helps in cutting down the size of a reachability tree (which is our ultimate goal) will be shown in the next section.

3 Parameterizing the dynamics

When constructing a reachability tree with ordinary markings a method for generating new markings from old ones by transition occurrences is needed. Therefore, to have a corresponding method for parameterized markings the transition rule has to be modified to cope with parameters. This means that parameters will also be introduced to the occurrence of a transition by possible assignment of parameters instead of individuals to the variables appearing in the tuples of A_F.

What should be the semantics of a parameterized occurrence of a transition which changes one parameterized marking into another ? What should its interpretation be ? Clearly this parameterized occurrence should stand for all those occurrences which may lead from the denotation of the one marking into the denotation of the other. Therefore we can speak of the denotation of a parameterized occurrence and present the following definition:

Definition 3.1 *Let $\widehat{M}$ and $\widehat{M}'$ be two parameterized markings of a PrT-net MN with $N = (S, T; F)$. Let $t \in T$ be a transition and $\hat{\alpha}$ a parameterized assignment replacing the variables in the index of t with parameters and individuals. Further, let β be a fixing $\beta : \hat{\mathcal{V}}(\widehat{M}) \cup \hat{\mathcal{V}}(\widehat{M}') \cup \hat{\mathcal{V}}(\hat{\alpha}) \rightarrow D$. Then*

$$\mathcal{V}(\widehat{M}[t\hat{\alpha}\rangle\widehat{M}') = \{t\hat{\alpha}\beta \mid \widehat{M}\beta[t\hat{\alpha}\beta\rangle\widehat{M}'\beta \wedge \widehat{M}\beta \in \mathcal{V}(\widehat{M}) \wedge \widehat{M}'\beta \in \mathcal{V}(\widehat{M}')\},$$

is the (strict) denotation of the parameterized transition occurrence $\widehat{M}[t\hat{\alpha}\rangle\widehat{M}'$.

The "ordinary" transition rule of Definition 1.5 uses the requirement that an assignment replacing the variables with individuals has to be both *feasible* and *permissible* as defined in Definitions 1.3 and 1.4. The former involves fulfilling static requirements which do not change as processes occur in the net. The requirements set by the latter depend, on the other hand, solely on the current marking of the net and are thus of a dynamic nature. When parameterized markings are involved, this distinction is still somewhat valid. The role of these requirements will be as significant as in the ordinary case. They alone should be enough to ensure that the denotation of a parameterized occurrence is not empty.

The feasibility requirement should guarantee that the assignment is such that there exists a fixing of the parameters in $\hat{\mathcal{V}}(\widehat{M})$ such that the requirements of Definition 1.3 are fulfilled. The feasibility can, however, be checked symbolically only in the case that the selector formula is restricted to being a conjunction of identities and their negations. This restriction, however, is not absolutely necessary and it may be dropped without hampering the use of parameterized markings as explained in [10, Section 5.3].

Definition 3.2 Feasible assignment of parameters *Let MN be a PrT-net with $N = (S, T; F)$, $\widehat{M}$ a parameterized marking of MN, t its transition and φ the selector formula annotating t being* *a conjuction of identities and their negations. Let* $\hat{\alpha} = [v_1 \leftarrow \hat{x}_1, \ldots, v_n \leftarrow \hat{x}_n]$ *be a parameterized assignment replacing variables in the index of t with individuals or parameters. Then* $\hat{\alpha}$ *is called feasible iff:*

1. $\hat{\alpha}$ *satisfies* φ
   (a) *if* $\varphi\hat{\alpha} \Rightarrow v_i\hat{\alpha} = v_j\hat{\alpha}$ *then* $\hat{\alpha}$ *must assign the same parameter or individual to variables* v_i *and* v_j.
   (b) *if* $\varphi\hat{\alpha} \Rightarrow v_i\hat{\alpha} \neq v_j\hat{\alpha}$ *then* $\hat{\alpha}$ *must assign different parameters or individuals to variables* v_i *and* v_j.
2. $\hat{\alpha}$ *does not generate an impurity; if* $(s,t) \in F$ *then for any pair* $\hat{\tau}_1, \hat{\tau}_2$ *of tuples such that* $\hat{\tau}_1 \in A_F(s,t)$ *and* $\hat{\tau}_2 \in A_F(t,s)$ *it holds that* $\hat{\tau}_1\hat{\alpha} \neq \hat{\tau}_2\hat{\alpha}$.
3. $\hat{\alpha}$ *does not generate a multiple arc: if* $\hat{\tau}_1, \hat{\tau}_2 \in A_F(s,t)$ *or* $A_F(t,s)$ *and* $\hat{\tau}_1 \neq \hat{\tau}_2$ *then* $\hat{\tau}_1\hat{\alpha} \neq \hat{\tau}_2\hat{\alpha}$.

The two last items of Definition 3.2 correspond directly to the items of Definition 1.3. Item 1 ensures that all dependencies that are set by the selector formula φ are taken explicitly into account and are reflected directly in the assignment. This way no hidden constraints are left in the parameterized marking resulting from an occurrence of a transition with a selector formula.

The permissibility requirement of Definition 1.4 ensures that the assignment is such that the result of the occurrence of the transition is a new marking. The permissibility requirement should, in the parameterized case, ensure that the denotation of the new parameterized marking produced by the parameterized transition occurrence is not empty. This then requires considering the parameterized marking of each s-element not separately but as one global entity.

Definition 3.3 Permissible assignment of parameters

Let MN be a PrT-net with $N = (S,T;F)$, $\widehat{M}$ *a parameterized marking of MN and t its transition. Let* $\hat{\alpha} = [v_1 \leftarrow \hat{x}_1, \ldots, v_n \leftarrow \hat{x}_n]$ *be a parameterized assignment replacing variables in the index of t with individuals or parameters. Then* $\hat{\alpha}$ *is called permissible iff:*

1. $\hat{x}_i, i = 1, \ldots, n$, *is an individual* $\hat{x}_i \in D$ *or an old parameter* $\hat{x}_i \in \hat{V}(\widehat{M})$ *iff:*
   (a) $\exists\, \tau \in A_F(s,t)$ *such that* $\tau(j) = v_i$ *and* $\forall\, \hat{\tau} \in \widehat{M}^+(s)$ *such that* $\hat{\tau} \simeq \tau\hat{\alpha} : \hat{\tau}(j) = \hat{x}_i$ *and*
   (b) $\forall \tau \in A_F(s',t)$ *such that* $\tau(k) = v_i\ \exists\, \hat{\tau} \in \widehat{M}^+(s')$ *such that* $\hat{\tau} \simeq \tau\hat{\alpha}$.
2. $\hat{x}_i, i = 1, \ldots, n$, *is a new parameter* $\hat{x}_i \notin \hat{V}(\widehat{M})$ *iff* $\forall\, \tau \in A_F(s,t)$ *such that* $\tau(j) = v_i\ \exists\, \hat{\tau}_1, \hat{\tau}_2$ *such that* $\hat{\tau}_1 \simeq \tau\hat{\alpha} \wedge \hat{\tau}_2 \simeq \tau\hat{\alpha}$ *and* $\hat{\tau}_1(j) \neq \hat{\tau}_2(j)$.
3. $\exists\, \hat{\beta} : \hat{V}(\widehat{M}) \cup \hat{V}(\hat{\alpha}) \rightarrow \hat{X}(\widehat{M})$ *such that*
   (a) $\forall\, s \in S\ \widehat{M}^+\hat{\beta}(s) \geq \widehat{M}^-\hat{\beta}(s)$ *and* $\neg\exists\, \hat{\tau}$ *such that* $\widehat{M}^+\hat{\beta}(s)[\hat{\tau}] - \widehat{M}^-\hat{\beta}(s)[\hat{\tau}] > 1$, *i.e.* $\widehat{M}\hat{\beta}(s)$ *is a set of parameterized tokens.*
   (b) $\forall\, s \in S$ *such that* $\tau \in A_F(s,t)\ \widehat{M}^+\hat{\beta}(s)[\tau\hat{\alpha}\hat{\beta}] - \widehat{M}^-\hat{\beta}(s)[\tau\hat{\alpha}\hat{\beta}] = 1$.
   (c) $\forall\, s \in S$ *such that* $\tau \in A_F(t,s)\ \widehat{M}^+\hat{\beta}(s)[\tau\hat{\alpha}\hat{\beta}] - \widehat{M}^-\hat{\beta}(s)[\tau\hat{\alpha}\hat{\beta}] = 0$.

We have now presented the feasibility and permissibility requirements for the parameterized case. The motivation for the feasibility requirement of Definition 3.2 should be quite clear but may seem rather cumbersome for the permissibility requirement of Definition 3.3. Therefore, its meaning will be studied somewhat more closely.

The meaning of items 1 and 2 of Definition 3.3 is to tell what the prerequisities are for assigning an individual, an old parameter, or a new parameter to a variable. It is easily motivated by studying the following example:

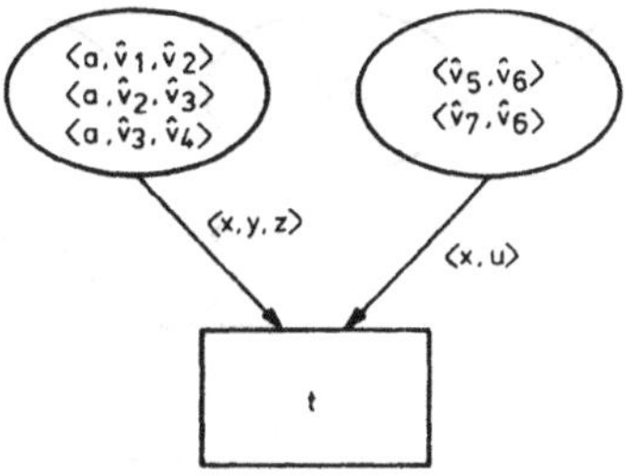

Figure 1: A transition of a PrT-net with its input s-elements and a parameterized marking $\widehat{M}$.

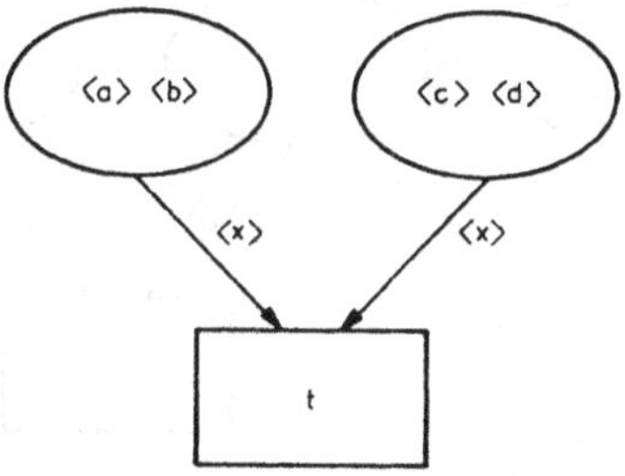

Figure 2: A situation where a permissible parameterized assignment does not exist.

Example 3.1 In the situation of Figure 1 items 1, 2 and 3 of Definition 3.3 require that the assignment $\hat{\alpha} = [u \leftarrow \hat{v}_6, x \leftarrow a, y \leftarrow \hat{v}_8, z \leftarrow \hat{v}_9]$, where $a \in D, \hat{v}_6 \in \hat{V}(\widehat{M})$ and $\hat{v}_8, \hat{v}_9 \notin \hat{V}(\widehat{M})$. For u we can only assign $\hat{v}_6$ since all tokens of s_2 contain it as their second component. For y and z we must take new parameters since there is more than one possibility for choosing the assignment for them. The only thing known is that the pair $\hat{v}_8, \hat{v}_9$ has the same value as the pair $\hat{v}_1, \hat{v}_2$ or $\hat{v}_2, \hat{v}_3$ or $\hat{v}_3, \hat{v}_4$ in any unfolding. The only possible assignment for x is individual a because of the tokens on s-element s_1. Additionally, the components which may be assigned to x in the tuple from s_2 to t are parameters and thus we can assume that either $\hat{v}_5$ or $\hat{v}_7$ will have the value a. If there were only individuals different from a as first components of tokens in s_2 a permissible assignment could not be found.

■

The rest of the items of Definition 3.3 are needed to ensure that both the markings involved in an occurrence of a transition, the source and the target so to speak, are still feasible after the occurrence. They are somewhat complex but unfortunately also unavoidable since the feasibility constraints put on a marking of some s-element effect all those markings of other s-elements which share the common parameters with it. This will become clear when studying the following examples. They are chosen to reflect those troublesome cases which require Definition 3.3 to be enforced all the way before the permissibility of an assignment can be ensured.

Example 3.2 In the situation of Figure 2 where $\widehat{M}(s_1) = \{\langle a\rangle, \langle b\rangle\}$ and $\widehat{M}(s_2) = \{\langle c\rangle, \langle d\rangle\}$ items 1 and 2 of Definition 3.3 would give, say, the following assignment $\hat{\alpha} = [x \leftarrow \hat{v}]$ where $\hat{v}$ is a new parameter. But there is no fixing β for $\hat{v}$ such that $\tau\hat{\alpha}\beta \in \widehat{M}\beta(s_1)$ and $\tau\hat{\alpha}\beta \in \widehat{M}\beta(s_2)$ since a, b, c and d are all different individuals. This problem arises with the new parameter introduced by the assignment $\hat{\alpha}$. It represents a set of possible parameters and individuals that could be assigned to the variables on the arcs. On different s-elements these sets may, however, be disjoint and thus in some cases no feasible fixing for the parameters exists. This also means that one cannot find a substitution $\hat{\beta}$ as required by item 3.b of Definition 3.3 and thus the assignment is not permissible.

■

The case in the previous example was still quite simple. However, already in this simple case we had

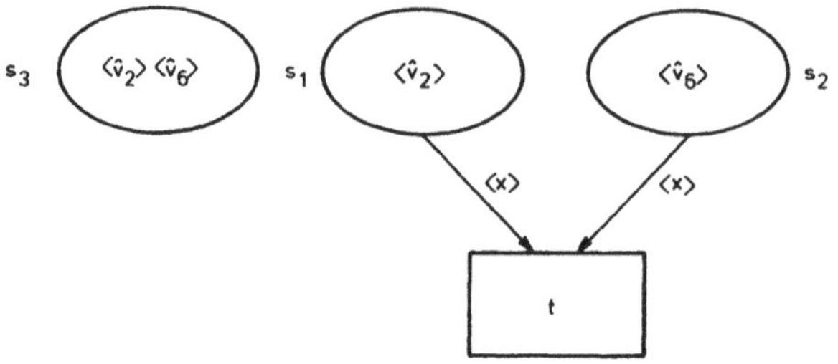

Figure 3: A situation where the occurrence of t causes $\widehat{M}(s_3)$ to become unfeasible under any possible assignment.

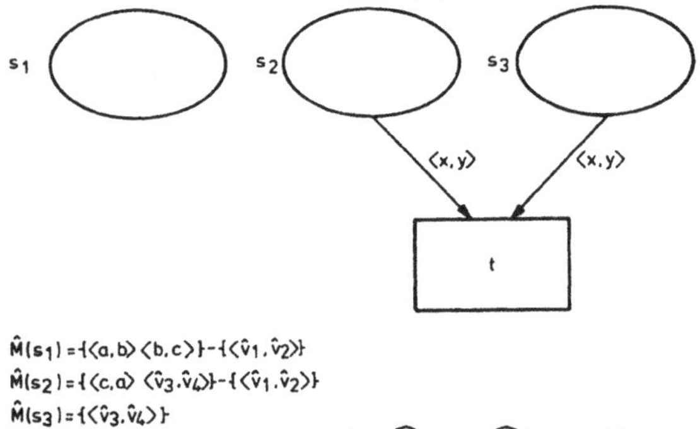

Figure 4: Transition t cannot occur because either $\widehat{M}(s_1)$ or $\widehat{M}(s_3)$ would become unfeasible.

to fall back on item 3 of Definition 3.3 in order to see that using a certain assignment in an occurrence of a transition would have produced a parameterized occurrence with an empty denotation. The next example shows that it is also necessary to consider the marking of s-elements which are not immediately connected to the transition which occurs:

Example 3.3 In Figure 3 the assignment $\hat{\alpha}$ assigns to variable x either $\hat{v}_2$ or $\hat{v}_6$. An implicit consequence of this is that for any fixing β it must be that $\hat{v}_2\beta = \hat{v}_6\beta$. Thus, any assignment causes the marking $\widehat{M}(s_3)$ to become unfeasible even if s_3 is not connected to the transition which occurs. It is also impossible to find a substitution such that items 3.a and 3.b of Definition 3.3 would be fulfilled and therefore a permissible assignment does not exist. And neither should it, since the denotation of a parameterized occurrence of t would necessarily be empty.

■

It is necessary to check the effect of the dependencies caused by the assignment. A variable appearing in more than one of the input tuples forces the parameters assigned for the different appearances to represent the same individual, like parameters $\hat{v}_2$ and $\hat{v}_6$ in the above example. One would very probably tend to think that it would be enough to check the feasibility of markings for only those s-elements which contain parameters involved in the assignment. But unfortunately that is not the case as shown in the next example.

Example 3.4 Consider the parameterized marking depicted in Figure 4. Parameters $\hat{v}_1$ and $\hat{v}_2$ are not involved in the assignment at all. However, since the token $\langle \hat{v}_3, \hat{v}_4 \rangle$ is necessarily removed from $\widehat{M}(s_2)$ by the occurrence of t we get that $\langle \hat{v}_1, \hat{v}_2 \rangle$ must be $\langle c, a \rangle$. But now we run into a problem since such a token is not present in $\widehat{M}^+(s_1)$ and the transition cannot occur without causing either $\widehat{M}(s_1)$ or $\widehat{M}(s_2)$ to become unfeasible. Therefore the assignment should not be permissible, and indeed, it is not, since it is impossible to fulfill items 3.a and 3.b of Definition 3.3.

We have now studied some examples which clearly show why the permissibility requirement of Definition 3.3 must be as exacting as it is. What it is ultimately about is that it tells when a new parameter expressing a possibility of choice has to be introduced. In addition this new parameter must stand for some old one and therefore at least one feasible parameterized marking where new parameters have been replaced with old ones must exist. In fact, this is quite similar to what the permissibility requirement of ordinary markings requires of variables and the values assigned to them.

In [10, pages 77–78] an algorithm to check the permissibility of a parameterized assignment is presented. Here we content ourselves with presenting the parameterized transition rule and some of its properties.

Definition 3.4 Parameterized transition rule:

Let $\widehat{M}$ and $\widehat{M}'$ be two parameterized markings of a PrT-net with $N = (S,T;F)$, t a transition and $\hat{\alpha} = [v_1 \leftarrow \hat{x}_1, \ldots v_n \leftarrow \hat{x}_n]$ a parameterized assignment replacing the variables in the index of t with parameters or individuals. Then $\widehat{M}[t\hat{\alpha}\rangle\widehat{M}'$ iff:

1. *$\hat{\alpha}$ is a permissible parameterized assignment,*
2. *$\hat{\alpha}\hat{\beta}$ is a feasible assignment, where $\hat{\beta} : \hat{V}(\widehat{M}) \cup \hat{V}(\hat{\alpha}) \to \hat{X}(\widehat{M})$ is a substitution as defined in Definition 3.3.*
3. *For all places $s \in S$:*
   (a) *If $(s,t) \in S$ then $\widehat{M}'^{-}(s) = \widehat{M}^{-}(s) + \{\tau\hat{\alpha} \mid \tau \in A_F(s,t)\}$.*
   (b) *If $(t,s) \in S$ then $\widehat{M}'^{+}(s) = \widehat{M}^{+}(s) + \{\tau\hat{\alpha} \mid \tau \in A_F(t,s)\}$.*
   (c) *$\widehat{M}'^{+}(s) = \widehat{M}^{+}(s)$ and $\widehat{M}'^{-}(s) = \widehat{M}^{-}(s)$ otherwise.*

We say that t is $\hat{\alpha}$ enabled in $\widehat{M}$ iff $\widehat{M}[t\hat{\alpha}\rangle\widehat{M}'$.

The transition rule for the parameterized case now gives the possibility of generating follower markings when an initial marking has been given. This already allows for generating a reachability tree consisting of parameterized markings. But before starting to study how this is done a theorem of central importance will be presented. It tells that using the transition rule of Definition 3.4 ensures that the denotation of the parameterized occurrence will be non empty:

Theorem 3.5 *Let $\widehat{M}$ and $\widehat{M}'$ be two parameterized markings of a PrT-net such that $\widehat{M}$ is feasible, t a transition and $\hat{\alpha}$ a parameterized assignment replacing the variables in the index of t with parameters and individuals. Suppose $|D|$ is sufficiently large[4] and the selector φ of t as in Definition 3.2.[5] Then*

$$\widehat{M}[t\hat{\alpha}\rangle\widehat{M}' \Leftrightarrow \mathcal{V}(\widehat{M}[t\hat{\alpha}\rangle\widehat{M}') \neq \emptyset.$$

Proof:

See Appendix 1.

We have now defined a parameterized transition rule and shown that its use ensures that the denotation of a parameterized occurrence is non empty. This, however, holds only under the assumption that the fixing is not limited by any other means but those resulting from the feasibility requirements of the two markings involved. Therefore we have added into the premises the assumption that D has enough members to allow for a fixing which fixes each parameter to a different individual. We also assumed that the selector formula contains only identities and their negations. For one direction of the proof this assumption was not needed and even for the other it is not always necessary but it is sufficient. Before starting with the introduction of parameterized reachability trees we have yet to present a theorem about parameterized occurrences telling more of their denotation:

[4] At most the maximum of $|\hat{V}(\widehat{M}'(s))|$ of all $s \in S$.

[5] The consequences of dropping this assumption has been delt with in Section 5.3 in [10].

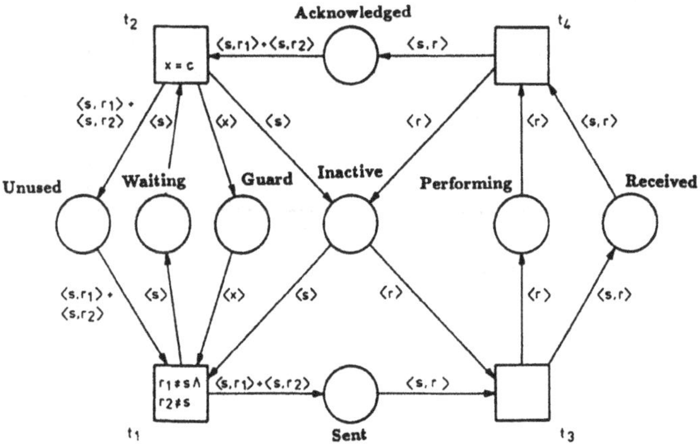

Figure 5: A system for maintaining multiple copies of a bata base.

Theorem 3.6 *Let M be a marking such that $M[t\alpha\rangle M'$ and $M \in \mathcal{V}(\widehat{M})$ where $\widehat{M}$ is a parameterized marking. Further, let D be the set of individuals and $\widehat{M}[t\hat{\alpha}\rangle\widehat{M}'$ be a parameterized occurrence according to Definition 3.4. Then $M[t\alpha\rangle M' \in \mathcal{V}(\widehat{M}[t\hat{\alpha}\rangle\widehat{M}')$.*

Proof: See Appendix 1.

We have now almost everything that is needed for constructing reachability trees with parameterized markings. One crucial concept, however, is still missing: that is the covering relation for parameterized markings. As we already mentioned at the end of previous section, the inclusion relation of parameterized markings can be used. The reason for this is shown by the next theorem:

Theorem 3.7 *Let $MN = (N, A, M_0)$ be a PrT-net with $N = (S, T; F)$ and $t \in T$ a transition of MN. Let $\widehat{M}, \widehat{M}'$ be two parameterized markings of MN and $\widehat{M} \subseteq \widehat{M}'$. Further, let $\hat{\alpha}, \hat{\alpha}'$ be two parameterized assignments such that t is $\hat{\alpha}$ enabled in $\widehat{M}$ and $\hat{\alpha}'$ enabled in $\widehat{M}'$. Then*

$$\mathcal{V}(\widehat{M}[t\hat{\alpha}\rangle\widehat{M}_1) \subseteq \mathcal{V}(\widehat{M}'[t\hat{\alpha}'\rangle\widehat{M}_1').$$

Proof:

See Appendix 1.

Theorem 3.7 shows that the denotation of a marking $\widehat{M}$ included in some other marking $\widehat{M}'$ can not have more followers than the denotation of $\widehat{M}'$. One immediate result of this is that everything that can be reached from $\widehat{M}$ can also be reached from $\widehat{M}'$. Therefore the use of the inclusion relation as the covering relation of parameterized markings is justified.

3.1 Parameterized reachability trees

We will start the study of parameterized reachability trees, PR-trees for short, by looking at an example involving a well known PrT-net model. Consider the net of Figure 5 describing a system maintaining multiple copies of a database [5]. Further, consider the case where there are three different agents, a_1, a_2 and a_3, in the system. The initial marking, denoted by $\widehat{M}_0$ is then the following:

$$\widehat{M}_0 \begin{cases} \text{Acknowledged} & \\ \text{Unused} & \{\langle a_1,a_2\rangle,\langle a_1,a_3\rangle,\langle a_2,a_1\rangle,\langle a_2,a_3\rangle,\langle a_3,a_1\rangle,\langle a_3,a_2\rangle\} = N \\ \text{Waiting} & \\ \text{Guard} & \{\langle c\rangle\} \\ \text{Inactive} & \{\langle a_1\rangle,\langle a_2\rangle,\langle a_3\rangle\} \\ \text{Performing} & \\ \text{Received} & \\ \text{Sent} & \end{cases}$$

The set of individuals is $D = \{a_1, a_2, a_3, c\}$. From here only transition t_1 may fire but it may fire with three different values assigned to variable s. We use parameter $\hat{s}_1$ to denote the possible values assignable to s, i. e. the values, or individuals a_1, a_2 or a_3. The selector formula φ of t_1 restricts the possible values assignable to variables r_1 and r_2 to be different from the value assigned to s.[6] We will denote these values with parameters $\hat{r}_1$ and $\hat{r}_2$. Since the only possibility is to assign individual c for x the parameterized assignment becomes $\hat{\alpha} = [s \leftarrow \hat{s}_1, r_1 \leftarrow \hat{r}_1, r_2 \leftarrow \hat{r}_2, x \leftarrow c]$. In this case it is trivial to find such a $\hat{\beta} : \hat{V}(\widehat{M}_0) \cup \hat{V}(\hat{\alpha}) \to \hat{X}(\widehat{M}_0)$ that $\hat{\alpha}$ is permissible, say $\hat{\beta} = [\hat{s}_1 \leftarrow a_1, \hat{r}_1 \leftarrow a_2, \hat{r}_2 \leftarrow a_3]$. Clearly $\hat{\alpha}\hat{\beta}$ is also feasible. Therefore t may occur under the parameterized assignment $\hat{\alpha}$ and a new parameterized marking $\widehat{M}_1$ is produced:

$$\widehat{M}_0$$

$$\Big\downarrow \begin{array}{ll} t_1: & \hat{\alpha} = [s \leftarrow \hat{s}_1, r_1 \leftarrow \hat{r}_1, r_2 \leftarrow \hat{r}_2, x \leftarrow c] \\ \varphi: & \hat{r}_1 \neq \hat{s}_1 \wedge \hat{r}_2 \neq \hat{s}_1 \end{array}$$

$$\widehat{M}_1 \begin{cases} \text{Acknowledged} & \\ \text{Unused} & N - \{\langle \hat{s}_1,\hat{r}_1\rangle,\langle \hat{s}_1,\hat{r}_2\rangle\} \\ \text{Waiting} & \hat{s}_1 \\ \text{Guard} & \{\langle c\rangle\} - \{\langle \hat{x}\rangle\} = \emptyset \\ \text{Inactive} & \{\langle a_1\rangle,\langle a_2\rangle,\langle a_3\rangle\} - \{\hat{s}_1\} \\ \text{Performing} & \\ \text{Received} & \\ \text{Sent} & \{\langle \hat{s}_1,\hat{r}_1\rangle,\langle \hat{s}_1,\hat{r}_2\rangle\} \end{cases}$$

The edge connecting $\widehat{M}_0$ to $\widehat{M}_1$ is labeled with the transition that occurred and the used parameterized assignment $\hat{\alpha}$. Also the selector formula φ of the transition is shown with its variables replaced by parameters and individuals in the way $\hat{\alpha}$ defines. This is to show the static restrictions that are put on all occurrences of t_1 regardless of the marking.

The complete parameterized reachability tree of the net of Figure 5 is depicted in Appendix 2. It is obtained by applying reasoning based on Definition 3.4 in a manner similar to that described above. This works nicely and no such complex considerations are necessary as in the examples presented in the previous section.

A reachability tree is made finite by the use of covering markings. This is also employed in PR-trees: consider the marking presented below. It is $\widehat{M}_6$ of the PR-tree depicted in Appendix 2. There it is claimed that $\widehat{M}_6$ is included in marking $\widehat{M}_5$. How this claim is justified is resolved in the following. To make it easier to follow the discourse the markings $\widehat{M}_6$ and $\widehat{M}_5$ are repeated below:

[6] We could actually do without the selector φ in this case.

$$\begin{array}{l} \widehat{M}_4 \\ \big\downarrow\ t_4 : \quad \hat{\alpha} = [s \leftarrow \hat{s}_1, r \leftarrow \hat{r}_6] \end{array}$$

$$\widehat{M}_6 \left\{ \begin{array}{ll} \text{Acknowledged} & \{\langle \hat{s}_1, \hat{r}_6 \rangle\} \\ \text{Unused} & N - \{\langle \hat{s}_1, \hat{r}_1 \rangle, \langle \hat{s}_1, \hat{r}_2 \rangle\} \\ \text{Waiting} & \hat{s}_1 \\ \text{Guard} & \\ \text{Inactive} & \{\langle \hat{r}_6 \rangle\} \\ \text{Performing} & \{\langle \hat{r}_3 \rangle, \langle \hat{r}_4 \rangle\} - \{\langle \hat{r}_6 \rangle\} = \{\langle \hat{r}_8 \rangle\} \\ \text{Received} & \{\langle \hat{s}_1, \hat{r}_3 \rangle, \langle \hat{s}_1, \hat{r}_4 \rangle\} - \{\langle \hat{s}_1, \hat{r}_6 \rangle\} = \{\langle \hat{s}_1, \hat{r}_8 \rangle\} \\ \text{Sent} & \end{array} \right.$$

$$\begin{array}{l} \widehat{M}_3 \\ \big\downarrow\ t_3 : \quad \hat{\alpha} = [s \leftarrow \hat{s}_1, r \leftarrow \hat{r}_3] \end{array}$$

$$\widehat{M}_5 \left\{ \begin{array}{ll} \text{Acknowledged} & \{\langle \hat{s}_1, \hat{r}_3 \rangle\} \\ \text{Unused} & N - \{\langle \hat{s}_1, \hat{r}_1 \rangle, \langle \hat{s}_1, \hat{r}_2 \rangle\} \\ \text{Waiting} & \hat{s}_1 \\ \text{Guard} & \\ \text{Inactive} & \{\langle a_1 \rangle, \langle a_2 \rangle, \langle a_3 \rangle\} - \{\langle \hat{s}_1 \rangle, \langle \hat{r}_5 \rangle\} = \{\langle \hat{r}_7 \rangle\} \\ \text{Performing} & \{\langle \hat{r}_5 \rangle\} \\ \text{Received} & \{\langle \hat{s}_1, \hat{r}_5 \rangle\} \\ \text{Sent} & \end{array} \right.$$

Looking at $\widehat{M}_5$ and $\widehat{M}_6$ we can immediately see that they are of the same cardinality and thus it might be possible that $\widehat{M}_6 \subseteq \widehat{M}_5$. If this were true then it should be possible according to Theorem 2.11 to construct a unifier $\hat{\beta} : \hat{V}(\widehat{M}_5) \to \hat{X}(\widehat{M}_6)$ such that $\widehat{M}_5\hat{\beta} = \widehat{M}_6$. The prerequisite for this is that for all s-elements $\widehat{M}_5^+(s) \geq \widehat{M}_6^+(s)$, which is not true for s-elements Performing and Received. We can, however, replace these markings with other ones so that this prerequisite would be satisfied [10, pages 70–71]. We use markings $\{\langle \hat{r}_8 \rangle\}$ and $\{\langle \hat{s}_1, \hat{r}_8 \rangle\}$ to stand for $\widehat{M}_6$(Performing) and $\widehat{M}_6$(Received), respectively, as can be seen above. But we still have problems with $\widehat{M}_5$(Inactive) since it has parameters only in $\widehat{M}_5^-$(Inactive) and thus no unifier unifying it with $\widehat{M}_6$(Inactive) can be found. But here again $\widehat{M}_5$(Inactive) can be replaced with $\{\langle \hat{r}_7 \rangle\}$ since the denotation of the marking remains intact. Now it is rather straightforward to find a unifier $\hat{\beta} : \hat{V}(\widehat{M}_5) \to \hat{X}(\widehat{M}_6)$ such that $\widehat{M}_5\hat{\beta} = \widehat{M}_6$. It is in this case

$$\hat{\beta} = [\hat{r}_3 \leftarrow \hat{r}_6, \hat{r}_5 \leftarrow \hat{r}_8, \hat{r}_7 \leftarrow \hat{r}_6].$$

It is easily seen that indeed $\widehat{M}_5\hat{\beta} = \widehat{M}_6$. Now we can use Theorem 2.11 and conclude that $\widehat{M}_6$ is included in $\widehat{M}_5$. Therefore we can conclude that all that can be reached from any marking in the denotation of $\widehat{M}_6$ can also be reached from a marking in the denotation of $\widehat{M}_5$ as shown by Theorem 3.7. Therefore there it is no use to developing $\widehat{M}_6$ further.

Returning to our example of the data base system of Figure 5 there is still one more marking to consider. That is the marking $\widehat{M}_8$ which is shown below:

$$\begin{array}{l} \widehat{M}_7 \\ \big\downarrow\ t_2 : \quad \hat{\alpha} = [s \leftarrow \hat{s}_1, r_1 \leftarrow \hat{r}_9, r_2 \leftarrow \hat{r}_{10}] \end{array}$$

$$\widehat{M}_8 \left\{ \begin{array}{ll} \text{Acknowledged} & \\ \text{Unused} & N + \{\langle \hat{s}_1, \hat{r}_9 \rangle, \langle \hat{s}_1, \hat{r}_{10} \rangle\} - \{\langle \hat{s}_1, \hat{r}_1 \rangle, \langle \hat{s}_1, \hat{r}_2 \rangle\} = N \\ \text{Waiting} & \\ \text{Guard} & \{\langle c \rangle\} \\ \text{Inactive} & \{\langle a_1 \rangle, \langle a_2 \rangle, \langle a_3 \rangle\} \\ \text{Performing} & \\ \text{Received} & \\ \text{Sent} & \end{array} \right.$$

This marking is equal to $\widehat{M}_0$, the initial marking, except on s-element Unused. This marking can, however, be reduced. Since we are dealing with strict parameterized markings we can delete all the tokens that are in excess of N since N is the complete denotation of each of these tokens. Therefore we obtain that $\widehat{M}_8 \subseteq \widehat{M}_0$ and the generation of the reachability tree has been completed.

To generate the reachability tree we have used reasoning based on several of the definitions and theorems presented earlier in this and the previous section. By pulling all this material together we can now present the algorithm for generating parameterized reachability trees. [7]

Algorithm 3.1 An algorithm to produce a parameterized reachability tree of a PrT-net with an initial marking $\widehat{M}_0$ under the strict interpretation. Symbol $\mathcal{U}$ denotes the set of unprocessed nodes, $\mathcal{N}$ the set of nodes in the tree and $\mathcal{E}$ edges connecting these nodes.

INPUT: A PrT-net MN with $N = (S, T; F)$.
The initial marking $\widehat{M}_0$ of MN.

OUTPUT: A parameterized reachability tree T of MN with the root $\widehat{M}_0$.

GENERATETREE($MN, \widehat{M}_0$, **VAR** T)

Let unprocessed nodes $\mathcal{U} := \{\widehat{M}_0\}; T := \widehat{M}_0$;
REPEAT
  Select some node $\widehat{M} \in \mathcal{U}$
  FORALL transitions t enabled at $\widehat{M}$ under some $\hat{\alpha}$
    according to Definition 3.4 **DO**
    Generate follower $\widehat{M}'$ of $\widehat{M}$ via $t\hat{\alpha}$ according to Definition 3.4
    Reduce the representation of $\widehat{M}'$ if possible
    Append $\widehat{M}'$ to $\mathcal{N}$ and $(\widehat{M}, \widehat{M}')$ labeled by $t\hat{\alpha}$ and $\varphi\hat{\alpha}$ into $\mathcal{E}$
    IF $\exists\ \widehat{M}'' \in \mathcal{N}$ such that $|\widehat{M}'(s)| = |\widehat{M}''(s)|\ \forall s \in S$
      THEN try to find a unifier $\hat{\beta}$ according to Theorem 2.11
      IF a unifier was found
        THEN $\widehat{M}' \subseteq \widehat{M}''$, add $\hat{\beta}$ to $\widehat{M}'$
        ELSE add $\widehat{M}'$ to $\mathcal{U}$
    ELSE add $\widehat{M}'$ to $\mathcal{U}$
  END FORALL
UNTIL $\mathcal{U} = \emptyset$.

We now have an algorithm to produce PR-trees.[8] It works in the way that was described with the example involving the net of Figure 5 and the PR-tree in Appendix 2. We are now able to produce reachability trees of PrT-nets such that the number of nodes in them is reduced. This reduction is achieved by using a folding such that one node in the tree represents not only one marking but a whole set of markings. It is clear that the number of nodes in a reachability tree of a PrT-net is strongly decreased using this method since one parameterized marking may represent a whole set of instances of ordinary markings in a reachability tree.

But before concluding the presentation we should still discuss what PR-trees are good for. After all, the crucial point is how a PR-tree can be used to deduce properties of the net it was generated from. This will be briefly addressed in the following section.

[7] It is a slightly simplified version of the one presented in [10].

[8] The reduction of the representation of a parameterised marking $\widehat{M}$ has not been discussed here. It has been studied in [10, pages 61–64]. However, the results concerning reduction are still somewhat initial. What is needed is a canonic representation of a parameterised marking.

4 How can PR-trees be used

In this section we will briefly state without further proof some properties of PR-trees and outline the method that can be used to deduce properties of the net they are derived from. For a detailed treatment with necessary theorems we refer to [10, pages 86–103].

First of all PR-trees are finite. One can also say a little about their size when compared to an underlying P/T-system [8]. If no selectors are involved and the tuples on arcs do not contain any individuals the lower limit to the size of a PR-tree of some net is the size of the reachability tree of the underlying P/T-net. If selectors are involved it can be even lower. Not very much can be said about the upper limit without some rather strong assumptions. This concerns the order in which markings of the same cardinality are generated: Suppose that the first generated marking of a certain cardinality always includes all the markings of the same cardinality that are generated later. In this case the size of the PR-tree is at most the size of the reachability tree of the underlying P/T-system. [10, pages 86–89]

The central thing now to ask is what the relation of a PR-tree and an ordinary reachability tree of a PrT-net is. What we naturally want is for them to be in some sense equivalent in their information content. A theorem addressing this question is presented in the following.

Theorem 4.1 *Let $MN = (N, A, \widehat{M}_0)$ be a PrT-net with $N = (S, T; F)$ and $\mathcal{T} = (\mathcal{N}, \mathcal{E})$ a PR-tree produced by Algorithm 3.1 under the strict interpretation. Then*

$$\exists \pi = M_0[t_1\alpha_1\rangle M_1 \dots M_{n-1}[t_n\alpha_n\rangle M_n$$
$$\Leftrightarrow$$
$$\exists \hat{\pi} = M_0[t_1\hat{\alpha}_1\rangle \widehat{M}_1 \dots \widehat{M}_{n-1}[t_n\hat{\alpha}_n\rangle \widehat{M}_n$$
$$\text{and a fixing } \beta : \hat{V}(\hat{\pi}) \to D \text{ such that}$$

1. $M_0, \widehat{M}_i \in \mathcal{N}, i = 1, \dots, n,$
2. $\widehat{M}_i\beta = M_i, i = 1, \dots, n$ *and*
3. $t_i\hat{\alpha}\beta = t_i\alpha, i = 1, \dots, n.$

Proof:

See Theorem 5.8 in [10].

Even though the $\Leftarrow$ direction of the above theorem seems rather trivial (what is on the left side is more or less qiven on the right side) the other direction shows that all that is in an ordinary reachability tree is represented in a PR-tree. But the converse is not true: a PR-tree may in some cases represent something that does not have an origin in the ordinary case, i.e. sometimes a PR-tree may contain parts that do not have any meaningful interpretation. In such cases no legal fixing β can be found for the path.[9]

Even though PR-trees may contain unnecessary information in the context of a given initial marking they have the nice property that everything contained in an ordinary reachability tree is represented in the corresponding PR-tree. Therefore PR-trees can be used to decide the reachability between two markings.

PR-trees often describe the behavior of a system modelled as a net on a more abstract level than is desirable. Consequently a PR-tree can be seen as an intermediate point between the net and statements expressing the properties of the net. An ordinary tree takes us considerably closer than a PR-tree towards being able to state these properties. The information of a PR-tree must be elaborated further in parts which seem interesting. This allows us to focus our effort more accurately than with ordinary reachability trees and concentrate only on what seems to be of importance.

The essential information in a reachability tree is that it tells what the states of a system are and how they are reached from each other. All the other properties can be seen as consequences of this

[9] For details see [10, pages 91–92]

reachability relation. Therefore one should investigate how this reachability relation can be decided from PR-trees. This involves unfolding a part of the reachability tree by fixing the parameters such that the reachability relation between the particular members of the denotations of the parameterized markings is revealed. Two markings are then reachable if one can find them in the denotation of two parameterized markings which are reachable in the PR-tree. In addition the fixing of parameters involved must not make the path between the two markings unfeasible. As before, for details we refer to [10, pages 92–99].

Conclusions

In this presentation parameterized markings were introduced as a means for folding reachability trees of Predicate/Transition nets into significantly conciser parameterized reachability trees, PR-trees for short.

In the beginning parameterized markings and central points of the formalism were introduced. The core of the matter was to study the relationship between a parameterized marking as a syntactical object and its meaning or denotation. Including markings were introduced to allow for an ordering of parameterized markings according to their denotation. The dynamics of Predicate/Transition nets was then parameterized. The validity of the parameterized transition rule was shown by numerous examples and by a theorem concerning its denotation: the denotation of a parameterized transition occurrence is always non empty provided that the selector can be evaluated without fixing the parameters. It was also shown that the use of including markings in the coverability relation was justified. Finally, parameterized reachability trees were introduced and an algorithm for producing them was presented. An example of generating a PR-tree for a well-known net was presented in detail.

In the last section, the properties and the use of parameterized reachability trees were discussed. A PR-tree of a finite Pr/T-net is finite and it covers the information of the corresponding ordinary reachability tree. Therefore PR-trees can be used to decide the reachability of a marking.

The work presented here introduces a new method for generating reachability trees for Predicate/Transition nets. It does the reachability analysis on a 'high level' all the way, i.e. one does not necessarily have to consider the actual unfolded markings while generating the reachability tree. In addition it is a method that does not require any specific properties of the analyzed net to be effective in the reduction. The method can also be applied to other higher level net models once it is generalized to deal with the weak interpretation.

Although the reachability trees or PR-trees produced by this method can be significantly smaller in size than those produced by ordinary methods it is premature to make claims concerning its practical value. The results are still somewhat initial when it comes to using PR-trees in proving properties of the analyzed net. The basic framework has, however, been built here which opens a door into a new and little explored area of research. This, in turn, may offer several possibilities for speeding up reachability analysis so as to make it an attractive analysis method even with nets of larger size.

The PR-tree method should not be taken as self contained. Quite on the contrary; possibilities to profitably combine the PR-tree method with other reduction methods to improve reachability analysis should be looked for. Therefore the different reachability tree reduction methods should not be thought of as mutually exclusive but rather complementary.

Acknowledgements

I am indebted to Dr. Hartmann Genrich for his valuable advice and constructive criticism he has presented over the time the work with parameterized reachability trees was conducted. I also thank the anynomous referees for their remarks and suggestions helping to improve the paper. Especially I am grateful to the "One anynomous referee" who helped me to eliminate several irksome mistakes.

A significant part of the work has been done under a grant from Academy of Finland.

References

[1] C. Chang, H. Keisler: *Model Theory*. North Holland, Amsterdam, (1973).

[2] C. Chang, R. Lee: *Symbolic Logic and Mechanical Theorem Proving*. Academic Press, New York, (1973).

[3] G. Chiola et al: *On Well-Formed Coloured Nets and their Symbolic Reachability Graph*. Proceedings of the Eleventh International Conference on Applications and Theory of Petri nets, Paris, June 1990.

[4] C. Dutheillet, S. Haddad: *Regular Stochastic Petri Nets*. Proceedings of the Tenth International Conference on Applications and Theory of Petri nets, Bonn, June 1989.

[5] H. Genrich: *Projections on C/E-systems*. Proceedings of Sixth European Workshop on Applications and Theory of Petri nets, Espoo, Finland, June 1985.

[6] H. Genrich: *Predicate/Transition nets*. Petri Nets: Central Models and Their Properties (eds. W. Brauer, W. Reisig, G. Rozenberg), Lecture Notes in Computer Science, Vol. 254, Springer-Verlag, Berlin (1987).

[7] K. Jensen: *Coloured Petri Nets*. Petri Nets: Central Models and Their Properties (eds. W. Brauer, W. Reisig, G. Rozenberg), Lecture Notes in Computer Science, Vol. 254, Springer-Verlag, Berlin (1987).

[8] P. Huber, A. Jensen, L. Jepsen, K. Jensen: *Reachability Trees for High Level nets*. Theoretical Computer Science, Nr. 45, (1986), pp. 261 - 292.

[9] R. Kujansuu, M. Lindqvist: *Efficient Algorithms for Computing S-invariants for Predicate/Transition Nets*. Proceedings of Fifth European Workshop on Applications and Theory of Petri Nets, Aarhus, Denmark, June 1984.

[10] M. Lindqvist: *Parameterized Reachability Trees for Predicate/transition Nets*. Acta Polytechnica Scandinavica, Mathematics and Computer Science Series No. 54, Helsinki, 1989, 120 pp.

[11] W. Reisig: *Petri Nets, An Introduction*. Springer-Verlag, Berlin, (1985).

[12] W. Reisig: *A Strong Part of Concurrency*. Advances in Petri Nets 1987 (ed. G. Rozenberg), Lecture Notes in Computer Science, Vol. 266, Springer-Verlag, Berlin (1987).

[13] A. Valmari: Error Detection by Reduced Reachability Graph Generation. Proceedings of 9th European Workshop on Applications and Theory of Petri Nets, Venice, June 1988.

Appendix 1

Proof of Theorem 3.5:

Since $\hat{\alpha}$ is permissible a substitution $\hat{\beta} : \hat{V}(\widehat{M}) \cup \hat{V}(\hat{\alpha}) \rightarrow \hat{X}(\widehat{M})$ exists such that for all $s \in S$ $\widehat{M}^+(s) \geq \widehat{M}^-(s)$. Therefore $\widehat{M}^-(s)$ can be removed from the presentation of the markings and let $\widehat{M}''(s)$ be such that $\mathcal{V}(\widehat{M}''(s)) = \mathcal{V}(\widehat{M}^+(s) - \widehat{M}^-(s))$. Since $\neg\exists\ \hat{\tau}$ such that $\widehat{M}^+(s)[\hat{\tau}] - \widehat{M}^-(s)[\hat{\tau}] > 1$ all $\widehat{M}''(s)$ are sets of parameterized tokens.

For all input places it holds that if $\tau \in A_F(s,t)$ then $\widehat{M}''(s)[\tau\hat{\alpha}\hat{\beta}] = 1$. Since $\hat{\alpha}\hat{\beta}$ is feasible there are no two $\tau_1, \tau_2 \in A_F(s,t)$ such that $\tau_1\hat{\alpha}\hat{\beta} = \tau_2\hat{\alpha}\hat{\beta}$. Therefore all $\tau_i\hat{\alpha}\hat{\beta}$ such that $\tau_i \in A_F(s,t), i = 1, \ldots n$ can be removed from $\widehat{M}''(s)$ and the resulting parameterized marking which is equivalent to $\widehat{M}'\hat{\beta}(s)$ is still a set of parameterized tokens.

For all output places it holds that if $\tau \in A_F(t,s)$ then $\widehat{M}''(s)[\tau\hat{\alpha}\hat{\beta}] = 0$. Since $\hat{\alpha}\hat{\beta}$ is feasible there are no two $\tau_1, \tau_2 \in A_F(t,s)$ such that $\tau_1\hat{\alpha}\hat{\beta} = \tau_2\hat{\alpha}\hat{\beta}$. Therefore all $\tau_i\hat{\alpha}\hat{\beta}$ such that $\tau_i \in A_F(t,s), i = 1, \ldots n$

can be added to $\widehat{M}''(s)$ and the resulting parameterized marking which is equivalent to $\widehat{M}'\hat{\beta}(s)$ is still a set of parameterized tokens.

Now we can conclude that for all $s \in S$ both $\widehat{M}\hat{\beta}(s)$ and $\widehat{M}'\hat{\beta}(s)$ are sets of parameterized tokens. Let $\beta = \hat{\beta}\beta'$ where β' is a fixing $\beta' : \hat{V}(\widehat{M}\hat{\beta}) \cup \hat{V}(\widehat{M}'\hat{\beta}) \to D$. Then $\widehat{M}\beta \in \mathcal{V}_S(\widehat{M})$ and $\widehat{M}'\beta \in \mathcal{V}_S(\widehat{M}')$. Also $\hat{\alpha}\beta$ is feasible and permissible according to Definitions 1.3 and 1.4 since we have assumed that there are no predicates or functions in the selector formula. Therefore

$$\exists \text{ a fixing } \beta \text{ such that } \widehat{M}\beta[t\hat{\alpha}\beta\rangle\widehat{M}'\beta$$

and $\widehat{M}\beta \in \mathcal{V}_S(\widehat{M})$ and $\widehat{M}'\beta \in \mathcal{V}_S(\widehat{M}')$. Consequently $\mathcal{V}(\widehat{M}[t\hat{\alpha}\rangle\widehat{M}')$ is non empty.

For the other direction: if $\mathcal{V}(\widehat{M}[t\hat{\alpha}\rangle\widehat{M}')$ is non empty then there exists a β such that $\widehat{M}\beta[t\hat{\alpha}\beta\rangle\widehat{M}'\beta$. Now, let $\hat{\beta} = \beta$ and the claim trivially follows even in the case when the selectors are not restricted in any way.

Proof of Theorem 3.6:

Since $M \in \mathcal{V}(\widehat{M})$ there must be a fixing β' such that $\widehat{M}\beta' = M$.

Suppose $\alpha = [v_1 \leftarrow d_1, \ldots, v_n \leftarrow d_n]$ and $\hat{\alpha} = [v_1 \leftarrow \hat{x}_1, \ldots, v_n \leftarrow \hat{x}_n]$. Then we can not find a fixing β'' such that $\hat{\alpha}\beta'' = \alpha$ if

1. $\hat{x}_i = d_k \in D$ and $d_k \neq d_i$ or
2. $\hat{x}_i = \hat{x}_j, i \neq j$ and $d_i \neq d_j$ where $i, j \in \{1, \ldots, n\}$.

But then from item 1.a of Definition 3.3 it would follow that either $M \notin \mathcal{V}(\widehat{M})$ or α is not permissible as defined by Definition 1.4. Since these are assumed we can conclude that $\exists \beta'' : \hat{\alpha}\beta'' = \alpha$. Since α is feasible and permissible it follows that $t\hat{\alpha}\beta''$ is enabled in $\widehat{M}\beta'$.

Next we have to show that there is no parameter $\hat{v}_i$ such that $\hat{v}_i\beta' \neq \hat{v}_i\beta''$. If $\hat{v}_i$ is a parameter such that $\hat{v}_i \notin \hat{V}(\widehat{M})$ or $\hat{v}_i \notin \hat{V}(\hat{\alpha})$ this naturally holds. But, if $\hat{v}_i = \hat{x}_i, i \in \{1, \ldots, n\}$, is not such a parameter then according to item 1.a of Definition 3.3

$$\begin{aligned}&\exists\, \tau \in A_F(s,t) \text{ for some } s \in S \text{ such that } \tau(j) = v_i, v_i \in V \text{ and}\\ &\forall\, \hat{\tau} \in \widehat{M}^+(s) \text{ such that } \hat{\tau} \simeq \tau\hat{\alpha} \Rightarrow\\ &\hat{\tau}(j) = \hat{x}_i.\end{aligned}$$

Suppose $\hat{x}_i\beta' \neq \hat{x}_i\beta''$. Then $t\alpha = t\hat{\alpha}\beta''$ could not be enabled in $M = \widehat{M}\beta'$ since there would be no token $\tau' \in M(s)$ such that $\tau' = \tau\alpha$: there is always a j such that $\tau'(j) \neq \tau\alpha(j)$. Since α is permissible it must be that $\hat{x}_i\beta' = \hat{x}_i\beta''$.

Now we have a $\beta = \beta'\beta''$ such that $\widehat{M}\beta = M$ and $t\hat{\alpha}\beta = t\alpha$. Since $M[t\alpha\rangle M'$ it must also be that $\widehat{M}\beta[t\hat{\alpha}\beta\rangle M'$. It still remains to show that $M' = \widehat{M}'\beta$. Since $\hat{V}(\widehat{M}') \subseteq (\hat{V}(\widehat{M}) \cup \hat{V}(\alpha))$ this directly follows and thus

$$M[t\alpha\rangle M' \in \mathcal{V}(\widehat{M}[t\hat{\alpha}\rangle\widehat{M}').$$

Proof of Theorem 3.7:

According to Theorem 3.6

$$M \in \mathcal{V}(\widehat{M}) \Rightarrow M[t\alpha\rangle M_1 \in \mathcal{V}(\widehat{M}[t\hat{\alpha}\rangle\widehat{M}_1).$$

Now, $\widehat{M} \subseteq \widehat{M}'$. Therefore $M[t\alpha\rangle M_1 \in \mathcal{V}(\widehat{M}'[t\hat{\alpha}'\rangle\widehat{M}_1')$. From this we can conclude that

$$\mathcal{V}(\widehat{M}[t\hat{\alpha}\rangle\widehat{M}_1) \subseteq \mathcal{V}(\widehat{M}'[t\hat{\alpha}'\rangle\widehat{M}_1').$$

Appendix 2

Initial marking

$$\widehat{M}_0 \left\{ \begin{array}{ll} \text{Acknowledged} & \\ \text{Unused} & \{\langle a_1, a_2\rangle, \langle a_1, a_3\rangle, \langle a_2, a_1\rangle, \langle a_2, a_3\rangle, \langle a_3, a_1\rangle, \langle a_3, a_2\rangle\} = N \\ \text{Waiting} & \\ \text{Guard} & \{\langle c\rangle\} \\ \text{Inactive} & \{\langle a_1\rangle, \langle a_2\rangle, \langle a_3\rangle\} \\ \text{Performing} & \\ \text{Received} & \\ \text{SentR} & \end{array} \right.$$

Marking 1

$$\Big\downarrow \begin{array}{ll} t_1: & \hat{\alpha} = [s \leftarrow \hat{s}_1, r_1 \leftarrow \hat{r}_1, r_2 \leftarrow \hat{r}_2, x \leftarrow c] \\ \varphi: & \hat{r}_1 \neq \hat{s}_1, \hat{r}_2 \neq \hat{s}_1 \end{array}$$

$$\widehat{M}_1 \left\{ \begin{array}{ll} \text{Acknowledged} & \\ \text{Unused} & N - \{\langle \hat{s}_1, \hat{r}_1\rangle, \langle \hat{s}_1, \hat{r}_2\rangle\} \\ \text{Waiting} & \{\langle \hat{s}_1\rangle\} \\ \text{Guard} & \\ \text{Inactive} & \{\langle a_1\rangle, \langle a_2\rangle, \langle a_3\rangle\} - \{\langle \hat{s}_1\rangle\} \\ \text{Performing} & \\ \text{Received} & \\ \text{SentR} & \{\langle \hat{s}_1, \hat{r}_1\rangle, \langle \hat{s}_1, \hat{r}_2\rangle\} \end{array} \right.$$

Marking 2

$$\Big\downarrow\ t_3: \quad \hat{\alpha} = [s \leftarrow \hat{s}_1, r \leftarrow \hat{r}_3]$$

$$\widehat{M}_2 \left\{ \begin{array}{ll} \text{Acknowledged} & \\ \text{Unused} & N - \{\langle \hat{s}_1, \hat{r}_1\rangle, \langle \hat{s}_1, \hat{r}_2\rangle\} \\ \text{Waiting} & \{\langle \hat{s}_1\rangle\} \\ \text{Guard} & \\ \text{Inactive} & \{\langle a_1\rangle, \langle a_2\rangle, \langle a_3\rangle\} - \{\langle \hat{s}_1\rangle, \langle \hat{r}_3\rangle\} \\ \text{Performing} & \{\langle \hat{r}_3\rangle\} \\ \text{Received} & \{\langle \hat{s}_1, \hat{r}_3\rangle\} \\ \text{SentR} & \{\langle \hat{s}_1, \hat{r}_1\rangle, \langle \hat{s}_1, \hat{r}_2\rangle\} - \{\langle \hat{s}_1, \hat{r}_3\rangle\} \end{array} \right.$$

Marking 3

$$\Big\downarrow\ t_4: \quad \hat{\alpha} = [s = \hat{s}_1, r = \hat{r}_3]$$

$$\widehat{M}3 \left\{ \begin{array}{ll} \text{Acknowledged} & \{\langle \hat{s}_1, \hat{r}_3\rangle\} \\ \text{Unused} & N - \{\langle \hat{s}_1, \hat{r}_1\rangle, \langle \hat{s}_1, \hat{r}_2\rangle\} \\ \text{Waiting} & \{\langle \hat{s}_1\rangle\} \\ \text{Guard} & \\ \text{Inactive} & \{\langle a_1\rangle, \langle a_2\rangle, \langle a_3\rangle\} - \{\langle \hat{s}_1\rangle\} \\ \text{Performing} & \\ \text{Received} & \\ \text{SentR} & \{\langle \hat{s}_1, \hat{r}_1\rangle, \langle \hat{s}_1, \hat{r}_2\rangle\} - \{\langle \hat{s}_1, \hat{r}_3\rangle\} \end{array} \right.$$

Marking 4

$$\Big\downarrow\; t_3 : \quad \hat{\alpha} = [s \leftarrow \hat{s}_1, r \leftarrow \hat{r}_4]$$

$$\widehat{M}_4 \left\{ \begin{array}{ll} \text{Acknowledged} & \\ \text{Unused} & N - \{\langle \hat{s}_1, \hat{r}_1\rangle, \langle \hat{s}_1, \hat{r}_2\rangle\} \\ \text{Waiting} & \{\langle \hat{s}_1\rangle\} \\ \text{Guard} & \\ \text{Inactive} & \\ \text{Performing} & \{\langle \hat{r}_3\rangle, \langle \hat{r}_4\rangle\} \\ \text{Received} & \{\langle \hat{s}_1, \hat{r}_3\rangle, \langle \hat{s}_1, \hat{r}_4\rangle\} \\ \text{SentR} & \end{array} \right.$$

Marking 5

$$\Big\downarrow\; t_3 : \quad \hat{\alpha} = [s \leftarrow \hat{s}_1, r \leftarrow \hat{r}_5]$$

$$\widehat{M}_5 \left\{ \begin{array}{ll} \text{Acknowledged} & \{\langle \hat{s}_1, \hat{r}_3\rangle\} \\ \text{Unused} & N - \{\langle \hat{s}_1, \hat{r}_1\rangle, \langle \hat{s}_1, \hat{r}_2\rangle\} \\ \text{Waiting} & \{\langle \hat{s}_1\rangle\} \\ \text{Guard} & \\ \text{Inactive} & \{\langle a_1\rangle, \langle a_2\rangle, \langle a_3\rangle\} - \{\langle \hat{s}_1\rangle, \langle \hat{r}_5\rangle\} = \{\langle \hat{r}_7\rangle\} \\ \text{Performing} & \{\langle \hat{r}_5\rangle\} \\ \text{Received} & \{\langle \hat{s}_1, \hat{r}_5\rangle\} \\ \text{SentR} & \end{array} \right.$$

Marking 6

$$\Big\downarrow\; t_4 : \quad \hat{\alpha} = [s \leftarrow \hat{s}_1, r = \hat{r}_6]$$

$$\widehat{M}_6 \left\{ \begin{array}{ll} \text{Acknowledged} & \{\langle \hat{s}_1, \hat{r}_6\rangle\} \\ \text{Unused} & N - \{\langle \hat{s}_1, \hat{r}_1\rangle, \langle \hat{s}_1, \hat{r}_2\rangle\} \\ \text{Waiting} & \{\langle \hat{s}_1\rangle\} \\ \text{Guard} & \\ \text{Inactive} & \{\langle \hat{r}_6\rangle\} \\ \text{Performing} & \{\langle \hat{r}_3\rangle, \langle \hat{r}_4\rangle\} - \{\langle \hat{r}_6\rangle\} = \{\langle \hat{r}_8\rangle\} \\ \text{Received} & \{\langle \hat{s}_1, \hat{r}_3\rangle, \langle \hat{s}_1, \hat{r}_4\rangle\} - \{\langle \hat{s}_1, \hat{r}_6\rangle\} = \{\langle \hat{s}_1, \hat{r}_8\rangle\} \\ \text{SentR} & \end{array} \right.$$

$$\widehat{M}_6 \subseteq \widehat{M}_5, \hat{\beta} = [\hat{r}_3 \leftarrow \hat{r}_6, \hat{r}_5 \leftarrow \hat{r}_8, \hat{r}_7 \leftarrow \hat{r}_6]$$

Marking 7

$$\Big\downarrow\; t_4 : \quad \hat{\alpha} = [s \leftarrow \hat{s}_1, r \leftarrow \hat{r}_5]$$

$$\widehat{M}_7 \left\{ \begin{array}{ll} \text{Acknowledged} & \{\langle \hat{s}_1, \hat{r}_3\rangle, \langle \hat{s}_1, \hat{r}_5\rangle\} \\ \text{Unused} & N - \{\langle \hat{s}_1, \hat{r}_1\rangle, \langle \hat{s}_1, \hat{r}_2\rangle\} \\ \text{Waiting} & \{\langle \hat{s}_1\rangle\} \\ \text{Guard} & \\ \text{Inactive} & \{\langle \hat{r}_5\rangle, \langle \hat{r}_7\rangle\} \\ \text{Performing} & \\ \text{Received} & \\ \text{SentR} & \end{array} \right.$$

Marking 8

$$\downarrow \begin{array}{ll} t_2: & \hat{\alpha} = [s \leftarrow \hat{s}_1, r_1 \leftarrow \hat{r}_9, r_2 \leftarrow \hat{r}_{10}, x = c] \\ \varphi: & x = c \end{array}$$

$$\widehat{M}_8 \left\{ \begin{array}{ll} \text{Acknowledged} & \\ \text{Unused} & N + \{\langle \hat{s}_1, \hat{r}_9\rangle, \langle \hat{s}_1, \hat{r}_{10}\rangle\} - \{\langle \hat{s}_1, \hat{r}_1\rangle, \langle \hat{s}_1, \hat{r}_2\rangle\} = N \\ \text{Waiting} & \{\langle \hat{s}_1\rangle\} - \{\langle \hat{s}_1\rangle\} = \emptyset \\ \text{Guard} & \{\langle c\rangle\} \\ \text{Inactive} & \{\langle \hat{r}_5\rangle, \langle \hat{r}_7\rangle, \langle \hat{s}_1\rangle\} = \{\langle a_1\rangle, \langle a_2\rangle, \langle a_3\rangle\} \\ \text{Performing} & \\ \text{Received} & \\ \text{SentR} & \end{array} \right.$$

$$\widehat{M}_8 = \widehat{M}_0$$

How the tree is put together:

$$\begin{array}{llllllll} \widehat{M}_0 \rightarrow & \widehat{M}_1 \rightarrow & \widehat{M}_2 \rightarrow & \widehat{M}_3 \rightarrow & \widehat{M}_5 \rightarrow & & \widehat{M}_7 \longrightarrow & \widehat{M}_8 = \widehat{M}_0 \\ & & \downarrow & & & & & \\ & & \widehat{M}_2 \rightarrow & \widehat{M}_4 \rightarrow & \widehat{M}_6 \subseteq \widehat{M}_5 & & & \end{array}$$

Iterative Decomposition and Aggregation of Stochastic Marked Graph Petri Nets

Yao Li and C. Murray Woodside

Telecommunications Research Institute of Ontario
Department of Systems and Computer Engineering
Carleton University
Ottawa, Ontario, Canada, K1S 5B6
email: li@sce.carleton.ca and cmw@sce.carleton.ca

Abstract— This paper addresses the problem of state explosion and computational complexity in solving marked graph Stochastic Petri Nets (SPNs). We first develop a simple and powerful Petri Nets (PNs) reduction technique that reduces the size of a marked graph PN. Then we propose an iterative delay equivalent reduction technique to solve the reduced SPN. This method iteratively tunes two or more partly aggregated auxiliary SPNs until they are approximately delay equivalent to the original SPN. It avoids the direct solution of the original SPN. In our experience the iteration usually converges and the accuracy is usually better than 5%, though there are exceptional cases. The technique is a step towards approximating more general SPNs.

Keywords— (Generalized) Stochastic Petri nets, Markov chain, marked graph, PN reduction and delay equivalent aggregation.

Contents

1. Introduction

Stochastic Petri nets [Moll82] and Generalized SPNs (or GSPNs) [Mars84] have proven to be extremely useful in modeling the performance of communicating concurrent systems such as protocols [Suzu90], distributed software [Wood88b] and flexible manufacturing systems [Hato91, Silv89]. A Marked Graph (MG) SPN is one in which every place has one input and one output arc. This is a limited but nontrivial class of SPNs which in particular are capable of representing interprocess synchronization. Many software models turn out to be marked graphs, such as the pipeline of tasks described later in this paper. Although SPNs are powerful in modelling and performance analysis, their use is impeded by the exponential growth of the state space of their underlying Markov Chain (MC), which quickly makes performance analysis by direct Markovian analysis impossible even for systems of modest size. The purpose of this paper is to approximate the solution of SPNs and GSPNs which are marked graphs, in a way which overcomes state explosion. The derivations in the paper are for SPNs, in the interests of simplicity. However they generalize in a direct and immediate way to GSPNs.

Various techniques have been used to cope with state explosion in Petri nets and also in Queueing Networks (QNs), which are closely related. First among these are product-form solutions which, if they can be found, offer enormous computational advantages. These were found first for QNs, and solutions for SPNs corresponding to product-form QNs were described in [Li89]. Some other special classes of SPN have also been shown to have a product-form solution [Flor91, Laza87, Mars86,87]. Norton's theorem [Chan75, Bals82] gives a simplified and exact representation for a subnet in a product-form QN or (as shown in [Li89]) in a product-form SPN. It also has been used to motivate approximations for non-product-form QNs. For non-product-form SPNs this approach can be applied, but it is often computationally expensive.

There are many other types of approximate techniques for SPNs, besides Norton's theorem. Giglmayr [Gigl87] decomposed the transition rate matrix of an SPN by using the concept of "nearly complete decomposability" [Cour77]. Along the same line, Ammar *et al* suggested a time scale decomposition method to hierarchically reduce the SPN [Amma87,89]. This method has good accuracy when transition firing rates differ by orders of magnitude, as required. Ciardo and Trivedi developed an approximate technique [Ciar91] that decomposes a GSPN into a set of subnets and solves each individual subnet separately. Because there exist dependences among the subnets, after solving each subnet, certain quantities need to be exported to other subnets, and this is conducted iteratively. Their decomposition is based on an assumption of near-independence among subnets and on special subnet structures which may not be present in a given system.

Approximations for QNs are also relevant to the present research, particularly the method surrogate delays which Jacobson and Lazowska invented for analyzing simultaneous resource possession [Jaco82]. It partitions queueing delay according to which of the simultaneously held resources is responsible, then iterates between two models, each of which includes an explicit representation of one of the simultaneously held resources and a "surrogate delay" to represent the congestion at the other resource. This iteration strategy is somewhat similar to that of Ciardo and Trivedi, and has been adopted also in the present work.

Petri net reduction is another approach to reducing the state space of a model. Berthelot *et al*, in [Bert76,79,85,86], defined reduction rules, and showed that a set of logical properties are exactly preserved under each reduction rule. The rules can be applied iteratively. However, they are not directly applicable to timed nets, for they do not deal with timing parameters, and some of the rules fuse unconnected vertices, which may not be desirable in a performance model. Murata *et al* have considered reduction of marked graphs in [Mura80, John81]. They defined some special net structure reductions of marked graphs (serial, parallel, YV, unique-circuit), and showed that the number of equivalent classes of the marked graph $\rho(G)$ is invariant under these reductions. However, their special reductions are not as general as the present approach. Lee *et al* defined several classes of reducible subnets such that the reduced net preserves liveness, boundedness and proper termination [Lee85,87]. Still, for those reducible subnets applicable to marked graph reduction, the reduction power is limited. Song *et al* defined two types of reducible subnets: a 'well-behaved place module' and a 'well-behaved transition module' [Song87]. The former can be aggregated to a single place, and the latter to a single transition while preserving some logical properties. There is a restriction on a reducible subnet that it must contain one and only one exit point, either a transition or a place, which is very limiting. Campos *et al* presented a kit of transformation rules that allows to fully reduce any live and bounded 1-cut marked graph [Camp91] (i.e., such that there exists at least one transition belonging to all circuits, which is not the condition of our reduction.)

The present paper reduces marked graphs in a new way that is most suitable for performance calculations, and then uses the reductions within an iterative approximation using surrogate rates, to overcome the state explosion problem. Because marked graphs may also occur as easily identifiable components in a more general SPN model, this approach may also, ultimately, be a component in a more general SPN reduction technique.

To approximately solve a large marked graph SPN, the proposed technique has a static phase and a dynamic phase. In the static phase, two or more identical duplicates of the model are created and then reduced in different ways to produce two or more smaller complementary auxiliary models. During this process, different parts of the original model are retained unaggregated in each auxiliary model, such that the union of unaggregated parts covers the original SPN. The major concern in the static phase is to ensure the logical equivalence between the reduced auxiliary models and the original SPN by preserving liveness and boundedness. In the dynamic phase, some parameters of the auxiliary SPN models are iteratively tuned, using a mean delay equivalence relationship, until the models are statistically approximately equivalent.

The present paper makes a number of original contributions. It gives a sound foundation for simplifying a MG by replacing an *internally connected* subnet by a single transition (including showing that the net is still live, and identifying traversing paths and traversable token counts). It describes a strategy of *complementary—model iteration*, with some novel features. Unlike [Ciar91], the aggregatable subnets allowed in our approach are defined purely on a general class of Petri net, regardless of special modelling structures. These subnets do not have to cover the entire net, and there is more freedom in choosing them, for example to correspond to known physical or logical subsystems. Finally a heuristic parameter-tuning approach based on the method of surrogate delays has three novel features: it incorporates a generalization of Littles' result to weighted token flows, it applies surrogate delays to multiple-input multiple-output systems, and it develops a multiple-rate approximation (rate as a function of internal population), which has not been attempted before.

This paper is organized in following way. Section 2 introduces some preliminaries on PNs, SPNs and marked graphs. Section 3 gives a new reduction of marked graph PNs. Section 4 presents the iterative delay equivalent approximation. Section 5 provides some examples illustrating the method and its applications. Section 6 concludes the paper.

2. Preliminaries

A formal definition of the PN used in this paper is

Definition 2.1. A *PN* is a quadruple of K places P, M transitions T, arcs A and an initial marking $\mathbf{M}_0$:

$$\begin{aligned} PN &= (P, T, A, \mathbf{M}_0) \\ P &= \{ p_1, p_2, \dots, p_K \} \\ T &= \{ t_1, t_2, \dots, t_M \} \\ A &\subset \{ P \times T \} \cup \{ T \times P \} \\ \mathbf{M}_0 &= (n_{01}, n_{02}, \dots, n_{0K}) \end{aligned} \tag{2.1}$$

The set of reachable markings from initial marking $\mathbf{M}_0$ is denoted by $R(\mathbf{M}_0)$. The sets of input and output places for transition t are denoted by ${}^\bullet t$ and $t^\bullet$ respectively, and the input and output transitions for place p are similarly ${}^\bullet p$ and $p^\bullet$.

Definition 2.2. The *multiplicity* of an arc defines the number of tokens that flow when a transitions fires; denoted by γ^+_{ij} the input multiplicity of the arc from p_j to t_i and by γ^-_{ij} the output multiplicity (of the arc from t_i to p_j). Then $\Gamma = (\gamma_{ij}) = (\gamma^+_{ij} - \gamma^-_{ij})$ for $1 \le i \le M$, $1 \le j \le K$ is the *incidence matrix* of the net.

Definition 2.3. A *stochastic Petri net* is augmented from a PN by associating a set of the transition firing rates $\mu = \{\mu_1, \mu_2, \dots, \mu_M\}$ (with exponentially distributed transition times) to all transitions. The mean time to fire t_i, once it is enabled, is μ_i^{-1}. A *generalized stochastic Petri net* is extended from SPN by splitting transitions into two classes: timed transitions and immediate transitions [Mars84]. Timed transitions are assigned finite firing rates. Immediate transitions are divided into groups, containing transitions which may be simultaneously enabled by the same marking, and their relative probabilities q_{ij} are in the ratio of their rates.

Definition 2.4. A *marked graph* is a Petri net $PN = (P, T, A, \mathbf{M}_0)$ such that for all $p \in P$, $|{}^\bullet p| = |p^\bullet| = 1$. That is, each place p has exactly one input transition and exactly one output transition.

It will be convenient to use some graphical terminologies in marked graph. Let *vertex* v in a PN be either a place p or a transition t. A *path* in a marked graph is a finite, alternating sequence of arcs and vertices:

$$x_0, \dots, a_1, v_1, a_2, v_2, \dots, a_j, v_j, \dots, a_{J-1}, v_{J-1}, \dots, x_J$$

beginning with element x_0 and ending with element x_J, such that

(1) elements x_0, x_J may be in types of place p, transition t, arc a, or partial arc $\tilde{a}$ (part of a);

(2) vertices are also in alternating sequence, i.e., for $i = 0,1,2,3,\dots$, there is either ($v_{2i} \in P$

and $v_{2i+1} \in T$) or ($v_{2i} \in T$ and $v_{2i+1} \in P$);

(3) places and transitions are in chaining relations, i.e., for $0 \le j \le J$, there are $v_j \in {}^\bullet v_{j+1}$ and $v_{j+1} \in v_j^\bullet$;

(4) no part of the path is repeatedly visited, i.e., (i) for $0 \le i < j \le J$, there are $v_i \ne v_j$ and $a_i \ne a_j$; (ii) if $x_0 = \tilde{a}_i$ and $x_J = \tilde{a}_j$, then $i \ne j$.

A *cycle* in a marked graph is a path such that it begins and ends with the same element x. In particular, if $x_0 = \tilde{a}_i$ then $x_J = \tilde{a}_i$ also. Two cycles are *independent* of each other if each of them contains at least one unique place that is not on the other cycle. Among all possible cycles in a marked graph, the *system cycles* are a set of independent cycles that cover all vertices and arcs of the net. Let C_s be the number of system cycles.

Definition 2.5. A PN is

- *live* if every transition in the net is ultimately firable by progressing through some firing sequence for every marking **M** in $R(\mathbf{M}_0)$;
- *k-bounded* or simply *bounded* if the number of tokens in each place does not exceed a finite number k for any marking reachable from initial marking $\mathbf{M}_0$;
- *safe* if it is 1-bounded;
- *structurally bounded* if it is bounded for any finite initial marking $\mathbf{M}_0$;
- *conservative* if there exists a positive integer (or rational) weighting vector **w**, such that $w_k > 0$ for $k = 1,2,...,K$ satisfy $\Gamma \cdot \mathbf{w} = \underline{0}$, where a weight w_k is associated with place p_k for all $p_k \in P$, denoted by $p_k \sim w_k$;
- *connected* if there is a path between any two vertices;
- *strongly connected* if there are two paths in opposite direction between any two vertices;
- *regular* if all arc multiplicities are unity, there is no inhibitor arc, and a transition firing depends only on its input marking;

The cycle concept has special importance in marked graph. Two theorems below from [Pete81] describe some properties based on the cycle concept. The third theorem links some important structural properties of the marked graph.

Theorem 2.1. The number of tokens on a cycle (the token count of a cycle) of a marked graph does not change as a result of transition firing.

Theorem 2.2. A marked graph is *live* iff the number of tokens on each cycle of the marked graph is at least one; and it is *safe* iff every place in the marked graph is in a cycle with a token count of one.

Theorem 2.3. For a connected marked graph the following structural properties: (a) strongly connected, (b) every place is in a cycle, (c) conservative, (d) structurally bounded, and (e) bounded, are all equivalent.

Proof: The equivalences of (b) and (d), and from (e) to (a) are shown in [Li91]. The rest are in the literature and are summarized in [Li91]. #

Corollary 2.1. For a connected marked graph PN, if every place is in a cycle, then every transition is also in a cycle.

Proof: A transition is not in a cycle only if its input and output places are not in a cycle. But this is excluded. #

Net Structures

Now let's define some net structures needed in marked graph reduction. A *link* consists of one or more paths connected in series regardless of their directions. A *subnet* $SN = (P_{SN}, T_{SN}, A_{SN}, \mathbf{M}_{0SN})$ in a marked graph PN is chosen such that its boundary is over the input arcs of places, and over the output arcs of transitions as in Figure 2.1. Furthermore, it is internally connected, i.e., there is at least one internal link between any two vertices within the subnet. For convenience, we may use *SN* for an original/unaggregated subnet, and *sn* for an aggregated subnet. A set of *redundant places* $P_R = \{p_r\}$ (Figure 2.2) are those places between a pair of transitions, which have no effect on enabling and firing the second transition; or more generally, are those places which may be removed without affecting the reachability graph of the entire net. For a complete definition, one may refer to [Bert85].

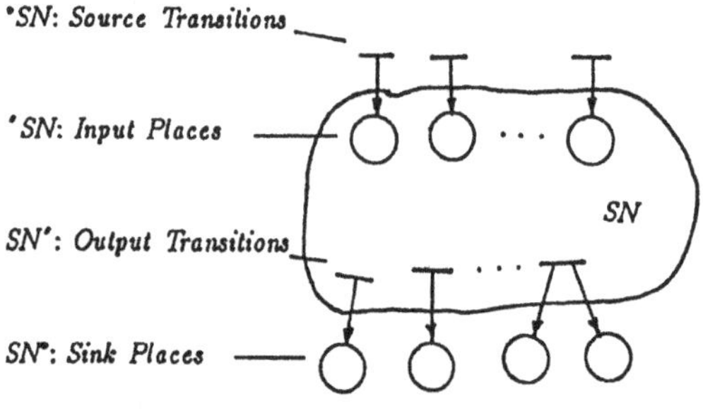

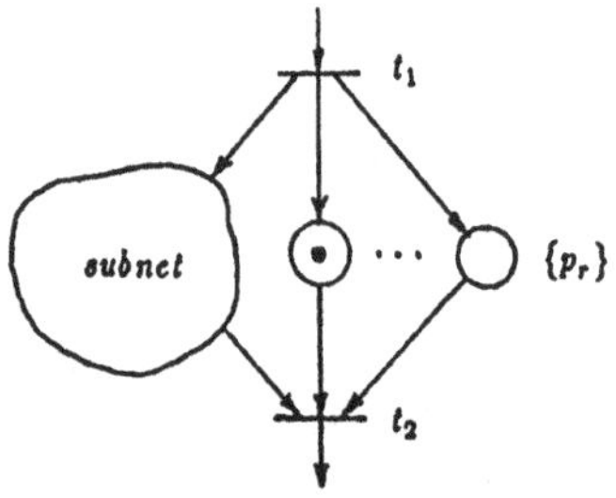

Figure 2.1 A General Subnet *SN* Figure 2.2

This paper considers marked graph PN, SPN and GSPN which are regular, live, bounded, and free of redundant places.

Relative to a subnet (as shown in Figure 2.3 on next page), a cycle is called an *internal cycle* if it is completely contained in the subnet; or a *traversing cycle* if it is partly contained in the subnet (across the subnet boundary). For each cycle in a MG we know the cycle token count is invariant. For a traversing cycle, the tokens may in general be inside or outside. However in some Petri nets, the part of the tokens inside *SN* never goes below some number, called the *residual token count* N_r of that cycle; from outside *SN* it is as if they did not exist except for their effect on firing rates. The (remaining) part of the cycle token count is seen to enter and leave *SN* and will be called the *traversable token count* N_t of the cycle; it is viewed (from outside *SN*) as a population for the traversing cycle. N_r may be calculated by finding a global marking $\mathbf{M}_1$ within $R(\mathbf{M}_0)$ such that $N_r = \min \sum_i M_1(i)$, where the summation is over the places on the concerned traversing cycle and inside the subnet. N_t is calculated by finding another global marking $\mathbf{M}_2$ within $R(\mathbf{M}_0)$ such that $N_t = max(\sum_i M_2(i)) - N_r$, where the summation is over the same set of places as above. Equivalently, let $p_o \in SN^\bullet$ be the *sink place* of the concerned traversing cycle, $M_{\max}(p_o)$ and $M_{\min}(p_o)$ be the maximum and minimum number of tokens containable in p_o at two markings of $R(\mathbf{M}_0)$, then $N_t = M_{\max}(p_o) - M_{\min}(p_o)$ is also the traversable token count of those traversing cycles with p_o as the common sink place.

A path is called a *traversing path* if it is delimited at both ends by the subnet boundary, and it is part of a traversing cycle. In this case, a traversing path begins and ends with two partial arcs (incident upon the subnet boundary). A path within a subnet of the marked graph may be *shared* by a traversing cycle and an internal cycle. But according to our definitions it is the part of a traversing path. Two paths are *distinct* if no parts of them are overlapping and intersecting.

Example 1. (Illustration of terminology). Figure 2.3 shows some instances of the structures defined above.

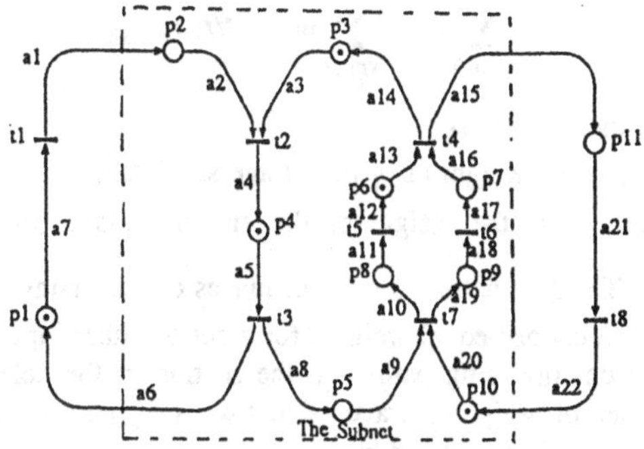

Figure 2.3 An Illustrating Example

Internal cycle: $p_3,t_2,p_4,t_3,p_5,t_7,p_8,t_5,p_6,t_4$ and associated arcs.

Traversing cycle: $p_{11},t_8,p_{10},t_7,p_8,t_5,p_6,t_4$ and associated arcs;

Residual token count of a traversing cycle: one token currently in p_6 for above traversing cycle.

Traversable token count of a traversing cycle: 1 for above traversing cycle.

Sink place of some traversing cycles: p_{11} for above traversing cycle.

Traversing paths: (1) $\tilde{a}_{22},p_{10},a_{20},t_7,a_{10},p_8,a_{11},t_5,a_{12},p_6,a_{13},t_4,\tilde{a}_{15}$ for above traversing cycle.

(2) $\tilde{a}_1,p_2,a_2,t_2,a_4,p_4,a_5,t_3,\tilde{a}_6$.

Shared path: t_2,a_4,p_4,a_5,t_3.

Distinct paths: traversing path (1) is distinct from (2).

When solving a SPN for performance measures, the throughput is a key figure to obtain. To be specific, let this throughput represent the rate of token flow. In marked graph SPN, there is a nice and simple result which seems to be new as stated below.

Theorem 2.4. In a live and strongly connected marked graph SPN, all cycles and arcs have the same throughput [Li91].

Thus we can call this common token throughput the *system throughput*. It is the function of, in addition to the net structure, the system initial marking $\mathbf{M}_0$ or $R(\mathbf{M}_0)$. Cycles play an important role, and there are usually more places than system cycles in marked graph. Therefore the system throughput can also be expressed as the function of, in addition to the net structure, the token vector of system cycles $\mathbf{N}_s = (N_1, N_2, \ldots, N_i, \ldots, N_{C_s})$ where $N_i > 0$ is the number of tokens on cycle i.

In section 4 of the mean delay equivalent aggregation, the mean total number of weighted tokens of a subnet will be used. The weights for places in *SN*, and the formula to calculate this weighted mean, are now defined:

Definition 2.6. For an original subnet *SN* in marked graph PN with respect to a set of independent cycles that cover its all vertices and arcs, the *constrained weights of places* in the *SN* are calculated by solving

$$\sum_{\forall p_i \in {}^{\bullet}t} w_i = \sum_{\forall p_j \in t^{\bullet}} w_j; \quad \forall t: t \in T_{SN} \tag{2.2}$$

subject to the following constraints

(i) $w_i > 0$ only if w_i is the weight of p_i on a traversing path;

(ii) $\sum_j w_j = 1$, where w_j is the weight of the entrance place (the first place) p_j on a traversing path. The summation is over all places on traversing paths.

It is convenient to choose equal weights for a set of either input or output places of a transition if they are on traversing paths. In the section of the delay equivalent aggregation, the mean number of weighted traversable tokens $\overline{N}'_{SN}$ in an original marked graph subnet will be used, and it is calculated by

$$\overline{N}'_{SN} = \sum_i \overline{n}'_i = \sum_i w_i \overline{n}_i \tag{2.3}$$

where the summation is over all places on all traversing paths. $\overline{n}_i$ is the mean number of tokens in place p_i excluding the residual traversing cycle tokens, and $\overline{n}'_i$ is the weighted mean.

The token split and merge caused by split and join transitions in *SN* will change the total number of tokens in *SN*. However, by introducing the above weights to places in *SN*, the sum of weighted traversable tokens N'_{SN} will conserve over the firings of local transitions in *SN* except $t \in SN^{\bullet}$. The mean of N'_{SN}, denoted by $\overline{N}'_{SN}$, is a measure of mean number of "customers" in *SN*. With these weights to places, the "customers" throughput can also be properly defined. Thus Little's result can be applied to marked graph SPN, or to more general SPN for calculating the mean delay [Wood91].

3. Reduction of Marked Graph Petri Nets

It is a key step to reduce the size of the SPN through aggregating some subnets *SN*'s to MPST (Multiple-Place-Single-Transition) subnets *sn*'s in our approximate analysis. By solving the size-reduced SPN, we can thus avoid solving the original entire SPN. The structure and marking of the reduced nets are a PN reduction problem. However, compared to the previous research listed earlier, our requirements are different. We wish to preserve fewer logical properties of the model (just liveness and boundedness), and to avoid special structural requirements on the model, besides being a marked graph.

Definition 3. The MPST aggregation of an internally connected subnet *SN* in a live and bounded marked graph PN is a single transition t_a such that $^{\cdot}t_a = {}^{*}SN$ and $t_a^{\cdot} = SN^{\cdot}$. The places $^{\cdot}t_a$ are marked as described in the procedure below. The MPST aggregation requires that

(i) the subnet *SN* be internally connected, as mentioned;

(ii) there should be no more than one traversing path in *SN* for any cycle in PN.

The requirements (i) and (ii) impose a certain degree of internal cohesion on what may be regarded as a suitable subnet for *SN*. They do no guarantee in themselves a good approximation. Figure 3.1 shows an example of a MPST aggregation.

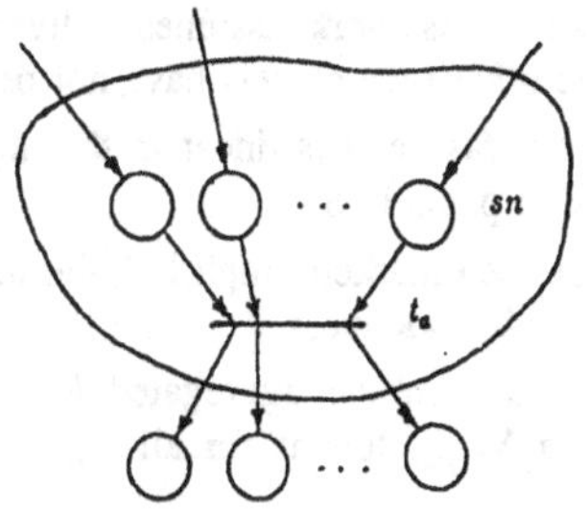

Figure 3.1 The Aggregated MPST Subnet *sn*

Structure: The source transitions $^{\cdot}sn$, input places $^{*}sn$, and sink places $sn^{\cdot}$ match one to one with $^{\cdot}SN$, $^{*}SN$ and $SN^{\cdot}$ respectively.

Markings: For each independent covering cycle of *SN*, there is a traversing cycle of *sn* with the same structure outside the subnet. A marking for $^{*}sn$ is to be determined which preserves the traversable token counts on these traversing cycles, where *SN* is replaced by *sn*. This is done by the following procedure:

Procedure for Marking sn in MPST Aggregation

begin

{exhaustively empty *SN*}

Disable all source transitions $t \in {}^{\cdot}SN$;

Exhaustively fire all $t \in T_{SN}$ until no more is enabled;

{preserve traversable token counts inside *SN*}

Do {for each input place $p_{in} \in {}^{*}SN$}

for each traversing path l_k within *SN*, and beginning with p_{in}

Find token sum $N_k = \sum_{i:\, p_i \in l_k} n_i$ along the path;

Choose the minimum token sum $N_{k,min}= min(N_k)$;

Add $N_{k,min}$ tokens into the corresponding input place $p_{in}\in {}^*sn$;

Until (all $p_{in}\in {}^*SN$ have been examined)

end.

Remarks:

(i) The rest of the net, including structure and marking, is unchanged by this procedure, i.e., $PN_{ori}-SN= PN_{agg}-sn$.

(ii) In the above aggregation, with respect to a covering set of independent cycles, all internal cycles and their cycle tokens will be suppressed. The number of traversing cycles may be changed, since traversing cycles which separate only within *SN* will be merged.

(iii) The above proposed procedure can make a nonlive net, such as a net with an empty internal cycle, live. Because this work assumes a live and bounded net, clauses to exclude or properly handle other type of nets have not been included for simplicity.

(iv) The above procedure is very fast, and is linear in the maximum traversing path length and the number of traversing paths in *SN*.

Theorem 3. For a live and bounded marked graph PN, the MPST reduction given in above definition preserves liveness and boundedness.

Proof: Liveness: Traversing cycles in the aggregated PN are through input places ${}^*sn$. These places are filled up with $N_{k,min}$ tokens for all $p_{in}\in {}^*sn$. Thus the aggregated net is live by Theorem 2.2.

Boundedness: The aggregation does not move any place off a cycle, thus the aggregated net is strongly connected, and must be bounded by Theorem 2.3. #

We note however that aggregation may alter the maximum enabling degree of some transitions.

4. Iterative Delay Equivalent Reduction of Stochastic Marked Graph Petri Nets

After PN reduction, only the rate μ_{sn} of the aggregated transition t_a remains to be determined. It could be a constant, or a function of the input place markings. In general μ_{sn} will depend not only on sn, but on the entire net, and will require solving the entire net.

Our goal in this work is to avoid solving the entire net, for example because it may be too large. This section describes an approach in which the PN is divided into a number of aggregated auxiliary nets and solved iteratively by a surrogate delay approach.

The basic idea of the iterative delay equivalent aggregation is quite simple. To analyze a large marked graph SPN approximately, we may partition the SPN into two (or more) nonoverlapped subnets; then establish two (or more) auxiliary SPN models, each with one subnet aggregated into a multiple-place-single-transition subnet. The firing rates of the composite transitions of these aggregated subnets are made marking-dependent, and are adjusted iteratively so as to make each aggregated subnet delay equivalent to its corresponding unaggregated subnet. In the case of product-form SPN, this type of delay equivalent aggregation gives the same marking-dependent transition firing rates and yields the same result as Norton's aggregation does [Li89]. To adjust two (or a set of) marking-dependent transition firing rates, the method of surrogate delays [Jaco82] will be generalized.

Now the iterative delay equivalent reduction of a marked graph SPN is presented. We study a simple case— a two-part partitioned SPN. There may be several types of connections between two subnets. The simplest case is the two-arc connection between two subnets as in following subsection. The most general case is the multiple arc connection between two subnets as in the subsection after.

4.1 Single-Input Single-Output Subnets

Figure 4.1 is the original model. The two partially aggregated auxiliary SPN models are in Figure 4.2.

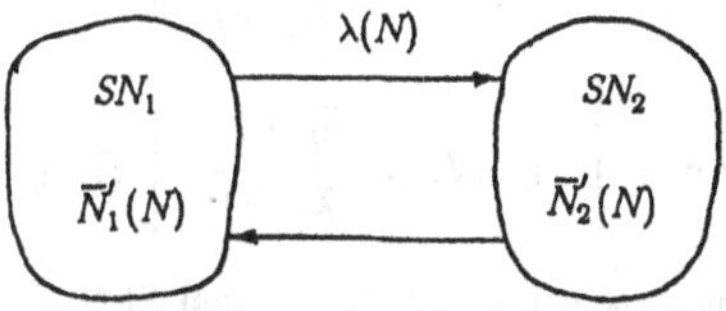

Figure 4.1 The Original Marked Graph SPN

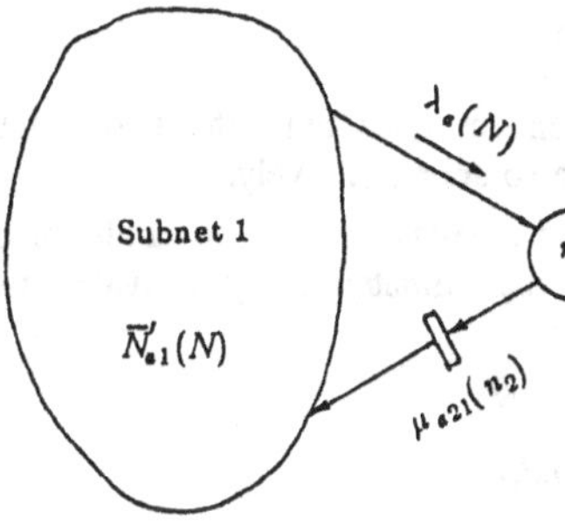

Figure 4.2 (a) Auxiliary Model a

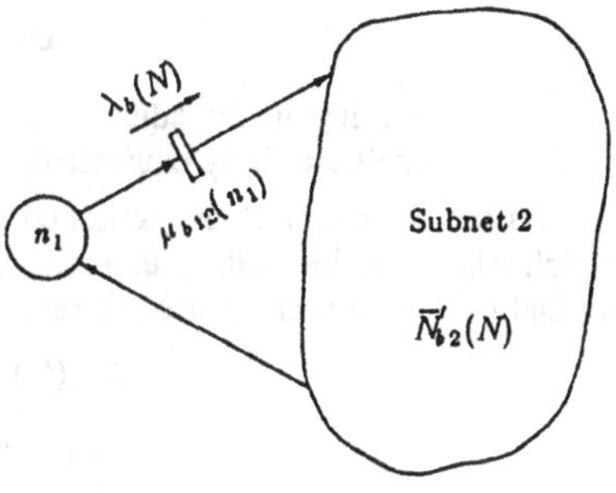

Figure 4.2 (b) Auxiliary Model b

More Notations and Definitions:

N: the number of traversable tokens to the partition or to either subnet;

n_1, n_2 : the number of instantaneous tokens in aggregated places p_1, p_2, $1 \leq n_1, n_2 \leq N$;

$\mu_{a21}(n_2)$, $\mu_{b12}(n_1)$: marking-dependent rates, to be found;

$\lambda_{a12}(N)$, $\lambda_{b12}(N)$, *etc* : throughputs while N tokens present;

For $N = 1,2,\ldots$, there exist $\lambda_{a12}(N) = \lambda_{a21}(N) = \lambda_a(N)$, and $\lambda_{b12}(N) = \lambda_{b21}(N) = \lambda_b(N)$.

$\overline{N}'_{a1}(N), \overline{N}'_{b2}(N)$: mean number of weighted traversable tokens to Subnet 1 and Subnet 2 of two auxiliary models respectively when N tokens flow between two subnets. They are calculated by (2.3);

$\overline{n}'_{a2}(N), \overline{n}'_{b1}(N)$: mean number of weighted tokens in aggregated places p_2, p_1, where their weights $w_1 = w_2 = 1$. Hence $\overline{n}'_{a2}(N) = \overline{n}_{a2}(N)$ and $\overline{n}'_{b1}(N) = \overline{n}_{b1}(N)$.

Also define some delays using Little's result

Delays in Model	Subnet 1	Subnet 2
Original	$D_1(N) = \dfrac{\overline{N}'_1(N)}{\lambda(N)}$	$D_2(N) = \dfrac{\overline{N}'_2(N)}{\lambda(N)}$
Auxiliary a	$D_{a1}(N) = \dfrac{\overline{N}'_{a1}(N)}{\lambda_a(N)}$	$d_{a2}(N) = \dfrac{\overline{n}'_{a2}(N)}{\lambda_a(N)}$
Auxiliary b	$d_{b1}(N) = \dfrac{\overline{n}'_{b1}(N)}{\lambda_b(N)}$	$D_{b2}(N) = \dfrac{\overline{N}'_{b2}(N)}{\lambda_b(N)}$

Goal: To obtain performance measures for the original SPN.

Approach: By enforcing delay equivalence between an aggregated subnet in one auxiliary model and the corresponding unaggregated subnet in the other auxiliary model, we get two nonlinear equations that relate two unknowns: $\mu_{a21}(N)$ and $\mu_{b12}(N)$

$$D_{a1}(N) = d_{b1}(N) \tag{4.1}$$

$$D_{b2}(N) = d_{a2}(N) \tag{4.2}$$

Then iteratively adjust the marking dependent rates until the two auxiliary models are delay equivalent, i.e., obtain the solution iteratively.

As the collection of unaggregated subnets in two auxiliary models cover the original model, when iteration halts both auxiliary models are approximately delay equivalent to the original model for every pair of corresponding subnets

$$D_{a1}(N) \approx d_{b1}(N) \approx D_1(N)$$

$$D_{b2}(N) \approx d_{a2}(N) \approx D_2(N)$$

Performance measures, as a by-product of the tuning process, are readily extractable from the unaggregated subnets in auxiliary models. In the sequel, we derive formulas used for tuning the marking dependent rates by delay equivalence, then give an algorithm that describes the tuning process.

Use superscript (k), such as $D_{a1}^{(k)}(N)$, to represent the delay from kth iteration.

Case 1. $N = 1$

$$d_{b1}^{(k)}(1) = \frac{\overline{n}_{b1}'^{(k)}(1)}{\lambda_b^{(k)}(1)} = \frac{1}{\mu_{b12}^{(k)}(1)}$$

From (4.1) it follows immediately that

$$d_{b1}^{(k)}(1) = D_{a1}^{(k)}(1)$$

To find $\mu_{b12}^{(k+1)}(1)$ for next iteration, we simply replace $\mu_{b12}^{(k)}(1)$ with $\mu_{b12}^{(k+1)}(1)$. Thus we have marking-dependent rate

$$\mu_{b12}^{(k+1)}(1) = \frac{1}{D_{a1}^{(k)}(1)} = \frac{\lambda_a^{(k)}(1)}{\overline{N}_{a1}^{\prime(k)}(1)} \tag{4.3}$$

and similarly

$$\mu_{a21}^{(k+1)}(1) = \frac{1}{D_{b2}^{(k)}(1)} = \frac{\lambda_b^{(k)}(1)}{\overline{N}_{b2}^{\prime(k)}(1)} \tag{4.4}$$

Case 2. $N > 1$

The above solution is the SPN version of the surrogate delay calculation of [Jaco82], and so is well known. However, difficulties arise when $N > 1$ if the aggregated transitions are not in type of infinite server, i.e., delay server in QN. In general for each parameter $m = N$, i.e., initially setting $m = N$ traversable tokens, there exist a set of marking dependent rates $\{\mu(n; m = N);\ n = 1,2,\ldots,N\}$ for an aggregated transition, as arranged in following table for different m's.

m \ n	1	2	3	...	N
1	$\mu(1;1)$				
2	$\mu(1;2)$	$\mu(2;2)$			
3	$\mu(1;3)$	$\mu(2;3)$	$\mu(3;3)$		
⋮	⋮	⋮	⋮	⋱	
N	$\mu(1;N)$	$\mu(2;N)$	$\mu(3;N)$	...	$\mu(N;N)$

In product-form SPN, rates on the same column are identical. In non-product form SPN, they are different, i.e.,

$$\mu(n; m_1) \neq \mu(n; m_2); \quad \text{for } 1 \leq m_1 < m_2 \leq N \text{ and } 1 \leq n \leq m_1$$

But for simplicity and practical reason, we use each rate on the top of a column to approximate other rates in the same column, i.e.,

$$\mu(n; m) \approx \mu(n; n); \quad \text{for } 1 \leq n < m \leq N$$

$\mu(n; n)$ can be simply denoted by $\mu(n)$. Therefore only rates on the diagonal will be actually obtained. Let $\mu_{b12}(n)$, $\mu_{a21}(n)$ (for $\mu_{b12}(n_1)$, $\mu_{a21}(n_2)$); $n = 1,2,\ldots,N-1$ be obtained rates from previous iterations, and $\mu_{b12}(N)$, $\mu_{a21}(N)$ be rates to be obtained. Then the mean delay

$$d_{b1}^{(k)}(N) = \frac{\overline{n}_{b1}^{\prime(k)}(N)}{\lambda_b^{(k)}(N)} = \overline{n}_{b1}^{\prime(k)}(N)\left[\sum_{n=1}^{N-1}\mu_{b12}(n)\cdot Prob_1^{(k)}(n) + \mu_{b12}^{(k)}(N)\cdot Prob_1^{(k)}(N)\right]^{-1}$$

where $Prob_1^{(k)}(n)$ is the marginal probability of n tokens being in place p_1. To find $\mu_{b12}^{(k+1)}(N)$ for next iteration, we substitute above expression into

$$D_{a1}^{(k)}(N) = d_{b1}^{(k)}(N) \tag{4.5}$$

and replace $\mu_{b12}^{(k)}(N)$ of the current iteration with $\mu_{b12}^{(k+1)}(N)$, then solve the equation for $\mu_{b12}^{(k+1)}(N)$ to give

$$\mu_{b12}^{(k+1)}(N) = \frac{1}{Prob_1^{(k)}(N)}\left[\frac{\bar{n}_{b1}^{\prime(k)}(N)}{D_{a1}^{(k)}(N)} - \sum_{n=1}^{N-1}\mu_{b12}(n)\cdot Prob_1^{(k)}(n)\right] \tag{4.6}$$

Similarly there is

$$\mu_{a21}^{(k+1)}(N) = \frac{1}{Prob_2^{(k)}(N)}\left[\frac{\bar{n}_{a2}^{\prime(k)}(N)}{D_{b2}^{(k)}(N)} - \sum_{n=1}^{N-1}\mu_{a21}(n)\cdot Prob_2^{(k)}(n)\right] \tag{4.7}$$

When $N=1$, (4.6) and (4.7) reduce to (4.3) and (4.4).

With above iteration formulas, two auxiliary models are solved iteratively until mean delay equivalent, and all marking dependent rates are recursively obtained for $n=1,2,\ldots,N$. Here is an algorithm describing this parameter tuning process.

Algorithm. Parameter tuning process for $N \geq 1$

for $n = 1$ *to* N *do* {*recursion*}

begin

{*Choose initial* $\mu_{b12}^{(0)}(n)$, $\mu_{a21}^{(0)}(n)$ *arbitrarily in principle, or*}

if $n = 1$ *then*

$\mu_{b12}^{(0)}(1) := \mu_{a21}^{(0)}(1) := 1;$

if $n > 1$ *then*

$\mu_{b12}^{(0)}(n) := \mu_{b12}(n-1);\ \mu_{a21}^{(0)}(n) := \mu_{a21}(n-1);$

$k := 0;$

do {*iteration*}

Use $\mu_{b12}^{(k)}(n)$, $\mu_{a21}^{(k)}(n)$ *to solve two auxiliary models for delays, probabilities, etc.;*

Calculate $\mu_{b12}^{(k+1)}(n)$, $\mu_{a21}^{(k+1)}(n)$ *for next iteration by formulas (4.6) and (4.7);*

$k := k+1;$

Until (The accuracy of $\mu_{b12}^{(k)}(n)$, $\mu_{a21}^{(k)}(n)$ *meet the stopping criterion.)*

$\mu_{b12}(n) := \mu_{b12}^{(k)}(n);\ \mu_{a21}(n) := \mu_{a21}^{(k)}(n);$

end.

Remarks. In the above algorithm, for ease of writing the method, the iteration uses simultaneous substitutions. This is analogous to Jacobi's method in solving a system of linear equations. For quick convergence, one may use successive substitutions for the iteration, an analogy to Gauss-Siedel's method for solving a system of linear equations. A variety of stopping criteria may be used, including the percentage change in the variables between iterations, and the percentage difference in throughput of the two models.

4.2 Multiple-Input Multiple-Output Subnets

The above development emphasized (1) how to iteratively tune a set of auxiliary SPN models to obtain the marking dependent rates, and (2) how to handle multiple traversing cycle tokens. In the following we establish the delay equivalent relations between the original subnet and the aggregated subnet for general interfacing connection, and only derive formulas used for adjusting marking dependent rates. The multivariate marking dependent rate $\mu(\mathbf{n}_a)$ in MPST subnet (Figure 4.3) is preferable for good aggregation accuracy, but may be difficult to obtain in practice. It is more convenient to find the single-variable quantities $Prob(n)$ and $\mu(n)$ in an MP2T (Multiple-Place-Two-Transition) subnet as a further approximation. The difference between the two aggregated subnets is that transition t_a in the MPST subnet is divided into two transitions: an immediate transition t_1 representing the synchronization delay, and a timed transition t_2.

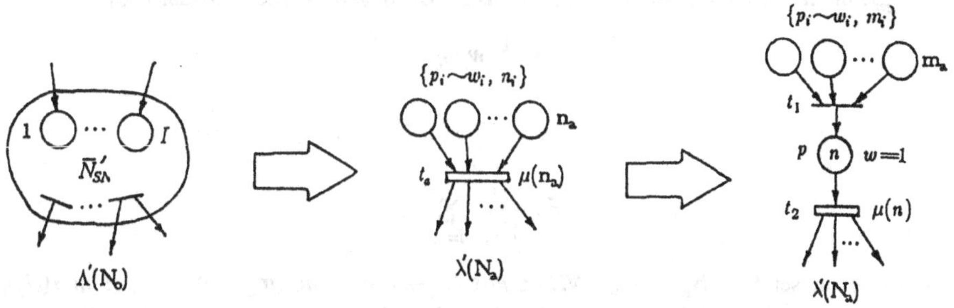

Figure 4.3 An Original Subnet SN, the Aggregated MPST Subnet and the MP2T Subnet sn

In Figure 4.3:

- $\mathbf{N}_o = (N_{o_1}, N_{o_2}, \ldots, N_{o_i}, \ldots, N_{o_{I_o}})$ for $I_o = |{}^*SN|$ is the traversable token vector of the original subnet, where N_{o_i} is the maximum number of tokens containable in p_i in a steady-state marking;
- $\mathbf{N}_a = (N_{a_1}, N_{a_2}, \ldots, N_{a_i}, \ldots, N_{a_{I_a}})$ for $I_a = |{}^*sn|$ is the traversable token vector for both aggregated subnets;
- $\mathbf{n}_a = (n_1, n_2, \ldots, n_i, \ldots, n_{I_a})$: the input place marking vector of the MPST sn;
- $\mathbf{m}_a = (m_1, m_2, \ldots, m_i, \ldots, m_{I_a})$: the input place marking vector of the MP2T sn;
- relations:
  - $I_o = I_a = I$, and $\mathbf{N}_o = \mathbf{N}_a$;
  - let $min(\mathbf{n}_a) = \min\{n_i;\ 1 \le i \le I\}$, and $min(\mathbf{m}_a) = \min\{m_i;\ 1 \le i \le I\}$, then

    $\mathbf{m}_a = \mathbf{n}_a - min(\mathbf{n}_a) \cdot \underline{1} = \mathbf{n}_a - n \cdot \underline{1}$, and $min(\mathbf{m}_a) = 0$;

The separation of t_a in MPST subnet to two transitions in MP2T subnet makes the approximation $\mu(\mathbf{n}_a) \approx \mu(min(\mathbf{n}_a)) = \mu(n)$ implementable. Combined with another approximation $\mu(\mathbf{n}_a | \mathbf{N}_a) \approx \mu(\mathbf{n}_a)$ where $\mu(\mathbf{n}_a | \mathbf{N}_a)$ is marking dependent rate of t_a for given $\mathbf{N}_a$, and restated for MP2T subnet, there is

$$\mu((n, \mathbf{m_a}) | \mathbf{N_a}) \approx \mu(n, \mathbf{m_a}) \approx \mu(n) \tag{4.8}$$

Next define

- $min(\mathbf{N_a}) = \min\{N_{a_i};\ 1 \le i \le I\}$;
- $Prob(n)$: the marginal probability of the place p in MP2T subnet over all $\mathbf{m_a}$'s for a given $\mathbf{N_a}$;
- $Prob(n, \mathbf{m_a})$: the joint probability over all places of the MP2T subnet for a given $\mathbf{N_a}$;
- $\Lambda'(\mathbf{N_o})$, $\lambda'(\mathbf{N_a})$: the weighted throughputs of subnets SN and sn;
- $\lambda'(n | \mathbf{N_a})$: the weighted throughput component for different level of enability n of t_2 of MP2T subnet for a given $\mathbf{N_a}$;
- $\overline{N}'_{SN}$: the mean number of weighted tokens in SN, obtained by (2.3);
- $\overline{N}'_{sn'}$: the mean number of weighted tokens in MP2T subnet, and is obtained by

$$\begin{aligned}
\overline{N}'_{sn'} &= w\overline{n} + \sum_{i=1}^{I} w_i \overline{m}_i \\
&= \overline{n} + w_i \sum_{i=1}^{I} \overline{m}_i; \text{ if } w_i = w_j \ for \ 1 \le i \ne j \le I \\
&= \overline{n} + \frac{1}{|{}^{\bullet}t_1|} \sum_{i=1}^{I} \overline{m}_i
\end{aligned}$$

- a domain set $S(n, \mathbf{N_a}) = \{\mathbf{m_a} | ((\forall i{:}\ 0 \le m_i \le N_{a_i} - n) \text{ and } (min(\mathbf{m_a}) = 0))\}$, $1 \le n \le min(\mathbf{N_a})$, that records all possible markings of $\mathbf{m_a}$'s in the MP2T subnet for given n and $\mathbf{N_a}$;

Then enforce delay equivalence $D(\mathbf{N_o}) = d(\mathbf{N_a})$ over the original subnet and the MP2T subnet, i.e.,

$$\begin{aligned}
\frac{\overline{N}'_{SN}}{\Lambda'(\mathbf{N_o})} &= \frac{\overline{N}'_{sn'}}{\lambda'(\mathbf{N_a})} \\
&= \frac{\overline{N}'_{sn'}}{\sum_{n=1}^{min(\mathbf{N_a})} \lambda'(n | \mathbf{N_a})} \\
&= \frac{\overline{N}'_{sn'}}{\sum_{n=1}^{min(\mathbf{N_a})} \sum_{\mathbf{m_a} \in S(n, \mathbf{N_a})} \mu((n, \mathbf{m_a}) | \mathbf{N_a}) \cdot Prob(n, \mathbf{m_a})}
\end{aligned}$$

which will be replaced by

$$\frac{\overline{N}'_{SN}}{\Lambda'(\mathbf{N_o})} \approx \frac{\overline{N}'_{sn'}}{\sum_{n=1}^{min(\mathbf{N_a})} \mu(n) \cdot Prob(n)} \quad \text{by (4.8)}$$

By rearranging this and solving for $\mu(min(\mathbf{N_a}))$ we obtain

$$\mu(min(\mathbf{N_a})) \approx \frac{1}{Prob(min(\mathbf{N_a}))}\left[\frac{\Lambda'(\mathbf{N_o})}{\overline{N}'_{SN}}\overline{N}'_{sn'} - \sum_{n=1}^{min(\mathbf{N_a})-1} \mu(n)\cdot Prob(n)\right] \tag{4.9}$$

$\mathbf{N_a}$ is arbitrary. In fact we want $\mu(n)$ for $n=1$ to $\min(\mathbf{N_a})$. Above equation gives such a recursive relation from $\mu(1)$ through $\mu(min(\mathbf{N_a}))$. For next iteration, it becomes

$$\mu^{(k+1)}(min(\mathbf{N_a})) \approx \frac{1}{Prob^{(k)}(min(\mathbf{N_a}))}\left[\frac{\Lambda'^{(k)}(\mathbf{N_o})}{\overline{N}'^{(k)}_{SN}}\overline{N}'^{(k)}_{sn'} - \sum_{n=1}^{min(\mathbf{N_a})-1} \mu(n)\cdot Prob^{(k)}(n)\right] \tag{4.10}$$

From this section, one may notice some similarity between the delay equivalent aggregation and the approximate Norton method. Both methods use the same form of marking dependent rate for the aggregated transition, and approximately obtain these rates by recursion on N. However, the delay equivalent aggregation solves a set of size-reduced auxiliary models iteratively, while the approximate Norton method solves the partly short-circuited original model noniteratively. When the net is not too large, and one or more single-input-single-output subnets can be aggregated, the Norton approach may be preferred. Even then it sometimes fails, as will be demonstrated. For larger nets the iteration procedure of this paper is preferred because it allows the use of a large number of aggregated subnets in one auxiliary model, so that smaller auxiliary models are solved. It is also simpler to apply for subnets with multiple inputs and outputs.

5. Illustrative and Application Examples

To illustrate the iterative aggregation, we develop the following two examples. In both examples, the iteration results are also compared with the results from applying the approximate Norton method. In the first example both methods give the similar good results, while in the second example, representing high synchronization, the approximate Norton method fails but the method of this paper succeeds.

Example 2. Figure 5.1 represents a cyclic structure with forking and joining of the flow, which is a marked graph. It has N tokens initially in p_1. Figure 5.2 shows two auxiliary models with aggregated subnets for the right and left halves of the cyclic structure. $\mu_1(n_1)$ and $\mu_5(n_6)$ are marking dependent rates to be tuned. For the initial values of these μ's when $N=1$, we set $\mu_5^{(0)}(1)=1$ and $\mu_1^{(0)}(1)=1$. For $N=2$ or the next N, the initial rates are set to the final rates obtained from $N=1$ or the previous N.

The iteration results obtained by using simultaneous substitutions are presented in Table 1, with exact results found by solving the original net. For $N=1$ the exact result is obtained in the first iteration and conferred in the second. For $N=2$ when the two throughputs converge to the same value with the specified precision eight iterations were required, with a relative error of

$$\frac{0.662788-0.663343}{0.663343} = -0.0836\%$$

An additional comparison is provided to a Norton-like flow equivalent aggregation method. One can aggregate either the left side or the right side of the model. For $N=1$ the results are also exact, while for $N=2$ the results in the row labelled "Norton-like" were obtained; the errors are similar in magnitude with -0.07% for the left model and -0.06% for the right model.

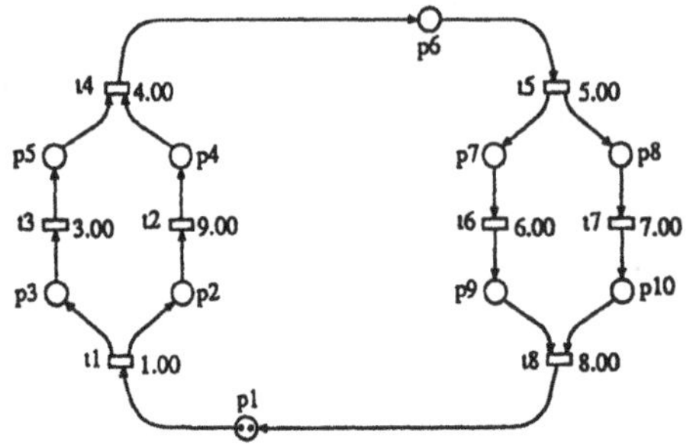

Figure 5.1 The Original SPN of Example 2

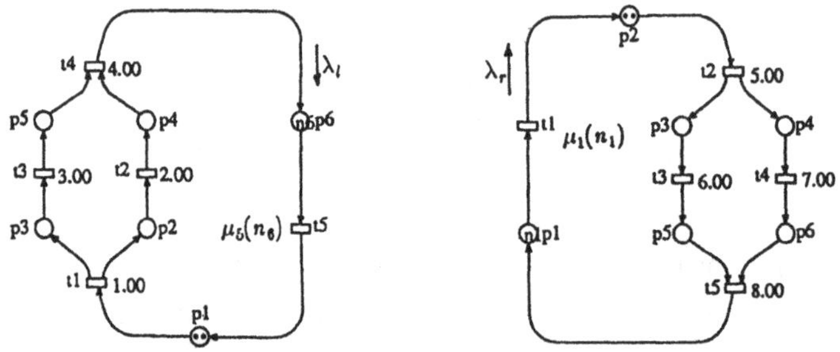

Figure 5.2 The Auxiliary SPN Models of Example 2

To examine the effect of more tokens in the net, two more sets of experiments have been conducted for N=1,2,...,7.

Set 1. Optimal Initialization

The initial rates of tuned transitions are initialized with rates from previous iterations, as carried out in Example 2. The largest relative errors of the throughput in two auxiliary models for N=3,4,5,6,7 are 0.69%, 0.31%, 0.62%, 0.052%, 0.021% at iteration 2; –0.08%, –0.068%, –0.044%, –0.025%, –0.014% at iteration 10.

Set 2. Non-Optimal Initialization

Rather than choosing initial rate values of current N from the previous iteration of $N-1$, a large range of rates, differed in up to 5 orders of magnitudes had been tested. The convergence behaviors of iteration processes were robust, especially for cases where the initial rate values are in the scale of the transition rates of the corresponding original subnet.

Table 1. Iteration Results

N	iterate	$\mu_5(N)$	$\lambda_l(N)$	$\lambda_r(N)$	$\mu_1(N)$
1	0	1	0.346821	0.642013	1
	1	1.793398	0.409679	0.409679	0.530973
	2	1.793399	0.409679	0.409679	0.530973
	exact	1.793399	0.409679	0.409679	0.530973
2	0	1.793399	0.643721	0.671815	0.530973
	1	2.992302	0.665264	0.662186	0.790032
	2	2.740963	0.662224	0.662828	0.772894
	3	2.793655	0.662904	0.662785	0.774028
	4	2.782611	0.662764	0.662788	0.773953
	5	2.784923	0.662793	0.662788	0.773958
	6	2.784438	0.662787	0.662788	0.773958
	7	2.784540	0.662788	0.662788	0.773958
	8	2.784519			0.773958
	Norton-like	2.791373	0.662875	0.662937	0.774222
	exact		0.663343	0.663343	

Example 3. Four task pipeline system.

Pipelines are used to increase throughput by overlapping successive operations on successive items of data. In concurrent software environments this often be a sequence of tasks operating as a pipeline on a stream of data. These task pipelines may have rather complex structure [Wood88a]. But to show the method, we use a four task pipeline as in Figure 5.3.

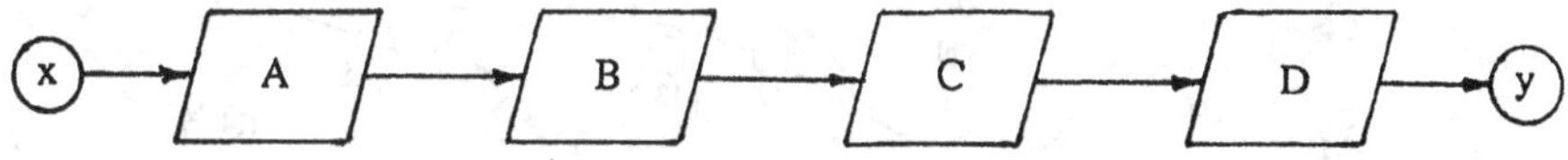

Figure 5.3 Four Task Pipeline

x is input data. It is processed sequentially by tasks A, B, C and D. The pipeline generates output y. Inter-task communications are in the form of rendezvous, i.e., a send-receive-reply sequence. A Petri net model is given in Figure 5.4, and an example with rate parameters (in sec^{-1}) is shown in Figure 5.5, where x and y_{ack} are assumed immediately available. The rate parameters are such chosen that in general the work transition is much fast than communication transitions for each task; for the present set of rates, from input to output task processing speed is slowing down.

To conduct the iterative surrogate delay equivalent aggregation, different partitions and aggregations may be chosen. One of them is presented in Figure 5.6 (a) and (b).

An aggregated transition rate μ_l or μ_r is initialized by choosing the rate of the bottleneck transition in its corresponding original subnet. When solving two auxiliary SPN

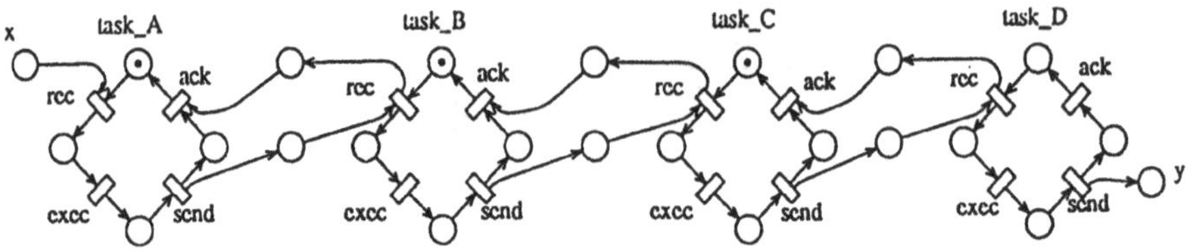

Figure 5.4 Petri Net Model of Four Task Pipeline

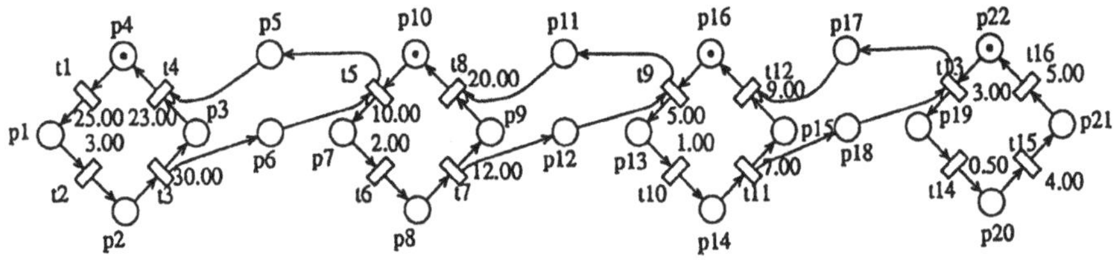

Figure 5.5 SPN Model of Four Task Pipeline

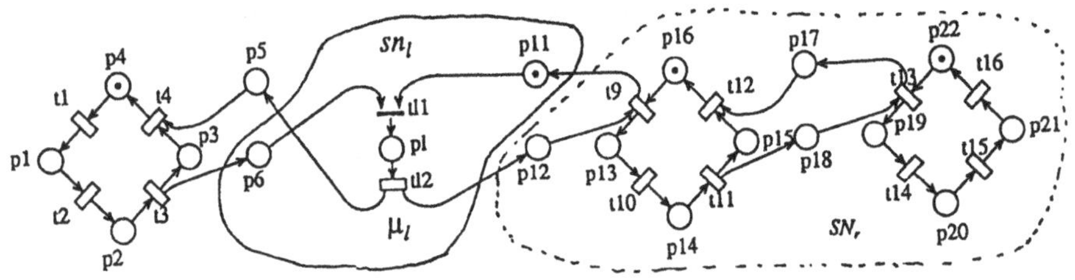

Figure 5.6 (a) The "Left" Auxiliary SPN Model: Task B Is Aggregated

models, the formulas used for statistics and results are

The left auxiliary model:

Throughput: $\lambda_l = \mu_2 \cdot Prob\{\#p1>0\}$

Mean number of weighted tokens in original subnet SN_r: $\overline{N'}_{SN_r} = \bar{n}_{12}$

Mean number of weighted tokens in aggregated subnet sn_l: $\overline{n'}_{sn_l} = \bar{n}_6 + \bar{n}_{11} + 2 \cdot \bar{n}_l$

The right auxiliary model:

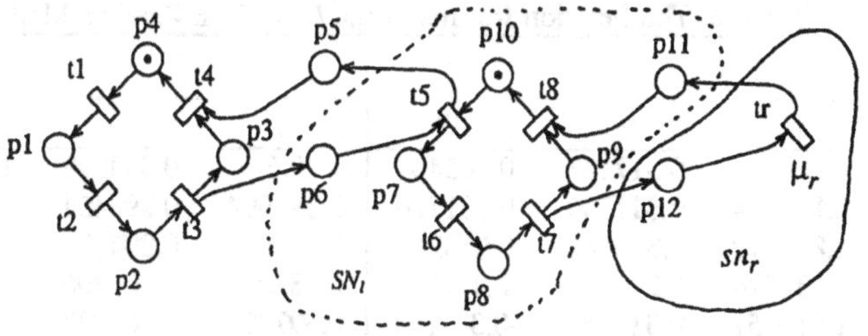

Figure 5.6 (b) The "Right" Auxiliary SPN Model: Task C and D Are Aggregated

Rate value for next iteration: $\mu_1 = \lambda_l / \overline{N}'_l$

Throughput: $\lambda_r = \mu_2 \cdot Prob\{\#p1>0\}$

Mean number of weighted tokens in original subnet SN_l: $\overline{N}'_{SN_l} = \overline{n}_6 + \overline{n}_{11} + \overline{n}_{10} + \overline{n}_7 + \overline{n}_8$

New rate values for the next iteration:

$$\mu_l = \frac{\overline{n}'_{sn_l}}{Prob\{\#pl>0\}} \cdot \frac{\lambda_r}{\overline{N}'_{SN_l}}$$

$$\mu_r = \frac{\lambda_r}{\overline{N}'_{SN_l}}$$

The iteration results are given in Table 2 for the set of parameters in the original model. Notice that in this table two sets of independent iteration results obtained by using successive substitutions are tabulated. The exact throughput: λ=0.316662. The iteration process is stopped when the largest relative difference between two successive tuned rates gets smaller than the prescribed threshold 0.001. In this case it is at the 9th iteration with a half percent relative error of the throughput.

When the approximate Norton method is applied to the same task pipeline model, the resulted right model (with the same structure as the right auxiliary model shown in Figure 5.6b) gives a throughput of 0.257165 with relative error −19.19%, an indication of failure. This error is due to the net being non-product form, since the method does not employ any iterative correction.

To further validate the approximate method on this model, additional nine sets of rate parameters have been chosen for transitions. They represent different processing and communicating speeds of all tasks in many reasonable variations. The iteration processes all converge to the correct or near correct solutions. The initial rates of tuned transitions were similarly chosen as the above. By the same stopping criterion, iteration processes took 6-22 steps to stop with the average 12 steps. By then the relative errors of the throughput are between 0.2-3% with the average of 1%. Iteration processes took an average 8 steps to achieve an average 2 percent accuracy; 6 steps for 3 percent accuracy.

Table 2 The Iteration Results of the Four Task Pipeline Model

k	μ_l	λ_l	$\delta_{\lambda_l}(\%)$	μ_r	λ_r	$\delta_{\lambda_r}(\%)$
0	2	0.317187	0.165404	0.5	0.363299	12.837191
1	2.114974	0.317366	0.221720	0.380994	0.296454	-6.816604
2	1.843170	0.316862	0.063261	0.377070	0.294085	-7.677158
3	1.634274	0.316213	-0.142078	0.387247	0.300206	-5.481509
4	1.513051	0.315659	-0.317861	0.397721	0.306428	-3.339652
5	1.452031	0.315309	-0.429139	0.405328	0.310899	-1.853791
6	1.425765	0.315140	-0.482847	0.409709	0.313455	-1.023228
7	1.416710	0.315080	-0.502246	0.411728	0.314628	-0.646442
8	1.414716	0.315066	-0.506590	0.412443	0.315043	-0.513892

6. Conclusions

An iterative decomposition and aggregation technique has been developed for reduction of marked graph SPNs. It includes PN reduction and iterative aggregation of SPN. In the first part, a reduction procedure was specified that replaces an original subnet with an MPST aggregated subnet, which preserves liveness and boundedness. In the second part, a mean delay equivalent technique was suggested that iteratively solves the set of size-reduced SPNs for performance measures. Its major use is in approximately analyzing large systems with acceptable accuracy.

This work promises to assist in the larger goal of solving large general SPNs by decomposition, by operating on marked graph subnets. Some researches along this line is reported in [Wood91].

Acknowledgements

This research was supported by the University Research Incentive Fund of the Province of Ontario, and by the Telecommunications Research Institute of Ontario through the Telecom Software Methods project. The use of the GreatSPN Petri-Net solving software of the University of Turin, Italy is gratefully acknowledged. We would like to also thank the three referees for their constructive comments.

References

[Amma87] Ammar, H.H., Y.F. Huang and R.W. Liu, "Hierarchical Models for Systems Reliability, Maintainability, and Availability," *IEEE Transactions on Circuits and Systems*, Vol. CAS-34, No. 6, June 1987, pp. 629-638.

[Amma89] Ammar, H.H. and S.M.R. Islam, "Time Scale Decomposition of A Class of Generalized Stochastic Petri Net Models," *IEEE Transactions on Software Eng.*, Vol. 15, No. 6, June 1989, pp. 809-820.

[Bals82] Balsamo, S. and G. Iazeolla, "An Extension of Norton's Theorem for Queueing Networks," *IEEE Trans. on Software Eng.*, Vol. SE-8, No. 4, July 1982, pp. 298-305.

[Bert76] Berthelot, G. and G. Roucairol, "Reduction of Petri-Nets," *Mathematical Foundations of Computer Science, Lecture Notes in Computer Science*, Vol. 45, 1976, pp. 202-209.

[Bert79] Berthelot, G. and G. Roucairol, "Reductions of Nets and Parallel Programs," *Net Theory and Applications, Lecture Notes in Computer Science*, Vol. 84, 1979, pp. 277-290.

[Bert85] Berthelot, G. and Lri-Iie, "Checking Properties of Nets Using Transformations," *Advances in Petri Nets, Lecture Notes in Computer Science*, Vol. 222, 1985, pp. 19-40.

[Bert86] Berthelot, G., Cham-Iie and Lri, "Transformations and Decompositions of Nets," *Advances in Petri Nets, Lecture Notes in Computer Science*, Vol. 254, Part 1, 1986, pp. 359-376.

[Best86] Best, E., "Structure Theory of Petri Nets: the Free Choice Hiatus," *Petri Nets: Central Models and Their Properties, Lecture Notes in Computer Science*, Vol. 254, Springer-Verlag, 1986, pp. 165-205.

[Camp91] Campos, J., B. Sanchez, and M. Silva, "Throughput Lower Bounds for Markovian Petri Nets: Transformation Techniques," *The 4th International Workshop of Petri Nets and Performance Models*, Melbourne, Australia, December 2-5, 1991, pp. 322-331.

[Chan75] Chandy, K.M., U. Herzog and L. Woo, "Parametric Analysis of Queueing Networks," *IBM Journal of the Research Development*, Vol. 19, No. 9, Jan. 1975, pp. 36-42.

[Ciar91] Ciardo, G. and K.S. Trivedi, "A Decomposition Approach for Stochastic Petri Net Models," *The 4th International Workshop of Petri Nets and Performance Models*, Melbourne, Australia, December 2-5, 1991, pp. 74-83.

[Cour77] Courtois, P.J., "Decomposability: Queueing and Computer Applications," *Academic Press, New York*, 1977.

[Flor91] Florin, G. and S. Natkin, "Generalization of Queueing Network Product Form Solutions to Stochastic Petri Nets," *IEEE Trans. on Software Eng.*, Vol. 17, No. 2, Feb. 1991, pp. 99-107.

[Gigl87] Giglmayr, J., "Analysis of Stochastic Petri Nets by the Decomposition of the Transition Rate Matrix," *NTZ Archiv* (Germany), Part 1: Vol. 9, No. 5, May 1987, pp. 115-120; Part 2: Vol. 9, No. 6, June 1987, pp. 147-152.

[Hato91] Hatono, I., K. Yamagata and H. Tamura, "Modeling and On-Line Scheduling of Flexible Manufacturing Systems Using Stochastic Petri Nets," *IEEE Trans. on Software Eng.*, Vol. 17, No. 2, Feb. 1991, pp. 126-132.

[Jaco82] Jacobson, P.A. and E.D. Lazouska, "Analyzing Queueing Networks with Simultaneous Resource Possession," *Communications of the ACM*, Vol. 25, No. 2, Feb., 1982, pp. 142-151.

[John81] Johnsonbaugh, R. and T. Murata, "Additional Methods for Reduction and Expansion of Marked Graphs," *IEEE Trans. on Circuits and Systems*, Vol. CAS-28, No. 10, Oct. 1981, pp. 1009-1014.

[Laza87] Lazar, A.A. and T.G. Robertazzi, "Markovian Petri Net Protocols with Product Form Solution," *The 6th Annual Conference on Computer Communications*,

IEEE INFOCOM'87, San Francisco, California, March 31 - April 2, 1987.

[Lee85] Lee, K.H. and J. Favrel, "Hierarchical Reduction Method for Analysis and Decomposition of Petri Nets," *IEEE Trans. on Systems, Man, and Cybernetics.*, Vol. SMC-15, No. 2, March/April 1985, pp. 272-280.

[Lee87] Lee, K.H., J. Favrel and P. Baptiste, "Generalized Petri Net Reduction Methods," *IEEE Trans. on Systems, Man, and Cybernetics.*, Vol. SMC-17, No. 2, March/April 1987, pp. 297-303.

[Li89] Li, Y. and C.M. Woodside, "Product Form Stochastic Petri Nets and Norton's Aggregation," *Technical Report*, 1989.

[Li91] Li, Y. and C.M. Woodside, "Iterative Decomposition and Aggregation of Stochastic Marked Graph Petri Nets," *The 12th International Conference on Application and Theory of Petri Nets*, Aarhus, Denmark, June 26-28, 1991, pp. 257-275.

[Lien76] Lien, Y.E., "Termination Properties of Generalized Petri Nets," *SIAM J. Comput.*, Vol. 5, No. 2, June 1976, pp. 251-265.

[Mars84] Marsan, M.A. and G. Balbo, "A Class of Generalized Stochastic Petri Nets for the Performance Evaluation of Multiprocessor Systems," *ACM Trans. on Computer Systems*, Vol. 2, No. 2, May 1984, pp. 93-122.

[Mars86] Marsan, M.A., G. Balbo, G. Chiola and S. Donatelli, "On the Product-Form Solution of A Class of Multiple-Bus Multiprocessor System Models," *The Journal of Systems and Software*, Vol. 1, No. 2, 1986, pp. 117-124.

[Mars87] Marsan, M.A., G. Balbo, G. Chiola and G. Conte, "Generalized Stochastic Petri Nets Revisited: Random Switches and Priorities," *International Workshop on Petri Nets and Performance Models*, Madison, Wisconsin, August 24-26, 1987, pp. 44-53.

[Mars87] Marsan, M.A. and G. Chiola, "On Petri Nets with Deterministic and Exponentially Distributed Firing Times," *Advances in Petri Nets 1987*, Lecture Notes in Computer Science 266, Springer-Verlag, 1987, pp. 132-145.

[Moll82] Molloy, M.K., "Performance Analysis Using Stochastic Petri Nets," *IEEE Trans. on Computers*, Vol. C-31, No. 9, Sept. 1982, pp. 913-917.

[Mura80] Murata, T. and J.Y. Koh, "Reduction and Expansion of Live and Safe Marked Graphs," *IEEE Trans. on Circuits and Systems*, Vol. CAS-27, No. 1, Jan. 1980, pp. 68-70.

[Mura80] Murata, T., "Synthesis of Decision-Free Concurrent Systems for Prescribed Resources and Performance," *IEEE Trans. on Software Eng.*, Vol. SE-6, No. 6, Nov. 1980, pp. 525-529.

[Mura89] Murata, T., "Petri Nets: Properties, Analysis and Applications," *Proceedings of the IEEE*, Vol. 77, No. 4, April 1989, 541-580.

[Pete81] Peterson, J.L., "Petri Net Theory and the Modeling of Systems," *Prentice-Hall, Inc.*, Englewood Cliffs, N.J., 1981.

[Silv87] Silva, M. and R. Valette, "Petri Nets and Flexible Manufacturing," *Advances in Petri Nets 1989*, *Lecture Notes in Computer Science*, Vol. 424, Springer-Verlag, 1989, pp. 374-417.

[Song87] Song, J-S., S. Satoh and C.V. Ramamoorthy, "The Abstraction of Petri Net," *Telcon 87*, Vol. 2 of 3, August 25-28, 1987, Seoul, Korea, pp. 467-471.

[Suzu90] Suzuki, T., S.M. Shatz and T. Murata, "A Protocol Modeling and Verification Approach Based on a Specification Language and Petri Nets," *IEEE Trans. on Software Eng.*, Vol. 16, No. 5, May 1990, pp. 523-536.

[Wood88a] Woodside, C.M., J.E. Neilson, J.W. Miernik, D.C. Petriu and R. Constantin, "Performance of Concurrent Rendezvous Systems with Complex Pipeline Structures," *Technical Report*, Dec. 1988.

[Wood88b] Woodside, C.M., "Throughput Calculation for Basic Stochastic Rendezvous Networks," *Performance Evaluation*, No. 9, 1988/89, pp. 143-160.

[Wood91] Woodside, C.M. and Y. Li, "Performance Petri Net Analysis of Communications Protocol Software by Delay-Equivalent Aggregation," *The 4th International Workshop of Petri Nets and Performance Models*, Melbourne, Australia, December 2-5, 1991, pp. 64-73.

Constraints and Extensions in a Calculus of EN Systems

Giorgio De Michelis

Dipartimento di Scienze dell'Informazione
Università degli Studi di Milano
via Comelico 39 - 20135 Milano (Italy)
e-mail: gdemich@hermes.dsi.unimi.it

Abstract

In this paper the domain of EN Systems is characterized as a Partial Order, by means of an injective morphism notion.
The partial order that is introduced has a behavioural interpretation in the sense that 'larger' Systems have 'larger' behavioural possibilities.
Then some unary operations are defined allowing to add Places and/or Transitions to an existing EN System. On the defined Partial Order the operation of adding a Transition is interpreted as enlarging the behaviour of the System (*Extension*), while the operation of adding a Place is interpreted as restricting it (*Constraint*).
Some properties of the two operation types are investigated.
The newly proposed order and operations are fully consistent with the semantics of EN Systems in terms of Elementary Transition Systems as defined in [NRT90].

Keywords

Elementary Net Systems, Elementary Transition Systems, Net Morphisms, unary operations on nets, Regions

1. Introduction

Many critics argue against Net Models of Concurrent Systems that Net Theory lacks of algebraic operations constituting the basis of a Calculus of Concurrent Systems, while other approaches to Concurrency Modeling are defined as algebraic calculi (e. g. CCS [Mil80])
The DEMON Basic Research Action of the EEC Esprit Program, poses the definition of a Design Calculus for Net Systems as one of its long term objectives [BDH90].

One way to face the problem of defining a calculus of Net Systems is that one to transfer on Net Systems the operations that were defined for well established calculi as CCS.
It is my opinion that this approach difficultly will generate a calculus that, from one hand, has better qualities than that one on which it is inspired and, on the other one, is able to fully exploit those specific attributes (explicit description of local states and events, explicit representation of concurrency, etc.) that have made Net Theory popular.
A different way to face the problem is that one to try to define in algebraic terms the operations that naturally arise from Net Theory, as: i) those that allow to add Places or Transitions (or more complex Structures, as Net Systems having boundaries defined through Transitions or Places) to a given Net System; ii) or those that allow to refine A Place or a Transition of a given Net system with a new Net System; iii) or, finally, those that allow to compose two Net Systems through some of their Places or of their Transitions.

In this paper we make a first step in this direction, facing the problem of defining the simplest unary operations on Elementary Net Systems: namely Place- and Transition-addition. This first step is sufficient to show that designing Net Systems we can follow two directions: either we can extend the behaviour of the target system, or we can constrain it. It is well known that algebraic Calculi of Concurrent Systems do not offer the same freedom.
The framework within which we define our operations, is based, on one hand, on the correspondence between Elementary Net (EN) Systems and a subclass of Transition Systems, namely Elementary Transition Systems, as it was defined by Ehrenfeucht and Rozenberg [ER90a, b] and further exploited by Nielsen, Rozenberg and Thiagarajan [NRT90], and, on the other one, on the work Pomello and Simone did (at the very beginning with the De Cindio and the author) on Local State Transformation Algebras

generated by EN Systems and on morphisms between EN Systems [DDPS88], [PS90], [PRS92]. This framework has been exploited in categorical terms in [BDDPRS91].

As first we introduce two equivalence notions, namely S-equivalence (relating Net Systems having isomorphic Graphs) and TS-equivalence (relating Net Systems having isomorphic associated Transition Systems).
As second we characterize the Quotient domain of EN Systems with respect to both the above mentioned equivalence notions, as a Partial Order, by means of an injective morphism notion.
The Partial Orders that are introduced have both a behavioural interpretation (in terms of Transition Systems) in the sense that 'larger' Systems have 'larger' behavioural possibilities, due to a larger set of possible events and/or smaller sets of local states constraining the occurrence of any event.
Then three unary operations are defined, allowing to add (Marked and/or Non-Marked) Places and/or Transitions to an existing EN System. On the defined Partial Order the operation of adding a Transition is interpreted as enlarging the behaviour of the System (*Extension*), while the operations of adding a Place are interpreted as restricting it (*Constraint*).
Some properties of the three operation types are finally investigated.

2. Basic Definitions

Let us as first recall some basic notations on Nets, in particular on Elementary Net Systems, and on Transition Systems, in particular on Elementary Transition Systems.

2.1. Elementary Net Systems

In this paper we will dedicate our attention to Elementary Net Systems (for more details, see [RT86], [Roz87], [Thi87]).

Definition 1 (Net)

A Net is a triple $N = (B, E, F)$ such that: B is a finite set of *Places*; E is a finite set of *Transitions*; $B \cap E = \emptyset$ and $F \subseteq (B \times E) \cup (E \times B)$ is the *flow relation*. F is such that $dom(F) \cup ran(F) = B \cup E$.
If $B = E = F = \emptyset$, the Net is called the Empty Net and we write $N = \emptyset$. ♦

Some further notations will be useful in the following pages.
Let $x \in E \cup B$, then $\bullet x =^{def} \{y | (y,x) \in F\}$ is the *preset* of x, $x\bullet =^{def} \{y | (x,y) \in F\}$ is the *postset* of y.
$N = (B, E, F)$ is said to be *E-Simple* (*B-Simple*) iff $\forall e_1, e_2 \in E$: $[\bullet e_1 = \bullet e_2$ and $e_1\bullet = e_2\bullet] \Rightarrow e_1 = e_2$ ($\forall b_1, b_2 \in B$: $[\bullet b_1 = \bullet b_2$ and $b_1\bullet = b_2\bullet] \Rightarrow b_1 = b_2$). $N = (B, E, F)$ is said *Simple* iff it is both E-Simple and B-Simple.

Definition 2 (Elementary Net System)

An Elementary Net (EN) System is a couple $\Sigma = (N_\Sigma, c_{in})$, where $N_\Sigma = (B, E, F)$ is a Net, the *underlying* Net of Σ, and $c_{in} \subseteq B$ is the *initial Case* of Σ. If $N_\Sigma = \emptyset$, then Σ is called the Empty (Elementary Net) System and we write $\Sigma = \emptyset$. ♦

Examples-1

As it is well known Petri Nets and Net Systems have an elegant graphic representation. In Figure 1 the EN System Σ_1 is presented.

Definition 3 (Transition rule)

Let $N = (B, E, F)$ be a Net, $e \in E$ be a Transition and $c \subseteq B$ be a set of Places: e is *enabled* in c, c[e>, iff $(c \supseteq \bullet e)$ and $(c \cap e\bullet = \emptyset)$; if e is enabled in c, then the *occurrence* of e leads the System from c to $c' = (c - \bullet e) \cup e\bullet$, c[e>c'. ♦

Definition 4 (Set of Cases)
Let $\Sigma = (N_\Sigma, c_{in})$ be an EN System, with $N_\Sigma = (B, E, F)$, then C, the *set of* all reachable *Cases* of Σ, is the minimal subset of 2^B such that:
i) $c_{in} \in C$;
ii) $\forall c \in C, \forall e \in E, \forall c' \subseteq B: c[e>c' \Rightarrow c' \in C$. ♦

Definition 5 (Dead Transition)
Let $\Sigma = (N_\Sigma, c_{in})$ be an EN System, with $N_\Sigma = (B, E, F)$, and let $e \in E$ be a Transition: e is *Dead* iff it is not enabled in any Case of Σ. ♦

Definition 6 (Normalized EN System)
Let $\Sigma = (N_\Sigma, c_{in})$ be an EN System, with $N_\Sigma = (B, E, F)$, then the EN System $\Sigma' = (N_\Sigma', c_{in}')$, with $N_{\Sigma'} = (B', E', F')$, defined as follows $E' = \{e \mid e \in E$ and e is not Dead in $\Sigma\}$; $F' = F \cap ((E' \times B) \cup (B \times E'))$; $B' = B \cap (dom(F') \cup ran(F'))$; $c_{in}' = c_{in} \cap B'$; is the *Normalized* version of Σ. ♦

$\Sigma_1 =$

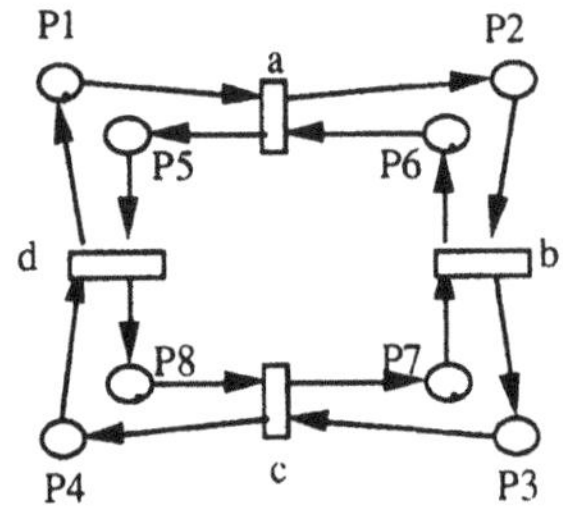

Figure 1

$TS_1 =$

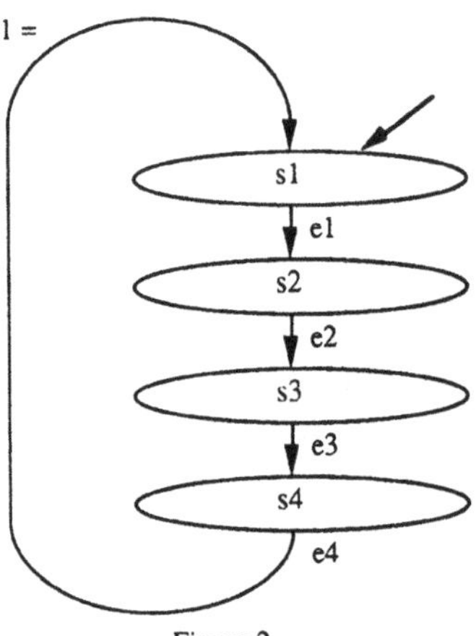

Figure 2

RTS1 = { r1={s1}, r2={s2}, r3={s3}, r4={s4}, r5={s1, s2}, r6={s1, s3}, r7={s1, s4}, r8={s2, s3}, r9={s2, s4}, r10={s3, s4}, r11={s1, s2, s3}, r12={s1, s2, s4}, r13={s1, s3, s4}, r14={s2, s3, s4} }.

$\bullet r5 = \{e4\}$, $r5\bullet = \{e2\}$; $°e2 = \{r2, r5, r9, r12\}$, $e2° = \{r3, r6, r10, r13\}$.

Figure 3

Definition 7 (B-Simplified EN System)
Let $\Sigma = (N_\Sigma, c_{in})$ be an EN System, with $N_\Sigma = (B, E, F)$. Let furthermore $\equiv_{BS}$ be the equivalence relation associated to B-Simplicity, ($\forall b_1, b_2$: $b_1 \equiv_{BS} b_2$ iff ($\bullet b_1 = \bullet b_2$ and $b_1\bullet = b_2\bullet$)). Then the EN System $\Sigma' = (N_\Sigma', c_{in}')$, with $N_{\Sigma'} = (B', E', F')$, defined as follows:
$E' = E$;
$B' = \{[b]_{/BS} \mid b \in B\}$;

$F' = \{([b]_{/BS}, e) | (b, e) \in F\} \cup \{(e, [b]_{/BS}) | (e, b) \in F\}$;

$c_{in}' = \{[b]_{/BS} | b \in c_{in}\}$;

is the *B-Simplified* version of Σ. ♦

Examples-2
The EN System Σ_1 of Figure 1 is Normalized and its underlying Net is Simple.

B-Simplification and Normalization do not commute. In the following pages we will consider B-Simplified versions of Normalized versions of, for short B-Simplified and Normalized, EN Systems, calling them simply EN Systems.

2.2 Elementary Transition Systems
Elementary Transition Systems have been introduced by Nielsen, Rozenberg and Thiagarajan in [NRT90]. Elementary Transition Systems are particular cases of Partial (Set) 2-Structures ([ER90a, b]). Elementary Transition Systems characterize in an elegant way the semantics of Elementary Net Systems. In the following pages we consider also the Empty Transition System.

Definition 8 (Transition System)
A Transition System TS is a quadruple (S, E, T, s_{in}), where: S is a finite set of *States*; E is a set of *Events*; $T \subseteq S \times E \times S$ is the *Transition Relation*; $s_{in} \in S$ is the *initial State*. If $S = \emptyset$, then E, T and s_{in} are also empty, and TS is called the Empty Transition System, $TS = \emptyset$. ♦

Some further notations will be useful in the following pages.
When TS is clear from the context we will often write $s \xrightarrow{e} s'$ instead of $(s, e, s') \in T$. We say that e is *enabled* at s, denoted by $s \xrightarrow{e}$, if there exists a State s' such that $s \xrightarrow{e} s'$.
For what concerns this paper we will assume that every Transition System $TS = (S, E, T, s_{in})$ satisfies the following axioms:

(A1) $\forall (s, e, s') \in T$: $s \neq s'$;

(A2) $\forall (s, e_1, s_1), (s, e_2, s_2) \in T$: $[s_1 = s_2 \Rightarrow e_1 = e_2]$;

(A3) $\forall e \in E$, $\exists (s, e, s') \in T$;

(A4) $\forall s \in S - \{s_{in}\}$, $\exists e_0, e_1, ..., e_{n-1} \in E$, $\exists s_0, s_1, ..., s_n \in S$: $s_0 = s_{in}$, $s_n = s$ and $(s_i, e_i, s_{i+1}) \in T$ for $0 \leq i < n$.

Remark
Axiom A1 does not allow self loops.
Axiom A2 does not allow more than one arc between two states.
Axiom A3 grants that each event may occurr.
Axiom A4 grants that each state is reachable from the initial one.

Definition 9 (G-isomorphism)
Let $TS_i = (S_i, E_i, T_i, s_{ini})$, i = 1, 2, be two Transition Systems. Then TS_1 is *G-isomorphic* to TS_2 iff $\exists \sigma: S_1 \to S_2$, $\exists \eta: E_1 \to E_2$, bijections: $[(s, e, s') \in T_1 \Leftrightarrow (\sigma(s), \eta(e), \sigma(s')) \in T_2$ and $\sigma(s_{in1}) = s_{in2}]$. ♦

Remark
Two G-isomorphic Transition Systems are identical, but for renaming States and Events.

Definition 10 (Region)
Let $TS = (S, E, T, s_{in})$ be a Transition System. Then $r \subseteq S$ is a Region of TS iff the following two conditions are satisfied:

i) $(s, e, s') \in T$ and $s \in r$ and $s' \notin r \Rightarrow \forall (s_1, e, s_1') \in T: [s_1 \in r$ and $s_1' \notin r]$;

ii) $(s, e, s') \in T$ and $s \notin r$ and $s' \in r \Rightarrow \forall (s_1, e, s_1') \in T: [s_1 \notin r$ and $s_1' \in r]$. ♦

Some additional notations and remarks will also be useful in what follows.
To each Region r of TS we can associate two subsets of E:

$\bullet r =^{def} \{e \mid \exists s \notin r, \exists s' \in r: (s, e, s') \in T\}$ (the set of *pre-Events* of r) and

$r \bullet =^{def} \{e \mid \exists s \in r, \exists s' \notin r: (s, e, s') \in T\}$ (the set of *post-Events* of r).

Let $TS = (S, E, T, s_{in})$ be a Transition System. Then it is easy to see that both S and $\emptyset$ are Regions. They will be called the *trivial* Regions. R_{TS} will denote the *set of non-trivial Regions* of TS. For each $s \in S$ we let R_s denote the *set of non-trivial Regions containing* s: i. e. $R_s =^{def} \{r \mid s \in r \in R_{TS}\}$.

To each Event e of TS we can associate two subsets of R_{TS}: $°e =^{def} \{r \mid r \in R_{TS}$ and $e \in r \bullet\}$ (the set of *pre-Regions* of e) and $e° =^{def} \{r \mid r \in R_{TS}$ and $e \in \bullet r\}$ (the set of *post-Regions* of e).

Definition 11 (Elementary Transition System)
Let $TS = (S, E, T, s_{in})$ be a Transition System. Then TS is said to be *Elementary* if it satisfies (in addition to Axioms (A1) - (A4)) the two regional axioms:

(A5) $\forall s, s' \in S: [R_s = R_{s'} \Rightarrow s = s']$;

(A6) $\forall s \in S, \forall e \in E: [°e \subseteq R_s \Rightarrow s\text{-}^{e}\text{->}]$. ♦

Examples-3
The Transition System TS_1 of Figure 2 is Elementary. Its Regions are listed in Figure 3.

2.3 Elementary Transition Systems as Semantics of EN Systems
Elementary Transition Systems are a simple and powerful formalism for explaining the operational behaviour of EN Systems [NRT90]. All the Theory developed in [NRT90] extends naturally to the Empty Elementary Net System and to Empty Transition System.

Definition 12 (Transition System associated to Σ)
Let $\Sigma = (N_\Sigma, c_{in})$ be an EN System, with $N_\Sigma = (B, E, F)$. Then the structure $TS_\Sigma =^{def} (C_\Sigma, E, \text{-->}_\Sigma, c_{in})$, where $\text{-->}_\Sigma \subseteq C_\Sigma \times E \times C_\Sigma$ is defined as follows: $(c, e, c') \in \text{-->}_\Sigma$ iff $c[e>c'$ in Σ, is called the *Transition System associated* with Σ. ♦

Proposition 1
Let $\Sigma = (N_\Sigma, c_{in})$ be an EN System, with $N_\Sigma = (B, E, F)$ and let $TS_\Sigma = (C_\Sigma, E, \text{-->}_\Sigma, c_{in})$ be the Transition System associated with Σ. Then the following hold:
i) TS_Σ is Elementary (see Definition 11).
ii) $\forall b \in B: r_b =^{def} \{c \mid b \in c$ and $c \in C_\Sigma\}$ is a (non-trivial) Region of TS_Σ (see Definition 10).

Proof.
See [NRT90]. ♦

Remark
Clause ii) of Proposition 1 shows also that each Place $b \in B$ of Σ, is associated with a Region r_b of TS_Σ. In particular it has to be observed that: $\bullet b = \bullet r_b$ and $b\bullet = r_b\bullet$.

Examples-4
The Transition System associated to the EN System Σ_1 (see Figure 1), TS_{Σ_1}, is presented in Figure 4. It is easy to see that TS_1 (see Figure 2) and TS_{Σ_1} are G-isomorphic.

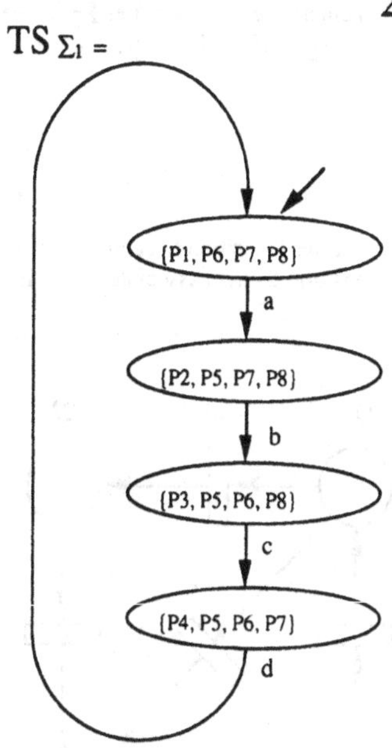

Figure 4

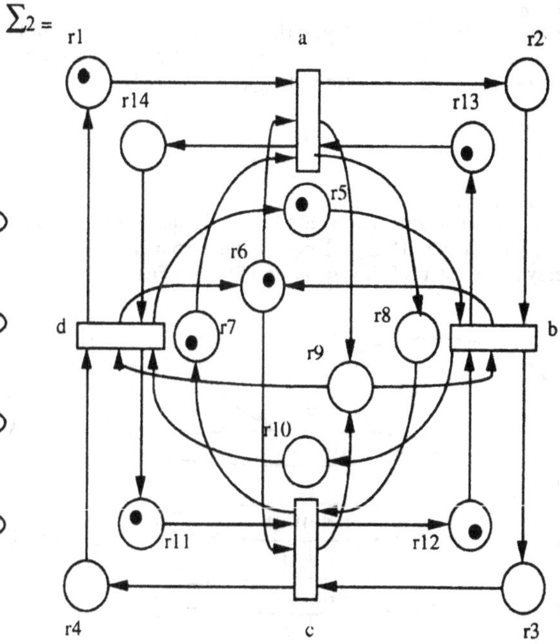

Figure 5

In [EhR90a, b] and [NRT90] it is shown that we can associate to any Elementary Transition System TS a unique EN System, Σ_{TS} that is its Regional version, i. e. the EN System having as Places the non-trivial Regions of TS.

Definition 13 (Regional version of TS)
Let TS = (S, E, T, s_{in}) be an Elementary Transition System. Then the EN System $\Sigma_{TS} = (N_{\Sigma TS}, R_{sin})$, with $N_{\Sigma TS} = (R_{TS}, E, F_{TS})$, where $F_{TS} =^{def} \{(r, e) \mid r \in R_{TS} \text{ and } e \in E \text{ and } r \in {}^{\circ}e\} \cup \{(e, r) \mid r \in R_{TS}$ and $e \in E$ and $r \in e^{\circ}\}$, is the *Regional version* of TS. ♦

Remark
The Regional version of an Elementary Transition System TS is both Normalized (because the Events of TS may all occurr, Axiom 3) and Simple (because if two of the Regions of TS have the same Pre- and Post-Events, then they coincide, Definition 10).

Proposition 2
Let TS = (S, E, T, s_{in}) be an Elementary Transition System and let $\Sigma_{TS} = (N_{\Sigma TS}, R_{sin})$ with $N_{\Sigma TS}$ = (R_{TS}, E, F_{TS}), be the Regional version of TS. Let finally $TS_{\Sigma TS}$ be the Transition System associated to Σ_{TS}. Then TS and $TS_{\Sigma TS}$ are G-isomorphic.
Proof.
See [NRT90]. ♦

Corollary
Let $\Sigma_i = (N_{\Sigma_i}, c_{in_i})$ with $N_{\Sigma_i} = (B_i, E_i, F_i)$, i = 1, 2, be a pair of Elementary Net Systems. Let Σ_2 be the Regional version of TS_{Σ_1}. Then TS_{Σ_1} and TS_{Σ_2} are G-isomorphic ($TS_{\Sigma_i} = (C_{\Sigma_i}, E_i, -->_{\Sigma_i}, c_{in_i})$ is the Transition System associated with Σ_i, i = 1, 2, see Definition 12).

Proof.
See [NRT90].

♦

Examples- 5
In Figure 5 it is presented the EN System Σ_2, that is Regional version of the Transition System associated to Σ_1 (see Figure 1), $\Sigma_2 = \Sigma_{TS_{\Sigma 1}}$. In Figure 6 it is presented the Transition System associated to it. It is easy to see that it is G-isomorphic to TS_{Σ_1} (see Figure 4).

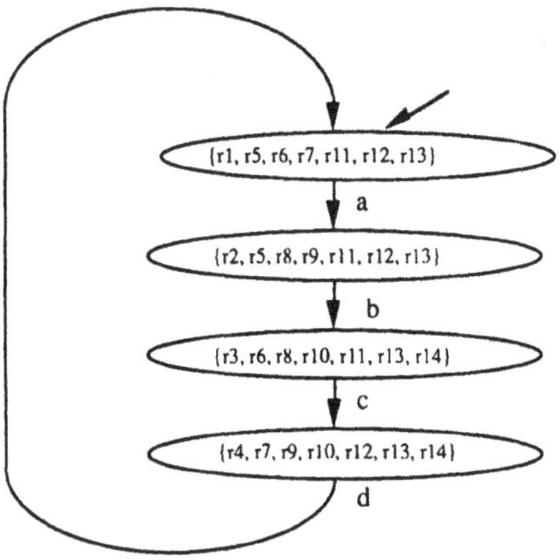

Figure 6

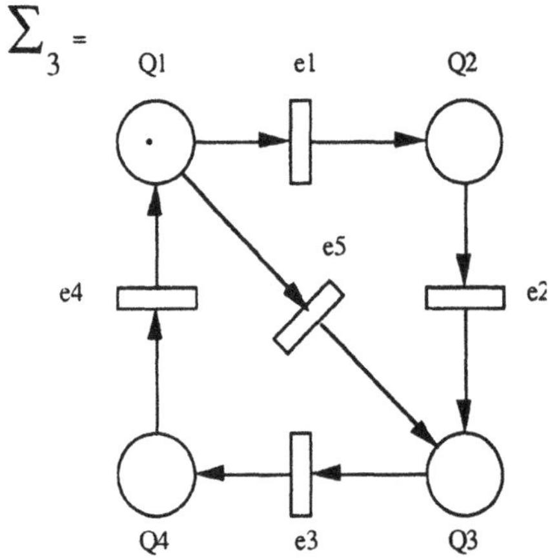

Figure 7

3. Partial orders of EN Systems

We are now ready to introduce a structure into the class of the EN Systems.
Let **EN** be the class of all the (Simple) EN Systems without Dead Transitions. Then we can define a partial order relation on **EN** (more precisely on the Quotients of **EN**, with respect to two equivalence notions; see below), through a well-suited morphism notion, namely Order Net (ON-)morphisms.

As first let us introduce two equivalence notions, called respectively Strong (S-)equivalence and Transition System (TS-)equivalence.

Definition 14 (S-equivalence)
Let $\Sigma_i = (N_{\Sigma_i}, c_{in_i})$ with $N_{\Sigma_i} = (B_i, E_i, F_i)$, i = 1, 2, be a pair of Elementary Net Systems.
Then Σ_1 and Σ_2 are *S-equivalent*, $\Sigma_1 \equiv_S \Sigma_2$, iff $\exists\beta: B_1 \text{-->} B_2$, $\exists\eta : E_1 \text{-->} E_2$, both bijective, such that:
i) $\forall b \in B_1$: $[b \in c_{in1} <=> \beta(b) \in c_{in2}]$.
ii) $(x, y) \in F_1 <=> (\beta \cup \eta\ (x), \beta \cup \eta\ (y)) \in F_2$. ♦

Remark
S-equivalence is based on Net isomorphism: i. e. two S-equivalent EN Systems are equivalent in a very Strong sense: they are identical but for renaming Places and Transitions.

Definition 15 (TS-equivalence)
Let $\Sigma_i = (N_{\Sigma_i}, c_{in_i})$ with $N_{\Sigma_i} = (B_i, E_i, F_i)$, i = 1, 2, be a pair of Elementary Net Systems.
Then Σ_1 and Σ_2 are *TS-equivalent*, $\Sigma_1 \cong_{TS} \Sigma_2$, iff
$TS_{\Sigma_1} = (C_{\Sigma_1}, E_1, \text{-->}_{\Sigma_1}, c_{in_1})$ and $TS_{\Sigma_2} = (C_{\Sigma_2}, E_2, \text{-->}_{\Sigma_2}, c_{in_2})$, the Transition Systems associated, respectively, with Σ_1 and Σ_2, are G-isomorphic (see Definition 9). ♦

Remarks
i) TS-equivalence is frequently called Sequential Case Graph (SCG-)equivalence. It has been widely used in [ER90a, b] and further studied in [NRT90].
ii) We can add some comments about the two equivalence notions introduced above.
S-equivalence is a very 'concrete' equivalence notion: two EN Systems are S-equivalent iff they are the 'same' system (in terms of local conditions, events and their relations), i. e. if they are structurally and behaviourally not distinguishable.
TS-equivalence is a very 'abstract' equivalence notion: two EN Systems are TS-equivalent iff they are behaviourally not distinguishable, without paying attention to their structure.

Examples-6
The EN-Systems Σ_1 (see Figure 1) and Σ_2 (see Figure 5) are TS-equivalent as their associated Transition Systems are G-isomorphic (see Figures 4 and 6, respectively).

Proposition 3
$\cong_S \;\; \Rightarrow \;\; \cong_{TS}$

Proof.
Let $\Sigma_i = (N_{\Sigma_i}, c_{in_i})$ with $N_{\Sigma_i} = (B_i, E_i, F_i)$, i = 1, 2, be a pair of Elementary Net Systems.
If $\Sigma_1 \cong_S \Sigma_2$, then TS_{Σ_1} is G isomorphic to TS_{Σ_2} as Σ_1 and Σ_2 are identical but for renaming Places and Transitions, and therefore $\Sigma_1 \cong_{TS} \Sigma_2$. ♦

In the following pages we will use $[\mathbf{EN}]_{/S}$ and $[\mathbf{EN}]_{/TS}$ to indicate the Quotients of the class of the EN Systems, $\mathbf{EN}$, with respect to, respectively, S-equivalence and TS-equivalence.We will use $[\Sigma]_{/S} \in [\mathbf{EN}]_{/S}$ and $[\Sigma]_{/TS} \in [\mathbf{EN}]_{/TS}$ to indicate the equivalence classes of the EN System Σ with respect to, respectively, S-equivalence and TS-equivalence.

Proposition 4
Let $\Sigma = (N_\Sigma, c_{in})$ be an EN System, with $N_\Sigma = (B, E, F)$, then $[\Sigma]_{/TS}$ contains a unique (up to S-equivalence) canonical version of Σ, Σ', that is the Regional version of the Transition System associated to Σ.

Proof.
The assertion is true by Proposition 2 and Definition 15. ♦

Definition 16 (ON-morphism)
Let $\Sigma_i = (N_{\Sigma_i}, c_{in_i})$ with $N_{\Sigma_i} = (B_i, E_i, F_i)$, i = 1, 2, be a pair of Elementary Net Systems. Then an ON-morphism from Σ_1 to Σ_2 is an ordered pair (β, η) where $\beta \subseteq B_1 \times B_2$ is a binary relation and $\eta: E_1 \text{-->} E_2$ is a total injective function such that:
i) β^{-1} is a partial function, $\beta^{-1}: B_2 \text{-->} B_1$;
ii) $\forall (b_1, b_2) \in \beta: [b_1 \in c_{in_1} \Leftrightarrow b_2 \in c_{in_2}]$;

iii) $\forall e_1 \in E_1$: $[\eta(e_1) = e_2 \Rightarrow (\beta(\bullet e_1) = \bullet e_2$ and $\beta(e_1\bullet) = e_2\bullet)]$. ♦

In the following pages we will write $\beta(b)$ for $\{b' \mid (b, b') \in \beta\}$ and $\beta(B')$ for $\cup_{b \in B'} \beta(b)$.

Remark

It is easy to see that ON-morphisms are N-morphisms, in the sense of [NRT90]. They require, in fact, only a restriction with respect to N-morphisms: η must be a total injective function instead of a partial function. In [BDDPRS91] ON-morphisms as well as another subclass of N-morphisms, namely PN-morphisms, are introduced and discussed in categorical terms. Both these sub-classes of N-morphism are closed with respect to composition [BDDPRS91]. For a discussion of the relations between N-morphism and the morphism introduced by Winskel see [NRT90].

Examples-7

The couple of functions β: $B_2 \dashrightarrow B_1$ and η: $E_2 \dashrightarrow E_1$, where β is defined as follows

$\beta = \{(r_1,P_1), (r_2,P_2), (r_3,P_3), (r_4,P_4), (r_{11},P_8), (r_{12},P_7), (r_{13},P_6), (r_{14},P_5)\}$ and η is the identity function, constitute an ON-morphism: $\Sigma_2 \dashrightarrow \Sigma_1$ (Σ_1 is presented in Figure 1 and Σ_2 is presented in Figure 5).

Let Σ_3 be the EN System presented in Figure 7, then the couple of functions β': $B_1 \dashrightarrow B_3$, η': $E_1 \dashrightarrow E_3$, defined as follows: $\beta' = \{ (P_1, Q_1), (P_2, Q_2), (P_3, Q_3), (P_4, Q_4)\}$, $\eta' = \{(a, e_1), (b, e_2), (c, e_3), (d, e_4)\}$, constitute an ON-morphism: $\Sigma_1 \dashrightarrow \Sigma_3$.

Proposition 5

Let $\Sigma_i = (N_{\Sigma_i}, c_{in_i})$ with $N_{\Sigma_i} = (B_i, E_i, F_i)$, $i = 1, 2$, be a pair of Elementary Net Systems, and let (β, η): $\Sigma_1 \dashrightarrow \Sigma_2$ be an ON-morphism. Let f_β: $C_{\Sigma_1} \dashrightarrow 2^{B_2}$ be given by: $\forall c \in C_{\Sigma_1}$:

$f_\beta(c) = \beta(c) \cup (c_{in2} - \beta(c_{in1}))$. Then the following hold:

i) $\forall c \in C_{\Sigma_1}$: $f_\beta(c) \in C_{\Sigma_2}$.

ii) $\forall c, c' \in C_{\Sigma_1}$, $\forall e \in E_1$: $c[e\rangle c'$ in $\Sigma_1 \Rightarrow f_\beta(c)[\eta(e)\rangle f_\beta(c')$ in Σ_2.

Proof.

ON-morphisms are N-morphisms, and therefore this Proposition is an easy Corollary of the similar Proposition Nielsen, Rozenberg and Thiagarajan proved for N-morphisms [NRT90]. ♦

The following Proposition 6 will be useful in the proof of Proposition 7, here below.

Proposition 6

Let $\Sigma_i = (N_{\Sigma_i}, c_{in_i})$ with $N_{\Sigma_i} = (B_i, E_i, F_i)$, $i = 1, 2$, be a pair of Elementary Net Systems, and let (β, η) be an ON-morphism from Σ_1 to Σ_2. Then the following holds:

$\forall b \in B_1, \forall b', b'' \in \beta(b)$: $\bullet b' \cap \eta(E_1) = \bullet b'' \cap \eta(E_1)$ and $b'\bullet \cap \eta(E_1) = b''\bullet \cap \eta(E_1))$.

Proof.

Per absurdum.

Let us suppose that (β, η) is an ON-morphism from Σ_1 to Σ_2 and $\exists b \in B_1, \exists b', b'' \in \beta(b)$: $\bullet b' \cap \eta(E_1) \neq \bullet b'' \cap \eta(E_1)$ (the case $b'\bullet \cap \eta(E_1) = b''\bullet \cap \eta(E_1)$ can be treated in the same way).

Then, without lack of generality, we can suppose that $\exists e' \in E_2$: $e' \in \eta(E_1) \cap \bullet b'$ and $e' \notin \eta(E_1) \cap \bullet b''$.

Let finally be $e = \eta^{-1}(e')$. Then either $e \in \bullet b$ or $e \notin \bullet b$.

If $e \in \bullet b$, then $\beta(e\bullet) \supseteq \{b', b''\}$, but $e' \notin \eta(E_1) \cap \bullet b'' \Rightarrow b'' \notin \beta(e\bullet)$ (Definition 16.iii). Contradiction.

If $e \notin \bullet b$, then $\beta(e\bullet) \cap \{b', b''\} = \emptyset$, but $e' \in \eta(E_1) \cap \bullet b' \Rightarrow b' \in \beta(e\bullet)$ (Definition 16.iii).

Contradiction. ♦

Proposition 7
Let $\Sigma_i = (N_{\Sigma_i}, c_{ini})$ with $N_{\Sigma_i} = (B_i, E_i, F_i)$, i = 1, 2, be a pair of Elementary Net Systems.
Then there exists a couple of ON-morphisms $(\beta_1, \eta_1): \Sigma_1 \to \Sigma_2$ and $(\beta_2, \eta_2): \Sigma_2 \to \Sigma_1$, iff $\Sigma_1 \equiv_S \Sigma_2$.

Proof.
The if part is very simple, because the two bijections characterizing S-equivalence, (β, η), and their inverses, (β^{-1}, η^{-1}), are both ON-morphisms.
The only if part requires more attention.
As first it is easy to see that η_1 is bijective, because $N_{\Sigma_i} = (B_i, E_i, F_i)$, i = 1, 2, are finite Nets and, being both η_1 and η_2 total injections, then both η_1 and η_2 are bijections. Moreover $\eta_2 \circ \eta_1$ is a permutation on E_1 and $\eta_1 \circ \eta_2$ is a permutation on E_2.
As second let us show that β_1 is a function and that it is a bijection.
Let us prove that β_1 is a function.
Let us suppose that $\exists b \in B_1, \exists b', b'': b', b'' \in \beta_1(b)$. Then, by Proposition 6, $\bullet b' \cap \eta_1(E_1) = \bullet b'' \cap \eta_1(E_1)$ and $b'\bullet \cap \eta_1(E_1) = b''\bullet \cap \eta_1(E_1)$.
But $\eta_1(E_1) = E_2$, because η_1 is a bijection (see above) and therefore: $\bullet b' = \bullet b''$ and $b'\bullet = b''\bullet$. By definition, Σ_2 is B-Simple, and therefore b' = b".
We can write, therefore, $\beta_1(b) = b'$ instead of $b' \in \beta_1(b)$.
Let us prove that β_1 is a bijection, also, per absurdum.
Let us suppose that $\exists b_1 \in B_1: \beta_1(b_1)$ = undefined. Σ_1, by Definition 1, has not isolated elements, therefore $\exists e_1 \in E_1: b_1 \in \bullet e_1$ (or $b_1 \in e_1\bullet$; we will not dedicate our attention to this second case, whose proof is identical to the previous one).
We can generate two sequences of elements, respectively, of E_1 and E_2, namely
$e_1^{(0)}, e_1^{(1)}, \ldots, e_1^{(n)}$ and $e_2^{(0)}, e_2^{(1)}, \ldots, e_2^{(n)}$ such that the following hold:
$e_1 = e_1^{(0)}$ and $\forall n \geq 0: \eta_1(e_1^{(n)}) = e_2^{(n)}$ and $\eta_2(e_2^{(n)}) = e_1^{(n+1)}$.
Being $\eta_1 \circ \eta_2$ a permutation on a finite set, then $\exists k \geq 1: e_1 = e_1^{(k)}$.
Being both β_1 and β_2 partial injections, and being, by property iii) in the Definition of ON-morphism, $\beta_i(\bullet e_i) = \bullet\eta_i(e_i)$, then the following holds: $\forall n \geq 0: |\bullet e_1^{(n)}| \geq |\bullet e_2^{(n)}|$ and $|\bullet e_2^{(n)}| \geq |\bullet e_1^{(n+1)}|$.
Moreover, being by hypothesis $\beta_1(b_1)$ = undefined and $b_1 \in \bullet e_1$, $|\bullet e_1| = |\bullet e_1^{(0)}| > |\bullet e_2^{(0)}|$.
We have therefore the following sequence of disequations:
$|\bullet e_1| = |\bullet e_1^{(0)}| > |\bullet e_2^{(0)}| \geq |\bullet e_1^{(1)}| \geq \ldots \geq |\bullet e_2^{(k-1)}| \geq |\bullet e_1^{(k)}| = |\bullet e_1|$,
and the contradiction, $|\bullet e_1| > |\bullet e_1|$, is generated.
As third let us show that $\forall b \in B_1: [b \in c_{in1} \Leftrightarrow \beta_1(b) \in c_{in2}]$.
Being β_1 a bijection, then it is total, and therefore property ii) in the Definition of ON-morphism, $(\forall b_1 \in B_1: \beta_1(b_1) = b_2 \in B_2 \Rightarrow [b_1 \in c_{in1} \Leftrightarrow b_2 \in c_{in2}])$, implies $\forall b \in B_1: [b \in c_{in1} \Leftrightarrow \beta_1(b) \in c_{in2}]$.
Finally it is easy to see that $\forall e_1 \in E_1: (\beta_1(\bullet e_1) = \bullet\eta_1(e_1)$ and $\beta_1(e_1\bullet) = \eta_1(e_1)\bullet)$ and
$\forall e_2 \in E_2: (\beta_1^{-1}(\bullet e_2) = \bullet\eta_1^{-1}(e_2)$ and $\beta_1^{-1}(e_2\bullet) = \eta_1^{-1}(e_2)\bullet)$ are both true because both β_1 and η_1 are bijections satisfying $\forall e_1 \in E_1: [\eta_1(e_1) = e_2 \Rightarrow \beta_1(\bullet e_1) = \bullet e_2$ and $\beta_1(e_1\bullet) = e_2\bullet]$. ♦

Definition 17 (≤)

i) Let $\mathcal{A}$ and $\mathcal{B}$ be two elements of $[\mathcal{EN}]/_S$. Then $\mathcal{A} \leq \mathcal{B}$ iff there exist two Elementary Net Systems $\Sigma_1 = (N_{\Sigma 1}, c_{in1})$ and $\Sigma_2 = (N_{\Sigma 2}, c_{in2})$, such that, respectively, $\Sigma_1 \in \mathcal{A}$ and $\Sigma_2 \in \mathcal{B}$ and there exists an ON-morphism (β, η): Σ_1 --> Σ_2.

ii) Let $\mathcal{A}$ and $\mathcal{B}$ be two elements of $[\mathcal{EN}]/_{TS}$. Then $\mathcal{A} \leq \mathcal{B}$ iff there exist two Elementary Net Systems $\Sigma_1 = (N_{\Sigma 1}, c_{in1})$ and $\Sigma_2 = (N_{\Sigma 2}, c_{in2})$, such that, respectively, $\Sigma_1 \in \mathcal{A}$ and $\Sigma_2 \in \mathcal{B}$ and there exists an ON-morphism (β, η): Σ_1 --> Σ_2. ♦

Remark

In Definition 17 we use the same symbol, ≤, for the order relation on two different classes, namely $[\mathcal{EN}]/_S$ and $[\mathcal{EN}]/_{TS}$. This choice does not lead to ambiguities as, always, the elements related by ≤ clearly identify the class that is taken into consideration.

Proposition 8

Let $\mathcal{A}$ and $\mathcal{B}$ be two elements of $[\mathcal{EN}]/_S$, and let $\mathcal{A} \leq \mathcal{B}$. Then $\forall \Sigma_1 \in \mathcal{A}$, $\forall \Sigma_2 \in \mathcal{B}$: there exists an ON-morphism (β, η): Σ_1 --> Σ_2.

Proof.

$\mathcal{A} \leq \mathcal{B}$ implies that there exist $\Sigma_1' \in \mathcal{A}$ and $\Sigma_2' \in \mathcal{B}$ such that there exists an ON-morphism (β', η'): Σ_1' --> Σ_2'.

$\Sigma_1' \in \mathcal{A}$ implies that Σ_1' is S-equivalent to Σ_1, and, by Proposition 7, there exists an ON-morphism (β_1, η_1): Σ_1 --> Σ_1'; $\Sigma_2' \in \mathcal{B}$ implies that Σ_2' is S-equivalent to Σ_2, and, by Proposition 7, there exists an ON-morphism (β_2, η_2): Σ_2' --> Σ_2.

The ON-morphism (β, η): Σ_1 --> Σ_2 can therefore be obtained by composition of (β_1, η_1), (β', η') and (β_2, η_2). ♦

Proposition 9

Let $\mathcal{A}$ and $\mathcal{B}$ be two elements of $[\mathcal{EN}]/_{TS}$, and let $\mathcal{A} \leq \mathcal{B}$. Let Σ_1' be the canonical version of $\mathcal{A}$ and Σ_2' be the canonical version of $\mathcal{B}$, then $\forall \Sigma_1'' \in [\Sigma_1']/_S$, $\forall \Sigma_2'' \in [\Sigma_2']/_S$: there exists an ON-morphism (β, η): Σ_1'' --> Σ_2''.

Proof.

By hypothesis, $\mathcal{A} \leq \mathcal{B}$. Then there exist two Elementary Net Systems $\Sigma_1 = (N_{\Sigma 1}, c_{in1})$, with $N_{\Sigma 1} = (B_1, E_1)$, and $\Sigma_2 = (N_{\Sigma 2}, c_{in2})$, with $N_{\Sigma 2} = (B_2, E_2)$, such that, respectively, $\Sigma_1 \in \mathcal{A}$ and $\Sigma_2 \in \mathcal{B}$ and there exists an ON-morphism (β, η): Σ_1 --> Σ_2.

Let also, respectively, Σ_1' be the Regional version of the Transition System associated to Σ_1, and Σ_2' be the Regional version of the Transition System associated to Σ_2.

Let the couple (β', η'), be defined as follows: η': E_1--> E_2 is a total injective function ($\eta' = \eta$) and $\beta' \subseteq B_1' \times B_2'$ is a relation such that $\beta' = \{(b_1, b_2) | r_{b1} \in R_{TS1}$ and $r_{b2} \in R_{TS2}$ and $\forall c \in C_{\Sigma 1}$: $c \in r_{b1}$ <=> $f_\beta(c) \in r_{b2}\}$, where R_{TSi} is the Transition System associated to Σ_i (i=1,2).

Let us prove that (β', η') is an ON-morphism between Σ_1' and Σ_2', i.e. that β' is a relation satisfying the conditions i)-iii) of Definition 16.

i) β'^{-1} is a partial function, as, by definition of β' and being Σ_1 B-Simple, $\forall b_2' \in B_2'$: $((\exists b_1', b_1'' \in B_1'$: $(b_1', b_2'), (b_1'', b_2') \in \beta') \Rightarrow b_1' = b_1'')$.

ii) $\forall (b_1', b_2') \in \beta'$: $(b_1' \in c_{in1}' \Leftrightarrow b_2' \in c_{in2}')$, by the definition of β'.

iii) $\forall e_1 \in E_1$: $[\eta(e_1) = e_2 \Rightarrow \beta'(\bullet e_1) = \bullet e_2$ and $\beta'(e_1\bullet) = e_2\bullet]$, as, if $b_2' \in \bullet e_2$, then $f_\beta^{-1}(b_2') = b_1'$ and $b_1' \in \bullet e_1$, because f_β^{-1} (see [NRT90]) preserves Regions. ♦

Remark

In [BDDPRS91] Proposition 9 is an immediate derivation of the constructed adjunction between the two Categories of, respectively, Simple EN Systems without Dead Transitions with ON-morphisms and Elementary Transitions Systems with OG-morphisms.

Proposition 10

i) Let $\mathcal{A}$ and $\mathcal{B}$ be two elements of $[\mathbf{EN}]_{/S}$, and let $\mathcal{A} \leq \mathcal{B}$ and $\mathcal{B} \leq \mathcal{A}$. Then $\mathcal{A} = \mathcal{B}$.

ii) Let $\mathcal{A}$ and $\mathcal{B}$ be two elements of $[\mathbf{EN}]_{/TS}$, and let $\mathcal{A} \leq \mathcal{B}$ and $\mathcal{B} \leq \mathcal{A}$. Then $\mathcal{A} = \mathcal{B}$.

Proof.

i) Immediate by Proposition 7 and Proposition 8.

ii) Let Σ_1' be the canonical version of $\mathcal{A}$ and Σ_2', be the canonical version of $\mathcal{B}$, then, by Proposition 9, $\forall \Sigma_1'' \in [\Sigma_1']_{/S}$, $\forall \Sigma_2'' \in [\Sigma_2']_{/S}$: there exist two ON-morphisms (β_1, η_1): $\Sigma_1'' \dashrightarrow \Sigma_2''$ and (β_2, η_2): $\Sigma_2'' \dashrightarrow \Sigma_1''$. Then, by Proposition 7, $\Sigma_1'' \equiv_S \Sigma_2''$ (and $\Sigma_1' \equiv_{TS} \Sigma_2'$, by Proposition 3), and the Proposition is proved. ♦

Theorem 1

$([\mathbf{EN}]_{/S}, \leq)$, $([\mathbf{EN}]_{/ST}, \leq)$ are both Partially Ordered Sets with a minimum.

Proof.

i) $([\mathbf{EN}]_{/S}, \leq)$.

The relation $\leq$ is an order relation on $[\mathbf{EN}]_{/S}$.

It is, in fact, transitive, thanks to the composability of ON-morphisms and to Proposition 8, reflexive, because (id_B, id_E) is an ON-morphism, and antisymmetric thanks to Proposition 10. $\{\emptyset\}$ is the minimal element of $[\mathbf{EN}]_{/S}$.

ii) $([\mathbf{EN}]_{/TS}, \leq)$.

The relation $\leq$ is a well defined relation on $[\mathbf{EN}]_{/TS}$.

Proposition 9 grants, in fact, that $\forall \mathcal{A}, \mathcal{B} \in [\mathbf{EN}]_{/TS}$, $\mathcal{A} \leq \mathcal{B}$ is univocally characterized. The Proof that $\leq$ is an order relation on $[\mathbf{EN}]_{/TS}$ is similar to the one sketched for $[\mathbf{EN}]_{/S}$. $\{\emptyset\}$ is the minimal element of $[\mathbf{EN}]_{/TS}$. ♦

Remarks

i) Let $\mathcal{A}$ and $\mathcal{B}$ be two elements of $[\mathbf{EN}]_{/S}$, and let $\mathcal{A} < \mathcal{B}$ ($\mathcal{A} \leq \mathcal{B}$ and $\mathcal{A} \neq \mathcal{B}$). Then for each $\Sigma_1 \in \mathcal{A}$ and for each $\Sigma_2 \in \mathcal{B}$, the following hold:

either Σ_2 admits a sequence of occurrences of Transitions that is not the image of any sequence of occurrences of Transitions of Σ_1, and therefore Σ_1 is minor of Σ_2 with respect to its possible behaviours, or (non disjunctive or) the preset (postset) of at least one Transition $\eta(e)$ of Σ_2 has a smaller number of Places than the preset (postset) of the corresponding Transition e of Σ_1.

ii) Let $\mathcal{A}$ and $\mathcal{B}$ be two elements of $[\mathcal{EN}]_{/TS}$, and let $\mathcal{A} < \mathcal{B}$ ($\mathcal{A} \leq \mathcal{B}$ and $\mathcal{A} \neq \mathcal{B}$). Then for each $\Sigma_1 \in \mathcal{A}$ and for each $\Sigma_2 \in \mathcal{B}$, the following hold:
Σ_2 admits a sequence of occurrences of Transitions that is not the image of any sequence of occurrences of Transitions of Σ_1, and therefore Σ_1 is minor of Σ_2 with respect to its possible behaviours .Nothing can be said about the relation between the numbers of Places of the two EN Systems Σ_1 and Σ_2.

4. Some operations of a Top-Down Calculus of EN Systems

A Top-Down Calculus can be characterized as a Calculus within which we can build new Objects from previously defined Objects, adding to them some elements and/or refining them through the replacement of an element by an Object.
In particular, with respect to Petri Nets, a Top-Down Calculus is a Calculus within which we can build Net Systems in two ways: i) adding a new Net System to a previously defined Net System, either connecting them through Places or through Transitions, ii) substituting (refining) a Place (or a Transition) by a Net System in previously defined Net Systems.
In this Section we disregard refinements, concentrating our attention to the most simple forms of addition of elements: Place- and Trasition-Addition. The Domains we introduced in the previous Section, allow us to get a deep understanding of these operations.
It is interesting to observe that, while adding new Transitions to an EN System extends (intuitively speaking) its behaviour, adding a new Place to an EN System restricts (always intuitively speaking) it. This difference needs a careful discussion.
The Partially Ordered sets ($[\mathcal{EN}]_{/S}$, $\leq$), ($[\mathcal{EN}]_{/TS}$, $\leq$) constitute a good framework within which defining the operations of adding Places and Transitions. As we will show in the following pages, adding a new Place, as well as adding a new Transition, to an existing EN System has natural interpretations in the two above Partial Orders.
Before introducing the Definitions of our unary Operations on EN Systems, let us recall that adding a new Transition (or a new Place) to an EN System means, as it is evident, to add it, together with the arcs connecting it to other elements of the System.

Definition 18 (Non-Marked and Marked Constraints)
Let $\Sigma = (N_\Sigma, c_{in})$ be an EN System, with $N_\Sigma = (B, E, F)$, and let $(b', F_{b'})$ be a new Place, defined as follows: $b' \notin B \cup E$ and $F_{b'} \subseteq (\{b'\} \times E) \cup (E \times \{b'\})$, then:
i) the B-Simplified and Normalized version (see Definitions 6 and x) of $\Sigma' = (N_{\Sigma'}, c_{in})$, with $N_{\Sigma'} = (B \cup \{b'\}, E, F \cup F_{b'})$, is the EN System obtained through the *non-Marked Constraint* $(b', F_{b'})$ from Σ;
ii) the B-Simplified and Normalized version of $\Sigma'' = (N_{\Sigma''}, c_{in} \cup \{b'\})$, with $N_{\Sigma''} = (B \cup \{b'\}, E, F \cup F_{b'})$, is the EN Systems obtained through the *Marked Constraint* $(b', F_{b'})$ from Σ. ♦

Remarks
i) Let us say that, if $\forall b \in B$: $\bullet b \neq \bullet b'$ or $b\bullet \neq b'\bullet$, then $(b', F_{b'})$ is *Simple* in Σ. Then, if $(b', F_{b'})$ is not Simple in Σ, i.e. $\exists b \in B$: $\bullet b = \bullet b'$ and $b\bullet = b'\bullet$, we have two interesting cases:
1) if $b \in c_{in}$ then the EN System obtained through the Marked Constraint $(b', F_{b'})$ from Σ, is Σ itself.
2) if $b \notin c_{in}$ then the EN System obtained through the non-Marked Constraint $(b', F_{b'})$ from Σ, is Σ itself.
ii) Definition 18 and Definition 19 here below are the only places where non B-Simplified and Normalized EN Systems are used. The fact that they are used only to generate B-Simplified and Normalized EN Systems grants the locality of their appearence.
iii) The Empty EN System has been introduced into the class of EN Systems to let it be closed with respect to the Constraint operations. In fact if the (Marked or non-Marked) new Place $(b', F_{b'})$ inhibits the enabling of any Transition of Σ in the initial Case, then the EN System obtained through the (Marked or non-Marked) Constraint from Σ, is the Empty EN System. By the Definition of Net (Definition 1), no

operation (neither Marked and non-Marked Constraint, nor - see below - Extension) is possible on the Empty EN System.

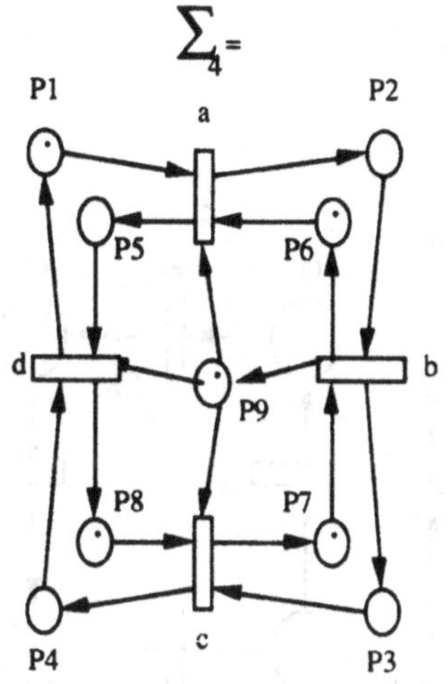

Figure 8

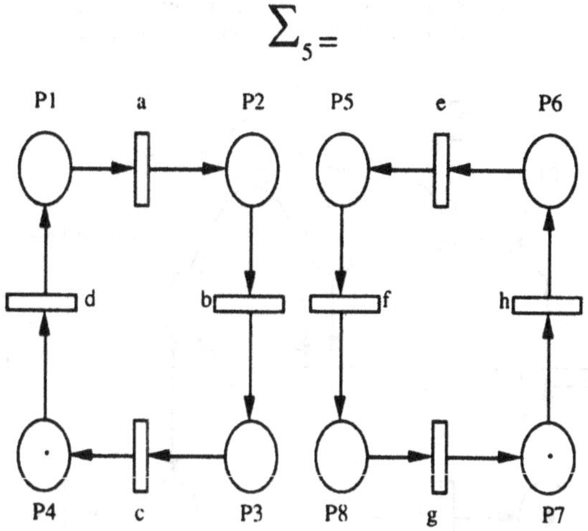

Figure 9

Examples-8
Let Σ_1 be defined as in Figure 1, and let (P_9, {(P_9, a), (P_9, c), (b, P_9), (d, P_9)}) be a new Place. Then Σ_4, presented in Figure 8, is the EN System obtained through the Marked Constraint (P_9, {(P_9, a), (P_9, c), (b, P_9), (d, P_9)}) from Σ_1. The Empty EN System, $\varnothing$, is the EN System obtained through the non-Marked Constraint (P_9, {(P_9, a), (P_9, c), (b, P_9), (d, P_9)}) from Σ_1, as no Transition can occur if P_9 is not marked. Let Σ_5 be defined as in Figure 9, and let (P_9, {(P_9, b), (P_9, f), (a, P_9), (e, P_9)}) be a new Place. Then Σ_6, presented in Figure 10, is the EN System obtained through the non-Marked Constraint (P_9, {(P_9, b), (P_9, f), (a, P_9), (e, P_9)}) from Σ_5.

Definition 19 (Extension)
Let $\Sigma = (N_\Sigma, c_{in})$ be an EN System, with $N_\Sigma = (B, E, F)$, and let (e', $F_{e'}$) be a new Transition, defined as follows: $e' \notin E \cup B$ and $F_{e'} \subseteq (B \times \{e'\}) \cup (\{e'\} \times B)$, then the Normalized version of $\Sigma' = (N_{\Sigma'}, c_{in})$, with $N_{\Sigma'} = (B, E \cup \{e'\}, F \cup F_{e'})$ is the EN System Σ' obtained through the *Extension* (e', $F_{e'}$) from Σ.

Remarks
i) Let us say that, if $\forall e \in E$: $\bullet e \neq \bullet e'$ or $e\bullet \neq e'\bullet$, then (e', $F_{e'}$) is Simple in Σ. Then, if (e', $F_{e'}$) is not Simple in Σ, the EN System obtained through the Extension (e', $F_{e'}$) from Σ, is Σ itself.
ii) It has to be recalled that if (e', $F_{e'}$) is Simple in Σ, then the Normalized version of Σ' is either Σ' itself, if e' is not Dead in Σ', or, otherwise, it is Σ, because the addition of a Transition to an EN System Σ can not provoke the death of any other Transition of Σ.

Examples-9
Let Σ_7 be the EN System presented in Figure 11, and let (e_5, {(Q_1, e_5), (e_5, Q_3)}) be a new Transition. Then the EN System obtained through the Extension (e_5, {(Q_1, e_5), (e_5, Q_3)}) from Σ_7, is Σ_3, presented in Figure 7.

Let, again, Σ_7 be the EN System presented in Figure 11, and let $(e_5, \{(Q_1, e_5), (e_5, Q_2)\})$ be a new Transition. Then the EN System obtained through the Extension $(e_5, \{(Q_1, e_5), (e_5, Q_2)\})$ from Σ_7, is Σ_7 itself, as $(e_5, \{(Q_1, e_5), (e_5, Q_2)\})$ is not Simple in Σ_7.
Finally, the EN System obtained through the Extension $(e_6, \{(Q_1, e_6), (Q_2, e_6), (e_6, Q_3)\}$ from Σ_7, is Σ_7 itself, as e_6 is Dead with respect to the the Initial Case of Σ_7.

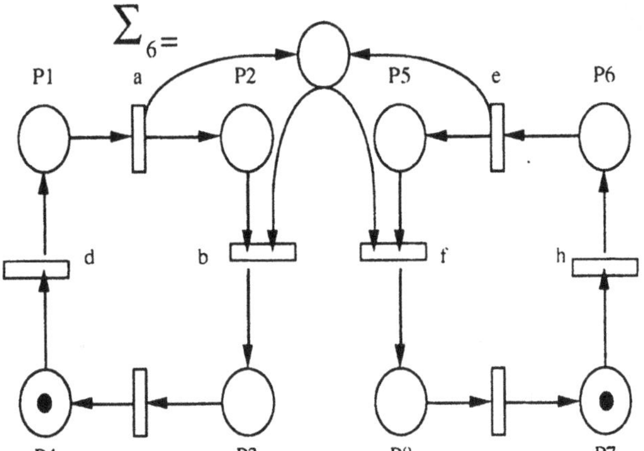

Figure 10

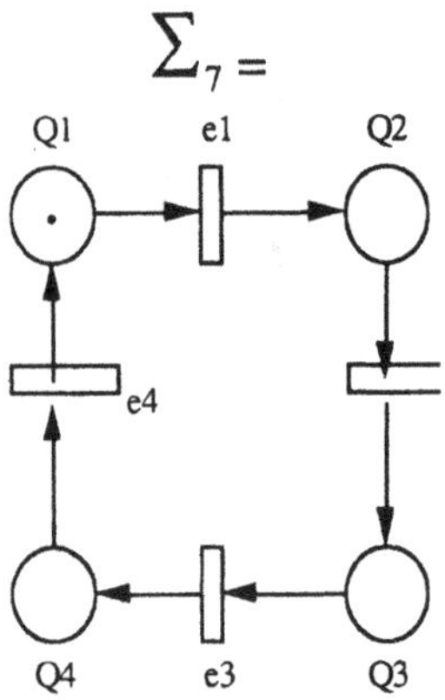

Figure 11

Proposition 11
Let $\Sigma = (N_\Sigma, c_{in})$ be an EN System, with $N_\Sigma = (B, E, F)$, and let $(b', F_{b'})$ be a new Place.
Then both $\Sigma' = (N_{\Sigma'}, c_{in}')$, with $N_{\Sigma'} = (B', E', F')$, and $\Sigma'' = (N_{\Sigma''}, c_{in}'')$, with $N_{\Sigma''} = (B'', E'', F'')$, the two EN Systems obtained, respectively, through the non-Marked and Marked Constraint $(b', F_{b'})$ from Σ, are such that: $[\Sigma']_{/S} \leq [\Sigma]_{/S}$ and $[\Sigma'']_{/S} \leq [\Sigma]_{/S}$.

Proof.
i) Let us consider the Thesis $[\Sigma']_{/S} \leq [\Sigma]_{/S}$.

Let $\beta' \subseteq B' \times B$ and η': $E' \dashrightarrow E$ be defined as follows:

$\beta' = \{(b_1, b_2) \mid b_1 = [b_2]_{/BS}\}$, where $[b_2]_{/BS}$ denotes the equivalence class of b_2 with respect to B-Simplicity in the Normalized version of the EN System obtained through the non-Marked Constraint $(b', F_{b'})$ from Σ, and η' is such that $\forall e \in E'$: $\eta'(e) = e$. Then (β', η') is an ON-morphism, because β' satisfies the three conditions i-iii of Definition 16, and therefore $[\Sigma']_{/S} \leq [\Sigma]_{/S}$ is proved.

ii) In the same way we can prove that $[\Sigma'']_{/S} \leq [\Sigma]_{/S}$. ♦

Corollary
Let $\Sigma = (N_\Sigma, c_{in})$ be an EN System, with $N_\Sigma = (B, E, F)$, and let $(b', F_{b'})$ be a new Place.
Then both Σ' and Σ'', the two EN Systems obtained, respectively, through the non-Marked and Marked Constraint $(b', F_{b'})$ from Σ, are such that:
$[\Sigma']_{/TS} \leq [\Sigma]_{/TS}$ and $[\Sigma'']_{/TS} \leq [\Sigma]_{/TS}$.

Proof.
The ON-morphism constructed in the proof of Proposition 11, is sufficient to prove the assertions of the Corollary (see Definition 17, comma ii)). ♦

Proposition 12
Let $\Sigma = (N_\Sigma, c_{in})$ be an EN System, with $N_\Sigma = (B, E, F)$, and let $(e', F_{e'})$ be a new Transition.
Then $\Sigma' = (N_{\Sigma'}, c_{in}')$, with $N_{\Sigma'} = (B', E', F')$, the EN System obtained through the Extension $(e', F_{e'})$ from Σ, is such that: $[\Sigma]/_S \leq [\Sigma']/_S$.

Proof.
Let β: B --> B' and η: E --> E' be two functions defined as follows: β is the identity function on B (it is easy to see that B' = B, by Definition 19); η is such that $\forall e \in E$: $\eta(e) = e$. Then it is easy to see that (β,η) is an ON-morphism, and therefore $[\Sigma]/_S \leq [\Sigma']/_S$ is proved. ♦

Corollary
Let $\Sigma = (N_\Sigma, c_{in})$ be an EN System, with $N_\Sigma = (B, E, F)$, and let $(e', F_{e'})$ be a new Transition.
Then Σ', the EN System obtained through the Extension $(e', F_{e'})$ from Σ, is such that:
$[\Sigma]/_{TS} \leq [\Sigma']/_{TS}$.

Proof.
See the proof of the Corollary of Proposition 11. ♦

Proposition 13
Let $\Sigma = (N_\Sigma, c_{in})$ be an EN System, with $N_\Sigma = (B, E, F)$, let $(b', F_{b'})$ be a new Place and let $TS_\Sigma = (C_\Sigma, E, \text{-->}_\Sigma, c_{in})$ be the Transition System associated with Σ.
Let $\Sigma' = (N_{\Sigma'}, c_{in}')$, with $N_{\Sigma'} = (B', E', F')$ and $\Sigma'' = (N_{\Sigma''}, c_{in}'')$, with $N_{\Sigma''} = (B'', E'', F'')$ (for the details see Definition 18) be respectively the EN Systems obtained through the non-Marked and Marked Constraint $(b', F_{b'})$ from Σ.
Let finally $TS_{\Sigma'} = (C_{\Sigma'}, E', \text{-->}_{\Sigma'}, c_{in}')$ and $TS_{\Sigma''} = (C_{\Sigma''}, E'', \text{-->}_{\Sigma''}, c_{in}'')$ be the Transition Systems associated respectively with Σ' and Σ''.
Then the following hold:
i) $[\exists r \in R_{TS_\Sigma}: {\bullet}r = {\bullet}b'$ and $r{\bullet} = b'{\bullet}$ and $c_{in} \notin r] \Leftrightarrow \Sigma \equiv_{TS} \Sigma'$.
ii) $[\exists r \in R_{TS_\Sigma}: {\bullet}r = {\bullet}b'$ and $r{\bullet} = b'{\bullet}$ and $c_{in} \in r] \Leftrightarrow \Sigma \equiv_{TS} \Sigma''$.

Proof.
Let us prove i). The proof of ii) is similar.
As first let us prove: $[\exists r \in R_{TS_\Sigma}: {\bullet}r = {\bullet}b'$ and $r{\bullet} = b'{\bullet}$ and $c_{in} \notin r] \Rightarrow \Sigma \equiv_{TS} \Sigma'$.
If b' is such that ${\bullet}r = {\bullet}b'$ and $r{\bullet} = b'{\bullet}$ and $c_{in} \notin r$, then the Transition System $TS_{\Sigma'}$ has the same Regions as the Transition System TS_Σ (because Regions characterize - see Definition 10 - causal dependencies between sets of Transitions as well as Places) and $R_{cin} = R_{cin'}$; therefore they are G-isomorphic (because their Regional versions are S-equivalent), and the assertion is proved.
Let us now consider: $\Sigma \equiv_{TS} \Sigma' \Rightarrow [\exists r \in R_{TS_\Sigma}: {\bullet}r = {\bullet}b'$ and $r{\bullet} = b'{\bullet}$ and $c_{in} \notin r]$.
If $\Sigma \equiv_{TS} \Sigma'$, then TS_Σ and $TS_{\Sigma'}$ are G-isomorphic, and therefore they have the same Regions and $R_{cin} = R_{cin'}$. By Proposition 1, $[\exists r \in R_{TS_\Sigma}: {\bullet}r = {\bullet}b'$ and $r{\bullet} = b'{\bullet}$ and $c_{in} \notin r]$, and the assertion is proved. ♦

Corollary
Let $\Sigma = (N_\Sigma, c_{in})$ be an EN System, with $N_\Sigma = (B, E, F)$, let $(b', F_{b'})$ be a new Place and let $TS_\Sigma = (C_\Sigma, E, \text{-->}_\Sigma, c_{in})$ be the Transition System associated with Σ.

Let finally $\Sigma' = (N_{\Sigma'}, c_{in}')$, with $N_{\Sigma'} = (B', E', F')$ and $\Sigma'' = (N_{\Sigma''}, c_{in}'')$, with $N_{\Sigma''} = (B'', E'', F'')$ (for the details see Definition 18) be respectively the EN Systems obtained through the non-Marked and Marked Constraint $(b', F_{b'})$ from Σ.

i) not $[\exists r \in R_{TS_\Sigma}: \bullet r = \bullet b'$ and $r\bullet = b'\bullet$ and $c_{in} \notin r] \Leftrightarrow [\Sigma']_{/TS} < [\Sigma]_{/TS}$.

ii) not $[\exists r \in R_{TS_\Sigma}: \bullet r = \bullet b'$ and $r\bullet = b'\bullet$ and $c_{in} \in r] \Leftrightarrow [\Sigma'']_{/TS} < [\Sigma]_{/TS}$.

Proof.
Let us prove i). The proof of ii) is similar.

By Proposition 13, not $[\exists r \in R_{TS_\Sigma}: \bullet r = \bullet b'$ and $r\bullet = b'\bullet$ and $c_{in} \notin r] \Leftrightarrow$ not $\Sigma \equiv_{TS} \Sigma'$, i. e. $[\Sigma']_{/TS} \neq [\Sigma]_{/TS}$. By the Corollary of Proposition 11, $[\Sigma']_{/TS} \leq [\Sigma]_{/TS}$.

Then: not $[\exists r \in R_{TS_\Sigma}: \bullet r = \bullet b'$ and $r\bullet = b'\bullet$ and $c_{in\ n} \notin r] \Leftrightarrow [\Sigma']_{/TS} < [\Sigma]_{/TS}$. ♦

Remark
The Corollary of Proposition 13 emphasizes that we have a real restriction of the behaviour, if and only if the Constraint adds a Place that is not associated to a Region (see Proposition 1 and the following Remark).

Proposition 14
Let $\Sigma = (N_\Sigma, c_{in})$ be an EN System, with $N_\Sigma = (B, E, F)$. Let $TS_\Sigma = (C_\Sigma, E, \dashrightarrow_\Sigma, c_{in})$ be the Transition System associated with Σ. Then $[\Sigma_{TS_\Sigma}]_{/S}$, the S-equivalence class of the Regional version of TS_Σ, is minimal in $[\Sigma]_{/TS}$.

Proof.
$\equiv_S \Rightarrow \equiv_{TS}$ and therefore $[\Sigma_{TS_\Sigma}]_{/S} \subseteq [\Sigma]_{/TS}$.

$[\Sigma_{TS_\Sigma}]_{/S}$ is minimal in $[\Sigma]_{/TS}$, because $\forall \Sigma' \in [\Sigma]_{/TS}$ there is an ON-morphism (β, η): $\Sigma_{TS_\Sigma} \dashrightarrow \Sigma'$, defined as follows:

η: $E_{TS_\Sigma} \dashrightarrow E'$is the bijection derivable from the proof of the TS-equivalence between Σ_{TS_Σ} and Σ';

β: $B_{TS_\Sigma} \dashrightarrow B'$ is such that $\beta(b) = b'$, if $\eta(\bullet b) = \bullet b'$ and $\eta(b\bullet) = b'\bullet$, undefined, otherwise.

Let us prove that (β, η) is an ON-morphism, i. e. that β satisfies the three conditions i-iii) of Definition 16.

As first let us say that β is injective (since Σ_{TS_Σ} is B-Simple) and that $\beta(B_{TS_\Sigma}) = B'$ (Proposition 1).

i) β has an inverse since it is injective.

ii) Proposition 1 grants also that $\forall b \in B_{TS_\Sigma}$: $b \in c_{in}TS_\Sigma \Leftrightarrow \beta(b) \in c_{in}'$, since b and $\beta(b)$ are associated to the same Region of TS_Σ.

iii) $\forall e_1 \in E_1$: $[\eta(e_1) = e_2 \Rightarrow (\beta(\bullet e_1) = \bullet e_2$ and $\beta(e_1\bullet) = e_2\bullet)]$, since all the Places of Σ' are associated to a Region of TS_Σ. ♦

Remark
Proposition 14 shows that the canonical form of a TS-equivalence class of EN Systems is the most detailed (the smallest with respect to our order relation) concrete model we can obtain of a System having that behaviour.

Examples-12
$[\Sigma_1]_{/S}$, where Σ_1 is presented in Figure 1, $[\Sigma_2]_{/S}$, where Σ_2 is presented in Figure 5, $[\Sigma_4]_{/S}$, where Σ_4 is presented in Figure 8, and $[\Sigma_7]_{/S}$, where Σ_7 is presented in Figure 11, are all contained in $[[\Sigma_1]_{/TS}]_{/S}$.
Moreover the following relations hold:
$[\Sigma_2]_{/S} \leq [\Sigma_4]_{/S} \leq [\Sigma_1]_{/S} \leq [\Sigma_7]_{/S}$, and $[\Sigma_2]_{/S}$ is minimal in $[[\Sigma_1]_{/TS}]_{/S}$ as Σ_2 is the Regional version of the Transition System associated to Σ_1.
$[\Sigma_8]_{/S}$, where Σ_8 is presented in Figure 12, is also contained in $[[\Sigma_1]_{/TS}]_{/S}$, but while the following relation hold:s $[\Sigma_2]_{/S} \leq [\Sigma_8]_{/S}$, no Order Relation holds between it and any of $[\Sigma_1]_{/S}$, $[\Sigma_4]_{/S}$, $[\Sigma_7]_{/S}$.

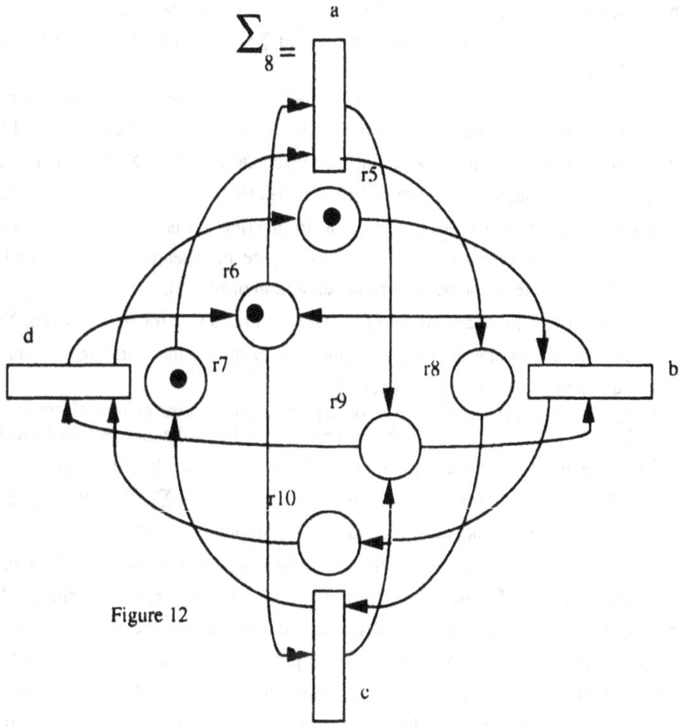

Figure 12

Theorem 2

Let $\Sigma_i = (N_{\Sigma_i}, c_{in_i})$ with $N_{\Sigma_i} = (B_i, E_i, F_i)$, i = 1, 2, be a pair of Elementary Net Systems and let (β, η) be an ON-morphism from Σ_1 to Σ_2.

Let Σ_1', Σ_1'', Σ_1''' be the EN-Systems obtained, respectively, through the Marked Constraint $(b', F_{b'})$, through the non-Marked Constraint $(b', F_{b'})$ and through the Extension $(e', F_{e'})$ from Σ_1, and Σ_2', Σ_2'' and Σ_2''' be the EN-Systems obtained, respectively, through the non-Marked Constraint $(b', \eta(F_{b'}))$, through the Marked Constraint $(b', \eta(F_{b'}))$ and through the Extension $(e', \beta(F_{e'}))$ from Σ_2, where $\eta(F_{b'}) = \{(b', \eta(e)) \mid (b', e) \in F_{b'}\} \cup \{(\eta(e), b') \mid (e, b') \in F_{b'}\}$ and $\beta(F_{e'}) = \{(e', b') \mid (b, b') \in \beta \text{ and } (e', b) \in F_{e'}\} \cup \{(b', e') \mid (b, b') \in \beta \text{ and } (b, e') \in F_{e'}\}$. Then the following hold:

i) $[\Sigma_1']_{/S} \leq [\Sigma_2']_{/S}$,
ii) $[\Sigma_1'']_{/S} \leq [\Sigma_2'']_{/S}$,
iii) $[\Sigma_1''']_{/S} \leq [\Sigma_2''']_{/S}$.

Proof.

i) Let us prove it by cases.

(1) Let us assume that $(b', F_{b'})$ is not Simple in Σ_1, i.e. (Remark i on Definition 18) $\exists b \in B_1$: $\bullet b = \bullet b'$ and $b\bullet = b'\bullet$, and that $b \notin c_{in1}$ then, either

(1.1) also (b', $\eta(F_{b'})$) is not Simple in Σ_2, i.e. $\exists b'' \in B_2$: $\bullet b'' = \bullet b'$ and $b\bullet'' = b'\bullet$, and $b'' \notin c_{in2}$ (if $b'' \in c_{in2}$ then we have not an ON-morphism between Σ_1 and Σ_2) , and therefore (β, η) is also an ON-morphism between Σ_1'and Σ_2', or

(1.2) (b', $\eta(F_{b'})$) is Simple in Σ_2. In this case the construction of Σ_2' does not require Normalization, as (b', $\eta(F_{b'})$) is restricted to $\eta(E_1)$, and therefore if a Transition of E_2 would be made Dead by b' in Σ_2', then its counter-image through η^{-1} in E_1 would also be made Dead by b' in Σ_1', contradicting hypothesis (1). Let $b \in B_1$ be the Place such that $\bullet b = \bullet b'$ or $b\bullet = b'\bullet$, then (β', η), where $\beta' = \beta \cup \{(b, b')\}$, is an ON-morphism, as it satisfies all the Properties of Definition 16 (the first one is true because β'^{-1} is the function extending β^{-1}, with $\beta^{-1}(b') = b$, the second one does not require any attention as b' does not belong to the initial Case, while the third one is true because of the definition of $\eta(F_{b'})$).

(2) Let us assume that (b', $F_{b'}$) is Simple in Σ_1, then the same is true for (b', $\eta(F_{b'})$) in Σ_2, as, by the definition of (b', $\eta(F_{b'})$), b' is connected only to Transitions of $\eta(E_1)$, and therefore the simplicity of (b', $\eta(F_{b'})$) in Σ_2 is granted by the Simplicity of (b', $F_{b'}$) in Σ_1.

(2.1) Let us assume also that the construction of Σ_1' does not require neither Normalization nor B-Simplification. Then the construction of Σ_2' requires either only Normalization or both Normalization and B-Simplification or neither Normalization nor B-Simplification, but all the Transitions of $\eta(E_1)$ are not Dead in Σ_2', as $\eta(F_{b'})$ grants that, for each $e \in \eta(E_1)$, if e is not dead in Σ_1', then $\eta(e)$ is not Dead in Σ_2', and b' belongs to B_2', because b' is not connected to any Transition in (E_2' - $\eta(E_1)$).

(2.1.1) If the construction of Σ_2' does not require neither Normalization nor B-simplification, then (β', η), where $\beta' = \beta \cup \{(b', b')\}$, is an ON-morphism as it satisfies all the Properties of Definition 16 (only the first and third ones need some attention, because the second one is immediate as (b', $F_{b'}$) and (b', $\eta(F_{b'})$) are non-Marked Constraints; β'^{-1} is a partial function as β^{-1} is a partial function and $\beta'^{-1}(b') = b'$, $\forall e_1 \in E_1$: $[\eta(e_1) = e_2 \Rightarrow \beta'(\bullet e_1) = \bullet e_2$ and $\beta'(e_1\bullet) = e_2\bullet]$ thanks to the way by which $\eta(F_{b'})$ is defined).

(2.1.2) If the construction of Σ_2' requires Normalization but not B-Simplification, then (β', η): Σ_1'--> Σ_2', where $\beta' = \beta \cup \{(b', b')\}$, is, therefore, an ON-morphism also (see the Proof of case (2.1.1)).

(2.1.3) If the construction of Σ_2' requires both Normalization and B-Simplification, then Σ_2' has as Places the equivalence classes of the Places of the Normalized version of (($B_2 \cup \{b'\}$, E_2, $F_2 \cup \eta(F_{b'})$), c_{in2}), with respect to B-Simplicity (Definition 7). All the equivalence classes containing Places of $\beta(B_1)$ are singletons since no Transition in $\eta(E_1)$ is Dead in Σ_2'. Then (β', η): Σ_1'--> Σ_2', where $\beta' = \{(b_1, [b_2]/_{BS}) | (b_1, b_2) \in \beta$ and $[b_2]/_{BS} \in \Sigma_2'\} \cup \{(b', b')\}$is an ON-morphism also.

(2.2) Let us assume that the construction of Σ_1' requires Normalization but not B-Simplification, then we can have two cases.

(2.2.1) If the construction of Σ_2' does not require B-simplification, then (β', η'): Σ_1'--> Σ_2', where β' is the restriction of $\beta \cup \{(b', b')\}$ to B_1', and η' is the restriction of η to E_1', is an ON-morphism (see the Proof of case (2.1.1)).

(2.2.2) If the construction of Σ_2' requires both Normalization and B-Simplification, then, with respect to $\beta(B_1')$ and to $\eta(E_1')$, we can apply the same arguments used in case (2.1.3).

(2.3) Let us assume that the construction of Σ_1' requires Normalization and B-Simplification, then B_1' is composed of the equivalence classes of the Places of the Normalized version of (($B_1 \cup \{b'\}$, E_1, $F_1 \cup F_{b'}$), c_{in1}), with respect to B-Simplicity . Let (β', η'): Σ_1'--> Σ_2', where $\beta' = \{([b_1]/_{BS}, b_2') | (b_1, b_2) \in \beta$ and $[b_1]/_{BS} \in B_1$'and $b_2 \in B_2'\}$and η' is the restriction of η to E_1', is an ON-morphism because each equivalence class of Places of B_1' is related by β' either to a set of Places of B_2' (if Σ_2' does not require B-Simplification) or to their equivalence classes (if Σ_2' requires B-Simplification). The proof follows the same line as case (2.2).

(3) Let us assume that (b', $F_{b'}$) is not Simple in Σ_1, i.e. (Remark i on Definition 18) $\exists b \in B_1$: •b = •b' and b• = b'•, and that b $\in c_{in1}$, then the construction of Σ_1'requires either only Normalization or both Normalization and B-Simplification. The Proof is carried on as in case (2).

ii) The proof follows the same line as the proof of i).

iii) We prove it also by cases.

(1) Let us assume that e' does not belong to E_1' (either because (e', $F_{e'}$) is not Simple in Σ_1, or because, for any case $c \in C_1$, it is not true that $c \supseteq$ •e and e• $\cap c = \emptyset$) then (β, η) is also an ON-morphism between Σ_1'and Σ_2', both if e' does belong to B_2' or not.

(2) Let us assume that e' belongs to E_1'(i. e. that (e', $F_{e'}$) is Simple and not Dead in Σ_1). Then, either

(2.1) (e', $\beta(F_{e'})$) is not Simple in Σ_2, and (β, η'), where η' extends η with η'(e') = e, where e is the Transition of E_2 such that •e = •e' and e• = e'• in Σ_2, is also an ON-morphism between Σ_1'and Σ_2', as it satisfies all the Properties of Definition 16 (only the third one requires some attention, as the first two ones do not regard η': (e', $\beta(F_{e'})$) is defined in such a way that also e' satisfies β(•e') = •η'(e') and β(e'•) = η'(e')•]), or

(2.2) (e', $\beta(F_{e'})$) is Simple in Σ_2 and (β, η'), where η' extends h with η'(e') = e'; η'(e) = e', is also an ON-morphism between Σ_1'and Σ_2', as it satisfies all the Properties of Definition 16 (also in this case only the third one requires some attention, as the first two ones do not regard η': (e', $\beta(F_{e'})$) is defined in such a way that also e' satisfies β(•e') = •η'(e') and β(e'•) = η'(e')•]). ♦

5. Conclusion

The Partial Orders, namely ([EN]/S, ≤), ([EN]/TS, ≤), defined in Section 3 as well as the Constraint and Extension unary operations defined in Section 4 are deeply based on Net Theory. On one hand, they emphasize characteristics of Net Systems, that are not immediately recognizable in other Concurrency models (a clear distinction between structural and behavioural properties of the System, an explicit definition of local states and events characterizing it, etc.). On the other hand, they are the formal characterization of concepts and operations that are natural for Net-based Systems, but they do not find corresponding notions in other calculi of concurrency as CCS.

Two are the main lines along which we intend to further develop this research:

1) The unary operations defined above, can be extended so that you can add more complex B-Structures and/or E-Structures (B-Structures are couples constituted by a Normalized EN System and a Boundary defined in terms of Transitions, while, conversely, E-structures are couples constituted by a Normalized EN System and a boundary defined in terms of Places), using instead of ON-morphisms, PN-morphisms, see [BDDPRS91])

The same classes of morphisms can be used as a basis to define refinements of Places and/or Transitions [Dem92].

2) The categorical characterization of the relations between EN Systems and Elementary Transition Systems given in [NRT90], [BDDPRS91], can be assumed as the basis to characterize in a more rich way the behavioural properties of both Constraints and Extensions.

Acknowledgments

This research has been conducted under the financial support of the Italian Ministero della Universita' e della Ricerca Scientifica, of the Progetto Finalizzato "Sistemi Informatici e Calcolo Parallelo" of CNR (Subproject 4, Task "Languages and Tools for Concurrent and Distributed Systems"), and of the ESPRIT-BRA DEMON (#3148).

The author wants to thank his colleagues Lucia Pomello and Carla Simone, as well as Luca Bernardinello and Aldo Restelli for the stimulating discussions and for their careful reading of the manuscript.
Some anonimous referees detected a serious error in the first version of this paper and proposed twice useful suggestions and remarks. Their help had a great impact on this final version.

References

LNCS stands for Lecture Notes in Computer Sciences, Springer Verlag, Berlin.

[BDDPRS91] L. Bernardinello, G. De Michelis, C. Diamantini, L. Pomello, A. Restelli, C. Simone, Relationships between Categories of "Elementary" Concurrent Systems, DSI Tech. Report, 1991
[BDH90] E. Best, F. De Cindio, R. P. Hopkins, DEMON - Design Methods Based on Nets. An ESPRIT Basic Research Action (no. 3148), Bullettin of the EATCS, nr. 41, 1991
[BRG87] W. Brauer, W. Reisig, G. Rozenberg (eds.), Petri Nets: Central Models and Their Properties, LNCS 254, 1987.
[DDPS88] F. De Cindio, G. De Michelis, L. Pomello, C. Simone, A State Transformation Equivalence for Concurrent Systems: Exhibited Functionality Equivalence, in F. H. Vogt (ed.), CONCURRENCY 88, LNCS 335, 1988.
[Dem92] G. De Michelis, Morphisms and Refinements for EN-Systems, DSI Tech. Report, 1992
[ER90a] A. Ehrenfeucht, G. Rozenberg, Partial (Set) 2-Structures - Part 1: Basic Notion and the Representation Problem, Acta Informatica vol. 26, 1990.
[ER90b] A. Ehrenfeucht, G. Rozenberg, Partial (Set) 2-Structures - Part 2: State Spaces of Concurrent Systems, Acta Informatica vol. 26, 1990.
[MM88] S. J. Meseguer, U. Montanari, Petri Nets are Monoids, SRI-CSL-88-3, january 1988.
[Mil80] R. Milner, A Calculus for Communicating Systems, LNCS 92, 1980
[NRT90] M. Nielsen, G. Rozenberg, P. S. Thiagarajan, Elementary Transition Systems, Tech. Report, Dept. of Computer Science, University of Leiden, 1990.
[PRS92] L. Pomello, C. Simone, A Survey of Equivalence Notions for Net based Systems, LNCS 609, 1992
[PS91] L. Pomello, C. Simone, A State Transformation Preorder over a class of EN-Systems, in APN'90, LNCS 483, 1991.
[PS92] L. Pomello, C. Simone, Concurrent Systems as Local State Transformation Algebras: the Case of Elementary Net Systems, Formal Aspects of Computing, 1992 (to appear).
[Roz87] G. Rozenberg, Behaviour of Elementary Net Systems, in [BRG87].
[RT86] G. Rozenberg, P.S. Thiagarajan, Petri Nets: basic notions, structure, behaviour, in J. W. de Bakker, W. P. de Roever, G. Rozenberg (eds.), Current Trends in Concurrency, LNCS 224, 1986.
[Thi87] P.S. Thiagarajan, Elementary Net Systems, in [BRG87].

Comparability Orders and Measurement

EINAR SMITH

GMD-I1.P, Schloß Birlinghoven
5205 St. Augustin, Germany
einar.smith@gmd.de

Abstract This paper is concerned with the relationship between continuous phenomena and discrete representations in measurement. Empirical indistinguishability is identified as a fundamental notion. We show that this relation is in general not transitive and discuss the consequences of this fact for the construction and application of ordinal measurement scales. In particular, we develop a normal form for the representation of empirical orderings. This includes the investigation of denseness notions compatible with discrete partial orders.

Keywords Intransitive indifference, Interval orders, Concurrency-theory, Ordinal scales.

Contents

1 Introduction

Measurement is fundamental to physics and technical matters, but also to economics and social sciences concerned with human behaviour[1]. Measurement is necessary for prediction as well as control of phenomena.

With the advances in computer technology it has become technically possible to delegate measuring and control to highly automated integrated systems. Reliable delegation to automata, however, requires a precise understanding of the nature of such processes when carried out by humans.

In practice, measurement always involves a *comparison* of the measurand with a known object of the same kind. Every measurement system provides a set of reference quantities and a method to determine equality. For instance, in weight measurement with a beam balance, a reference set consists of a suitable collection of known unit weights. Two objects are considered to be of equal weight if and only if the weighbeam balances in equilibrium.

The first problem of measurement theory is to identify and characterize the relevant abstract properties of empirical comparison procedures, in particular properties that may be assumed to hold for equality determined through empirical observations. It is generally agreed that this relation is *reflexive* and *symmetric*. The empirical status of the axiom of *transitivity* is, however, not equally uncontroversial.

Some approaches assume without question that transitivity holds also for empirical observations. For instance, in his seminal paper on measurement theory, H. v. Helmholtz [11, p. 99] asserts:

> Finally it is confirmed that, if the weight of a is equal not only to the weight of b, but also to the weight of c, then so is $b = c$. Equilibrium of the weights on a true balance, therefore, indeed establishes a method to determine equality.[2]

Similarly R. Carnap [7, p. 55] claims:

> We find that if a balances with b on the scales, and b balances with c, then a will balance with c.

Now, although plausible at first sight, these assertions are actually *not* in accordance with experience. Practical experiments rather tend to confirm the opposite. With a common balance we may probably not observe any difference between n and $n+1$ grains of rice for any single $n = 10.000, \ldots, 20.000$, but very well between 10.000 grains on one side and 20.000 on the other.[3]

---

[1]The interest in a proper measurement theory for these disciplines derive in large part from the work of J. v. Neumann and O. Morgenstern [16] where it is recognized that the mathematics developed for the physical sciences, which describes the workings of a disinterested nature, is a poor model for economics.

[2]Translated by the author from the German original: Endlich bestätigt sich, dass, wenn das Gewicht von a nicht blos dem Gewichte von b, sondern auch dem von c gleich ist, dann auch $b = c$ ist. Das Gleichgewicht der Gewichte an einer richtigen Waage begründet also in der That eine Methode, eine Gleichheit zu bestimmen.

[3]Cf. the question posed by Zeno of Elea, why a single falling grain of millet makes no sound, whereas a whole sack does, see e.g. [14, p. 228ff].

Many authors pointing to "imperfect powers of discrimination of the human mind" [3][4] admit non-transitivity as an empirical phenomenon, but do not consider it a matter of major theoretical importance, assuming that 'genuine equality' may be logically reconstructed from the observations. For instance, N. Wiener [32] remarks that two observations may be indistinguishable, i.e. *seem* equal, but not necessarily *be* equal. He then claims (p. 184):

> We regard two intervals as genuinely equal when and only when all the intervals that are indistinguishable from one are indistinguishable from the other. Genuine equality is, as may readily be seen, a reflexive, symmetrical and transitive relation.

Similarly, J. Pfanzagl [22, p. 59] distinguishes between equivalence and empirical indifference. As a reasonable method to refine indifference to equivalence he suggests

> to eliminate from the set of all elements that are indifferent to a all elements which are indifferent to an element which is preferred or postponed to a and to consider these elements as preferred to a or postponed to a, respectively.

In the present paper we shall show that non-transitivity of observational indifference is in fact unavoidable in the practice of measurement. Moreover, in contrast to the approaches mentioned above, we shall advocate that in general it is *not* possible to deduct genuine equality by mathematical interpolation techniques. Such formal manipulations rather pave the way for incorrect or contradicting interpretations. We shall indicate that non-transitivity even has attractive consequences that can profitably be exploited for the construction, calibration and evaluation of empirical measuring scales.

The paper is organized as follows. In Section 2 we collect some terminology and recall some basic facts concerning partial orders. Section 3 examines *interval orders* and *comparability orders* (known also as *semiorders* in the literature). In particular, we characterize exact conditions under which indifference can formally be refined to mathematical equivalence. These results are then interpreted in the context of technical applications. Much of the material here is related to ideas and methods in [15, 24, 26], cf. also [10].

Section 4 studies *coherent* and *combinatoric* orders and develops partial-order representations for *ordinal measuring scales*. Section 5 investigates the resolution power of empirical ordinal scales. This includes a discussion of *K-density*, a denseness concept compatible with discrete orders. In Section 6, formal methods for the construction of K-dense orders are examined and discussed in measurement applications. Many concepts and notions in this part of the paper are based on C. A. Petri's *concurrency-theory* [19, 20], a theory of partial orders mainly developed in connection with non-sequential processes in distributed systems, see e.g. [5], but also profitably applicable within the general context of empirical order relations [18, 21].

---

[4] A quite similar remark can for example be found in [25]: "Unfortunately human powers of discrimination often lead to cases where indifference is intransitive."

2 Prerequisites

In this section we collect some basic terminology, notation and facts concerning partial orders that will be used throughout.

We shall use standard notations for handling sets. In particular, the complement of B in A will be denoted by $A \setminus B$. We write $A \subseteq B$ if A is a subset of B, and $A \subset B$ if A is a proper subset. For a family $\mathcal{F}$ of sets, $\bigcup \mathcal{F}$ is the union of all sets belonging to $\mathcal{F}$. The cardinality of a set A is denoted by $|A|$. As symbols for the set of natural numbers (including 0), integers and real numbers we use $\mathbf{N}$, $\mathbf{Z}$ and $\mathbf{R}$, respectively.

For a binary relation $R \subseteq X \times Y$ we shall often use infix-notation and write $x\,R\,y$ instead of $(x,y) \in R$. If A is a subset of X we use $R \restriction A$, or simply R if there is no danger of confusion, to denote the restriction $R \cap (A \times Y)$. The complement $(X \times Y) \setminus R$ of a relation R is written as $\overline{R}$. As usual, R^{-1} denotes the inverse of R. The identity relation on a set X will be denoted by id_X or simply id, if the set X is clear from the context. The concatenation, or *relational product*, of two relations R and S is written as $R \circ S$. For a relation R and natural numbers n, R^n is defined inductively by $R^0 := \mathrm{id}$ and $R^{n+1} := R^n \circ R$. We denote the transitive closure $\bigcup_{n \geq 1} R^n$ of R by R^+ and the reflexive and transitive closure $\bigcup_{n \geq 0} R^n$ by R^*.

By a (partial) *ordering* or *order* we shall understand an irreflexive and transitive relation. If $<$ is an ordering of a set X, the pair $(X, <)$ – and for convenience also the set X – will be called a *(partially) ordered set* (*poset* for short). By abuse of language we sometimes also use the term 'order' for the pair $(X, <)$. The inverse $<^{-1}$ of an ordering will also be written as $>$. If $<$ is an order we denote its reflexive extension $< \cup \mathrm{id}$ by $\leq$.

Notation 2.1 For an order (occasionally also for an arbitrary relation) $<$ we write $\lessdot$ for the relation $< \setminus <^2$ expressing direct neighbourhood. □

Notation 2.2 The symmetric complement $X^2 \setminus (< \cup >)$ of an order $<$ will be denoted by co. Note that the co-relation of an order is always reflexive and symmetric (i.e. a *similarity* relation) but in general not transitive. Occasionally the symbol co will also be used for the symmetric complement of an arbitrary relation. By way of speaking we shall often use formulations such as "x is co to y" instead of "x co y" etc. It will usually be clear from the context to which relation the symbol co refers, if not, we use self-explanatory subscripts as identifiers. □

In a poset $(X, <)$ two elements $x, y \in X$ are said to be *comparable* if $x < y$ or $y < x$, *incomparable* if x co y. An order is *total* or *linear* if any two elements are comparable, i.e. if co = id.

On the sets $\mathbf{N}$, $\mathbf{Z}$ and $\mathbf{R}$, unless specified otherwise, the symbol $<$ denotes the usual linear order.

By an *interval* in $\mathbf{Z}$ we understand any convex subset, i.e. a set $I \subseteq \mathbf{Z}$ such that $x, y \in I \wedge x < z < y \Rightarrow z \in I$, in particular $\mathbf{Z}$ itself is an interval.

Definition 2.3 A totally ordered subset A of a poset $(X, <)$ is a *chain*. A chain of the form $\{ x_i \mid i \in I \}$ where I is an interval in $\mathbf{Z}$ will be called a $\lessdot$-*chain* if $x_i \lessdot x_{i+1}$ for all $i, i+1 \in I$. A maximal chain (a chain not properly contained in a larger one) will be called a *line*. Dually, a subset consisting only of pairwise incomparable elements is an *antichain*. A maximal antichain will be called a *cut*. □

For two posets $(X, <)$ and $(Y, <)$, a mapping $f: X \to Y$ is called *increasing* if $x < y \Rightarrow f(x) \leq f(y)$, *strictly increasing* if it is also injective. If f is increasing and bijective it is an *isomorphism*. Note that the same symbol $<$ is used for the orders on X and Y, respectively. We shall usually follow this convention if there is no danger of confusion.

In the graphical representation of posets we use arrows to indicate order as usual. Thus, unless specified otherwise, two elements will be incomparable iff they are not connected by a directed path. For finite posets this representation is essentially unique: Any finite directed acyclic graph defines a poset when the edges are interpreted as the neighbourhood-relation.

3 Comparability Orders

Empirical order structures are concerned with comparative concepts such as "noticeably larger", "definitely heavier" or "preferable" and the complementary relations "indistinguishability" or "indifference"[5]. As indicated in the introduction, observational indifference will usually not be transitive. In this section we investigate two basic *comparability axioms* which appear to characterize reasonably tight bounds for the deviation from transitivity. On the other hand we shall show that these axioms also reflect the upper limit of precision that can realistically be expected.

As running example we take the comparison of weights by means of a beam balance. Let $x < y$ denote that y is noticeably heavier than x. We may assume the relation $<$ to be transitive and thus to be a partial ordering. Then $x \text{ co } y$ indicates that x and y are indistinguishable in this setting of the experiment.

If x and y are indistinguishable, whereas v is noticeably lighter than x, and y lighter than w, then it is natural to assume that in direct comparison v will be lighter than w, in symbols

(C1) $$v < x \text{ co } y < w \Rightarrow v < w.$$

This axiom has been noted independently by various authors in different contexts, e.g. [22, 27, 28, 31], cf. also [29].

Whenever two objects are separated by another one noticeably different from either of them, it is not plausible that there might also exist a common object indistinguishable to both. A failure of this axiom could rather indicate a malfunction of the experiment setting, cf. [10]. This postulate also has been noted independently by various authors, e.g. [15, 27]. Formally:

(C2) $$x < y < z \Rightarrow \neg \exists v : (x \text{ co } v \land v \text{ co } z).$$

[5]These terms reflect the fact that initially interest in empirical order structures arose mainly from various sources in the social sciences, such as experiments concerning psychophysical measurements of perceptions of length, mass and so forth; or from the analysis of consumer preference relations in the economical sciences. We shall mostly use the noun "indifference" and the adjective "indistinguishable".

Figure 1 below illustrates both axioms by the configurations they *exclude*. The connection between (C2) and (b) is immediate. Likewise, it is clear that (a) is excluded by (C1). Conversely, observe that if (C1) is *not* satisfied, then there are x, y, v, w such that $v < x$ co $y < w$ and *not* $(v < w)$. But then, in addition to the assumption x co y, also the other relations (v co w), (v co y) and (x co w) in (a) hold. This is seen as follows: Clearly w co v, since otherwise $y < w < v < x$, and thus $y < x$, contradicting x co y. Therefore v co y, since $v < y$ would imply $v < w$, and $y < v$ would imply $y < x$. A symmetrical argument shows x co w.

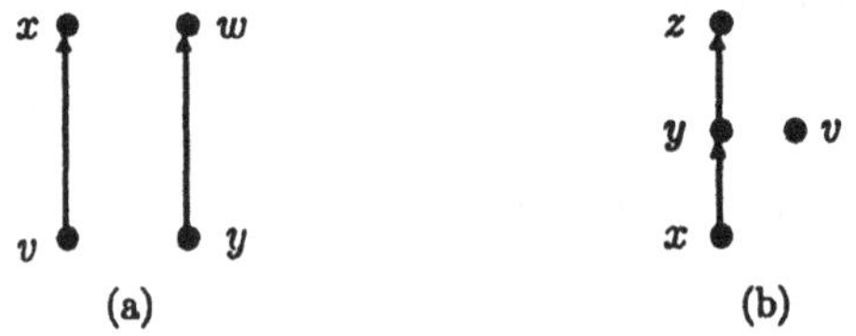

Figure 1 (a) Excluded by (C1). (b) Excluded by (C2).

The following notions will be central:

Definition 3.1 A partial ordering $<$ of a set X will be called a

(i) *comparability order* iff it satisfies both of the postulates (C1) and (C2).

(ii) *interval order* iff it satisfies (C1).

(iii) (C2)-*order* iff it satisfies (C2).

From now on we assume every order arising from empirical comparisons to be a comparability order. □

In the literature comparability orders and (C2)-orders are sometimes called *semiorders* and *partial semiorders*, respectively.[6] The term *interval order* derives from the fact that every such order is representable by a canonic order defined on the set of intervals of a linear ordering, see e.g. [10]. A typical case is illustrated in the following example.

Example 3.2 Let $\mathcal{I}$ be the set of open intervals of $\mathbf{R}$. Let $\lhd$ denote the ordering of $\mathcal{I}$ defined by

$$I \lhd J :\Leftrightarrow \forall x \in I \forall y \in J : x < y.$$

For the co-relation co of $\lhd$, clearly I co $J \Leftrightarrow I \cap J \neq \emptyset$, hence in particular co is not transitive. It is also readily verified that $\lhd$ is an interval order: Assume $I_1 \lhd I_2$ co $I_3 \lhd I_4$. Choose any $v \in I_2 \cap I_3$. Then for all $x \in I_1$, $y \in I_4$ we have $x < v < y$, hence $x < y$. Therefore $I_1 \lhd I_4$, as required. However, $\lhd$ is not a comparability order: Assume $I_1 \lhd I_2 \lhd I_3$. Now choose $x \in I_1$, $y \in I_3$. Then the interval $I := (x, y)$ is co to I_1 and I_3.

If we only allow intervals of a fixed length, say 1, it is not possible to choose any such I that intersects both I_1 and I_3, hence with $\mathcal{I}_1 := \{(r, r+1) \mid r \in \mathbf{R}\}$ the pair $(\mathcal{I}_1, \lhd)$ *is* a comparability poset. □

[6] We avoid these terms since they tend to suggest that comparability orders are some kind of defective real orders.

Note 3.3 'Real' interval orders as in Example 3.2 are often used for the representation of temporal events of non-zero duration [23, 24, 31]. Two events are considered contemporaneous if their time spans overlap. Unlike contemporaneity between pointlike instants, this notion of contemporaneity is not transitive. In computer science interest in durational events arises naturally in the analysis of distributed system behaviour, see e.g. [1, 2, 12]. □

Note 3.4 Readers familiar with *Petri-nets*, see e.g. [5], may find it interesting to note that the order F^+ in an occurrence net $(S, T; F)$ is an interval order if and only if F^+ restricted to the set of event-occurrences T is total [27]. □

The following example illustrates how common procedures to deal with inaccuracies of measurement naturally lead to the consideration of interval orders and comparability orders. The idea is that measurement values are given together with a surrounding 'inaccuracy-interval'. Two measurements are considered to be significantly different only if their respective intervals do not overlap.

Example 3.5 Let $\ll$ be the partial ordering of $\mathbf{R}$ defined by

$$x \ll y :\Leftrightarrow x + 1 < y,$$

where $<$ denotes the standard order of $\mathbf{R}$.[7] We prove that $\ll$ is a comparability order such that its co-relation co is intransitive. First, note that

$$x \text{ co } y \Leftrightarrow |x - y| \leq 1. \tag{1}$$

To establish (C1), assume $v \ll x \text{ co } y \ll w$. Hence by definition, $v + 1 < x$, $|x - y| \leq 1$ and $y + 1 < w$, and thus

$$\begin{aligned} v + 1 < x &= x - y + y \\ &\leq 1 + y < w, \end{aligned}$$

i.e. $v \ll w$, as required.

To verify (C2), by contradiction suppose there are $x, y, z, v \in \mathbf{R}$ such that

$$\text{(a)}\quad x \ll y \ll z \qquad \text{and} \qquad \text{(b)}\quad x \text{ co } v \text{ co } z. \tag{2}$$

From (2a) we obtain $2 < |x - z|$, whereas (2b) to the contrary implies

$$\begin{aligned} |x - z| &= |x - v + v - z| \\ &\leq |x - v| + |v - z| \leq 2. \end{aligned}$$

It remains to show that co is not transitive. But this is immediate. We have for instance 1 co 2 co 3 but $1 \ll 3$.

For later reference we remark that also $(\mathbf{Z}, \ll)$ is a comparability poset. The relation co restricted to $\mathbf{Z}$ remains intransitive; two integers are incomparable with respect to $\ll$ iff they are immediate neighbours. □

Note 3.6 An early discussion of the poset $(\mathbf{R}, \ll)$ can be found in the article [26] by D. Scott and P. Suppes, where it is shown, among others, that every finite interval order is isomorphic to an interval order $(X, \ll)$ with $X \subseteq \mathbf{R}$, cf. also [25]. □

---

[7] The number 1 in the definition of $\ll$ has no special significance. We might just as well use any other constant > 0.

Refinement and Weak Orders

Situations in which measurement data are believed to give only a partial picture of the underlying order because of limited discriminatory power of the measurement process suggest to seek to uncover this order with the help of mathematical order extensions. In the following we shall try to indicate that this is in general not possible, however; it is not realistic to expect any reliable increase in accuracy through formal a-posteriori deductions. For definiteness we base the discussion on the approach [32, 22] mentioned in the introduction.

Wiener and Pfanzagl regard any of the two observations

$$x < y \text{ co } z \quad \text{or} \quad x \text{ co } y < z$$

as an indication that x is in reality smaller than z. Therefore, so their argument, the observed order $<$ can be formally *refined* to

$$\prec := (\text{co} \circ <) \cup (< \circ \text{ co}), \tag{3}$$

such that the co-relation of $\prec$ becomes genuine transitive equality.

Now, although this reasoning may look convincing at first sight, it is not tenable in general. We shall demonstrate that refinement does not reliably improve empirical accuracy but rather paves the way for inconsistent interpretations.

First however, we discuss the relationship between an order $<$ and the refinement (3) from a structural point of view. In particular, in Theorem 3.14 below we show that $\prec$ defines an order relation at all (then in fact with a transitive co-relation) if and only if $<$ satisfies both of the axioms (C1) and (C2).

The following characterizations of the comparability-axioms in terms of relational products will be useful:

Clearly,

$$(\text{C1}) \Leftrightarrow (< \circ \text{ co} \circ <) \subseteq <. \tag{4}$$

For (C2) we have:

Lemma 3.7 *For a poset* $(X, <)$ *the following are equivalent:*

(i) $<$ *is a* (C2)*-order.*

(ii) $\text{co}^2 \cap <^2 = \emptyset$.

(iii) $(< \circ < \circ \text{ co}) \subseteq <$.

(iv) $(\text{co} \circ < \circ <) \subseteq <$.

Proof. Straightforward. ∎

Using (4) and Lemma 3.7 we can characterize comparability orders in terms of symbol occurrences in "words over the alphabet $\{\text{co}, <\}$".

Notation 3.8 Let α be a relational product of the form $r_1 \circ \cdots \circ r_n$, where each r_i is either co or $<$. We let $\Psi_{\text{co}}(\alpha)$ and $\Psi_<(\alpha)$ be the *Parikh-mappings* denoting the number of occurrences of co and $<$ in α, respectively. □

Proposition 3.9 *For a poset $(X,<)$ the following are equivalent:*

(i) *$<$ is a comparability order.*

(ii) *For every product α over $\{\text{co},<\}$, if $\Psi_{\text{co}}(\alpha) < \Psi_<(\alpha)$, then $\alpha \subseteq <$.*

Proof. (i) $\Rightarrow$ (ii). By induction on $\Psi_{\text{co}}(\alpha)$. For $\Psi_{\text{co}}(\alpha) = 0$ the claim holds trivially. Now assume $0 < \Psi_{\text{co}}(\alpha) < \Psi_<(\alpha)$. Then α can be decomposed into a product $\alpha_1 \circ \alpha' \circ \alpha_2$, where α' is one of the following: $(< \circ < \circ \text{co})$, $(< \circ \text{co} \circ <)$ or $(\text{co} \circ < \circ <)$. Observing (4) and Lemma 3.7, in all three cases $\alpha' \subseteq <$, and hence, using transitivity of $<$ and the induction hypothesis, $\alpha \subseteq (\alpha_1 \circ < \circ \alpha_2) \subseteq <$.

(ii) $\Rightarrow$ (i). Consider the relational products $(< \circ \text{co} \circ <)$, $(< \circ < \circ \text{co})$ and $(\text{co} \circ < \circ <)$. The claim again follows with (4) and Lemma 3.7. ∎

Note 3.10 Proposition 3.9 is due to the fact that adjacent occurrences of co and $<$ can be reduced to a single $<$ in the context of another occurrence of $<$. If this reduction is possible independent of the context, then co is transitive. In fact, if co is transitive, a single occurrence of $<$ is enough to imply $\alpha \subseteq <$; it is easily verified that the following are equivalent:

(i) co is transitive.

(ii) For every product α, if $\Psi_{\text{co}}(\alpha) \leq \Psi_<(\alpha)$, then $\alpha \subseteq <$.

(iii) For every product α, if $\Psi_<(\alpha) > 0$, then $\alpha \subseteq <$. □

Definition 3.11 In accordance with common terminology, an order with a transitive co-relation will be called *weak*. □

A weak ordering induces a partition into a set of strata consisting of pairwise equivalent elements such that all elements in a lower stratum are smaller than all elements in a higher one. Every weak order is a fortiori a comparability order.[8] This is an immediate consequence of the following proposition:

Proposition 3.12 *An order $<$ is weak iff it satisfies the postulate*

$$x \text{ co } y < w \Rightarrow x < w \quad \textit{and} \quad v < x \text{ co } y \Rightarrow v < y,$$

or equivalently

$$(\text{co} \circ <) \subseteq < \quad \textit{and} \quad (< \circ \text{co}) \subseteq <.$$

Proof. Straightforward. ∎

In analogy to the comparability axioms (C1) and (C2) we shall refer to either of the postulates in Proposition 3.12 as (C0).

[8] Since the point of reference in the context of this paper are *comparability* orders rather than *total* orders, 'strong' would perhaps be a more suggestive term than 'weak'. We concede to established usage, however.

Definition 3.13 If co is the co-relation of a relation $<$ (usually a partial order), then we use $\widetilde{\text{co}}$ to denote the relation given by

$$x \;\widetilde{\text{co}}\; y :\Leftrightarrow (\forall z : z \text{ co } x \Leftrightarrow z \text{ co } y).$$

If $<$ is an order, then $\widetilde{\text{co}}$ is an equivalence contained in co. In this case we call $\widetilde{\text{co}}$ the *transitive kernel* of co. □

We are now ready to prove that the relation $\prec$ in (3) defines a partial ordering if and only if the empirical observations constitute a comparability order. If this is the case, the resulting order is *weak*. An early proof can be found in [15]. We shall follow [27].

Theorem 3.14 *Let $(X, <)$ be a poset. Then the relation $\prec := (\text{co} \circ <) \cup (< \circ \text{ co})$ defines a partial order on X if and only if $<$ is a comparability order. Moreover, if $\prec$ is an order, then it is weak.*

Proof. We start with the first equivalence.

"$\Rightarrow$". We have to establish (C1) and (C2). For (C1) assume $v < x \text{ co } y < w$. Then either $v < w$ or $v \text{ co } w$. The second alternative can be ruled out because it implies $w \prec^2 w$, which is impossible, since by assumption $\prec$ is an order. For (C2) assume $x < y < z$. Similar to above, from the existence of an element v such that $x \text{ co } v \text{ co } z$ we could conclude $v \prec^2 v$.

"$\Leftarrow$". Irreflexitivity of $\prec$ is trivial, since $(\prec \cap \text{id}) \subseteq (\overline{\text{co}} \cap \text{co}) = \emptyset$. It remains to verify $\prec^2 \subseteq \prec$. By definition, $\prec^2$ can be written as a relational product α built from two occurrences each of $<$ and co. Clearly there are 6 possible combinations. From these, 5 can be reduced to $\prec$ immediately using transitivity of $<$ and Proposition 3.9. It remains to consider the case $\alpha = (< \circ \text{ co} \circ \text{co} \circ <)$. Since $(< \circ \text{ co} \circ \text{co}) \cap > = \emptyset$ because of (C2), we have either $\alpha \subseteq (\text{co} \circ <)$ or $\alpha \subseteq <^2$. But both alternatives imply $\alpha \subseteq \prec$, as required.

For the remaining claim assume that $\prec$ is an order. Consider the transitive kernel $\widetilde{\text{co}}$ of co. We prove that $\widetilde{\text{co}}$ is the co-relation of $\prec$ by showing $\overline{\widetilde{\text{co}}} = \prec \cup \prec^{-1}$:

"$\subseteq$". Assume that *not* $(x \;\widetilde{\text{co}}\; y)$. Then without loss of generality there is v such that $x \text{ co } v \;\overline{\text{co}}\; y$, hence $x \prec y$ or $y \prec x$.

"$\supseteq$". Both $\prec \not\subseteq \widetilde{\text{co}}$ and $\prec^{-1} \not\subseteq \widetilde{\text{co}}$ are immediate by definition. ∎

Example 3.15

(i) We begin with a counter-example. Consider the poset $(\mathcal{I}, \lhd)$ of open $\mathbf{R}$-intervals as defined in Example 3.2. Let $\prec := (\text{co} \circ \lhd) \cup (\lhd \circ \text{ co})$. Choose $I_1 \lhd I_2 \lhd I_3$, and let I be an interval which intersects both I_1 and I_3. Then $I \text{ co } I_1 \lhd I_2$, hence $I \prec I_2$, but conversely also $I_2 \prec I$ since $I_2 \lhd I_3 \text{ co } I$. Therefore $\prec$ cannot be an order.

(ii) In contrast, in the comparability poset $(\mathcal{I}_1, \lhd)$ consisting only of intervals of the form $(r, r+1)$, we clearly have $(r, r+1) \prec (s, s+1)$ iff $r < s$ in the standard order on the reals. Hence $\prec$ restricted to $\mathcal{I}_1$ is even a linear order.

(iii) We continue with the comparability poset $(\mathbf{R}, \ll)$ from Example 3.5. Consider the derived weak order $\prec := (\text{co} \circ \ll) \cup (\ll \circ \text{co})$. As in the proof of Theorem 3.14, the transitive kernel $\widetilde{\text{co}}$ is the co-relation of $\prec$. Using equation (1) in Example 3.5, we note that $x \,\widetilde{\text{co}}\, y$ iff

$$\forall z : (|x - z| \leq 1 \Leftrightarrow |y - z| \leq 1),$$

which clearly is the case iff $x = y$. It follows that $\widetilde{\text{co}} = \text{id}$. Hence $\prec$ is a linear order, which moreover obviously coincides with the standard order on $\mathbf{R}$. □

Example 3.15(iii) apparently confirms the view that reconstruction of genuine order and equality from imprecise observations is possible. But note that, by definition, an infinite number of comparisons is required to compute the relation $\widetilde{\text{co}}$ from co. Moreover, the relation co itself depends on a precise knowledge of the limits of the inaccuracy intervals, which in practice are as unavailable as 'exact' measurement values themselves.[9] The refinement of $<$ to $\prec$ above must therefore be regarded as a mathematical construction only, and should in particular not be confounded with a 'real' executable process.

Accuracy and Refinement in Technical Applications

After these formal considerations we shall now demonstrate that application of technical devices in measurement naturally results in proper – i.e. non-weak – comparability orders. Moreover, we shall indicate that mathematical refinement of the observed order relations does not increase measurement accuracy.

Example 3.16 Consider a device M for sorting steel balls according to size into consecutively numbered adjacent boxes. A run S of M on a set of balls X induces an empirical ordering $<_S$ by

$$x <_S y :\Leftrightarrow S(x) < S(y),$$

where $S(x)$ stands for the number of the box into which x is sorted by S.

For a reliable ordering of X a single run S is not sufficient, however: By nature, no matter how carefully M is made, the possibility of border line cases among the balls is unavoidable. Hence it cannot be excluded that two runs may have a different outcome; a ball might be put into one box by S and into an adjacent one in another run S'. In fact, for two balls x and y it is even possible that the two runs result in the converse observations $x <_S y$ and $y <_{S'} x$, respectively.

This suggests to base an ordering of X on a *set* $\mathcal{S}$ of repeated observations, such that x is regarded as smaller than y if and only if

(i) $\mathcal{S}$ provides positive evidence $S \in \mathcal{S}$ such that $S(x) < S(y)$, and moreover,

(ii) the possibility of an observation "y smaller than x" can be excluded, i.e. for any conceivable run S'' of M it can be guaranteed that $S''(y) \not< S''(x)$.

[9] We cannot agree with the following remark in [25]: "The question is then to find numerical assignments in which the boundary between preference and indifference is made explicit: the arithmetic relation $\alpha \geq \beta + 1$ is an obvious candidate for performing this service."

Observe that requirement (ii) refers to situations not known in advance. We can, however, formulate a sufficient criterium in terms of the actual observations in $\mathcal{S}$. To this end we define a relation on X by

$$x <_{\mathcal{S}} y :\Leftrightarrow \exists S, S' \in \mathcal{S} : S(x) + 1 < S'(y). \tag{5}$$

We shall show that $<_{\mathcal{S}}$ is a comparability order which satisfies requirements (i) and (ii) above. This relies crucially on the fact that even if we cannot exclude border cases altogether, we clearly *may* assume that a border case between two boxes will never be sorted into a third one, i.e. for any two conceivable runs S, S' we may assume

$$\forall x \in X : |S(x) - S'(x)| \leq 1. \tag{6}$$

Using (6) we can now verify requirements (i) and (ii): Assume $x <_{\mathcal{S}} y$. Choose $S, S' \in \mathcal{S}$ such that $S(x) + 1 < S'(y)$. An easy computation shows $S(x) < S(y)$, which proves (i). For (ii), in any conceivable run S'' we get $S''(y) \not< S''(x)$ from

$$\begin{aligned} S''(x) &\leq S(x) + 1 \\ &\leq S'(y) - 1 \leq S''(y). \end{aligned}$$

Conversely, if the set $\mathcal{S}$ does *not* establish $x <_{\mathcal{S}} y$, then in particular we do not possess sufficient information to guarantee requirement (ii). This is seen as follows: First observe that by definition, *not* $(x <_{\mathcal{S}} y)$ is equivalent to

$$\forall S, S' \in \mathcal{S} : S'(y) \leq S(x) + 1.$$

Now let $\underline{S}(x) := \min \{ S(x) \mid S \in \mathcal{S} \}$ and similarly $\overline{S}(y) := \max \{ S'(y) \mid S' \in \mathcal{S} \}$. Then a run S'' of M with $S''(x) = \underline{S}(x) + 1$ and $S''(y) = \overline{S'}(y) - 1$ is not excluded by (6). For such an S'', clearly $S''(y) < S''(x)$, which contradicts (ii).

We have thus shown that the relation $<_{\mathcal{S}}$ meets the requirements (i) and (ii). Moreover, note that the precision of $<_{\mathcal{S}}$ increases with the information contained in the observation set: Assume there are $x, y \in X$ and a number i such that $S(x) = i$ and $S(y) = i + 1$ for all $S \in \mathcal{S}$. Then $x \operatorname{co}_{\mathcal{S}} y$. If now $\mathcal{S}'$ is an extension of $\mathcal{S}$ such that there is $S^- \in \mathcal{S}'$ with $S^-(x) = i - 1$, then $x <_{\mathcal{S}'} y$, i.e. in particular $<_{\mathcal{S}} \subset <_{\mathcal{S}'}$.

We still have to prove that

$$<_{\mathcal{S}} \text{ is a comparability order.} \tag{7}$$

To this end first observe that the co-relation $\operatorname{co}_{\mathcal{S}}$ of $<_{\mathcal{S}}$ can be expressed by

$$x \operatorname{co}_{\mathcal{S}} y \Leftrightarrow \forall S, S' \in \mathcal{S} : |S(x) - S'(y)| \leq 1. \tag{8}$$

Now (8) and (6) put together imply $\mathrm{id} \subseteq \operatorname{co}_{\mathcal{S}}$, hence irreflexitivity of $<_{\mathcal{S}}$ follows immediately.

Using $\mathrm{id} \subseteq \operatorname{co}_{\mathcal{S}}$ again, we take care of (C1) as well as transitivity of $<_{\mathcal{S}}$ by showing that

$$v <_{\mathcal{S}} x \operatorname{co}_{\mathcal{S}} y <_{\mathcal{S}} w \Rightarrow v <_{\mathcal{S}} w.$$

To see this, assume $S_1, \ldots, S_4 \in \mathcal{S}$ such that

$$S_1(v) + 1 < S_2(x) \quad \text{and} \quad S_3(y) + 1 < S_4(w).$$

We obtain

$$S_1(v) + 1 \;<\; S_2(x) \;\leq\; S_3(y) + 1 \;<\; S_4(w),$$

where the inner inequality follows by (8). Hence $v <_{\mathcal{S}} w$, as was to be shown.

For (C2) suppose there are x, y, z, v, such that

$$\text{(a)} \quad x <_{\mathcal{S}} y <_{\mathcal{S}} z \qquad \text{and} \qquad \text{(b)} \quad x \text{ co}_{\mathcal{S}}\ v \text{ co}_{\mathcal{S}}\ z. \tag{9}$$

Because of (9a) we can choose $S_1, S_2 \in \mathcal{S}$ such that

$$S_1(x) + 2 \;<\; S_2(z).$$

By (9b), however, $|S_1(x) - S(v)|$, $|S(v) - S_2(z)| \leq 1$ for every $S \in \mathcal{S}$, and therefore

$$\begin{aligned} |S_1(x) - S_2(z)| \;&=\; |S_1(x) - S(v) + S(v) - S_2(z)| \\ &\leq\; |S_1(x) - S(v)| + |S(v) - S_2(z)| \;\leq\; 2. \end{aligned}$$

Hence (9a) and (9b) are incomparable. Thus also (C2) holds. This proves (7).

In general, (7) cannot be improved, i.e. $<_{\mathcal{S}}$ cannot universally be assumed to be a weak order: Consider for instance a situation where X consists of three balls v, x, y. Assume that every run $S \in \mathcal{S}$ results in

$$S(v) = 1, \;\; S(x) = 2, \;\; S(y) = 3.$$

With respect to the observation set $\mathcal{S}$ we thus get $v \text{ co}_{\mathcal{S}}\ x \text{ co}_{\mathcal{S}}\ y$, but $v <_{\mathcal{S}} y$.

This three-ball-situation also may serve to illustrate that the refined order

$$\prec_{\mathcal{S}} \;:=\; (\text{co}_{\mathcal{S}} \circ <_{\mathcal{S}}) \cup (<_{\mathcal{S}} \circ \text{co}_{\mathcal{S}})$$

is not empirically reliable. We get $v \prec_{\mathcal{S}} x$, even though *not* $(v <_{\mathcal{S}} x)$, and likewise for x and y. Trusting in $\prec_{\mathcal{S}}$, we thus would conclude that x is genuinely smaller than y. But note that the information contained in $\mathcal{S}$ is not sufficient to exclude the possibility of a whole set $\mathcal{S}'$ of experiments, in which $S'(v) = 1$, $S'(x) = 3$ and $S'(y) = 2$ for all $S' \in \mathcal{S}'$. Now, from $\mathcal{S}'$ we could equally well draw the contrary conclusion "y is smaller than x".

To sum up: It turns out that the ordering $<_{\mathcal{S}}$ is the most accurate one reliably derivable from a set $\mathcal{S}$ of experiments. Logical manipulation of the observations does not result in more accurate order statements. More precise order information may only be obtained by repeating the experiments. Still, however, there will remain an insuperable '±1-accuracy-limit'. □

Example 3.17 A related phenomenon arises in technical devices for analogue-to-digital conversion, which convert the physical position of a pointer on a scale into a digital value. Commonly this is done by dividing the scale into segments each representing a discrete value. Since the pointers are of finite width, they will overlap the change in segments, and no matter how carefully it is made, the coder will have erroneous outputs in several positions. To circumvent this difficulty, generally two pointers are used either one displaced slightly from the other. By logically choosing from the outputs available, ambiguity may be eliminated at a slight cost in accuracy. For further details see e.g. [4].

Instead of applying *two* displaced pointers on *one* scale it is clearly conceptually equivalent to consider *one* pointer on *two* displaced scales. This is illustrated in Figure 2, where without loss of generality we use integers as digital values.[10]

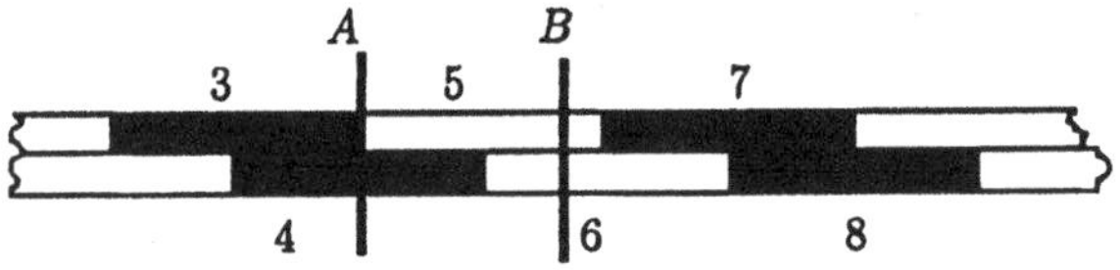

Figure 2 Two displaced scales.

The pointer in position A does not permit the reading of an unambiguous value on the upper scale. However, it is now possible to read off the unambiguous value 4 on the lower scale. In general, for *every* analogue signal x we can choose a definite digital value $D(x)$ on one of the partial scales. (Some positions of the pointer, e.g. B, indicate a definite value on both scales. In such situations *either* reading is valid. We shall return to this later.)

For two analogue values x and y, if $D(x)+1 < D(y)$ we may draw the conclusion that x is definitely smaller than y, whereas digital values $|D(x) - D(y)| \leq 1$ are within the range of measurement uncertainty. The prima facie reading precision induces a partial order on the set of digital values, in which i represents a measurement value definitely smaller than j if and only if $i + 1 < j$, in other words, iff $i \ll j$ in the comparability order $(\mathbf{Z}, \ll)$ from Example 3.5.

As in the previous example, we may use Theorem 3.14 to formally construct a refined weak order. For instance, assume that an input x generates B and is read as $D(x) = 5$. Suppose another input y results in a pointer position B' slightly to the left of B. As long as the two measurements are performed independently of each other it cannot be excluded that B' is interpreted as $D(y) = 6$. If this is the case, it is obviously not advisable to conclude "x smaller than y" from $D(x) < D(y)$. This, however, is precisely what the refined order suggests. We conclude that, as before, mathematical refinement does not reliably increase measurement accuracy. □

In both of the examples above, ambiguity and along with it intransitive indifference arose from the conversion of analogue values to digital data. In general, similar uncertainty phenomena are in fact unavoidable in every context where processes of continuous-to-discrete conversion are involved.

[10]The considerations concerning displaced scales are based on [18].

In measurement this will always be the case. To be more precise, measurement is in practice always concerned with the classification of continuous values into a *finite* number of alternatives. This is for instance emphasized by Scott and Suppes [26, p. 117]:

> No natural scientific situation would seem strictly to require the consideration of sets of infinite data. This state of affairs suggests that theories of measurement containing only finite relational systems would suffice for empirical purposes. The problem is delicate, however, for the measurement of a quantity such as temperature by an automatic recording device is usually treated as continuous both in its own scale and in time. Yet the important problem of measurement does not really lie in the correct use of such recording devices but rather in their initial calibration, a process proceeding from a finite number of qualitative decisions.

They conclude that when infinite models for measurement are preferred, it is often only for reasons of mathematical simplicity due to the "awkwardness of the uniform application of finite relational systems".

As indicated, non-transitivity follows by necessity if finite models are considered. If for mathematical convenience infinite models are preferred,[11] non-transitivity must usually be required explicitly. In the following sections we discuss possible axioms and their practical implications.

4 Coherence and Doublescales

In the preceding section we argued that non-transitivity of indifference is an unavoidable fact in the practice of measurement. We shall now show that this phenomenon, usually seen only as an unfortunate limitation to infinite precision, may have positive implications for the construction and evaluation of measurement instruments.

Suppose we want to construct a system for weight measurement using a beam balance B as a device to determine equality. Then, in addition to B, we need a suitable collection X of known objects as measurement references. In order to exploit the resolution power of B, the set X should provide reference weights to balance any possible measurand.[12]

Now, it is clear that such a set is conceivable only because of non-transitivity, since otherwise it would be impossible to cover the whole measurement range with a *finite* number of references. Observe that, similar to the situation in the ball-sorting example 3.16, the granulation requirement cannot be verified directly as it refers to situations not known in advance. But also here an appropriate testable criterium may be characterized in terms of B and X alone: It is intuitively clear (and will be formally proved below) that X is sufficiently fine grained if it can be traversed in a sequence of 'indistinguishability steps', more precisely, if

$$\forall x, y \in X\, \exists x_1, \ldots, x_n \in X : x \text{ co } x_1 \text{ co} \cdots \text{co } x_n \text{ co } y, \tag{10}$$

where co denotes indistinguishability with respect to B.

[11] In many contexts this supposed convenience appears rather as a Greek gift. For instance, difficulties with the formal semantics of 'floating point' operations in digital computers are not least due to the discrepancy between ideally infinite value sets and finite representation.

[12] It is sufficient that every measurand may be matched by a *combination* of weights in X. This distinction is, however, not essential for the following discussion, since also a combination of weights may again be regarded as one single object.

For reasons of practicability it is desirable that the set of references should not be larger than necessary. One way to approach this, is to require that each 'indistinguishability class', i.e. maximal set of pairwise indistinguishable objects should be represented by as few elements as possible.

In the present section we shall discuss these granularity criteria in the framework of comparability orders, where particular emphasis will be put on the 'coherence'-postulate (10). We take care of the minimality requirement by considering 'narrow' orders – measured in terms of antichain cardinality. As a result we shall derive certain orders of breadth 2 as canonic models for empirical ordinal scales.

Coherent and Combinatoric Posets

Definition 4.1 A poset $(X, <)$ is *coherent* iff it satisfies (10) above,[13] in brief

(C3) $$X^2 = \mathrm{co}^* .$$

To avoid trivial cases we shall always assume $|X| \geq 2$. □

Example 4.2

(i) All the posets $(\mathcal{I}, \lhd)$, $(\mathcal{I}_1, \lhd)$, $(\mathbf{R}, \ll)$ and $(\mathbf{Z}, \ll)$ are easily seen to be coherent.

(ii) No weak order $< \neq \emptyset$ is coherent. □

The next proposition provides a formal proof of the fact that a coherent set of references is sufficiently fine grained, in the sense that any measurand (within a certain range) will be matched by one of the references.

Proposition 4.3 *Suppose $(X, <)$ is a coherent poset. Let c be a new element, and let $(X \cup \{c\}, <_c)$ be an extension of $(X, <)$ – i.e. $<_c\restriction X = <$ – such that c is neither minimal nor maximal in $<_c$. Then there is $z \in X$ such that z co_c c.*

Proof. By assumption there are $x, y \in X$ such that $x <_c c <_c y$. Since $<$ is coherent, x and y are connected by a co-sequence

$$x \ \mathrm{co} \ x_1 \ \mathrm{co} \ \cdots \ \mathrm{co} \ x_n \ \mathrm{co} \ y.$$

We show that c is co_c to one of the x_i. By contradiction, suppose $c \ \overline{\mathrm{co}_c} \ x_i$ for all i, $1 \leq i \leq n$. Then it is clear that $x_1 <_c c$, because from $c <_c x_1$ it follows that $x <_c x_1$, hence $x < x_1$, contradicting the choice of x_1. Extending this argument inductively we successively obtain

$$x_2 <_c c, \quad \ldots \quad , x_n <_c c.$$

But the last inequality $x_n <_c c$ implies $x_n < y$, contrary to x_n co y. ∎

In combination with comparability orders, coherence turns out to be a rather strong concept. We shall show below that every coherent comparability order is finitary in the sense that it is spanned by the relation of direct neighbourhood. This latter property is captured by the following definition:

[13] Note that this requirement corresponds to the axiom (A6) in [20], where the term 'coherent' is used only if any two elements are additionally also connected by a $\overline{\mathrm{co}}$-sequence.

Definition 4.4 A poset $(X, <)$ is called *combinatoric* iff $\lessdot^+ = <$. □

Example 4.5

(i) The poset $(\mathbf{R}, \ll)$ is combinatoric since a real number y is a direct successor of another one x with respect to $\ll$ iff $x + 1 < y \leq x + 2$. The same is a fortiori also true for $(\mathbf{Z}, \ll)$.

(ii) Both $(\mathcal{I}, \lhd)$ and $(\mathcal{I}_1, \lhd)$ are easily seen to be combinatoric.

(iii) Assume $c \notin \mathbf{R}$. Consider the poset $(\mathbf{R} \cup \{c\}, <)$, where the order $<$ on $\mathbf{R}$ is extended trivially such that c is incomparable to every element of $\mathbf{R}$. It is immediately verified that $(\mathbf{R} \cup \{c\}, <)$ is a non-combinatoric coherent interval order. □

Note that in (iii) above, the postulate (C2) is not satisfied. The following proposition shows that this is no coincidence.

Proposition 4.6 *Every coherent* (C2)*-order, hence a fortiori every coherent comparability order, is combinatoric.*

Proof. Let $x < y$, and consider a co-sequence

$$x \text{ co } x_1 \text{ co } \cdots \text{ co } x_n \text{ co } y$$

connecting x and y. As in the proof of Proposition 4.3 it can be verified that for every $z \in X$:

$$x < z < y \Rightarrow \exists i : z \text{ co } x_i. \tag{11}$$

Application of (11) asserts that in a chain of the form

$$x < v_1 < \cdots < v_m < y$$

every v_j is co to one of the x_i. The axiom (C2), however, implies that x_i cannot be co to more than two of the v_j. Hence we obtain the estimate $m \leq 2n$, which in particular yields $x \lessdot^+ y$. ∎

Note 4.7 Closer examination of the proof shows that every coherent (C2)-poset $(X, <)$ is even *bounded discrete* (cf. [5]), i.e. for all $x, y \in X$ there is a constant which uniformly bounds the length of any chain from x to y. □

Remark 4.8 Empirical order structures derived from a finite number of comparisons are obviously combinatoric. The immediate-neighbourhood relation $\lessdot$ must, however, be interpreted with care; in particular it should not be confounded with "just noticeable difference". If y actually happens to be just noticeably larger than x, then clearly $x \lessdot y$ holds in any set of objects containing x and y, but not necessarily vice versa; $x \lessdot y$ only means that within the set *presently under consideration* there is no element that properly fits between x and y. For this reason we prefer *not* to consider $\lessdot$ as a basic notion. We shall return to this question later. □

Doublescales

As mentioned above, for the construction of measurement scales partial order structures with tightly bounded cuts are desirable. Every cut in a coherent order must contain at least two elements (except in the trivial case that the poset itself consists of a single point). We shall demonstrate that coherent orders with the minimal possible breadth 2 are of particular interest both from a theoretical and application point of view.

The following notion of *doublescale* will be central. As we shall show, it essentially comprises all minimal breadth coherent comparability posets.

Definition 4.9 A poset $(X, <)$ is called a *doublescale* iff X can be enumerated in the form $\{x_i\}_I$, where I is an interval of $\mathbf{Z}$, such that

$$x_i < x_j \Leftrightarrow i + 1 < j \quad \text{for all } i, j \in I.$$

To avoid tedious trivial cases we shall always assume that $|I| \geq 2$. The structure of a doublescale is illustrated in Figure 3. □

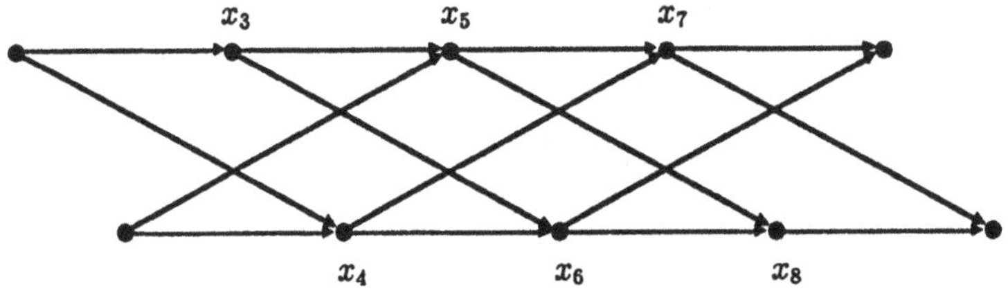

Figure 3 Doublescale. Arrows denote $\lessdot$.

Proposition 4.10 *Every doublescale is a coherent comparability order such that every cut consists of two elements.*

Proof. Note that cuts in a doublescale $(\{x_i\}_I, <)$ are precisely those sets $\{x_i, x_{i+1}\}$ where $i, i+1 \in I$. The postulates (C1), (C2) und (C3) are easily verified. ∎

Example 4.11 The poset $(\mathbf{Z}, \ll)$ is a doublescale. Moreover, $(\mathbf{Z}, \ll)$ structurally embodies all doublescales, because clearly an arbitrary doublescale $(\{x_i\}_I, <)$ is isomorphically mapped onto the substructure $(I, \ll)$ of $(\mathbf{Z}, \ll)$ by $x_i \mapsto i$. In particular, two doublescales may structurally differ from each other only in length. □

Remark 4.12 Recall that in Example 3.17 we showed that the structure $(\mathbf{Z}, \ll)$ arises naturally from considerations of measurement accuracy in analogue-to-digital conversion. Similarly, every ordering of the form $<_S$ in Example 3.16 can be embedded into a doublescale. □

The fact that $(\mathbf{Z}, \ll)$ is a doublescale, is a special case of the following:

Proposition 4.13 *A substructure* $(\{x_i\}_I, \lessdot)$ *of* $(\mathbf{R}, \lessdot)$*, where* I *is an interval in* $\mathbf{Z}$*, is a doublescale iff for all indices in* I*:*

$$x_{i+1} \leq x_i + 1 < x_{i+2}.$$

Proof. By elementary arithmetic. ∎

The next theorem shows that doublescales are canonic representatives of coherent comparability orders of minimal breadth. For this we need a lemma, interesting in its own right:

Lemma 4.14 *If* $(X, <)$ *is a poset, then* $\lessdot \cap \text{co}^* \subseteq \text{co}^3$.

Proof. Assume $x < y$ and $x \text{ co}^* y$. Let $n \in \mathbf{N}$ be the least number such that $x \text{ co}^n y$. Assume $n > 3$. We show that y is not a direct successor of x.

Let

$$x = x_0 \text{ co } x_1 \text{ co } \ldots \text{ co } x_n = y, \quad n > 3,$$

be a co-sequence of minimal length connecting x and y.

By choice of n we have $x_i \overline{\text{co}}\, y$ for all $i \leq n-2$. By induction on i we show:

$$x_i < y \quad \text{for} \quad 1 \leq i \leq n-2: \tag{12}$$

Clearly $x_1 < y$, since $y < x_1$ implies $x < x_1$, contradicting $x \text{ co } x_1$. Now assume $i < n-2$ and $x_i < y$. Using the same argument once more we see that $x_{i+1} > y$ is not possible, from which we may conclude $x_{i+1} < y$.

Dually to (12) we have

$$x < x_i \quad \text{for} \quad 2 \leq i \leq n-1. \tag{13}$$

Now (12) and (13) put together imply $x < x_i < y$ for $2 \leq i \leq n-2$, whence in particular $x \lessdot y$ is not true. ∎

Theorem 4.15 *A poset* $(X, <)$ *is representable as a doublescale iff it is a coherent comparability order in which all cuts have precisely two elements.*

Proof. Because of Proposition 4.10, it remains to prove "$\Leftarrow$". Assume $|X| \geq 3$, since otherwise there is nothing to show. For $x \in X$ we use $\Uparrow x$ as an abbreviation for the set $\{y \in X \mid x < y\}$, and dually $\Downarrow x$ for $\{y \in X \mid y < x\}$.

We start by proving the following claim:

> For every cut $\{x, y\}$ with $\Uparrow x \cup \Uparrow y \neq \emptyset$ there is $z \in X$ such that $x \lessdot z \text{ co } y$ or $y \lessdot z \text{ co } x$. (14)

By symmetry, without loss of generality we assume $\Uparrow x \neq \emptyset$. Since $(X, <)$ according to Proposition 4.6 is combinatoric there is $v \in X$ with $x \lessdot v$. If $v \text{ co } y$, the claim (14) holds for $z := v$. Otherwise we have

$$y < v. \tag{15}$$

Then by Lemma 4.14 there is a co-sequence of one of the following forms:

$$x \text{ co } x_1 \text{ co } v \quad \text{or} \quad x \text{ co } x_1 \text{ co } x_2 \text{ co } v \ \text{ with } \ x < x_2.$$

In the first case we choose $z := x_1$. Using (15) it follows that $z \not\leq y$. Since all cuts in X consist of only two elements, z cannot be co to y. Thus $y < z$, and hence $y \lessdot z$ by (C2). In the second alternative, (C2) implies $x \lessdot x_2$. For $z := x_2$ we again obtain $y \lessdot z$. This proves (14). Note that we can obviously also make use of (14) in the dual form where $\Uparrow$ is replaced by $\Downarrow$ and $\lessdot$ by $\gtrdot$.

Next, we shall inductively define an increasing sequence

$$I_0 \subseteq I_1 \subseteq \cdots \subseteq I_n \subseteq \cdots$$

of finite intervals of $\mathbf{Z}$ such that for every n the following holds:

$$\forall i, j \in I_n \exists x_i, x_j \in X : x_i < x_j \Leftrightarrow i + 1 < j. \tag{16}$$

Let $I_0 := \{-1, 0, 1\}$. Since every cut contains only two elements and $|X| \geq 3$, we can apply (14) to find $x, y, z \in X$ such that $x \lessdot z$ co y. It is readily verified that (16) holds for $i = 0$ with $x_{-1} := x$, $x_0 := y$ and $x_1 := z$.

Now let $n \geq 0$, and assume I_n to be defined such that (16) is satisfied. As an abbreviation we write l for $\max(I_n)$. By induction, $\{x_{l-1}, x_l\}$ is a cut. If (14) is applicable to this cut we choose a corresponding element z, and set $x_{l+1} := z$. By induction hypothesis and (C2), we get $x_{l-1} \lessdot x_{l+1}$ co x_l. With (C1) we obtain $x_{l-2} < x_{l+1}$.

Dually we let k denote $\min(I_n)$. If $\Downarrow x_k \cup \Downarrow x_{k+1} \neq \emptyset$ we choose an element $x_{k-1} \lessdot x_{k+1}$.

The interval I_{n+1} can now be defined by

$$I_{n+1} := \begin{cases} I_n \cup \{k-1, l+1\} & \text{if } x_{k-1} \text{ and } x_{l+1} \text{ are defined} \\ I_n \cup \{k-1\} & \text{if } x_{k-1} \text{ is defined, but not } x_{l+1} \\ I_n \cup \{l+1\} & \text{if } x_{l+1} \text{ is defined, but not } x_{k-1} \\ I_n & \text{otherwise.} \end{cases}$$

To verify that $(X, <)$ is a doublescale it remains to show

$$X \subseteq \{x_i \mid i \in I\}, \quad \text{where } I := \bigcup_n I_n :$$

Suppose the contrary. Then we may choose an element $x \in X \setminus \{x_i \mid i \in I\}$. Since cuts in X consist of two elements, x cannot possibly be co to all x_i. Hence, without loss of generality, we can choose an element x_i such that $x_i < x$. Since X is combinatoric we can even assume that $x_i \lessdot x$ and, moreover, that there is no $j > i$ with $x_j < x$. By definition of the sequence $\{I_n\}$ there exist elements x_{i+1} and x_{i+2}. With x co x_{i+1} co x_{i+2} co x we therefore obtain an antichain with three elements, contradicting the assumption. ∎

The concept of doublescales appears as a natural choice for the characterization of empirical measurement. An attractive property of a reference set with a doublescale structure is that any measurand will be matched by a reference. Moreover, doublescales are the narrowest partial orders where this property can structurally be guaranteed a priori.

A further advantage is that the construction of a 'real-world' (as opposed to mathematical models) doublescale is generally straightforward. Essentially one may proceed as in the proof of Theorem 4.15 above. For example, assume a doublescale $x_1, \ldots, x_n$ of reference weights for a beam balance has been constructed. Then, in particular, x_n is noticeably heavier than x_{n-2} but indistinguishable from x_{n-1}. Any object that is just noticeably heavier than x_{n-1} will then be indistinguishable from x_n, and may serve as reference weight x_{n+1} extending the doublescale.

5 Saturated and K-dense Orders

In the previous section we tried to indicate that proper partial orderings arise naturally in the characterization of measurement accuracy. For actual use in practice, however, references that are only partially ordered are clearly not very convenient. Here it is customary to use *totally* ordered sets. As an approach to meet both conceptual and practical requirements this suggests to construct reference sets in two steps. First a coherent – hence only partially ordered – collection of references is put together. In a second step then a suitable totally ordered subset is extracted. 'Suitable' here means that the subset still contains enough objects to match the whole range of possible measurands. In the present section we shall examine the structural framework for this construction.

Let $(X, <)$, with $X = \{x_i\}_I$, be a reference set with the structure of a doublescale as in Figure 3. Assume we extract the totally ordered $\lessdot$-chain

$$l = \cdots \lessdot x_1 \lessdot x_3 \lessdot x_5 \lessdot x_7 \lessdot \cdots. \tag{17}$$

Then for any pair of immediate neighbours x_i and x_{i+2} in l, there is x_{i+1} in X indistinguishable to both. This x_{i+1} may be interpreted as a "witness" to the fact that there is no 'gap' between x_i and x_{i+2}, into which some additional element could fall.

Unfortunately such a witness is not always available. Consider the sequence

$$l' = \cdots \lessdot x_1 \lessdot x_3 \lessdot x_6 \lessdot x_8 \lessdot \cdots. \tag{18}$$

For l' it cannot a priori be excluded that a measurand might fit in a gap between x_3 and x_6. The reason is that these two references are only bridged by an 'indistinguishability-path' of length 3. This observation reflects the distinction between the relation $\lessdot$ and the notion of 'just noticeable difference' discussed in Remark 4.8.

Because of the above, we shall be particularly interested in sets that are structurally *saturated* with witnesses. Formally this is captured by the following definition:

Definition 5.1 A poset $(X, <)$ is *saturated* iff

$$\forall x, y \in X : x \lessdot y \Rightarrow \exists z : x \text{ co } z \text{ co } y, \quad \text{or equivalently} \quad \lessdot \subseteq \text{co}^2 . \qquad \square$$

Note that every dense order is trivially saturated because the relation of direct neighbourhood is empty. On the other hand, in combinatoric orders saturation is a rather strong requirement, which immediately implies coherence. This is in fact the situation we shall mainly be interested in.

Example 5.2

(i) The posets $(\mathcal{I}, \lhd)$, $(\mathcal{I}_1, \lhd)$ and $(\mathbf{R}, \ll)$ are saturated (and also combinatoric, recall Example 4.5).

(ii) The doublescale $(\mathbf{Z}, \ll)$ is not saturated. Note that although the order $\ll$ is inherited from $(\mathbf{R}, \ll)$, the relations of immediate neighbourhood are different in the two posets. In fact, by Theorem 4.15, *no* coherent comparability order with breadth 2 is saturated. □

The next proposition shows that if a set of measurement references is saturated, then any maximal linearly ordered subset results in a scale that retains the desired granularity (cf. Proposition 4.3 above).

Proposition 5.3 *Suppose $(X, <)$ is a saturated poset. Let c be a new element and let $(X \cup \{c\}, <_c)$ be an extension of $(X, <)$ satisfying* (C2). *Assume*

$$l = \cdots \lessdot x_{i-1} \lessdot x_i \lessdot x_{i+1} \lessdot \cdots$$

is a $\lessdot$-chain in X such that the element c is neither minimal nor maximal in $(l \cup \{c\}, <_c)$. Then there is $x \in l$ such that $x \operatorname{co}_c c$.

Proof. Suppose the contrary. Then there is an index i such that $x_i <_c c <_c x_{i+1}$. Now, by hypothesis X contains a witness y for $x_i \lessdot x_{i+1}$. By definition of $<_c$, therefore also $x_i \operatorname{co}_c y \operatorname{co}_c x_{i+1}$, contradicting (C2). ∎

Proposition 5.3 indicates that saturation is certainly an attractive property. However, it is still formulated in terms of $\lessdot$, which in light of Remark 4.8 is not altogether satisfactory. If we look at the difference between the chains (17) and (18) from a slightly different angle we arrive at a characterization which does not rely explicitly on the notion of direct neighbourhood:

Observe that the chain l is 'dense' within $(X, <)$ in the sense that it meets every indistinguishability-class (to recall: maximal set of pairwise indistinguishable objects). In contrast, the chain l' is not dense since it 'tunnels' through the class $\{x_4, x_5\}$ without intersection. We take this as an indication that the gap between x_3 and x_6 in l' might be too large.

In order to avoid such tunneling phenomena we are interested in coherent sets in which *every* line contains a representative from *every* indistinguishability-class, since then the choice of linear scale becomes uncritical as it can be guaranteed a priori that it will cover the whole range of measurands, without gaps. Formally this is captured by the following definition:

Definition 5.4 Following Petri [17] we shall call a poset *K-dense* iff every line intersects every cut. Since an antichain and a chain cannot possibly have more than one point in common, this is equivalent to the condition that the intersection of *every* line with *every* cut contains *exactly* one element. □

Clearly every *linear* order $(X, <)$ is K-dense since the whole set X itself is the only line and every point constitutes its own cut. Incidentally, every weak order is K-dense. This will follow as an immediate consequence of Proposition 5.11 below.

Both K-density and saturation were introduced as criteria to evaluate measurement references in empirical orders. The following theorem shows that in *coherent* sets, K-density is the stronger property (coherence is of course necessary, the standard order on **Z** is K-dense but not saturated):

Theorem 5.5 *Every K-dense coherent comparability order* $<$ *is saturated.*

Proof. Let $x \lessdot y$. By contradiction, suppose that *not* $(x \text{ co}^2\, y)$. By Lemma 4.14 there is a co-sequence x co v co w co y of length 3 connecting x and y. As in the proof of that lemma, one can easily verify that $x < w$ and $v < y$. Let C be a cut containing v and w, and let l be a line containing x and y. K-density asserts that there exists an element $z \in l \cap C$. Clearly, $x < z < y$, which contradicts $x \lessdot y$. ∎

Note 5.6 Closer examination of the proof shows it to be sufficient that every *local* configuration x co v co w co y with $x < w$ and $v < y$ is K-dense. This local form of K-density is usually called *N-density*, see e.g. [5, 27]. □

The following example shows that the converse of Theorem 5.5 does not hold:

Example 5.7 Figure 4 defines a saturated comparability poset $(X, <)$, which is not K-dense since the line $\{v, w\}$ is disjoint from the cut $\{x, y, z\}$. □

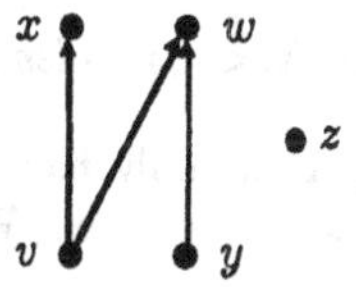

Figure 4 Saturated, not K-dense. Arrows denote $\lessdot$.

The general definition of K-density is formulated in terms of cuts *and* lines. We shall show below that in comparability orders, K-density is equivalently characterized by cut-properties alone.

Notation 5.8 For a poset $(X, <)$ we let $\mathcal{C}(X)$, or simply $\mathcal{C}$ if there is no danger of confusion, denote the set of cuts. □

Definition 5.9 Let $(X, <)$ be a poset. A cut $A \in \mathcal{C}(X)$ is called *free* iff it cannot be covered by any collection of cuts that does not contain A itself; in symbols:

$$A \not\subseteq \bigcup\{B \in \mathcal{C} \mid A \neq B\}.$$

If A is a cut, any element $a \in A$ that does not belong to any other cut will be said to be *private* to that cut. Hence a cut is free iff it contains a private element. □

Example 5.10
(i) In a weak order every cut consists exclusively of private elements and is therefore trivially free.
(ii) In a doublescale no cut is free. □

Proposition 5.11 *Every poset $(X, <)$ containing only free cuts is K-dense.*

Proof. By contraposition, suppose X is *not* K-dense. Then we can choose a cut A and a line l such that $A \cap l = \emptyset$. Let a be an arbitrary element in A. By maximality, l contains a point x such that x co a. Let B be a cut containing both x and a. Since $x \notin A$, clearly $B \neq A$. ∎

Corollary 5.12 *Every weak order is K-dense.*

Proof. See Example 5.10(i) above. ∎

The converse of Proposition 5.11 is not true in general:

Example 5.13 Consider Figure 1(a). Assume the arrows denote direct neighbourhood. The resulting poset $(X, <)$ is K-dense although the cut $\{x, v\}$ is not free. Observe that $<$ is not an interval order. □

In *interval orders* – hence a fortiori in *comparability orders* – also the converse of Proposition 5.11 holds:

Theorem 5.14 *An interval poset $(X, <)$ is K-dense iff all cuts in X are free.*

Proof. Because of Proposition 5.11, we only have to show "$\Rightarrow$". By contraposition, suppose there is a cut $A \in \mathcal{C}$ which is not free. We shall construct a cut and a line disjoint from each other.

Let

$$\mathcal{B} := \{B \in \mathcal{C} \mid B \cap A \neq \emptyset \wedge B \neq A\},$$

and consider a chain $l_0 \subseteq \bigcup \mathcal{B} \setminus A$, which is maximal within this subset, i.e.

$$\forall a \in \bigcup \mathcal{B} \setminus A \; \exists x \in l_0 : x \text{ co } a.$$

Case 1. Assume that every $a \in A$ is co to an element of l_0. Let l be a line in X extending l_0. We show that $A \cap l = \emptyset$. By contradiction, suppose A and l have an element x in common. Then, in particular, x must be comparable to every element of l_0, which, however, by the assumption is not possible.

Case 2. We turn to the case that A contains an element a comparable to all $x \in l_0$. Observe that then $a \notin l_0$. We use a as a pivot element to partition l_0 into

$$l^- = \{x \in l_0 \mid x < a\} \quad \text{and} \quad l^+ = \{x \in l_0 \mid a < x\}.$$

Since A is not free, there is $B \in \mathcal{B}$ with $a \in B$. This will be our desired cut.

Choose an arbitrary element $c \in A \setminus B$. This is possible because, by maximality, a cut cannot be contained in another one. Using maximality again, there is $b \in B$ comparable to c. By symmetry, without loss of generality we may assume $b < c$. Thus, for every $x \in l^-$ we have $x < a$ co $b < c$. Together with (C1) this implies $x < c$. Hence in particular:

$$l_1 := l^- \cup \{c\} \text{ is a chain.} \tag{19}$$

Since $c \notin B$ we have $x < a$ co b for $x \in l^-$, and hence $x \notin B$. Therefore

$$B \cap l_1 = \emptyset. \tag{20}$$

We shall shortly prove that

$$\forall b \in B \, \exists x \in l_1 : x \text{ co } b. \tag{21}$$

Similar to Case 1, we can then use (19), (20) and (21) to show that every line l in X that extends l_1 is disjoint from B.

It thus remains to verify (21). Let $b \in B$. If $b \in A$, then b co $c \in l_1$. Otherwise $b \in B \setminus A$. Dually to the proof of (19), observe that $b < x$ for all $x \in l^+$. By contradiction, suppose b is also comparable to all elements in l^-. By maximality of l_0, then b itself must be an element of l_1. Because of (20), this is absurd, however. We conclude that b is co to an element in l^-, which proves (21) and hence the theorem. ∎

Theorem 5.14 can often conveniently be applied to establish non-K-density. Some examples follow.

Example 5.15 An antichain in $(\mathbf{R}, \ll)$ is a set $A \subseteq \mathbf{R}$ such that $x, y \in A \Rightarrow |x-y| \leq 1$. Cuts are thus precisely all closed intervals of length 1. In particular, no $x \in \mathbf{R}$ belongs exclusively to only one cut. This implies that no cut is free. Hence $(\mathbf{R}, \ll)$ is not K-dense. In fact, it is even 'nowhere' K-dense in the sense that for *every* cut there is a line disjoint from it. □

Example 5.16 A cut in $(\mathcal{I}, \lhd)$ is a class of intervals such that any two overlap, and no interval outside this class overlaps with all of them. For instance, the class A of all intervals containing 0 is a cut, and so is the class B of all intervals (x, y) such that $x \leq 1 < y$.

As in the previous example we show that also in $(\mathcal{I}, \lhd)$ no element of $\mathcal{I}$ belongs to only one cut, which then implies that $(\mathcal{I}, \lhd)$ is nowhere K-dense. To this end let $I \in \mathcal{I}$, and choose $I_1, I_2 \in \mathcal{I}$ such that $I_1 \lhd I_2$ and both of them overlap I. Let C_1 be a cut containing I and I_1, and likewise C_2 a cut containing I and I_2. By choice of I_1 and I_2, clearly $C_1 \neq C_2$. □

Note 5.17 An early investigation of non-K-density of the poset $(\mathcal{I}, \lhd)$ can be found in [17], where for instance implications for the Achilles- and dichotomy-paradoxa of Zeno are discussed. □

To summarize the development in this section: We first established saturation as an intuitive test for measurement accuracy. We then considered the concept of K-density, which in coherent empirical orders implies saturation, but unlike saturation is not formulated in terms of the empirically problematic relation of direct neighbourhood. We showed that in the case of interval orders it is possible to characterize K-density in terms of cuts alone. In the next section we shall make use of this result for the construction of K-dense – hence also saturated – measurement scales.

6 K-Densification and Saturated Ordinal Scales

According to Theorem 5.14, a necessary and sufficient condition for K-density in interval orders is that all cuts have private elements. In this section we shall show that every interval poset can formally be 'densified' through appropriate insertion of new elements. In particular, densification applied to *doublescales* will result in *comparability posets*. We conclude with an assessment of the formal construction for measurement practice.

Densification of Interval Orders

Suppose $(X, <)$ is an interval poset. The idea is to extend this into a poset $(X', <')$ with a distinguished new element a for every cut A in $(X, <)$, such that $A' := A \cup \{a\}$ is a cut in X' and every line in X disjoint from A is contained in a line in X' that meets A' in the point a.

Example 6.1 In Figure 5(a) the cuts are $A = \{v, y\}$, $B = \{x, y\}$ and $C = \{x, w\}$. B is disjoint from the line $l = \{v, w\}$. The picture (b) shows an extended poset, which contains new points a, b, c, corresponding to the respective cuts from X. The extension is K-dense, in particular the line $l \cup \{b\}$ intersects the cut $B \cup \{b\}$. □

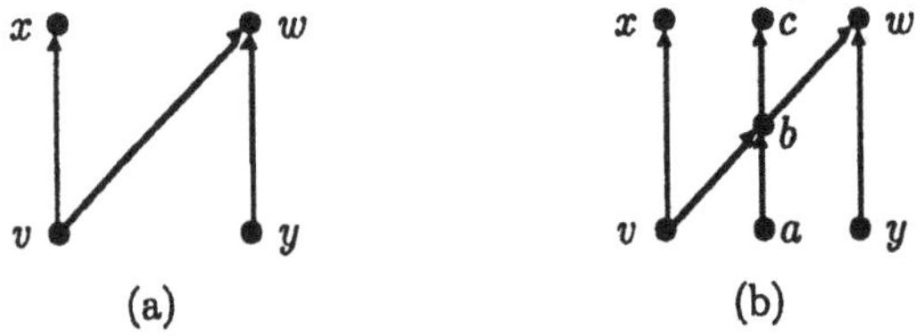

Figure 5 (a) An interval poset. (b) A K-dense extension of (a). Arrows denote $\lessdot$.

In the formal construction of $(X', <')$, for technical simplicity we shall use cuts of X as *elements* in X'. We always assume the sets X and $\mathcal{C}(X)$ to be disjoint. If necessary this is achieved through a suitable renaming of the original elements in X. The order $<'$ will be an immediate extension of $<$ and a canonic ordering $\sqsubset$ of the cut-class $\mathcal{C}(X)$.

Notation 6.2 If $(X,<)$ is a poset, we define a relation $\sqsubset$ on $\mathcal{C}(X)$ by

$$A \sqsubset B :\Leftrightarrow \exists a \in A \exists b \in B : a < b.$$

Without danger of confusion we may use this symbol throughout, since it will always be clear from the context to which basic order it refers. □

Clearly, $\sqsubset$ is irreflexive. As in the following example, $\sqsubset$ is in general not transitive, hence not an order:

Example 6.3 Suppose $(X,<)$ is the poset from Example 5.13. Then $\{v,w\} \sqsubset \{x,y\} \sqsubset \{v,w\}$, but $\{v,w\} \not\sqsubset \{v,w\}$. □

Example 6.4 We continue with Example 5.15. For two cuts A, B in $(\mathbf{R}, \ll)$ we have

$$A \sqsubset B \Leftrightarrow \exists x \in A \exists y \in B : x+1 < y.$$

This can equivalently be expressed by $\min(A) < \min(B)$, which shows that $\sqsubset$ is a linear order. Note that $\ll$ is an interval order, in contrast to the order $<$ in the previous example. □

Proposition 6.5 *For a poset $(X,<)$ the following are equivalent:*

(i) $<$ *is an interval order.*

(ii) $\sqsubset$ *is an order.*

Moreover, if $\sqsubset$ is an order, it is total.

Proof. (i) $\Rightarrow$ (ii). We only have to show transitivity. Assume $A \sqsubset B \sqsubset C$. By definition there are $v \in A$, $x,y \in B$, $w \in C$ such that $v < x$ co $y < w$. Application of (C1) yields $v < w$, hence $A \sqsubset C$.

(ii) $\Rightarrow$ (i). Assume $v < x$ co $y < w$ in X. We can immediately exclude $w < v$. It remains to show that v co w is impossible. Suppose the contrary, and let A be a cut containing v, w. Let B be a cut containing x, y. Then $A \sqsubset B$ as well as $B \sqsubset A$, which contradicts (ii).

Now, for the totality claim let A, B be two distinct cuts. By maximality, we can choose elements $x \in A \setminus B$ and $y \in B \setminus A$. Obviously $x < y$ or $y < x$, hence either $A \sqsubset B$ or $B \sqsubset A$. ∎

Note 6.6 The idea behind the order $\sqsubset$ can be traced to B. Russel [23]. He defines point-like temporal instants in terms of maximal clusters of contemporaneous *events* of non-zero duration (cf. Note 3.3). An instant is considered to precede another one if the first contains an event occurring wholly before an event belonging to the second. □

Example 6.7 Consider the interval poset $(\mathcal{I}, \lhd)$, and let A and B be the two cuts defined in Example 5.16. Then $A \sqsubset B$ since for instance the interval $(-1,1)$ from A precedes $(1,2)$ from B. □

Note 6.8 For an arbitrary poset $(X, <)$ an ordering $\sqsubset'$ of $\mathcal{C}(X)$, often called Egli-Milner ordering, see e.g. [9], can be defined by

$$A \sqsubset' B :\Leftrightarrow \forall x \in A \, \exists y \in B : x < y, \qquad \text{or equivalently} \qquad \forall y \in B \, \exists x \in A : x < y.$$

For interval posets the two orderings coincide, in fact $(X, <)$ is an interval poset if and only if $\sqsubset = \sqsubset'$, see [27]. □

Notation 6.9 If $(X, <)$ is a poset, we put $X_{\mathcal{C}} := X \cup \mathcal{C}(X)$. Let $<_{\mathcal{C}}$ stand for the following extension of $<$ and $\sqsubset$ to a relation on $X_{\mathcal{C}}$:

$$\alpha <_{\mathcal{C}} \beta :\Leftrightarrow \begin{cases} \alpha < \beta & \text{if } \alpha, \beta \in X \\ \alpha \sqsubset \beta & \text{if } \alpha, \beta \in \mathcal{C} \\ \exists x \in \alpha : x < \beta & \text{if } \alpha \in \mathcal{C}, \beta \in X \\ \exists y \in \beta : \alpha < y & \text{if } \alpha \in \mathcal{C}, \beta \in X. \end{cases}$$

The co-relation belonging to $<_{\mathcal{C}}$ will be denoted by $\mathrm{co}_{\mathcal{C}}$. □

For the next three lemmas we fix $(X, <)$ to be an interval order.

Lemma 6.10 *$<_{\mathcal{C}}$ is a partial order on $X_{\mathcal{C}}$.*

Proof. Since $<$ and $\sqsubset$ are partial orders (by assumption and Proposition 6.5, respectively), only the "mixed" expressions have to be considered. We shall show that (a) $x <_{\mathcal{C}} A \Rightarrow A \not<_{\mathcal{C}} x$ and (b) $x <_{\mathcal{C}} A <_{\mathcal{C}} y \Rightarrow x <_{\mathcal{C}} y$, where $x, y \in X, A \in \mathcal{C}$. The other cases can be treated similarly.

(a). If $A <_{\mathcal{C}} x$ and $x <_{\mathcal{C}} A$, there are $a, b \in A$ with $a < x < b$, which is not possible because A is an antichain.

(b). There are $a, b \in A$ such that $x < a$ and $b < y$. Since $<$ is an interval order we obtain $x < y$, hence $x <_{\mathcal{C}} y$. ∎

The following lemma gives a characterization of $\mathrm{co}_{\mathcal{C}}$:

Lemma 6.11

(i) $\mathrm{co}_{\mathcal{C}} \restriction X = \mathrm{co}$.

(ii) $\mathrm{co}_{\mathcal{C}} \restriction \mathcal{C}(X) = \mathrm{id}$.

(iii) *For $x \in X$, $A \in \mathcal{C}(X)$: $x \ \mathrm{co}_{\mathcal{C}} \ A \Leftrightarrow x \in A$.*

Proof. (i). Immediate, since $< \, = \, <_{\mathcal{C}} \restriction X$.

(ii). Immediate, since $\sqsubset$ by Proposition 6.5 is a total order on $\mathcal{C}(X)$.

(iii). We have the following chain of equivalences:

$$\begin{aligned} x \ \mathrm{co}_{\mathcal{C}} \ A &\Leftrightarrow \neg (x <_{\mathcal{C}} A \vee A <_{\mathcal{C}} x) \\ &\Leftrightarrow \neg \exists a \in A : (x < a \vee a < x) \\ &\Leftrightarrow \forall a \in A : \neg (x < a \vee a < x) \\ &\Leftrightarrow \forall a \in A : x \ \mathrm{co} \ a \\ &\Leftrightarrow x \in A. \end{aligned}$$

∎

Observing Lemma 6.11, we may now characterize cuts in $X_{\mathcal{C}}$ as follows:

Lemma 6.12 *Cuts in $(X_C, <_C)$ are precisely all the sets of the form $A \cup \{A\}$ where $A \in \mathcal{C}(X)$.*

Proof. "$\Rightarrow$". First assume $A \subseteq X_C$ to be an arbitrary co_C-set. If $A \subseteq X$, there is a cut $B \in \mathcal{C}(X)$ such that $A \subseteq B$. Then $A \cup \{B\}$ is a co_C-set properly containing A, hence A is not maximal.

Now, let C be a cut in X_C. Then, as just seen, there are an antichain A and a cut B in X, such that $A \cup \{B\} \subseteq C$. By Lemma 6.11(ii), C cannot contain any further element from $\mathcal{C}(X)$. Hence $C = A \cup \{B\}$. Since a co_C B for every $a \in A$, we obtain $A \subseteq B$ with Lemma 6.11(iii). Now $A = B$ follows by maximality of C.

"$\Leftarrow$". By simple verification. ∎

Corollary 6.13 *$\mathcal{C}(X)$ is a line in X_C which, moreover, intersects every cut.*

Proof. Immediate. ∎

We are now ready to show that our extension always yields K-dense orders:

Theorem 6.14 *Suppose $(X, <)$ is an interval order. Let the extension $(X_C, <_C)$ be defined as in* 6.9. *Then $<_C$ is a K-dense order.*

Proof. Because of Lemma 6.10 it remains to prove K-density. Let C be a cut and l a line in X_C, respectively. By Lemma 6.12 there is $A \in \mathcal{C}(X)$ such that $C = A \cup \{A\}$. For non-triviality assume $l \cap A = \emptyset$. We prove that $A \in l$. By maximality of l, it suffices to show that every element of l is comparable to A (interpreted as an *element* of X_C).

Now, let $\alpha \in l$. Assume first that α belongs to X. Then there is $a \in A$ such that $\alpha < a$ or $a < \alpha$. Hence $\alpha <_C A$ or $A <_C \alpha$, as required. Finally, assume α is an element of $\mathcal{C}(X)$. Because $A \in \mathcal{C}(X)$, we have either $\alpha = A$, $\alpha \sqsubset A$ or $A \sqsubset \alpha$, since $\sqsubset$ by Proposition 6.5 is a total order on $\mathcal{C}(X)$. ∎

Our main interest is in coherent comparability orders. The question thus naturally arises whether (C1), (C2) and (C3) are respected by K-densification. The following proposition shows that for (C1) and (C3) this is the case, whereas (C2) requires more attention.

Proposition 6.15 *Suppose $(X, <)$ is an interval poset, and let $(X_C, <_C)$ be as above.*

(i) *Then $(X_C, <_C)$ is also an interval poset.*

(ii) *If $(X, <)$ is coherent, then so is $(X_C, <_C)$.*

(iii) *If $(X, <)$ is a comparability poset such that every cut has at most two elements, then $(X_C, <_C)$ is also a comparability poset.*

Proof. (i). By simple verification of the different cases. For instance, assume $x, y \in X$ and $A, B \in \mathcal{C}(X)$ with $x <_C A \text{ co}_C\ y <_C B$. We have to show $x <_C B$. By definition of $<_C$ there are $a \in A$, $b \in B$ such that

$$x < a \quad \text{and} \quad y < b. \tag{22}$$

Moreover, $y \in A$ because of Lemma 6.11(iii), and thus

$$a \text{ co } y. \tag{23}$$

Using (C1) we obtain $x < b$ from (22) and (23). Now $x <_C B$ follows by choice of b and definition of $<_C$.

(ii). Use Lemma 6.11 to check the different cases.

(iii). Because of the preceding we only have to verify that (C2) holds in $(X_C, <_C)$. Suppose to the contrary that there are $\alpha, \beta, \gamma, \delta \in X_C$ such that $\alpha <_C \beta <_C \gamma$ and $\alpha \text{ co}_C\ \delta \text{ co}_C\ \beta$. By definition of $(X_C, <_C)$ we can choose points a, b_1, b_2, c, d in X such that $a < b_1 \text{ co } b_2 < c$ and $a \text{ co } d \text{ co } c$. Since (C2) holds in X it follows that $b_1 \neq b_2$. Moreover, d is co to – and obviously also distinct from – both b_1 and b_2. Hence we obtain an antichain with 3 elements, contrary to assumption. ∎

The following example shows that the restriction to cuts of breadth 2 in (iii) above is necessary:

Example 6.16 Consider the comparability poset $(X, <)$ defined by Figure 4 in Example 5.7. Let $A := \{x, y, z\}$. Clearly $v <_C A <_C w$. But also $v \text{ co}_C\ z \text{ co}_C\ w$. Hence (C2) does not hold in $(X_C, <_C)$. □

Remark 6.17 As mentioned, the particular choice of *cuts* as additional elements in X_C was merely for technical simplicity. From now on we shall often discard the distinction between the two types of points within X_C. □

Note 6.18 According to Proposition 6.15(i), the extension $(X_C, <_C)$ of an interval poset $(X, <)$ is again an interval poset. It is therefore possible to iterate the construction. This does not result in any new interesting structure, however; the only difference between $(X_C, <_C)$ and the 'level 2'-extension $(X_{CC}, <_{CC})$ is that X_{CC} contains one more private point for every cut from X; in other words, only the breadth of the cuts in $(X_C, <_C)$ are increased by 1. □

Minimal Saturated Measurement Scales

From the general discussion we now return to the particular case of *doublescales*. We first establish a representation theorem similar to Theorem 4.15, which says that extension of doublescales by K-densification yields precisely all K-dense comparability orders with the minimal possible breadth 3. We then discuss possible interpretations of such extended doublescales in the context of measurement applications.

Theorem 6.19

(i) *The extension* $(X_C, <_C)$ *of a doublescale* $(X, <)$ *is a*

(a) *K-dense coherent comparability poset such that*

(b) *every cut consists of precisely three elements.*

(ii) *Conversely, every poset* $(X', <')$ *satisfying* (a) *and* (b) *is isomorphic to the extension* $(X_C, <_C)$ *of a doublescale* $(X, <)$.

Proof. (i). (C1), (C2) and (C3) follow from Proposition 6.15. By construction it is immediate that every cut in X_C consists of three elements.

(ii). Since $(X', <')$ is a K-dense interval order, Theorem 5.14 asserts that every cut contains a private element. Let Y denote the collection of these. Consider the restriction $<$ of $<'$ to $X := X' \setminus Y$. It is immediately verified that $(X, <)$ is a comparability poset, which moreover is coherent, since the private elements in Y by definition do not contribute to the coherence of X'. Clearly all cuts in X have precisely two elements. Hence $(X, <)$ is a doublescale by Theorem 4.15. Let $f: X' \to X_C$ be the following mapping: if $x \in X$ then $f(x) := x$, and if $y \in Y$ then $f(y) := C \setminus \{y\}$, where C is the unique cut in X' containing y. It is immediately verified that f induces an isomorphism between $(X', <')$ and $(X_C, <_C)$. ∎

Definition 6.20 Because of Theorem 6.19, the term *extended doublescale* will be used for any K-dense coherent comparability poset in which every cut consists of precisely three elements. The general structure of an extended doublescale is illustrated in Figure 6. □

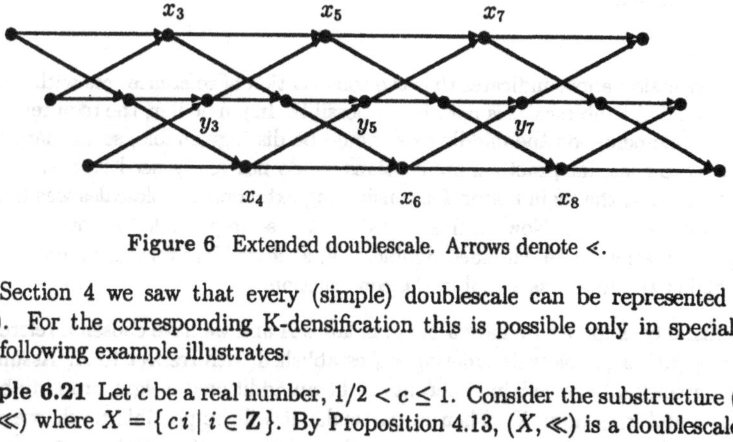

Figure 6 Extended doublescale. Arrows denote $<$.

In Section 4 we saw that every (simple) doublescale can be represented within $(\mathbf{R}, \ll)$. For the corresponding K-densification this is possible only in special cases, as the following example illustrates.

Example 6.21 Let c be a real number, $1/2 < c \leq 1$. Consider the substructure $(X, \ll)$ of $(\mathbf{R}, \ll)$ where $X = \{ci \mid i \in \mathbf{Z}\}$. By Proposition 4.13, $(X, \ll)$ is a doublescale.

(i) Suppose $c = 1$. Then $X = \mathbf{Z}$. The doublescale $(\mathbf{Z}, \ll)$ is expandable to an extended doublescale $(X \cup Y, \ll)$ within $\mathbf{R}$: Let $g: \mathbf{Z} \to (0, 1) \subseteq \mathbf{R}$ be strictly increasing. For $i \in \mathbf{Z}$ set $y_i := i + g(i)$. Then $Y = \{y_i \in \mathbf{R} \mid i \in \mathbf{Z}\}$ is as required.

(ii) Suppose $1/2 < c < 1$. Then it is not possible to choose any such set Y within $\mathbf{R}$, since the distance between the y_i would have to grow faster than the distance between the x_i. □

In Section 4 we also remarked that the construction of 'real' doublescales for practical applications is straightforward. Example 6.21 suggests that this might no longer hold for the additional elements in an extended doublescale. The following example confirms this view.

Example 6.22 Consider the analogue-to-digital converter from Example 3.17. Recall that the division of the scale into discrete segments *in general* only permits to classify analogue inputs with the accuracy of the doublescale $(\mathbf{Z}, \ll)$, cf. Remark 4.12. However, in many particular cases an unambiguous "double precision" reading on *both* partial scales is possible. For instance, the analogue input x corresponding to the pointer position B in Figure 2 may be recorded as a discrete value "$D(x) = 5\&6$". This suggests that the accuracy of the converter may be increased significantly if all such $i\&(i+1)$ are included in the value set. For example, suppose $D(x) = 3\&4$ and $D(y) = 4\&5$. Then x is definitely smaller than y, and similarly if $D(x) = 3\&4$ and $D(y) = 5$, etc. Thus it might seem as if the converter could be used for classifications with the resolution power of an *extended* doublescale as in Figure 6 (with nodes $x_i := i$ and $y_i := i\&(i+1)$).

This is not possible, however, since the inherent uncertainty due to finite pointer width – which led us to consider displaced scales in the first place – remains. Just as the transition between segments 3 and 5 is fuzzy, it is not possible to localize definite borders between "3&4", "only 4 but neither 3 nor 5" and "4&5" (cf. pointer position A in Figure 2). Order statements are only reliable if they respect a certain 'safety distance', whose bounds, in turn, also cannot be fixed with exactitude, cf. the remarks after Example 3.15.[14] □

The discussion above indicates that the construction of reference sets with the structure of extended doublescales is not always possible. In particular, the requirement that any two 'Y-elements' on the middle axis should be distinguishable, seems hard to realize. But note that, for practical applications we do not really need it in such a strict form. Recall that the main reason for considering extended doublescales was the desire to guarantee saturation. Now, in this respect it *does* seem possible to provide a satisfactory approximation to an extended doublescale, at least if we may use a second device with a higher resolution as a tool in the construction.

For instance, suppose we have a beam balance A and we have chosen a reference set $X = \{x_i\}_I$ with a doublescale ordering $<_A$ established with respect to A. Assume B is a higher precision balance which permits to fit an additional weight properly between every x_{i-1} and x_{i+2} from X. Then in particular it will be possible to choose weights y_i such that always $x_{i-1} <_B y_i <_B x_{i+2}$ and $x_i \lesssim_B y_i \lesssim_B x_{i+1}$, where $<_B$ stands for "noticeably lighter than (*with respect to* B)", and similarly $\lesssim_B$ is short for "noticeably lighter than *or* indistinguishable". We may then expect that the collection of all weights $\{x_i\}_I \cup \{y_i\}_I$ will form a saturated scale for the balance A.

---

[14] A similar reasoning might be applied in the *stadium-argument* of Zeno, which investigates infinite subdivisibility of time by iterative displacement of a given discrete timescale, cf. [30, p. 190ff].

7 Concluding Remarks

Measurement is often considered synonymous to assignment of numerical values, since in technical applications quantitative aspects are generally in the centre of interest. On the other hand, in dealing with matters that are essentially comparative in nature, such as economical utility theory or decision theory,[15] the use of numbers is often rather artificial and tends to obscure the underlying structure. Here attention is naturally attracted to qualitative and comparative models that permit to " 'measure' without acting quantitatively" [8][16]. The discussion of qualitative orderings conversely may also contribute to a comprehensive foundation of quantitative models. For instance, in the discussion of timing issues in distributed computer systems, there is a growing trend to regard causal order between events as an indispensable structural basis for reliable numerical evaluations.

In the approach presented in this paper we tried to avoid a-priori hypotheses altogether, admitting only observable properties of empirical comparisons and orderings. We indicated that empirical comparison permits to establish *equality* only in form of *intransitive* similarity relations. This motivated the introduction of certain proper partial order structures where non-transitivity is formulated as a basic axiom; specifically *coherent posets* and *doublescales*.

Measurement involves continuous phenomena. It is often assumed without question that continuous order may be identified with the continuum of real numbers. However, it should be noted that this assumption cannot be derived from actual experience.[17] Moreover, as indicated in Section 3, measurement processes are in practice invariably concerned with discrete classification.[18] This suggests to consider discrete mathematical domains as possible alternatives to the real numbers in the development of empirically based measurement models. A central problem to be solved in this approach is clearly the representation of continuity-phenomena. In this respect, the notion of K-density investigated in Sections 5 and 6 can be seen as an attempt to formulate the essential idea of density in a form consistent with discrete partial orders. For a further discussion we refer to [21, 27] where, moreover, also discrete forms of Dedekind-completeness are investigated.

Acknowledgements

I want to express my gratitude to C. A. Petri for all the discussions and all the inspirations throughout the years without which this paper would not have been written.

[15] For a detailed discussion of comparative vs. quantitative concepts we refer to [6], cf. also [13].

[16] Translation by the author.

[17] Again it was in the modelling of time that the adequacy of real numbers was first put in doubt, namely in the discussion whether the sensation of duration may be described by an ensemble of extensionless points. We refer to [30].

[18] It is a well known curiosity that infinite precision measurement would allow to represent the contents of a whole library by a single mark on, say, a rod of metal. The texts are coded into a Gödel-number n. This is then recorded by a mark dividing the rod in the ratio $1 : n$. Through precise measurement the number n may be regained and decoded.

References

[1] U. ABRAHAM, S. BEN-DAVID, M. MADIGOR: *On Global-Time and Inter-Process Communication.* Workshops in Computing: Semantics for Concurrency, Leicester 1990. M. Z. Kwiatkowska, M. W. Shields, R. M. Thomas (eds.). Berlin: Springer (1990), 311–323.

[2] V. S. ALAGAR, G. RAMANATHAN: *Functional Specification and Proof of Correctness for Time Dependent Behaviour of Reactive Systems.* Formal Aspects of Computing **3** (1991), 253–283.

[3] W. E. ARMSTRONG: *A note on the Theory of Consumer's Behaviour.* Oxford Economical Papers **2** (1950), 119–122.

[4] T. C. BARTEE: *Digital Computer Fundamentals.* (6th ed.). New York: McGraw-Hill (1985).

[5] E. BEST, C. FERNÁNDEZ C.: *Nonsequential Processes. A Petri Net View.* EATCS Series "Monographs in Theoretical Computer Science" **13**. Berlin: Springer (1988).

[6] R. CARNAP: *Logical Foundations of Probability.* (2nd ed.). Chicago: University Press (1962).

[7] R. CARNAP: *Philosophical Foundations of Physics.* New York: Basic Books (1966).

[8] K. EGLE: *Graphen und Präordnungen.* Mannheim: Bibliographisches Institut (1977).

[9] C. FERNÁNDEZ, P. S. THIAGARAJAN: *A Lattice Theoretic View of K-Density.* Lecture Notes in Computer Science **188**, Berlin: Springer (1985), 139–153.

[10] F. FISHBURN: *Interval Orders and Interval Graphs.* New York: John Wiley & Sons (1985).

[11] H. V. HELMHOLTZ: *Zählen und Messen, erkenntnistheoretisch betrachtet,* in: Philosophische Aufsätze Eduard Zeller gewidmet. Leipzig (1887).

[12] M. JOSEPH, A. GOSWAMI: *Relating Computation and Time.* Univ. Warwick: Research Report 138, Dep. Comp. Scie. (1989).

[13] J. M. KEYNES: *A Treatise on Probability* (2nd ed.). New York: Mac Millan (1929).

[14] D. LAUGWITZ: *Zahlen und Kontinuum.* Mannheim: Bibliographisches Institut (1986).

[15] R. D. LUCE: *Semiorders and a Theory of Utility Discrimination.* Econometrica **24** (1956), 178–191.

[16] J. V. NEUMANN, O. MORGENSTERN: *Theory of Games and Economic Behavior.* Princeton: University Press (1944).

[17] C. A. PETRI: *Non-Sequential Processes.* St. Augustin: Internal Report of the GMD-ISF 77-5 (1977).

[18] C. A. PETRI: *Modelling as a Communication Discipline.* Unpublished manuscript; abstract in: H. Beilner, E. Gelenbe (eds.): Measuring, Modelling and Evaluating Computer Systems. Amsterdam: North Holland (1977), 435.

[19] C. A. PETRI: *Concurrency.* LNCS **84** (1980), 251–260.

[20] C. A. PETRI: *Concurrency Theory.* LNCS **254** (1987), 4–24.

[21] C. A. PETRI, E. SMITH: *Concurrency and Continuity.* LNCS **266** (1987), 273–292.

[22] J. PFANZAGL: *Theory of Measurement.* Würzburg: Physica-Verlag (1971).

[23] B. RUSSELL: *Our Knowledge of the External World,* Lecture IV. London: Allen and Unwin (1914).

[24] B. RUSSELL: *On Order in Time.* Proc. Cambridge Philosophical Society **32** (1936), 216–228.

[25] D. SCOTT: *Measurement Structures and Linear Inequalities.* Journal of Mathematical Psychology **1** (1964), 233–247.

[26] D. SCOTT, P. SUPPES: *Foundational Aspects of Theories of Measurement.* Journal of Symbolic Logic **23** (1958), 113–128.

[27] E. SMITH: *Zur Bedeutung der Concurrency-Theorie für den Aufbau hochverteilter Systeme.* Bericht der GMD 180. München: Oldenbourg (1989).

[28] A. G. WALKER: *Durée et Instants.* Revue Scientifique **85** (1947), 131–134.

[29] A. G. WALKER: *Foundations of Relativity: Parts I and II.* Proc. Roy. Soc. Edinburgh **62** (1948), 319–35.

[30] G. J. WHITROW: *The Natural Philosophy of Time* (2nd ed.). Oxford: Clarendon (1980).

[31] N. WIENER: *A Contribution to the Theory of Relative Position.* Proc. Cambridge Phil. Soc. **17** (1914), 441–449.

[32] N. WIENER: *A New Theory of Measurement: A Study in the Logics of Mathematics.* Proc. London Math. Soc. **19** (1921), 181–205.

Deterministic Systems of Sequential Processes : a class of structured Petri nets [1]

Younes SOUISSI
Institut National des Télécommunications
9 rue Charles Fourrier. 91011 Evry cedex. FRANCE
e-mail : souissi@vaxu.int-evry.fr

Abstract : In this paper, we define deterministic systems of sequential processes (DSSP), a class of Petri nets which generalizes the one introduced by Wolfgang Reisig in 1979. In studying this class of Petri nets, we have two aims. Our first aim is to give efficient and formal methods for the validation of a class of systems of sequential processes cooperating by message passing and resource sharing. Our second aim is to show that the modular structure of DSSPs allows us to fully use compositions of nets in the specification and the validation steps of the parallel applications that we describe through DSSPs. Indeed, we give several rules for building, in a bottom-up and modular way, a live DSSP. We also give for DSSPs an inexpensive method of liveness validation. Finally, we show that the liveness of a DSSP is monotonic, and that the minimal resources configurations ensuring the liveness are computable. This work is a contribution to the approach which involves developing classes of structured nets in order to specify and validate systems in a modular way via compositions and refinements.

Keywords : Deterministic system of sequential processes, liveness, boundedness, monotonicity, modularity, composition, properties preservation.

CONTENTS

---

[1] Part of this work has been done within the context of the DEMON project (ESPRIT II n° 3148)

1. INTRODUCTION

Many simple and less simple classes of Petri nets have been defined [Hack 73], [Commoner 72], [Lien 76], [Lautenbach 79], [Reisig 79], [Memmi 83] in order to find some structures, behaviours and methods which would allow the validation of more complex classes of Petri nets. This method has had limited success because it seems to be too difficult to go from these simple classes to more complex ones.

There is however a method which is favoured by a large number of researchers in Petri nets theory (Esprit project n° 3148). This method is based on the following two points. The first point consists in developing some classes of structured nets for which validation of properties can be mastered, and in developing rules for combining the nets of these classes (compositions, refinements and abstractions), while preserving certain properties. This is done in order to specify and to validate systems in modularly. The second point consists in developing equivalences for comparing the nets of these classes in order to go from one specification to another, ensuring that they describe the same system.

Among all the classes defined in the literature, we see two classes which could bear the label of structuration. The first one is the set of state machines decomposable nets [Hack 73]. The problem with this class is that it reflects a total synchronization between tasks. The second one is the set of deterministic buffer synchronization of sequential processes (DBSSP) [Reisig 79]. This class is defined as a set of cooperating sequential components, where the cooperation is ensured by an asynchronous communication via a set of buffers. Three papers have been written about this class of nets [Reisig 79], [Reisig 82], [Berthelot...83]. Two sufficient conditions and one necessary condition for liveness are given in these papers. One sufficient condition for liveness was based on Commoner's property [Commoner 72] and the other was based on a similar result for the marked directed graphs of [Commoner 72]. A first decomposition of DBSSP was proposed in [Berthelot...83].

In this paper, a more general class is presented, namely Deterministic Systems of Sequential Processes (DSSP). The generalization comes from an extension of the notion of a sequential process [Reisig 79] (see definition 3.1). A sequential process is a Petri net which is made up of by two parts. The first being a state machine which represents the internal structure of the process, the second being a set of buffers connected to the state machine and representing the interface with the environment of the process.

Since the methods used by Reisig are not applicable for our extended class of nets, the first question which naturally follows this extensions is : are we able to preserve the results obtained in Reisig's class? The answer is yes and the principal result is given in theorem 4.26.

Our main aim in this paper is to show how to use all the modularity possibilities involved in this class of nets, and how to consider it as a part of a more complex model. Indeed we present three rules for constructing a DSSP in a modular way. First, we show that a DSSP can be built starting from a simple class of nets. Then we show that a large part of the analysis methods for DSSPs is a direct extension of the methods that we develop for this simple class of nets. A second way to build a DSSP is by connecting them via buffers in such way as to construct a circuitless graph of DSSPs and buffers. Finally, the third rule is the step by step construction of a DSSP by adding buffers between the sequential processes.
For all these rules of construction we ensure the liveness preservation.

In addition to these modularity results, we recall that the liveness is monotonic for a class of marked DSSPs [Souissi...88]. We also show that the liveness of a DSSP can be validated via the search of a sink vertex (a vertex without successor) in any coverability graph of the DSSP (see definition 2.2 and [Brams...83] for a precise construction of a coverability graph). This result gives us a way to validate liveness in a much cheaper way than in the general case [Kosaraju 82], [Mayr 84], [Lambert 86].

Finally, we show that the composition via a sequential process [Souissi...89], [Souissi 90] can be applied in order to compose a DSSP with another net.

We suggest two conjectures, the resolution of which would probably permit to go one step further by generalizing the methods presented in this article to more general classes of nets.

2. BASIC DEFINITIONS AND NOTATIONS OF PETRI NETS

In this section we recall the definition of a Petri net and definitions of liveness and boundedness, two main properties which contribute to the validation of a system through its model in Petri nets. We introduce some notations which allow us to easily manipulate the notions that we often use in this paper.

Definition 2.1: A *Petri net* (or *net* for short) is a triplet N=<P,T,W> where P and T are two finite sets such that $P \cap T = \emptyset$ and $W : (P \times T) \cup (T \times P) \rightarrow \mathbf{N}$ (**N** is the set of natural numbers). P is the set of places, T the set of transitions and W the flow function of N.

For X included in $P \cup T$:
we note $|X|$ the number of elements of X and we define $\Gamma^-(X)=\{y \in P \cup T \,/\, \exists x \in X, W(y,x)>0\}$, $\Gamma^+(X)=\{y \in P \cup T \,/\, \exists x \in X, W(x,y)>0\}$ and $\Gamma(X)=\Gamma^-(X) \cup \Gamma^+(X)$.
Let N=<P,T,W> be a net. We say that N' is the subnet of N generated by (P',T'), where P' is a subset of P and T' a subset of T, if and only if N'=<P',T',W'> is the net such that for every $(x,y) \in (P' \times T') \cup (T' \times P')$, $W'(x,y)=W(x,y)$.

Let N=<P,T,W> be a net and let M be a marking of N (M is a function of $P \rightarrow \mathbf{N}$). Using the usual definitions of an enabled sequence (or a firing sequence) $\sigma \in T^*$ at M (noted $M(\sigma>$) and occurrence of σ changing M into a new marking M' (noted $M(\sigma> M'$), we recall that $L(N,M)=\{\sigma \in T^* : M(\sigma>\}$ is the free language of (N,M) and that $[N,M>=\{M' : \exists \sigma \in T^*, M(\sigma> M'\}$ is the reachability set of (N,M) (i.e. the set of reachable markings of (N,M)). For $\sigma \in T^*$ and $t \in T$ we note : $|\sigma|$ the length of σ (the number of transitions in σ), $|\sigma|_t$ the number of occurrences of the transition t in σ and $im(\sigma)=\{t \in T / |\sigma|_t > 0\}$. $\underline{\sigma}$ is the vector of $\mathbf{N}^{|T|}$ representing σ (the Parikh mapping of σ). This means that the coordinate $\underline{\sigma}[t]$ (representing t) of $\underline{\sigma}$ is defined by $\underline{\sigma}[t]=|\sigma|_t$.

Definition 2.2 : Let (N,M)=(<P,T,W>,M) be a marked net. A transition *t of T is quasi-live* at M iff : $\exists M' \in [N,M>$ such that $t \in L(N,M')$. *(N,M) is quasi-live* (or also that M is quasi-live) iff every transition of T is quasi-live at M. A transition *t of T is live* iff $\forall M' \in [N,M>$ t is quasi-live at M'. *(N,M) is live* (or also that M is live) iff every transition of T is live. *(N,M) is bounded* iff : $\exists n \in \mathbf{N}$ such that $\forall M' \in [N,M>, \forall p \in P, M'(p) \leq n$. If (N,M) is unbounded, the reachability set of (N,M) is infinite. Nevertheless, with the price of losing some information a coverability tree, named a reduced reachability tree in [Peterson 81], can be constructed. A coverability graph can be obtained from the coverability tree by merging the nodes having the same label.

3. DETERMINISTIC SYSTEMS OF SEQUENTIAL PROCESSES

Deterministic systems of sequential processes is a class of Petri nets that has been introduced in [Souissi...88]. Actually, it is a generalization of Reisig's DBSSP [Reisig 79]. Here we directly give our definition of a sequential process, a definition from which this generalization arises. From the semantic point of view, a DSSP can be seen as modeling a system of cooperating sequential components. This structuration into sequential components is directly given by definitions 3.1 and 3.2 which describe this class (see figure 3.3). The cooperation is made by an asynchronous communication (by message passing) through a set of buffers.

3.1. DEFINITIONS

Definition 3.1 : A net $R=< (P \cup K),T,W >$ is a *sequential process* (SP) if and only if :

i) $P \cap K=\emptyset$, P is the set of internal states, K is the set of buffers

ii) The subnet generated by (P,T) is a state machine (i.e. $\forall t\in T$, $|\Gamma^+(t)\cap P| = |\Gamma^-(t)\cap P| =1$).

iii) $\forall$ p $\in$ P if $|\Gamma^+(p)| > 1$ then $\forall$ t,t'$\in \Gamma^+(p)$,$\forall q\in K$, $W(q,t)=W(q,t')$.

$C=p_0t_0...p_{n-1}t_{n-1}$ is an *elementary circuit* of R iff :

for $0\leq i\leq n-1$, $t_i\in\Gamma^+(p_i)$, $p_{i+1}\in\Gamma^+(t_i)$ and $p_0\in\Gamma^+(t_{n-1})$ ($\{p_0,\ldots,p_{n-1}\}$ and $\{t_0,\ldots,t_{n-1}\}$ are subsets of P and T respectively).

This definition of a sequential process is a generalization of Reisig's. A first generalization is based on the free choice notion [Commoner 72], [Hack 72]. Indeed this extension is similar to the one which consists in going from free choice nets [Hack 72] to extended free choice nets [Commoner 72]. The second generalization is the extension of the flow function of the sequential process from the set {0,1} to N (the natural numbers) for the connection of the buffers to the transitions (structure of the state machine generated by (P,T) is not changed). It is clear that the values associated with the arrows, given by the flow function, are important with regard to the analysis of a net. Indeed, almost all results on the liveness of a net are constrained by a hypothesis governing these values (see the analysis of Petri nets classes in [Memmi 83], [Barkaoui 89]). In section 4, we present a new approach for liveness analysis of DSSPs.

Let us now introduce deterministic systems of sequential processes as a class of nets constructed by making the SPs share, in a certain manner, their buffers.

Definition 3.2 : Let $R=\{ R_i = < P_i\cup K_i , T_i , W_i > , i=1,\ldots,s \; s\in N\}$ be a set of sequential processes. $S=<P\cup K,T,W>$ is the *deterministic system of sequential processes* (DSSP) associated with R (see figure 3.3) if and only if :

i) $P= \cup P_i$; $K= \cup K_i$; $T= \cup T_i$; $\forall i\in [1\ldots s]$, $\forall x\in P_i\cup K_i$,$\forall t\in T_i$, $W(x,t) = W_i (x,t)$ and $W(t,x)=W_i (t,x)$ and for all the other pairs $(x,t)\in (P\cup K,T)$: $W(x,t)=W(t,x)=0$

ii) Two distinct processes of S can only have buffers in common

i.e $\forall R_i,R_j \in R \;\; i\neq j \Rightarrow (P_i \cup T_i \cup K_i) \cap (P_j \cup T_j \cup K_j) = K_i \cap K_j$

iii) A buffer can support the communication of, at the most, two sequential processes R_i and R_j

i.e $\forall k\in K, \exists! \, i : T_i \supset \Gamma^-(k)$; $\exists! \; j : T_j \supset \Gamma^+(k)$

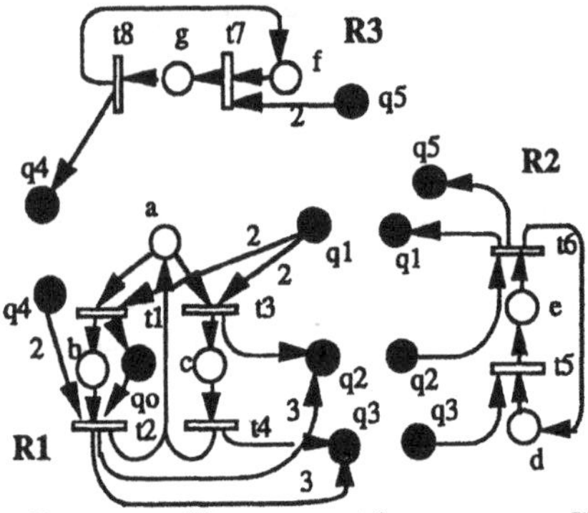

Figure 3.3 a : Three sequential processes

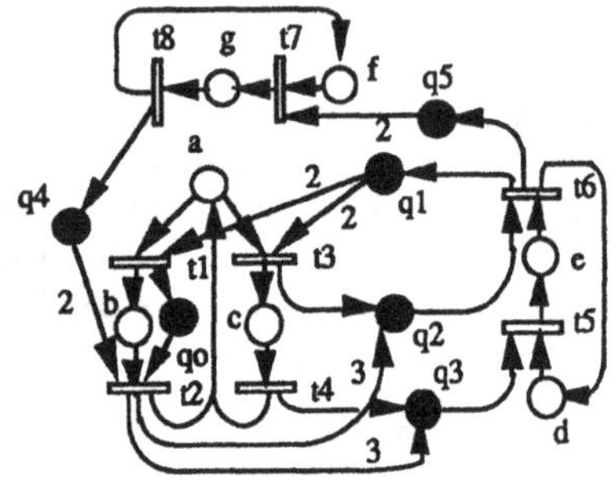

Figure 3.3 b : DSSP S_1 associated with the SPs

In figure 3.3 a : a,b,...,g , t1, t2,..., t8 and q1,q2,...,q5 are the internal states, the transitions and the buffers of the SPs respectively.

Remarks : If some place of a net N has no input transition, then N can not be live regardless of the initial markings. If some place has no output transition its removal has no effect on the liveness of the net (the only effect can be on the boundedness of the net). From this point on, we assume that every place (buffer or internal state) of a DSSP has at least one input and one output transition. This hypothesis makes the state machine associated with a sequential process be strongly connected.

The cooperation of the SPs from which a DSSP is constructed can be seen as a sharing of resources and an asynchronous communication (via the buffers). It seems clear that the number of tokens SPs can put into and remove from the buffers is very important with regard to liveness. We state definitions of the quantities that reflect the cooperation of the SPs (definitions 3.4 and 3.5).

Definition 3.4 : Let R=<P∪K,T,W> be a sequential process. Let τ be a subset of T and let q be a buffer of R ($q \in K$), then we define: $in(\tau,q)=\Sigma_{t\in\tau}W(q,t)$ and $out(\tau,q)=\Sigma_{t\in\tau}W(t,q)$
Let q_1 be an *input buffer* of R (i.e. ($in(T,q_1)>0$) and q_2 be an *output buffer* of R (i.e. ($out(T,q_2)>0$), then $mcc(q_2,q_1) = \min_Y\{\ out(Y,q_2)/in(Y,q_1)$, Y is the set of transitions of an elementary circuit of R$\}$ is the minimal characteristic (q_2,q_1) constant of R (mcc). A buffer which is an input as well as an output buffer of an SP is called an *internal buffer*.

Using this definition of an mcc we can state definitions of a ring and a small ring which are the direct extensions of [Reisig 79] and which allow us to define well-structured DSSPs (see definition 3.5).

Definition 3.5 : Let S be the DSSP associated with a set R of sequential processes. The string $Z=q_0R_0q_1R_1\ldots q_{n-1}R_{n-1}$ is a *ring* of S if and only if :
$\forall R_i, R_j$, i,j=0,...,n-1 two processes of R : $i\neq j \Rightarrow R_i \neq R_j$,
$\forall$ i=0,...,n-1, $q_i \in \Gamma^-(T_{Ri})$ and $q_{i+1} \in \Gamma^+(T_{Ri})$ (+ is modulo n).
If $\alpha(Z) = \Pi_{i=0,\ldots,n-1}mcc(q_{i+1},q_i) < 1$ then this ring is called a *small ring*.
S is said to be *well-structured* if and only if it does not contain a small ring.

As an illustration of definitions 3.4 and 3.5, let us consider the SPs and DSSP of figure 3.3. In R_1, for $\tau_1=\{t_1,t_2\}$: $in(\tau_1,q_1)=2$, $out(\tau_1,q_2)=3$ and for $\tau_2=\{t_3,t_4\}$: $in(\tau_2,q_1)=2$, $out(\tau_2,q_2)=1$. Since τ_1 and τ_2 are the set of transitions of the two elementary circuits of R_1, we have $mcc(q_2,q_1)=Min\{1/2,3/2\}=1/2$. In R_2, for $\tau_3=\{t_5,t_6\}$: $in(\tau_3,q_2)=1$, $out(\tau_3,q_1)=1$. Since τ_3 is the set of transitions of the elementary circuit of R_1, we have $mcc(q_1,q_2)=1$. If we consider the ring $Z=q_1R_1q_2R_2$ we get $\alpha(Z)=1\cdot(1/2)=1/2$ and therefore we can conclude that Z is a small ring and that S_1 is not well-structured (definition 3.5).

A DSSP can be seen as a set of sites connected by communicating buffers. On each site (modeled by a sequential process) one or several tasks can be executed. This brings us to introduce a definition used to distinguish between the two cases :

1) On each site, only one task is executed and therefore, only one token will be able to run through the different internal states (elements of P) of the process (S-marking).

2) On a site, any number of tasks can be executed (usual marking).

Definition 3.6 : $M\in N^{|P|+|K|}$ is an S-marking of the DSSP S associated with the set $R=\{R_i=<P_i\cup K_i, T_i, W_i>, i=1,\ldots,s\ \ s\in N\}$ of SPs ((S,M) is then called an S-marked DSSP) if and only if for every process R_i there is only one internal state (place of P_i) marked by one token (i.e. $\forall i\in[1..s]$, $\Sigma_{p\in P_i} M(p)=1$). However there is no restriction to the marking of the buffers.

3.2. LIVENESS MONOTONICITY OF DSSPs AND ITS CONSEQUENCES

A property Π of a marked Petri Net (N,M) is said to be monotonic if $\Pi(N,M)$ and $M'\geq M$ imply $\Pi(N,M')$. Liveness is known to be monotonic for state machines and event graphs. For DSSPs we do not have such a property for arbitrary markings but only for S-markings. The interpretation of this property for DSSPs could be : if a system modeled by a DSSP is live then it remains live when we give it more resources.

Theorem 3.7 [Souissi...88] : Let S be a DSSP and let M and M' be two S-markings of S. If (S,M) is live and $M'\geq M$ then (S, M') is live.

The liveness monotonicity of S-marked DSSPs allows us to separate DSSPs into two classes. Those for which there exists a live S-marking, the S-structurally live DSSPs and the others.

Definition 3.8 : A DSSP S is said to be ***structurally*** (respectively ***S-structurally***) ***live*** if and only if there exists a marking (respespectively S-marking) M such that (S,M) is live.

An interesting result that can be deduced from the theorem of liveness monotonicity is : for every S-structurally live DSSP and every initial state of its processes (marking of the process internal states), there is an initial configuration of the resources (marking of the buffers) such that the net is live.

Corollary 3.9 : Let S be an S-structurally live DSSP. $\forall$ M S-marking of S, $\exists$ M' S-marking of S such that $M'\geq M$ and (S,M') is live.

Example 3.10

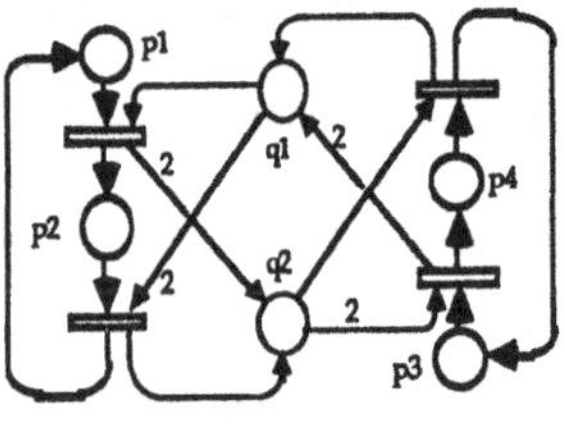

	p1	p2	q1	q2	p3	p4	LIVENESS
m1	1	0	1	0	1	0	yes
m2	1	1	1	0	1	0	yes
m3	1	0	2	0	1	0	yes
m4	1	1	2	0	1	0	no

This example shows that the liveness monotonicity is not true for two markings of a DSSP S, when these two markings are not S-markings. Nevertheless, we think that the property is true for a larger class of markings. Let us introduce this class. We say that two markings m and m' of a DSSP S=<P∪K,T,W> are *compatible* if and only if these markings have the same restriction on P (i.e. $m/_P = m'/_P$). We conjecture that :

Conjecture 3.11 : Let S be an S-structurally live DSSP. Let μ be a marking of S such that there exists an S-marking μ' meeting μ≥μ'. Let *M* be the set of markings of S compatible to μ. There exists μ"∈ *M* such that ∀m∈ *M* , m≥μ" ⇒ (S,m) is live.

To illustrate this conjecture, let us consider the net of example 3.10. Let *M*= {m∈ N^6 : m(p1)=1, m(p_2)=1, m(p_3)=1 and m(p_4)=0}. Let μ be the marking of *M* such that μ(q_2)=4. Then for every marking m of *M* such that m≥μ, (S,m) is live.
It is clear that the liveness monotonicity can not be true for incompatible markings (see markings m_3 and m_4 in example 3.10). Notice that this conjecture 3.11 is weaker than Theorem 3.7, in the sense that we do not say that for two compatible markings m, m' of a DSSP S, m'≥m and (S,m) live imply that (S,m') is live. This last property is false. Indeed, if we consider the DSSP S of example 3.10 , (S,m_2) is live but (S,m_4) is not.

As a final result of this section we recall that using [Valk...85] result concerning closed set residue we can prove that the set of live and minimal S-markings of a DSSP is computable :

Theorem 3.12 : Let S be an S-structurally live DSSP. The set of live and minimal S-markings of S is computable (see [Souissi 90] or [Souissi 92]).

These first results on the liveness of DSSPs, lead us to ask the question :

how to recognize the S-structurally live DSSPs ?

This question is very important for the liveness analysis. Indeed, Corollary 3.9 allows us to increase the markings of the buffers, in the hope of obtaining a live DSSP, when for the initial marking the DSSP is not live. But what we need to obtain is a structural characterization of S-structurally live DSSPs. This is the main result of section IV-5.

To solve this problem we will try to concentrate on the smallest relevant substructure of DSSPs. This means that we want to take advantage as much as possible of the modularity of this class of nets. In the following chapter, we show how to use compositions and bottom up constructions with DSSPs.

4. THE STRUCTURATION OF DSSPs

Firstly, we introduce deterministic systems of linear processes (DSLP) as a subclass of DSSPs. Then we give, for DSLPs, algebraic analysis methods for liveness and boundedness properties. These methods can support the analysis of DSSPs. Indeed, we show that every DSSP can be constructed by composing DSLPs and can be analyzed through the analysis of the DSLPs of which it is composed.

The other notions of structuration come directly from the way in which the state machines are connected via buffers in a DSSP. A first and simple way to decompose a DSSP is to split it into its components of interdependent sequential processes (DSISP). This is just an application of the decomposition via a separation line of [Souissi...89]. In the case of DSSPs, this decomposition allows us to validate liveness of a DSISP by testing the absence of sinks (nodes without successors) in any coverability graph of the DSISP. In subsection IV-4 we give a rule for constructing DSSPs step by step by adding buffers to the system. Finally, using these methods of decomposition, we are able to concentrate on the smallest relevant substructure of DSSPs to characterize in subsection IV-5, the S-structurally live DSSPs.

4.1. DETERMINISTIC SYSTEMS OF LINEAR PROCESSES

We begin our work on the structure of DSSPs by studying the deterministic systems of linear processes DSLPs. This class of nets was introduced in [Lautenbach...79]. We study this class not only because it is a subclass of DSSPs, but also because every DSSP can be obtained by composing DSLPs, and can be analyzed by analyzing these DSLPs. Briefly, deterministic systems of linear processes is a class of nets built modularly by connecting linear processes via their buffers. A linear process is made up of two parts. The first is an elementary circuit , that is a state machine where every place has exactly one output transition [Lien 76]. In other terms it is simultaneously a state machine and an event graph (see figure 4.2a). The second is a set of buffers, that is a set of places which are connected to the transitions of the elementary circuit.

Point (1) of definition 4.1 presents LPs and DSLPs as particular classes of SPs and DSSPs respectively. We can also present an SP as formed by LPs and a DSSP as formed by DSLPs. Indeed, we can consider an SP R=<P∪K,T,W> as the composition of a set of linear processes, namely those which are obtained by taking from the state machine generated by P∪T the elementary circuits C_i (a finite number) and from K the buffers connected to C_i (see figure 4.4).

Point (2) of definition 4.1 presents a DSSP S as a composition of DSLPs. These DSLPs are said to be included in S (see point (2) of definition 4.1 and figure 4.6).

Definition 4.1 : (1) A SP R=<P∪K,T,W> is a *linear process* (LP) iff the subnet of R generated by (P,T) is an elementary circuit of R (see definition 3.1). Let $R=\{ R_i = < P_i \cup K_i , T_i , W_i > , i=1,...,s$ $s \in N\}$ be a set of SPs and let S be the DSSP associated with R. S is the *deterministic system of linear processes* associated with R iff every SP of R is an LP.

(2) Let $R=\{ R_i =<P_i \cup K_i,T_i,W_i >, i=1,...,s$ $s \in N\}$ be a set of SPs and let S be the DSSP associated with R. Let $R'=\{ R'_i = < P'_i \cup K'_i , T'_i , W'_i > , i=1,...,s$ $s \in N\}$ be a set of linear processes and S' the DSLP associated with R'. We say that *S' is included in S* iff :

(a) $\forall i \in [1..s]$, the subnet generated by (P'_i,T'_i) is an elementary circuit of R_i (which implies that

P'_i, T'_i are particular subsets of P_i, T_i respectively).

(b) $K'_i = K_i \cap \Gamma_i(T'_i)$ and $\forall q \in K'_i, \forall t \in T'_i$, $W'_i(q,t) = W_i(q,t)$ and $W'_i(t,q) = W_i(t,q)$.

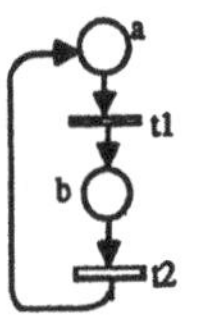

figure 4.2a : an elementary circuit

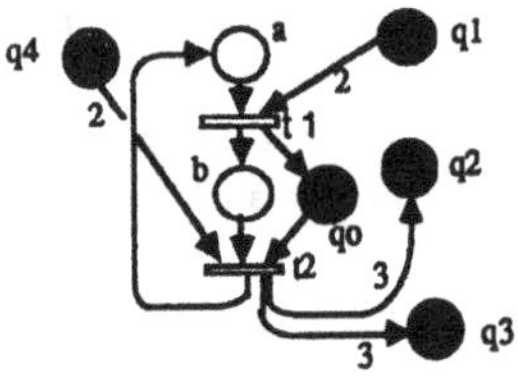

figure 4.2b : a linear process

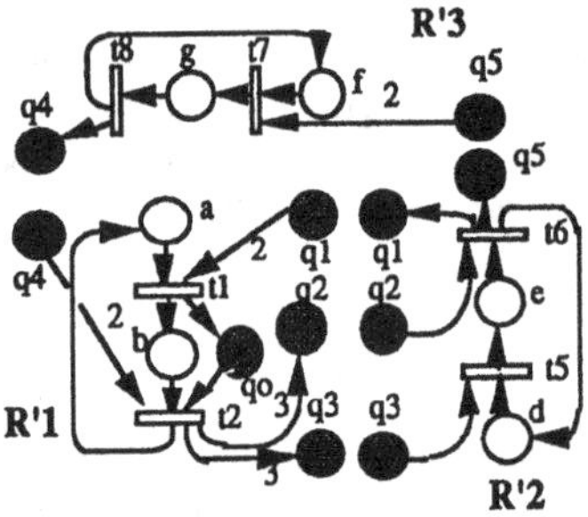

figure 4.3a : three LPs

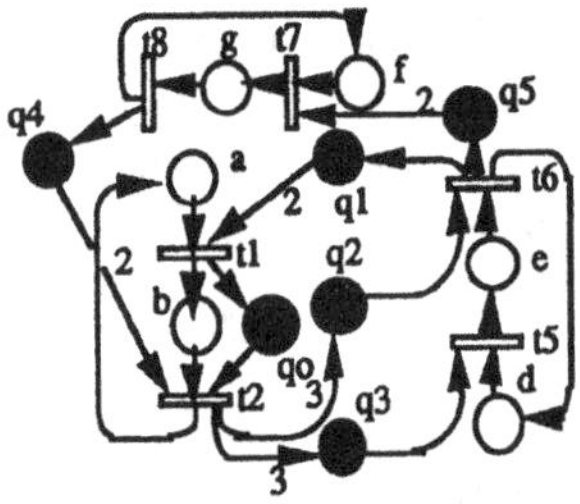

figure 4.3b : a DSLP

For the LP of figure 4.2b, {a,b} is the set of internal states, $\{t_1, t_2\}$ is the set of transitions $\{q_0, q_1, q_2, q_3, q_4\}$ is the set of buffers, where q_0 is an internal buffer. Figure 4.3b shows the deterministic system of linear processes associated with the set of linear processes of figure 4.3a.

Let us point out that all the notions of input, output and internal buffers, mcc, ring, small ring, and well-structuration apply to DSLP (since DSLP is a subclass of DSSPs by definition 4.1 (1)).

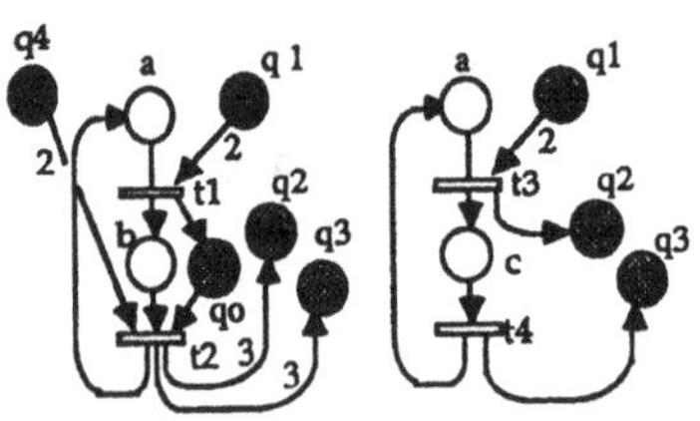

figure 4.4a : two linear processes

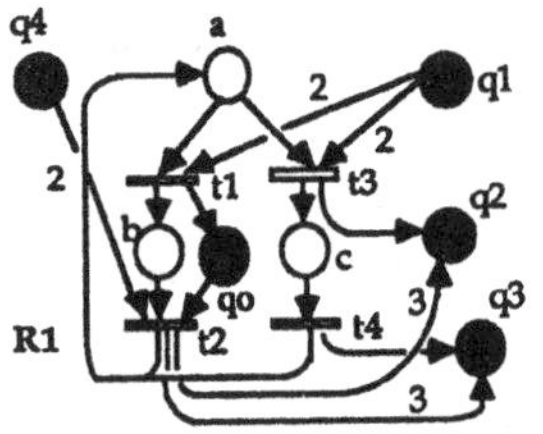

figure 4.4b : a sequential process

We can also point out that the $mcc(q_2, q_1)$ in an SP is the minimal value of the set of $mcc(q_2, q_1)$ of the linear processes from which the sequential process is built (see figure 4.4).

Given the way in which we could build a DSSP by putting DSLPs together (definition 4.1 (2)) we can propose the following :

Proposition 4.5 : Let S be a DSSP and let $S_1,\ldots,S_m$ be the DSLPs included in S. Let M be an S-marking of S. The two following properties hold :
(1) S is well-structured $\Leftrightarrow$ $S_1,\ldots S_m$ are well-structured.
(2) (S,M) is live $\Rightarrow$ ($\forall M' \in [S,M>, \forall i \in [1\ldots m]$, (S_i,M'_i) S-marked $\Rightarrow$ (S_i,M'_i) is live)
where M'_i is the restriction of M' to the DSLP S_i.

Proof : Straightforward using the definitions ♦

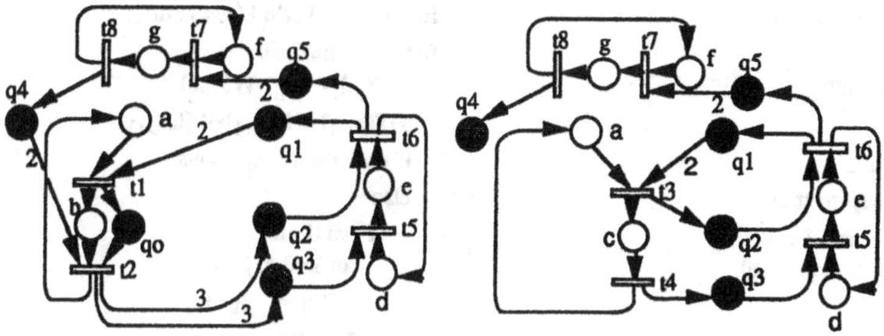

figure 4.6 : The two DSLPs which are included in the DSSP S_1 of figure 3.3 b

4.2. LIVENESS AND BOUNDEDNESS VALIDATION FOR DSLPs

It is clear that a Petri net formed by an elementary circuit is live if one of its places contains one token. If we consider a linear process, we also have to take care of its buffers. The analysis of DSLPs will be done through the analysis of the net's rings. We can detect bad structures of DSLPs through operations that are classic in the world of Petri nets and algebra. Indeed, theorem 4.8 gives a total connection between the rings of a DSLP S and the P-Flow of S (i.e. solutions of $F^T{*}C=0$, $F^T{*}C<0$ or $F^T{*}C>0$ where C is the incidence matrix of S and $F \in N^{|P|+|K|}$).

Example 4.7 : DSLP of figure 4.3b, contains five rings : $Z_0=q_0R'_1$, $Z_1=q_1R'_1q_2R'_2$, $Z_2=q_1R'_1q_3R'_2$, $Z_3=q_4R'_1q_2R'_2q_5R'_3$ and $Z_4=q_4R'_1q_3R'_2q_5R'_3$ for which we have:
$mcc(q_0,q_0)=1/1$ and then $\alpha(Z_0)=1$, $mcc(q_2,q_1)=3/2$;
$mcc(q_1,q_2)=1/1$ and then $\alpha(Z_1)=3/2$,
$mcc(q_3,q_1)=3/2$; $mcc(q_1,q_3)=1/1$ and then $\alpha(Z_2)=3/2$,
$mcc(q_4,q_5)=1/2$; $mcc(q_2,q_4)=3/2$; $mcc(q_5,q_2)=1/1$ and then $\alpha(Z_3)=3/4$,
$mcc(q_3,q_4)=3/2$; $mcc(q_5,q_3)=1/1$ and then $\alpha(Z_4)=3/4$, therefore the DSLP contains two small rings.

Theorem 4.8 : Let $S=\langle P \cup K,T,W \rangle$ be a DSLP, then to each ring $Z=q_0R_0q_1R_1\ldots q_{n-1}R_{n-1}$ we can associate a vector $F \in N^{|P|+|K|}$ such that:

$F^T{*}C<0 \Leftrightarrow \alpha(Z)<1$, $F^T{*}C=0 \Leftrightarrow \alpha(Z)=1$, $F^T{*}C>0 \Leftrightarrow \alpha(Z)>1$,

where C is the incidence matrix of S [Brams...83] [Peterson 81] (see [Souissi 90] or [Souissi 92]).

For DSLPs, we present an algorithm which associates a vector F_Z to each ring Z. This algorithm allows us to prove theorem 4.8 by constructing F_Z.
For the sake of readability, we split this algorithm into two parts (algorithm_1 and algorithm_2). Algorithm_1 gives weight $F_Z(q_i)$ to every q_i of Q(Z) the set of buffers involved in Z. Algorithm_2

gives for every process R_i weight $F_Z(p)$ to every p of P_i.

Algorithm_1 and algorithm_2 compute vector F_Z associated to the ring $Z=q_0R_0q_1R_1...q_{n-1}R_{n-1}$. For every process $R_i=<P_i \cup K_i, T_i, W_i>$ ($i \in [0...n-1]$) involved in Z, $p_0t_0p_1t_1...p_{mi-1}t_{mi-1}$ is the elementary circuit generated by (P_i,T_i).

Algorithm_1

```
begin    Begin
for i=0 to n-2 do
  f1(qi)=out(Ti,qi+1)
  F(qi)=out(Ti,qi+1)
  f2(qi+1)=in(Ti,qi)
end_do
for i=1 to n-2 do
  if f1(qi)≠f2(qi) then
    for j=0 to i-1 do
      F(qj)=F(qj)*f1(qi)
    end_do
    F(qi)=F(qi)*f2(qi)
    f2(qi+1)=f2(qi+1)*f2(qi)
  end_if
end_do
F(qn-1)=f2(qn-1)
end
```

Algorithm_2

```
for i=0 to n-1 do
  for any p ∈ Pi do F(p)=0 end_do
  for j=0 to mi-2 do
    e=F(pj) + F(qi)*W(qi,tj)
    s=F(pj+1) + F(qi+1)*W(tj,qi+1)
    if e > s then F(pj+1)=e-s
    else
      if e<s then
        for k=0 to j do
          F(pk)=F(pk) + s-e
        end_do
      end_if
    end_if
  end_do
end_do
end
```

Example 4.9 : For the rings Z_0, Z_1, Z_2, Z_3 and Z_4 of example 4.7 (taken from figure 4.3 b) we have :

	a	b	d	e	f	g	q_0	q_1	q_2	q_3	q_4	q_5
F_{Z0}	1	0	0	0	0	0	1	0	0	0	0	0
F_{Z1}	0	6	0	2	0	0	0	3	2	0	0	0
F_{Z2}	0	6	0	2	0	0	0	3	0	2	0	0
F_{Z3}	0	0	0	0	0	4	0	0	2	0	3	2
F_{Z4}	0	0	0	2	0	4	0	0	0	2	3	2

Using the following [Memmi 83] result:

if there is $f \gneq 0$ $f^T * C < 0$ then $\exists M$ such that (R,M) is live (C is the incidence matrix of R). We can state a result which gives a necessary condition for a DSLP to have a live marking :

Corollary 4.10 : Let S be a DSLP. If S contains a small ring, then there exists no marking m of S such that (S,m) is live (see [Souissi...88]).

In terms of graph theory, we build for any ring Z, a set of places : $||F||=\{x \in P \cup K, F(x)>0\}$, the support of F. If Z is a small ring, then $||F||$ is both a deadlock [Commoner 72] and a leakage set [Memmi 83] . We then have given ourselves a means of correcting the structure default of the net. Indeed, we can increase the valuation of input edges of Z buffers, or decrease the valuation of output edges of Z buffers. Therefore, it is sufficient to change the values of the edges cited above in such a way that $\alpha(Z) \geq 1$ in order to obtain a DSLP without small rings.

Corollary 4.11 : Let $S=<P \cup K,T,W>$ be the DSLP associated with the set $R=\{ R_i=<P_i \cup K_i,T_i,W_i>, i=1,...,s\ s \in N\}$ of LPs. Let M_0 be an S-marking of S verifying :
For every ring $Z = q_0R_0q_1R_1...q_{n-1}R_{n-1}$,

$F_z^T * M_0 > \Sigma_{q \in Q(Z)} \max_{t \in \Gamma^+(q)} \{(W(q,t)-1)*F_z(q) + F_z(p_t)\}$ (p_t is the only element of $\Gamma^-(t) \cap P$).

If S is well-structured then (S,M_0) is live (see [Souissi 90] or [Souissi 92]).

Sketch of the proof : Suppose that (S,M_0) is not live (by contradiction). First we prove that $\exists\ T_i$ and $M \in [S,M_0>$ such that $\forall t \in T_i$, t cannot be enabled in (S,M), then we prove that $\exists\ M' \in [S,M>$ and $Z=q_0R_0q_1R_1...q_{n-1}R_{n-1}$ such that $\forall q \in Q(Z)$: $M'(q) \leq W(q,t_q)-1$ where t_q is the only transition of $T \cap \Gamma^+(q)$ such that $M'(\Gamma^-(t_q) \cap P)=1$. Since well-structuration of S implies : $F_z^T * M' \geq F_z^T * M_0$, we get a contradiction with the fact that : $F_z^T * M' > \Sigma_{q \in Q(Z)} \max_{t \in \Gamma^+(q)} \{(W(q,t)-1)*F_z(q) + F_z(p_t)\}$. ♦

Another necessary condition of liveness for Petri nets is the repetitivity of the net [Brams...83]. Let $N=<P,T,W>$ be a net, a sequence $\sigma \in T^*$ is *repetitive* if and only if $C*\underline{\sigma} \geq 0$ (C being the incidence matrix of N). N is said to be *repetitive* if and only if there exists a repetitive sequence $\sigma \in T^*$ such that for every $t \in T$, $|\sigma|_t > 0$ (σ is said to be complete). We show that for DSLPs this condition is also a sufficient condition for DSLPs structural liveness.

Theorem 4.12 : Let S be a DSLP. The three following propositions are equivalent:
(1) S is well-structured.
(2) there is a marking m of S such that (S,m) is live.
(3) S is repetitive.

Proof : (1)⇒(2) Corollary 4.11
(2)⇒(3) If there exists a marking m such that (S,m) is live then S is repetitive [Brams...83] (it is a general result in Petri nets).
(3)⇒(1) Let $Z=q_0R_0q_1R_1...q_{n-1}R_{n-1}$ be a ring of S. Let $\sigma \in T^*$ be a complete (containing every transition of T) and repetitive sequence of S.
Then there exists $x_0,x_1...,x_{n-1} \in N$ such that : $\forall i \in [0...n-1]$, $\forall t,t' \in T_i$ $|\sigma|_t = |\sigma|_{t'} = x_i$ (because of the structure of a linear process and the fact that σ is a repetitive sequence)
Therefore we have :

$x_0 * in(T_0,q_0) \leq x_{n-1} * out(T_{n-1},q_0)$
$x_1 * in(T_1,q_1) \leq x_0 * out(T_0,q_1)$
" "
$x_{n-1} * in(T_{n-1},q_{n-1}) \leq x_{n-2} * out(T_{n-2},q_{n-1})$

$\Rightarrow \alpha(Z) \geq 1$. ♦

Corollary 4.13 : Let S be a strongly connected DSLP. Then we have :
S is bounded for every initial marking ⇔ $\exists$ Z such that $\alpha(Z)<1$ or $\forall Z$, $\alpha(Z) \leq 1$ (see [Souissi 90] or [Souissi 92]).

4.3. DETERMINISTIC SYSTEMS OF INTERDEPENDENT SEQUENTIAL PROCESSES

In [Souissi...89] we have shown that, in some cases, a non strongly connected net can be broken down into strongly connected components, and that the liveness validation of the whole net can be done by validating the liveness of each component. The non strongly connected DSSPs belong to the kind of nets to which we can apply this decomposition rule. Moreover, we recall that a strongly connected DSSP is live if and only if its coverability graph does not contain a vertex without successor, a vertex that we name a sink. This result decreases effectively the liveness validation cost of DSSPs.

Definition 4.14 : Let S be a DSSP. S is called a ***deterministic system of interdependent sequential processes*** (DSISP), if and only if it is strongly connected.

When a DSSP is not strongly connected we can apply the decomposition rule introduced in [Souissi...89] (decomposition via a separation line). Application of this rule leads to the decomposition of a non strongly connected DSSP S into two components, two DSSPs. By application of this rule to the components of S, and after to the components of the components of S and so on, we obtain a decomposition of S into deterministic systems of interdependent sequential processes DSISPs (see figures 4.15). We can then apply the theorem of [Souissi...89] which says in this case that a marked DSSP (S,M) is live if and only if every marked DSISP (obtained by decomposition of S into strongly connected components) is live .

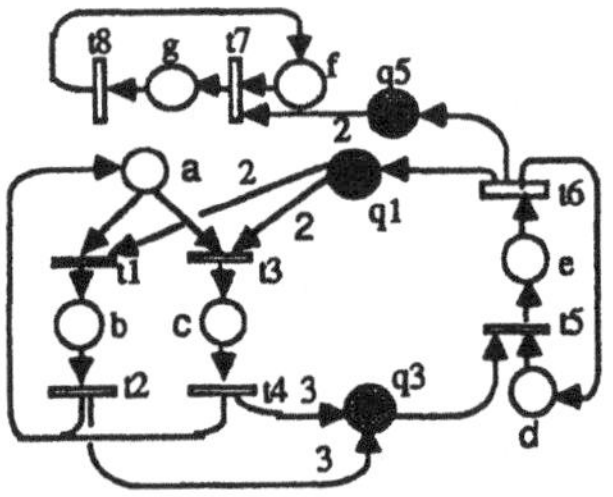

figure 4.15a : a DSSP S3

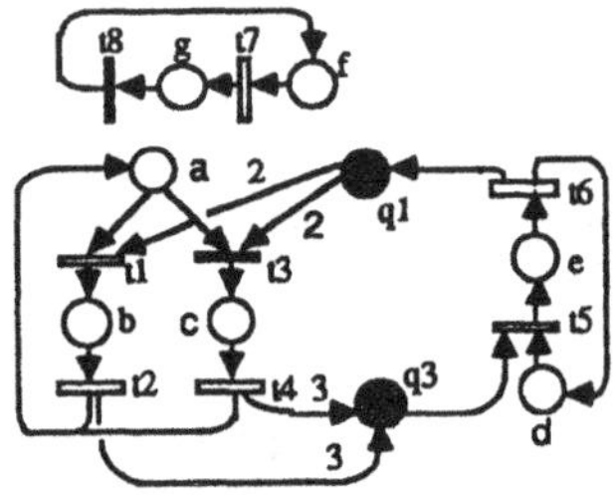

figure 4.15b : the result of the separation of S3

For every Petri net we can build a finite graph (coverability graph CG) , with the price of losing some information about the reachable markings (if the set of reachable marking is infinite). It is well known that this loss of information makes liveness validation much more expensive for unbounded nets [Kosaraju 82], [Lambert 86]. For S-marked DSSPs, liveness can be analysed simply by using the following theorem.

Theorem 4.16 : Let (S,M) be an S-marked DSISP then :
(1) (S,M) is live if and only if its reachability graph RG(S,M) does not contain a sink,
(2) a shortest firing sequence leading to a sink does not contain a repetitive subsequence (but the empty word),
(3) (S,M) is live if and only if any of its coverability graphs CG(S,M) does not contain a sink,
(see [Souissi 90] or [Souissi 92]).

4.4. STEP BY STEP CONSTRUCTION OF A DSSP

Starting from a DSSP S that contains rings $Z_1,...,Z_m$, we show that S can be analyzed through the analysis of the DSSPs S_i that are obtained from S by removing all the buffers except those involved in Z_i (namely $Q(Z_i)$).

First, let us introduce the notion of a DSSP containing another DSSP and the notion of a 1-constrained DSSP. A DSSP S from which we remove some buffers to get another DSSP S' is said to contain S'. A 1-constrained DSSP is a DSSP which has only one constraint, that is only one ring which contains all the buffers.

Definition 4.17 : Let $S=<P \cup K, T, W>$ and $S^1= <P^1 \cup K^1, T^1, W^1>$ be two DSSPs. We say that S *contains* S^1 (or that S^1 *is contained in* S) if and only if S^1 meets : $P^1=P$; $T^1=T$; $K \supset K^1$ and $\forall x \in P^1 \cup K^1$, $\forall t \in T^1$, $W^1(x,t)=W(x,t)$ and $W^1(t,x)=W(t,x)$.

Definition 4.18 : Let $S=<P \cup K, T, W>$ be a DSSP. S is said to be *1-constrained* if and only if there exists a ring $Z=q_0R_0q_1R_1...q_{n-1}R_{n-1}$ of S, such that $K=Q(Z)$, where $Q(Z)=\{q_0,q_1,...,q_{n-1}\}$ is the set of buffers involved in the ring Z.

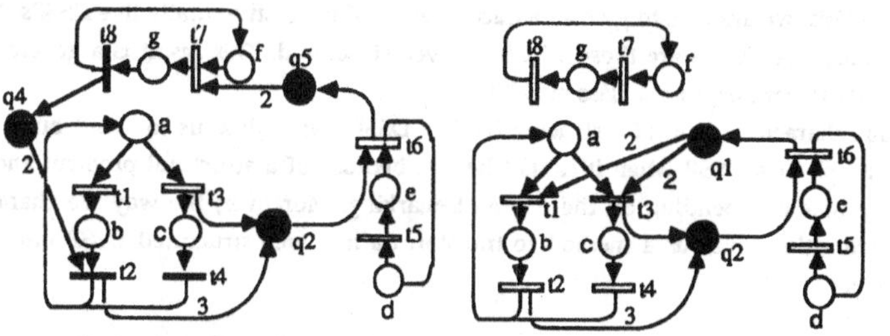

figure 4.19 : Two of the five 1-constrained DSSPs contained in DSSP S_1 of figure 3.3 b

We can now state the result which makes the connection between the liveness of a DSSP S and the liveness of the 1-constrained DSSPs contained in S.

Theorem 4.20 : Let S be a DSISP. Let $\Sigma=\{S^1,S^2,...,S^l\}$ be the set of the 1-constrained DSSPs contained in S. Let M be an S-marking of S and M_i the restrictions of M to the places of S^i. The following property holds : (S,M) live $\Leftrightarrow \forall i \in [1...l]$ (S^i,M_i) live.

Proof : First, let us notice that Σ is a finite set (since K and the set of rings of S are two finite sets).
($\Rightarrow$)Let us prove that if $\exists i \in [1...l]$ such that (S^i,M_i) is not live then (S,M) is not live.
Let $Z=q_0R_0q_1R_1...q_{n-1}R_{n-1}$ be the ring associated with S^i.
Let σ be an enabled sequence at M_i such that $M_i (\sigma > M'_i$ and every transition of every sequential process in Z is non quasi-live at M'_i (existence due to theorem 4.16 (1)).
Assume that (S,M) is live (by contradiction), then $\exists$ M_0 S-marking of S such that :

$\forall p \in P$: $M_0(p)=M(p)$

$\forall q \in K^i$: $M_0(q)=M(q)$

$\forall q \in K-K^i$: $M_0(q) \geq \max(M(q),\Sigma_{t\in im(\sigma)} |\sigma|_t * W(q,t))$.

The existence of M_0 is due to the liveness monotonicity (theorem 3.7).
σ is then an enabled sequence of (S,M_0) and σ allows us to reach the same blocking as the one reached in (S^i,M_i) by the firing of σ. This is in contradiction with the liveness of S.
($\Leftarrow$) Assume that (S,M) is not live. This implies that:
there exists σ enabled at M such that $M (\sigma > M'$ with no transition enabled at M (theorem 4.16(1)).
Therefore, there exists a ring $Z= q_0R_0q_1R_1...q_{n-1}R_{n-1}$ of S such that M' verifies : $\forall i \in [0...n-1]$

$M'(q_i)<W(q_i,t)$ for every $t\in\Gamma^+(p_i)$ (p_i is the internal state of P_i marked at M'). Let S^j be the 1-constrained DSSP contained in S and having Q(Z) as set of buffers. (S^j,M'_j) is not live. ♦

This theorem can be used to analyse a DSSP that is constructed by refinements. Indeed a DSSP S' can be constructed starting from a DSSP S to which a buffer q is added. This addition must conform to the definition 3.1 point (iii) in order to obtain a DSSP. As S' contains one more buffer than S, S' contains more rings than S. Therefore if S has been successfully analysed, to analyse S' it is sufficient to analyse the DSSP obtained from S' by removing all the buffers that do not belong to the same rings as q.

4.5. CHARACTERIZATION OF S-STRUCTURALLY LIVE DSSPs

Taking advantage of all the previous results which allow us in particular to focus on 1-constrained DSSPs, we are able to give a characterization of the S-structurally live DSSPs. Indeed, the S-structurally live DSSPs are those which are well-structured. This result is a generalization of the one of [Berthelot...83] to our class of DSSPs.
The structural characterization of S-structurally live DSSPs will allow us to avoid building the reachability graph of a DSSP when it cannot be live because of a structural problem and not a behavioural problem depending on the chosen S-marking. Moreover, the way we characterize the well-structuration gives us a method to transform a non well-structured DSSP into a well-structured one.

As we did for deterministic systems of linear processes, we show that the well-structuration implies the repetitivity for DSSPs. But unlike for DSLPs the converse is false (see DSSP S_1 of figure 3.3b). First we define the notion of a free circuit in a sequential process.

Definition 4.21 : Let $R=<P\cup K,T,W>$ be a sequential process. Let Ω be an elementary circuit of R, Ω is a *free circuit* of R if and only if : $\Gamma^-(T_\Omega)\cap K=\varnothing$ (T_Ω is the set of transitions that belong to Ω).

Proposition 4.22 : Let S be a 1-constrained and well-structured DSISP. For every process R_0 of S and every elementary circuit Ω_0 of R_0 we have :
- either Ω_0 is a free circuit then $T_{\Omega 0}$ is a support of a minimal repetitive sequence of S .
- or there exists an s-tuple of elementary circuits $(\Omega_0,\Omega_1,\dots,\Omega_{s-1})$ of $(R_0,R_1,\dots,R_{s-1})$ such that $(\cup T_{\Omega i})$ is the support of a minimal repetitive sequence of S (see [Souissi 90] or [Souissi 92]).

Remark 4.23 : (1) Let S be a DSSP and let $\Sigma=\{S_1,\dots,S_n\}$ be the set of DSISP obtained by decomposition of S. Then we have : S is well-structured $\Leftrightarrow \forall i\in [1\dots n]$ S_i is well-structured.
(2) Let S be a DSSP and let $\Sigma=\{S_1,\dots,S_m\}$ be the set of 1-constrained DSSP contained in S. Then we have : S is well-structured $\Leftrightarrow \forall i\in [1\dots m]$ S_i is well-structured (comes from definitions).

Using the equivalence between the liveness of a DSISP S and the absence of sinks in the reachability graph of S and the fact that the shortest firing sequences leading to a sink do not contain repetitive subsequences (theorem 4.16), we are able, by the repetitivity of a well-structured DSISP to get a live S-marking. First, we introduce the class of S-markings and the class of enabled sequences of a Petri net which allow us to prove that a well-structured DSSP is S-structurally live.

Let S be a 1-constrained and well-structured DSISP. Let g be the set of minimal vectors representing the set of repetitive sequences of minimal support of S . For every circuit Ω_i^k of a sequential process R_k of S, let X_i^k be the maximal value of the coefficients of the transitions of $T_{\Omega_i k}$ in g.

Let μ be an S-marking of S such that :

$\forall k \in [0...s\text{-}1], \forall q \in \Gamma^{-}(T_k), \mu(q)=\Sigma_i (\Sigma_{t \in T_{\Omega_i k}} W(q,t) * (X_i^k+1))$.

Let $L^{\infty}(S,\mu)$ be the set of infinite firing sequences of (S,μ) and let $\underline{L}(S,\mu)= \{ \sigma \in T^* : \mu(\sigma > M$ and M is a sink $\} \cup L^{\infty}(S,\mu)$.

μ has been constructed in such a way that for any sequence $\sigma \in \underline{L}(S,\mu)$, there exists a repetitive sequence α of L(S,M) such that $\underline{\sigma} \leq \underline{\alpha}$.

Lemma 4.24 : Let S be a 1-constrained and well-structured DSISP. For the S-marking μ of S defined above we have : $\forall \sigma \in \underline{L}(S,\mu)$, $\exists \alpha \in L(S,M)$ with $C*\underline{\alpha}=0$ such that $\underline{\sigma} \leq \underline{\alpha}$.

Proof : straightforward using definition of μ. ♦

Theorem 4.16 and lemma 4.24 allow us to bring the liveness problem of a DSSP to a problem of graph theory. Indeed, when using the marking μ, in a well-structured DSSP, we are able to show that every firing sequence which is supposed to reach a sink is long enough. By graph theory we show that a long path in a graph like a DSSP can be ordered in such way that it generates a path corresponding to a repetitive subsequence of the DSSP (see appendix). Finally by using theorem 4.16 we give a contradiction between the fact that a firing sequence σ leads to a sink and that this sequence contains a repetitive subsequence.

It is more convenient to work on a 1-constrained DSSP. Then, by theorem 4.20 and the result on liveness preservation by decomposition of a DSSP into DSISPs, the result will also work for a general DSSP.

Theorem 4.25 : Let S be a well-structured and 1-constrained DSSP. Let μ be the S-marking defined above. (S,μ) is live.

Proof : Let $\sigma \in \underline{L}(S,\mu)$ then there exists $\sigma_1 \in \underline{L}(S, \mu)$ such that:
$\underline{\sigma_1} = \underline{\sigma}$ and $\sigma_1 = \delta_1 \delta_2 ... \delta \gamma$ where $\delta_i \in T_i^*$ and $\gamma \in T^*$ with :
$\forall k=1,...,s \ \exists \Omega_i^k \in R_k$ such that $\forall t \in T_{\Omega_i k} \ |\delta_i|_t > X_i^k + 1$ (lemma 4.24) and the δ_i using, for their occurrence the tokens available at μ.
We can write:
$\forall i=1, ... , s \quad \delta_i = \alpha_i \beta_i$ where β_i fulfil the hypothesis of corollary A1 (see appendix).
Besides, $\sigma_2 = \alpha_1 \alpha_2 ... \alpha_s \beta_1 \beta_2 ... \beta_s \gamma \in \underline{L}(S, \mu)$ and $\underline{\sigma_2}=\underline{\sigma}$ (because of the definition of μ)
We apply corollary A1 (see appendix) to each β_i to obtain ζ_i :
$\sigma_3 = \alpha_1 \alpha_2 ... \alpha_s \zeta_1 \zeta_2 ... \zeta_s \gamma$ belongs to $\underline{L}(S, \mu)$ and $\underline{\sigma_3} = \underline{\sigma}$.
Let then δ be the repetitive sequence such that $\underline{\delta} \leq \underline{\zeta_1 \zeta_2 ... \zeta_s}$ (lemma 4.24 and proposition 4.22).
Without any loss of generality, we can write $\delta = \phi_1 ... \phi_n$ where $n \in [1...s]$, and $\phi_i \in T_i^*$.
Then we can split the ζ_i into ϕ_i and ψ_i where $\zeta_i = \phi_i \psi_i$ and $\phi_1 \phi_2 ... \phi v$ is a repetitive sequence.
Once more, we have : $\sigma_4 = \alpha_1 \alpha_2 ... \alpha_s \phi_1 \phi_2 ... \phi_s \psi_1 \psi_2 ... \psi_s \gamma$ belonging to $\underline{L}(S,\mu)$ and $\underline{\sigma_4} = \underline{\sigma}$. This implies (by point (3) of theorem 4.16) that $\underline{L}(S, \mu)=L^{\infty}(S, \mu)$ and therefore, that (S, μ) is live. ♦

Theorem 4.26 : Let $S=< P\cup K, T,W >$ be a DSSP. The following property holds:
S is S-structurally live $\Leftrightarrow$ S is well-structured.

Proof : ($\Rightarrow$) By contradiction we prove that : S not well-structured $\Rightarrow$ S not S-structurally live.
Assume that there exists an S-marking M such that (S,M) is live.
Let $Z=q_0R_0q_1R_1...q_{n-1}R_{n-1}$ be a small ring of S. Let S_1 be the DSISP that contains Z, and let M_1 be the restriction of M to places of S_1, (S_1,M_1) is live (liveness preservation by decomposition into strongly connected components [Souissi...89]). Let $\Omega_0,\Omega_1,...,\Omega_{n-1}$ be circuits of $R_0,R_1,...,R_{n-1}$ such that for $i\in[0...n-1]$ $mcc(q_{i+1},q_i)=out(T_{\Omega i},q_{i+1})/in(T_{\Omega i},q_i)$ (i.e. $\Omega_0,\Omega_1,...,\Omega_{n-1}$ are relevant for the computation of $\alpha(Z)$). These circuits may not be unique, from each sequential process, we take one which can be involved in the computation of $\alpha(Z)$. Let $S_2=<P_2,T_2,W_2>$ be the 1-constrained DSSP contained in S_1 and having Q(Z) as a set of buffers. Let M_2 be the restriction of M_1 to places of S_2, (S_2,M_2) is live (theorem 4.20). Let M'_2 be a reachable marking of (S_2,M_2) such that the DSLP $S'=<P'\cup K',T',W'>$ generated by $(\cup P(\Omega_i)\cup Q(Z),\cup T(\Omega_i))$ is S-marked, i.e. the restriction M' of M'_2 to places of S' is an S-marking. (S',M') is live because of proposition 4.5 point (2). S' is not well-structured since it contains Z and then there exists no marking M_0 such that (S,M_0) is live, and then we get a contradiction.
($\Leftarrow$) Let S_0 be one of the DSISPs obtained by the decomposition of S into strongly connected components. Let $\Sigma=\{S^1,...,S^l\}$ be the set of the 1-constrained DSSPs contained in S_0.
If S is well structured then every $S^i\in\Sigma$ is well-structured.
By theorem 4.25, for every $S^i\in\Sigma$ there exists a marking m_i such that (S^i,m_i) is live. Using corollary 3.9, we can choose live S-markings (one per $S^i\in\Sigma$) having the same restriction on P. More formally, we can build a set $\psi=\{M_1,...,M_l\}$ of markings verifying :

- M_i S-marking of S^i
- $\forall p\in P, \forall i,j\in[1...l], M_i(p)=M_j(p)$
- (S^i,M_i) live.

Using theorem 3.7 we can choose live S-markings having the same restriction on the same buffers. More formally, we can build a set $\Phi=\{M'_1,...,M'_l\}$ verifying:

- $\forall p\in P\ \forall i\in[1...l]\ M'_i(p)=M_i(p)$.
- $\forall i\in[1...l]\ \forall q\in K^i\ M'_i(q)=\max_j\{M_j(q) / q\in K^j\}$.
- (S^i,M'_i) live.

Let M_0 be the S-marking of S_0 defined by:

- $\forall p\in P\ \ M_0(p)=M'_i(p)$ where $i\in[1...l]$
- $\forall q\in K\ \ M_0(q)=M'_i(q)$ with K^i containing q.

From theorem 4.20 (S_0,M_0) is live.
Let $S_1,...S_k$ be the other DSISPs obtained from the decomposition of S into DSISPs. We can find (as done for S_0), for $i\in[1..k]$, an S-marking M_i such that (S_i,M_i) is live. Using the liveness equivalence between a marked DSSP (S,M) and the S-marked DSISPs obtained by decomposition of (S,M) [Souissi...89], we can conclude that (S,M) is live. Indeed, we define M as follows : for each buffer q of K_i ($i\in[0..k]$) $M(q)=M_i(q)$ and for every buffer q' that connects the strongly connected components (in S) $M(q')=0$. ♦

We think that the well-structuration can be a more general characterization of DSSPs liveness.

Conjecture 4.27 : Let (S,M) be a marked DSSP. If (S,M) is live then S is well-structured (see [Souissi 92] for a discussion of this conjecture).

The notion of a ring can also be used in order to characterize the behavioural link between the buffers of a ring. Indeed, for a well S-structured DSSP, we can concentrate on only one buffer of each ring, in such a way that by suitably marking these buffers we can get a live S-marking and this without paying attention the other buffers of the DSSP. This result is given for 1-constrained DSSPs by the following theorem, and can be extended to a general DSSP by using theorem 4.20 and liveness preservation by decomposition of a DSSP into DSISPs.

Theorem 4.28 : Let $S=<P\cup K,T,W>$ be a 1-constrained and well-structured DSSP. Let M be an S-marking of S and let $q\in K$. $\exists r\in N$, such that $M(q)\geq r \Rightarrow (S,M)$ is live

Sketch of the proof : Let $Z=q_0R_0q_1R_1...q_{n-1}R_{n-1}$ be the ring of S. Without any loss of generality, assume that $q=q_{n1}$.
The idea is to start from a live S-marking M_0 with $M_0\geq M$ (existence by corollary 3.9) and to add some tokens in K-{q}, obtaining a live marking M' (by theorem 3.7) in order to be able to fire a sequence σ (from M') that reaches a marking M" where all buffers but q are empty and $\forall p\in P$ $M''(p)=M(p)$. Since M" is reachable from M', M" is a live marking. M" has the same restriction as M on P. We take $r=M''(q)$ which concludes the proof.
So what we must prove is the existence of M". We proceed step by step, in the first step we empty q_0, in the second we empty q_1 and so on.
In the first step we add to $M_0(q_0)$, $x(q_0)\in N$ such that

$M_0(q_0)+x(q_0)= y(q_0) * in(T_0,q_0)$ and $x(q_0)\leq in(T_0,q_0)$, where $y(q_0)\in N$

We get an S-marking M_1 that allows to reach (by firing $y(q_0)$ times all transitions of T_0) a marking M_2 that differs from M_1 only by the fact that q_0 is empty and q_1 contains more tokens.
In the second step : we add to $M_2(q_1)$, $x(q_1)\in N$ such that

$M_2(q_1)+x(q_1)= y(q_1) * in(T_1,q_1)$ and $x(q_1)\leq in(T_1,q_1)$, where $y(q_1)\in N$

We get an S-marking M_3 that allows to reach (by firing $y(q_1)$ times all transitions of T_1) a marking M_4 that differs from M_3 only by the fact that q_1 is empty and q_2 contains more tokens.
The same schema can be repeated for $q_2,..., q_{n-2}$. Finally, r is the number of tokens in q_{n-1} (in the last marking). ♦

5. DISCUSSION

Deterministic systems of sequential processes is a non trivial class of structured nets for which we have detailed analysis and composition methods.

A first version of some of these validation methods had been implemented in an expert system for Petri nets analysis [Beldiceanu 88], [Souissi...88]. In particular one of the first steps of the package is to check if the net belongs to a known class of nets (e.g. DSSP or DSLP) in which case special methods can be applied (e.g. decompositions, computation of rings). Recognition of the structure of DSSPs which means separation of the places into two sets (buffers and internal states) and separation of the transitions into sets (of processes) is done quickly without any help from the user.

Let us notice that composition of nets via a sequential process [Souissi...89] obviously applies to the construction of DSSPs or the composition of a DSSP with other nets.

For DSSPs liveness is a monotonic property. Refereeing to F-monotonicity defined in

[Souissi 90], it would be fruitful to explore the application of this notion (or an extended definition of it) to the buffers belonging to a ring.

In this article, we have proposed two conjectures that, in our opinion would facilitate (if they are solved) the extension of the class of DSSPs and the analysis methods which have been developed around it. One can easily believe that our results hold mainly because of hypothesis (iii) of definition 3.2 which expresses the fact that the buffers of a DSSP are "not shared" (exactly one producer and one consumer per buffer). But if conjectures 3.11 and 4.27 hold, then the well-structuration will completely characterize the structural liveness (as it currently characterizes S-structural liveness). This simply expresses the fact that some of our results could be extended by changing hypothesis (iii) of definition 3.2 with a less constraining hypothesis with regard to buffer sharing.

Finally, an interesting question which has been suggested to me by one of the referees is : Is it more efficient to split and decompose a DSSP into its relevant components (from which it can be analyzed) and analyze the components or is it more efficient to directly analyze the DSSP? I would say that it is more efficient to construct a DSSP modularly thus not having to put much computation power into looking for the components. From the complexity point of view, I agree that it will be interesting to compare the two approaches. As the decomposition rules only need to operate on the net structure it seems to be less costly to decompose the DSSP and only analyze its components.

Acknowledgements : I would like to thank the 3 anonymous referees whose comments helped me in improving this paper. Particular thanks go to 2 of them, for having detected some elements lacking in a previous version of this paper.

6. REFERENCES

[Barkaoui...89] K. Barkaoui and B. Lemaire : *An effective characterization of minimal deadlocks and traps in Petri nets based on graph theory,* Proc. of the Xth Int. Conf. on Application and Theory of Petri Nets, Bonn, 1989.

[Berge 83] C. Berge : *Graphes,* Gauthiers-villars, Paris 1983.

[Berthelot...83] G. Berthelot, W. Reisig, and G. Memmi : *A control structure for sequential processes synchronized by buffers,* Proc. of the 4th European Work. on App. and Th. of Petri nets, Toulouse, 1983.

[Berthelot 85] G. Berthelot : *Transformations and decompositions of nets,* Advances in Petri Nets, LNCS 254, pp 359-376, 1986.

[Beldiceanu 88] N.H. Beldiceanu : *Language de règles et moteur d'inférence basé sur des contraintes et des actions. Application aux réseaux de Petri,* Doctoral report, Paris VI, January 1988.

[BRAMS...83] G.W. Brams : *Réseaux de Petri : théorie et pratique,* Masson, Paris, 1983.

[Commoner 72] F. Commoner : *Deadlock in Petri nets,* Applied Data Research Inc. Wakefiels Mass. CA 7206-2311, 1972.

[Hack 72] M. Hack : *Analysis of production schemata by Petri nets,* M.S. thesis, D.E.E. M.I.T. Cambridge Mass. Project MAC-TR 94, 1972.

[Hack 73] M. Hack : *Extended state-machine allocatable nets, an extension of free-choice nets*, M.I.T Cambridge Mass. Project Mac, CSG-Memo 78-1, 1973.

[Kosaraju 82] S.R. Kosaraju : *Decidability of reachability in vector addition systems*, in Proc. 14th Ann ACM Symp. on Theo. of Comp. 1982.

[Lambert 86] J.L. Lambert : *Consequences of the decidablity of the reachability problem for Petri nets*, Université Paris Sud. Rapport de recherche LRI 313, 1986.

[Lautenbach...79] K. Lautenbach and P.S. Thiagarajan : *Analysis of resource allocation problem using Petri nets*, 1st Euro. Conference on Parallel and Distributed Processing, J.C. Syre (Ed.) Cepadues edition, 1979

[Lien 76] Y.E. Lien : *Termination properties of generalized Petri nets*, SIAM J. Comput. v. 5, n° 2,pp 251-265, Jun 1976.

[Memmi 83] G. Memmi : *Methodes d'analyse des réseaux de Petri, réseaux à files et application aux systèmes temps réels*, thèse d'état, Paris VI, 1983.

[Mayr 84] W. Mayr : *An algorithm for the general Petri net reachability problem*, in SIAM J. Comp. vol 13 (3), August 1984.

[Peterson 81] J.L Peterson : *Petri net theory and the modeling of systems*, Prentice Hall, 1981.

[Reisig 79] W. Reisig : *On a Class of co-operating sequential processors*, 1st European conference on parallel and distributed processing, Toulouse, February 1979.

[Reisig 82] W. Reisig : *Deterministic buffer synchronization of sequential processes*, Acta Informatica 18, 1982.

[Souissi...88] Y. Souissi and N. Beldiceanu : *Deterministic systems of sequential processes: theory and tools*, Concurrency 88, LNCS 335, pp 380-400, Springer-Verlag, 1988.

[Souissi...89] Y. Souissi and G. Memmi : *Compositions of nets via a communication medium*, Advances in Petri nets '90, G. Rozenberg (Ed.) 1990.

[Souissi 90] Y. Souissi : *Préservation de propriétés par composition de réseaux de Petri, extension aux réseaux à files et application aux protocoles de communication*, thèse de l'Université Paris VI , February 1990.

[Souissi 92] Y. Souissi : *Deterministic systems of sequential processes : a class of structured Petri nets*, Internal INT report, to appear.

[Valk...85] R.Valk and M. Jantzen : *The residue of vectors sets with application to decidability problems in Petri nets*, Acta Informatica 21: 643-674, 1985.

APPENDIX

Definition A.1 [1] Euler's path and Euler's circuit

Let G=(X,U) be a strongly connected graph. Let P be a path of G, P is a Euler's path if and only if it contains, each arrow of U once. Let C be a circuit of G, C is a Euler's circuit if and only if C contains each arrow of U once .

Theorem A.1 [1] Euler's theorem

Let G=(X,U) be a strongly connected graph , G contains :

(1) a Euler's circuit if and only if $\forall x \in X$, $|\Gamma^+(x)| = |\Gamma^-(x)|$,

(2) a Euler's path from a to b if and only if $\forall x \in X$ $x \neq a$ or $x \neq b$

$|\Gamma^+(x)| = |\Gamma^-(x)|$ and $|\Gamma^+(a)| = |\Gamma^-(a)|+1$ and $|\Gamma^+(b)|+1 = |\Gamma^-(b)|$.

Corollary A.1

Let G=(X,U) be a graph. Let c be a circuit of G and let p be a path (respectively a circuit) of G verifying that :

(1) p starts at an arrow of c ,

(2) p contains at least n+1 occurrences of each arrow of c,

Then there exists a path (respectively a circuit) p' which verifies that :

(1) p' starts at the same arrow as p,

(2) p' starts with n occurrences of circuit c,

(3) p' ends at the same nodes as p,

(4) $\underline{p} = \underline{p'}$.

Proof

Let $a_1, a_2, \ldots, a_t$ be the arrows of c and $b_1, b_2, \ldots, b_u$ be the other arrows of p. We remove from G all the nodes and arrows which are not in p. If a_i (resp. b_i) occurs many times in p then we note $a_i^1, a_i^2, \ldots$ (respectively $b_i^1, b_i^2, \ldots$) its different occurrences in p. We remove from G the arrows $a_1, a_2, \ldots, a_t$ and we add the arrows $a_i^1, a_i^2, \ldots$ and $b_i^1, b_i^2, \ldots$. We obtain a new graph G_1, where each arrow of G has been repeated as often as it appears in p . Moreover we have built an Euler's path or an Euler's circuit p_1 (according to the fact that p is a path or a circuit) of G_1 . We remove from G_1 the arrows $a_1^1, \ldots a_1^n, a_2^1, \ldots, a_2^n, \ldots, a_t^1, \ldots, a_t^n$, to obtain a new graph G_2 which meets the hypothesis of Euler's theorem in the same conditions as G_1 (i.e. Euler's path or circuit). G_2 contains an Euler's path or an Euler's circuit p_3 (depending on whether p_1 is a path or a circuit). Let $p' = p_2 p_3$ be the path obtained by the concatenation of p_2 (the n occurrences of c starting at the same arrow as p) and p_3. By coming back to the first names of the arrows p' becomes the path or circuit that we are looking for. ♦

COMPOSITIONAL STATE SPACE GENERATION

Antti Valmari

Technical Research Centre of Finland
Computer Technology Laboratory
PO Box 201, SF–90571 OULU
FINLAND
Tel. int. +358 81 5512 111

ABSTRACT Compositional state space generation means the generation of a condensed version of the state space of a system in a compositional manner. The system is divided to parts. The state spaces of the parts are generated, condensed and composed to get a state space of the system. The method may be applied recursively; that is, the state spaces of the parts may have been generated compositionally. The generated condensed state space is in a certain sense equivalent with the ordinary state space, thus it can be used for the analysis of certain properties of the system.

Compositional state space generation is a very desirable goal because it has the potential to significantly increase the size of systems analysable with given computer resources. In this paper the theoretical and technical prerequisites of compositional state space generation methods are discussed. Then one particular method is developed. The method guarantees that the composed state spaces are equivalent in the sense of the theory of Communicating Sequential Processes (CSP) with the corresponding ordinary state spaces. Therefore the method is suitable for the analysis of the language and deadlock properties of systems which are not expected to execute infinite sequences of invisible transitions. The method is demonstrated with the aid of an example.

Keywords system verification, analysis of behaviour of nets, state space, compositionality, Communicating Sequential Processes

CONTENTS

1. INTRODUCTION

The analysis and verification of properties of concurrent systems is a topic of intensive research. The research is well motivated: it is very difficult to eliminate concurrency oriented problems from system designs without automatic aids, but, on the other hand, the performance of the analysis techniques and tools available today is often unsatisfactory. It is known that the poor performance has deep reasons. It has been proven that the problem of deciding non-trivial behavioural properties of concurrent systems is virtually always at least polynomial space complete, and it tends to be undecidable if the concurrency formalism in question allows unbounded queues [Brand & 83] [Jantzen 87] [Kanellakis & 85] [Räuchle & 85] [Valmari 88b]. But unpleasant complexity results do not guarantee that practical solutions to the analysis problems cannot be found. By taking advantage of special properties of the analysis problems it might be possible to develop analysis techniques which give reasonable performance for systems of practical size. In this paper we develop an analysis method which takes advantage of the fact that concurrent systems are often designed in a compositional way. We will briefly mention some other examples of analysis speed-up techniques based on special properties of concurrent systems in this introduction.

We concentrate on the group of analysis techniques which can be collectively called *state space generation*, *occurrence graph generation*, *reachability analysis* or *exhaustive simulation*, depending on what particular details of the techniques are emphasised. The basic step of the techniques is the generation of a directed graph called *reachability graph*, *occurrence graph*, *state space* or *labelled transition system* consisting of all global states the system can reach from its given initial state. Then the state space is investigated to decide various properties of the system. It is also possible to collect information about the behaviour of the system during the state space generation phase.

The performance problem of concurrent system analysis is demonstrated in state space generation by the fact that the state spaces of systems tend to grow exponentially in the number of processes of the systems. The state spaces of other than the smallest systems are typically far too large for processing in a real computer. It is thus obvious that to analyse medium scale or large systems with state space generation techniques, the size of the state space must somehow be reduced. Several approaches have been suggested, including: the aggregation of "similar" system states into one data object as in the *covering marking* or ω-technique of Karp and Miller ([Karp & 69]; [Peterson 81] and [Reisig 85, 87] are more recent sources, see also [Finkel 90] for optimisation and [Vuong & 87] for an extension to protocols), *equivalent marking method* of [Jensen 87] and *parameterized markings* of [Lindqvist 90], *parameterized expansion* in the Lotos Laboratory tool [Quemada & 89], and *state schema* technique of [Valmari 89c]; the collapsing of a set of identical processes to an indistinguishable single (or fewer) process(es) as in the *indexed computation tree logic* of Clarke and others [Clarke & 86, 87]; and the elimination of redundant interleavings as in the classic *virtual coarsening method* (see [Pnueli 86]), Overman's two tree pruning rules [Overman 81] and the *stubborn set method* [Valmari 88c, 89a, 89b, 91c] (applied to linear temporal logic in [Valmari 90] and to CSP semantics in [Valmari & 91b]).

The *divide-and-conquer* technique is a general approach to solving large instances of problems. Its application to state space generation would imply the division of the system under analysis into parts, the generation and analysis of the state spaces of the parts, and the combination of the analysis results. This is a natural idea, in particular because recent system design techniques tend to promote hierarchical or decompositional approach to system specification. The idea has been applied in temporal logic by Clarke with his colleagues, among others. They have developed a compositional verification technique for properties specified in their Computation Tree Logic Star [Clarke & 89]. The technique uses so-called *interface processes* to replace the environments of system components when they are separated from the system.

Process algebras are compositional by their very nature. As a consequence, one would expect them to lend themselves naturally to compositional verification techniques. Explicit discussion of the idea seems to be rare, though. Graf and Steffen have pointed out that the straightforward compositionality outlined above is not always satisfactory, because a process isolated from its environment may exhibit spurious behaviour, leading to a state space which may even be larger than the state space of the system as a whole [Graf & 90]. They present a technique based on the use of interface processes specified by the operator. The tighter the interface processes are the better reduction the method gives. If they are too tight the method fails and indicates it.

The *Concurrency Workbench* tool by Cleaveland and others [Cleaveland & 89] contains algorithms for finding a minimal process satisfying certain requirements and being equivalent (in some sense) with a given process. The minimisation algorithm could be used as a condensation algorithm of a compositional state space generation method as discussed in Chapter 2, and most of the other requirements of compositional state space generation are automatically met by process algebraic approaches. However, [Cleaveland & 89] does not explicitly refer to this possibility. Instead, compositional reasoning somewhat along the lines of Clarke and others has been mentioned as a possible future extension of the tool. This is perhaps because the tool stresses the *verification* of equivalence and the minimisation algorithms arise as a side product of the verification algorithms.

Not much has been written on compositional reachability analysis in the domain of Petri nets either. [Souissi & 89] and [Souissi 90] contain some results about the composition of nets so that the liveness and/or boundedness of the composed net can be decided from the properties of the original nets. Because reachability graph generation is one possible technique for deciding boundedness and a possible intermediate step in deciding liveness, the results can be applied to compositional reachability analysis of boundedness and liveness. However, this is not compositional state space generation in our sense of the word, because there is no hierarchy of nested composition levels. [Vogler 89] uses the earlier version of the semantic theory of CSP [Brookes & 84] in order to define the equivalence of two nets. He then analyses the deadlock properties of nets in a compositional way. However, he does not give any condensation algorithm in the sense of Section 2.3 or 3.4 of this paper.

In Chapter 2 we discuss the prerequisites of compositional state space generation. We argue that a good basis for compositional state space generation is a black-box semantics for the components of the system with the property that the corresponding semantic equivalence is a congruence with respect to the operations needed to build up the system. We discuss the desirable properties of the semantics. Based on our discussion, in Chapter 3 we choose suitable semantics from the process algebra world, namely the semantic model of the theory of *Communicating Sequential Processes* (*CSP*) of Brookes, Hoare and Roscoe [Brookes & 85] [Hoare 85]. We transport the semantics to the Petri net world and develop a compositional reachability analysis method. Chapter 4 is devoted to an example, and the conclusions follow in Chapter 5.

2. PREREQUISITES OF COMPOSITIONAL STATE SPACE GENERATION

Compositional state space generation assumes that the system under analysis can be seen as a collection of smaller systems connected together. The component systems are composed of yet smaller systems and so on as long as necessary. The semantics of the system and its components are defined in such a way that there is an *equivalence notion* which is a *congruence* with respect to the operations used in building up an upper level system from lower level systems. More formally, let S be a system, which is composed of the lower level systems $S_1, S_2, \ldots, S_n$ by a composition function f. That is, $S = f(S_1, \ldots, S_n)$. Let "$\cong$" be the equivalence notion. We require that for every f constructed using the composition operators, if $S'_i \cong S_i$ for every $i \in \{1, \ldots, n\}$, then $S' = f(S'_1, \ldots, S'_n) \cong S$. In other words, replacing system components by "$\cong$"-equivalent components should lead to a system which is "$\cong$"-equivalent with the original one.

In compositional state space generation systems are represented by their state spaces or, to be more accurate, by their *labelled transition systems* (*LTS*, for short). First, the LTSs $L_1, \ldots, L_n$ of the lowest-level systems are generated. Then they are *condensed* respecting the equivalence notion. That is, for every L_i a (preferably significantly smaller) LTS L'_i is generated such that $L'_i \cong L_i$. Then LTSs of the next level systems are generated by composing together the condensed LTSs L'_i of the previous level systems. The resulting LTSs are again condensed and so on, until we have a condensed LTS L of the whole system. Because of the congruence property, L is equivalent with the ordinary LTS of the whole system, and can thus be used to verify the properties of the system within the limits of the equivalence notion.

We distinguish the following ingredients of a compositional state space generation method:

- The equivalence notion.
- The operations used in the composition of lower level systems to upper level systems.
- The generation of the LTSs of the lowest level systems.
- The LTS condensation algorithm.
- The combination of the lower level LTSs to an upper level LTS.

The remainder of this chapter is devoted to an informal discussion of the requirements stated to the equivalence notion, the choice of the composition operators and the condensation algorithm. In the next chapter we take a more formal approach and develop a concrete compositional state space generation method.

2.1 Equivalence Notion

There are several requirements to the equivalence notion. First, it has to preserve the properties we want to analyse or verify. For instance, if we want to verify that a system is free from deadlocks, then either all or none of a set of systems which are equivalent according to the chosen notion should contain a deadlock. In general, the more distinctions the equivalence notion makes between systems, the more properties it preserves. In this respect, the stronger the equivalence notion is, the better.

Second, in order to get good LTS condensation results, it is necessary to find a small LTS which is equivalent to a given LTS. If the equivalence notion makes too many distinctions, the chances of finding a small equivalent LTS are limited. Therefore, regarding the condensation results, the weaker the equivalence notion is, the better.

These two requirements are clearly in contradiction with each other. The best compromise would be to use an equivalence which is exactly strong enough to preserve the properties we want to verify, but not any stronger. We assume that we want to verify the properties of the system as a whole. Component systems are important only as far as they contribute to the behaviour of the whole system. In other words, we are not interested in the interior of systems, but only their interfaces with the rest of the world. To keep our equivalence weak it is thus desirable that the equivalence refers to the interfaces only, that is, we take the *black-box* approach to system semantics. An interesting discussion of the motivation of black-box semantic models is found in [Olderog 87 Chapter 5].

Third, as already mentioned, the equivalence notion must be a congruence with respect to the operations used to compose upper level systems from lower level systems. Otherwise the hierarchical application of composition and condensation would not be justified. To satisfy the congruence property it might be necessary to take an equivalence which preserves more properties than what we want to verify.

2.2 Composition of Subsystems

The main composition operator in compositional state space generation is the *parallel composition*. There are two reasons for this.

First, parallel composition is a widely used "top-level" operator. A compositional state space generation method has to contain all the operators used at the topmost levels of the composition of the system, because the method can be used only as far down the system structure hierarchy as no composition operators disallowed by the method are encountered. Large concurrent systems are usually structured as a collection of (often relatively small) interconnected processes running in parallel.

Second, the exponential growth of the sizes of the LTSs of systems in the sizes of the systems is mainly due to parallel composition. The size of the LTS of the parallel composition of P_1, ..., P_n is at worst the product of the sizes of the LTSs of each P_i. If each of the individual LTSs is condensed by a factor of k, the biggest possible size of the composed LTS reduces by the factor of k^n. Consequently, condensation immediately before parallel composition can prove very advantageous.

When a system is composed from subsystems, some interface events of the subsystems become internal to the system as a whole. To maintain the black-box view to system semantics we want to hide the internal events. The *hiding* operator is used for this purpose.

We adopt also a *renaming* operator. With it similar subsystems can be used in different contexts just like the same procedure of a Pascal program can be called with different parameters.

Exploiting more composition operators is possible, but it may be expensive. The chosen equivalence must be a congruence with respect to all composition operators in use, and this is more difficult to ensure when there are many operators. In the remainder of this paper we restrict the available composition operators to the above mentioned parallel composition, hiding and renaming.

2.3 Condensation Algorithm

The two main requirements of the LTS condensation algorithm are that it should be reasonably fast and it should produce small condensed LTSs. Both requirements are only efficiency concerns. In particular, the correctness of compositional state space generation is not violated if the condensation results are not optimal. If efficient algorithms for producing optimal condensation results prove too difficult to find, then algorithms producing worse results but running fast can be used instead. The algorithm to be presented in this paper is relatively fast, but the condensation results achieved using it are not the best possible.

3. COMPOSITIONAL METHOD BASED ON CSP SEMANTICS

Most of the literature speaking about the state space generation or reachability analysis of Petri nets does not talk explicitly about black-box semantics of nets or subnets. The goal of reachability analysis has usually been the detection of properties such as deadlocks, boundedness of places, liveness of transitions, and violations of assertions represented as fact transitions. To find a black-box semantics suitable for compositional state space generation, we take advantage of the extensively studied relationship between Petri nets and process algebras (e.g. [Pomello 86] [Nielsen 87] [Best 87] [Olderog 87] [Vogler 89]). We build upon the CSP theory [Brookes & 85] [Hoare 85]. In particular we take advantage of the operational semantics of CSP as developed in [Olderog & 86].

3.1 Composition of Nets

To be able to define a black-box semantics for nets suitable for compositional state space generation we first define *labelled place/transition systems.* Let $\mathbb{N} = (\mathbb{P}, \mathbb{T}, \mathbb{W}, \mathbb{M}_0)$ be a place/transition system, where, as usual, $\mathbb{P}$ is the finite set of *places*, $\mathbb{T}$ is the finite set of *transitions*, $\mathbb{P} \cap \mathbb{T} = \varnothing$, $\mathbb{W}$ is a function from $(\mathbb{P} \times \mathbb{T}) \cup (\mathbb{T} \times \mathbb{P})$ to non-negative integers specifying the *arcs* and their *weights*, and $\mathbb{M}_0$ is the initial marking, which is a function from $\mathbb{P}$ to the set of non-negative integers. The assumption that $\mathbb{T}$ is finite will be used in Section 3.3.

We attach names or *labels* to the transitions of the P/T-system $\mathbb{N}$ in a common way. First, we associate with $\mathbb{N}$ a finite *alphabet* denoted by Σ. The alphabet is a set of symbols called *labels*. There is a special symbol or label "τ" which is not a member of the alphabet of any net. As usual in the process algebra literature, τ denotes an invisible or silent transition occurrence. Labels are attached to transitions with the aid of a *labelling function* α, $\alpha: \mathbb{T} \to \Sigma \cup \{\tau\}$.

Definition 3.1 Let $\mathbb{N} = (\mathbb{P}, \mathbb{T}, \mathbb{W}, \mathbb{M}_0)$ be a P/T-system, Σ a finite collection of symbols not containing τ, and α a function from $\mathbb{T}$ to $\Sigma \cup \{\tau\}$. A *labelled P/T-system* is the 6-tuple $(\mathbb{P}, \mathbb{T}, \mathbb{W}, \mathbb{M}_0, \Sigma, \alpha)$. Σ is called the *alphabet* of $\mathbb{N}$. We say that $t \in \mathbb{T}$ is *invisible* if and only if $\alpha(t) = \tau$, otherwise t is *visible*. □

We will define the black-box semantics of a labelled P/T-system in the next section. In the remainder of this section we define three composition operators which we will use in building larger nets from smaller ones: *parallel composition*, *hiding* and *renaming*.

Before the formal definition of the parallel composition operator we give an intuitive description of it. The alphabet of the composition is the union of the alphabets of the individual labelled P/T-systems. The individual subsystems communicate with each other by executing transitions with a common label. The labels can thus be thought of as communication channels. A subsystem may or may not be connected to a particular communication channel. It is the task of the alphabet of the subsystem to specify the channels the subsystem is connected to. Communication is synchronous: it can take place only if every subsystem connected to the channel in question is ready to communicate, and it affects all of the communicating subsystems. This notion of parallel composition is equivalent to the parallel composition in CSP as presented in [Hoare 85] or, in an operational form, in [Olderog & 86 p. 56].

For simplicity we assume that the sets of places of subsystems are disjoint, and similarly with the sets of transitions. The set of places of the composed system is simply the union of the sets of places of the subsystems. An invisible transition corresponds to local activity of the subsystem it belongs to, therefore invisible transitions and the arcs adjacent to them are left as they are. To achieve synchronization visible transitions are "fused" (see [Huber & 89]) in all possible combinations picking one transition from each subsystem having the label in question in its alphabet.

Definition 3.2 Let $\mathbb{L}_i = (\mathbb{P}_i, \mathbb{T}_i, \mathbb{W}_i, \mathbb{M}_{0i}, \Sigma_i, \alpha_i)$ where $i \in \{1, \ldots, n\}$ be labelled P/T-systems such that all the $\mathbb{P}_i$ and all the $\mathbb{T}_i$ are disjoint. Let $a \in \Sigma_1 \cup \ldots \cup \Sigma_n$. The *parallel composition* of $\mathbb{L}_1$ to $\mathbb{L}_n$, denoted by $\mathbb{L}_1 \parallel \ldots \parallel \mathbb{L}_n$, is the labelled P/T-system $\mathbb{L} = (\mathbb{P}, \mathbb{T}, \mathbb{W}, \mathbb{M}_0, \Sigma, \alpha)$ defined as follows:

- $\Sigma = \Sigma_1 \cup \ldots \cup \Sigma_n$
- $\mathbb{P} = \mathbb{P}_1 \cup \ldots \cup \mathbb{P}_n$

- $\mathbf{T}_{i\tau} = \{t \in \mathbf{T}_i \mid \alpha_i(t) = \tau\}$
- $\mathbf{T}_\tau = \mathbf{T}_{1\tau} \cup \ldots \cup \mathbf{T}_{n\tau}$
- $uses(a) = \{i \in \{1,\ldots,n\} \mid a \in \Sigma_i\}$
- $\mathbf{T}_{ia} = \{t \in \mathbf{T}_i \mid \alpha_i(t) = a\}$, if $i \in uses(a)$
- $\mathbf{T}_a = \underset{i \in uses(a)}{\times} \mathbf{T}_{ia}$ (i.e. the Cartesian product of those $\mathbf{T}_{ia}$ where $a \in \Sigma_i$)
- $\mathbf{T} = \mathbf{T}_\tau \cup \bigcup_{a \in \Sigma} \mathbf{T}_a$
- Let $p \in \mathbf{P}$, i be chosen such that $p \in \mathbf{P}_i$ and $t \in \mathbf{T}_\tau$. If $t \in \mathbf{T}_i$ then $\mathbf{W}(p,t) = \mathbf{W}_i(p,t)$, otherwise $\mathbf{W}(p,t) = 0$. $\mathbf{W}(t,p)$ is defined similarly.
- Let p and i be as above and $t \in \mathbf{T}_a$. If $i \in uses(a)$ then $\mathbf{W}(p,t) = \mathbf{W}_i(p,t_i)$, where t_i is the component of t belonging to $\mathbf{T}_i$. Otherwise $\mathbf{W}(p,t) = 0$. $\mathbf{W}(t,p)$ is defined similarly.
- If $p \in \mathbf{P}_i$, then $\mathbf{M}_0(p) = \mathbf{M}_{0i}(p)$.
- $\alpha(t) = \tau$, if $t \in \mathbf{T}_\tau$, and
- $\alpha(t) = a$, if $t \in \mathbf{T}_a$. □

The fact that the parallel composition of labelled P/T-systems corresponds to the parallel composition operator of CSP is implied by the following proposition, which is a direct consequence of Definition 3.2:

Proposition 3.3 Let $\mathbf{L} = (\mathbf{P},\mathbf{T},\mathbf{W},\mathbf{M}_0,\Sigma,\alpha) = \mathbf{L}_1 \parallel \ldots \parallel \mathbf{L}_n$, where $\mathbf{L}_i = (\mathbf{P}_i,\mathbf{T}_i,\mathbf{W}_i,\mathbf{M}_{0i},\Sigma_i,\alpha_i)$ for $1 \le i \le n$. Let M and M' satisfy $M(p) = M_i(p)$ and $M'(p) = M'_i(p)$ for all i and $p \in \mathbf{P}_i$.

(1) $\exists t \in \mathbf{T}: \alpha(t) = \tau \wedge M\,[t\!>\,M'$ in $\mathbf{L}$ iff
$\exists i \in \{1,\ldots,n\}: \exists t_i \in \mathbf{T}_i$:
$\alpha(t_i) = \tau \wedge M_i\,[t_i\!>\,M'_i$ in $\mathbf{L}_i \wedge \forall j \in \{1,\ldots,i-1,i+1,\ldots,n\}: M_j = M'_j$.

(2) $\exists t \in \mathbf{T}: \alpha(t) = a \neq \tau \wedge M\,[t\!>\,M'$ in $\mathbf{L}$ iff
$\forall i \in uses(a): \exists t_i \in \mathbf{T}_i: \alpha(t_i) = a \neq \tau \wedge M_i\,[t_i\!>\,M'_i$ in $\mathbf{L}_i \wedge$
$\forall j \in \{1,\ldots,n\} - uses(a): M_j = M'_j$. □

Note that it makes a significant difference whether symbol a not labelling any transition of subsystem $\mathbf{L}_i$ belongs to the alphabet Σ_i of $\mathbf{L}_i$. If $a \notin \Sigma_i$, $\mathbf{L}_i$ does not contribute to the fusing of "a"-transitions i.e. to $\mathbf{T}_a$ of Definition 3.2. If $a \in \Sigma_i$, the contribution of $\mathbf{L}_i$ to the Cartesian product $\mathbf{T}_a$ is $\mathbf{T}_{ia} = \varnothing$, implying that there are no merged transitions at all. This reflects the intuitive idea that the subnet is connected to the channel, but is never ready — never able, as a matter of fact — to actually communicate via it. Instead, it prevents everyone from using the channel.

In addition to the parallel composition we need the operations of *hiding* and *renaming*. These affect only the labels of transitions, not the net itself. As in CSP, hiding changes a set of transition labels to the invisible symbol τ. Renaming replaces some transition labels by new labels which need not be drawn from the alphabet of the original system.

Definition 3.4 Let $\mathbf{L} = (\mathbf{P},\mathbf{T},\mathbf{W},\mathbf{M}_0,\Sigma,\alpha)$ be a labelled P/T-system and A a set of symbols not containing τ. $\mathbf{L}\backslash A$ is the labelled P/T-system $(\mathbf{P},\mathbf{T},\mathbf{W},\mathbf{M}_0,\Sigma',\alpha')$, where

- $\Sigma' = \Sigma - A$

- $\alpha'(t) = \tau$, if $\alpha(t) \in A$, and
- $\alpha'(t) = \alpha(t)$, if $\alpha(t) \notin A$. □

Definition 3.5 Let $\mathbb{L} = (\mathbb{P}, \mathbb{T}, \mathbb{W}, \mathbb{M}_0, \Sigma, \alpha)$ be a labelled P/T-system, $a_1, \ldots, a_n \in \Sigma$, $a_i \neq a_j$ if $i \neq j$, and $b_1, \ldots, b_n \neq \tau$. $\mathbb{L}[a_1 \leftarrow b_1, \ldots, a_n \leftarrow b_n]$ is the labelled P/T-system $(\mathbb{P}, \mathbb{T}, \mathbb{W}, \mathbb{M}_0, \Sigma', \alpha')$, where

- $\Sigma' = (\Sigma - \{a_1, \ldots, a_n\}) \cup \{b_1, \ldots, b_n\}$
- $\alpha'(t) = b_i$, if $\alpha(t) = a_i$ for some $i \in \{1, \ldots, n\}$, and
- $\alpha'(t) = \alpha(t)$, otherwise. □

3.2 Semantics of Subnets

Consider again the P/T-system $\mathbf{N} = (\mathbb{P}, \mathbb{T}, \mathbb{W}, \mathbb{M}_0)$ and an associated labelled P/T-system $\mathbb{L} = (\mathbb{P}, \mathbb{T}, \mathbb{W}, \mathbb{M}_0, \Sigma, \alpha)$. The reachability graph of a P/T-system is a representation of its interleaving semantics. As was mentioned in Section 2.1, we want our semantic model to be a black-box semantics. The reachability graph is not a black-box semantics, because transitions are represented by themselves and markings are known as such. As an intermediate step in constructing a black-box semantics we define a *labelled transition system* of a labelled P/T-system.

Definition 3.6 A *labelled transition system* (*LTS*, for short) is a quadruple $(\mathbb{S}, \Sigma \cup \{\tau\}, \Delta, \mathbf{s}_0)$, where $\mathbb{S}$ is a set of *states*, Σ is (as before) a finite set of symbols not containing the *invisible event* symbol τ, $\Delta \subseteq \mathbb{S} \times (\Sigma \cup \{\tau\}) \times \mathbb{S}$ and $\mathbf{s}_0 \in \mathbb{S}$ is the *initial state*. Σ is called the *alphabet* and its elements are *event* names. □

Definition 3.7 Let $\mathbb{L} = (\mathbb{P}, \mathbb{T}, \mathbb{W}, \mathbb{M}_0, \Sigma, \alpha)$ be a labelled P/T-system. The labelled transition system of $\mathbb{L}$ is the quadruple $\text{LTS}(\mathbb{L}) = (\mathbb{S}, \Sigma \cup \{\tau\}, \Delta, \mathbf{s}_0)$, where

- $\mathbb{S} = [\mathbb{M}_0>$ is the set of reachable markings
- Σ and τ are as before
- $\Delta = \{ (M, a, M') \in \mathbb{S} \times (\Sigma \cup \{\tau\}) \times \mathbb{S} \mid \exists t \in \mathbb{T}: \alpha(t) = a \wedge M\, [t> M' \}$
- $\mathbf{s}_0 = \mathbb{M}_0$ □

The LTS of a labelled P/T-system is in close relationship with the ordinary reachability graph of the system. The almost only difference is the labelling of edges. If an edge of the reachability graph is labelled by $t \in \mathbb{T}$, then the corresponding edge of the LTS is labelled by $\alpha(t) \in \Sigma \cup \{\tau\}$. Actually several edges of a reachability graph map to one edge of the LTS if the edges share their start and end markings and the corresponding transitions have the same label; this is why we added the word "almost" to the previous statement.

We see that in the LTS the exact identities of the transitions are hidden and only their roles as communicating entities are retained. This is a step towards black-box semantics. It is not sufficient alone, however. To take the next step we abstract from occurrences of invisible transitions by defining *traces* as follows.

Definition 3.8 Let $(\mathbb{S}, \Sigma \cup \{\tau\}, \Delta, \mathbf{s}_0)$ be a labelled transition system, $s, s' \in \mathbb{S}$, $n \geq 0$, a, a_1, $a_2, \ldots, a_n \in \Sigma \cup \{\tau\}$ and $b_1, b_2, \ldots, b_n \in \Sigma$.

- $s -a\rightarrow s' \Leftrightarrow (s, a, s') \in \Delta$

- $s -a_1a_2...a_n\rightarrow s' \Leftrightarrow \exists\, s_0, ..., s_n \in \mathbf{S}: s = s_0 \wedge s_n = s' \wedge \forall\, i \in \{1, ..., n\}: s_{i-1} -a_i\rightarrow s_i$
- $s =b_1b_2...b_n\Rightarrow s'$, iff there are non-negative integers $i(0)$, ..., $i(n)$ such that $s -\tau^{i(0)}b_1\tau^{i(1)}b_2\tau^{i(2)}...\tau^{i(n-1)}b_n\tau^{i(n)}\rightarrow s'$, where τ^i denotes the string of i τ-symbols
- $s -a_1a_2...a_n\rightarrow \;\Leftrightarrow\; \exists\, s' \in \mathbf{S}: s -a_1a_2...a_n\rightarrow s'$, and
  $s =b_1b_2...b_n\Rightarrow \;\Leftrightarrow\; \exists\, s' \in \mathbf{S}: s =b_1b_2...b_n\Rightarrow s'$
- $tr(s) = \{\sigma \in \Sigma^* \mid s =\sigma\Rightarrow\}$ is the set of *traces* of s. □

Let $\mathbf{M}_0$ be the initial marking of the labelled P/T-system $\mathbb{L}$. $\mathbf{M}_0$ is the initial state of LTS($\mathbb{L}$) and $tr(\mathbf{M}_0)$ is the set of traces of $\mathbf{M}_0$ in LTS($\mathbb{L}$). $tr(\mathbf{M}_0)$ has a natural interpretation: it is the language generated by all finite transition sequences of $\mathbb{L}$ starting at $\mathbf{M}_0$. The word generated by a transition sequence is the sequence of the labels of the transitions with all τ-symbols removed.

We define the *trace semantics* of the labelled P/T-system $\mathbb{L}$ as the pair $(\Sigma, tr(\mathbf{M}_0))$. Accordingly, two systems are *trace equivalent* if they have the same alphabet and the same set of traces. Trace semantics is a black-box semantics. It is known that trace equivalence is a congruence with respect to parallel composition, hiding and renaming. On the other hand, it is also known that trace semantics is not strong enough for many purposes, because it does not record the deadlock behaviour of nets. Let ε denote the empty string. Both of the two labelled P/T-systems in Figure 1 have $\{\varepsilon, a, aa, ...\}$ as their set of traces, but the rightmost one can deadlock, while the other can not.

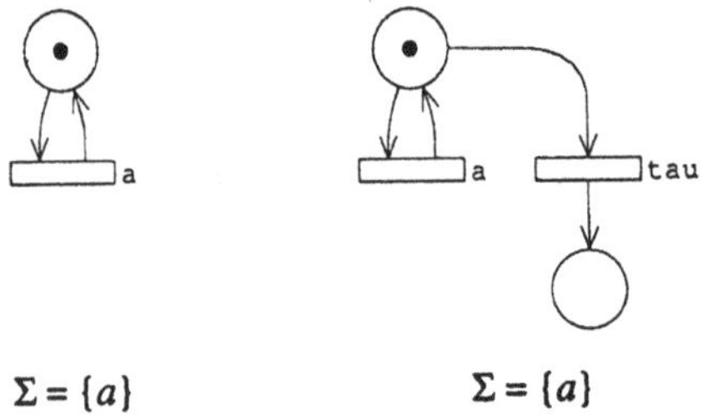

Figure 1 Two labelled P/T-systems with same traces and different deadlocks

Several stronger equivalences and corresponding semantic models have been defined in the process algebra world. The most important are the *observation equivalence*, *observation congruence* [Milner 80, 89] and the equivalence induced by the denotational model of CSP based on the notions of *failures* and *divergence traces* [Brookes & 85] [Hoare 85]. (A version of CSP without divergence traces is discussed in [Brookes & 84].) Observation congruence is stronger than observation equivalence in the sense that if two systems are observation congruent, then they are observation equivalent, but the reverse does not always hold [Milner 80, 89]. In the absence of infinite sequences of occurrences of invisible transitions, observation equivalence is stronger than CSP-equivalence and CSP-equivalence is stronger than trace equivalence.

All of these notions are congruences with respect to parallel composition, hiding and renaming. We have chosen to use the equivalence of CSP in our compositional state space generation method because weaker equivalences lead to better condensation results, as discussed in Section 2.1. We will soon present a formal definition of CSP-equivalence. Instead of following the treatment in [Brookes & 85] or [Hoare 85] which is based on defining a structurally inductive mapping from CSP expressions to a given semantic domain, we follow the treatment in [Olderog 87] and build the definition upon the LTS concepts we have already introduced. This way we can relate the operational concepts arising naturally from labelled P/T-systems (traces etc.) to the related concepts in [Brookes & 85], [Hoare 85].

We take deadlock properties into account in the form of *failures*.

Definition 3.9 Let $(\mathbf{S}, \Sigma \cup \{\tau\}, \Delta, \mathbf{s}_0)$ be a labelled transition system, $s \in \mathbf{S}$, $A \subseteq \Sigma$ and $\sigma \in \Sigma^*$. (σ, A) is a *failure* of s, iff $\exists\, s' \in \mathbf{S}$: $s = \sigma \Rightarrow s' \wedge \forall\, a \in A: \neg\,(s' = a \Rightarrow)$. The set of the failures of s is denoted by $fail(s)$. □

Obviously $\forall\, s \in \mathbf{S}: \forall\, a \in \varnothing: \neg\,(s = a \Rightarrow)$. As a consequence, $(\sigma, \varnothing) \in fail(s)$ if and only if $\sigma \in tr(s)$. The set of failures thus determines the set of traces. We call two systems *f-equivalent* if they have the same alphabet and the same set of failures. Because of the above, f-equivalence is stronger than trace equivalence.

Unfortunately f-equivalence is not a congruence with respect to the hiding operator. Hiding an event a of the LTS L means the replacement of all occurrences of a in L by the invisible event symbol τ. The result is denoted by $L \backslash \{a\}$. Consider the two LTSs L_1 and L_2 in Figure 2. Both have all the pairs $(a^n, [\{b\}])$ and $(a^n b, [\{a, b\}])$ and nothing else as their failures, where a^n is a string of n $(n \geq 0)$ a's and $[X]$ denotes any subset of X. However, if a is hidden, $(\varepsilon, \{b\})$ is a failure of the leftmost system $L_1 \backslash \{a\}$ but not of the rightmost system $L_2 \backslash \{a\}$.

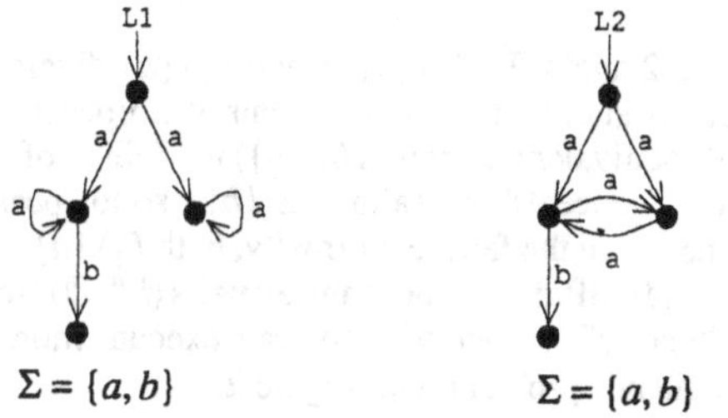

Figure 2 Demonstrating that f-equivalence is not a congruence

As discussed in Section 2.2, the hiding operator is important to compositional state space generation. It has turned out that the congruence problem with the hiding operator is due to the fact that it can introduce infinite sequences of occurrences of invisible transitions. A trace such that after executing it the system may perform an infinite sequence of invisible transitions is called a *divergence trace*:

Definition 3.10 Let $(\mathbf{S}, \Sigma \cup \{\tau\}, \Delta, \mathbf{s}_0)$ be a labelled transition system, $s \in \mathbf{S}$ and $\sigma \in \Sigma^*$. σ is a *divergence trace* of s, iff $\exists\, s' \in \mathbf{S}$: $s = \sigma \Rightarrow s' \wedge s' - \tau^\infty \rightarrow$, where τ^∞ denotes an infinite sequence of τ-symbols. The set of the divergence traces of s is denoted by $div(s)$. □

Divergence traces make it very difficult to relate the failures of a system after hiding to the failures of the system before the hiding. As a consequence, it is not trivial to design a congruent failure-based semantic model coping with the hiding operator. The developers of CSP adopted a solution which might seem brutal at the first sight: the behaviour of a process after divergence is just ignored. In other words, we can get information about the behaviour of a process up to the point where the process diverges, but not after that. This is called the *catastrophic* interpretation of divergence. It is encoded into the formalism by interpreting every continuation of a divergence trace as a divergence trace, and assuming that after executing a divergence trace a process may fail just anything. The next definition shows how this is done.

Definition 3.11 Let $(\mathbb{S}, \Sigma \cup \{\tau\}, \Delta, \mathbf{s}_0)$ be a labelled transition system, $s \in \mathbb{S}$, $\sigma \in \Sigma^*$ and $A \subseteq \Sigma$.

(1) σ is a *CSP-divergence* of s, iff $\sigma = \sigma_1\sigma_2$ where $\sigma_1 \in div(s)$. The set of CSP-divergences of s is denoted by $CSPdiv(s)$.

(2) (σ, A) is a *CSP-failure* of s, iff $(\sigma, A) \in fail(s)$ or $\sigma \in CSPdiv(s)$. The set of CSP-failures of s is denoted by $CSPfail(s)$.

(3) σ is a *CSP-trace* of s, iff $(\sigma, \emptyset) \in CSPfail(s)$. The set of CSP-traces of s is denoted by $CSPtr(s)$.

(4) The *CSP-semantics* of $(\mathbb{S}, \Sigma \cup \{\tau\}, \Delta, \mathbf{s}_0)$ is the triple $(\Sigma, CSPfail(\mathbf{s}_0), CSPdiv(\mathbf{s}_0))$. The *CSP-semantics* of a labelled P/T-system $\mathbb{L}$ is the CSP-semantics of LTS($\mathbb{L}$).

(5) The labelled transition systems $(\mathbb{S}, \Sigma \cup \{\tau\}, \Delta, \mathbf{s}_0)$ and $(\mathbb{S}', \Sigma' \cup \{\tau\}, \Delta', \mathbf{s}'_0)$ are *CSP-equivalent*, iff $\Sigma = \Sigma'$, $CSPfail(\mathbf{s}_0) = CSPfail(\mathbf{s}'_0)$ and $CSPdiv(\mathbf{s}_0) = CSPdiv(\mathbf{s}'_0)$, where *CSPfail* and *CSPdiv* are evaluated in the corresponding LTS. The labelled P/T-systems $\mathbb{L}$ and $\mathbb{L}'$ are CSP-equivalent, if LTS($\mathbb{L}$) and LTS($\mathbb{L}'$) are CSP-equivalent. □

Let us consider the example in Figure 2 again. Both $L_1 \backslash \{a\}$ and $L_2 \backslash \{a\}$ diverge initially. Because the CSP-semantics does not pay attention to the behaviour of a process when it has diverged, $L_1 \backslash \{a\}$ and $L_2 \backslash \{a\}$ are CSP-equivalent, although $(\varepsilon, \{b\})$ is a failure of $L_1 \backslash \{a\}$ but not of $L_2 \backslash \{a\}$. The divergence trace ε "conceals" the failure $(\varepsilon, \{b\})$, so to speak, because the divergence trace ε is a prefix of the "ε" in the failure. Formally, both $L_1 \backslash \{a\}$ and $L_2 \backslash \{a\}$ have all strings b^n as their CSP-traces and CSP-divergences and all pairs $(b^n, \emptyset)$ and $(b^n, \{b\})$ as their CSP-failures, although in "reality" neither of them can execute more than one b-transition. This eliminates the congruence problem with Figure 2.

We will use CSP-equivalence as the equivalence notion in our compositional state space generation method. We will show in Section 3.3 that it indeed is a congruence with respect to the parallel composition, hiding and renaming operators. In the remainder of this section we investigate its relation to the theory in [Hoare 85], justify the term "CSP-semantics", and discuss the properties of systems deducible from their CSP-semantics.

In the theory of CSP a process is defined as a formal triple consisting of the alphabet Σ of the process and two sets denoted by $\mathbb{F}$ and $\mathbb{D}$. The definition is abstract in the sense that $\mathbb{F}$ and $\mathbb{D}$ need no interpretation. However, they are required to posses some properties which are listed as conditions C0 to C6 in the below definition.

Definition 3.12 [Hoare 85 p. 130] A *process* is a triple $(\Sigma, \mathbb{F}, \mathbb{D})$ where Σ is a finite set of symbols called the *alphabet*, $\mathbb{F} \subseteq \Sigma^* \times 2^\Sigma$ and $\mathbb{D} \subseteq \Sigma^*$ such that

C0 $(\varepsilon,\varnothing) \in \mathbb{F}$

C1 $(\sigma\rho,A) \in \mathbb{F} \Rightarrow (\sigma,\varnothing) \in \mathbb{F}$

C2 $(\sigma,A) \in \mathbb{F} \wedge B \subseteq A \Rightarrow (\sigma,B) \in \mathbb{F}$

C3 $(\sigma,A) \in \mathbb{F} \wedge a \in \Sigma \Rightarrow (\sigma,A \cup \{a\}) \in \mathbb{F} \vee (\sigma a,\varnothing) \in \mathbb{F}$

C4 $\mathbb{D} \subseteq \{ \sigma \mid \exists A \subseteq \Sigma: (\sigma,A) \in \mathbb{F} \}$

C5 $\sigma \in \mathbb{D} \wedge \rho \in \Sigma^* \Rightarrow \sigma\rho \in \mathbb{D}$

C6 $\sigma \in \mathbb{D} \wedge A \subseteq \Sigma \Rightarrow (\sigma,A) \in \mathbb{F}$ □

We prove next that if we interpret $\mathbb{F}$ and $\mathbb{D}$ as the CSP-failures and CSP-divergences of a LTS, then all of the conditions in Definition 3.12 are satisfied. Therefore, the triple (Σ, *CSPfail*($\mathbf{s}_0$), *CSPdiv*($\mathbf{s}_0$)) is a process in the sense of the theory of CSP, and we can indeed call our semantic model "CSP-semantics".

Theorem 3.13 Let $\mathbb{L} = (\mathbb{P}, \mathbb{T}, \mathbb{W}, \mathbb{M}_0, \Sigma, \alpha)$ be a labelled P/T-system and LTS($\mathbb{L}$) = ($\mathbf{S}$, $\Sigma \cup \{\tau\}$, Δ, $\mathbf{s}_0$). (Σ, *CSPfail*($\mathbf{s}_0$), *CSPdiv*($\mathbf{s}_0$)) is a process in the sense of the theory of CSP (Definition 3.12).

Proof Σ is a finite set of symbols, *CSPfail*($\mathbf{s}_0$) $\subseteq \Sigma^* \times 2^\Sigma$ and *CSPdiv*($\mathbf{s}_0$) $\subseteq \Sigma^*$ by Definitions 3.1 and 3.11. $(\varepsilon,\varnothing) \in$ *fail*($\mathbf{s}_0$) by Definition 3.9, because $\mathbf{s}_0 = \varepsilon \Rightarrow \mathbf{s}_0$ by Definition 3.8. Thus Definition 3.11 (2) implies that C0 is satisfied. Regarding C1, if $(\sigma\rho,A) \in$ *CSPfail*($\mathbf{s}_0$) then $(\sigma\rho,A) \in$ *fail*($\mathbf{s}_0$) or $\sigma\rho \in$ *CSPdiv*($\mathbf{s}_0$). In the former case the claim follows from Definitions 3.8 and 3.9. In the latter case $\sigma\rho$ has a prefix $\sigma' \in$ *div*($\mathbf{s}_0$). If σ' is a prefix of σ then $\sigma \in$ *CSPdiv*($\mathbf{s}_0$) implying the claim. If σ is a prefix of σ' then $(\sigma,\varnothing) \in$ *fail*($\mathbf{s}_0$) by Definitions 3.10 and 3.9. C2 follows directly from Definitions 3.9 and 3.11 (2). To prove C3, if $\sigma \in$ *CSPdiv*($\mathbf{s}_0$) then $(\sigma, A \cup \{a\}) \in$ *CSPfail*($\mathbf{s}_0$). Let $(\sigma,A) \in$ *fail*($\mathbf{s}_0$). There is s such that $\mathbf{s}_0 = \sigma \Rightarrow s$. If there is s such that $\mathbf{s}_0 = \sigma \Rightarrow s -a\rightarrow$ then $(\sigma a,\varnothing) \in$ *fail*($\mathbf{s}_0$) $\subseteq$ *CSPfail*($\mathbf{s}_0$). Otherwise $(\sigma, A \cup \{a\}) \in$ *fail*($\mathbf{s}_0$). C4 and C6 follow immediately from Definition 3.11 (2) and C5 from Definition 3.11 (1). □

Let us discuss the system properties which are present in the CSP-semantics of labelled P/T-systems. If there are no divergence traces then CSP-equivalence reduces to f-equivalence. This implies that if the system cannot perform infinite sequences of invisible events, the semantics preserve complete information about the sequences of visible events the system may participate, that is, the language generated by the system. The deadlock behaviour after participating a given sequence is also preserved by the semantics. The system may deadlock after executing σ if and only if it has (σ,Σ) as its failure. Also the possibility of the system to deadlock in a given environment is extensively shown in the failure sets, all the time assuming that the system cannot perform infinite sequences of invisible events.

If the system can enter a state from which it can execute an infinite sequence of invisible events then we still obtain the event sequence and deadlock behaviour information up to (but not including) the point where the system *may* be capable of executing an infinite sequence of invisible events. We are also told when we have reached this point. From then on we get absolutely no information of the behaviour of the system. Whether the system really is in a state where it could start an infinite sequence of invisible events is immaterial; no information of the future behaviour of the system is obtained if it *could* be in such a state after executing the visible events it has executed.

These kind of semantics are adequate if we require that the system always produces its responses in finite time, since extensive information of the black-box behaviour of the system is obtained as long as response times are guaranteed to remain finite, and the semantics reveal when this assumption is violated. There are systems, however, where this assumption is too strict. A protocol with unbounded retransmission is an obvious example, as there is no limit to how many times the retransmission may take place before the transmission succeeds. "Legal" divergence traces may arise also if we for some reason want to investigate a system from a narrow point of view. For instance, if we investigate a system serving many customers from the point of view of one customer only, then the activity of other customers appears as divergences.

Recently a CSP-like semantic model has been introduced which coincides with the CSP model in the absence of divergences, but keeps on recording appropriate information about failures and (true) divergence traces even after the system may have diverged. The new model is a congruence with respect to parallel composition, hiding and renaming and many other useful composition operators. It is thus well-suited for compositional analysis of systems. The so far reported form of the model is valid for finite-state systems only [Valmari & 91a], but that is sufficient for compositional state space generation. What is more, an extension of it to infinite-state systems is known.

3.3 Composition of LTSs

In this section we define the parallel composition, hiding and renaming of labelled transition systems and relate them to the corresponding operators of labelled P/T-systems. We also show that CSP-equivalence is a congruence with respect to these operators. This congruence property was proven already in [Olderog & 86] in a somewhat different setting.

Definition 3.14 Let $L_1 = (\mathbf{S}_1, \Sigma_1 \cup \{\tau\}, \Delta_1, \mathbf{s}_{01}), \ldots, L_n = (\mathbf{S}_n, \Sigma_n \cup \{\tau\}, \Delta_n, \mathbf{s}_{0n})$ be labelled transition systems. Let $\Sigma = \Sigma_1 \cup \ldots \cup \Sigma_n$, $a \in \Sigma \cup \{\tau\}$, $s = (s_1, \ldots, s_n) \in \mathbf{S}_1 \times \ldots \times \mathbf{S}_n$ and $s' = (s'_1, \ldots, s'_n) \in \mathbf{S}_1 \times \ldots \times \mathbf{S}_n$.

- $s -a\rightarrow s'$ iff
  - $a = \tau \wedge \exists i \in \{1, \ldots, n\}: s_i -\tau\rightarrow s'_i \wedge \forall j \in \{1, \ldots, i-1, i+1, \ldots, n\}: s'_j = s_j$, or
  - $a \in \Sigma \wedge \forall i \in \{1, \ldots, n\}: (a \in \Sigma_i \wedge s_i -a\rightarrow s'_i) \vee (a \notin \Sigma_i \wedge s'_i = s_i)$

  Let $\rho \in (\Sigma \cup \{\tau\})^*$ and $\sigma \in \Sigma^*$. $s -\rho\rightarrow s'$, $s =\sigma\Rightarrow s'$, $s -\rho\rightarrow$ and $s =\sigma\Rightarrow$ are defined using $s -a\rightarrow s'$ as in Definition 3.8.
- $L_1 \parallel \ldots \parallel L_n$ is the labelled transition system $(\mathbf{S}, \Sigma \cup \{\tau\}, \Delta, \mathbf{s}_0)$ such that
  - $\Sigma = \Sigma_1 \cup \ldots \cup \Sigma_n$
  - $\mathbf{s}_0 = (\mathbf{s}_{01}, \ldots, \mathbf{s}_{0n})$
  - $\mathbf{S} = \{s \in \mathbf{S}_1 \times \ldots \times \mathbf{S}_n \mid \exists \rho \in (\Sigma \cup \{\tau\})^*: \mathbf{s}_0 -\rho\rightarrow s\}$
  - $\Delta = \{(s, a, s') \in \mathbf{S} \times (\Sigma \cup \{\tau\}) \times \mathbf{S} \mid s -a\rightarrow s'\}$ □

Definition 3.15 Let $L = (\mathbf{S}, \Sigma \cup \{\tau\}, \Delta, \mathbf{s}_0)$ be a labelled transition system.

- Let $A \subseteq \Sigma$. $L \backslash A$ is the labelled transition system $(\mathbf{S}, \Sigma' \cup \{\tau\}, \Delta', \mathbf{s}_0)$ where
  - $\Sigma' = \Sigma - A$, and
  - $\Delta' = \{(s, a, s') \in \mathbf{S} \times (\Sigma' \cup \{\tau\}) \times \mathbf{S} \mid (s, a, s') \in \Delta \wedge a \notin A\} \cup$
    $\{(s, \tau, s') \in \mathbf{S} \times (\Sigma' \cup \{\tau\}) \times \mathbf{S} \mid \exists a \in A: (s, a, s') \in \Delta\}$

- Let $\{a_1,\ldots,a_n\} \subseteq \Sigma$ and $\tau \notin \{b_1,\ldots,b_n\}$. $L[a_1 \leftarrow b_1,\ldots,a_n \leftarrow b_n]$ is the labelled transition system $(\mathbf{S}, \Sigma' \cup \{\tau\}, \Delta', \mathbf{s}_0)$ where
  - $\Sigma' = (\Sigma - \{a_1,\ldots,a_n\}) \cup \{b_1,\ldots,b_n\}$, and
  - $\Delta' = \{(s,a,s') \in \mathbf{S} \times (\Sigma' \cup \{\tau\}) \times \mathbf{S} \mid (s,a,s') \in \Delta \wedge a \notin \{a_1,\ldots,a_n\}\} \cup$
    $\{(s,b,s') \in \mathbf{S} \times (\Sigma' \cup \{\tau\}) \times \mathbf{S} \mid \exists i \in \{1,\ldots,n\}: b = b_i \wedge (s,a_i,s') \in \Delta\}$ □

The first part of Definition 3.14 specifies the reachability relation on $L_1 \parallel \ldots \parallel L_n$. It turns out that $L_1 \parallel \ldots \parallel L_n$ can be computed in a similar way to ordinary reachability graph generation. The operations specified by Definition 3.15 are simple name replacements and duplicate edge deletions in the LTS. Therefore the LTS composition operations are not hard to compute.

According to the following theorem, the parallel composition, hiding and renaming of labelled transition systems are consistent with the corresponding operations of labelled P/T-systems.

Theorem 3.16 Let $\mathbb{L}_1, \ldots, \mathbb{L}_n$ be labelled P/T-systems.

- $\mathrm{LTS}(\mathbb{L}_1 \parallel \ldots \parallel \mathbb{L}_n)$ is isomorphic with $\mathrm{LTS}(\mathbb{L}_1) \parallel \ldots \parallel \mathrm{LTS}(\mathbb{L}_n)$
- $\mathrm{LTS}(\mathbb{L}_1 \backslash A) = \mathrm{LTS}(\mathbb{L}_1) \backslash A$
- $\mathrm{LTS}(\mathbb{L}_1[a_1 \leftarrow b_1,\ldots,a_n \leftarrow b_n]) = \mathrm{LTS}(\mathbb{L}_1)[a_1 \leftarrow b_1,\ldots,a_n \leftarrow b_n]$

Proof The first claim follows from Definitions 3.2 and 3.14 and Proposition 3.3. The latter two claims follow directly from Definitions 3.4, 3.5 and 3.15. □

Theorem 3.16 gives us the permission to generate a LTS of a composition of labelled P/T-systems by generating and composing the LTSs of the individual labelled P/T-systems. This way we can avoid the construction of the composed labelled P/T-system. However, no verification effort is saved as yet, because the composition of the LTSs of subsystems is isomorphic to and thus as big as the LTS generated directly from the composed labelled P/T-system. Savings of effort are obtained by condensing the LTSs of subsystems before their composition. That the repeated application of condensation and composition does not modify the CSP-semantics of the system arises from the fact that CSP-equivalence is a congruence with respect to "$\parallel$", "$\backslash A$" and "$[a_1 \leftarrow b_1,\ldots,a_n \leftarrow b_n]$", as discussed in Chapter 2. We now prove this congruence property.

We prove the required congruence property by demonstrating that Σ, $CSPfail(\mathbf{s}_0)$ and $CSPdiv(\mathbf{s}_0)$ can be uniquely derived from Σ_i, $CSPfail(\mathbf{s}_{0i})$ and $CSPdiv(\mathbf{s}_{0i})$, where $L_1, \ldots, L_n$ are labelled transition systems; $\Sigma_1, \ldots, \Sigma_n$ are their alphabets; $\mathbf{s}_{01}, \ldots, \mathbf{s}_{0n}$ are their initial states; L is $L_1 \parallel \ldots \parallel L_n$, $L_1 \backslash A$ or $L_1[a_1 \leftarrow b_1,\ldots,a_n \leftarrow b_n]$; Σ is the alphabet of L; and $\mathbf{s}_0$ is the initial state of L. Note that by Definition 3.11 (3), $CSPtr(\mathbf{s}_{0i})$ can be uniquely derived from $CSPfail(\mathbf{s}_{0i})$.

Theorem 3.17 Let $L_1 = (\mathbf{S}_1, \Sigma_1 \cup \{\tau\}, \Delta_1, \mathbf{s}_{01})$ and ... and $L_n = (\mathbf{S}_n, \Sigma_n \cup \{\tau\}, \Delta_n, \mathbf{s}_{0n})$ be labelled transition systems. Let $L_\parallel = L_1 \parallel \ldots \parallel L_n$, $L_\backslash = L_1 \backslash A$ and $L_\leftarrow = L_1[a_1 \leftarrow b_1,\ldots,a_n \leftarrow b_n]$, where $A \subseteq \Sigma_1$, $\{a_1,\ldots,a_n\} \subseteq \Sigma_1$ and $\tau \notin \{b_1,\ldots,b_n\}$. Let $\Sigma_\parallel$, $\Sigma_\backslash$, $\Sigma_\leftarrow$, $\mathbf{s}_{0\parallel}$, $\mathbf{s}_{0\backslash}$ and $\mathbf{s}_{0\leftarrow}$ be the alphabets and initial states of $L_\parallel$, $L_\backslash$ and $L_\leftarrow$, respectively. Let $restr(\sigma, A)$ and $\sigma_\leftarrow$ denote the strings constructed by deleting all symbols not in A from σ, and by replacing all symbols a_i by b_i in σ, respectively. We write $\sigma' \leq \sigma$, if σ' is a prefix of σ, and $|\sigma|$ denotes the length of σ.

(1) $\Sigma_\parallel = \Sigma_1 \cup \ldots \cup \Sigma_n$, $\Sigma_\backslash = \Sigma_1 - A$ and $\Sigma_\leftarrow = (\Sigma_1 - \{a_1,\ldots,a_n\}) \cup \{b_1,\ldots,b_n\}$

(2) $CSPdiv(\mathbf{s}_{0\parallel}) = \{\, \sigma \in \Sigma_\parallel{}^* \mid \exists \sigma' \leq \sigma: \forall i \in \{1,\ldots,n\}: restr(\sigma', \Sigma_i) \in CSPtr(\mathbf{s}_{0i}) \wedge$
$\exists i \in \{1,\ldots,n\}: restr(\sigma', \Sigma_i) \in CSPdiv(\mathbf{s}_{0i}) \,\}$

(3) $CSPdiv(\mathbf{s}_{0\backslash}) = \{\ \sigma \in \Sigma_\backslash^* \mid \exists\, \sigma' \in \Sigma_1^*\colon restr(\sigma', \Sigma_1 - A) \le \sigma\ \wedge$
$(\ \sigma' \in CSPdiv(\mathbf{s}_{01}) \vee \forall\, k \ge 0\colon \exists\, \rho_k \in A^*\colon |\rho_k| \ge k \wedge \sigma'\rho_k \in CSPtr(\mathbf{s}_{01})\ )\ \}$

(4) $CSPdiv(\mathbf{s}_{0\leftarrow}) = \{\ \sigma_\leftarrow \mid \sigma \in CSPdiv(\mathbf{s}_{01})\ \}$

(5) $CSPfail(\mathbf{s}_{0\|}) = \{\ (\sigma,B) \in \Sigma_\|^* \times 2^{\Sigma_\|} \mid \sigma \in CSPdiv(\mathbf{s}_{0\|})\ \} \cup \{\ (\sigma,B) \in \Sigma_\|^* \times 2^{\Sigma_\|} \mid$
$\forall\, i \in \{1,\ldots,n\}\colon \exists\, B_i \subseteq \Sigma_i\colon B = B_1 \cup \ldots \cup B_n \wedge (restr(\sigma, \Sigma_i), B_i) \in CSPfail(\mathbf{s}_{0i})\ \}$

(6) $CSPfail(\mathbf{s}_{0\backslash}) = \{\ (\sigma,B) \in \Sigma_\backslash^* \times 2^{\Sigma_\backslash} \mid \sigma \in CSPdiv(\mathbf{s}_{0\backslash})\ \} \cup$
$\{\ (restr(\sigma, \Sigma_1 - A), B) \mid B \subseteq \Sigma_\backslash \wedge (\sigma, A \cup B) \in CSPfail(\mathbf{s}_{01})\ \}$

(7) $CSPfail(\mathbf{s}_{0\leftarrow}) = \{\ (\sigma,B) \in \Sigma_\leftarrow^* \times 2^{\Sigma_\leftarrow} \mid \sigma \in CSPdiv(\mathbf{s}_{0\leftarrow})\ \}\ \cup\ \{\ (\sigma_\leftarrow, B) \mid$
$\exists\, (\sigma, C) \in CSPfail(\mathbf{s}_{01})\colon B \subseteq \Sigma_\leftarrow - (\Sigma_1 - C - \{a_1,\ldots,a_n\}) - \{b_i \mid a_i \notin C\}\ \}$

Proof The proof of Theorem 3.17 is lengthy, so we do not give it in full, but concentrate on the most difficult claims (3) and (7) (see also [Olderog & 86]). (1) follows directly from Definitions 3.14 and 3.15.

To prove (3) assume $\sigma \in CSPdiv(\mathbf{s}_{0\backslash})$. σ has a prefix $\pi \in div(\mathbf{s}_{0\backslash})$. There are $s_0, s_1, \ldots \in \mathbf{S}_\backslash = \mathbf{S}_1$, $a_1, a_2, \ldots \in \Sigma_1 \cup \{\tau\}$ and $b_1, b_2, \ldots \in \Sigma_\backslash \cup \{\tau\}$ such that $\pi = restr(b_1 b_2 \ldots, \Sigma_\backslash)$, $s_0 = \mathbf{s}_{0\backslash} = \mathbf{s}_{01}$, $s_{i-1} -b_i\rightarrow s_i$ (in $L_\backslash$), $s_{i-1} -a_i\rightarrow s_i$ (in L_1), $b_i = a_i$ if $a_i \notin A$, and $b_i = \tau$ if $a_i \in A$. There is n such that $b_i = \tau$ for every $i > n$. If there is j such that $a_i = \tau$ for every $i \ge j$, then let $\sigma' = restr(a_1 a_2 \ldots, \Sigma_1)$. σ' is finite and $\sigma' \in div(\mathbf{s}_{01}) \subseteq CSPdiv(\mathbf{s}_{01})$ (in L_1). Otherwise there are $\sigma' = restr(a_1 a_2 \ldots a_n, \Sigma_1)$, $m(k) \ge k$ and $\rho_k = restr(a_{n+1} a_{n+2} \ldots a_{n+m(k)}, \Sigma_1)$ for every $k \ge 0$ such that $a_{n+i} \ne \tau$ for at least k values of i, $\rho_k \in A^*$ and $\sigma'\rho_k \in tr(\mathbf{s}_{01})$ (in L_1). In both cases $restr(\sigma', \Sigma_1 - A) = \pi \le \sigma$. Therefore $CSPdiv(\mathbf{s}_{0\backslash})$ is a subset of the set at right in (3).

If $\sigma' \in CSPdiv(\mathbf{s}_{01})$ (in L_1) then there is $\pi \le \sigma'$ such that $\pi \in div(\mathbf{s}_{01})$ (in L_1). Therefore $\sigma \in CSPdiv(\mathbf{s}_{0\backslash})$ if $restr(\pi, \Sigma_1 - A) \le \sigma$, and, consequently, also if $restr(\sigma', \Sigma_1 - A) \le \sigma$. If there are the ρ_k of (3) then either $\sigma'\rho_k \in CSPdiv(\mathbf{s}_{01})$ for some k, which reduces to the previous case, or $\sigma'\rho_k \in tr(\mathbf{s}_{01})$ for every $k \ge 0$. In the latter case we have arbitrarily long paths in a graph which is finitely branching by the assumption that **T** is finite. By König's Lemma there is an infinite path whose restriction to $\Sigma_1 - A$ is $restr(\sigma', \Sigma_1 - A)$, giving the claim.

In order to prove (7) we show that $fail(\mathbf{s}_{0\leftarrow}) = \{\ (\sigma_\leftarrow, B) \mid \exists\, (\sigma, C) \in fail(\mathbf{s}_{01})\colon B \subseteq \Sigma_\leftarrow - (\Sigma_1 - C - \{a_1,\ldots,a_n\}) - \{b_i \mid a_i \notin C\}\ \}$. (7) then follows by Definition 3.11 (2). If $(\sigma, C) \in fail(\mathbf{s}_{01})$ then there is s such that $\mathbf{s}_{01} =\sigma\Rightarrow s$ and, furthermore, if $s =a\Rightarrow$, then $a \in \Sigma_1 - C$ (in L_1). We have $\mathbf{s}_{0\leftarrow} =\sigma_\leftarrow\Rightarrow s$ (in $L_\leftarrow$). By Definition 3.15, if $s =b\Rightarrow$ (in $L_\leftarrow$), then $b \in X = (\Sigma_1 - C - \{a_1,\ldots,a_n\}) \cup \{b_i \mid a_i \notin C\}$. Therefore $(\sigma_\leftarrow, B) \in fail(\mathbf{s}_{0\leftarrow})$ if $B \subseteq \Sigma_\leftarrow - X$.

Assume now $(\pi, B) \in fail(\mathbf{s}_{0\leftarrow})$. There is s such that $\mathbf{s}_{0\leftarrow} =\pi\Rightarrow s$ and, furthermore, if $s =b\Rightarrow$, then $b \in \Sigma_\leftarrow - B$ (in $L_\leftarrow$). By Definition 3.15 there is σ such that $\sigma_\leftarrow = \pi$, $\mathbf{s}_{01} =\sigma\Rightarrow s$ (in L_1), and if $s =a\Rightarrow$ (in L_1), then $a \in Y = (\Sigma_1 - B - \{a_1,\ldots,a_n\}) \cup \{a_i \mid b_i \notin B\}$. Let $C = \Sigma_1 - Y$ and $X = (\Sigma_1 - C - \{a_1,\ldots,a_n\}) \cup \{b_i \mid a_i \notin C\} = (Y - \{a_1,\ldots,a_n\}) \cup \{b_i \mid a_i \in Y\}$. Obviously $Y - \{a_1,\ldots,a_n\} = \Sigma_1 - B - \{a_1,\ldots,a_n\} \subseteq \Sigma_\leftarrow - B$, and $\{b_i \mid a_i \in Y\} = \{b_i \mid b_i \notin B\} \subseteq \Sigma_\leftarrow - B$. Therefore $X \subseteq \Sigma_\leftarrow - B$ and $B \subseteq \Sigma_\leftarrow - X$. □

3.4 Condensation of LTSs

Recalling the discussion in Section 2.3, it is good if the LTS condensation algorithm runs fast and gives nearly optimum results, but it need not give absolutely optimum results. The algorithm we suggest in this section has been designed with this in mind. The reduction it gives is not the best possible, but the algorithm is fast, easy to implement and easy to understand.

The algorithm has two features: the elimination of states at which an infinite sequence of invisible events can be started (Algorithm 3.19), and the elimination of states with only invisible transitions occurring immediately (Algorithm 3.20). We assume that the LTS is finite.

We call state s *divergent* if and only if $s -\tau^{\infty}\rightarrow$. Because the CSP-semantics do not keep track of the behaviour of a system after it has executed a divergence trace, the CSP-semantics of a LTS are not changed if all of its divergent states are fused together and their output edges are discarded, provided that the resulting fused state is marked divergent. Furthermore, the deletion of unreachable states and their adjacent edges of a LTS obviously does not modify the CSP-semantics of the LTS. These claims are stated more formally in the following proposition.

Proposition 3.18 Let $L = (\mathbf{S}, \Sigma \cup \{\tau\}, \Delta, \mathbf{s}_0)$ be a LTS. Let s_d be a new state (i.e. $s_d \notin \mathbf{S}$), and let $L_1 = (\mathbf{S}_1, \Sigma \cup \{\tau\}, \Delta_1, \mathbf{s}_{01})$ such that

- $\mathbf{S}_1 = (\mathbf{S} - \{s \in \mathbf{S} \mid s -\tau^{\infty}\rightarrow\}) \cup \{s_d\}$, iff $\exists\, s \in \mathbf{S}$: $s -\tau^{\infty}\rightarrow$, and otherwise $\mathbf{S}_1 = \mathbf{S}$
- $\Delta_1 = (\Delta - DE) \cup D\tau \cup DN$, where
  - $DE = \{\ (s, a, s') \in \Delta \mid s -\tau^{\infty}\rightarrow \vee s' -\tau^{\infty}\rightarrow\ \}$
  - $D\tau = \{\ (s_d, \tau, s_d)\ \}$ iff $\exists\, s \in \mathbf{S}$: $s -\tau^{\infty}\rightarrow$, and otherwise $D\tau = \emptyset$
  - $DN = \{\ (s, a, s_d) \in \mathbf{S} \times \Sigma \times \{s_d\} \mid \neg (s -\tau^{\infty}\rightarrow) \wedge \exists\, s'\colon (s, a, s') \in \Delta \wedge s' -\tau^{\infty}\rightarrow\ \}$
- $\mathbf{s}_{01} = s_d$, iff $\mathbf{s}_0 -\tau^{\infty}\rightarrow$, and otherwise $\mathbf{s}_{01} = \mathbf{s}_0$.

Let $L_2 = (\mathbf{S}_2, \Sigma \cup \{\tau\}, \Delta_2, \mathbf{s}_{02})$ such that

- $\mathbf{S}_2 = \{s \in \mathbf{S}_1 \mid \exists\, \sigma \in \Sigma^*\colon \mathbf{s}_{01} =\sigma\Rightarrow s\}$
- $\Delta_2 = \Delta_1 \cap (\mathbf{S}_2 \times (\Sigma \cup \{\tau\}) \times \mathbf{S}_2)$
- $\mathbf{s}_{02} = \mathbf{s}_{01}$

CSPdiv($\mathbf{s}_0$) (in L) = *CSPdiv*($\mathbf{s}_{01}$) (in L_1) = *CSPdiv*($\mathbf{s}_{02}$) (in L_2) and *CSPfail*($\mathbf{s}_0$) (in L) = *CSPfail*($\mathbf{s}_{01}$) (in L_1) = *CSPfail*($\mathbf{s}_{02}$) (in L_2).

Proof That *CSPdiv*($\mathbf{s}_{01}$) (in L_1) = *CSPdiv*($\mathbf{s}_{02}$) (in L_2) and *CSPfail*($\mathbf{s}_{01}$) (in L_1) = *CSPfail*($\mathbf{s}_{02}$) (in L_2) is obvious. We show first that *CSPdiv*($\mathbf{s}_0$) (in L) = *CSPdiv*($\mathbf{s}_{01}$) (in L_1). Consider a minimal element σ of *div*($\mathbf{s}_0$) (in L). That is, $\sigma \in$ *div*($\mathbf{s}_0$) (in L) and if σ' is a proper prefix of σ, then $\sigma' \notin$ *div*($\mathbf{s}_0$) (in L). If $\sigma = \varepsilon$ then $\mathbf{s}_0 -\tau^{\infty}\rightarrow$ and $\mathbf{s}_{01} = s_d -\tau^{\infty}\rightarrow$ by the construction, thus $\varepsilon \in$ *div*($\mathbf{s}_{01}$) (in L_1). Assume $\sigma \neq \varepsilon$. By Definition 3.10 $\exists\, s \in \mathbf{S}$: $\mathbf{s}_0 =\sigma\Rightarrow s -\tau^{\infty}\rightarrow$. By the minimality of σ there are $n > 0$, $s_0, s_1, \ldots, s_n \in \mathbf{S}$ and $a_1, \ldots, a_n \in \Sigma \cup \{\tau\}$ such that $a_n \neq \tau$, $\mathbf{s}_0 = s_0$, $s_0 -a_1\rightarrow s_1 -a_2\rightarrow \ldots -a_n\rightarrow s_n$, $s_n =\varepsilon\Rightarrow s$, $a_1 a_2 \ldots a_n$ produces σ if all τ-symbols are removed from it, and none of $s_0, \ldots, s_{n-1}$ is divergent. By the construction $(s_d, \tau, s_d) \in \Delta_1$, $s_0, \ldots, s_{n-1} \in \mathbf{S}_1$, $(s_0, a_1, s_1), \ldots, (s_{n-2}, a_{n-1}, s_{n-1}) \in \Delta_1$ and $(s_{n-1}, a_n, s_d) \in \Delta_1$. Therefore $\sigma \in$ *div*($\mathbf{s}_{01}$) (in L_1).

Assume $\sigma \in$ *div*($\mathbf{s}_{01}$) (in L_1). If $\sigma = \varepsilon$ then $\mathbf{s}_{01} = s_d$, thus by the construction $\mathbf{s}_0 -\tau^{\infty}\rightarrow$ and $\varepsilon \in$ *div*($\mathbf{s}_0$) (in L). Otherwise $\exists\, s_0, s_1, \ldots, s_n \in \mathbf{S}_1$ and $a_1, \ldots, a_n \in \Sigma \cup \{\tau\}$ such that $a_n \neq \tau$, $s_0 = \mathbf{s}_{01}$, $s_n = s_d \neq s_{n-1}$, $s_0 -a_1\rightarrow s_1 -a_2\rightarrow \ldots -a_n\rightarrow s_n$ and the deletion of τ-symbols from $a_1 a_2 \ldots a_n$ produces σ. Thus $\exists\, s'_n$ such that $s_{n-1} -a_n\rightarrow s'_n -\tau^{\infty}\rightarrow$ (in L), and $\sigma \in$ *div*($\mathbf{s}_0$) (in L). By Definition 3.11 (1) this implies that *CSPdiv*($\mathbf{s}_0$) (in L) = *CSPdiv*($\mathbf{s}_{01}$) (in L_1).

To prove $CSPfail(\mathbf{s}_0)$ (in L) = $CSPfail(\mathbf{s}_{01})$ (in L_1) it is sufficient to consider failures (σ, A) such that σ is not a CSP-divergence because we have already shown that $CSPdiv(\mathbf{s}_0)$ (in L) = $CSPdiv(\mathbf{s}_{01})$ (in L_1). If $(\sigma, A) \in CSPfail(\mathbf{s}_0)$ (in L) and $\sigma \notin CSPdiv(\mathbf{s}_0)$ (in L), then $\exists\, s$: $\mathbf{s}_0 = \sigma \Rightarrow s \wedge \forall\, a \in A: \neg\,(s = a \Rightarrow)$ (in L). Because $\sigma \notin CSPdiv(\mathbf{s}_0)$ (in L) we conclude $s \in \mathbf{S}_1$ and $\mathbf{s}_{01} = \sigma \Rightarrow s$ (in L_1). If $s = a \Rightarrow$ (in L_1), then $s = a \Rightarrow$ (in L), thus $(\sigma, A) \in CSPfail(\mathbf{s}_{01})$ (in L_1). We can apply a similar argument to show that if $(\sigma, A) \in CSPfail(\mathbf{s}_{01})$ (in L_1) and $\sigma \notin CSPdiv(\mathbf{s}_{01})$ (in L_1), then $(\sigma, A) \in CSPfail(\mathbf{s}_0)$ (in L), giving the claim. □

The following algorithm computes first the L_1 and then the L_2 of Proposition 3.18. The computation of L_1 is based on performing a depth-first search starting at every so far unprocessed state and traversing via τ-edges only. Because we assumed that the LTS L is finite, infinite sequences of τ-transitions correspond to cycles with only τ-labelled edges. Such cycles are found with the aid of the set "onpath" of states. "onpath" contains exactly the states on the path from the start state of the current search to the current state. A cycle is found whenever the search tries to enter a state which is already in "onpath". The states belonging to the cycle are processed as required by Proposition 3.18, and information of divergence is backtracked via the parameter "child-div".

The LTS L_2 can be computed by first performing a search marking the states encountered during the search, and then deleting the unmarked states and their adjacent edges. This is standard technology, so we assume the existence of a procedure "delete-unreachable" which performs the task.

Algorithm 3.19
Input: A finite LTS $L = (\mathbf{S}, \Sigma \cup \{\tau\}, \Delta, \mathbf{s}_0)$
Output: The LTS L changes to by the following algorithm; it is the LTS L_2 of Proposition 3.18.

```
procedure main;

var is-div : Boolean; unprocessed, divset, onpath : set of S;

unprocessed := S; divset := ∅;
while unprocessed ≠ ∅ do
      pick s ∈ unprocessed; onpath := ∅; check( s, is-div )
endwhile;
if divset ≠ ∅ then
      create( s_d ); S := S ∪ {s_d} − divset; Δ := Δ ∪ { (s_d, τ, s_d) };
      for each s ∈ S − {s_d} do
            for each a ∈ Σ, s′ ∈ divset such that (s, a, s′) ∈ Δ do
                  Δ := Δ − { (s, a, s′) } ∪ { (s, a, s_d) }
            endfor
      endfor;
      if s0 ∈ divset then s0 := s_d
      endif;
endif;
delete-unreachable( S, Δ, s0 )
endproced
```

```
procedure check( s : state; var is-div : Boolean );

var child-div : Boolean;

(* Check whether s diverges *)
onpath := onpath ∪ {s}; is-div := false;
for each s' such that s –τ→ s' do
    if s' ∈ unprocessed then
        if s' ∈ onpath then is-div := true  (* s'∈ onpath ⇒ s' –τ*→ s *)
        else  check( s', child-div ); is-div := is-div ∨ child-div
        endif
    else
        if s' ∈ divset then is-div := true
        endif
    endif
endfor;   (* now is-div knows whether s diverges *)
if is-div then divset := divset ∪ {s}
endif;
onpath := onpath – {s}; unprocessed := unprocessed – {s}
endproced
```

□

The elimination of divergent states makes the LTS smaller only if the system has divergences, which we often want not to be the case. Therefore the elimination of divergent states cannot be the only condensation method. This is why our condensation algorithm contains another step: the elimination of states with only invisible transitions occurring immediately. This step is executed after the elimination of divergent states and is as follows.

Algorithm 3.20
Input: The LTS $L = (\mathbf{S}, \Sigma \cup \{\tau\}, \Delta, \mathbf{s}_0)$ produced by Algorithm 3.19
Output: The LTS L changes to by the following algorithm.

```
for each s ∈ S – {s₀, s_d} do
    if s –τ→ ∧ ¬∃ a ∈ Σ: s –a→ then
        Δ := Δ ∪ { (s₁, a, s₂) | a ∈ Σ∪{τ} ∧ (s₁, a, s) ∈ Δ ∧ (s, τ, s₂) ∈ Δ };
        Δ := Δ – { (s₁, a, s) | a ∈ Σ∪{τ} ∧ (s₁, a, s) ∈ Δ } –
                { (s, τ, s₂) | (s, τ, s₂) ∈ Δ };
        S := S – {s}
    endif
endfor
```

□

Algorithm 3.20 consists of the deletion of certain kind of states and their adjacent edges. The deleted states have at least one output edge each, and all of their output edges are τ-edges. The following proposition implies that one execution of the **for**-loop of Algorithm 3.20 does not modify the CSP-semantics of the LTS. As a result, Algorithm 3.20 preserves the CSP-semantics.

Proposition 3.21 Let $L = (\mathbf{S}, \Sigma \cup \{\tau\}, \Delta, \mathbf{s}_0)$, $s \in \mathbf{S} - \{\mathbf{s}_0\}$, $s -\tau\rightarrow$, $\neg(s -\tau\rightarrow s)$ and $\forall a \in \Sigma: \neg(s -a\rightarrow)$. $CSPdiv(\mathbf{s}_0)$ (in L) = $CSPdiv(\mathbf{s}_0)$ (in L') and $CSPfail(\mathbf{s}_0)$ (in L) = $CSPfail(\mathbf{s}_0)$ (in L'), where $L' = (\mathbf{S}', \Sigma \cup \{\tau\}, \Delta', \mathbf{s}_0)$ such that

- $\mathbf{S}' = \mathbf{S} - \{s\}$, and

- $\Delta' = (\Delta \cup \{ (s_1,a,s_2) \in \mathbf{S}' \times (\Sigma \cup \{\tau\}) \times \mathbf{S}' \mid (s_1,a,s) \in \Delta \wedge (s,\tau,s_2) \in \Delta \}) -$
$\{ (s_1,a,s) \in \mathbf{S} \times (\Sigma \cup \{\tau\}) \times \{s\} \mid (s_1,a,s) \in \Delta \} -$
$\{ (s,\tau,s_1) \in \{s\} \times \{\tau\} \times \mathbf{S} \mid (s,\tau,s_1) \in \Delta \}$.

Proof If $\sigma \in div(\mathbf{s}_0)$ (in L), then $\exists\, s_1, s_2, \ldots \in \mathbf{S}$: $\mathbf{s}_0 = \sigma \Rightarrow s_1 - \tau \rightarrow s_2 - \tau \rightarrow \ldots$ (in L). Because $\neg\,(s - \tau \rightarrow s)$, at most every second state in the sequence $s_1 s_2 \ldots$ is s. Together with the assumption $s \neq \mathbf{s}_0$ this implies $\mathbf{s}_0 = \sigma \Rightarrow s'_1 - \tau \rightarrow s'_2 - \tau \rightarrow \ldots$ (in L') where $s'_1 s'_2 \ldots$ is $s_1 s_2 \ldots$ with all instances of s removed. Therefore $\sigma \in div(\mathbf{s}_0)$ (in L'). If $\sigma \in div(\mathbf{s}_0)$ (in L') then obviously $\exists\, s' \in \mathbf{S}'$: $\mathbf{s}_0 = \sigma \Rightarrow s' - \tau^\infty \rightarrow$ (in L'), thus $\mathbf{s}_0 = \sigma \Rightarrow s' - \tau^\infty \rightarrow$ (in L) and $\sigma \in div(\mathbf{s}_0)$ (in L). As a result $CSPdiv(\mathbf{s}_0)$ (in L) = $CSPdiv(\mathbf{s}_0)$ (in L').

Assume $(\sigma, A) \in CSPfail(\mathbf{s}_0)$ (in L) and $\sigma \notin CSPdiv(\mathbf{s}_0)$ (in L). There is s' such that $\mathbf{s}_0 = \sigma \Rightarrow s'$ (in L) and $\forall\, a \in A$: $\neg\,(s' = a \Rightarrow)$ (in L). If $s' = s$ then there is $s_1 \neq s$ such that $s' - \tau \rightarrow s_1$, otherwise let $s_1 = s'$. If $s_1 = a \Rightarrow$ (in L) then $s' = a \Rightarrow$ (in L), therefore we conclude that $s_1 \in \mathbf{S}'$, $\mathbf{s}_0 = \sigma \Rightarrow s_1$ (in L and L') and $\forall\, a \in A$: $\neg\,(s_1 = a \Rightarrow)$ (in L and L'). Consequently $(\sigma, A) \in CSPfail(\mathbf{s}_0)$ (in L'). The proof that $CSPfail(\mathbf{s}_0)$ (in L') $\subseteq CSPfail(\mathbf{s}_0)$ (in L) is similar, but slightly simpler. □

We would like to remark that Algorithm 3.20 does not preserve the observation equivalence of [Milner 80, 89]. However, it does preserve observation equivalence if its application is limited to states with only one adjacent output edge. This is an example of the fact that CSP-equivalence offers more potential to LTS condensation than observation equivalence because it is less discriminating.

A typically significantly more powerful but also much more complicated condensation algorithm is given in [Valmari & 91a]. It has been designed for the new semantic model discussed towards the end of Section 3.2, but it can be applied to the CSP-semantics simply by running Algorithm 3.19 of this section before it. The new algorithm is based on well known techniques for the determinisation and minimisation of finite automata. The theoretical worst-case complexity of the new algorithm is exponential, and it even sometimes *increases* the size of an LTS instead of decreasing it. This happens seldom in practice, however. Often the new algorithm gives really excellent results. A comparison of the performances of the new algorithm and the algorithm in this paper on the example of Chapter 4 is given towards the end of Chapter 4.

4. EXAMPLE: PROTOCOL

In this chapter we demonstrate the compositional state space generation method developed in the previous chapter with the aid of an example. The example is a version of the alternating bit protocol with retransmission in the case of acknowledgement not arriving in time, and success/error indication to the customer in the sending end. The channels between the protocol entities can lose messages but they cannot do any other harm. The capacity of the channels is one. The example protocol is not very intricate, but it is nevertheless a bit too complicated for demonstration purposes. Therefore we have chosen to divide its treatment to two stages: the composition of the sender and the composition of the protocol as a whole.

We specify the protocol processes as labelled place/transition systems. It is difficult to represent the retransmission counter in the specification of the sender because the retransmission counter has to be reset back to zero after a transmission session has been finished, and place/transition nets do not allow for a simple reset operation. (This problem has been discussed in detail in [Valmari & 87].) Therefore we have chosen to model the sender as two processes: the sender proper, and a counter. In Section 4.2 we compose the sender proper and the counter together to get a LTS of the sender. The composition of the sender proper and the counter is a small and illustrative enough example for the demonstration of the compositional state space generation method.

In Section 4.3 we build a condensed LTS of the whole system by first composing together the condensed LTSs of the sender and data channel in one hand and the condensed LTSs of the receiver and acknowledgement channel in the other. This is a more realistic application, but we cannot show all the LTSs because of their size and complexity. However, we give numerical results demonstrating the performance of the method.

4.1 Description of the Protocol

The protocol is shown in Figure 3. It has two clients: the local sender and the local receiver. The local sender communicates with the protocol sender, the local receiver with the protocol receiver, and the protocol sender and receiver communicate with each other via two noisy channels, one for data and the other for acknowledgements. The local sender starts a session by executing the event **s** (send). The message to be sent should be thought of as a parameter to the **s** event, but it is not shown in the model. The protocol tries to transmit the message and eventually tells the local sender whether the attempt was successful via the events **ok** (success) and **e** (failure). The protocol receiver delivers the arrived data to the local receiver via the event **r** (reception). The clients see no other events, that is, the alphabet of the protocol is {**e**, **ok**, **r**, **s**}.

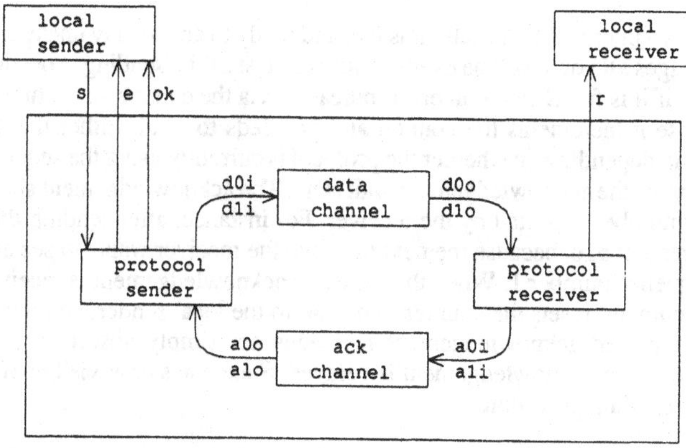

Figure 3 Example Protocol

As discussed above, the protocol sender consists of two processes, the counter C(N) and the sender proper S. N is the greatest number the counter can count to, and it will be used as the maximum number of transmission attempts the sender performs before giving up. The counter is specified as a labelled place/transition system in Figure 4. It has two modes: the *count mode* and the *reset mode*. The mode is represented by a token in the corresponding place. When in the count mode, the counter can participate at most N **inc**-events in succession. After

N **inc**-events, the counter can participate the event **full** which takes it back to its initial state. At any time when in the count mode the counter is ready to participate the event **reset** which takes it to the reset mode. In the reset mode the counter cannot participate any visible events, but there are invisible transitions which one by one decrement the count of the counter from whatever it was to zero and then automatically resume the count mode. The alphabet of the counter is {**full, inc, reset**}.

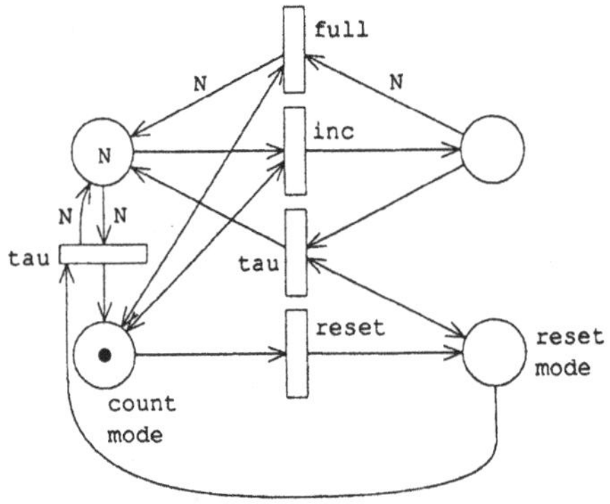

Σ_C = {**full, inc, reset**}

Figure 4 Counter C(*N*)

The sender proper is shown in Figure 5. Initially it is idle and ready to absorb any unexpected acknowledgement messages **a0o** or **a1o**. The event **s** causes it to start the sending procedure. First it tests the counter: if it is full S sends an error indication via the event **e** and returns to the initial state, otherwise it increments the counter and proceeds to send. Either the data message **d0i** or **d1i** is sent, depending on whether the protocol is currently using the sequence number 0 or 1. Then S enters the acknowledgement wait state. The acknowledgement should carry the next sequence number expected by the receiver. For instance, after sending **d0i** S expects the acknowledgement **a1o**, because the next message the receiver wants to see after receiving **d0** has the sequence number 1. When the expected acknowledgement is received, S changes its sequence number, resets the counter, sends **ok** to the local sender, and returns to the initial state. Unexpected acknowledgement messages are simply absorbed. If no acknowledgement arrive or the acknowledgement is delayed, S executes an invisible event **timeout** and restarts the sending procedure.

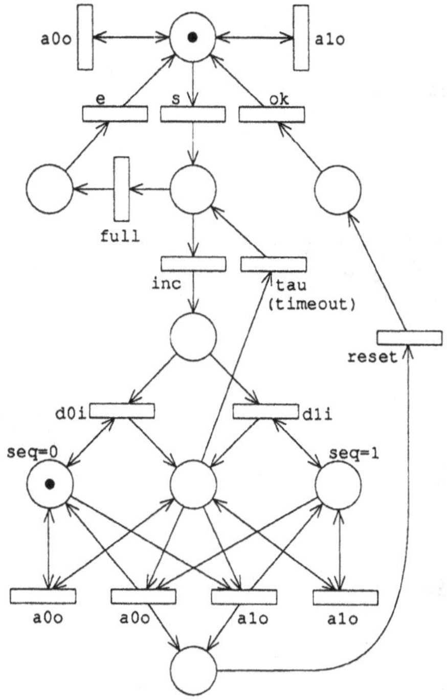

Σ_S = {**a0o, a1o, d0i, d1i, e, full, inc, ok, reset, s**}

Figure 5 Sender proper **S**

Figure 6 shows the receiver **R**. Initially it is ready to receive both an expected and an unexpected data message. If the expected one arrives, **R** changes its sequence number, delivers the data to the local customer via the event **r**, and sends an acknowledgement. If the wrong data message arrives **R** only sends the acknowledgement.

The data channel **D** is shown in Figure 7; the acknowledgement channel **A** is similar. Initially the channel is ready to input both kinds of data messages via the events **d0i** and **d1i.** Upon reception, **D** enters a state where it keeps the data message. Then it can either deliver the message to **R** via the event **d0o** or **d1o**, or it can lose the message. The loss of a message is represented by an invisible transition which takes the channel back to the initial state. **A** can be specified as **A = D[d0i←a0i, d0o←a0o, d1i←a1i, d1o←a1o]**.

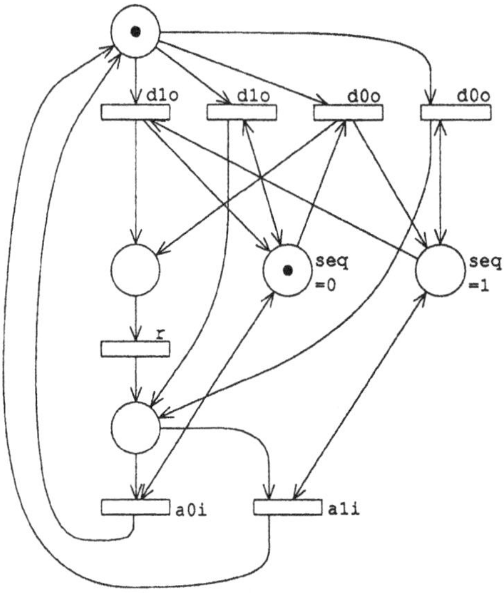

Σ_R = {**a0i, a1i, d0o, d1o, r**}

Figure 6 Receiver **R**

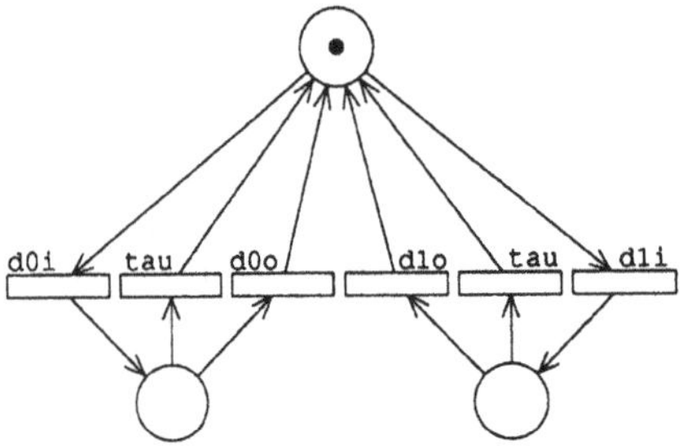

Σ_D = {**d0i, d0o, d1i, d1o**}

Figure 7 Data channel **D**
(acknowledgement channel **A = D[d0i←a0i, d0o←a0o, d1i←a1i, d1o←a1o]**)

4.2 Composing the Sender

The sender process SC is built by composing S and C(*N*) in parallel and then hiding the events in the alphabet of the counter, that is, SC = (S || C(*N*)) \ Σ_C. For demonstration purposes, we assume *N* = 2. In other words, the sender makes two attempts to send the data before giving up.

The LTS of the counter C(2) is shown at left in Figure 8. There are three states with only τ-events enabled. The elimination of them using the algorithm of Section 3.4 results in the condensed LTS at right in Figure 8.

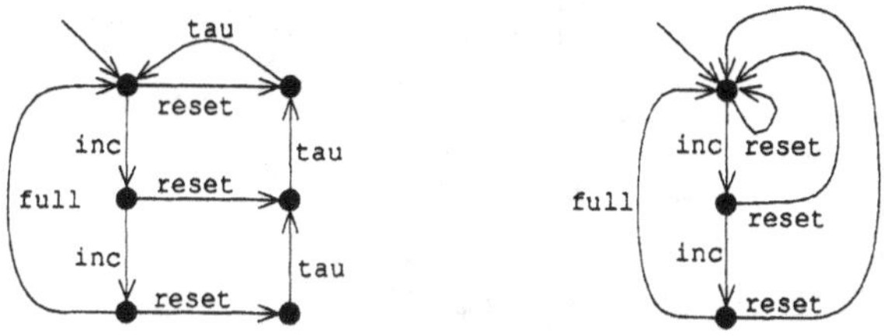

Figure 8 Ordinary and condensed LTS of C(2)

The LTS of the sender proper is shown in Figure 9. The condensation algorithm does not remove any states, as the timeout states can accept visible events, namely **a0o** and **a1o.**

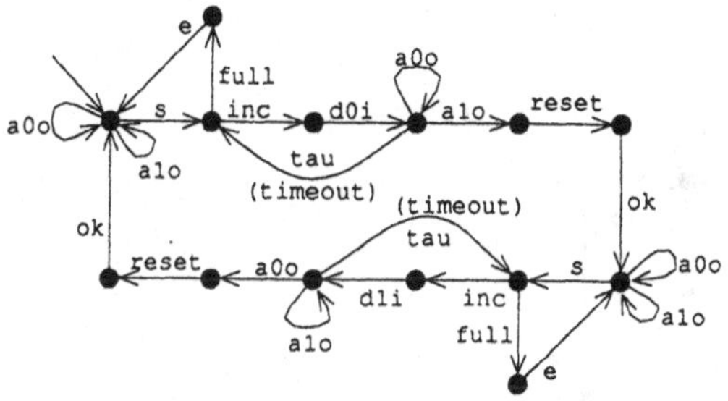

Figure 9 LTS of S

Figure 10 shows the composed LTS of the sender process SC = (S || C(2)) \ Σ_C achieved by composing the LTS at right in Figure 8 with the LTS in Figure 9. It has 24 states and 36 edges. If the LTS of C(2) had not been condensed before the composition, the six specially marked states towards the top of the figure would have been replaced by four states each, leading to an LTS with 18 more states and 42 more edges.

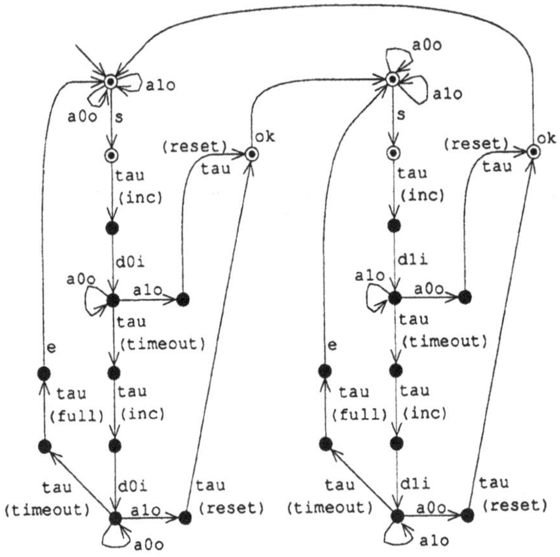

Figure 10 LTS of SC

The hiding of the events **full**, **inc** and **reset** introduces new τ-edges. In preparation for the next step, we apply again the condensation algorithm and end up with the LTS in Figure 11. It has only 14 states and 26 edges.

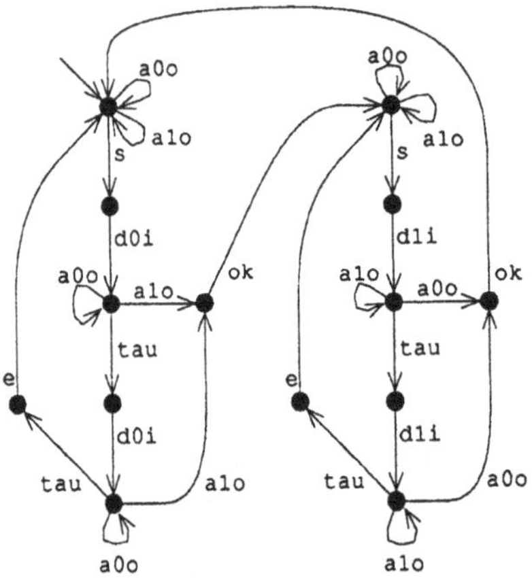

Figure 11 Condensed LTS of SC

4.3 Assembling the Whole Protocol

We generated a LTS of the whole protocol **P** = (**S** || **C**(2) || **D** || **R** || **A**) \ ($\Sigma_C \cup \Sigma_D \cup \Sigma_A$) by composing the LTSs of Figure 11 and **D** in one hand and **R** and **A** in the other hand, condensed the results, and composed them again. This procedure corresponds to the grouping of the protocol as ((**SC** || **D**) \ {**d0i**, **d1i**}) || ((**R** || **A**) \ {**a0i**, **a1i**}) \ {**a0o**, **a1o**, **d0o**, **d1o**}. For comparison, we also generated a LTS corresponding to the grouping (**SC** || **D** || **R** || **A**) \ ($\Sigma_D \cup \Sigma_A$). This is a realistic grouping, because the sender is taken as if it were one process, not a parallel composition of the two processes counter and sender proper. We denote the LTSs by ((**SC**)**D**)(**RA**) and (**SC**)**DRA**, respectively.

The LTS of **R** has 6 states and 8 edges and the LTSs of **D** and **A** have 3 states and 6 edges each. The condensation algorithm does not make them smaller. As was mentioned, the condensed LTS of **SC** has 14 states and 26 edges.

The LTS (**SC**)**D** has 32 states and 90 edges. The condensation algorithm eliminates four states and four edges. The LTS **RA** has 14 states and 30 edges. This time the condensation algorithm gets rid of two states and edges. These LTSs were generated manually and checked using two separate state space generator tools: PC-Rimst [Valmari 88a] and ARA, a new tool being developed by the Technical Research Centre of Finland [Kemppainen & 92]. The composed LTS ((**SC**)**D**)(**RA**) generated by PC-Rimst or ARA has 198 states and 524 edges, or 582 edges if duplicate edges are not removed. The total numbers of states and edges generated are thus 244 and 702. We do not include the sizes of the lowest level LTSs **SC**, **R**, **D** and **A** in the total numbers, because the lowest level LTS generation is applied to individual processes, not their LTSs, and in a realistic model **SC** would be one process. However, we do include the duplicate edges into the totals, because they are indeed generated, although they are eliminated afterwards.

The comparison LTS (**SC**)**DRA** was generated by PC-Rimst and ARA. It has 290 states and 724 edges (782 before duplicate edge removal). Thus the savings achieved by the compositional method are 46 states and 80 edges. This is not a huge number, but neither is the example huge. It is interesting to note that the condensation stages eliminated only a total of six states and six edges from the intermediate LTSs, but this small elimination led to a total saving of 46 states and 80 edges — about 8 and 13 times the number of eliminated states and edges. If this multiplication of savings proves to be the general case, the compositional method is very attractive.

We expect that in general, as the example grows, so do the savings. To test this we generated by PC-Rimst and ARA the state space **SCDRA** where the sender is modelled as the two parallel processes counter and sender proper. This grouping corresponds to a naive approach to the modelling of the counter but we hope it can be used as an example of a somewhat larger system. The LTS has 582 states and 1544 edges (1620 before duplicate removal), which is more than twice as much as the 268 states and 738 edges resulting as the total of the compositional method (now the size of the LTS **SC** is included in the total).

Towards the end of Section 3.4 we mentioned the new condensation algorithm described in [Valmari & 91a]. It gives the same results as the algorithm in this paper when applied to the process **SC**, that is, it produces 14 states and 26 edges. From (**SC**)**D** it eliminates two states and 12 edges which is two less states but eight more edges than eliminated by the algorithm in this paper. When applied to **RA** its performance is really bad: it eliminates no edges and introduces two *more* states! However, when given the whole system **SCDRA** or any of its compositionally generated reduced forms **(SC)DRA** or **((SC)D)(RA)** as input it produces an LTS of only *eight states* and *eleven edges*, which in the case of **SCDRA** means the elimination of 574 states and 1533 edges! This is a very remarkable and useful result if the protocol is later used as a component of a bigger system.

5. CONCLUDING REMARKS

We have discussed the general requirements and properties of a compositional state space generation method, and have developed one particular method. We have demonstrated with the aid of an example that our method can lead to savings in the number of states even when analysing a relatively small system. We do not claim that the presented method is the best, quite the opposite. It should be seen as a proof of the existence of reasonably implementable working compositional state space generation methods. We believe it is possible to design several good methods suited to various purposes by modifying the set of composition operators, the black-box semantics and the condensation algorithm. We hope our discussion in Chapter 2 is helpful in making the necessary trade-offs.

A compositional state space generation method with a larger set of composition operators, a more adequate equivalence notion and a more powerful condensation algorithm than the method in this paper possesses has been recently presented in [Valmari & 91a]. The improved equivalence is otherwise the same as the CSP-equivalence used in this paper, but it gives meaningful and extensive information of the behaviour of the system even after divergence traces. Incidentally, Algorithm 3.20 in this paper can be applied to the new model by removing the reference to s_d and adding the extra condition $\neg\,(s -\tau\rightarrow s)$ to the test of the **if**-statement within it.

The paper [Valmari & 91a] also introduces a new condensation algorithm. It is very powerful in the sense that most of the time it gives truly good condensation results. On the other hand, its theoretical worst case performance is exponential and it can even *increase* the size of the LTS instead of decreasing it. This is because the algorithm is based on the determinisation of the LTSs and sometimes the size of an LTS may grow (even exponentially) during determinisation. We have implemented the new algorithm and run it on various LTSs. Excluding the LTSs which we have constructed deliberately for demonstrating the exponential complexity and LTS size growth, the new algorithm has always been pleasingly fast and most of the time it has given good reduction.

ACKNOWLEDGEMENTS

The anonymous persons who refereed an earlier version of this paper for the 11th International Conference on Application and Theory of Petri Nets, and the four persons who refereed this for the "Advances in Petri Nets", gave important comments which have led to an increase in the quality of this paper. This work was funded by the Technical Research Centre of Finland and the Technology Development Centre of Finland (TEKES).

REFERENCES

[Best 87] Best, E.: *COSY: Its Relation to Nets and to CSP*. [Brauer & 87b] pp. 416–440.

[Brand & 83] Brand, D. & Zafiropulo, P.: *On Communicating Finite State Machines.* Journal of the ACM 30 (2) 1983 pp. 323–342.

[Brauer & 87a] Brauer, W., Reisig, W. & Rozenberg, G. (ed.): *Petri Nets, Central Models and Their Properties.* Lecture Notes in Computer Science 254, Springer-Verlag 1987, 480 p.

[Brauer & 87b] Brauer, W., Reisig, W. & Rozenberg, G. (ed.): *Petri Nets, Applications and Relationships to Other Models of Concurrency.* Lecture Notes in Computer Science 255, Springer-Verlag 1987, 516 p.

[Brookes & 84] Brookes, S. D., Hoare, C. A. R. & Roscoe, A. W.: *A Theory of Communicating Sequential Processes.* Journal of the ACM, Vol 31. No 3 July 1984, pp. 560–599.

[Brookes & 85] Brookes, S. D. & Roscoe, A. W.: *An Improved Failures Model for Communicating Sequential Processes.* Proceedings of the NSF-SERC Seminar on Concurrency, Lecture Notes in Computer Science 197, Springer-Verlag 1985, pp. 281–305.

[Clarke & 86] Clarke, E. M., Grümberg, O. & Browne, M. C.: *Reasoning about Networks with Many Identical Finite-State Processes.* Carnegie-Mellon University, Department of Computer Science, Report CMU-CS-86-155, Pittsburgh 1986, 18 p.

[Clarke & 87] Clarke, E. M. & Grümberg, O.: *Avoiding the State Explosion Problem in Temporal Logic Model Checking Algorithms.* Conference Record of the 6th ACM Symposium on Principles of Distributed Computing 1987, pp. 294–303.

[Clarke & 89] Clarke, E. M., Long, D. E. & McMillan, K. L.: *Compositional Model Checking.* Proceedings of the Fourth IEEE Symposium on Logic in Computer Science, June 4–8, 1989, Asilomar, California, USA.

[Cleaveland & 89] Cleaveland, R., Parrow, J. & Steffen, B.: *The Concurrency Workbench.* Proceedings of the Workshop on Automatic Verification Methods for Finite State Systems 1989, Lecture Notes in Computer Science 407, Springer-Verlag 1990, pp. 24–37.

[Finkel 90] Finkel, A.: *The Minimal Coverability Graph for Petri Nets.* Proceedings of the 11th International Conference on Application and Theory of Petri Nets, Paris, France, pp. 1–21.

[Graf & 90] Graf, S. & Steffen, B: *Compositional Minimization of Finite State Processes.* Computer-Aided Verification '90 (Proceedings of the Workshop on Computer-Aided Verification, Princeton, New Jersey, USA), AMS-ACM DIMACS Series in Discrete Mathematics and Theoretical Computer Science, Vol. 3, 1991, pp. 57–73. (Earlier version in DIMACS Technical Report 90-31, June 1990.)

[Hoare 85] Hoare, C. A. R.: *Communicating Sequential Processes.* Prentice-Hall International 1985, 256 p.

[Huber & 89] Huber, P., Jensen, K. & Shapiro, R. M.: *Hierarchies in Coloured Petri Nets.* Advances in Petri Nets 1990, Lecture Notes in Computer Science 483, Springer-Verlag 1991, pp. 313–341. (Earlier version in Proceedings of the 10th International Conference on Application and Theory of Petri Nets, Bonn, West Germany 1989, pp. 192–209.)

[Jantzen 87] Jantzen, M.: *Complexity of Place/Transition Nets.* [Brauer & 87a] pp. 413–434.

[Jensen 87] Jensen, K.: *Coloured Petri Nets.* [Brauer & 87a] pp. 248–299.

[Kanellakis & 85] Kanellakis, P. C. & Smolka, S. A.: *On the Analysis of Cooperation and Antagonism in Networks of Communicating Processes.* Proceedings of the 4th Annual ACM Symposium on Principles of Distributed Computing, 1985, pp. 23–38.

[Karp & 69] Karp, R. M. & Miller, R. E.: *Parallel Program Schemata.* Journal of Computer and System Sciences 3 (1969) pp. 147–195.

[Kemppainen & 92] Kemppainen, J., Levanto, M., Valmari, A. & Clegg, M.: *"ARA" Puts Advanced Reachability Analysis Techniques together.* Proceedings of the 5th Nordic Workshop on Programming Environment Reserach, Tampere University of Technology, Software Systems Laboratory Report 14, Tampere, Finland 1992.

[Lindqvist 90] Lindqvist, M.: *Parameterized Reachability Trees for Predicate/Transition Nets*. Proceedings of the 11th International Conference on Application and Theory of Petri Nets, Paris, France, pp. 22–42.

[Milner 80] Milner, R.: *A Calculus of Communicating Systems*. Lecture Notes in Computer Science 92, Springer-Verlag 1980.

[Milner 89] Milner, R.: *Communication and Concurrency*. Prentice-Hall 1989. 260 p.

[Nielsen 87] Nielsen, M.: *CCS – And Its Relationship to Net Theory*. [Brauer & 87b] pp. 393–415.

[Olderog & 86] Olderog, E.-R. & Hoare, C. A. R.: *Specification-Oriented Semantics for Communicating Processes*. Acta Informatica 23 (1986) pp. 9–66.

[Olderog 87] Olderog, E.-R.: *TCSP: Theory of Communicating Sequential Processes*. [Brauer & 87b] pp. 441–465.

[Overman 81] Overman, W. T.: *Verification of Concurrent Systems: Function and Timing*. Ph.D. Dissertation, University of California Los Angeles 1981, 174 p.

[Peterson 81] Peterson, J. L.: *Petri Net Theory and the Modeling of Systems*. Prentice-Hall 1981, 290 p.

[Pnueli 86] Pnueli, A.: *Applications of Temporal Logic to the Specification and Verification of Concurrent Systems: A Survey of Current Trends*. Current Trends in Concurrency, Lecture Notes in Computer Science 224, Springer-Verlag 1986, pp. 510–584.

[Pomello 86] Pomello, L.: *Some Equivalence Notions for Concurrent Systems*. Advances in Petri Nets 1985, Lecture Notes in Computer Science 222, Springer-Verlag 1986, pp. 381–400.

[Quemada & 89] Quemada, J., Pavón, S. & Fernández, A.: *State Exploration by Transformation with LOLA*. Proceedings of the Workshop on Automatic Verification Methods for Finite State Systems 1989, Lecture Notes in Computer Science 407, Springer-Verlag 1990, pp. 294–302.

[Räuchle & 85] Räuchle, T. & Toueg, S.: *Exposure to Deadlock for Communicating Processes is Hard to Detect*. Information Processing Letters 21 (1985) pp. 63–68.

[Reisig 85] Reisig, W.: *Petri Nets: An Introduction*. EATCS Monographs on Theoretical Computer Science 4, Springer-Verlag 1985, 161 p.

[Reisig 87] Reisig, W.: *Place/Transition Systems*. [Brauer & 87a] pp. 117–141.

[Souissi & 89] Souissi, Y. & Memmi, G.: *Compositions of Nets via a Communication Medium*. Advances in Petri Nets 1990, Lecture Notes in Computer Science 483, Springer-Verlag 1991, pp. 457–470. (Earlier version in Proceedings of the 10th International Conference on Application and Theory of Petri Nets, Bonn, West Germany 1989, pp. 292–311.)

[Souissi 90] Souissi, Y.: *On Liveness Preservation by Composition of Nets via a Set of Places*. Proceedings of the 11th International Conference on Application and Theory of Petri Nets, Paris, France, pp. 104–122.

[Valmari & 87] Valmari, A. & Tiusanen, M. *A Graph Model for Efficient Reachability Analysis of Description Languages*. Proceedings of the 8th European Workshop on Application and Theory of Petri Nets, Zaragoza, Spain, 1987, pp. 349–366.

[Valmari 88a] Valmari, A.: *PC-Rimst — A Tool for Validating Concurrent Program Designs*. Microprocessing and Microprogramming 24 (1988) 1–5 (Proceedings of the EUROMICRO '88) pp. 809–818.

[Valmari 88b] Valmari, A.: *Some Polynomial Space Complete Concurrency Problems*. Tampere University of Technology, Software Systems Laboratory Report 4, 1988, 34 p.

[Valmari 88c] Valmari, A.: *Error Detection by Reduced Reachability Graph Generation*. Proceedings of the 9th European Workshop on Application and Theory of Petri Nets, Venice, Italy 1988, pp. 95–112.

[Valmari 89a] Valmari, A.: *Eliminating Redundant Interleavings during Concurrent Program Verification*. Proceedings of the PARLE '89, Parallel Architectures and Languages Europe, Eindhoven, Vol. II, Lecture Notes in Computer Science 366, pp. 89–103.

[Valmari 89b] Valmari, A.: *Stubborn Sets for Reduced State Space Generation.* Advances in Petri Nets 1990, Lecture Notes in Computer Science 483, Springer-Verlag 1991, pp. 491–515. (Earlier version in Proceedings of the 10th International Conference on Application and Theory of Petri Nets, Bonn, West Germany 1989, Vol II, pp. 1–22.

[Valmari 89c] Valmari, A.: *State Space Generation with Induction (Short Version).* Scandinavian Conference on Artificial Intelligence -89, Frontiers in Artificial Intelligence and Applications, IOS, Amsterdam, Netherlands 1989, pp. 99–115.

[Valmari 90] Valmari, A.: *A Stubborn Attack on State Explosion.* Computer-Aided Verification '90 (Proceedings of the Workshop on Computer-Aided Verification, Princeton, New Jersey, USA), AMS-ACM DIMACS Series in Discrete Mathematics and Theoretical Computer Science, Vol. 3, 1991, pp. 25–41. (Earlier version in DIMACS Technical Report 90-31, June 1990.)

[Valmari & 91a] Valmari, A. & Tienari, M.: *An Improved Failures Equivalence for Finite-State Systems with A Reduction Algorithm.* Proceedings of the 11th International IFIP WG 6.1 Symposium on Protocol Specification, Testing and Verification, Stockholm, Sweden, June 1991, pp. 1–16. To appear in the North-Holland Protocol Specification, Testing and Verification series.

[Valmari & 91b] Valmari, A. & Clegg, M.: *Reduced Labelled Transition Systems Save Verification Effort.* Proceedings of the CONCUR '91, Amsterdam, Lecture Notes in Computer Science 527, Springer-Verlag 1991, pp. 526–540.

[Valmari 91b] Valmari, A.: *Stubborn Sets of Coloured Petri Nets.* Proceedings of the 12th International Conference on Application and Theory of Petri Nets, Gjern, Denmark 1991, pp. 102–121.

[Vogler 89] Vogler, W.: *Failures Semantics and Deadlocking of Modular Petri Nets.* Acta Informatica 26 (1989) pp. 333–348.

[Vuong & 87] Vuong, S. T., Hui, D. D. & Cowan, D. D.: *Valira — A Tool for Protocol Validation via Reachability Analysis.* Protocol Specification, Testing and Verification VI, North-Holland 1987, pp. 35–41.

Lecture Notes in Computer Science

For information about Vols. 1–595
please contact your bookseller or Springer-Verlag

Vol. 596: L.-H. Eriksson, L. Hallnäs, P. Schroeder-Heister (Eds.), Extensions of Logic Programming. Proceedings, 1991. VII, 369 pages. 1992. (Subseries LNAI).

Vol. 597: H. W. Guesgen, J. Hertzberg, A Perspective of Constraint-Based Reasoning. VIII, 123 pages. 1992. (Subseries LNAI).

Vol. 598: S. Brookes, M. Main, A. Melton, M. Mislove, D. Schmidt (Eds.), Mathematical Foundations of Programming Semantics. Proceedings, 1991. VIII, 506 pages. 1992.

Vol. 599: Th. Wetter, K.-D. Althoff, J. Boose, B. R. Gaines, M. Linster, F. Schmalhofer (Eds.), Current Developments in Knowledge Acquisition - EKAW '92. Proceedings. XIII, 444 pages. 1992. (Subseries LNAI).

Vol. 600: J. W. de Bakker, C. Huizing, W. P. de Roever, G. Rozenberg (Eds.), Real-Time: Theory in Practice. Proceedings, 1991. VIII, 723 pages. 1992.

Vol. 601: D. Dolev, Z. Galil, M. Rodeh (Eds.), Theory of Computing and Systems. Proceedings, 1992. VIII, 220 pages. 1992.

Vol. 602: I. Tomek (Ed.), Computer Assisted Learning. Proceedings, 1992. X, 615 pages. 1992.

Vol. 603: J. van Katwijk (Ed.), Ada: Moving Towards 2000. Proceedings, 1992. VIII, 324 pages. 1992.

Vol. 604: F. Belli, F.-J. Radermacher (Eds.), Industrial and Engineering Applications of Artificial Intelligence and Expert Systems. Proceedings, 1992. XV, 702 pages. 1992. (Subseries LNAI).

Vol. 605: D. Etiemble, J.-C. Syre (Eds.), PARLE '92. Parallel Architectures and Languages Europe. Proceedings, 1992. XVII, 984 pages. 1992.

Vol. 606: D. E. Knuth, Axioms and Hulls. IX, 109 pages. 1992.

Vol. 607: D. Kapur (Ed.), Automated Deduction – CADE-11. Proceedings, 1992. XV, 793 pages. 1992. (Subseries LNAI).

Vol. 608: C. Frasson, G. Gauthier, G. I. McCalla (Eds.), Intelligent Tutoring Systems. Proceedings, 1992. XIV, 686 pages. 1992.

Vol. 609: G. Rozenberg (Ed.), Advances in Petri Nets 1992. VIII, 472 pages. 1992.

Vol. 610: F. von Martial, Coordinating Plans of Autonomous Agents. XII, 246 pages. 1992. (Subseries LNAI).

Vol. 611: M. P. Papazoglou, J. Zeleznikow (Eds.), The Next Generation of Information Systems: From Data to Knowledge. VIII, 310 pages. 1992. (Subseries LNAI).

Vol. 612: M. Tokoro, O. Nierstrasz, P. Wegner (Eds.), Object-Based Concurrent Computing. Proceedings, 1991. X, 265 pages. 1992.

Vol. 613: J. P. Myers, Jr., M. J. O'Donnell (Eds.), Constructivity in Computer Science. Proceedings, 1991. X, 247 pages. 1992.

Vol. 614: R. G. Herrtwich (Ed.), Network and Operating System Support for Digital Audio and Video. Proceedings, 1991. XII, 403 pages. 1992.

Vol. 615: O. Lehrmann Madsen (Ed.), ECOOP '92. European Conference on Object Oriented Programming. Proceedings. X, 426 pages. 1992.

Vol. 616: K. Jensen (Ed.), Application and Theory of Petri Nets 1992. Proceedings, 1992. VIII, 398 pages. 1992.

Vol. 617: V. Mařík, O. Štěpánková, R. Trappl (Eds.), Advanced Topics in Artificial Intelligence. Proceedings, 1992. IX, 484 pages. 1992. (Subseries LNAI).

Vol. 618: P. M. D. Gray, R. J. Lucas (Eds.), Advanced Database Systems. Proceedings, 1992. X, 260 pages. 1992.

Vol. 619: D. Pearce, H. Wansing (Eds.), Nonclassical Logics and Information Proceedings. Proceedings, 1990. VII, 171 pages. 1992. (Subseries LNAI).

Vol. 620: A. Nerode, M. Taitslin (Eds.), Logical Foundations of Computer Science – Tver '92. Proceedings. IX, 514 pages. 1992.

Vol. 621: O. Nurmi, E. Ukkonen (Eds.), Algorithm Theory – SWAT '92. Proceedings. VIII, 434 pages. 1992.

Vol. 622: F. Schmalhofer, G. Strube, Th. Wetter (Eds.), Contemporary Knowledge Engineering and Cognition. Proceedings, 1991. XII, 258 pages. 1992. (Subseries LNAI).

Vol. 623: W. Kuich (Ed.), Automata, Languages and Programming. Proceedings, 1992. XII, 721 pages. 1992.

Vol. 624: A. Voronkov (Ed.), Logic Programming and Automated Reasoning. Proceedings, 1992. XIV, 509 pages. 1992. (Subseries LNAI).

Vol. 625: W. Vogler, Modular Construction and Partial Order Semantics of Petri Nets. IX, 252 pages. 1992.

Vol. 626: E. Börger, G. Jäger, H. Kleine Büning, M. M. Richter (Eds.), Computer Science Logic. Proceedings, 1991. VIII, 428 pages. 1992.

Vol. 628: G. Vosselman, Relational Matching. IX, 190 pages. 1992.

Vol. 629: I. M. Havel, V. Koubek (Eds.), Mathematical Foundations of Computer Science 1992. Proceedings. IX, 521 pages. 1992.

Vol. 630: W. R. Cleaveland (Ed.), CONCUR '92. Proceedings. X, 580 pages. 1992.

Vol. 631: M. Bruynooghe, M. Wirsing (Eds.), Programming Language Implementation and Logic Programming. Proceedings, 1992. XI, 492 pages. 1992.

Vol. 632: H. Kirchner, G. Levi (Eds.), Algebraic and Logic Programming. Proceedings, 1992. IX, 457 pages. 1992.

Vol. 633: D. Pearce, G. Wagner (Eds.), Logics in AI. Proceedings. VIII, 410 pages. 1992. (Subseries LNAI).

Vol. 634: L. Bougé, M. Cosnard, Y. Robert, D. Trystram (Eds.), Parallel Processing: CONPAR 92 – VAPP V. Proceedings. XVII, 853 pages. 1992.

Vol. 635: J. C. Derniame (Ed.), Software Process Technology. Proceedings, 1992. VIII, 253 pages. 1992.

Vol. 636: G. Comyn, N. E. Fuchs, M. J. Ratcliffe (Eds.), Logic Programming in Action. Proceedings, 1992. X, 324 pages. 1992. (Subseries LNAI).

Vol. 637: Y. Bekkers, J. Cohen (Eds.), Memory Management. Proceedings, 1992. XI, 525 pages. 1992.

Vol. 639: A. U. Frank, I. Campari, U. Formentini (Eds.), Theories and Methods of Spatio-Temporal Reasoning in Geographic Space. Proceedings, 1992. XI, 431 pages. 1992.

Vol. 640: C. Sledge (Ed.), Software Engineering Education. Proceedings, 1992. X, 451 pages. 1992.

Vol. 641: U. Kastens, P. Pfahler (Eds.), Compiler Construction. Proceedings, 1992. VIII, 320 pages. 1992.

Vol. 642: K. P. Jantke (Ed.), Analogical and Inductive Inference. Proceedings, 1992. VIII, 319 pages. 1992. (Subseries LNAI).

Vol. 643: A. Habel, Hyperedge Replacement: Grammars and Languages. X, 214 pages. 1992.

Vol. 644: A. Apostolico, M. Crochemore, Z. Galil, U. Manber (Eds.), Combinatorial Pattern Matching. Proceedings, 1992. X, 287 pages. 1992.

Vol. 645: G. Pernul, A M. Tjoa (Eds.), Entity-Relationship Approach – ER '92. Proceedings, 1992. XI, 439 pages, 1992.

Vol. 646: J. Biskup, R. Hull (Eds.), Database Theory – ICDT '92. Proceedings, 1992. IX, 449 pages. 1992.

Vol. 647: A. Segall, S. Zaks (Eds.), Distributed Algorithms. X, 380 pages. 1992.

Vol. 648: Y. Deswarte, G. Eizenberg, J.-J. Quisquater (Eds.), Computer Security – ESORICS 92. Proceedings. XI, 451 pages. 1992.

Vol. 649: A. Pettorossi (Ed.), Meta-Programming in Logic. Proceedings, 1992. XII, 535 pages. 1992.

Vol. 650: T. Ibaraki, Y. Inagaki, K. Iwama, T. Nishizeki, M. Yamashita (Eds.), Algorithms and Computation. Proceedings, 1992. XI, 510 pages. 1992.

Vol. 651: R. Koymans, Specifying Message Passing and Time-Critical Systems with Temporal Logic. IX, 164 pages. 1992.

Vol. 652: R. Shyamasundar (Ed.), Foundations of Software Technology and Theoretical Computer Science. Proceedings, 1992. XIII, 405 pages. 1992.

Vol. 653: A. Bensoussan, J.-P. Verjus (Eds.), Future Tendencies in Computer Science, Control and Applied Mathematics. Proceedings, 1992. XV, 371 pages. 1992.

Vol. 654: A. Nakamura, M. Nivat, A. Saoudi, P. S. P. Wang, K. Inoue (Eds.), Prallel Image Analysis. Proceedings, 1992. VIII, 312 pages. 1992.

Vol. 655: M. Bidoit, C. Choppy (Eds.), Recent Trends in Data Type Specification. X, 344 pages. 1993.

Vol. 656: M. Rusinowitch, J. L. Rémy (Eds.), Conditional Term Rewriting Systems. Proceedings, 1992. XI, 501 pages. 1993.

Vol. 657: E. W. Mayr (Ed.), Graph-Theoretic Concepts in Computer Science. Proceedings, 1992. VIII, 350 pages. 1993.

Vol. 658: R. A. Rueppel (Ed.), Advances in Cryptology – EUROCRYPT '92. Proceedings, 1992. X, 493 pages. 1993.

Vol. 659: G. Brewka, K. P. Jantke, P. H. Schmitt (Eds.), Nonmonotonic and Inductive Logic. Proceedings, 1991. VIII, 332 pages. 1993. (Subseries LNAI).

Vol. 660: E. Lamma, P. Mello (Eds.), Extensions of Logic Programming. Proceedings, 1992. VIII, 417 pages. 1993. (Subseries LNAI).

Vol. 661: S. J. Hanson, W. Remmele, R. L. Rivest (Eds.), Machine Learning: From Theory to Applications. VIII, 271 pages. 1993.

Vol. 662: M. Nitzberg, D. Mumford, T. Shiota, Filtering, Segmentation and Depth. VIII, 143 pages. 1993.

Vol. 663: G. v. Bochmann, D. K. Probst (Eds.), Computer Aided Verification. Proceedings, 1992. IX, 422 pages. 1993.

Vol. 664: M. Bezem, J. F. Groote (Eds.), Typed Lambda Calculi and Applications. Proceedings, 1993. VIII, 433 pages. 1993.

Vol. 665: P. Enjalbert, A. Finkel, K. W. Wagner (Eds.), STACS 93. Proceedings, 1993. XIV, 724 pages. 1993.

Vol. 666: J. W. de Bakker, W.-P. de Roever, G. Rozenberg (Eds.), Semantics: Foundations and Applications. Proceedings, 1992. VIII, 659 pages. 1993.

Vol. 667: P. B. Brazdil (Ed.), Machine Learning: ECML – 93. Proceedings, 1993. XII, 471 pages. 1993. (Subseries LNAI).

Vol. 668: M.-C. Gaudel, J.-P. Jouannaud (Eds.), TAPSOFT '93: Theory and Practice of Software Development. Proceedings, 1993. XII, 762 pages. 1993.

Vol. 669: R. S. Bird, C. C. Morgan, J. C. P. Woodcock (Eds.), Mathematics of Program Construction. Proceedings, 1992. VIII, 378 pages. 1993.

Vol. 670: J. C. P. Woodcock, P. G. Larsen (Eds.), FME '93: Industrial-Strength Formal Methods. Proceedings, 1993. XI, 689 pages. 1993.

Vol. 671: H. J. Ohlbach (Ed.), GWAI-92: Advances in Artificial Intelligence. Proceedings, 1992. XI, 397 pages. 1993. (Subseries LNAI).

Vol. 672: A. Barak, S. Guday, R. G. Wheeler, The MOSIX Distributed Operating System. X, 221 pages. 1993.

Vol. 673: G. Cohen, T. Mora, O. Moreno (Eds.), AAECC-10: Applied, Algebra, Algebraic Algorithms and Error-Correcting Codes. Proceedings, 1993. X, 355 pages 1993.

Vol. 674: G. Rozenberg (Ed.), Advances in Petri Nets 1993. VII, 457 pages. 1993.

Vol. 675: A. Mulkers, Live Data Structures in Logic Programs. VIII, 220 pages. 1993.